Europe

PHRASEBOOK & DICTIONARY

Acknowledgments
Editors Branislava Vladisavljevic, Tracy Whitmey
Production Support Chris Love
Cartographer Wayne Murphy
Cover Researcher Naomi Parker

Thanks
James Hardy, Colin Rowe, Angela Tinson, Tony Wheeler

Published by Lonely Planet Publications Pty Ltd
ABN 36 005 607 983

5th Edition – September 2015
ISBN 978 1 74321 435 0
Text © Lonely Planet 2015
Cover Image Convento de Santo Domingo, Jerez de la Frontera,
Spain – Philippe Lissac/Corbis

Printed in China 10 9 8 7 6 5 4 3 2 1

Contact lonelyplanet.com/contact

MIX
Paper from
responsible sources
FSC™ C021741

acknowledgments

This book is based on existing editions of Lonely Planet's phrasebooks. It was developed with the help of the following people:

- Ronelle Alexander for the Bulgarian chapter
- Gordana Ivetac for the Croatian chapter
- Richard Nebeský for the Czech chapter
- Michael Janes for the French chapter
- Gunter Muehl for the German chapter
- Thanasis Spilias for the Greek chapter
- Christina Mayer for the Hungarian chapter
- Karina Coates, Pietro Iagnocco and Susie Walker for the Italian chapter
- Piotr Czajkowski for the Polish chapter
- Robert Landon and Anabela de Azevedo Teixeira Sobrinho for the Portuguese chapter
- Anamaria Beligan and Dana Lovinesku for the Romanian chapter
- James Jenkin and Grant Taylor for the Russian chapter
- Marta López for the Spanish chapter
- Emma Koch for the Swedish chapter
- Arzu Kürklü for the Turkish chapter

contents

contents

contents

europe – at a glance

One of the most rewarding things about travelling through Europe is the rich variety of cuisine, customs, architecture and history. Adding to this variety is the number of very different languages you'll encounter on your travels. Most languages spoken in Europe, including English, belong to what's known as the Indo-European language family, believed to have originally developed from one language spoken thousands of years ago. A number of European languages are represented in Roman script, which can make them a little more accessible for English-speaking travellers. Other alphabets in use include Cyrillic (used for Russian, for example) and Greek. They can be a little confusing, given their vaguely (and often misleadingly) recognisable shapes, but learning their scripts is easily achievable.

The Romance languages (French, Italian, Spanish and Portuguese) all developed from Vulgar Latin, which spread through Western Europe during the rule of the Roman Empire. The freedom with which English has borrowed Latin-based vocabulary means you'll quickly recognise many words from these languages. The Germanic languages – Dutch and German – are more closely related to English. The Scandinavian languages form the northern branch of the Germanic languages tree, having developed from Old Norse, the language of the Vikings. Their big advantage is that, being so closely related, once you've got the hang of one language, the others should seem quite familiar. Greek, the language of the Iliad and the Odyssey, forms a single branch of the Indo-European language family and uses Greek script.

The Slavic languages are a branch of the Indo-European language family and share a large amount of basic vocabulary. They originated north of the Carpathian mountains and are now divided into Eastern (Russian), Western (Czech and Polish) and Southern (Bulgarian and Croatian) subgroups. The languages traditionally associated with the Orthodox Church (Russian, Bulgarian and Macedonian) use Cyrillic alphabet, while those influenced by the Catholic Church (Czech, Slovak, Polish, Croatian and Slovene) use Roman alphabet. Romanian, the only representative of the Romance languages in Eastern Europe, is more closely related to French, Italian or Spanish.

Finally, Turkish and Hungarian are part of the Ural-Altaic language family, which includes languages spoken from the Balkan Peninsula to northeast Asia.

Bulgarian

bulgarian alphabet

А а a	Б б buh	В в vuh	Г г guh	Д д duh
Е е e	Ж ж zhuh	З з zuh	И и ee	Й й ee *krat*·ko
К к kuh	Л л luh	М м muh	Н н nuh	О о o
П п puh	Р р ruh	С с suh	Т т tuh	У у oo
Ф ф fuh	Х х huh	Ц ц tsuh	Ч ч chuh	Ш ш shuh
Щ щ shtuh	Ъ ъ uh	ь er *ma*·luhk	Ю ю yoo	Я я ya

■ bulgarian

БЪЛГАРСКИ

about Bulgarian

Surprisingly, the name of the oldest South Slavic literary language, Bulgarian (български *buhl·gar·skee*), isn't of Slavic origin. It's one of a handful of words remaining in Bulgarian from the language of the Bulgars, a Turkic people who invaded the eastern Balkans in the late 7th century. Together with their language, they were assimilated by the local Slavs, who had crossed the Danube and settled in the peninsula at the start of the 6th century.

As a member of the South Slavic group of languages, Bulgarian has Macedonian and Serbian as its closest relatives. However, it also shows similarities with the non-Slavic languages in the so-called Balkan linguistic union (Romanian, Albanian and Greek), as a result of multilingualism and interaction among the Balkan nations. These foreign influences explain many of its grammatical features – for example, the lack of noun cases, which sets Bulgarian (and Macedonian) apart from the other Slavic languages. In addition, numerous Turkish words entered the Bulgarian vocabulary during five centuries of Ottoman rule. During the 19th century, many of the loanwords from Turkish were eliminated from the language. Their place was partially filled by Russian words, as Russian has influenced Bulgarian through both Bulgaria's ties with the Orthodox Church and long-standing cultural ties with Russia.

Old Bulgarian (also known as Old Church Slavonic) was the first Slavic language recorded in written form, in religious literature from the 9th century. The central figures in the development of the Slavic literary language were Saints Cyril and Methodius, Byzantine Orthodox missionaries who invented the Glagolitic alphabet around 863 AD and used it to translate Greek liturgical texts into Old Church Slavonic. Their disciples devised the Cyrillic alphabet (based on Greek and Glagolitic) in which Bulgarian has been written ever since. In its modern version, standardised after the last spelling reform in 1945, it's very similar to the Russian Cyrillic alphabet. Today, Bulgarians celebrate St Cyril and Methodius Day as a national holiday on 24 May (also known as the Day of Bulgarian Culture or the Cyrillic Alphabet Day).

Modern Bulgarian has about 9 million speakers and is the official language of Bulgaria, with Bulgarian-speaking minorities in Ukraine, Moldova, Romania, Serbia, Hungary, Greece and Turkey. The literary standard is based on the northeastern dialects. The transitional dialects spoken around the borders between Bulgaria, Serbia and Macedonia are very similar and the political issues arising from this linguistic similarity have been sensitive throughout history.

pronunciation

vowel sounds

The vowels in Bulgarian all have equivalents in English, so you shouldn't have any problems. To make yourself sound like a native, just remember that in Bulgarian, vowels in unstressed syllables are generally pronounced shorter and weaker than they are in stressed syllables.

symbol	english equivalent	bulgarian example	transliteration
a	father	дата	*da*·ta
ai	aisle	май	mai
e	bet	лек	lek
ee	see	бира	*bee*·ra
o	pot	вода	vo·*da*
oo	zoo	тук	took
uh	ago	къде	kuh·*de*

word stress

There's no general rule regarding word stress in Bulgarian — it can fall on any syllable and sometimes changes in different grammatical forms of the same word. Just follow our coloured pronunciation guides, in which the stressed syllable is always in italics.

consonant sounds

The consonant sounds in Bulgarian are pretty straightforward, as they all have equivalents in English. The only sound you might trip over is ts, which can occur at the start of words. Try saying 'cats', then 'ats', then 'ts' to get the idea.

symbol	english equivalent	bulgarian example	transliteration
b	bed	брат	brat
ch	cheat	чист	cheest
d	dog	душ	doosh
f	fat	фенерче	fe·ner·che
g	go	гума	goo·ma
h	hat	хотел	ho·tel
k	kit	карта	kar·ta
l	lot	билет	bee·let
m	man	масло	mas·lo
n	not	нула	noo·la
p	pet	грип	greep
r	run	утро	oot·ro
s	sun	син	seen
sh	shot	шест	shest
t	top	сто	sto
ts	hats	крадец	kra·dets
v	very	вчера	vche·ra
y	yes	брой	broy
z	zero	зад	zad
zh	pleasure	плаж	plazh

tools

language difficulties

Do you speak English?
Говорите ли английски? go·*vo*·ree·te lee ang·*lees*·kee

Do you understand?
Разбирате ли? raz·*bee*·ra·te lee

I (don't) understand.
(Не) разбирам. (ne) raz·*bee*·ram

What does (механа) mean?
Какво значи (механа)? kak·*vo* zna·chee (me·ha·*na*)

How do you …? Как се …? kak se …
  pronounce this произнася това pro·eez·*nas*·ya to·*va*
  write (спирка) пише (спирка) *pee*·she (*speer*·ka)

Could you please …? Моля …? *mol*·ya …
  repeat that повторете това pov·to·*re*·te to·*va*
  speak more slowly говорете бавно go·vo·*re*·te *bav*·no
  write it down напишете това na·pee·*she*·te to·*va*

essentials

Yes.	Да.	da
No.	Не.	ne
Please.	Моля.	*mol*·ya
Thank you	Благодаря	bla·go·dar·*ya*
(very much).	(много).	(*mno*·go)
You're welcome.	Няма защо.	*nya*·ma zash·*to*
Excuse me.	Извинете.	iz·vee·*ne*·te
Sorry.	Съжалявам.	suh·zhal·*ya*·vam

numbers

0	нула	*noo*·la	15	петнайсет	pet·*nai*·set
1	един/една m/f	ed·*een*/ed·*na*	16	шеснайсет	shes·*nai*·set
	едно n	ed·*no*	17	седемнайсет	se·dem·*nai*·set
2	два/две m/f&n	dva/dve	18	осемнайсет	o·sem·*nai*·set
3	три	tree	19	деветнайсет	de·vet·*nai*·set
4	четири	che·tee·ree	20	двайсет	*dvai*·set
5	пет	pet	21	двайсет и едно	*dvai*·set ee ed·*no*
6	шест	shest	22	двайсет и две	*dvai*·set ee dve
7	седем	se·dem	30	трийсет	*tree*·set
8	осем	o·sem	40	четирийсет	che·*tee*·ree·set
9	девет	de·vet	50	петдесет	pet·de·*set*
10	десет	de·set	60	шестдесет	shest·de·*set*
11	единайсет	e·dee·*nai*·set	70	седемдесет	se·dem·de·*set*
12	дванайсет	dva·*nai*·set	80	осемдесет	o·sem·de·*set*
13	тринайсет	tree·*nai*·set	90	деветдесет	de·vet·de·*set*
14	четири-	che·tee·ree·	100	сто	sto
	найсет	*nai*·set	1000	хиляда	hee·*lya*·da

time & dates

What time is it?	Колко е часът?	*kol*·ko e cha·*suht*
It's one o'clock.	Часът е един.	cha·*suht* e e·*deen*
It's (two) o'clock.	Часът е (два).	cha·*suht* e (dva)
Quarter past (one).	(Един) и петнайсет.	(e·*deen*) ee pet·*nai*·set
Half past (one).	(Един) и половина.	(e·*deen*) ee po·lo·*vee*·na
Quarter to (eight).	(Осем) без петнайсет.	(o·sem) bez pet·*nai*·set
At what time ...?	В колко часа ...?	v *kol*·ko cha·*suh* ...
At ...	В ...	v ...
am	сутрин	*soo*·treen
pm	следобед	sle·*do*·bed
Monday	понеделник	po·ne·*del*·neek
Tuesday	вторник	*vtor*·neek
Wednesday	сряда	*srya*·da
Thursday	четвъртък	chet·*vuhr*·tuhk
Friday	петък	*pe*·tuhk
Saturday	събота	*suh*·bo·ta
Sunday	неделя	ne·*del*·ya

January	януари	ya·noo·*a*·ree
February	февруари	fev·roo·*a*·ree
March	март	mart
April	април	ap·*reel*
May	май	mai
June	юни	*yoo*·nee
July	юли	*yoo*·lee
August	август	*av*·goost
September	септември	sep·*tem*·vree
October	октомври	ok·*tom*·vree
November	ноември	no·*em*·vree
December	декември	de·*kem*·vree

What date is it today?
Коя дата е днес? ko·*ya da*·ta e dnes

It's (15 December).
Днес е (петнайсти декември). dnes e (pet·*nai*·stee de·*kem*·vree)

| since (May) | от (май) | ot (mai) |
| until (June) | до (юни) | do (*yoo*·nee) |

last/	миналата/	*mee*·na·la·ta/
next ...	следващата ...	*sled*·vash·ta·ta ...
night	вечер	*ve*·cher
week	седмица	*sed*·mee·tsa
year	година	go·*dee*·na

| last month | миналия месец | *mee*·na·lee·ya *me*·sets |
| next month | следващия месец | *sled*·vash·tee·ya *me*·sets |

yesterday/	вчера/утре ...	*vche*·ra/*oot*·re ...
tomorrow ...		
morning	сутринта	soot·reen·*ta*
afternoon	следобед	sle·*do*·bed
evening	вечерта	ve·cher·*ta*

weather

What's the weather like?	Какво е времето?	kak·*vo* e *vre*·me·to

It's ...	... е.	... e
cloudy	Облачно	*ob*·lach·no
cold	Студено	stoo·*de*·no
hot	Горещо	go·*resh*·to
raining	Дъждовно	duhzh·*dov*·no
snowing	Снеговито	sne·go·*vee*·to
sunny	Слънчево	*sluhn*·che·vo
warm	Топло	*top*·lo
windy	Ветровито	vet·tro·*vee*·to

spring	пролет f	*pro*·let
summer	лято n	*lya*·to
autumn	есен f	*e*·sen
winter	зима f	*zee*·ma

border crossing

I'm here ...	Тука съм ...	*too*·ka suhm ...
on business	по работа	po *ra*·bo·ta
on holiday	във ваканция	vuhv va·*kan*·tsee·ya

I'm here for ...	Тука съм за ...	*too*·ka suhm za ...
(10) days	(десет) дена	(*de*·set) *de*·na
(two) months	(два) месеца	(dva) me·*se*·tsa
(three) weeks	(три) седмици	(tree) *sed*·mee·tsee

I'm going to (Gabrovo).
Отивам в (Габрово).　　　　o·*tee*·vam v (*gab*·ro·vo)

I'm staying at the (Serdika).
Отседнал/Отседнала　　　　ot·*sed*·nal/ot·*sed*·na·la
съм в (Сердика). m/f　　　　suhm v (*ser*·dee·ka)

I have nothing to declare.
Нямам нищо да декларирам.　　*nya*·mam *neesh*·to da dek·la·*ree*·ram

I have something to declare.
Имам нещо да декларирам.　　*ee*·mam *nesh*·to da dek·la·*ree*·ram

That's (not) mine.
Това (не) е мое.　　　　to·*va* (ne) e *mo*·ye

transport

tickets & luggage

Where can I buy a ticket?
Къде мога да си купя билет?   kuh-*de mo*-ga da see *koop*-ya bee-*let*

Do I need to book a seat?
Трябва ли да запазя място?   *tryab*-va lee da za-*paz*-ya *myas*-to

One ... ticket	Един билет ...	e-*deen* bee-*let* ...
(to Varna), please.	(за Варна), моля.	(za *var*-na) *mol*-ya
one-way	в едната посока	v ed-*na*-ta po-*so*-ka
return	за отиване	za o-*tee*-va-ne
	и връщане	ee *vruhsh*-ta-ne
I'd like to ... my	Искам да ...	*ees*-kam da ...
ticket, please.	своя билет, моля.	*svo*-ya bee-*let mol*-ya
cancel	върна	*vuhr*-na
change	сменя	smen-*ya*
collect	взема	*vze*-ma
confirm	потвърдя	pot-*vuhr*-*dya*
I'd like a ... seat,	Искам място ...,	*ees*-kam *myas*-to ...
please.	моля.	*mol*-ya
nonsmoking	за непушачи	za ne-poo-*sha*-chee
smoking	за пушачи	za poo-*sha*-chee

How much is it?
Колко струва?   *kol*-ko *stroo*-va

Is there air conditioning?
Има ли климатична   *ee*-ma lee klee-ma-*teech*-na
инсталация?   een-sta-*la*-tsee-ya

Is there a toilet?
Има ли тоалетна?   *ee*-ma lee to-a-*let*-na

How long does the trip take?
Колко трае пътуването?   *kol*-ko *tra*-ye puh-*too*-va-ne-to

Is it a direct route?
Има ли прекачване?   *ee*-ma lee pre-*kach*-va-ne

I'd like a luggage locker.
Искам да оставя багажа   *ees*-kam da os-*tav*-ya ba-*ga*-zha
си на гардероб.   see na gar-de-*rob*

My luggage has been ...	Багажът ми е ...	ba·*ga*·zhuht mee e ...
damaged	повреден	po·vre·*den*
lost	загубен	za·*goo*·ben
stolen	откраден	ot·*kra*·den

getting around

Where does flight (355) arrive?
Къде пристига полет (355)?   kuh·*de* prees·*tee*·ga *po*·let (tree pet pet)

Where does flight (355) depart?
Откъде тръгва полет (355)?   ot·kuh·*de* *truhg*·va *po*·let (tree pet pet)

Where's (the) ...?	Къде се намира ...?	kuh·*de* se na·*mee*·ra ...
arrivals hall	терминал	ter·mee·*nal*
	'пристигане'	pree·*stee*·ga·ne
departures hall	терминал	ter·mee·*nal*
	'заминаване'	za·mee·*na*·va·ne
duty-free shop	безмитен магазин	bez·*mee*·ten ma·ga·*zeen*
gate (12)	изход (дванайсет)	ees·hod (dva·*nai*·set)

Is this the ...	Това ли е ...	to·*va* lee e ...
to (Burgas)?	за (Бургас)?	za (boor·*gas*)
boat	корабът	ko·*ra*·buht
bus	автобусът	av·to·*boo*·suht
plane	самолетът	sa·mo·*le*·tuht
train	влакът	*vla*·kuht

What time's	В колко часа	v *kol*·ko cha·*suh*
the ... bus?	е ... автобус?	e ... av·to·*boos*
first	първият	*puhr*·vee·yat
last	последният	po·*sled*·nee·yat
next	следващият	*sled*·vash·tee·yat

At what time does it arrive/leave?
В колко часа пристига/тръгва?   v *kol*·ko cha·*suh* prees·*tee*·ga/*truhg*·va

How long will it be delayed?
Колко закъснение има?   *kol*·ko za·kuhs·*ne*·nee·ye *ee*·ma

What station/stop is this?
Коя е тази гара/спирка?   ko·*ya* e *ta*·zee *ga*·ra/*speer*·ka

Does it stop at (Plovdiv)?
Спира ли в (Пловдив)?   *spee*·ra lee v (*plov*·deev)

Please tell me when we get to (Smoljan).

Кажете ми моля когато
пристигнем в (Смолян).

ka-*zhe*-te mee *mol*-ya ko-*ga*-to
prees-*teeg*-nem v (*smol*-yan)

How long do we stop here?

След колко време тръгваме оттук?

sled *kol*-ko *vre*-me *truhg*-va-me ot-*took*

Is this seat available?

Това място свободно ли е?

to-*va myas*-to svo-*bod*-no lee e

That's my seat.

Това е моето място.

to-*va* e *mo*-ye-to *myas*-to

I'd like a taxi …	Искам да поръчам такси …	ees-kam da po-*ruh*-cham *tak*-see …
at (9am)	в (девет часа сутринта)	v (*de*-vet cha-*sa* soo-treen-*ta*)
now	сега	se-*ga*
tomorrow	за утре	za *oot*-re

Is this taxi available?

Такситото свободно ли е?

tak-*see*-to svo-*bod*-no lee e

How much is it to …?

Колко струва до …?

kol-ko *stroo*-va do …

Please put the meter on.

Моля да включите таксиметъра.

mol-ya da *vklyoo*-chee-te tak-see-*me*-tuh-ra

Please take me to (this address).

Моля да ме докарате
до (този адрес).

mol-ya da me do-*ka*-ra-te
do (*to*-zi ad-*res*)

Please …	Моля …	*mol*-ya …
slow down	намалете	na-ma-*le*-te
stop here	спрете тук	*spre*-te took
wait here	чакайте тук	*cha*-kai-te took

car, motorbike & bicycle hire

I'd like to hire a …	Искам да взема под наем …	ees-kam da vze-ma pod *na*-em …
bicycle	един велосипед	e-*deen* ve-lo-see-*ped*
car	една кола	e-*dna* ko-*la*
motorbike	един мотопед	e-*deen* mo-to-*ped*

with ...	с ...	s ...
a driver	шофьор	sho·*fyor*
air conditioning	климатична	klee·ma·*teech*·na
	инсталация	een·sta·*la*·tsee·ya
antifreeze	антифриз	an·tee·*freez*
snow chains	вериги за сняг	ve·*ree*·gee za snyag
How much for	Колко струва на ...	*kol*·ko *stroo*·va na ...
... hire?	да се наеме?	da se na·*e*·me
hourly	час	chas
daily	ден	den
weekly	седмица	*sed*·mee·tsa
air	въздух m	*vuhz*·dooh
oil	масло n	*mas*·lo
petrol	бензин m	ben·*zeen*
tyres	гуми f pl	*goo*·mee

I need a mechanic.
Трябва ми монтьор.   *tryab*·va mee mon·*tyor*

I've run out of petrol.
Нямам бензин.   *nya*·mam ben·*zeen*

I have a flat tyre.
Пукнала ми се е гумата.   *pook*·na·la mee se e *goo*·ma·ta

directions

Where's the ...?	Къде се намира ...?	kuh·*de* se na·*mee*·ra ...
bank	банката	*ban*·ka·ta
city centre	центърът на града	*tsen*·tuh·ruht na gra·*duh*
hotel	хотелът	ho·*te*·luht
market	пазарът	pa·*za*·ruht
police station	полицейският	po·lee·*tsey*·skee·uht
	участък	oo·*chas*·tuhk
post office	пощата	*po*·shta·ta
public toilet	една градска	ed·*na grad*·ska
	тоалетна	to·a·*let*·na
tourist office	бюрото за	*byoo*·ro·to za
	туристическа	too·*ree*·stee·*ches*·ka
	информация	een·for·*ma*·tsee·ya

Is this the road to (Rila)?

Това ли е пътят за (Рила)? · to-*va* lee e *puh*-tyat za (*ree*-la)

Can you show me (on the map)?

Можете ли да ми покажете (на картата)? · *mo*-zhe-te lee da mee po-*ka*-zhe-te (na *kar*-ta-ta)

What's the address?

Какъв е адресът? · ka-*kuhv* e ad-*re*-suht

How far is it?

На какво разстояние е? · na kak-*vo* ras-to-*ya*-nee-e e

How do I get there?

Как се ходи до там? · kak se *ho*-dee do tam

Turn ...	Завийте ...	za-*veey*-te ...
at the corner	на следващия ъгъл	na *sled*-vash-tee-ya *uh*-guhl
at the traffic lights	при светофара	pree sve-to-*fa*-ra
left/right	наляво/надясно	na-*lya*-vo/na-*dyas*-no

It's ...	Това е ...	to-*va* e ...
behind ...	зад ...	zad ...
far away	далече	da-*le*-che
here	тука	*too*-ka
in front of ...	пред ...	pred ...
left	наляво	na-*lya*-vo
near (to ...)	близо (до ...)	*blee*-zo (do ...)
next to ...	до ...	do ...
on the corner	на ъгъла	na *uh*-guh-luh
opposite ...	срещу ...	*sresh*-too ...
right	надясно	na-*dyas*-no
straight ahead	право	*pra*-vo
there	там	tam

by bus	с автобус	s av-to-*boos*
by taxi	с такси	s tak-*see*
by train	с влак	s vlak
on foot	пеша	pe-*sha*

north	север	*se*-ver
south	юг	yoog
east	изток	*ees*-tok
west	запад	*za*-pad

20

signs

Вход/Изход	vhod/*ees*-hod	**Entrance/Exit**
Отворено/Затворено	ot-*vo*-re-no/zat-*vo*-re-no	**Open/Closed**
Свободни стаи	svo-*bod*-nee *sta*-yee	**Rooms Available**
Няма стаи	*nya*-ma *sta*-yee	**No Vacancies**
Информация	een-for-*ma*-tsee-ya	**Information**
Полиция	po-*lee*-tsee-ya	**Police Station**
Забранено	za-bra-*ne*-no	**Prohibited**
Тоалетни	to-a-*let*-nee	**Toilets**
Мъже	muh-*zhe*	**Men**
Жени	zhe-*nee*	**Women**
Горещо/Студено	go-*resh*-to/stoo-*de*-no	**Hot/Cold**

accommodation

finding accommodation

Where's a ...?	Къде има ...?	kuh-*de ee*-ma ...
camping ground	къмпинг	*kuhm*-peeng
guesthouse	пансион	pan-see-*on*
hotel	хотел	ho-*tel*
youth hostel	общежитие	ob-shte-*zhee*-tee-ye

Can you	Можете ли	*mo*-zhe-te lee
recommend	да препоръчате	da pre-po-*ruh*-cha-te
somewhere ...?	нещо ...?	*nesh*-to ...
cheap	евтино	*ev*-tee-no
good	хубаво	*hoo*-ba-vo
nearby	наблизо	na-*blee*-zo

I have a reservation.
Имам резервация.   *ee*-mam re-zer-*va*-tsee-ya

My name's ...
Казвам се ...   *kaz*-vam se ...

I'd like to book a room, please.
Искам да взема една стая, моля.   *ees*-kam da *vze*-ma ed-*na sta*-ya *mol*-ya

21

Do you have a ... room?	Имате ли стая с ...?	ee·ma·te lee sta·ya s ...
single	едно легло	ed·no leg·lo
double	едно голямо легло	ed·no go·lya·mo leg·lo
twin	две легла	dve leg·la

How much is it per ...?	Колко е на ...?	kol·ko e na ...
night	вечер	ve·cher
person	човек	cho·vek

Can I pay ...?	Мога ли да платя ...?	mo·ga lee da pla·tya ...
by credit card	с кредитна карта	s kre·deet·na kar·ta
with a travellers	с пътнически	s puht·nee·ches·kee
cheque	чекове	che·ko·ve

I'd like to stay for (two) nights.
Искам стаята за (две) нощи.
ees·kam sta·ya·ta za (dve) nosh·ti

From (2 July) to (6 July).
От (втори юли) до (шести юли).
ot (vto·ree yoo·lee) do (shes·tee yoo·lee)

Can I see it?
Мога ли да я видя?
mo·ga lee da ya vee·dya

Am I allowed to camp here?
Мога ли да си сложа
палатката тук?
mo·ga lee da see slo·zha
pa·lat·ka·ta took

Is there a camp site nearby?
Има ли къмпинг наблизо?
ee·ma lee kuhm·peeng na·blee·zo

requests & queries

When/Where is breakfast served?
Кога/Къде сервират закуската?
ko·ga/kuh·de ser·vee·rat za·koos·ka·ta

Please wake me at (seven).
Моля събудете ме в (седем).
mol·ya suh·boo·de·te me v (se·dem)

Could I have my key, please?
Дайте ми ключа, моля.
dai·te mee klyoo·cha mol·ya

Can I get another (blanket)?
Дайте ми моля още едно
(одеяло).
dai·te mee mol·ya osh·te ed·no
(o·de·ya·lo)

Is there an elevator/a safe?
Има ли асансьор/сейф?
ee·ma lee a·san·syor/seyf

The room is too ...	Стаята е прекалено ...	sta-ya-ta e pre-ka-le-no ...
expensive	скъпа	skuh-pa
noisy	шумна	shoom-na
small	малка	mal-ka

The ... doesn't work.	Не работи ...	ne ra-bo-tee ...
air conditioning	климатичната	klee-ma-teech-na-ta
	инсталация	een-sta-la-tsee-ya
fan	вентилаторът	ven-tee-la-to-ruht
toilet	тоалетната	to-a-let-na-ta

This ... isn't clean.	Тази ... не е чиста.	ta-zee ... ne e chees-ta
pillow	възглавница	vuhz-glav-nee-tsa
towel	кърпа	kuhr-pa

| This sheet isn't clean. | Този чаршаф не е чист. | to-zee char-shaf ne e cheest |

checking out

What time is checkout?
Кога трябва да напусна стаята?   ko-ga tryab-va da na-poos-na sta-ya-ta

Can I leave my luggage here?
Мога ли да оставя своя
багаж тук?   mo-ga lee da os-tav-ya svo-ya
ba-gazh took

Could I have my ...?	Дайте ми ..., моля.	dai-te mee ... mol-ya
deposit	моя депозит	mo-ya de-po-zeet
passport	моя паспорт	mo-ya pas-port
valuables	моите ценности	mo-yee-te tsen-nos-tee

communications & banking

the internet

Where's the local Internet café?
Къде се намира най-близкият
интернет?   kuh-de se na-mee-ra nai-blees-kee-yat
een-ter-net

How much is it per hour?
Колко се плаща на час?   kol-ko se pla-shta na chas

I'd like to ...	Искам да ...	*ees*·kam da ...
check my email	проверя и-мейла си	pro·*ver*·ya ee·*mey*·la see
get Internet access	използвам интернета	iz·*polz*·vam een·ter·*ne*·ta
use a printer	използвам принтер	iz·*polz*·vam *preen*·ter
use a scanner	използвам скенер	iz·*polz*·vam *ske*·ner

mobile/cell phone

I'd like a ...	Искам ...	*ees*·kam ...
mobile/cell phone for hire	да взема под наем един мобилен телефон	da *vze*·ma pod *na*·em e·*deen* mo·*bee*·len te·le·*fon*
SIM card for your network	предплатена карта за мобилни телефони за вашата мрежа	pred·pla·*te*·na *kar*·ta za mo·*beel*·nee te·le·*fo*·nee za *va*·sha·ta *mre*·zha
What are the rates?	Какви са цените?	kak·*vee* sa tse·*nee*·te

telephone

What's your phone number?
Какъв е вашият телефонен номер?
ka·*kuhv* e *va*·shee·yat te·le·*fo*·nen *no*·mer

The number is ...
Номерът е ...
no·me·ruht e ...

Where's the nearest public phone?
Къде се намира най-близката телефонна будка?
kuh·*de* se na·*mee*·ra nai·*blees*·ka·ta te·le·*fon*·na *bood*·ka

I'd like to buy a phonecard.
Искам да си купя една телефонна карта.
ees·kam da see *koop*·ya ed·*na* te·le·*fon*·na *kar*·ta

I want to ...	Искам да ...	*ees*·kam da ...
call (Singapore)	се обадя в (Сингапур)	se o·*bad*·ya v (seen·ga·*poor*)
make a local call	се обадя някъде в града	se o·*bad*·ya *nya*·kuh·de v gra·*duh*
reverse the charges	се обадя на тяхната сметка	se o·*bad*·ya na *tyah*·na·ta *smet*·ka

How much does ... cost?	Колко струва ...?	kol·ko stroo·va ...
a (three)-minute call	разговор от (три) минути	raz·go·vor ot (tree) mee·noo·tee
each extra minute	всяка допълнителна минута	vsya·ka do·puhl·nee·tel·na mee·noo·ta

| (Five) leva per minute. | | |
| (Пет) лева една минута. | | (pet) le·va ed·na mee·noo·ta |

post office

I want to send a ...	Искам да изпратя ...	ees·kam da eez·prat·ya ...
letter	едно писмо	ed·no pees·mo
parcel	един колет	e·deen ko·let
postcard	една пощенска картичка	ed·na posh·ten·ska kar·teech·ka

I want to buy a/an ...	Искам да купя ...	ees·kam da koop·ya ...
envelope	един плик	e·deen pleek
stamp	една марка	ed·na mar·ka

Please send it (to Australia) by ...	Моля да се изпрати (в Австралия) ...	mol·ya da se eez·pra·tee (v av·stra·lee·ya) ...
airmail	с въздушна поща	s vuhz·doosh·na posh·ta
express mail	с бърза поща	s buhr·za posh·ta
registered mail	препоръчано	pre·po·ruh·cha·no
surface mail	с обикновена поща	s o·beek·no·ve·na posh·ta

| Is there any mail for me? | | |
| Има ли писма за мене? | | ee·ma lee pees·ma za me·ne |

bank

Where's a/an ...?	Къде има ...?	kuh·de ee·ma ...
ATM	банкомат	ban·ko·mat
foreign exchange office	обмяна на валута	ob·mya·na na va·loo·ta

I'd like to ...	Искам да ...	ees·kam da ...
Where can I ...?	Къде мога да ...?	kuh·de mo·ga da ...
arrange a transfer	уредя да ми се	oo·red·ya da mee se
	изпратят пари	eez·prat·yat pa·ree
	чрез банков превод	chrez ban·kov pre·vod
cash a cheque	осребря чек	os·reb·ryuh chek
change a travellers	осребря	os·reb·ryuh
cheque	пътнически чек	puht·nee·ches·kee chek
change money	обменя пари	ob·men·ya pa·ree
get a cash advance	изтегля пари от	eez·teg·lya pa·ree ot
	кредитната си карта	kre·deet·na·ta see kar·ta
withdraw money	тегля пари в брой	teg·lya pa·ree v broy
What's the ...?	Каква е ...?	kak·va e ...
charge for that	таксата	ko·mee·see·on·na
commission	комисионна	tak·sa·ta
It's ...	... е.	... e
(10) leva	(Десет) лева	(de·set) le·va
free	Безплатно	bez·plat·no

What's the exchange rate?
Какъв е валутен курс? — ka·kuhv e va·loo·ten koors

What time does the bank open?
В колко часа се отваря банката? — v kol·ko cha·suh se ot·var·ya ban·ka·ta

Has my money arrived yet?
Парите ми пристигнаха ли вече? — pa·ree·te mee prees·teeg·na·ha lee ve·che

sightseeing

getting in

What time does it open/close?
В колко часа се отваря/затваря? — v kol·ko cha·suh se ot·var·ya/zat·var·ya

What's the admission charge?
Каква е входната такса? — kak·va e vhod·na·ta tak·sa

Is there a discount for students/children?
Има ли намаление за — ee·ma lee na·ma·le·nee·ye za
студенти/деца? — stoo·den·tee/det·sa

26

I'd like a …	Искам …	*ees*·kam …
catalogue	един каталог	e·*deen* ka·ta·*log*
guide	един гид	e·*deen* geed
map	една карта на района	ed·*na kar*·ta na ra·*yo*·na

I'd like to see …	Искам да видя …	*ees*·kam da *veed*·ya …
What's that?	Какво е онова?	kak·*vo* e o·no·*va*
Can I take a photo?	Мога ли да направя снимка?	*mo*·ga lee da na·*prav*·ya *sneem*·ka

tours

When's the next …?	Кога тръгва следващата …?	ko·*ga truhg*·va *sled*·vash·ta·ta …
day trip	еднодневна екскурзия	ed·no·*dnev*·na eks·*koor*·zee·ya
tour	обиколка	o·*bee*·kol·ka

Is … included?	Включена ли е …?	*vklyoo*·che·na lee e …
accommodation	нощувката	nosh·*toov*·ka·ta
the admission charge	входната такса	*vhod*·na·ta *tak*·sa
food	храната	hra·*na*·ta

Is transport included?
Включен ли е транспортът? — *vklyoo*·chen lee e trans·*por*·tuht

How long is the tour?
Колко трае екскурзията? — *kol*·ko *tra*·e eks·*koor*·zee·ya·ta

What time should we be back?
В колко часа ще се върнем? — v *kol*·ko cha·*suh* shte se *vuhr*·nem

sightseeing		
church	църква f	*tsuhrk*·va
main square	централен площад m	tsen·*tra*·len plosh·*tad*
monastery	манастир m	ma·nas·*teer*
monument	паметник m	*pa*·met·nik
museum	музей m	moo·*zey*
old city	старият град m	*sta*·ree·yuht grad
palace	дворец m	dvo·*rets*
ruins	развалини f pl	raz·va·lee·*nee*
stadium	стадион m	sta·dee·*on*
statue	статуа f	*sta*·too·a

shopping

enquiries

Where's a ... ?	Къде има ...?	kuh-de ee-ma ...
bank	банка	ban-ka
bookshop	книжарница	knee-zhar-nee-tsa
camera shop	магазин за	ma-ga-zeen za
	фотоапарати	fo-to-a-pa-ra-tee
department store	универсален	oo-nee-ver-sa-len
	магазин	ma-ga-zeen
grocery store	гастроном	gas-tro-nom
market	пазар	pa-zar
newsagency	киоск	kee-osk
supermarket	супермаркет	soo-per-mar-ket

Where can I buy ...?
Къде мога да си купя
(един катинар)?
kuh-de mo-ga da see koop-ya
(e-deen ka-nee-tar)

I'm looking for ...
Търся ...
tuhr-sya ...

Can I look at it?
Мога ли да го разгледам?
mo-ga lee da go raz-gle-dam

Do you have any others?
Имате ли още?
ee-ma-te lee osh-te

Does it have a guarantee?
Има ли гаранция?
ee-ma lee ga-ran-tsee-ya

Can I have it sent abroad?
Можете ли да го изпратите
в чужбина?
mo-zhe-te lee da go eez-pra-tee-te
v choozh-bee-na

Can I have my ... repaired?
Можете ли да поправите
моя ...?
mo-zhe-te lee da po-pra-vee-te
mo-ya ...

It's faulty.
Не е на ред.
ne e na red

БЪЛГАРСКИ – shopping

I'd like ..., please.	Искам ..., моля.	ees·kam ... mol·ya
a bag	един плик	e·deen pleek
a refund	да ми се вратят	da mee se vrat·yuht
	парите	pa·ree·te
to return this	да върна това нещо	da vuhr·na to·va nesh·to

paying

How much is it?
Колко струва? — *kol·ko stroo·va*

Can you write down the price?
Моля, напишете цената. — *mol·ya na·pee·she·te tse·na·ta*

That's too expensive.
Скъпо е. — *skuh·po e*

What's your lowest price?
Каква е най-низката ви цена? — *kak·va e nai·neez·ka·ta vee tse·na*

I'll give you (five) euros.
Ще ви дам (пет) евро. — shte vee dam (pet) *ev·ro*

I'll give you (15) leva.
Ще ви дам (петнайсет) лева. — shte vee dam (pet·*nai*·set) *le·va*

There's a mistake in the bill.
Има грешка в сметката. — *ee·ma gresh·ka v smet·ka·ta*

Do you accept ...?	Приемате ли ...?	pree·e·ma·te lee ...
credit cards	кредитни карти	kre·deet·nee kar·tee
debit cards	дебитни карти	de·beet·nee kar·tee
travellers cheques	пътнически	puht·nee·ches·kee
	чекове	che·ko·ve

I'd like ..., please.	Дайте ми моля ...	dai·te mee mol·ya ...
a receipt	квитанция	kvee·tan·tsee·ya
my change	ресто	res·to

clothes & shoes

Can I try it on?
Мога ли да го пробвам? — *mo*·ga lee da go *prob*·vam

My size is (42).
Номерът ми е — *no*·me·ruht mee e
(четирийсет и два). — (che·*tee*·ree·set ee dva)

It doesn't fit.
Не ми става. — ne mee *sta*·va

small	малко	*mal*·ko
medium	средно	*sred*·no
large	голямо	gol·*ya*·mo

books & music

I'd like a ...	Искам ...	*ees*·kam ...
newspaper	един вестник	e·*deen* vest·neek
(in English)	(на английски)	(na an·*glee*·skee)
pen	една писалка	ed·*na* pee·*sal*·ka

Is there an English-language bookshop?
Има ли книжарница с | *ee*·ma lee knee·*zhar*·nee·tsa s
книги на английски? | *knee*·gee na ang·*lees*·kee

I'm looking for something by (Ivan Vazov).
Търся нещо от (Иван Вазов). | *tuhr*·sya *nesh*·to ot (ee·*van* va·zov)

Can I listen to this?
Мога ли да слушам това? | *mo*·ga lee da *sloo*·sham to·*va*

photography

Can you ...?	Можете ли да ...?	*mo*·zhe·te lee da ...
burn a CD from	запишете на	za·*pee*·she·te na
my memory card	компактен диск от	kom·*pak*·ten deesk ot
	моя флешдрайв	*mo*·ya *flesh*·draiv
develop this film	проявите този филм	pro·*ya*·vee·te *to*·zee film
load my film	заредите моя филм	za·*re*·dee·te *mo*·ya film

I need a ... film	Трябви ми ... филм	*tryab*·va mee ... film
for this camera.	за този фотоапарат.	za *to*·zee fo·to·a·pa·*rat*
APS	АПС	a puh suh
B&W	черно-бял	*cher*·no·*byal*
colour	цветен	*tsve*·ten

I need a ... film	Трлбви ми филм ...	*tryab*·va mee film ...
for this camera.	за този фотоапарат.	za *to*·zee fo·to·a·pa·*rat*
slide	за диапозитиви	za dee·a·po·zee·*tee*·vee
(200) speed	за скорост (двеста)	za *sko*·rost (*dve*·sta)

| When will it be ready? | Кога ще бъде готов? | ko·*ga* shte *buh*·de go·*tov* |

meeting people

greetings, goodbyes & introductions

Hello/Hi.	Здравейте/Здравей.	zdra·*vey*·te/zdra·*vey*
Good night.	Лека нощ.	*le*·ka nosht
Goodbye/Bye.	Довиждане/Чао.	do·*veezh*·da·ne/*cha*·o
Mr/Mrs	господин/госпожа	gos·po·*deen*/gos·*po*·zha
Miss	госпожица	gos·*po*·zhee·tsa
How are you?	Как си/сте? inf/pol	kak si/ste
Fine, thanks.	Добре, благодаря.	do·*bre* bla·go·da·*rya*
And you?	А ти/вие? inf/pol	a te/*vee*·e
What's your name?	Как се казваш/	kak se *kaz*·vash/
	казвате? inf/pol	*kaz*·va·te
My name is ...	Казвам се ...	*kaz*·vam se ...
I'm pleased to	Приятно ми е да се	pree·*yat*·no mee e da se
meet you.	запозная с вас.	za·poz·*na*·ya s vas
This is my ...	Това е ...	to·*va* e ...
boyfriend	моят приятел	*mo*·yat pree·*ya*·tel
brother	моят брат	*mo*·yat brat
daughter	моята дъщеря	*mo*·ya·ta duh·shter·*ya*
father	моят баща	*mo*·yat bash·*ta*
friend	мой приятел m	moy pree·*ya*·tel
	моя приятелка f	*mo*·ya pree·*ya*·tel·ka
girlfriend	моята приятелка	*mo*·ya·ta pree·*ya*·tel·ka
husband	моят съпруг	*mo*·yat suh·*proog*
mother	моята майка	*mo*·ya·ta *mai*·ka
partner (intimate)	моят приятел m	*mo*·yat pree·*ya*·tel
	моята приятелка f	*mo*·ya·ta pree·*ya*·tel·ka
sister	моята сестра	*mo*·ya·ta ses·*tra*
son	моят син	*mo*·yat seen
wife	моята съпруга	*mo*·ya·ta suh·*proo*·ga
Here's my ...	Ето моя ...	e·to *mo*·ya ...
What's your ...?	Какъв е вашият ...?	ka·*kuhv* e va·shee·yat ...
(email) address	(и-мейл) адрес	(*ee*·meyl) a·*dres*
fax number	факс	faks
phone number	телефонен номер	te·le·*fo*·nen *no*·mer

occupations

What's your occupation?	Какво работите?	kak·*vo* ra·*bo*·tee·te
I'm a/an ...	Аз съм ...	az suhm ...
artist	художник m	hoo·*dozh*·neek
	художничка f	hoo·*dozh*·neech·ka
businessperson	бизнесмен m	beez·nes·*men*
	бизнесменка f	beez·nes·*men*·ka
farmer	фермер m	*fer*·mer
	фермерка f	*fer*·mer·ka
office worker	чиновник m	chee·*nov*·neek
	чиновничка f	chee·*nov*·neech·ka
scientist	учен m&f	*oo*·chen

background

Where are you from?	Откъде сте?	ot·kuh·*de* ste
I'm from ...	Аз съм от ...	az suhm ot ...
Australia	Австралия	av·*stra*·lee·ya
Canada	Канада	*ka*·na·da
England	Англия	*ang*·lee·ya
New Zealand	Нова Зеландия	*no*·va ze·*lan*·dee·ya
the USA	Съединените	suh·e·dee·*ne*·nee·te
	Щати	*sha*·tee
Are you married?	Женен/Омъжена	*zhe*·nen/o·*muh*·zhe·na
	ли сте? m/f	lee ste
I'm married.	Женен/Омъжена	*zhe*·nen/o·*muh*·zhe·na
	съм. m/f	suhm
I'm single.	Не съм женен/	ne suhm *zhe*·nen/
	омъжена. m/f	o·*muh*·zhe·na

age

How old ...?	На колко години ...?	na *kol*·ko go·*dee*·nee ...
are you	си/сте inf/pol	si/ste
is your daughter	е дъщеря	e duhsh·ter·*ya*
	ти/ви inf/pol	tee/vee
is your son	е синът ти/ви inf/pol	e see·*nuht* tee/vee

| I'm ... years old. | На ... години съм. | na ... go·dee·nee suhm |
| He/She is ... years old. | Той/Тя е на ... години. | toy/tya e na ... go·dee·nee |

feelings

I'm ...	Аз съм ...	az suhm ...
I'm not ...	Не съм ...	ne suhm ...
happy	щастлив	shtast·*leev*
hungry	гладен	*gla*·den
sad	тъжен	*tuh*·zhen
thirsty	жаден	*zha*·den
tired	уморен	oo·mo·*ren*

I'm ...	На мене ми е ...	na *me*·ne mee e ...
I'm not ...	Не ми е ...	ne mee e ...
cold	студено	stoo·*de*·no
hot	топло	*top*·lo
OK	добре	do·*bre*

Are you ...?	... ли ви е?	... lee vee e
cold	Студено	stoo·*de*·no
hot	Топло	*top*·lo
OK	Добре	do·*bre*

entertainment

going out

Where can I find ...?	Къде има ...?	kuh·*de* ee·*ma* ...
clubs	нощни заведения	*nosht*·nee za·ve·*de*·nee·ya
gay venues	гей клубове	gey *kloo*·bo·ve
pubs	кръчми	*kruhch*·mee

I feel like going to a/the ...	Ходи ми се на ...	*ho*·dee mee se na ...
concert	концерт	kon·*tsert*
movies	кино	*kee*·no
party	един купон	e·*deen* koo·*pon*
restaurant	ресторант	res·to·*rant*
theatre	театър	te·*a*·tuhr

interests

Do you like ...?	Харесвате ли ...?	ha-*res*-va-te lee ...
I (don't) like ...	(Не) Харесвам ...	(ne) ha-*res*-vam ...
art	изкуството	iz-*koost*-vo-to
movies	киното	*kee*-no-to
reading	четенето	*che*-te-ne-to
sport	спорта	*spor*-tuht
travelling	пътуването	puh-*too*-va-ne-to

Do you like to ...?	Обичате ли да ...?	o-*bee*-cha-te lee da ...
dance	танцувате	tan-*tsoo*-va-te
go to concerts	ходите на концерти	*ho*-dee-te na kon-*tser*-tee
listen to music	слушате музика	*sloo*-sha-te *moo*-zee-ka

food & drink

finding a place to eat

Can you recommend a ...?	Можете ли да препоръчате ...?	*mo*-zhe-te lee da pre-po-*ruh*-cha-te ...
bar	един бар	e-*deen* bar
café	едно кафене	ed-*no* ka-fe-*ne*
restaurant	един ресторант	e-*deen* res-to-*rant*

I'd like ..., please.	Искам ..., моля.	*ees*-kam ... *mol*-ya
a table for (four)	една маса за (четирма)	ed-*na ma*-sa za (che-*teer*-ma)
the (non)smoking section	в залата за (не)пушачи	v *za*-la-ta za (ne-)poo-*sha*-chee

ordering food

breakfast	закуска f	za-*koos*-ka
lunch	обед m	o-bed
dinner	вечеря f	ve-*cher*-ya
snack	закуска f	za-*koos*-ka

| What would you recommend? | Какво ще препоръчате? | kak-*vo* shte pre-po-*ruh*-cha-te |

I'd like (the) ..., please.	Дайте ми ..., моля.	*dai*·te mee ... *mol*·ya
bill	сметката	*smet*·ka·ta
drink list	листата с напитките	*lees*·ta·ta s na·*peet*·kee·te
menu	менюто	men·*yoo*·to
that dish	онова блюдо	o·no·*va blyoo*·do

drinks

(cup of) coffee/tea ...	(чаша) кафе/чай ...	(*chas*·ha) ka·*fe*/chai ...
with milk	с мляко	s *mlya*·ko
without sugar	без захар	bez *za*·har
(orange) juice	(портокалов) сок m	(por·to·*ka*·lov) sok
soft drink	безалкохолна напитка f	bez·al·ko·*hol*·na na·*peet*·ka
... water	... вода	... vo·*da*
boiled	преварена	pre·va·*re*·na
mineral	минерална	mee·ne·*ral*·na

in the bar

I'll have ...	Ще взема ...	shte *vze*·ma ...
I'll buy you a drink.	Ще ти/ви	shte tee/vee
	почерпя. inf/pol	po·*cher*·pya
What would you like?	Какво ще вземеш/	kak·*vo* shte *vze*·mesh/
	вземете? inf/pol	*vze*·me·te
Cheers!	Наздраве!	na·*zdra*·ve
brandy	ракия f	ra·*kee*·ya
cocktail	коктейл m	kok·*teyl*
cognac	коняк m	kon·*yak*
a shot of (whisky)	едно малко (уиски)	ed·*no mal*·ko (oo·*ees*·kee)
a ... of beer	... бира	... *bee*·ra
bottle	едно шише	ed·*no* shee·*she*
glass	една чаша	ed·*na* cha·*sha*
a bottle of ... wine	едно шише ... вино	ed·*no* shee·*she* ... *vee*·no
a glass of ... wine	една чаша ... вино	ed·*na* cha·*sha* ... *vee*·no
red	червено	cher·*ve*·no
sparkling	шумящо	shoo·*myash*·to
white	бяло	*bya*·lo

self-catering

What's the local speciality?

Има ли някакъв
местен специалитет?

ee·ma lee *nya*·ka·kuhv
mes·ten spe·tsee·a·lee·*tet*

How much is (a kilo of cheese)?

Колко струва (един
килограм кашкавал)?

kol·ko *stroo*·va (e·*deen*
kee·lo·*gram* kash·ka·*val*)

I'd like ...	Дайте ми ...	*dai*·te mee ...
(100) grams	(сто) грама	(sto) *gra*·ma
(two) kilos	(два) килограма	(dva) kee·lo·*gra*·ma
(three) pieces	(три) парчета	(tree) par·*che*·ta
(six) slices	(шест) парчета	(shest) par·*che*·ta

Less.	По-малко.	*po*·mal·ko
Enough.	Достатъчно.	dos·*ta*·tuch·no
More.	Повече.	*po*·ve·che

special diets & allergies

Is there a vegetarian restaurant near here?

Има ли наблизо
вегетериански ресторант?

ee·ma lee nab·*lee*·zo
ve·ge·te·ree·*an*·skee res·to·*rant*

Do you have vegetarian food?

Имате ли вегетерианска храна?

ee·ma·te lee ve·ge·te·ree·*an*·ska hra·*na*

Could you	Можете ли да	*mo*·zhe·te lee da
prepare a meal	приготвите	pree·*got*·vee·te
without ...?	яденето без ...?	*ya*·de·ne·to bez ...
butter	краве масло	*kra*·ve *mas*·lo
eggs	яйца	yai·*tsa*
meat stock	месен бульон	*me*·sen bool·*yon*

I'm allergic to ...	Алергичен/Алергична	a·ler·*gee*·chen/a·ler·*geech*·na
	съм към ... m/f	suhm kuhm ...
dairy produce	млечни продукти	*mlech*·nee pro·*dook*·tee
gluten	глутен	*gloo*·ten
MSG	МСГ	muh suh guh
nuts	ядки	*yad*·kee
seafood	морски продукти	*mor*·skee pro·*dook*·tee

emergencies

basics

Help!	Помощ!	*po*-mosht
Stop!	Стоп!	stop
Go away!	Махайте се!	*ma*-hai-te se
Thief!	Крадец!	kra-*dets*
Fire!	Пожар!	po-*zhar*
Watch out!	Внимавайте!	vnee-*ma*-vai-te

Call ...!	Повикайте ...!	po-*vee*-kai-te ...
a doctor	лекар	*le*-kar
an ambulance	бърза помощ	*buhr*-za po-mosht
the police	полицията	po-*lee*-tsee-ya-ta

It's an emergency!
Има спешен случай!   *ee*-ma *spe*-shen *sloo*-chai

Could you help me, please?
Бихте ли ми помогнали?   *beeh*-te lee mee po-*mog*-na-lee

I have to use the telephone.
Трябва да телефонирам.   *tryab*-va da te-le-fo-*nee*-ram

I'm lost.
Загубих се.   za-*goo*-beeh se

Where are the toilets?
Къде има тоалетни?   kuh-*de* ee-ma to-a-*let*-nee

police

Where's the police station?
Къде е полицейският участък?   kuh-*de* e po-lee-*tsey*-skee-yat oo-*chas*-tuhk

I want to report an offence.
Искам да съобщя за едно   *ees*-kam da suh-obsh-*tya* ed-*no*
нарушение.   na-roo-*she*-nee-ye

I have insurance.
Имам застраховка.   *ee*-mam za-stra-*hov*-ka

I've been ...	... ме.	... me
assaulted	Нападнаха	na-*pad*-na-ha
raped	Изнасилиха	eez-na-*see*-lee-ha
robbed	Ограбиха	o-*gra*-bee-ha

I've lost my ...	Изгубих си ...	eez-*goo*-beeh see ...
My ... was/were stolen.	Откраднаха ми ...	ot-*krad*-na-ha mee ...
backpack	раница	*ra*-nee-tsa
bags	чантите	*chan*-tee-te
credit card	кредитната карта	kre-*deet*-na-ta *kar*-ta
handbag	чантата	*chan*-ta-ta
jewellery	бижутата	bee-*zhoo*-ta-ta
money	парите	pa-*ree*-te
passport	паспорта	pas-*por*-ta
travellers	пътническите	puht-*nee*-ches-kee-te
cheques	чекове	*che*-ko-ve
wallet	портфейла	port-*fey*-la

I want to contact	Искам да се свържа	*ees*-kam da se *svuhr*-zha
my ...	с нашето ...	s *na*-she-to ...
consulate	консулство	*kon*-sools-tvo
embassy	посолство	po-*sols*-tvo

health

medical needs

Where's the	Къде е най-близкият/	kuh-*de* e nai-*bleez*-kee-yat/
nearest ...?	най-близката ...? m/f	nai-*bleez*-ka-ta ...
dentist	зъболекар m	zuh-bo-*le*-kar
doctor	лекар m	*le*-kar
hospital	болница f	*bol*-nee-tsa
(night) pharmacist	(нощна) аптека f	(*nosht*-na) a-po-*te*-ka

I need a doctor (who speaks English).
Трябва ми лекар
(говорещ английски).
tryab-va mee *le*-kar
(go-*vo*-resht ang-*lees*-kee)

Could I see a female doctor?
Може ли да ме прегледа лекарка?
mo-zhe lee da me pre-*gle*-da *le*-kar-ka

I've run out of my medication.
Свърши ми се е лекарството.
svuhr-shee mee se e le-*karst*-vo-to

conditions, symptoms & allergies

I'm sick.	Болен/Болна съм. m/f	bo·len/bol·na suhm
It hurts here.	Тук ме боли.	took me bo·lee
I have a headache/ toothache.	Боли ме глава/ зъб.	bo·lee me gla·va/ zuhb

I have (a) ...	Имам ...	ee·mam ...
asthma	астма	ast·ma
bronchitis	бронхит	bron·heet
constipation	запек	za·pek
cough	кашлица	kash·lee·tsa
diarrhoea	диария	dee·a·ree·ya
fever	температура	tem·pe·ra·too·ra
heart condition	болно сърце	bol·no suhr·tse
pain	болки	bol·kee
sore throat	възпалено гърло	vuhz·pa·le·no guhr·lo

I'm allergic to ...	Алергичен/Алергична съм на. m/f	a·ler·gee·chen/a·ler·geech·na suhm na ...
antibiotics	антибиотици	an·tee·bee·o·tee·tsee
anti-inflammatories	противо-възпалителни лекарства	pro·tee·vo·vuhz·pa·lee·tel·nee le·karst·va
aspirin	аспирин	as·pee·reen
bees	пчели	pche·lee
codeine	кодеин	ko·de·een
penicillin	пеницилин	pe·nee·tsee·leen

antiseptic	антисептичен m	an·tee·sep·tee·chen
bandage	бинт m	beent
condoms	презервативи m pl	pre·zer·va·tee·vee
contraceptives	противозачатъчни средства n pl	pro·tee·vo·za·cha·tuhch·nee sred·stva
diarrhoea medicine	лекарство против разтройство n	le·karst·vo pro·teev raz·troyst·vo
insect repellent	средство срещу насекоми n	sredst·vo pro·teev na·se·ko·mee
laxatives	пургатив m	poor·ga·teev
painkillers	обезболяващо n	o·bez·bo·lya·va·shto
rehydration salts	соли за оводняване f pl	so·lee za o·vod·nya·va·ne
sleeping tablets	приспивателно n	pree·spee·va·tel·no

english–bulgarian dictionary

Bulgarian nouns in this dictionary have their gender indicated by ⓜ (masculine), ⓕ (feminine) or ⓝ (neuter). If it's a plural noun, you'll also see pl. Adjectives are given in the masculine form only. Words are also marked as a (adjective), v (verb), sg (singular), pl (plural), inf (informal) or pol (polite) where necessary.

A

accident катастрофа ⓕ ka-tas-*tro*-fa
accommodation нощувка ⓕ nosh-*toov*-ka
adaptor адаптер ⓜ a-*dap*-ter
address адрес ⓜ ad-*res*
after след sled
air-conditioned с климатична инсталация
s klee-ma-*teech*-na een-sta-*la*-tsee-ya
airplane самолет ⓜ sa-mo-*let*
airport летище ⓝ le-*teesh*-te
alcohol алкохол ⓜ al-ko-*hol*
all всичко *vseech*-ko
allergy алергия ⓕ a-*ler*-gee-ya
ambulance линейка ⓕ lee-*ney*-ka
and и ee
ankle глезен ⓜ *gle*-zen
arm ръка ⓕ ruh-*ka*
ashtray пепелница ⓕ pe-pel-*nee*-tsa
ATM банкомат ⓜ ban-ko-*mat*

B

baby бебе ⓝ *be*-be
back (body) гръб ⓜ gruhb
backpack раница ⓕ *ra*-nee-tsa
bad лош losh
bag чанта ⓕ *chan*-ta
baggage claim подаване на багаж ⓝ
po-*da*-va-ne na ba-*gazh*
bank банка ⓕ *ban*-ka
bar бар ⓜ bar
bathroom баня ⓕ *ban*-ya
battery батерия ⓕ ba-te-*ree*-ya
beautiful красив kra-*seev*
bed легло ⓝ leg-*lo*
beer бира ⓕ *bee*-ra
before пред pred
behind зад zad
bicycle колело ⓝ ko-le-*lo*
big голям gol-*yam*
bill банкнота ⓕ bank-*no*-ta

black черен *che*-ren
blanket одеяло ⓝ o-de-*ya*-lo
blood group кръвна група ⓕ *kruhv*-na *groo*-pa
blue син seen
boat кораб ⓜ *ko*-rab
book (make a reservation) v запазвам za-*paz*-vam
bottle шише ⓝ shee-*she*
bottle opener отварачка ⓕ ot-va-*rach*-ka
boy момче ⓝ mom-*che*
brakes (car) спирачки ⓕ pl spee-*rach*-kee
breakfast закуска ⓕ za-*koos*-ka
broken (faulty) развален raz-va-*len*
Bulgaria България ⓕ buhl-*ga*-ree-ya
Bulgarian (language) български ⓜ *buhl*-gar-skee
Bulgarian a български *buhl*-gar-skee
bus автобус ⓜ av-to-*boos*
business търговия ⓕ tuhr-go-*vee*-ya
buy купувам koo-*poo*-vam

C

café кафене ⓝ ka-fe-*ne*
camera фотоапарат ⓜ fo-to-a-pa-*rat*
camp site къмпинг ⓜ *kuhm*-peeng
cancel отказвам ot-*kaz*-vam
can opener отварачка ⓕ ot-va-*rach*-ka
car кола ⓕ ko-*la*
cash пари ⓕ pa-*ree*
cash (a cheque) v осребрявам os-reb-*rya*-vam
cell phone мобилен телефон ⓜ mo-*bee*-len te-le-*fon*
centre център ⓜ *tsen*-tuhr
change (money) v сменям *smen*-yam
cheap евтин *ev*-teen
check (bill) сметка ⓕ *smet*-ka
check-in регистрация ⓕ re-gees-*tra*-tsee-ya
chest гърди ⓕ guhr-*dee*
child дете ⓝ de-*te*
cigarette цигара ⓕ tsee-*ga*-ra
city град ⓜ grad
clean a чист cheest
closed затворен zat-*vo*-ren
coffee кафе ⓝ ka-*fe*
coins монети ⓕ pl mo-*ne*-tee

cold a студен stoo-*den*
collect call обаждане за тяхна цметка ⓕ
  o-*bazh*-da-ne na *tyah*-na *smet*-ka
come идвам *eed*-vam
computer компютър ⓜ kom-*pyoo*-tuhr
condom презерватив ⓜ pre-zer-va-*teev*
contact lenses контактни лещи ⓕ pl
  kon-*takt*-nee *lesh*-tee
cook v готвя *got*-vya
cost цена ⓕ tse-*na*
credit card кредитна карта ⓕ *kre*-deet-na *kar*-ta
cup чаша ⓕ *cha*-sha
currency exchange обмяна на валута ⓕ
  ob-*mya*-na na va-*loo*-ta
customs (immigration) митница ⓕ *meet*-neet-sa

D

dangerous опасен o-*pa*-sen
date (time) дата ⓕ *da*-ta
day ден den
delay закъснение ⓝ za-kuhs-*ne*-nee-ye
dentist зъболекар ⓜ zuh-bo-le-*kar*
depart тръгвам *truhg*-vam
diaper пелена ⓕ pe-le-*na*
dictionary речник ⓜ *rech*-neek
dinner вечеря ⓕ ve-*cher*-ya
direct пряк pryak
dirty мръсен *mruh*-sen
disabled (person) инвалид ⓜ een-va-*leed*
discount намаление ⓝ na-ma-le-*nee*-ye
doctor лекар ⓜ *le*-kar
double bed двойно легло ⓝ *dvoy*-no leg-*lo*
double room стая с две легла ⓕ *sta*-ya s dve leg-*la*
drink пия ⓕ *pee*-ya
drive v карам *ka*-ram
drivers licence шофьорска книжка ⓕ
  sho-*fyor*-ska *kneesh*-ka
drug (illicit) наркотик ⓜ nar-ko-*teek*
dummy (pacifier) биберон ⓜ bee-be-*ron*

E

ear ухо ⓝ *oo*-ho
east изток ⓜ *eez*-tok
eat ям yam
economy class втора класа ⓕ *vto*-ra *kla*-sa
electricity електричество ⓝ e-lek-*tree*-chest-vo
elevator асансьор ⓜ a-san-*syor*
email и-мейл ⓜ *ee*-meyl
embassy посолство ⓝ po-*sols*-tvo

emergency спешен случай ⓜ *spe*-shen *sloo*-chai
English (language) английски ⓜ ang-*lees*-kee
entrance вход ⓜ vhod
evening вечер ⓕ *ve*-cher
exchange rate валутен курс ⓜ va-*loo*-ten koors
exit изход ⓜ *eez*-hod
expensive скъп skuhp
express mail бърза поща ⓕ *buhr*-za *posh*-ta
eye око ⓝ o-*ko*

F

far далече da-*le*-che
fast бърз buhrz
father баща ⓜ bash-*ta*
film (camera) филм ⓜ feelm
finger пръст ⓜ pruhst
first-aid kit първа помощ ⓕ *puhr*-va *po*-mosht
first class първа класа ⓕ *puhr*-va *kla*-sa
fish риба ⓕ *ree*-ba
food храна ⓕ hra-*na*
foot крак ⓜ krak
fork вилица ⓕ *vee*-lee-tsa
free (of charge) безплатно bez-*plat*-no
friend приятел/приятелка ⓜ/ⓕ
  pree-*ya*-tel/pree-*ya*-tel-ka
fruit плод ⓜ plod
full пълен *puh*-len
funny смешен *sme*-shen

G

gift подарък ⓜ po-*da*-ruhk
girl момиче ⓝ mo-*mee*-che
glass (drinking) чаша ⓕ *cha*-sha
glasses очила ⓝ pl o-chee-*la*
go отивам o-*tee*-vam
good добър do-*buhr*
green зелен ze-*len*
guide гид ⓜ geed

H

half половина ⓕ po-lo-*vee*-na
hand ръка ⓕ ruh-*ka*
handbag дамска чанта ⓕ *dam*-ska chan-*ta*
happy щастлив shtast-*leev*
have имам *ee*-mam
he той toy
head глава ⓕ gla-*va*

heart сърце ⑩ suhr-*tse*
heat горещина ① go-resh-tee-*na*
heavy тежък *te*-zhuk
help v помагам po-*ma*-gam
here тука *too*-ka
high висок vee-*sok*
highway шосе ⑩ sho-*se*
hike v ходя пеш *hod*-ya pesh
holiday ваканция ① va-*kan*-tsee-ya
homosexual a хомосексуален ho-mo-sek-soo-*a*-len
hospital болница ① *bol*-nee-tsa
hot горещ go-*resht*
hotel хотел ⑩ ho-*tel*
hungry гладен *gla*-den
husband мъж ⑩ muhzh

I

I аз az
identification (card) легитимация ①
le-gee-tee-*ma*-tsee-ya
ill болен *bo*-len
important важен *va*-zhen
included включен *vklyoo*-chen
injury щета ① shte-*ta*
insurance застраховка ① za-stra-*hov*-ka
Internet интернет ⑩ een-ter-*net*
interpreter преводач ⑩ pre-vo-*dach*

J

jewellery бижутерия ① bee-zhoo-*te*-ree-ya
job работа ① *ra*-bo-ta

K

key ключ ⑩ klyooch
kilogram килограм ⑩ kee-lo-*gram*
kitchen кухня ① *kooh*-nya
knife нож ⑩ nozh

L

laundry (place) пералня ① pe-*ral*-nya
lawyer адвокат ⑩ ad-vo-*kat*
left (direction) ляво *lya*-vo
left-luggage office гардероб ⑩ gar-de-*rob*
leg крак ⑩ krak
lesbian a лезбийски lez-*bee*-skee

less по-малко po-*mal*-ko
letter (mail) писмо ⑩ pees-*mo*
lift (elevator) асансьор ⑩ a-san-*syor*
light светлина ① svet-lee-*na*
like v харесвам ha-*res*-vam
lock брава ① bra-*va*
long дълъг *duh*-luhg
lost загубен za-*goo*-ben
lost-property office бюро за загубени вещи ⑩
byoo-*ro* za za-*goo*-be-nee *vesh*-tee
love v обичам o-*bee*-cham
luggage багаж ⑩ ba-*gazh*
lunch обяд ⑩ o-*byad*

M

mail поща ① *posh*-ta
man мъж ⑩ muhzh
map карта ① *kar*-ta
market пазар ⑩ pa-*zar*
matches кибрит ⑩ kee-*breet*
meat месо ⑩ me-*so*
medicine лекарство ⑩ le-*karst*-vo
menu меню ⑩ men-*yoo*
message съобщение ① suh-ob-*shte*-nee-ye
milk мляко ⑩ *mlya*-ko
minute минута ① mee-*noo*-ta
mobile phone мобилен телефон ⑩
mo-*bee*-len te-le-*fon*
money пари ① pa-*ree*
month месец ⑩ *me*-sets
morning сутрин ① *soot*-reen
mother майка ① *mai*-ka
motorcycle мотоциклет ⑩ mo-to-tseek-*let*
motorway магистрала ① ma-gee-*stra*-la
mouth уста ① oos-*ta*
music музика ① *moo*-zee-ka

N

name име ⑩ *ee*-me
napkin салфетка ① sal-*fet*-ka
nappy пелена ① pe-le-*na*
near близък *blee*-zuhk
neck врат ⑩ vrat
new нов nov
news новина ① no-vee-*na*
newspaper вестник ⑩ *vest*-neek
night нощ ① nosht
no не ne

noisy шумен *shoo*-men
nonsmoking за непушачи za ne-poo-*sha*-chee
north север ⓜ *se*-ver
nose нос ⓜ nos
now сега se-*ga*
number число ⓕ chees-*lo*

O

oil (engine) масло ⓕ *mas*-lo
old стар star
one-way ticket еднопосочен билет ⓜ
   ed-no-po-*so*-chen bee-*let*
open a отворен ot-*vo*-ren
outside навън na-*vuhn*

P

package колет ⓜ ko-*let*
paper хартия ⓕ har-*tee*-ya
park (car) v паркирам par-*kee*-ram
passport паспорт ⓜ pas-*port*
pay плащам *plash*-tam
pen писалка ⓕ pee-*sal*-ka
petrol бензин ⓜ ben-*zeen*
pharmacy аптека ⓕ ap-*te*-ka
phonecard телефонна карта ⓕ te-le-*fon*-na *kar*-ta
photo снимка ⓕ *sneem*-ka
plate чиния ⓕ chee-*nee*-ya
police полиция ⓕ po-*leet*-see-ya
postcard пощенска карта ⓕ *posh*-ten-ska *kar*-ta
post office поща ⓕ *posh*-ta
pregnant бременна *bre*-men-na
price цена ⓕ tse-*na*

Q

quiet тих teeh

R

rain дъжд ⓜ duhzhd
razor самобръсначка ⓕ sa-mo-bruhs-*nach*-ka
receipt квитанция ⓕ kvee-*tan*-tsee-ya
red червен cher-*ven*
refund връщане на парите ⓝ
   vruhsh-ta-ne na pa-*ree*-te
registered mail препоръчано писмо ⓝ
   pre-po-*ruh*-cha-no pees-*mo*
rent v вземам под наем *vze*-mam pod *na*-em

repair v поправям po-*prav*-yam
reservation резервация ⓕ re-zer-*va*-tsee-ya
restaurant ресторант ⓜ res-to-*rant*
return v връщам *vruhsh*-tam
return ticket билет за отиване и връщане ⓜ
   bee-*let* za o-*tee*-va-ne e *vruhsh*-ta-ne
right (direction) дясно *dyas*-no
road път ⓜ puht
room стая ⓕ *sta*-ya

S

safe a безопасен be-zo-*pa*-sen
sanitary napkin дамска превръзка ⓕ
   dam-ska pre-*vruh*-zka
seat място ⓝ *myas*-to
send пращам *prash*-tam
service station бензиностанция ⓕ
   ben-zee-no-*stan*-tsee-ya
sex секс ⓜ seks
shampoo шампоан ⓜ sham-po-*an*
share a room живея в една стая с
   zhe-*ve*-ya v ed-*na sta*-ya s
shaving cream крем за бръснене ⓜ
   krem za *bruhs*-ne-ne
she тя *tya*
sheet (bed) чаршаф ⓜ char-*shaf*
shirt риза ⓕ *ree*-za
shoes обувки ⓕ pl o-*boov*-kee
shop магазин ⓜ ma-ga-*zeen*
short къс kuhs
shower душ ⓜ doosh
single room стая с едно легло ⓕ *sta*-ya s ed-*no* leg-*lo*
skin кожа ⓕ *ko*-zha
skirt пола ⓕ po-*la*
sleep v спя spyuh
slowly бавно *bav*-no
small малък *mal*-uhk
smoke (cigarettes) v пуша *poo*-sha
soap сапун ⓜ sa-*poon*
some някои *nya*-ko-yee
soon скоро *sko*-ro
south юг ⓜ yoog
souvenir shop магазин за сувенири ⓜ
   ma-ga-*zeen* za soo-ve-*nee*-ree
speak говоря go-*vor*-ya
spoon лъжица ⓕ luh-*zhee*-tsa
stamp марка ⓕ *mar*-ka
stand-by ticket билет на търси се ⓜ
   bee-*let* na *tuhr*-see se
station (train) гара ⓕ *ga*-ra
stomach стомах ⓜ sto-*mah*

english–bulgarian

43

stop v спря spryuh
stop (bus) спирка ⓕ *speer*-ka
street улица ⓕ *oo*-leet-sa
student студент/студентка ⓜ/ⓕ
   stoo-*dent*/stoo-*dent*-ka
sun слънце ⓝ *sluhn*-tse
sunscreen крем против загаряне ⓜ
   krem pro-teev za-*ga*-rya-ne
swim v плувам *ploo*-vam

T

tampons тампони ⓜ pl tam-*po*-nee
taxi такси ⓝ tak-*see*
teaspoon лъжичка ⓕ luh-*zheech*-ka
teeth зъби ⓝ pl *zuh*-bee
telephone телефон ⓜ te-le-*fon*
television телевизия ⓕ te-le-*vee*-zee-ya
temperature (weather) температура ⓕ
   tem-pe-ra-*too*-ra
tent палатка ⓕ pa-*lat*-ka
that (one) онова o-no-*va*
they те te
thirsty жаден zha-*den*
this (one) това to-*va*
throat гърло *guhr*-lo
ticket билет ⓜ bee-*let*
time време ⓝ *vre*-me
tired уморен oo-mo-*ren*
tissues хартийни носни кърпички ⓕ pl
   har-*teey*-nee nos-nee kuhr-*peech*-kee
today днес dnes
toilet тоалетна ⓕ to-a-*let*-na
tomorrow утре *oot*-re
tonight довечера do-*ve*-che-ra
toothbrush четка за зъби ⓕ *chet*-ka za *zuh*-bee
toothpaste паста за зъби ⓕ *pas*-ta za *zuh*-bee
torch (flashlight) фенерче ⓝ fe-*ner*-che
tour екскурзия eks-*koor*-zee-ya
tourist office бюро за туристическа информация ⓝ
   byoo-*ro* za too-rees-*tee*-ches-ka een-for-*ma*-tsee-ya
towel кърпа ⓕ *kuhr*-pa
train влак ⓜ vlak
translate превеждам pre-*vezh*-dam
travel agency туристическа агенция ⓕ
   too-rees-*tee*-ches-ka a-*gen*-tsee-ya
travellers cheque пътнически чек ⓜ
   puht-*nee*-ches-kee chek
trousers панталони ⓜ pl pan-ta-*lo*-nee
twin beds двойни легла ⓝ pl *dvoy*-nee leg-*la*
tyre гума ⓕ *goo*-ma

U

underwear бельо ⓝ bel-*yo*
urgent спешен spe-*shen*

V

vacant свободен svo-*bo*-den
vacation ваканция ⓕ va-*kan*-tsee-ya
vegetable зеленчук ⓝ ze-len-*chook*
vegetarian a вегетериански ve-ge-te-ree-*an*-skee
visa виза ⓕ *vee*-za

W

waiter сервитьор ⓜ ser-vee-*tyor*
walk v ходя *ho*-dya
wallet портфейл ⓜ port-*feyl*
warm a топъл *to*-puhl
wash (something) мия *mee*-ya
watch часовник ⓜ cha-*sov*-neek
water вода ⓕ vo-*da*
we ние *nee*-ye
weekend събота и неделя ⓕ suh-bo-ta ee ne-*del*-ya
west запад ⓜ *za*-pad
wheelchair инвалидна количка ⓕ
   een-va-*leed*-na ko-*leech*-ka
when кога ko-*ga*
where къде kuh-*de*
white бял byal
who кой koy
why защо zash-*to*
wife жена ⓕ zhe-*na*
window прозорец ⓝ pro-zo-rets
wine вино ⓝ *vee*-no
with с/със s/suhs
without без bez
woman жена ⓕ zhe-*na*
write пиша *pee*-sha

Y

yellow жълт zhult
yes да da
yesterday вчера *vche*-ra
you sg inf ти tee
you sg pol & pl вие *vee*-ye

Croatian

croatian & serbian alphabets

croatian	serbian	croatian	serbian	croatian	serbian	croatian	serbian
A a a	А а	*E e* e	Е е	*Lj lj* l'	Љ љ	*Š š* sh	Ш ш
B b be	Б б	*F f* ef	Ф ф	*M m* em	М м	*T t* te	Т т
C c tse	Ц ц	*G g* ge	Г г	*N n* en	Н н	*U u* u	У у
Č č tch	Ч ч	*H h* ha	Х х	*Nj nj* n'	Њ њ	*V v* ve	В в
Ć ć ch	Ћ ћ	*I i* i	И и	*O o* o	О о	*Z z* zed	З з
D d de	Д д	*J j* y	Ј ј	*P p* pe	П п	*Ž ž* zh	Ж ж
Dž dž dzh	Џ џ	*K k* ka	К к	*R r* er	Р р		
Đ đ j	Ђ ђ	*L l* el	Л л	*S s* es	С с		

croatian/serbian

HRVATSKI

about Croatian

Did you know that the words *Dalmatian* and *cravat* come from Croatian (*hrvatski* hr·vat·ski)? Linguists commonly refer to the languages spoken in Croatia, Serbia, Montenegro and Bosnia-Hercegovina as members of the macrolanguage Serbo-Croatian while acknowledging differences between the individual languages. Croats, Serbs, Bosnians and Montenegrins themselves generally maintain that they speak different languages, however – a reflection of their desire to retain separate ethnic identities.

As the language of about 5 million people in one of the world's newer countries, Croatian has an intriguing, cosmopolitan and at times fraught history. Its linguistic ancestor was brought to the region in the sixth and seventh centuries AD by the South Slavs, who may have crossed the Danube from the area now known as Poland. This ancestral language split off into two branches: East South Slavic, which later evolved into Bulgarian and Macedonian, and West South Slavic, of which Slovene, Serbian and Croatian are all descendants.

Croatia may be a peaceful country today but the Balkan region to which it belongs has a long history of invasion and conflict. These upheavals have enriched and po-liticised the language. The invasion by Charlemagne's armies and the conversion of Croats to the Roman Church in AD 803 left its mark on Croatian in the form of words borrowed from Latin and the adoption of the Latin alphabet rather than the Cyrillic alphabet (with which Serbian is written). Subsequent invasions by the Hapsburg, Ottoman and Venetian empires added vibrancy to the language through an influx of German, Turkish and Venetian dialect words. Many words from the standard Italian of Croatia's neighbour Italy have also been absorbed.

The good news is that if you venture into Serbia, Bosnia or Montenegro, you'll be able to enrich your travel experience there by using this chapter -- Croatian, Serbian and Montenegrin are all mutually comprehensible, and it's an official lan-guage in Bosnia-Herzegovina. In case of the most common differences between Croatian and Serbian, both translations are given and indicated with ©/⑤. The Cyrillic alphabet (used in Serbia, Bosnia and often in Montenegro) is also included on the page opposite. People in Macedonia and Slovenia, who speak closely re-lated languages, generally understand Croatian. In other words (often heard throughout this region) – *nema problema* ne·ma pro·ble·ma (no problem)!

pronunciation

vowel sounds

In written Croatian, vowels that appear next to each other don't run together as in English. When you see two or more vowels written next to each other in a Croatian word, pronounce them separately.

symbol	english equivalent	croatian example	transliteration
a	father	*zdravo*	*zdra*-vo
ai	aisle	*ajvar*	*ai*-var
e	bet	*pet*	pet
i	hit	*sidro*	*si*-dro
o	pot	*brod*	brod
oy	toy	*tvoj*	tvoy
u	put	*skupo*	*sku*-po

word stress

As a general rule, in two-syllable words in Croatian stress usually falls on the first syllable. In words of three or more syllables, stress may fall on any syllable except the last. In our pronunciation guides, the stressed syllable is italicised.

Croatian also has what's known as 'pitch accent'. A stressed vowel may have either a rising or a falling pitch and be long or short. The combination of stress, pitch and vowel length in a given syllable occasionally affects the meaning of a word, but you don't need to worry about reproducing this feature of Croatian and we haven't indicated it in this book. In the few cases where it's important, it should be clear from the context what's meant. You may notice though that the speech of native speakers has an appealing musical lilt to it.

consonant sounds

Croatian consonant sounds all have close equivalents in English. The rolled r sound can be pronounced in combination with other consonants as a separate syllable – eg *Hrvat* hr·vat (Croat). If the syllables without vowels look a bit intimidating, try inserting a slight 'uh' sound before the r to help them run off your tongue more easily.

symbol	english equivalent	croatian example	transliteration
b	**bed**	*glazba*	*glaz*·ba
ch	**ch**eat	*četiri, ćuk*	*che*·ti·ri, chuk
d	**d**og	*doručak*	*do*·ru·chak
f	**f**at	*fotograf*	fo·*to*·graf
g	**g**o	*jagoda*	*ya*·go·da
h	**h**at	*hodnik*	*hod*·nik
j	**j**oke	*džep, đak*	jep, jak
k	**k**it	*krov*	krov
l	**l**ot	*lutka*	*lut*·ka
ly	mi**lli**on	*nedjelja*	*ned*·ye·lya
m	**m**an	*mozak*	*mo*·zak
n	**n**ot	*nafta*	*naf*·ta
ny	ca**ny**on	*kuhinja*	*ku*·hi·nya
p	**p**et	*petak*	*pe*·tak
r	**r**un (rolled)	*radnik*	*rad*·nik
s	**s**un	*sastanak*	*sas*·ta·nak
sh	**sh**ot	*košta*	*kosh*·ta
t	**t**op	*sat*	sat
ts	ha**ts**	*prosinac*	*pro*·si·nats
v	**v**ery	*viza*	*vi*·za
y	**y**es	*svjetlost*	*svyet*·lost
z	**z**ero	*zec*	zets
zh	plea**s**ure	*koža*	*ko*·zha
'	a slight y sound	*kašalj, siječanj*	*ka*·shal', si·ye·chan'

tools

language difficulties

Do you speak English?
Govorite/Govoriš li engleski? **pol/inf**   go·vo·ri·te/go·vo·rish li en·gle·ski

Do you understand?
Da li razumijete/razumiješ? **pol/inf**   da li ra·zu·mi·ye·te/ra·zu·mi·yesh

I (don't) understand.
Ja (ne) razumijem.   ya (ne) ra·zu·mi·yem

What does (*dobro*) mean?
Što znači (dobro)?   shto zna·chi (do·bro)

How do you ...?	*Kako se ...?*	*ka·ko se ...*
pronounce this	*ovo izgovara*	*o·vo iz·go·va·ra*
write (*dobro*)	*piše (dobro)*	*pi·she (do·bro)*

Could you please ...?	*Možete li ...?* **pol**	*mo·zhe·te li ...*
	Možeš li ...? **inf**	*mo·zhesh li ...*
repeat that	*to ponoviti*	to po·no·vi·ti
speak more slowly	*govoriti sporije*	go·vo·ri·ti spo·ri·ye
write it down	*to napisati*	to na·pi·sa·ti

essentials

Yes.	*Da.*	da
No.	*Ne.*	ne
Please.	*Molim.*	*mo*·lim
Thank you (very much).	*Hvala vam/ti (puno).* **pol/inf**	*hva*·la vam/ti (*pu*·no)
You're welcome.	*Nema na čemu.*	ne·ma na *che*·mu
Excuse me.	*Oprostite.*	o·*pro*·sti·te
Sorry.	*Žao mi je.*	zha·o mi ye

numbers

0	*nula*	*nu*-la	14	*četrnaest*	che-*tr*-na-est	
1	*jedan* m	*ye*-dan	15	*petnaest*	*pet*-na-est	
	jedna f	*yed*-na	16	*šesnaest*	*shes*-na-est	
	jedno n	*yed*-no	17	*sedamnaest*	se-*dam*-na-est	
2	*dva* m&n	dva	18	*osamnaest*	o-*sam*-na-est	
	dvije f	*dvi*-ye	19	*devetnaest*	de-*vet*-na-est	
3	*tri*	tri	20	*dvadeset*	*dva*-de-set	
4	*četiri*	che-ti-ri	21	*dvadeset jedan*	*dva*-de-set *ye*-dan	
5	*pet*	pet	30	*trideset*	*tri*-de-set	
6	*šest*	shest	40	*četrdeset*	che-*tr*-de-set	
7	*sedam*	se-*dam*	50	*pedeset*	pe-*de*-set	
8	*osam*	o-*sam*	60	*šezdeset*	shez-*de*-set	
9	*devet*	de-*vet*	70	*sedamdeset*	se-*dam*-*de*-set	
10	*deset*	de-*set*	80	*osamdeset*	o-sam-*de*-set	
11	*jedanaest*	ye-*da*-na-est	90	*devedeset*	de-ve-*de*-set	
12	*dvanaest*	*dva*-na-est	100	*sto*	sto	
13	*trinaest*	*tri*-na-est	1000	*tisuću/hiljadu* ©/⑤	*ti*-su-chu/*hi*-lya-du	

time & dates

What time is it?	*Koliko je sati?*	ko-*li*-ko ye *sa*-ti
It's one o'clock.	*Jedan je sat.*	*ye*-dan ye *sa*-t
It's (10) o'clock.	*(Deset) je sati.*	(*de*-set) ye *sa*-ti
Quarter past (10).	*(Deset) i petnaest.*	(*de*-set) i *pet*-na-est
Half-past (10).	*(Deset) i po.*	(*de*-set) i *po*
Quarter to (10).	*Petnaest do (deset).*	*pet*-na-est do (*de*-set)
At what time?	*U koliko sati?*	u ko-*li*-ko *sa*-ti
At ...	*U ...*	u ...
am	*prijepodne*	*pri*-ye-*pod*-ne
pm	*popodne*	po-*pod*-ne
Monday	*ponedjeljak*	po-*ne*-dye-lyak
Tuesday	*utorak*	*u*-to-rak
Wednesday	*srijeda*	sri-*ye*-da
Thursday	*četvrtak*	chet-*vr*-tak
Friday	*petak*	*pe*-tak
Saturday	*subota*	*su*-bo-ta
Sunday	*nedjelja*	*ne*-dye-lya

tools – CROATIAN

January	*siječanj*	si·ye·chan'
February	*veljača*	ve·lya·cha
March	*ožujak*	o·zhu·yak
April	*travanj*	tra·van'
May	*svibanj*	svi·ban'
June	*lipanj*	li·pan'
July	*srpanj*	sr·pan'
August	*kolovoz*	ko·lo·voz
September	*rujan*	ru·yan
October	*listopad*	li·sto·pad
November	*studeni*	stu·de·ni
December	*prosinac*	pro·si·nats

What date is it today?	*Koji je danas datum?*	ko·yi ye da·nas da·tum
It's (18 October).	*(Osamnaesti listopad).*	(o·sam·na·e·sti li·sto·pad)
since (May)	*od (svibnja)*	od (svib·nya)
until (June)	*do (lipnja)*	do (lip·nya)
last night	*sinoć*	si·noch
last week	*prošlog tjedna* ©	prosh·log tyed·na
	prošle nedelje ⓢ	prosh·le ne·de·lye
last month	*prošlog mjeseca*	prosh·log mye·se·tsa
last year	*prošle godine*	prosh·le go·di·ne
next week	*idućeg tjedna* ©	i·du·cheg tyed·na
	iduće nedelje ⓢ	i·du·che ne·de·lye
next month	*idućeg mjeseca*	i·du·che mye·se·tsa
next year	*iduće godine*	i·du·che go·di·ne
yesterday/	*jučer/*	yu·cher/
tomorrow ...	*sutra ...*	su·tra ...
morning	*ujutro*	u·yu·tro
afternoon	*popodne*	po·pod·ne
evening	*uvečer*	u·ve·cher

weather

What's the weather like?	Kakvo je vrijeme?	*kak*·vo ye vri·*ye*·me
It's ...	... je.	... ye
cloudy	Oblačno	o·blach·no
cold	Hladno	*hlad*·no
hot	Vruće	*vru*·che
raining	Kišovito	ki·*sho*·vi·to
snowing	Snjegovito	snye·*go*·vi·to
sunny	Sunčano	*sun*·cha·no
warm	Toplo	*to*·plo
windy	Vjetrovito	vye·*tro*·vi·to
spring	proljeće n	pro·*lye*·che
summer	ljeto n	*lye*·to
autumn	jesen f	*ye*·sen
winter	zima f	*zi*·ma

border crossing

I'm here ...	Ja sam ovdje ...	ya sam *ov*·dye ...
in transit	u prolazu	u *pro*·la·zu
on business	poslovno	*po*·slov·no
on holiday	na odmoru	na *od*·mo·ru
I'm here for ...	Ostajem ovdje ...	o·sta·yem *ov*·dye ...
(10) days	(deset) dana	(*de*·set) *da*·na
(two) months	(dva) mjeseca	(dva) *mye*·se·tsa
(three) weeks	(tri) tjedna ©	(tri) *tyed*·na
	(tri) nedelje Ⓢ	(tri) *ne*·de·lye

I'm going to (Zagreb).
Ja idem u (Zagreb).   ya *i*·dem u (*za*·greb)

I'm staying at the (Intercontinental).
Odsjesti ću u (Interkontinentalu).   *od*·sye·sti chu u (*in*·ter·kon·ti·nen·*ta*·lu)

I have nothing to declare.
Nemam ništa za prijaviti.   *ne*·mam *nish*·ta za pri·*ya*·vi·ti

I have something to declare.
Imam nešto za prijaviti.   *i*·mam *nesh*·to za pri·*ya*·vi·ti

That's (not) mine.
To (ni)je moje.   to (*ni*·)ye *mo*·ye

transport

tickets & luggage

Where can I buy a ticket?
Gdje mogu kupiti kartu?   gdye *mo*-gu *ku*-pi-ti *kar*-tu

Do I need to book a seat?
Trebam li rezervirati mjesto?   *tre*-bam li re-zer-*vi*-ra-ti *myes*-to

One ... ticket	*Jednu ... kartu*	*yed*-nu ... *kar*-tu
(to Split), please.	*(do Splita), molim.*	(do *spli*-ta) *mo*-lim
one-way	*jednosmjernu*	*yed*-no-smyer-nu
return	*povratnu*	*po*-vrat-nu

I'd like to ... my	*Želio/Željela bih ...*	*zhe*-li-o/*zhe*-lye-la bih ...
ticket, please.	*svoju kartu, molim.* m/f	*svoy*-u *kar*-tu *mo*-lim
cancel	*poništiti*	po-ni-shti-ti
change	*promijeniti*	pro-mi-*ye*-ni-ti
collect	*uzeti*	*u*-ze-ti
confirm	*potvrditi*	pot-*vr*-di-ti

I'd like a ...	*Želio/Željela bih ...*	*zhe*-li-o/*zhe*-lye-la bih ...
seat, please.	*sjedište, molim.* m/f	*sye*-dish-te *mo*-lim
nonsmoking	*nepušačko*	*ne*-pu-shach-ko
smoking	*pušačko*	*pu*-shach-ko

How much is it?
Koliko stoji?   ko-*li*-ko *stoy*-i

Is there air conditioning?
Imate li klima-uređaj?   *i*-ma-te li *kli*-ma-*u*-re-jai

Is there a toilet?
Imate li zahod/toalet? ©/⑤   *i*-ma-te li *za*-hod/to-a-*let*

How long does the trip take?
Koliko traje putovanje?   ko-*li*-ko *trai*-e pu-to-*va*-nye

Is it a direct route?
Je li to direktan pravac?   ye li to di-*rek*-tan *pra*-vats

Where can I find a luggage locker?
Gdje se nalazi pretinac/sanduče   gdye se *na*-la-zi *pre*-ti-nats/*san*-du-che
za odlaganje prtljage? ©/⑤   za od-*la*-ga-nye prt-*lya*-ge

My luggage has been ...	Moja prtljaga je ...	moy·a prt·lya·ga ye ...
damaged	oštećena	osh·te·che·na
lost	izgubljena	iz·gub·lye·na
stolen	ukradena	u·kra·de·na

getting around

Where does flight (10) arrive?
Gdje stiže let (deset)?
gdye *sti*·zhe let (*de*·set)

Where does flight (10) depart?
Odakle kreće let (deset)?
o·dak·le *kre*·che let (*de*·set)

Where's (the) ...?	Gdje se nalazi ...?	gdye se na·la·zi ...
arrivals hall	dvorana za dolaske	dvo·ra·na za do·las·ke
departures hall	dvorana za odlaske	dvo·ra·na za od·las·ke
duty-free shop	duty-free	dyu·ti·fri
	prodavaonica	pro·da·va·o·ni·tsa
gate (12)	izlaz (dvanaest)	iz·laz (dva·na·est)

Which ... goes to (Dubrovnik)?	Koji ... ide za (Dubrovnik)?	koy·i ... i·de za (du·brov·nik)
boat	brod	brod
bus	autobus	a·u·to·bus
plane	zrakoplov/avion ©/Ⓢ	zra·ko·plov/a·vi·on
train	vlak/voz ©/Ⓢ	vlak/voz

What time's the ... bus?	Kada ide ... autobus?	ka·da i·de ... a·u·to·bus
first	prvi	pr·vi
last	zadnji	zad·nyi
next	slijedeći	sli·ye·de·chi

At what time does it arrive/leave?
U koliko sati stiže/kreće?
u ko·li·ko sa·ti sti·zhe/kre·che

How long will it be delayed?
Koliko kasni?
ko·li·ko kas·ni

What station/stop is this?
Koja stanica je ovo?
koy·a sta·ni·tsa ye o·vo

What's the next station/stop?
Koja je slijedeća stanica?
koy·a ye sli·ye·de·cha sta·ni·tsa

Does it stop at (Zadar)?
Da li staje u (Zadru)?
da li sta·ye u (zad·ru)

Please tell me when we get to (Pula).
Molim vas recite mi   *mo*·lim vas *re*·tsi·te mi
kada stignemo u (Pulu).   *ka*·da *stig*·ne·mo u (*pu*·lu)

How long do we stop here?
Koliko dugo ostajemo ovdje?   ko·*li*·ko *du*·go o·*stai*·e·mo *ov*·dye

Is this seat available?
Da li je ovo sjedište slobodno?   da li ye *o*·vo *sye*·dish·te *slo*·bod·no

That's my seat.
Ovo je moje sjedište.   *o*·vo ye *moy*·e *sye*·dish·te

I'd like a taxi ...	*Trebam taksi ...*	*tre*·bam *tak*·si ...
at (9am)	*u (devet prijepodne)*	u (*de*·vet *pri*·ye·*pod*·ne)
now	*sada*	*sa*·da
tomorrow	*sutra*	*su*·tra

Is this taxi available?
Da li je ovaj taksi slobodan?   da li ye *o*·vai *tak*·si *slo*·bo·dan

How much is it to ...?
Koliko stoji prijevoz do ...?   ko·*li*·ko *stoy*·i pri·*ye*·voz do ...

Please put the meter on.
Molim uključite taksimetar.   *mo*·lim uk·*lyu*·chi·te *tak*·si·*me*·tar

Please take me to (this address).
Molim da me odvezete   *mo*·lim da me *od*·ve·ze·te
na (ovu adresu).   na (*o*·vu a·*dre*·su)

Please ...	*Molim vas ...*	*mo*·lim vas ...
slow down	*usporite*	u·*spo*·ri·te
stop here	*stanite ovdje*	*sta*·ni·te *ov*·dye
wait here	*pričekajte ovdje*	pri·*che*·kai·te *ov*·dye

car, motorbike & bicycle hire

I'd like to	*Želio/Željela*	*zhe*·li·o/*zhe*·lye·la
hire a ...	*bih iznajmiti ...* m/f	bih iz·*nai*·mi·ti ...
bicycle	*bicikl*	bi·*tsi*·kl
car	*automobil*	a·u·to·*mo*·bil
motorbike	*motocikl*	mo·to·*tsi*·kl
with ...	*sa ...*	sa ...
a driver	*vozačem*	vo·*za*·chem
air conditioning	*klima-uređajem*	*kli*·ma·u·re·jai·em

How much for ... hire?	*Koliko stoji najam po ...?*	ko·*li*·ko *stoy*·i *nai*·am po ...
hourly	*satu*	*sa*·tu
daily	*danu*	*da*·nu
weekly	*tjednu/nedelji* ©/⑤	*tyed*·nu/*ne*·de·lyi

air	*zrak/vazduh* m ©/⑤	zrak/*vaz*·duh
oil	*ulje* n	*u*·lye
petrol	*benzin* m	*ben*·zin
tyres	*gume* f pl	*gu*·me

I need a mechanic.
  Trebam automehaničara.   *tre*·bam *a*·u·to·me·*ha*·ni·cha·ra

I've run out of petrol.
  Nestalo mi je benzina.   *ne*·sta·lo mi ye ben·*zi*·na

I have a flat tyre.
  Imam probušenu gumu.   *i*·mam *pro*·bu·she·nu *gu*·mu

directions

Where's the ...?	*Gdje je ...?*	gdye ye ...
bank	*banka*	*ban*·ka
city centre	*gradski centar*	*grad*·ski *tsen*·tar
hotel	*hotel*	*ho*·tel
market	*tržnica/pijaca* ©/⑤	*trzh*·ni·tsa/*pi*·ya·tsa
police station	*policijska stanica*	po·*li*·tsiy·ska *sta*·ni·tsa
post office	*poštanski ured*	*po*·shtan·ski *u*·red
public toilet	*javni zahod/toalet* ©/⑤	*yav*·ni za·hod/to·a·*let*
tourist office	*turistička agencija*	tu·*ris*·tich·ka a·*gen*·tsi·ya

Is this the road to (Pazin)?
  Je li ovo cesta/put za (Pazin)? ©/⑤   ye li *o*·vo *tse*·sta/put za (*pa*·zin)

Can you show me (on the map)?
  Možete li mi to   *mo*·zhe·te li mi to
  pokazati (na karti)?   po·*ka*·za·ti (na *kar*·ti)

What's the address?
  Koja je adresa?   *koy*·a ye a·*dre*·sa

How far is it?
  Koliko je udaljeno?   ko·*li*·ko ye *u*·da·lye·no

How do I get there?
  Kako mogu tamo stići?   *ka*·ko *mo*·gu *ta*·mo *sti*·chi

Turn ...	Skrenite ...	skre·ni·te ...
at the corner	na uglu	na u·glu
at the traffic lights	na semaforu	na se·ma·fo·ru
left/right	lijevo/desno	li·ye·vo/de·sno

It's ...	Nalazi se ...	na·la·zi se ...
behind ...	iza ...	i·za ...
far away	daleko	da·le·ko
here	ovdje	ov·dye
in front of ...	ispred ...	i·spred ...
left	lijevo	li·ye·vo
near ...	blizu ...	bli·zu ...
next to ...	pored ...	po·red ...
on the corner	na uglu	na u·glu
opposite ...	nasuprot ...	na·su·prot ...
right	desno	de·sno
straight ahead	ravno naprijed	rav·no na·pri·yed
there	tamo	ta·mo

by bus	autobusom	a·u·to·bu·som
by taxi	taksijem	tak·si·yem
by train	vlakom/vozom ©/⑤	vla·kom/vo·zom
on foot	pješke	pyesh·ke

north	sjever m	sye·ver
south	jug m	yug
east	istok m	is·tok
west	zapad m	za·pad

signs

Ulaz/Izlaz	u·laz/iz·laz	**Entrance/Exit**
Otvoreno/Zatvoreno	ot vo·re·no/zat vo·re·no	**Open/Closed**
Slobodna Mjesta	slo·bod·na mye·sta	**Rooms Available**
Bez Slobodnih Mjesta	bez slo·bod·nih mye·sta	**No Vacancies**
Informacije	in·for·ma·tsi·ye	**Information**
Policijska Stanica	po·li·tsiy·ska sta·ni·tsa	**Police Station**
Zabranjeno	za·bra·nye·no	**Prohibited**
WC	ve·tse	**Toilets**
Muški	mush·ki	**Men**
Ženski	zhen·ski	**Women**
Toplo/Hladno	to·plo/hlad·no	**Hot/Cold**

accommodation

finding accommodation

Where's a ...?	Gdje se nalazi ...?	gdye se *na*-la-zi ...
camping ground	kamp	kamp
guesthouse	privatni smještaj	*pri*-vat-ni *smyesh*-tai
	za najam	za *nai*-am
hotel	hotel	*ho*-tel
youth hostel	prenočište za	pre-no-*chish*-te za
	mladež	*mla*-dezh

Can you recommend	Možete li	*mo*-zhe-te li
somewhere ...?	preporučiti negdje ...?	pre-po-*ru*-chi-ti *neg*-dye ...
cheap	jeftino	*yef*-ti-no
good	dobro	*do*-bro
nearby	blizu	*bli*-zu

I'd like to book a room, please.
Želio/Željela bih rezervirati *zhe*-li-o/*zhe*-lye-la bih re-zer-*vi*-ra-ti
sobu, molim. m/f *so*-bu *mo*-lim

I have a reservation.
Imam rezervaciju. *i*-mam re-zer-*va*-tsi-yu

My name's ...
Moje ime je ... *moy*-e *i*-me ye ...

Do you have a ...	Imate li ...?	*i*-ma-te li ...
room?		
single	jednokrevetnu sobu	*yed*-no-*kre*-vet-nu *so*-bu
double	sobu sa duplim	*so*-bu sa *dup*-lim
	krevetom	*kre*-ve-tom
twin	dvokrevetnu sobu	*dvo*-kre-vet-nu *so*-bu

How much is it per ...?	Koliko stoji po ...?	ko-*li*-ko *sto*-yi po ...
night	noći	*no*-chi
person	osobi	*o*-so-bi

Can I pay by ...?	Mogu li platiti sa ...?	*mo*-gu li *pla*-ti-ti sa ...
credit card	kreditnom	*kre*-dit-nom
	karticom	*kar*-ti-tsom
travellers cheque	putničkim čekom	*put*-nich-kim *che*-kom

For (three) nights.
Na (tri) noći. na (tri) *no*·chi

From (2 July) to (6 July).
Od (drugog srpnja) do od (*dru*·gog *srp*·nya) do
(šestog srpnja). (*she*·stog *srp*·nya)

Can I see it?
Mogu li je vidjeti? *mo*·gu li ye *vi*·dye·ti

Am I allowed to camp here?
Mogu li ovdje kampirati? *mo*·gu li *ov*·dye kam·*pi*·ra·ti

Where can I find the nearest camp site?
Gdje se nalazi najbliže gdye se *na*·la·zi *nai*·bli·zhe
mjesto za kampiranje? *mye*·sto za kam·*pi*·ra·nye

requests & queries

When/Where is breakfast served?
Kada/Gdje služite doručak? *ka*·da/gdye *slu*·zhi·te *do*·ru·chak

Please wake me at (seven).
Probudite me u (sedam), molim. pro·*bu*·di·te me u (*se*·dam) *mo*·lim

Could I have my key, please?
Mogu li dobiti moj *mo*·gu li *do*·bi·ti moy
ključ, molim? klyuch *mo*·lim

Could I have another (blanket)?
Mogu li dobiti jednu dodatnu *mo*·gu li *do*·bi·ti *yed*·nu *do*·dat·nu
(deku)? (*de*·ku)

Is there a/an ...?	*Imate li ...?*	*i*·ma·te li ...
elevator	*dizalo/lift* ©/Ⓢ	*di*·za·lo/lift
safe	*sef*	sef

The room is too ...	*Suviše je ...*	*su*·vi·she ye ...
expensive	*skupo*	*sku*·po
noisy	*bučno*	*buch*·no
small	*malo*	*ma*·lo

The ... doesn't work.	*... je neispravan.*	... ye ne·i·spra·van
air conditioning	*Klima-uređaj*	*kli*·ma·u·re·jai
fan	*Ventilator*	ven·ti·*la*·tor
toilet	*Zahod/Toalet* ©/Ⓢ	*za*·hod/to·a·let

This ... isn't clean.	Ova ... nije čista.	o·va ... ni·ye chis·ta
blanket	deka	de·ka
sheet	plahta ©	plah·ta

This ... isn't clean.	Ovaj ... nije čist.	o·va ... ni·ye chist
sheet	čaršav ⑤	char·shav
towel	ručnik/peškir ©/⑤	ruch·nik/pesh·kir

checking out

What time is checkout?
U koliko sati treba napustiti sobu?   u ko·li·ko sa·ti tre·ba na·pu·sti·ti so·bu

Can I leave my luggage here?
Mogu li ovdje ostaviti svoje torbe?   mo·gu li ov·dye o·sta·vi·ti svoy·e tor·be

Could I have	Mogu li dobiti	mo·gu li do·bi·ti
my ..., please?	..., molim?	... mo·lim
deposit	svoj depozit	svoy de·po·zit
passport	svoju putovnicu/	svoy·u pu·tov·ni·tsu/
	pasoš ©/⑤	pa·sosh
valuables	svoje dragocjenosti	svo·ye dra·go·tsye·no·sti

communications & banking

the internet

Where's the local Internet café?
Gdje je mjesni internet kafić?   gdye ye mye·sni in·ter·net ka·fich

How much is it per hour?
Koja je cijena po satu?   koy·a ye tsi·ye·na po sa·tu

I'd like to ...	Želio/Željela bih ... m/f	zhe·li·o/zhe·lye·la bih ...
check my email	provjeriti svoj email	pro·vye·ri·ti svoy i·meyl
get Internet access	pristup internetu	pri·stup in·ter·ne·tu
use a printer	koristiti pisač/	ko·ri·sti·ti pi·sach/
	štampač ©/⑤	shtam·pach
use a scanner	koristiti skener	ko·ri·sti·ti ske·ner

mobile/cell phone

I'd like a ...
Trebao/Trebala bih ... m/f
tre·ba·o/tre·ba·la bih ...

| mobile/cell phone for hire | *iznajmiti mobilni telefon* | iz·nai·mi·ti mo·bil·ni te·le·fon |
| SIM card for your network | *SIM karticu za vašu mrežu* | sim kar·ti·tsu za va·shu mre·zhu |

What are the rates?
Koje su cijene telefoniranja?
ko·ye su tsi·ye·ne te·le·fo·ni·ra·nya

telephone

What's your phone number?
Koji je vaš/tvoj broj telefona? pol/inf
koy·i ye vash/tvoy broy te·le·fo·na

The number is ...
Broj je ...
broy ye ...

Where's the nearest public phone?
Gdje je najbliži javni telefon?
gdye ye nai·bli·zhi yav·ni te·le·fon

I'd like to buy a phonecard.
Želim kupiti telefonsku karticu.
zhe·lim ku·pi·ti te·le·fon·sku kar·ti·tsu

I want to ...
Želim ...
zhe·lim ...

call (Singapore)	*nazvati (Singapur)*	naz·va·ti (sin·ga·pur)
make a (local) call	*obaviti (lokalni) poziv*	o·ba·vi·ti (lo·kal·ni) po·ziv
reverse the charges	*obaviti poziv na račun pozvanog*	o·ba·vi·ti po·ziv na ra·chun poz·va·nog

How much does ... cost?
Koliko košta ...?
ko·li·ko kosh·ta ...

| a (three)-minute call | *poziv od (tri) minute* | po·ziv od (tri) mi·nu·te |
| each extra minute | *svaka naknadna minuta* | sva·ka nak·nad·na mi·nu·ta |

| (3 kuna) per (30) seconds. | *(3 kune) po (30) sekundi.* | (tri ku·ne) po (tri·de·set) se·kun·di |

post office

I want to send a ...	Želim poslati ...	zhe·lim po·sla·ti ...
fax	telefaks	te·le·faks
letter	pismo	pi·smo
parcel	paket	pa·ket
postcard	dopisnicu	do·pi·sni·tsu

I want to buy a/an ...	Želim kupiti ...	zhe·lim ku·pi·ti ...
envelope	omotnicu/koverat ©/ⓢ	o·mot·ni·tsu/ko·ve·rat
stamp	poštansku marku	posh·tan·sku mar·ku

Please send it by ... to (Australia).	Molim da pošaljete to ... u (Australiju).	mo·lim da po·sha·lye·te to ... u (a·u·stra·li·yu)
airmail	zračnom/vazdušnom poštom ©/ⓢ	zrach·nom/vaz·dush·nom posh·tom
express mail	ekspres poštom	eks·pres posh·tom
registered mail	preporučenom poštom	pre·po·ru·che·nom posh·tom
surface mail	običnom poštom	o·bich·nom posh·tom

Is there any mail for me?
Ima li bilo kakve pošte za mene?   i·ma li bi·lo kak·ve posh·te za me·ne

bank

Where's a/an ...?	Gdje se nalazi ...?	gdye se na·la·zi ...
ATM	bankovni automat	ban·kov·ni a·u·to·mat
foreign exchange office	mjenjačnica za strane valute	mye·nyach·ni·tsa za stra·ne va·lu·te

Where can I ...?	Gdje mogu ...?	gdye mo·gu ...
I'd like to ...	Želio/Željela bih ... m/f	zhe·li·o/zhe·lye·la bih ...
arrange a transfer	obaviti prijenos novca	o·ba·vi·ti pri·ye·nos nov·tsa
cash a cheque	unovčiti ček	u·nov·chi·ti chek
change a travellers cheque	zamijeniti putnički ček	za·mi·ye·ni·ti put·nich·ki chek
change money	zamijeniti novac	za·mi·ye·ni·ti no·vats
get a cash advance	uzeti predujam/avans u gotovini ©/ⓢ	u·ze·ti pre·du·yam/a·vans u go·to·vi·ni
withdraw money	podignuti novac	po·dig·nu·ti no·vats

What's the …?	Koji/Kolika je …? m/f	koy·i/ko·li·ka ye …
charge for that	pristojba/tarifa	pri·stoy·ba/ta·ri·fa
	za to f ©/⑤	za to
exchange rate	tečaj/kurs	te·chai/kurs
	razmjene m ©/⑤	raz·mye·ne

It's …	To je …	to ye …
(50) kuna	(pedeset) kuna	(pe·de·set) ku·na
free	besplatno	bes·plat·no

What time does the bank open?
U koliko sati se otvara banka? u ko·li·ko sa·ti se ot·va·ra ban·ka

Has my money arrived yet?
Da li je moj novac stigao? da li ye moy no·vats sti·ga·o

sightseeing

getting in

What time does it open/close?
U koliko sati se otvara/zatvara? u ko·li·ko sa·ti se ot·va·ra/zat·va·ra

What's the admission charge?
Koliko stoji ulaznica? ko·li·ko stoy·i u·laz·ni·tsa

Is there a discount for students/children?
Imate li popust za i·ma·te li po·pust za
studente/djecu? stu·den·te/dye·tsu

I'd like a …	Želio/Željela bih … m/f	zhe·li·o/zhe·lye·la bih …
catalogue	katalog	ka·ta·log
guide	turistički vodič	tu·ri·stich·ki vo·dich
local map	kartu mjesta	kar·tu mye·sta

I'd like to see …
Želio/Željela bih vidjeti … m/f zhe·li·o/zhe·lye·la bih vi dye·ti …

What's that?
Što je to? shto ye to

Can I take a photo?
Mogu li slikati? mo·gu li sli·ka·ti

tours

When's the next ...?	*Kada je idući/ iduća ...?* m/f	*ka*·da ye *i*·du·chi/ *i*·du·cha ...
day trip	*dnevni izlet* m	*dnev*·ni *iz*·let
tour	*turistička ekskurzija* f	tu·*ri*·stich·ka ek·*skur*·zi·ya
Is ... included?	*Da li je ... uključen/ uključena?* m/f	da li ye ... uk·lyu·chen/ uk·lyu·che·na
accommodation	*smještaj* m	*smye*·shtai
the admission charge	*ulaznica*	u·*laz*·ni·tsa
food	*hrana* f	*hra*·na
transport	*prijevoz* m	pri·*ye*·voz

How long is the tour?

Koliko traje ekskurzija?		ko·*li*·ko *trai*·e ek·*skur*·zi·ya

What time should we be back?

U koje bi se vrijeme trebali vratiti?		u *koy*·e bi se vri·*ye*·me *tre*·ba·li *vra*·ti·ti

sightseeing

castle	*dvorac* m	*dwa*·rats
cathedral	*katedrala* f	ka·te·*dra*·la
church	*crkva* f	*tsr*·kva
main square	*glavni trg* m	*glav*·ni trg
monastery	*samostan/manastir* m ©/⑤	sa·mo·stan/*ma*·nas·tir
monument	*spomenik* m	*spo*·me·nik
museum	*muzej* m	*mu*·zey
old city	*stari grad* m	*sta*·ri grad
palace	*palača* f	*pa*·la·cha
ruins	*ruševine* f pl	*ru*·she·vi·ne
stadium	*stadion* m	*sta*·di·on
statue	*kip* m	kip

shopping

enquiries

Where's a ...?	Gdje je ...?	gdye ye ...
bank	banka	*ban*·ka
bookshop	knjižara	*knyi*·zha·ra
camera shop	prodavaonica	pro·da·va·*o*·ni·tsa
	fotoaparata	*fo*·to·a·pa·*ra*·ta
department store	robna kuća	*rob*·na *ku*·cha
grocery store	prodavaonica	pro·da·va·*o*·ni·tsa
	namirnica	*na*·mir·ni·tsa
market	tržnica/pijaca ©/⑤	*tr*·zhni·tsa/*pi*·ya·tsa
newsagency	prodavaonica	pro·da·va·*o*·ni·tsa
	novina	*no*·vi·na
supermarket	supermarket	su·per·*mar*·ket

Where can I buy (a padlock)?
Gdje mogu kupiti (lokot)?   gdye *mo*·gu *ku*·pi·ti (*lo*·kot)

I'm looking for ...
Tražim ...   *tra*·zhim

Can I look at it?
Mogu li to pogledati?   *mo*·gu li to po·*gle*·da·ti

Do you have any others?
Imate li bilo kakve druge?   *i*·ma·te li *bi*·lo *kak*·ve *dru*·ge

Does it have a guarantee?
Ima li ovo garanciju?   *i*·ma li *o*·vo ga·*ran*·tsi·yu

Can I have it sent abroad?
Možete li mi to   *mo*·zhe·te li mi to
poslati u inozemstvo?   po·*sla*·ti u i·no·*zemst*·vo

Can I have my (backpack) repaired?
Mogu li popraviti svoj (ranac)?   *mo*·gu li po·*pra*·vi·ti svoy (*ra*·nats)

It's faulty.
Neispravno je.   ne·*is*·prav·no ye

I'd like ..., please.	Želio/Željela bih ... m/f	zhe·li·o/zhe·lye·la bih ...
a bag	vrećicu	*vre*·chi·tsu
a refund	povrat novca	*pov*·rat *nov*·tsa
to return this	ovo vratiti	*o*·vo *vra*·ti·ti

paying

How much is it?
Koliko stoji/košta? ©/⑤
ko·*li*·ko *sto*·yi/*kosh*·ta

Can you write down the price?
Možete li napisati cijenu?
mo·zhe·te li na·*pi*·sa·ti tsi·*ye*·nu

That's too expensive.
To je preskupo.
to ye *pre*·sku·po

Do you have something cheaper?
Imate li nešto jeftinije?
i·ma·te li *nesh*·to yef·*ti*·ni·ye

I'll give you (five kuna).
Dati ću vam (pet kuna).
da·ti chu vam (pet *ku*·na)

There's a mistake in the bill.
Ima jedna greška na računu.
i·ma yed·na *gresh*·ka na ra·*chu*·nu

Do you accept ...?	*Da li prihvaćate ...?*	da li *pri*·hva·cha·te ...
credit cards	*kreditne kartice*	*kre*·dit·ne *kar*·ti·tse
debit cards	*debitne kartice*	*de*·bit·ne *kar*·ti·tse
travellers cheques	*putničke čekove*	*put*·nich·ke *che*·ko·ve

I'd like ..., please.	*Želio/Željela bih ...* **m/f**	zhe·li·o/zhe·lye·la bih ...
a receipt	*račun*	*ra*·chun
my change	*moj ostatak novca*	moy o·*sta*·tak *nov*·tsa

clothes & shoes

Can I try it on?	*Mogu li to probati?*	*mo*·gu li to *pro*·ba·ti
My size is (40).	*Moja veličina je (četrdeset).*	*moy*·a ve·li·*chi*·na ye (che·tr·*de*·set)
It doesn't fit.	*Ne odgovara mi to.*	ne od·*go*·va·ra mi to
small	*sitna*	*sit*·na
medium	*srednja*	*sred*·nya
large	*krupna*	*krup*·na

books & music

I'd like (a) ...	*Želio/Željela bih ...* m/f	*zhe·li·o/zhe·lye·la bih ...*
newspaper	*novine*	*no·vi·ne*
(in English)	*(na engleskom)*	*(na en·gles·kom)*
pen	*kemijsku*	*ke·miy·sku*

Is there an English-language bookshop?
Postoji li knjižara za — *po·stoy·i li knyi·zha·ra za*
engleski jezik? — *en·gle·ski ye·zik*

I'm looking for something by (Oliver Dragojević).
Tražim nešto od — *tra·zhim nesh·to od*
(Olivera Dragojevića). — *(o·li·ve·ra dra·goy·e·vi·cha)*

Can I listen to this?
Mogu li ovo poslušati? — *mo·gu li o·vo po·slu·sha·ti*

photography

Can you ...?	*Možete li ...?*	*mo·zhe·te li ...*
develop this film	*razviti ovaj film*	*raz·vi·ti o·vai film*
load my film	*staviti moj film*	*sta·vi·ti moy film*
	u foto-aparat	*u fo·to·a·pa·rat*
transfer photos	*prebaciti*	*pre·ba·tsi·ti*
from my	*fotografije sa*	*fo·to·gra·fi·ye sa*
camera to CD	*mog aparata na CD*	*mog a·pa·ra·ta na tse de*

I need a/an ... film	*Trebam ... film*	*tre·bam ... film*
for this camera.	*za ovaj foto-aparat.*	*za o·vai fo·to·a·pa·rat*
APS	*APS*	*a pe es*
B&W	*crno-bijeli*	*tsr·no·bi·ye·li*
colour	*kolor*	*ko·lor*

I need a ... film	*Trebam film ...*	*tre·bam film ...*
for this camera.	*za ovaj foto-aparat.*	*za o·vai fo·to·a·pa·rat*
slide	*za dijapozitive*	*za di·ya·po·zi·ti·ve*
(200) speed	*brzine (dvijesto)*	*br·zi·ne (dvi·ye·sto)*

When will it	*Kada će to biti*	*ka·da che to bi·ti*
be ready?	*gotovo?*	*go·to·vo*

meeting people

greetings, goodbyes & introductions

Hello.	*Bog/Zdravo.* ©/⑤	bog/*zdra*·vo
Hi.	*Ćao.*	*cha*·o
Good night.	*Laku noć.*	*la*·ku noch
Goodbye.	*Zbogom.*	*zbo*·gom
Bye.	*Ćao.*	*cha*·o
See you later.	*Doviđenja.*	do·vi·*je*·nya
Mr	*Gospodin*	go·*spo*·din
Mrs	*Gospođa*	go·*spo*·ja
Miss	*Gospođica*	go·spo·ji·tsa
How are you?	*Kako ste/si?* pol/inf	*ka*·ko ste/si
Fine. And you?	*Dobro. A vi/ti?* pol/inf	*do*·bro a vi/ti
What's your name?	*Kako se zovete/zoveš?* pol/inf	*ka*·ko se zo·ve·te/zo·vesh
My name is ...	*Zovem se ...*	*zo*·vem se ...
I'm pleased to	*Drago mi je da smo se*	*dra*·go mi ye da smo se
meet you.	*upoznali.*	u·*poz*·na·li

This is my ...	*Ovo je moj/moja ...* m/f	*o*·vo ye moy/*moy*·a ...
boyfriend	*dečko*	*dech*·ko
brother	*brat*	brat
daughter	*ćerka*	*cher*·ka
father	*otac*	*o*·tats
friend	*prijatelj/prijateljica* m/f	pri·ya·*tel'*/pri·ya·*te*·lyi·tsa
girlfriend	*cura/devojka* ©/⑤	*tsu*·ra/*de*·voy·ka
husband	*muž*	muzh
mother	*majka*	*mai*·ka
partner (intimate)	*suprug/supruga* m/f	*su*·prug/*su*·pru·ga
sister	*sestra*	*ses*·tra
son	*sin*	sin
wife	*žena*	*zhe*·na

Here's my ...	*Ovo je moj/moja ...* m/f	*o*·vo ye moy/*moy*·a ...
What's your ...?	*Koji je tvoj ...?* m	*koy*·i ye tvoy ...
	Koja je tvoja ...? f	*koy*·a ye tvoy·a ...
(email) address	*(email) adresa* f	(i·meyl) a·*dre*·sa
fax number	*broj faksa* m	broy *fak*·sa
phone number	*broj telefona* m	broy te·le·*fo*·na

occupations

What's your occupation?	Čime se bavite?	*chi*·me se *ba*·vi·te
I'm a/an ...	Ja sam ...	ya sam ...
artist	umjetnik m	*um*·yet·nik
	umjetnica f	*um*·yet·ni·tsa
businessperson	poslovna osoba	po·*slo*·vna *o*·so·ba
farmer	poljodjelac ©	po·lyo·*dye*·lats
	zemljoradnik ⓢ	zem·lyo·*rad*·nik
office worker	službenik m	*sluzh*·be·nik
	službenica f	*sluzh*·be·ni·tsa
scientist	znanstvenik ©	*znans*·tve·nik
	naučnik ⓢ	*na*·uch·nik
tradesperson	zanatlija	za·*nat*·li·ya

background

Where are you from?	Odakle ste?	o·*da*·kle ste
I'm from ...	Ja sam iz ...	ya sam iz ...
Australia	Australije	a·u·*stra*·li·ye
Canada	Kanade	ka·na·de
England	Engleske	*en*·gles·ke
New Zealand	Novog Zelanda	*no*·vog ze·lan·da
the USA	Amerike	a·*me*·ri·ke
Are you married?	Jeste li vi vjenčani?	*ye*·ste li vi *vyen*·cha·ni
I'm married.	Ja sam u braku.	ya sam u *bra*·ku
I'm single.	Ja sam neoženjen. m	ya sam ne·*o*·zhe·nyen
	Ja sam neudata. f	ya sam *ne*·u·da·ta

age

How old ...?	Koliko ... godina?	ko·*li*·ko ... *go*·di·na
are you	imate/imaš pol/inf	*i*·ma·te/*i*·mash
is your daughter	vaša kći ima	*va*·sha k·*chi i*·ma
is your son	vaš sin ima	vash sin *i*·ma
I'm ... years old.	Imam ... godina.	*i*·mam ... *go*·di·na
He/She is ... years old.	On/Ona ima ... godina.	on/*o*·na *i*·ma ... *go*·di·na

feelings

I'm (not) ...	Ja (ni)sam ...	ya (ni·)sam ...
Are you ...?	Jeste li ...?	ye·ste li ...
happy	sretni	sret·ni
hungry	gladni	glad·ni
OK	dobro	dob·ro
sad	tužni	tuzh·ni
thirsty	žedni	zhed·ni
tired	umorni	u·mor·ni

Are you hot/cold?
Je li vam toplo/hladno?   ye li vam to·plo/hlad·no

I'm (not) hot/cold.
Meni (ni)je toplo/hladno.   me·ni (ni·)ye to·plo/hlad·no

entertainment

going out

Where can	Gdje mogu	gdye mo·gu
I find ...?	pronaći ...?	pro·na·chi ...
clubs	noćne klubove	noch·ne klu·bo·ve
gay venues	gay lokale	gey lo·ka·le
pubs	gostionice	go·sti·o·ni·tse

I feel like going to a/the ...	Želim otići ...	zhe·lim o·ti·chi ...
concert	na koncert	na kon·tsert
movies	u kino/bioskop ©/⑤	u ki·no/bi·os·kop
party	na zabavu	na za·ba·vu
restaurant	u restoran	u re·sto·ran
theatre	u kazalište	u ka·za·lish·te

interests

Do you like ...?	Volite li ...?	vo·li·te li ...
I (don't) like ...	Ja (ne) volim ...	ya (ne) vo·lim ...
art	umjetnost	um·yet·nost
cooking	kuhanje	ku·ha·nye
movies	filmove	fil·mo·ve
reading	čitanje	chi·ta·nye
shopping	kupovanje	ku·po·va·nye
sport	sport	sport
travelling	putovanja	pu·to·va·nya
Do you like to ...?	Da li volite da ...?	da li vo·li·te da ...
dance	plešete	ple·she·te
listen to music	slušate glazbu/	slu·sha·te glaz·bu/
	muziku ©/Ⓢ	mu·zi·ku

food & drink

finding a place to eat

Can you recommend a ...?	Možete li preporučiti neki ...?	mo·zhe·te li pre·po·ru·chi·ti ne·ki ...
bar	bar	bar
café	kafić	ka·fich
restaurant	restoran	re·sto·ran
I'd like ...	Želim ...	zhe·lim ...
a table for (five)	stol za (petoro)	stol za (pe·to·ro)
the (non)smoking section	(ne)pušačko mjesto	(ne·)pu·shach·ko mye·sto

ordering food

breakfast	doručak m	do·ru·chak
lunch	ručak m	ru·chak
dinner	večera f	ve·che·ra
snack	užina f	u·zhi·na
today's special	specijalitet dana m	spe·tsi·ya·li·tet da·na

What would you recommend?	Što biste nam preporučili?	shto *bi*·ste nam pre·po·*ru*·chi·li
I'd like (the) ..., please.	Mogu li dobiti ..., molim?	*mo*·gu li *do*·bi·ti ... *mo*·lim
bill	račun	*ra*·chun
drink list	cjenik pića	*tsye*·nik *pi*·cha
menu	jelovnik	*ye*·lov·nik
that dish	ono jelo	*o*·no *ye*·lo

drinks

coffee/tea ...	kava/čaj ...	*ka*·va/chai ...
with milk	sa mlijekom	sa mli·*ye*·kom
without sugar	bez šećera	bez *she*·che·ra
(orange) juice	sok (od naranče) m	sok (od *na*·ran·che)
mineral water	mineralna voda f	*mi*·ne·ral·na *vo*·da
soft drink	bezalkoholno piće m	be·zal·ko·hol·no *pi*·che
(hot) water	(topla) voda f	(*to*·pla) *vo*·da

in the bar

I'll have ...	Želim naručiti ...	*zhe*·lim na·*ru*·chi·ti ...
I'll buy you a drink.	Častim vas/te pićem. pol/inf	*cha*·stim vas/te *pi*·chem
What would you like?	Što želite/želiš? pol/inf	shto *zhe*·li·te/*zhe*·lish
Cheers!	Živjeli!	*zhi*·vye·li

brandy	rakija f	*ra*·ki·ya
champagne	šampanjac m	sham·*pa*·nyats
cocktail	koktel m	kok·*tel*
plum brandy	šljivovica f	*shlyi*·vo·vi·tsa

| a bottle/glass of beer | boca/čaša piva | *bo*·tsa/*cha*·sha *pi*·va |
| a shot of (whiskey) | jedna čašica (viskija) | *yed*·na *cha*·shi·tsa (*vi*·ski·ya) |

a bottle/glass of ... wine	boca/čaša ... vina	*bo*·tsa/*cha*·sha ... *vi*·na
red	crnog	*tsr*·nog
sparkling	pjenušavog	pye·*nu*·sha·vog
white	bijelog	bi·*ye*·log

self-catering

What's the local speciality?
Što je ovdje područni/lokalni　ⓒ/ⓢ
specijalitet?

shto ye *ov*·dye *po*·druch·ni/*lo*·kal·ni
spe·tsi·ya·*li*·tet

What's that?
Što je to?

shto ye to

How much is (a kilo of cheese)?
Koliko stoji/košta (kila sira)?　ⓒ/ⓢ

ko·*li*·ko *sto*·yi/*kosh*·ta (*ki*·la *si*·ra)

I'd like ...	*Želim ...*	zhe·lim ...
(200) grams	*(dvijesto) grama*	(dvi·ye·sto) *gra*·ma
(two) kilos	*(dvije) kile*	(dvi·ye) *ki*·le
(three) pieces	*(tri) komada*	(tri) ko·*ma*·da
(six) slices	*(šest) krišaka*	(shest) *kri*·sha·ka

Less.	*Manje.*	*ma*·nye
Enough.	*Dosta.*	*do*·sta
More.	*Više.*	vi·she

special diets & allergies

Is there a vegetarian restaurant near here?
Da li znate za vegetarijanski
restoran ovdje blizu?

da li *zna*·te za ve·ge·ta·*ri*·yan·ski
re·*sto*·ran *ov*·dye *bli*·zu

Do you have vegetarian food?
Da li imate vegetarijanski obrok?

da li *i*·ma·te ve·ge·ta·*ri*·yan·ski *o*·brok

Could you prepare a meal without ...?	*Možete li prirediti obrok koji ne sadrži ...?*	mo·zhe·te li pri·*re*·di·ti *o*·brok koy·i ne *sa*·dr·zhi ...
butter	*maslac*	*ma*·slats
eggs	*jaja*	*yai*·a
meat stock	*mesni bujon*	*mes*·ni *bu*·yon

I'm allergic to ...	*Ja sam alergičan/ alergična na ...* m/f	ya sam a·*ler*·gi·chan/ a·*ler*·gich·na na ...
dairy produce	*mliječne proizvode*	mli·*yech*·ne pro·*iz*·vo·de
gluten	*gluten*	*glu*·ten
MSG	*glutaminat*	glu·ta·mi·*nat*
nuts	*razne orahe*	*raz*·ne o·ra·he
seafood	*morske plodove*	*mor*·ske *plo*·do·ve

emergencies

basics

Help!	*Upomoć!*	*u*·po·moch
Stop!	*Stanite!*	*sta*·ni·te
Go away!	*Maknite se!*	*mak*·ni·te se
Thief!	*Lopov!*	*lo*·pov
Fire!	*Požar!*	*po*·zhar
Watch out!	*Pazite!*	*pa*·zi·te

Call ...!	*Zovite ...!*	*zo*·vi·te ...
a doctor	*liječnika/lekara* ©/ⓢ	li·*yech*·ni·ka/le·*ka*·ra
an ambulance	*hitnu pomoć*	*hit*·nu *po*·moch
the police	*policiju*	po·*li*·tsi·yu

It's an emergency!
Imamo hitan slučaj.   *i*·ma·mo *hi*·tan *slu*·chai

Could you help me, please?
Molim vas, možete li mi pomoći?   *mo*·lim vas *mo*·zhe·te li mi *po*·mo·chi

Can I use your phone?
Mogu li koristiti vaš telefon?   *mo*·gu li ko·*ri*·sti·ti vash te·*le*·fon

I'm lost.
Izgubio/Izgubila sam se. m/f   iz·*gu*·bi·o/iz·*gu*·bi·la sam se

Where are the toilets?
Gdje se nalaze zahodi/toaleti? ©/ⓢ   gdye se *na*·la·ze *za*·ho·di/to·a·*le*·ti

police

Where's the police station?
Gdje se nalazi policijska stanica?   gdye se *na*·la·zi po·*li*·tsiy·ska *sta*·ni·tsa

I want to report an offence.
Želim prijaviti prekršaj.   *zhe*·lim pri·*ya*·vi·ti *pre*·kr·shai

I have insurance.
Imam osiguranje.   *i*·mam o·si·gu·*ra*·nye

I've been ...	*Ja sam bio/bila ...* m/f	ya sam *bi*·o/*bi*·la ...
assaulted	*napadnut/napadnuta* m/f	na·*pad*·nut/na·*pad*·nu·ta
raped	*silovan/silovana* m/f	*si*·lo·van/*si*·lo·va·na
robbed	*opljačkan* m	op·*lyach*·kan
	opljačkana f	op·*lyach*·ka·na

My ... was/were stolen.	*Ukrali su mi ...*	u·kra·li su mi ...
I've lost my ...	*Izgubio/Izgubila*	iz·gu·bi·o/iz·gu·bi·la
	sam ... m/f	sam ...
backpack	*svoj ranac*	svoy ra·nats
bags	*svoje torbe*	svoy·e tor·be
credit card	*svoju kreditnu*	svoy·oo kre·dit·nu
	karticu	kar·ti·tsu
jewellery	*svoj nakit*	svoy na·kit
money	*svoj novac*	svoy no·vats
passport	*svoju putovnicu* ⓒ	svoy·oo pu·tov·ni·tsu
	svoj pasoš ⓢ	svoy pa·sosh
travellers cheques	*svoje putničke*	svoy·e put·nich·ke
	čekove	che·ko·ve
I want to contact	*Želim stupiti u*	zhe·lim stu·pi·ti u
my ...	*kontakt sa ...*	kon·takt sa ...
consulate	*svojom ambasadom*	svoy·om am·ba·sa·dom
embassy	*svojim konzulatom*	svoy·im kon·zu·la·tom

health

medical needs

Where's the	*Gdje je najbliži/*	gdye ye nai·bli·zhi/
nearest ...?	*najbliža ...?* m/f	nai·bli·zha ...
dentist	*zubar* m	zu·bar
doctor	*liječnik/lekar* m ⓒ/ⓢ	li·yech·nik/le·kar
hospital	*bolnica* f	bol·ni·tsa
(night) pharmacist	*(noćna) ljekarna/*	(noch·na) lye·kar·na
	apoteka f ⓒ/ⓢ	a·po·te·ka

I need a doctor (who speaks English).
Trebam liječnika/lekara   tre·bam li·yech·ni·ka/le·ka·ra
(koji govori engleski). ⓒ/ⓢ   (koy·i go·vo·ri en·gle·ski)

Could I see a female doctor?
Mogu li dobiti ženskog   mo·gu li do·bi·ti zhen·skog
liječnika/lekara? ⓒ/ⓢ   li·yech·ni·ka/le·ka·ra

I've run out of my medication.
Nestalo mi je lijekova.   ne·sta·lo mi ye li·ye·ko·va

symptoms, conditions & allergies

I'm sick.	*Ja sam bolestan/*	ya sam *bo·le·*stan/
	bolesna. m/f	*bo·le·*sna
It hurts here.	*Boli me ovdje.*	*bo·*li me *ov·*dye
I have ...	*Imam ...*	*i·*mam ...
asthma	*astma* f	*ast·*ma
bronchitis	*bronhitis* m	bron·*hi·*tis
constipation	*zatvorenje* n	zat·vo·*re·*nye
cough	*kašalj* m	*ka·*shal'
diarrhoea	*proljev* m	*pro·*lyev
fever	*groznica* f	*gro·*zni·tsa
headache	*glavobolja* f	gla·*vo·*bo·lya
heart condition	*poremećaj srca* m	*po·*re·me·chai *sr·*tsa
nausea	*mučnina* f	much·*ni·*na
pain	*bol* m	bol
sore throat	*grlobolja* f	gr·*lo·*bo·lya
toothache	*zubobolja* f	zu·*bo·*bo·lya
I'm allergic to ...	*Ja sam alergičan/*	ya sam a·*ler·*gi·chan/
	alergična na ... m/f	a·*ler·*gich·na na ...
antibiotics	*antibiotike*	*an·*ti·bi·o·ti·ke
anti-inflammatories	*lijekove protiv upale*	li·*ye·*ko·ve *pro·*tiv *u·*pa·le
aspirin	*aspirin*	a·*spi·*rin
bees	*pčele*	*pche·*le
codeine	*kodein*	ko·*de·*in
penicillin	*penicilin*	pe·ni·*tsi·*lin
antiseptic	*antiseptik* m	an·ti·*sep·*tik
bandage	*zavoj* m	*za·*voy
contraceptives	*sredstva za*	*sreds·*tva za
	spriječavanje	spri·ye·*cha·*va·nye
	trudnoće n pl	trud·*no·*che
diarrhoea medicine	*lijekovi protiv*	li·*ye·*ko·vi *pro·*tiv
	proljeva m pl	*pro·*lye·va
insect repellent	*sredstvo za odbijanje*	*sreds·*tvo za od·*bi·*ya·nye
	insekata n	*in·*se·ka·ta
laxatives	*laksativi* m pl	*lak·*sa·ti·vi
painkillers	*tablete protiv bolova* f pl	ta·*ble·*te *pro·*tiv *bo·*lo·va
rehydration salts	*soli za rehidrataciju* f	*so·*li za re·hi·dra·*ta·*tsi·yu
sleeping tablets	*tablete za spavanje* f pl	ta·*ble·*te za *spa·*va·nye

english–croatian dictionary

Croatian nouns in this dictionary have their gender indicated by ⓜ (masculine), ⓕ (feminine) or ⓝ (neuter). If it's a plural noun, you'll also see pl. Adjectives are given in the masculine form only. Words are also marked as a (adjective), v (verb), sg (singular), pl (plural), inf (informal), pol (polite), ⓒ (Croatian) or ⓢ (Serbian) where necessary.

A

accident *nezgoda* ⓕ *nez*-go-da
accommodation *smještaj* ⓜ *smye*-shtai
adaptor *konverter* ⓜ kon-*ver*-ter
address *adresa* ⓕ a-*dre*-sa
after *poslije* po-sli-ye
air-conditioned *klimatiziran* kli-ma-*ti*-zi-ran
airplane *zrakoplov/avion* ⓜ
   zra-ko-plov/a-vi-on ⓒ/ⓢ
airport *zračna luka* ⓕ */aerodrom* ⓜ
   zrach-na *lu*-ka/a-e-ro-drom ⓒ/ⓢ
alcohol *alkohol* ⓜ *al*-ko-hol
all *sve* sve
allergy *alergija* ⓕ a-*ler*-gi-ya
ambulance *hitna pomoć* ⓕ *hit*-na po-moch
and *i* i
ankle *gležanj/članak* ⓜ gle-zhan'/*chla*-nak ⓒ/ⓢ
arm *ruka* ⓕ *ru*-ka
ashtray *pepeljara* ⓕ pe-pe-*lya*-ra
ATM *bankovni automat* ⓜ *ban*-kov-ni a-u-*to*-mat

B

baby *beba* ⓕ *be*-ba
back (body) *leđa* ⓝ pl *le*-ja
backpack *ranac* ⓜ *ra*-nats
bad *loš* losh
bag *torba* ⓕ *tor*-ba
baggage claim *šalter za podizanje prtljage* ⓜ
   shal-ter za po-di-za-nye prt-*lya*-ge
bank *banka* ⓕ *ban*-ka
bar *bar* ⓜ bar
bathroom *kupaonica* ⓕ ku-pa-o-*ni*-tsa
battery (car) *akumulator* ⓜ a-ku-mu-*la*-tor
battery (general) *baterija* ⓕ ba-*te*-ri-ya
beautiful *lijep* li *yep*
bed *krevet* ⓜ *kre*-vet
beer *pivo* ⓝ *pi*-vo
before *prije* *pri*-ye
behind *iza* i-za
bicycle *bicikl* ⓜ bi-*tsi*-kl
big *velik* ve-lik
bill *račun* ⓜ *ra*-chun

black *crn* tsrn
blanket *deka* ⓕ *de*-ka
blood group *krvna grupa* ⓕ *krv*-na *gru*-pa
blue *plav* plav
boat (ship) *brod* ⓜ brod
boat (smaller/private) *čamac* ⓜ *cha*-mats
book (make a reservation) v *rezervirati* re-zer-*vi*-ra-ti
Bosnia-Hercegovina *Bosna i Hercegovina* ⓕ
   bos-na i *her*-tse-go-vi-na
Bosnian (language) *bosanski jezik* ⓜ bo-*san*-ski *ye*-zik
bottle *boca* ⓕ *bo*-tsa
bottle opener *otvarač za boce* ⓜ ot-*va*-rach za *bo*-tse
boy *dječak* ⓜ *dye*-chak
brakes (car) *kočnice* ⓕ pl *koch*-ni-tse
breakfast *doručak* ⓜ *do*-ru-chak
broken (faulty) *pokvaren* po-*kva*-ren
bus *autobus* ⓜ a-u-to-bus
business *biznis* ⓜ *biz*-nis
buy *kupiti* *ku*-pi-ti

C

café *kafić/kavana* ⓜ/ⓕ ka-fich/ka-*va*-na
camera *foto-aparat* ⓜ fo-to-*a*-pa-rat
camp site *mjesto za kampiranje* ⓜ
   mye-sto za kam-*pi*-ra-nye
cancel *poništiti* po-*ni*-shti-ti
can opener *otvarač za limenke/konzerve* ⓜ
   ot-*va*-rach za *li*-men-ke/*kon*-zer-ve ⓒ/ⓢ
car *automobil* ⓜ a-u-to-*mo*-bil
cash *gotovina* ⓕ go-to-*vi*-na
cash (a cheque) v *unovčiti* u-nov-*chi*-ti
cell phone *mobilni telefon* ⓜ *mo*-bil-ni te-*le*-fon
centre *centar* ⓜ *tsen*-tar
change (money) v *zamijeniti* za-mi-*ye*-ni-ti
cheap *jeftin* *yef*-tin
check (bill) *račun* ⓜ *ra*-chun
check-in *prijemni šalter* ⓜ pri-*yem*-ni *shal*-ter
chest *prsa/grudi* ⓝ pl *pr*-sa/*gru*-di ⓒ/ⓢ
child *dijete* ⓝ di-*ye*-te
cigarette *cigareta* ⓕ tsi-ga-*re*-ta
city *grad* ⓜ grad
clean a *čist* chist
closed *zatvoren* *zat*-vo-ren
coffee *kava* ⓕ *ka*-va

coins *novčići* ⓜ pl nov-chi-chi
cold a *hladan* hla-dan
collect call *poziv na račun nazvane osobe* ⓜ
  po-ziv na ra-chun naz-va-ne o-so-be
come *doći* do-chi
computer *računalo* ⓝ/*kompjuter* ⓜ
  ra-chu-na-lo/komp-yu-ter ©/ⓢ
condom *prezervativ* ⓜ pre-zer-va-tiv
contact lenses *kontakt leće* ① pl/*kontaktna sočiva*
  ⓝ pl *kon-takt le-che/kon-takt-na so-chi-va* ©/ⓢ
cook v *kuhati* ku-ha-ti
cost *cijena* ① tsi-ye-na
credit card *kreditna kartica* ① kre-dit-na kar-ti-tsa
Croatia *Hrvatska* ① hr-vat-ska
Croatian (language) *hrvatski* ⓜ hr-vat-ski
Croatian a *hrvatski* hr-vat-ski
cup *šalica/šoljica* ① sha-li-tsa/sho-l'i-tsa ©/ⓢ
currency exchange *tečaj/kurs stranih valuta* ⓜ
  te-chai/kurs stra-nih va-lu-ta ©/ⓢ
customs (immigration) *carinarnica* ① tsa-ri-nar-ni-tsa

D

dangerous *opasan* o-pa-san
date (time) *datum* ⓝ *da-*tum
day *dan* ⓜ dan
delay *zakašnjenje* ⓝ za-kash-nye-nye
dentist *zubar* ⓜ zu-bar
depart *otići* o-ti-chi
diaper *pelene* ① pl *pe-*le-ne
dictionary *rječnik* ⓜ ryech-nik
dinner *večera* ① ve-che-ra
direct *direktan* di-rek-tan
dirty *prljav* pr-lyav
disabled *onesposobljen* o-ne-spo-sob-lyen
discount *popust* ⓜ po-pust
doctor *liječnik/lekar* ⓜ li-yech-nik/le-kar ©/ⓢ
double bed *dupli krevet* ⓜ du-pli kre-vet
double room *dvokrevetna soba* ① dvo-kre-vet-na so-ba
drink *piće* ⓝ pi-che
drive v *voziti* vo-zi-ti
drivers licence *vozačka dozvola* ① vo-zach-ka doz-vo-la
drug (illicit) *droga* ① dro-ga
dummy (pacifier) *duda/cucla* ① du-da/tsu-tsla ©/ⓢ

E

ear *uho* ⓝ *u-*ho
east *istok* ⓜ *i-*stok
eat *jesti* ye-sti
economy class *drugi razred* ⓜ dru-gi raz-red
electricity *struja* ① stru-ya
elevator *dizalo* ⓝ/*lift* ⓜ di-za-lo/lift ©/ⓢ

email *e-mail* ⓜ i-me-il
embassy *ambasada* ① am-ba-sa-da
emergency *hitan slučaj* ⓜ hi-tan slu-chai
English (language) *engleski* ⓜ en-gle-ski
entrance *ulaz* ⓜ u-laz
evening *večer* ① ve-cher
exchange rate *tečaj/kurs razmjene* ⓜ
  te-chai/kurs raz-mye-ne ©/ⓢ
exit *izlaz* ⓜ iz-laz
expensive *skup* skup
express mail *ekspres pošta* ① eks-pres posh-ta
eye *oko* ⓝ o-ko

F

far *daleko* da-le-ko
fast *brz* brz
father *otac* ⓜ o-tats
film (camera) *film* ⓜ film
finger *prst* ⓜ prst
first-aid kit *pribor za prvu pomoć* ⓜ
  *pri-*bor za pr-vu po-moch
first class *prvi razred* ⓜ pr-vi raz-red
fish *riba* ① ri-ba
food *hrana* ① hra-na
foot *stopalo* ⓝ sto-pa-lo
fork *viljuška* ① vi-lyush-ka
free (of charge) *besplatan* be-spla-tan
friend *prijatelj/prijateljica* ⓜ/①
  *pri-*ya-tel'/pri-ya-te-lyi-tsa
fruit *voće* ⓝ vo-che
full *pun* pun
funny *smješan* smye-shan

G

gift *dar/poklon* ⓜ dar/pok-lon ©/ⓢ
girl *djevojčica* ① dye-voy-chi-tsa
glass (drinking) *čaša* ① cha-sha
glasses *naočale* ① pl na-o-cha-le
go *ići* i-chi
good *dobar* do-bar
green *zelen* ze-len
guide *vodič* ⓜ vo-dich

H

half *polovina* ① po-lo-vi-na
hand *ruka* ① ru-ka
handbag *ručna torbica* ① ruch-na tor-bi-tsa
happy *sretan* sre-tan
have *imati* i-ma-ti
he *on* on

head *glava* ① gla-va
heart *srce* ⑪ sr-tse
heat *vrućina* ① vru-chi-na
heavy *težak* te-zhak
help v *pomoći* po-mo-chi
here *ovdje* ov-dye
high *visok* vi-sok
highway *autoput* ⑫ a-u-to-put
hike v *pješačiti* pye-sha-chi-ti
holidays *praznici* ⑫ pl praz-ni-tsi
homosexual *homoseksualac/homoseksualka* ⑫/①
ho-mo-sek-su-a-lats/ho-mo-sek-su-al-ka
hospital *bolnica* ① bol-ni-tsa
hot *vruć* vruch
hotel *hotel* ⑫ ho-tel
hungry *gladan/gladna* ⑫/① gla-dan/gla-dna
husband *muž* ⑫ muzh

I

I *ja* ya
identification (card) *osobna iskaznica/lična karta* ①
o-sob-na i-skaz-ni-tsa/lich-na kar-ta ⑥/⑤
ill *bolestan* bo-le-stan
important *važan* va-zhan
included *uključen* uk-lyu-chen
injury *povreda* ① po-vre-da
insurance *osiguranje* ① o-si-gu-ra-nye
Internet *internet* ⑫ in-ter-net
interpreter *tumač* ⑫ tu-mach

J

jewellery *nakit* ⑫ na-kit
job *posao* ⑫ po-sa-o

K

key *ključ* ⑫ klyuch
kilogram *kilogram* ⑫ ki-lo-gram
kitchen *kuhinja* ① ku-hi-nya
knife *nož* ⑫ nozh

L

laundry (place) *praonica* ① pra-o-ni-tsa
lawyer *pravnik* ⑫ prav-nik
left (direction) *lijevi* li-ye-vi
left-luggage office *ured za odlaganje prtljage* ⑫
u-red za od-la-ga-nye prt-lya-ge
leg *noga* ① no-ga
lesbian *lezbijka* ① lez-biy-ka
less *manje* ma-nye

letter (mail) *pismo* ⑪ pi-smo
lift (elevator) *dizalo* ⑪/*lift* ⑫ di-za-lo/lift ⑥/⑤
light *svjetlost* ① svyet-lost
like v *dopadati se* do-pa-da-ti se
lock *brava* ① bra-va
long *dugačak* du-ga-chak
lost *izgubljen* iz-gub-lyen
lost-property office *ured za izgubljene stvari* ⑫
u-red za iz-gub-lye-ne stva-ri
love v *voljeti* vo-lye-ti
luggage *prtljaga* ① prt-lya-ga
lunch *ručak* ⑫ ru-chak

M

mail *pošta* ① posh-ta
man *čovjek* ⑫ cho-vyek
map (of country) *karta* ① kar-ta
map (of town) *plan grada* ⑫ plan gra-da
market *tržnica/pijaca* ① trzh-ni-tsa ⑥/⑤
matches *šibice* ① pl shi-bi-tse
meat *meso* ⑪ me-so
medicine *lijekovi* ⑫ pl li-ye-ko-vi
menu *jelovnik* ⑫ ye-lov-nik
message *poruka* ① po-ru-ka
milk *mlijeko* ⑪ mli-ye-ko
minute *minuta* ① mi-nu-ta
mobile phone *mobilni telefon* ⑫ mo-bil-ni te-le-fon
money *novac* ⑫ no-vats
Montenegro *Crna Gora* ① tsr-na go-ra
month *mjesec* ⑫ mye-sets
morning *jutro* ⑪ yu-tro
mother *majka* ① mai-ka
motorcycle *motocikl* ⑫ mo-to-tsi-kl
motorway *autoput* ⑫ a-u-to-put
mouth *usta* ⑪ pl u-sta
music *glazba* ① glaz-ba

N

name *ime* ⑪ i-me
napkin *salveta* ① sal-ve-ta
nappy *pelene* ① pl pe-le-ne
near *blizu* bli-zu
neck *vrat* ⑫ vrat
new *nov* nov
news *vijesti* ① pl vi-ye-sti
newspaper *novine* ① pl no-vi-ne
night *noć* ① noch
no *ne* ne
noisy *bučan* bu-chan
nonsmoking *nepušački* ⑫ ne-pu-shach-ki
north *sjever* ⑫ sye-ver

nose *nos* ⓜ nos
now *sada* sa·da
number *broj* ⓜ broy

O

oil (engine) *ulje* ⓝ u·lye
old *star* star
one-way ticket *jednosmjerna karta* ⓕ
  yed·no·smyer·na kar·ta
open a *otvoren* ot·vo·ren
outside *vani/napolju* va·ni/na·po·l'u ©/Ⓢ

P

package *paket* ⓜ pa·ket
paper *papir* ⓜ pa·pir
park (car) v *parkirati* par·ki·ra·ti
passport *putovnica* ⓕ/*pasoš* ⓜ
  pu·tov·ni·tsa/pa·sosh ©/Ⓢ
pay *platiti* pla·ti·ti
pen *kemijska* ⓕ ke·miy·ska
petrol *benzin* ben·zin
pharmacy *ljekarna/apoteka* ⓕ
  lye·kar·na/a·po·te·ka ©/Ⓢ
phonecard *telefonska kartica* ⓕ
  te·le·fon·ska kar·ti·tsa
photo *fotografija* ⓕ fo·to·gra·fi·ya
plate *tanjur* ⓜ ta·nyur
police *policija* ⓕ po·li·tsi·ya
postcard *dopisnica* ⓕ do·pi·sni·tsa
post office *poštanski ured* ⓜ posh·tan·ski u·red
pregnant *trudna* trud·na
price *cijena* ⓕ tsi·ye·na

Q

quiet *tih* tih

R

rain *kiša* ⓕ ki·sha
razor *brijač* ⓜ bri·yach
receipt *račun* ⓜ ra·chun
red *crven* tsr·ven
refund *povrat novca* ⓜ pov·rat nov·tsa
registered mail *preporučena pošta* ⓕ
  pre·po·ru·che·na posh·ta
rent v *iznajmiti* iz·nai·mi·ti
repair v *popraviti* po·pra·vi·ti
reservation *rezervacija* ⓕ re·zer·va·tsi·ya
restaurant *restoran* ⓜ re·sto·ran
return v *vratiti se* vra·ti·ti se

return ticket *povratna karta* ⓕ po·vra·tna kar·ta
right (direction) *desno* de·sno
road *cesta* ⓕ/*put* ⓜ tse·sta/put ©/Ⓢ
room *soba* ⓕ so·ba

S

safe a *siguran* si·gu·ran
sanitary napkin *higijenski uložak* ⓜ
  hi·gi·yen·ski u·lo·zhak
seat *sjedište* ⓝ sye·dish·te
send *poslati* po·sla·ti
Serbia *Srbija* ⓕ sr·bi·ya
Serbian (language) *srpski jezik* ⓜ srp·ski ye·zik
service station *benzinska stanica* ⓕ
  ben·zin·ska sta·ni·tsa
sex *seks* ⓜ seks
shampoo *šampon* ⓜ sham·pon
share (a dorm) *dijeliti* di·ye·li·ti
shaving cream *pjena za brijanje* ⓕ
  pye·na za bri·ya·nye
she *ona* o·na
sheet (bed) *plahta* ⓕ/*čaršav* ⓜ
  pla·hta/char·shav ©/Ⓢ
shirt *košulja* ⓕ ko·shu·lya
shoes *cipele* ⓕ pl tsi·pe·le
shop *prodavaonica* ⓕ pro·da·va·o·ni·tsa
short *kratak* kra·tak
shower *tuš* ⓜ tush
single room *jednokrevetna soba* ⓕ
  yed·no·kre·vet·na·so·ba
skin *koža* ⓕ ko·zha
skirt *suknja* ⓕ suk·nya
sleep v *spavati* spa·va·ti
slowly *sporo* spo·ro
small *mali* ma·li
smoke (cigarettes) v *pušiti* pu·shi·ti
soap *sapun* ⓜ sa·pun
some *malo* ma·lo
soon *uskoro* u·sko·ro
south *jug* ⓜ yug
souvenir shop *prodavaonica suvenira* ⓕ
  pro·da·va·o·ni·tsa su·ve·ni·ra
speak *govoriti* go·vo·ri·ti
spoon *žlica/kašika* ⓕ zhli·tsa/ka·shi·ka ©/Ⓢ
stamp *poštanska marka* ⓕ posh·tan·ska mar·ka
stand-by ticket *uvjetna/uslovna karta* ⓕ
  uv·yet·na/us·lov·na kar·ta ©/Ⓢ
station (train) *stanica* ⓕ sta·ni·tsa
stomach *želudac* ⓜ zhe·lu·dats
stop v *zaustaviti* za·u·sta·vi·ti
stop (bus) *stanica* ⓕ sta·ni·tsa
street *ulica* ⓕ u·li·tsa

student *student* ⓜ & ⓕ *stu*-dent
sun *sunce* ⓝ *sun*-tse
sunscreen *losion za zaštitu od sunca* ⓜ
　lo-si-on za *zash*-ti-tu od *sun*-tsa
swim v *plivati* *pli*-va-ti

T

tampon *tampon* ⓜ *tam*-pon
taxi *taksi* ⓜ *tak*-si
teaspoon *žličica/kašičica* ⓕ
　zhli-chi-tsa/*ka*-shi-chi-tsa ©/Ⓢ
teeth *zubi* ⓜ pl *zu*-bi
telephone *telefon* ⓜ te-*le*-fon
television *televizija* ⓕ te-le-*vi*-zi-ya
temperature (weather) *temperatura* ⓕ tem-pe-ra-*tu*-ra
tent *šator* ⓜ *sha*-tor
that (one) *ono* *o*-no
they *oni/one/ona* ⓜ/ⓕ/ⓝ *o*-ni/*o*-ne/*o*-na
thirsty *žedan* zhe-dan
this (one) *ovo* *o*-vo
throat *grlo* ⓝ *gr*-lo
ticket *karta* ⓕ *kar*-ta
time *vrijeme* ⓝ vri-*ye*-me
tired *umoran* u-mo-ran
tissues *papirnati rupčići* ⓜ pl *pa*-pir-na-ti *rup*-chi-chi ©
　papirne maramice ⓕ pl *pa*-pir-ne *ma*-ra-mi-tse Ⓢ
today *danas* da-nas
toilet *zahod/toalet* ⓜ za-*hod*/to-a-*let* ©/Ⓢ
tomorrow *sutra* su-tra
tonight *večeras* ve-che-ras
toothbrush *četkica za zube* ⓕ *chet*-ki-tsa za zu-be
toothpaste *pasta za zube* ⓕ *pa*-sta za zu-be
torch (flashlight) *ručna svjetiljka* ⓕ *ruch*-na svye-*til'*-ka
tour *ekskurzija* ⓕ ek-skur-zi-ya
tourist office *turistička agencija* ⓕ
　tu-*ri*-stich-ka a-*gen*-tsi-ya
towel *ručnik/peškir* ⓜ *ruch*-nik/*pesh*-kir ©/Ⓢ
train *vlak/voz* ⓜ vlak/voz ©/Ⓢ
translate *prevesti* pre-ve-sti
travel agency *putna agencija* ⓕ *put*-na a-*gen*-tsi-ya
travellers cheque *putnički ček* ⓜ *put*-nich-ki chek
trousers *hlače/pantalone* ⓕ pl
　hla-che/pan-ta-*lo*-ne ©/Ⓢ
twin beds *dva kreveta* ⓜ pl dva *kre*-ve-ta
tyre *guma* ⓕ *gu*-ma

U

underwear *donje rublje* ⓝ *do*-nye *rub*-lye
urgent *hitan* *hi*-tan

V

vacant *prazan* *pra*-zan
vacation *praznici* ⓜ pl *praz*-ni-tsi
vegetable *povrće* ⓝ *po*-vr-che
vegetarian a *vegetarijanski* ve-ge-ta-*ri*-yan-ski
visa *viza* ⓕ *vi*-za

W

waiter *konobar* ⓜ *ko*-no-bar
walk v *hodati* ho-da-ti
wallet *novčanik* ⓜ *nov*-cha-nik
warm a *topao* *to*-pa-o
wash (something) *oprati* o-pra-ti
watch *sat* ⓜ sat
water *voda* ⓕ *vo*-da
we *mi* mi
weekend *vikend* ⓜ *vi*-kend
west *zapad* ⓜ za-pad
wheelchair *invalidska kolica* ⓕ pl in-*va*-lid-ska ko-*li*-tsa
when *kada* ka-da
where *gdje* gdye
white *bijel* bi-yel
who *tko* tko
why *zašto* zash-to
wife *žena* ⓕ zhe-na
window *prozor* ⓜ *pro*-zor
wine *vino* ⓝ *vi*-no
with *sa* sa
without *bez* bez
woman *žena* ⓕ zhe-na
write *napisati* na-*pi*-sa-ti

Y

yellow *žut* zhut
yes *da* da
yesterday *jučer* yu-cher
you sg inf *ti* ti
you sg pol & pl *vi* vi

Czech

czech alphabet

A a uh	*Á á* a	*B b* bair	*C c* tsair	*Č č* chair
D d dair	*Ď ď* dyair	*E e* e	*É é* *dloh*-hair air	*Ě ě* e s *hach*·kem
F f ef	*G g* gair	*H h* ha	*Ch ch* cha	*I i* ee
Í í *dloh*-hair ee	*J j* yair	*K k* ka	*L l* el	*M m* em
N n en	*Ň ň* en'	*O o* o	*P p* pair	*Q q* kair
R r er	*Ř ř* erzh	*S s* es	*Š š* esh	*T t* tair
Ť ť tyair	*U u* u	*Ú ú* *dloh*-hair u	*Ů ů* u s *krohzh*·kem	*V v* vair
W w *dvo*·yi·tair vair	*X x* iks	*Y y* *ip*·si·lon	*Ý ý* *dloh*-hee *ip*·si·lon	*Z z* zet
Ž ž zhet				

ČEŠTINA

czech

about Czech

Czech (*čeština* chesh-tyi-nuh), the language which gave us words such as *dollar*, *pistol* and *robot*, has a turbulent history. The Czech Republic may now be one of the most stable and well-off Eastern European countries, but over the centuries the land and the language have been regularly swallowed and regurgitated by their neighbours. In 1993 the Velvet Divorce ended the patched-together affair that was Czechoslovakia, and allowed Czech to go its own way after being tied to Slovak for over 70 years.

Both Czech and Slovak belong to the western branch of the Slavic language family, pushed westward with the Slavic people by the onslaught of the Huns, Avars, Bulgars and Magyars in the 5th and 6th centuries. Czech is also related to Polish, though not as closely as to Slovak – adults in Slovakia and the Czech Republic can generally understand one another, although younger people who have not been exposed to much of the other language may have more difficulty.

The earliest written literature dates from the 13th century upswing in Czech political power, which continued for several centuries. In the 17th century, however, the Thirty Years War nearly caused literature in Czech to become extinct. Fortunately, the national revival of the late 18th century brought it to the forefront again, at least until the 20th century, when first Nazi and then Communist rule pressed it into a subordinate position once more.

Many English speakers flinch when they see written Czech, especially words like *prst* prst (finger) and *krk* krk (neck) with no apparent vowels, and the seemingly unpronounceable clusters of consonants in phrases like *čtrnáct dní* chtr-natst dnyee (fortnight). Don't despair! With a little practice and the coloured pronunciation guides in this chapter you'll be enjoying the buttery mouthfeel of Czech words in no time. Czech also has one big advantage in the pronunciation stakes – each Czech letter is always pronounced exactly the same way, so once you've got the hang of the Czech alphabet you'll be able to read any word put before you with aplomb. Thank religious writer and martyr Jan Hus for this – he reformed the spelling system in the 15th and 16th centuries and introduced the *háček* ha-chek (ˇ) and the various other accents you'll see above Czech letters.

So, whether you're visiting the countryside or marvelling at Golden Prague, launch into this Czech chapter and your trip will be transformed into a truly memorable one.

pronunciation

vowel sounds

The Czech vowel system is relatively easy to master and most sounds have equivalents in English.

symbol	english equivalent	czech example	transliteration
a	father	*já*	ya
ai	aisle	*krajka*	*krai*-kuh
air	hair	*veliké*	*ve*-lee-kair
aw	law	*balcón*	*bal*-kawn
e	bet	*pes*	pes
ee	see	*prosím*	pro-seem
ey	hey	*dej*	dey
i	bit	*kolik*	*ko*-lik
o	pot	*noha*	*no*-huh
oh	oh	*koupit*	*koh*-pit
oo	zoo	*ústa*	*oo*-stuh
oy	toy	*výstroj*	*vee*-stroy
ow	how	*autobus*	*ow*-to-bus
u	put	*muž*	muzh
uh	run	*nad*	nuhd

word stress

Word stress in Czech is easy – it's always on the first syllable of the word. Stress is marked with italics in the pronunciation guides in this chapter as a reminder.

consonant sounds

The consonants in Czech are mostly the same as in English, with the exception of the kh sound, the r sound (which is rolled as it is in Spanish) and the rzh sound.

symbol	english equivalent	czech example	transliteration
b	bed	*bláto*	*bla*-to
ch	cheat	*odpočinek*	ot-po-*chi*-nek
d	dog	*nedávný*	ne-*dav*-nee
f	fat	*vyfotit*	*vi*-fo-tit
g	go	*vegetarián*	ve-ge-tuh-ri-an
h	hat	*zahrady*	zuh-*hruh*-di
k	kit	*navěky*	na-vye-ki
kh	loch	*kuchyně*	ku-*khi*-nye
l	lot	*loni*	*lo*-nyi
m	man	*menší*	*men*-shee
n	not	*nízký*	*nyeez*-kee
p	pet	*dopis*	*do*-pis
r	run (rolled)	*rok*	rok
rzh	rolled r followed by zh	*řeka*	*rzhe*-kuh
s	sun	*slovo*	*slo*-vo
sh	shot	*pošta*	*posh*-tuh
t	top	*fronta*	*fron*-tuh
ts	hats	*co*	tso
v	very	*otvor*	ot-vor
y	yes	*již*	yizh
z	zero	*zmiz*	zmiz
zh	pleasure	*už*	uzh
'	a slight y sound	*promiňte*	pro-min'-te

tools

language difficulties

Do you speak English?
Mluvíte anglicky?   mlu·vee·te uhn·glits·ki

Do you understand?
Rozumíte?   ro·zu·mee·te

I understand.
Rozumím.   ro·zu·meem

I don't understand.
Nerozumím.   ne·ro·zu·meem

What does (*knedlík*) mean?
Co znamená (knedlík)?   tso znuh·me·na (kned·leek)

How do you ...?	*Jak se ...?*	yuhk se ...
pronounce this	*toto vyslovuje*	toh·to vis·lo·vu·ye
write (*krtek*)	*píše (krtek)*	pee·she (kr·tek)

Could you please ...?	*Prosím, můžete ...?*	pro·seem moo·zhe·te ...
repeat that	*to opakovat*	to o·puh·ko·vuht
speak more slowly	*mluvit pomaleji*	mlu·vit po·muh·le·yi
write it down	*to napsat*	to nuhp·suht

essentials

Yes.	*Ano.*	uh·no
No.	*Ne.*	ne
Please.	*Prosím.*	pro·seem
Thank you	*(Mnohokrát)*	(mno·ho·krat)
(very much).	*Děkuji.*	dye·ku·yi
You're welcome.	*Prosím.*	pro·seem
Excuse me.	*Promiňte.*	pro·min'·te
Sorry.	*Promiňte.*	pro·min'·te

numbers

0	*nula*	*nu*·luh		16	*šestnáct*	*shest*·natst
1	*jeden* m	*ye*·den		17	*sedmnáct*	*se*·dm·natst
	jedna f	*yed*·na		18	*osmnáct*	*o*·sm·natst
	jedno n	*yed*·no		19	*devatenáct*	*de*·vuh·te·natst
2	*dva/dvě* m/f&n	dvuh/dvye		20	*dvacet*	*dvuh*·tset
3	*tři*	trzhi		21	*dvacet jedna*	*dvuh*·tset *yed*·nuh
4	*čtyři*	*chti*·rzhi			*jednadvacet*	*yed*·nuh·dvuh·tset
5	*pět*	pyet		22	*dvacet dva*	*dvuh*·tset dvuh
6	*šest*	shest			*dvaadvacet*	*dvuh*·uh·dvuh·tset
7	*sedm*	*se*·dm		30	*třicet*	*trzhi*·tset
8	*osm*	*o*·sm		40	*čtyřicet*	*chti*·rzhi·tset
9	*devět*	*de*·vyet		50	*padesát*	*puh*·de·sat
10	*deset*	*de*·set		60	*šedesát*	*she*·de·sat
11	*jedenáct*	*ye*·de·natst		70	*sedmdesát*	*se*·dm·de·sat
12	*dvanáct*	*dvuh*·natst		80	*osmdesát*	*o*·sm·de·sat
13	*třináct*	*trzhi*·natst		90	*devadesát*	*de*·vuh·de·sat
14	*čtrnáct*	*chtr*·natst		100	*sto*	sto
15	*patnáct*	*puht*·natst		1000	*tisíc*	*tyi*·seets

time & dates

What time is it?	*Kolik je hodin?*	*ko*·lik ye *ho*·dyin
It's one o'clock.	*Je jedna hodina.*	ye *yed*·nuh *ho*·dyi·nuh
It's (10) o'clock.	*Je (deset) hodin.*	ye (*de*·set) *ho*·dyin
Quarter past (10).	*Čvrt na (jedenáct).*	chtvrt nuh (*ye*·de·natst)
	(lit: quarter of eleven)	
Half past (10).	*Půl (jedenácté).*	pool (*ye*·de·nats·tair)
	(lit: half eleven)	
Quarter to (eleven).	*Třičtvrtě na (jedenáct).*	*trzhi*·chtvr·tye nuh (*ye*·de·natst)
At what time?	*V kolik hodin?*	f *ko*·lik *ho*·dyin
At …	*V …*	f …
am (midnight–8am)	*ráno*	*ra*·no
am (8am–noon)	*dopoledne*	*do*·po·led·ne
pm (noon–7pm)	*odpoledne*	*ot*·po·led·ne
pm (7pm–midnight)	*večer*	*ve*·cher

Monday	*pondělí*	pon·dye·lee
Tuesday	*úterý*	oo·te·ree
Wednesday	*středa*	strzhe·duh
Thursday	*čtvrtek*	chtvr·tek
Friday	*pátek*	pa·tek
Saturday	*sobota*	so·bo·tuh
Sunday	*neděle*	ne·dye·le
January	*leden*	le·den
February	*únor*	oo·nor
March	*březen*	brzhe·zen
April	*duben*	du·ben
May	*květen*	kvye·ten
June	*červen*	cher·ven
July	*červenec*	cher·ve·nets
August	*srpen*	sr·pen
September	*září*	za·rzhee
October	*říjen*	rzhee·yen
November	*listopad*	li·sto·puht
December	*prosinec*	pro·si·nets

What date is it today?
   Kolikátého je dnes?   ko·li·ka·tair·ho ye dnes

It's (18 October).
   Je (osmnáctého října).   ye (o·sm·nats·tair·ho rzheey·nuh)

last night	*včera v noci*	fche·ruh v no·tsi
last week/month	*minulý týden/měsíc*	mi·nu·lee tee·den/mye·seets
last year	*vloni*	vlo·nyi
next ...	*příští ...*	przheesh·tyee ...
week	*týden*	tee·den
month	*měsíc*	mye·seets
year	*rok*	rok
tomorrow/yesterday ...	*zítra/včera ...*	zee·truh/fche·ruh ...
morning (early/late)	*ráno/dopoledne*	ra·no/do·po·led·ne
afternoon	*odpoledne*	ot·po·led·ne
evening	*večer*	ve·cher

weather

What's the weather like?	*Jaké je počasí?*	yuh-kair ye po-chuh-see
It's ...		
cloudy	*Je zataženo.*	ye zuh-tuh-zhe-no
cold	*Je chladno.*	ye khluhd-no
hot	*Je horko.*	ye hor-ko
raining	*Prší.*	pr-shee
snowing	*Sněží.*	snye-zhee
sunny	*Je slunečno.*	ye slu-nech-no
warm	*Je teplo.*	ye tep-lo
windy	*Je větrno.*	ye vye-tr-no
spring	*jaro* n	yuh-ro
summer	*léto* n	lair-to
autumn	*podzim* m	pod-zim
winter	*zima* f	zi-muh

border crossing

I'm here ...	*Jsem zde ...*	ysem zde ...
in transit	*v tranzitu*	f truhn-zi-tu
on business	*na služební cestě*	nuh slu-zheb-nyee tses-tye
on holiday	*na dovolené*	nuh do-vo-le-nair
I'm here for ...	*Jsem zde na ...*	ysem zde nuh ...
(10) days	*(deset) dní*	(de-set) dnyee
(three) weeks	*(tři) týdny*	(trzhi) teed-ni
(two) months	*(dva) měsíce*	(dvuh) mye-see-tse

I'm going to (Valtice).
Jedu do (Valtic). — ye-du do (vuhl-tyits)

I'm staying at the (Hotel Špalíček).
Jsem ubytovaný/á v — ysem u-bi-to-vuh-nee/a v
(Hotelu Špalíček). m/f — (ho-te-lu shpuh-lee-chek)

I have nothing to declare.
Nemám nic k proclení. — ne-mam nyits k prots-le-nyee

I have something to declare.
Mám něco k proclení. — mam nye-tso k prots-le-nyee

That's not mine.
To není moje. — to ne-nyee mo-ye

transport

tickets & luggage

Where can I buy a ticket?
Kde koupím jízdenku? — gde *koh*·peem *yeez*·den·ku

Do I need to book a seat?
Potřebuji místenku? — pot·rzhe·bu·yi *mees*·ten·ku

One ... ticket to (Telč), please.	... do (Telče), prosím.	... do (*tel*·che) *pro*·seem
one-way	Jednosměrnou jízdenku	*yed*·no·smyer·noh *yeez*·den·ku
return	Zpáteční jízdenku	zpa·tech·nyee *yeez*·den·ku

I'd like to ... my ticket, please. m/f	Chtěl/Chtěla bych ... mojí jízdenku, prosím. m/f	khtyel/*khtye*·luh bikh ... *mo*·yee *yeez*·den·ku *pro*·seem
cancel	zrušit	*zru*·shit
change	změnit	*zmye*·nyit
collect	vyzvednout	*vi*·zved·noht
confirm	potvrdit	*pot*·vr·dyit

I'd like a ... seat, please. m/f	Chtěl/Chtěla bych ... m/f	khtyel/*khtye*·luh bikh ...
nonsmoking	nekuřácké místo	*ne*·ku·rzhats·kair *mees*·to
smoking	kuřácké místo	*ku*·rzhats·kair *mees*·to

How much is it?
Kolik to stojí? — *ko*·lik to *sto*·yee

Is there a toilet?
Je tam toaleta? — ye tuhm *to*·uh·le·tuh

Is there air conditioning?
Je tam klimatizace? — ye tuhm *klí*·muh·ti·zuh·tse

How long does the trip take?
Jak dlouho trvá cesta? — yuhk *dloh*·ho *tr*·va *tses*·tuh

Is it a direct route?
Je to přímá cesta? — ye to *przhee*·ma *tses*·tuh

Where can I find a luggage locker?
Kde mohu najít zavazadlová schránka? — gde *mo*·hu *nuh*·yeet zuh·vuh·zuhd·lo·va *skhran*·kuh

My luggage	*Moje zavazadlo*	*mo·ye zuh·vuh·zuhd·lo*
has been ...	*bylo ...*	*bi·lo ...*
damaged	*poškozeno*	*posh·ko·ze·no*
lost	*ztraceno*	*ztruh·tse·no*
stolen	*ukradeno*	*u·kruh·de·no*

getting around

Where does flight (OK25) arrive?
Kam přiletí let (OK25)? kuhm *przhi·le·tyee let (aw·ka dvuh·tset pyet)*

Where does flight (OK25) depart?
Kde odlítá let (OK25)? gde *od·lee·ta let (aw·ka dvuh·tset pyet)*

Where's (the) ...?	*Kde je ...?*	gde ye ...
arrivals hall	*příletová hala*	*przhe·le·to·va huh·luh*
departures hall	*odletová hala*	*od·le·to·va huh·luh*
duty-free shop	*prodejna*	*pro·dey·nuh*
	bezcelního zboží	*bez·tsel·nyee·ho zbo·zhee*
gate (12)	*východ k letadlu*	*vee·khod k le·tuhd·lu*
	(dvanáct)	*(dvuh·natst)*

Is this the ...	*Jede tento/tato ...*	ye·de ten·to/tuh·to ...
to (Mělník)?	*do (Mělníka)?* m/f	do *(myel·nyee·kuh)*
bus	*autobus* m	*ow·to·bus*
train	*vlak* m	vluhk
tram	*tramvaj* f	*truhm·vai*
trolleybus	*trolejbus* m	*tro·ley·bus*

When's the	*V kolik jede*	f ko·lik ye·de
... bus?	*... autobus?*	... *ow·to·bus*
first	*první*	*prv·nyee*
last	*poslední*	*po·sled·nyee*
next	*příští*	*przhee·shtyee*

At what time does the bus/train leave?
V kolik hodin odjíždí f ko·lik ho·dyin od·yeezh·dyee
autobus/vlak? ow·to·bus/vluhk

How long will it be delayed?
Jak dlouho bude mít zpoždění? yuhk dloh·ho bu·de meet zpozh·dye·nyee

What's the next station/stop?
Která je příští stanice/zastávka? kte·ra ye przheesh·tyee stuh·nyi·tse/zuhs·taf·kuh

Does it stop at (Cheb)?
    Zastaví to v (Chebu)?   zuhs·tuh·vee to f (*khe*·bu)

Please tell me when we get to (Přerov).
    Prosím vás řekněte mi   pro·seem vas *rzhek*·nye·te mi
    kdy budeme v (Přerově).   kdi *bu*·de·me f (*przhe*·ro·vye)

How long do we stop here?
    Jak dlouho zde budeme stát?   yuhk *dloh*·ho zde *bu*·de·me stat

Is this seat available?
    Je toto místo volné?   ye *to*·to *mees*·to *vol*·nair

That's my seat.
    To je mé místo.   to ye mair *mees*·to

I'd like a taxi …	*Potřebuji taxíka …*	po·trzhe·bu·yi *tuhk*·see·kuh …
at (9am)	*v (devět hodin*	f (*de*·vyet *ho*·dyin
	dopoledne)	*do*·po·led·ne)
now	*teď*	teď
tomorrow	*zítra*	*zee*·truh

Is this taxi available?
    Je tento taxík volný?   ye *ten*·to *tuhk*·seek *vol*·nee

How much is it to …?
    Kolik stojí jízdenka do …?   ko·lik *sto*·yee *yeez*·den·kuh do …

Please put the meter on.
    Prosím zapněte taxametr.   pro·seem *zuhp*·nye·te *tuhk*·suh·me·tr

Please take me to (this address).
    Prosím odvezte mě na (tuto adresu).   pro·seem od·ves·te mye na (*tu*·to *uh*·dre·su)

Please …	*Prosím …*	pro·seem …
slow down	*zpomalte*	*spo*·muhl·te
stop here	*zastavte zde*	zuhs·tuhf·te zde
wait here	*počkejte zde*	poch·key·te zde

car, motorbike & bicycle hire

I'd like to hire	*Chtěl/Chtěla bych*	khtyel/khtye·luh bikh
a …	*si půjčit …* m/f	si *pooy*·chit …
bicycle	*kolo*	*ko*·lo
car	*auto*	*ow*·to
motorbike	*motorku*	*mo*·tor·ku

with ...	s ...	s ...
a driver	řidičem	rzhi·dyi·chem
air conditioning	klimatizací	kli·muh·ti·zuh·tsee
antifreeze	nemrznoucí směsí	ne·mrz·noh·tsee smye·see
snow chains	sněhovými řetězy	snye·ho·vee·mi rzhe·tye·zi

How much for	Kolik stojí	ko·lik sto·yee
... hire?	půjčení na ...?	pooy·che·nyee nuh ...
hourly	hodinu	ho·dyi·nu
daily	den	den
weekly	týden	tee·den

air	vzduch m	vz·dukh
oil	olej m	o·ley
petrol	benzin m	ben·zin
tyre	pneumatika f	pne·u·muh·ti·kuh

I need a mechanic.	Potřebuji mechanika.	pot·rzhe·bu·yi me·khuh·ni·kuh
I've run out of petrol.	Došel mi benzin.	do·shel mi ben·zin
I have a flat tyre.	Mám defekt.	mam de·fekt

directions

Where's the ...?	Kde je ...?	gde ye ...
bank	banka	buhn·kuh
city centre	centrum	tsen·trum
hotel	hotel	ho·tel
market	trh	trh
police station	policejní stanice	po·li·tsey·nyee stuh·nyi·tse
post office	pošta	posh·tuh
public toilet	veřejný záchod	ve·rzhey·nee za·khod
tourist office	turistická informační kancelář	tu·ris·tits·ka in·for·muhch·nyee kuhn·tse·larzh

Is this the road to (Cheb)?
Vede tato silnice do (Chebu)? ve·de tuh·to sil·ni·tse do (khe·bu)

Can you show me (on the map)?
Můžete mi to ukázat (na mapě)? moo·zhe·te mi to u·ka·zuht (nuh muh·pye)

What's the address?
Jaká je adresa? — yuh·ka ye uh·dre·suh

How far is it?
Jak je to daleko? — yuhk ye to duh·le·ko

How do I get there?
Jak se tam dostanu? — yuhk se tuhm dos·tuh·nu

Turn ...	Odbočte ...	od·boch·te ...
at the corner	za roh	zuh rawh
at the traffic lights	u semaforu	u se·muh·fo·ru
left/right	do leva/prava	do le·vuh/pruh·vuh

It's ...	Je to ...	ye to ...
behind ...	za ...	zuh ...
far away	daleko	duh·le·ko
here	zde	zde
in front of ...	před ...	przhed ...
left	na levo	nuh le·vo
near	blízko	bleez·ko
next to ...	vedle ...	ved·le ...
on the corner	na rohu	nuh ro·hu
opposite ...	naproti ...	nuh·pro·tyi ...
right	na pravo	nuh pruh·vo
straight ahead	přímo	przhee·mo
there	tam	tuhm

by bus	autobusem	ow·to·bu·sem
by taxi	taxikem	tuhk·si·kem
by train	vlakem	vluh·kem
on foot	pěšky	pyesh·ki

north	sever	se·ver
south	jih	yih
east	východ	vee·khod
west	západ	za·puhd

Vchod/Východ	vkhod/*vee*·khod	**Entrance/Exit**
Otevřeno/Zavřeno	o·te·vrzhe·no/*zuh*·vrzhe·no	**Open/Closed**
Volné pokoje	vol·nair po·ko·ye	**Rooms Available**
Obsazeno	op·suh·ze·no	**No Vacancies**
Informace	in·for·muh·tse	**Information**
Policejní stanice	po·li·tsey·nyee *stuh*·nyi·tse	**Police Station**
Zakázáno	zuh·ka·za·no	**Prohibited**
Záchody	za·kho·di	**Toilets**
Páni	pa·nyi	**Men**
Ženy	zhe·ni	**Women**
Horké/Studené	hor·kair/*stu*·de·nair	**Hot/Cold**

accommodation

finding accommodation

Where's a ...?	*Kde je ...?*	gde ye ...
camping ground	*tábořiště*	ta·bo·rzhish·tye
guesthouse	*penzion*	pen·zi·on
hotel	*hotel*	ho·tel
youth hostel	*mládežnická*	mla·dezh·nyits·ka
	ubytovna	u·bi·tov·nuh

Can you recommend	*Můžete mi doporučit*	moo·zhe·te mi do·po·ru·chit
somewhere ...?	*něco ...?*	nye·tso ...
cheap	*levného*	lev·nair·ho
good	*dobrého*	dob·rair·ho
nearby	*nejbližšího*	ney·blizh·shee·ho

I'd like to book a room, please.
Chtěl/Chtěla bych   khtyel/*khtye*·luh bikh
rezervovat pokoj, prosím. m/f   re·zer·vo·vuht po·koy pro·seem

I have a reservation.
Mám rezervaci.   mam re·zer·vuh·tsi

My name is ...
Mé jméno je ...   mair *ymair*·no ye ...

Do you have a double room?
Máte pokoj s manželskou postelí?   ma·te po·koy s *muhn*·zhels·koh pos·te·lee

Do you have a ... room?	*Máte ... pokoj?*	*ma*·te ... *po*·koy
single	*jednolůžkový*	*yed*·no·loozh·ko·vee
twin	*dvoulůžkový*	*dvoh*·loozh·ko·vee

How much is it per ...?	*Kolik to stojí ...?*	*ko*·lik to *sto*·yee ...
night	*na noc*	nuh nots
person	*za osobu*	zuh *o*·so·bu

Can I pay ...?	*Mohu zaplatit ...?*	*mo*·hu zuh·*pluh*·tyit ...
by credit card	*kreditní kartou*	*kre*·dit·nyee *kuhr*·toh
with a travellers cheque	*cestovním šekem*	*tses*·tov·nyeem *she*·kem

For (three) nights/weeks.
Na (tři) noci/týdny.   nuh (trzhi) *no*·tsi/*teed*·ni

From (2 July) to (6 July).
Od (druhého července)   od (*dru*·hair·ho *cher*·ven·tse)
do (šestého července).   do (*shes*·tair·ho *cher*·ven·tse)

Can I see it?
Mohu se na něj podívat?   *mo*·hu se na nyey *po*·dyee·vuht

Am I allowed to camp here?
Mohu zde stanovat?   *mo*·hu zde *stuh*·no·vuht

Where can I find a camping ground?
Kde mohu najít stanový tábor?   gde *mo*·hu *nuh*·yeet *stuh*·no·vee *ta*·bor

requests & queries

When's breakfast served?
V kolik se podává snídaně?   f *ko*·lik se *po*·da·va *snyee*·duh·nye

Where's breakfast served?
Kde se podává snídaně?   gde se *po*·da·va *snyee*·duh·nye

Please wake me at (seven).
Prosím probuďte mě v (sedm).   *pro*·seem *pro*·bud'·te mye f (*se*·dm)

Could I have my key, please?
Můžete mi dát můj klíč, prosím?   *moo*·zhe·te mi dat mooy kleech *pro*·seem

Can I get another (blanket)?
Mohu dostat další (deku)?   *mo*·hu *dos*·tuht *duhl*·shee (*de*·ku)

Do you have a/an ...?	Máte ...?	ma·te ...
elevator	výtah	vee·tah
safe	trezor	tre·zor

The room is too ...	Je moc ...	ye mots ...
expensive	drahý	druh·hee
noisy	hlučný	hluch·nee
small	malý	muh·lee

The ... doesn't work.	... nefunguje.	... ne·fun·gu·ye
air conditioning	Klimatizace	kli·muh·ti·zuh·tse
fan	Větrák	vye·trak
toilet	Toaleta	to·uh·le·tuh

This ... isn't clean.	Tento ... neni čistý.	ten·to ... ne·nyi chis·tee
pillow	polštář	pol·shtarzh
towel	ručník	ruch·nyeek

checking out

What time is checkout?
V kolik hodin máme vyklidit pokoj? f ko·lik ho·dyin ma·me vi·kli·dyit po·koy

Can I leave my luggage here?
Mohu si zde nechat zavazadla? mo·hu si zde ne·khuht zuh·vuh·zuhd·luh

Could I have my ..., please?	Můžete mi vratit ..., prosím?	moo·zhe·te mi vra·tyit ... pro·seem
deposit	zálohu	za·lo·hu
passport	pas	puhs
valuables	cennosti	tse·nos·tyi

communications & banking

the internet

Where's the local Internet café?
Kde je místní internetová kavárna? gde ye meest·nyee in·ter·ne·to·va kuh·var·nuh

How much is it per hour?
Kolik to stojí na hodinu? ko·lik to sto·yee nuh ho·dyi·nu

I'd like to ...	Chtěl/Chtěla bych ... m/f	khtyel/khtye·luh bikh ...
check my email	zkontrolovat	skon·tro·lo·vuht
	můj email	mooy ee·meyl
get Internet access	přístup na internet	przhees·tup nuh in·ter·net
use a printer	použít tiskárnu	po·u·zheet tyis·kar·nu
use a scanner	použít skener	po·u·zheet ske·ner

mobile/cell phone

I'd like a ...	Chtěl/Chtěla bych ... m/f	ktyel/khtye·luh bikh ...
mobile/cell phone for hire	si půjčit mobil	si pooy·chit mo·bil
SIM card for your network	SIM kartu pro vaší síť	sim kuhr·tu pro vuh·shee seet'

| What are the rates? | Jaké jsou tarify? | yuh·kair ysoh tuh·ri·fi |

telephone

What's your phone number?
Jaké je vaše telefonní číslo? yuh·kair ye vuh·she te·le·fo·nyee chees·lo

The number is ...
Číslo je ... chees·lo ye ...

Where's the nearest public phone?
Kde je nejbližší veřejný telefon? gde ye ney·blizh·shee ve·rzhey·nee te·le·fon

I'd like to buy a phonecard.
Chtěl/Chtěla bych koupit ktyel/khtye·luh bikh koh·pit
telefonní kartu. m/f te·le·fo·nyee kuhr·tu

I want to ...	Chtěl/Chtěla bych ... m/f	ktyel/khtye·luh bikh ...
call (Singapore)	telefonovat do (Singapůru)	te·le·fo·no·vuht do sin·guh·poo·ru
make a local call	si zavolat místně	si zuh·vo·luht meest·nye
reverse the charges	telefonovat na účet volaného	te·le·fo·no·vuht na oo·chet vo·luh·nair·ho

How much does ... cost?	Kolik stojí ...?	ko-lik sto-yee ...
a (three)-minute	(tří) minutový	(trzhee) mi-nu-to-vee
call	hovor	ho-vor
each extra minute	každá další	kuhzh-da duhl-shee
	minuta	mi-nu-tuh

(Seven crowns) per minute.
(Sedm korun) za jednu minutu.   (se-dm ko-run) zuh yed-nu mi-nu-tu

post office

I want to send a ...	Chci poslat ...	khtsi po-sluht ...
fax	fax	fuhks
letter	dopis	do-pis
parcel	balík	buh-leek
postcard	pohled	po-hled

I want to buy a/an ...	Chci koupit ...	khtsi koh-pit ...
envelope	obálku	o-bal-ku
stamp	známku	znam-ku

Please send it by	Prosím vás pošlete	pro-seem vas po-shle-te
... to (Australia).	to ... do (Austrálie).	to ... do (ow-stra-li-ye)
airmail	letecky poštou	le-tets-ki posh-toh
express mail	expresní poštou	eks-pres-nyee posh-toh
registered mail	doporučenou poštou	do-po-ru-che-noh posh-toh
surface mail	obyčejnou poštou	o-bi-chey-noh posh-toh

Is there any mail for me?
Mám zde nějakou poštu?   mam zde nye-yuh-koh posh-tu

bank

I'd like to ...	Chtěl/Chtěla bych ... m/f	kthyel/khtye-luh bikh ...
Where can I ...?	Kde mohu ...?	gde mo-hu ...
arrange a transfer	převést peníze	przhe-vairst pe-nyee-ze
cash a cheque	proměnit šek	pro-mye-nyit shek
change a travellers	proměnit	pro-mye-nyit
cheque	cestovní šek	tses-tov-nyee shek
change money	vyměnit peníze	vi-mye-nyit pe-nyee-ze
get a cash advance	zálohu v hotovosti	za-lo-hu v ho-to-vos-tyi
withdraw money	vybrat peníze	vi-bruht pe-nyee-ze

Where's a/an ...?	Kde je ...?	gde ye ...
ATM	bankomat	buhn·ko·muht
foreign exchange office	směnárna	smye·nar·nuh

What's the ...?	Jaký je ...?	yuh·kee ye ...
charge for that	poplatek za to	po·pluh·tek zuh to
exchange rate	devizový kurz	de·vi·zo·vee kurz

It's ...	Je to ...	ye to ...
(12) crowns	(dvanáct) korun	(dvuh·natst) ko·run
(five) euros	(pět) eur	(pyet) e·ur
free	bez poplatku	bez po·pluht·ku

What time does the bank open?
Jaké jsou úřední hodiny? yuh·kair ysoh oo·rzhed·nyee ho·dyi·ni

Has my money arrived yet?
Přišly už moje peníze? przhi·shli uzh mo·ye pe·nyee·ze

sightseeing

getting in

What time does it open/close?
V kolik hodin otevírají/zavírají? f ko·lik ho·dyin o·te·vee·ruh·yee/zuh·vee·ruh·yee

What's the admission charge?
Kolik stojí vstupné? ko·lik sto·yee vstup·nair

Is there a discount for students/children?
Máte slevu pro studenty/děti? ma·te sle·vu pro stu·den·ti/dye·tyi

I'd like a ...	Chtěl/Chtěla bych ... m/f	khtyel/khtye·luh bikh ...
catalogue	katalog	kuh·tuh·log
guide	průvodce	proo·vod·tse
local map	mapu okolí	ma·pu o·ko·lee

I'd like to see ...
   Chtěl/Chtěla bych vidět ... m/f   khtyel/*khtye*·luh bikh *vi*·dyet ...

What's that?
   Co je to?   tso ye to

Can I take a photo of this?
   Mohu toto fotografovat?   *mo*·hu *to*·to *fo*·to·gruh·fo·vuht

Can I take a photo of you?
   Mohu si vás vyfotit?   *mo*·hu si vas *vi*·fo·tyit

tours

When's the next ...?	*Kdy je příští ...?*	gdi ye *przheesh*·tyee ...
day trip	*celodenní výlet*	*tse*·lo·de·nye *vee*·let
tour	*okružní jízda*	*o*·kruzh·nye *yeez*·duh

Is ... included?	*Je zahrnuto/a ...?* n/f	ye *zuh*·hr·nu·to/a ...
accommodation	*ubytování* n	*u*·bi·to·va·nyee
the admission charge	*vstupné* n	*fstup*·nair
food	*strava* f	*struh*·vuh
transport	*doprava* f	*do*·pruh·vuh

How long is the tour?
   Jak dlouho bude trvat   yuhk *dloh*·ho *bu*·de *tr*·vuht
   tento zájezd?   *ten*·to za·yezd

What time should we be back?
   V kolik hodin se máme vrátit?   f *ko*·lik *ho*·dyin se *ma*·me *vra*·tyit

sightseeing

castle	*hrad* m	hruhd
cathedral	*katedrála* f	*kuh*·te·dra·luh
church	*kostel* m	*kos*·tel
main square	*hlavní náměstí* n	*hluhv*·nyee na·myes·tyee
monastery	*klášter* m	*klash*·ter
monument	*památník* m	*puh*·mat·nyeek
museum	*muzeum* f	*mu*·ze·um
old city	*staré město* n	*stuh*·rair *myes*·to
palace	*palác* m	*puh*·lats
ruins	*zříceniny* f pl	*zrzhee*·tse·nyi·ni
stadium	*stadion* m	*stuh*·di·yon
statue	*socha* f	*so*·khuh

shopping

enquiries

Where's a ...?	Kde je ...?	gde ye ...
bank	banka	*buhn*-kuh
bookshop	knihkupectví	*knyikh*-ku-pets-tvee
camera shop	foto potřeby	*fo*-to *pot*-rzhe-bi
department store	obchodní dům	*op*-khod-nyee doom
grocery store	smíšené zboží	*smee*-she-nair *zbo*-zhee
market	tržnice	*tr*-zhnyi-tse
newsagency	tabák	*tuh*-bak
supermarket	samoobsluha	*suh*-mo-op-slu-huh

Where can I buy (a padlock)?
Kde si mohu koupit (zámek)?   gde si *mo*-hu *koh*-pit (*za*-mek)

I'm looking for ....
Hledám ...   *hle*-dam ...

Can I look at it?
Mohu se na to podívat?   *mo*-hu se nuh to *po*-dyee-vuht

Do you have any others?
Máte ještě jiné?   *ma*-te *yesh*-tye *yi*-nair

Does it have a guarantee?
Je na to záruka?   ye nuh to *za*-ru-kuh

Can I have it sent abroad?
Můžete mi to poslat   *moo*-zhe-te mi to *pos*-luht
do zahraničí?   do *zuh*-hruh-nyi-chee

Can I have my ... repaired?
Můžete zde opravit ...?   *moo*-zhe-te zde *o*-pruh-vit ...

It's faulty.
Je to vadné.   ye to *vuhd*-nair

I'd like ..., please.	Chtěl/Chtěla bych ..., prosím. m/f	khtyel/*khtye*-la bikh ... *pro*-seem
a bag	tašku	*tuhsh*-ku
a refund	vrátit peníze	*vra*-tyit *pe*-nyee-ze
to return this	toto vrátit	*to*-to *vra*-tyit

paying

How much is it?
Kolik to stojí? — ko·lik to sto·yee

Can you write down the price?
Můžete mi napsat cenu? — moo·zhe·te mi nuhp·suht tse·nu

That's too expensive.
To je moc drahé. — to ye mots druh·hair

What's your lowest price?
Jaká je vaše konečná cena? — yuh·ka ye vuh·she ko·nech·na tse·nuh

I'll give you (200 crowns).
Dám vám (dvěstě korun). — dam vam (dvye·stye ko·run)

There's a mistake in the bill.
Na účtu je chyba. — nuh ooch·tu ye khi·buh

Do you accept ...? — *Mohu platit ...?* — mo·hu pluh·tyit ...
   credit cards — *kreditními kartami* — kre·dit·nyee·mi kuhr·tuh·mi
   debit cards — *platebními kartami* — pluh·teb·nyee·mi kuhr·tuh·mi
   travellers cheques — *cestovními šeky* — tses·tov·nyee·mi she·ki

I'd like ..., please. — *Můžete mi dát ..., prosím?* — moo·zhe·te mi dat ... pro·seem
   a receipt — *účet* — oo·chet
   my change — *mé drobné* — mair drob·nair

clothes & shoes

Can I try it on? — *Mohu si to zkusit?* — mo·hu si to sku·sit
My size is (40). — *Mám číslo (čtyřicet).* — mam chee·slo (chti·rzhi·tset)
It doesn't fit. — *Nepadne mi to.* — ne·puhd·ne mi to

small — *malý* — muh·le
medium — *střední* — strzhed·nyee
large — *velký* — vel·keeh

books & music

I'd like a ...   *Chtěl/Chtěla bych ... m/f*   khtyel/*khtye*·luh bikh ...
 newspaper   *noviny*   *no*·vi·ni
  (in English)   *(v angličtině)*   (f *uhn*·glich·tyi·nye)
 pen   *propisovací pero*   pro·pi·so·vuh·tsee *pe*·ro

Is there an English-language bookshop?
 Je tam knihkupectví   ye tuhm *knyih*·ku·pets·tvee
 s anglickýma knihama?   s *uhn*·glits·kee·muh *knyi*·huh·muh

I'm looking for something by (Kabát).
 Hledám něco od (Kabátu).   *hle*·dam *nye*·tso od (*kuh*·ba·tu)

Can I listen to this?
 Mohu si to poslechnout?   *mo*·hu si to *po*·slekh·noht

photography

Can you ...?   *Můžete ...?*   *moo*·zhe·te ...
 develop this film   *vyvolat tento film*   vi·vo·luht *ten*·to film
 load my film   *vložit můj film*   *vlo*·zhit mooy film
 transfer photos   *uložit fotografie*   u·lo·zhit *fo*·to·gruh·fi·ye
  from my camera   *z mého*   z *mair*·ho
  to CD   *fotoaparátu*   *fo*·to·uh·puh·ra·tu
     na CD   nuh *tsair*·dairch·ko

I need a/an ... film   *Potřebuji ... film*   pot·rzhe·bu·yi ... film
for this camera.   *pro tento fotoaparát.*   pro *ten*·to *fo*·to·uh·puh·rat
 APS   *APS*   a·*pair*·es
 B&W   *černobílý*   *cher*·no·bee·lee
 colour   *barevný*   *buh*·rev·nee
 slide   *diapozitivní*   *di*·uh·po·zi·tiv·nyee
 (200) speed   *film s citlivostí*   film s *tsit*·li·vos·tyee
     (dvěstě)   (*dvye*·stye)

When will it be ready?   *Kdy to bude hotové?*   gdi to *bu*·de *ho*·to·vair

meeting people

greetings, goodbyes & introductions

Hello/Hi.	*Ahoj/Čau.*	uh·hoy/chow
Good night.	*Dobrou noc.*	do·broh nots
Goodbye.	*Na shledanou.*	nuh·skhle·duh·noh
Bye.	*Ahoj/Čau.*	uh·hoy/chow
See you later.	*Na viděnou.*	nuh *vi*·dye·noh
Mr/Mrs	*pan/paní*	puhn/*puh*·nyee
Miss	*slečna*	*slech*·nuh
How are you?	*Jak se máte/máš?* pol/inf	yuhk se *ma*·te/mash
Fine. And you?	*Dobře. A vy/ty?* pol/inf	*dob*·rzhe a vi/ti
What's your name?	*Jak se jmenujete/*	yuhk se *yme*·nu·ye·te/
	jmenuješ? pol/inf	*yme*·nu·yesh
My name is ...	*Jmenuji se ...*	*yme*·nu·yi se ...
I'm pleased to meet you.	*Těší mě.*	*tye*·shee mye
This is my ...	*To je můj/moje ...* m/f	to ye mooy/*mo*·ye ...
boyfriend	*přítel*	*przhee*·tel
brother	*bratr*	*bruh*·tr
daughter	*dcera*	*dtse*·ruh
father	*otec*	*o*·tets
friend	*přítel* m	*przhee*·tel
	přítelkyně f	*przhee*·tel·ki·nye
girlfriend	*přítelkyně*	*przhee*·tel·ki·nye
husband	*manžel*	*muhn*·zhel
mother	*matka*	*muht*·kuh
partner (intimate)	*partner/partnerka* m/f	*puhrt*·ner/*puhrt*·ner·kuh
sister	*sestra*	*ses*·truh
son	*syn*	sin
wife	*manželka*	*muhn*·zhel·kuh
Here's my ...	*Zde je moje ...*	zde ye *mo*·ye ...
What's your ...?	*Jaké/Jaká je*	*yuh*·kair/*yuh*·ka ye
	vaše ...? n/f	*vuh*·she ...
(email) address	*(email) adresa* f	(*ee*·meyl) uh·dre·suh
fax number	*faxové číslo* n	*fuhk*·so·vair *chees*·lo
phone number	*telefonní číslo* n	te·le·fo·nyee *chees*·lo

occupations

What's your occupation?
Jaké je vaše povolání? yuh-kair ye *vuh*-she *po*-vo-la-nyee

I'm a/an ...	*Jsem ...*	ysem ...
artist	*umělec/umělkyně* m/f	*u*-mye-lets/*u*-myel-ki-nye
businessperson	*obchodník* m&f	*ob*-khod-nyeek
farmer	*zemědělec* m	ze-mye-dye-lets
	zemědělkyně f	ze-mye-dyel-ki-nye
manual worker	*dělník* m&f	*dyel*-nyeek
office worker	*úředník* m	oo-rzhed-nyeek
	úřednice f	oo-rzhed-nyi-tse
scientist	*vědec/vědkyně* m/f	*vye*-dets/*vyed*-ki-nye

background

Where are you from?	*Odkud jste?*	ot-kud yste
I'm from ...	*Jsem z ...*	ysem s ...
Australia	*Austrálie*	*ow*-stra-li-ye
Canada	*Kanady*	*kuh*-nuh-di
England	*Anglie*	*uhn*-gli-ye
New Zealand	*Nového Zélandu*	*no*-vair-ho *zair*-luhn-du
the USA	*Ameriky*	*uh*-meh-ri-ki

Are you married?	*Jste ženatý/vdaná?* m/f	yste zhe-nuh-tee/*fduh*-na
I'm married.	*Jsem ženatý/vdaná.* m/f	ysem zhe-nuh-tee/*fduh*-na
I'm single.	*Jsem svobodný/á.* m/f	ysem *svo*-bod-nee/a

age

How old ...?	*Kolik ...?*	ko-lik ...
are you	*je vám let* pol	ye vam let
	ti je let inf	ti ye let
is your daughter	*let je vaší dceři*	let ye *vuh*-shee *dtse*-rzhi
is your son	*let je vašemu synovi*	let ye *vuh*-she-mu *si*-no-vi

I'm ... years old.	*Je mi ... let.*	ye mi ... let
He's ... years old.	*Je mu ... let.*	ye mu ... let
She's ... years old.	*Jí je ... let.*	yee ye ... let

feelings

Are you ...?	Jste ...?	yste ...
I'm/I'm not ...	Jsem/Nejsem ...	ysem/ney·sem ...
happy	šťastný/šťastná m/f	shtyuhst·nee/shtyuhst·na
hungry	hladový/hladová m/f	hluh·do·vee/hluh·do·va
sad	smutný/smutná m/f	smut·nee/smut·na
thirsty	žíznivý/žíznivá m/f	zheez·nyi·vee/zheez·nyi·va

Are you ...?	Je vám ...?	ye vam ...
I'm/I'm not ...	Je/Neni mi ...	ye/ne·nyi mi ...
cold	zima	zi·muh
hot	horko	hor·ko

entertainment

going out

Where can I find ...?	Kde mohu najít ...?	gde mo·hu nuh·yeet ...
clubs	kluby	klu·bi
gay venues	homosexuální	ho·mo·sek·su·al·nyee
	zábavné podniky	za·buhv·nair pod·ni·ki
pubs	hospody	hos·po·di

I feel like going	Rád bych šel ... m	rad bikh shel ...
to a/the ...	Ráda bych šla ... f	ra·duh bikh shluh ...
concert	na koncert	nuh kon·tsert
movies	do kina	do ki·nuh
party	na mejdan/	nuh mey·duhn/
	večírek	ve·chee·rek
theatre	na hru	nuh hru
restaurant	do restaurace	do res·tow·ruh·tse

interests

Do you like to ...?		
go to concerts	Chodíte na koncerty?	kho·dyee·te nuh kon·tser·ti
dance	Tancujete?	tuhn·tsu·ye·te
listen to music	Posloucháte hudbu?	po·sloh·kha·te hud·bu

Do you like …?	Máte rád/ráda …? m/f	ma·te rad/ra·duh …
I like …	Mám rád/ráda … m/f	mam rad/ra·duh …
I don't like …	Nemám rád/ráda … m/f	ne·mam rad/ra·duh …
art	umění	u·mye·nyee
cooking	vaření	vuh·rzhe·nyee
movies	filmy	fil·mi
reading	čtení	chte·nyee
sport	sport	sport
travelling	cestování	tses·to·va·nyee

food & drink

finding a place to eat

Can you	Můžete	moo·zhe·te
recommend a …?	doporučit …?	do·po·ru·chit …
café	kavárnu	kuh·var·nu
pub	hospodu	hos·po·du
restaurant	restauraci	res·tow·ruh·tsi
I'd like …, please.	Chtěl/Chtěla bych	khtyel/khtye·luh bikh
	…, prosím. m/f	… pro·seem
a table for (five)	stůl pro (pět)	stool pro (pyet)
the nonsmoking	nekuřáckou	ne·ku·rzhats·koh
section	místnost	meest·nost
the smoking section	kuřáckou místnost	ku·rzhats·koh meest·nost

ordering food

breakfast	snídaně f	snee·duh·nye
lunch	oběd m	o·byed
dinner	večeře f	ve·che·rzhe
snack	občerstvení n	ob·cherst·ve·nyee
What would you	Co byste doporučil/	tso bis·te do·po·ru·chil/
recommend?	doporučila? m/f	do·po·ru·chi·luh

I'd like (the) ...,	Chtěl/Chtěla bych	khtyel/khtye·luh bikh
please.	..., prosím. m/f	... pro·seem
bill	účet	oo·chet
drink list	nápojový lístek	na·po·yo·vee lees·tek
menu	jídelníček	yee·del·nye·chek
that dish	ten pokrm	ten po·krm

drinks

(cup of) coffee ...	(šálek) kávy ...	(sha·lek) ka·vi ...
(cup of) tea ...	(šálek) čaje ...	(sha·lek) chuh·ye ...
with milk	s mlékem	s mlair·kem
without sugar	bez cukru	bez tsu·kru
(orange) juice	(pomerančový) džus m	(po·me·ruhn·cho·vee) dzhus
soft drink	nealkoholický nápoj m	ne·uhl·ko·ho·lits·kee na·poy
(hot) water	(horká) voda f	(hor·ka) vo·duh
... mineral water	... minerální voda	... mi·ne·ral·nyee vo·duh
sparkling	perlivá	per·li·va
still	neperlivá	ne·per·li·va

in the bar

I'll have a ...	Dám si ...	dam si ...
I'll buy you a drink.	Zvu vás/tě na	zvu vas/tye nuh
	sklenku. pol/inf	sklen·ku
What would you like?	Co byste si přál/	tso bis·te si przhal/
	přála? m/f	przha·la
Cheers!	Na zdraví!	nuh zdruh·vee
brandy	brandy f	bruhn·di
champagne	šampaňské n	shuhm·puhn'·skair
cocktail	koktejl m	kok·teyl
a shot of (whisky)	panák (whisky)	puh·nak (vis·ki)
a bottle/jug of beer	láhev/džbán piva	la·hef/dzhban pi·vuh
a bottle/glass	láhev/skleničku	la·hef/skle·nyich·ku
of ... wine	... vína	... vee·nuh
red	červeného	cher·ve·nair·ho
sparkling	šumivého	shu·mi·vair·ho
white	bílého	bee·lair·ho

self-catering

What's the local speciality?
Co je místní specialita?   tso ye *meest*·nyee *spe*·tsi·uh·li·tuh

What's that?
Co to je?   tso to ye

How much is (500 grams of cheese)?
Kolik stojí (padesát   *ko*·lik *sto*·yee (*puh*·de·sat
deka sýra)?   *de*·kuh see·ruh)

I'd like ...	*Chtěl/Chtěla bych ...* m/f	khtyel/*khtye*·luh bikh ...
200 grams	*dvacet deka*	*dvuh*·tset *de*·kuh
(two) kilos	*(dvě) kila*	(dvye) *ki*·luh
(three) pieces	*(tři) kusy*	(trzhi) *ku*·si
(six) slices	*(šest) krajíců*	(shest) *kruh*·yee·tsoo

Less.	*Méně.*	*mair*·nye
Enough.	*Stačí.*	*stuh*·chee
More.	*Trochu více.*	*tro*·khu *vee*·tse

special diets & allergies

Is there a vegetarian restaurant near here?
Je zde blízko vegetariánská   ye zde *blees*·ko *ve*·ge·tuh·ri·ans·ka
restaurace?   *res*·tow·ruh·tse

Do you have vegetarian food?
Máte vegetariánská jídla?   *ma*·te *ve*·ge·tuh·ri·ans·ka *yeed*·luh

Could you prepare a meal without ...?
Mohl/Mohla by jste   *mo*·hl/*mo*·hluh bi yste
připravit jídlo bez ...? m/f   *przhi*·pruh·vit *yeed*·lo bez ...

butter	*máslo* n	*mas*·lo
eggs	*vejce* n pl	*vey*·tse
meat stock	*bujón* m	*bu*·yawn

I'm allergic to ...	*Mám alergii na ...*	mam *uh*·ler·gi·yi nuh ...
dairy produce	*mléčné výrobky*	*mlair*·chnair *vee*·rob·ki
gluten	*lepek*	*le*·pek
MSG	*glutaman sodný*	*glu*·tuh·muhn sod·nee
nuts	*ořechy*	*o*·rzhe·khi
seafood	*plody moře*	*plo*·di *mo*·rzhe

emergencies

basics

Help!	*Pomoc!*	*po*-mots
Stop!	*Zastav!*	*zuhs*-tuhf
Go away!	*Běžte pryč!*	*byezh*-te prich
Thief!	*Zloděj!*	*zlo*-dyey
Fire!	*Hoří!*	*ho*-rzhee
Watch out!	*Pozor!*	*po*-zor
Call ...!	*Zavolejte ...!*	*zuh*-vo-ley-te ...
a doctor	*lékaře*	*lair*-kuh-rzhe
an ambulance	*sanitku*	*suh*-nit-ku
the police	*policii*	*po*-li-tsi-yi

It's an emergency.
To je naléhavý případ.
to ye *nuh*-lair-huh-vee *przhee*-puhd

Could you help me, please?
Můžete prosím pomoci?
moo-zhe-te *pro*-seem po-mo-tsi

Can I use the phone?
Mohu si zatelefonovat?
mo-hu si *zuh*-te-le-fo-no-vuht

I'm lost.
Zabloudil/Zabloudila jsem. m/f
zuh-bloh-dyil/*zuh*-bloh-dyi-luh ysem

Where are the toilets?
Kde jsou toalety?
gde ysoh *to*-uh-le-ti

police

Where's the police station?
Kde je policejní stanice?
gde ye *po*-li-tsey-nyee *stuh*-nyi-tse

I want to report an offence.
Chci nahlásit trestný čin.
khtsi *nuh*-hla-sit *trest*-nee chin

I have insurance.
Jsem pojištěný/pojištěná. m/f
ysem *po*-yish-tye-nee/*po*-yish-tye-na

I've been ...	... *mě.*	... mye
assaulted	*Přepadli*	*przhe*-puhd-li
raped	*Znásilnili*	*zna*-sil-nyi-li
robbed	*Okradli*	*o*-kruhd-li

I've lost my ...	Ztratil/Ztratila	ztruh·tyil/ztruh·tyi·luh
	jsem ... m/f	ysem ...
My ... was/were stolen.	Ukradli mě ...	u·kruhd·li mye ...
backpack	batoh	buh·tawh
credit card	kreditní kartu	kre·dit·nyee kuhr·tu
bag	zavazadlo	zuh·vuh·zuhd·lo
handbag	kabelku	kuh·bel·ku
jewellery	šperky	shper·ki
money	peníze	pe·nyee·ze
passport	pas	puhs
travellers cheques	cestovní šeky	tses·tov·nyee she·ki
wallet	peněženku	pe·nye·zhen·ku
I want to contact my ...	Potřebuji se obrátit na ...	pot·rzhe·bu·yi se o·bra·tyit nuh ...
consulate	můj konzulát	mooy kon·zu·lat
embassy	mé velvyslanectví	mair vel·vi·sluh·nets·tvee

health

medical needs

Where's the nearest ...?	Kde je nejbližší ...?	gde ye ney·blizh·shee ...
dentist	zubař	zu·buhrzh
doctor	lékař	lair·kuhrzh
hospital	nemocnice	ne·mots·nyi·tse
(night) pharmacist	(non-stop) lékárník	(non-stop) lair·kar·nyeek

I need a doctor (who speaks English).

Potřebuji (anglickomluvícího)   pot·rzhe·bu·yi (uhn·glits·kom·lu·vee·tsee·ho)
doktora.   dok·to·ruh

Could I see a female doctor?

Mohla bych být vyšetřená   mo·hluh bikh beet vi·shet·rzhe·na
lékařkou?   lair·kuhrzh·koh

I've run out of my medication.

Došly mi léky.   dosh·li mi lair·ki

symptoms, conditions & allergies

I'm sick.	Jsem nemocný/ nemocná. m/f	ysem ne·mots·nee/ ne·mots·na
It hurts here.	Tady to bolí.	tuh·di to bo·lee
I have (a) ...	Mám ...	mam ...

asthma	astma n	uhst·muh
bronchitis	zánět průdušek m	za·nyet proo·du·shek
constipation	zácpa f	zats·puh
cough n	kašel m	kuh·shel
diarrhoea	průjem m	proo·yem
fever	horečka f	ho·rech·kuh
headache	bolesti hlavy f	bo·les·tyi hluh·vi
heart condition	srdeční porucha f	sr·dech·nyee po·ru·khuh
nausea	nevolnost f	ne·vol·nost
pain n	bolest f	bo·lest
sore throat	bolest v krku f	bo·lest f kr·ku
toothache	bolení zubu n	bo·le·nyee zu·bu

I'm allergic	Jsem alergický/	ysem uh·ler·gits·kee/
to ...	alergická na ... m/f	uh·ler·gits·ka nuh ...
antibiotics	antibiotika	uhn·ti·bi·o·ti·kuh
anti-inflammatories	protizánětlivé léky	pro·tyi·za·nyet·li·vair lair·ki
aspirin	aspirin	uhs·pi·rin
bees	včely	fche·li
codeine	kodein	ko·deyn
penicillin	penicilin	pe·ni·tsi·lin

antiseptic	antiseptický prostředek m	uhn·ti·sep·tits·kee prost·rzhe·dek
bandage	obvaz m	ob·vuhz
condoms	prezervativy m pl	pre·zer·vuh·ti·vi
contraceptives	antikoncepce f	uhn·ti·kon·tsep·tse
diarrhoea medicine	lék na průjem m	lairk nuh proo·yem
insect repellent	prostředek na hubení hmyzu m	pros·trzhe·dek nuh hu·be·nyee hmi·zu
laxatives	projímadla m pl	pro·yee·muhd·la
painkillers	prášky proti bolesti m pl	prash·ki pro·tyi bo·les·tyi
rehydration salts	iontový nápoj m	yon·to·vee na·poy
sleeping tablets	prášky na spaní m pl	prash·ki nuh spuh·nyee

english–czech dictionary

Czech nouns in this dictionary have their gender indicated by ⓜ (masculine), ⓕ (feminine) or ⓝ (neuter). If it's a plural noun, you'll also see pl. Adjectives are given in the masculine form only. Words are also marked as a (adjective), v (verb), sg (singular), pl (plural), inf (informal) or pol (polite) where necessary.

A

A

accident *nehoda* ⓕ *ne-ho-duh*
accommodation *ubytování* ⓝ
  u-bi-to-va-nyee
adaptor *adaptor* ⓜ *uh-duhp-tor*
address *adresa* ⓕ *uh-dre-suh*
after *po* po
air-conditioned *klimatizovaný kli-*muh-ti-zo-vuh-nee
airplane *letadlo* ⓝ *le-tuhd-lo*
airport *letiště* ⓝ *le-tyish-tye*
alcohol *alkohol* ⓜ *uhl-ko-hol*
all a *všichni vshikh-*nyi
allergy *alergie* ⓕ *uh-ler-gi-ye*
ambulance *ambulance* ⓕ *uhm-*bu-luhn-tse
and *a* uh
ankle *kotník* ⓜ *kot-*nyeek
arm *paže* ⓕ *puh-*zhe
ashtray *popelník* ⓜ *po-*pel-nyeek
ATM *bankomat* ⓜ *buhn-*ko-muht

B

baby *nemluvně* ⓝ *nem-*luv-nye
back (body) *záda* ⓕ *za-*duh
backpack *batoh* ⓜ *buh-*tawh
bad *špatný shpuht-*nee
bag *taška* ⓕ *tuhsh-*kuh
baggage claim *výdej zavazadel* ⓜ
  vee-dey zuh-vuh-zuh-del
bank *banka* ⓕ *buhn-*kuh
bar *bar* ⓜ buhr
bathroom *koupelna* ⓕ *koh-*pel-nuh
battery *baterie* ⓕ *buh-*te-ri-ye
beautiful *krásný kras-*nee
bed *postel* ⓕ *pos-*tel
beer *pivo* ⓝ *pi-*vo
before *před* przhed
behind *za* zuh
bicycle *kolo* ⓝ *ko-*lo
big *velký vel-*kee
bill *účet* ⓜ *oo-*chet
black *černý cher-*nee

blanket *deka* ⓕ *de-*kuh
blood group *krevní skupina* ⓕ
  krev-nyee sku-pi-nuh
blue *modrý mod-*ree
book (make a reservation) v *objednat* ob-yed-nuht
bottle *láhev* ⓕ *la-*hef
bottle opener *otvírák na láhve* ⓜ
  ot-vee-rak nuh lah-ve
boy *chlapec* ⓜ *khluh-*pets
brakes (car) *brzdy* ⓕ pl *brz-*di
breakfast *snídaně* ⓕ *snee-*duh-nye
broken (faulty) *zlomený zlo-*me-nee
bus *autobus* ⓜ *ow-*to-bus
business *obchod* ⓜ *op-*khod
buy *koupit koh-*pit

C

café *kavárna* ⓕ *kuh-*var-nuh
camera *fotoaparát* ⓜ *fo-*to-uh-puh-rat
camp site *autokempink* ⓜ *ow-*to-kem-pink
cancel *zrušit zru-*shit
can opener *otvírák na konzervy* ⓜ
  ot-vee-rak nuh kon-zer-vi
car *auto* ⓝ *ow-*to
cash *hotovost* ⓕ *ho-*to-vost
cash (a cheque) v *inkasovat šek in-*kuh-so-vuht shek
cell phone *mobil* ⓜ *mo-*bil
centre *střed* ⓜ strzhed
change (money) v *vyměnit vi-*mye-nyit
cheap *levný lev-*nee
check (bill) *účet* ⓜ *oo-*chet
check-in *recepce* ⓕ *re-*tsep-tse
chest *hruď* ⓕ hrudy
child *dítě* ⓝ *dyee-*tye
cigarette *cigareta* ⓕ *tsi-*guh-re-tuh
city *město* ⓝ *myes-*to
clean a *čistý chis-*tee
closed *zavřený zuh-*vrzhe-nee
coffee *káva* ⓕ *ka-*vuh
coins *mince* ⓕ *min-*tse
cold a *chladný khluhd-*nee
collect call *hovor na účet volaného* ⓜ
  ho-vor nuh oo-chet vo-luh-nair-ho

DICTIONARY

come přijít *przhi-yeet*
computer počítač ⓜ *po-chee-tuhch*
condom prezervativ ⓜ *pre-zer-vuh-tif*
contact lenses kontaktní čočky ⓕ pl
  kon-tuhkt-nyee choch-ki
cook v vařit *vuh-rzhit*
cost cena ⓕ *tse-nuh*
credit card kreditní karta ⓕ
  kre-dit-nyee kuhr-tuh
cup šálek ⓜ *sha-lek*
currency exchange směnárna ⓕ *smye-nar-nuh*
customs (immigration) celnice ⓕ *tsel-ni-tse*
Czech a český *ches-kee*
Czech (language) čeština ⓕ *chesh-tyi-nuh*
Czech Republic Česká republika ⓕ
  ches-ka re-pu-bli-kuh

D

dangerous nebezpečný *ne-bez-pech-nee*
date (time) schůzka ⓕ *skhooz-kuh*
day den ⓜ *den*
delay zpoždění ⓕ *zpozh-dye-nyee*
dentist zubař/zubařka ⓜ/ⓕ *zu-buhrzh/zu-buhrzh-kuh*
depart odjet *od-yet*
diaper plénka ⓕ *plain-kuh*
dictionary slovník ⓜ *slov-nyeek*
dinner večeře ⓕ *ve-che-rzhe*
direct přímý *przhee-mee*
dirty špinavý *shpi-nuh-vee*
disabled invalidní *in-vuh-lid-nyee*
discount sleva ⓕ *sle-vuh*
doctor doktor/doktorka ⓜ/ⓕ *dok-tor/dok-tor-kuh*
double bed manželská postel ⓕ *muhn-zhels-ka pos-tel*
double room dvoulůžkový pokoj ⓜ
  dvoh-loozh-ko-vee po-koy
drink nápoj ⓜ *na-poy*
drive v řídit *rzhee-dyit*
drivers licence řidičský průkaz ⓜ
  rzhi-dyich-skee proo-kuhz
drugs (illicit) drogy ⓕ pl *dro-gi*
dummy (pacifier) dudlík ⓜ *dud-leek*

E

ear ucho ⓝ *u-kho*
east východ ⓜ *vee-khod*
eat jíst *yeest*
economy class turistická třída ⓕ *tu-ris-tits-ka trzhee-duh*
electricity elektřina ⓕ *e-lek-trzhi-nuh*
elevator výtah ⓜ *vee-tuh*
email email ⓜ *ee-meyl*

embassy velvyslanectví ⓝ *vel-vi-sluh-nets-tvee*
emergency pohotovost ⓕ *po-ho-to-vost*
English (language) angličtina ⓕ *uhn-glich-tyi-nuh*
entrance vstup ⓜ *vstup*
evening večer ⓜ *ve-cher*
exchange rate směnný kurs ⓜ *smye-nee kurz*
exit východ ⓜ *vee-khod*
expensive drahý *druh-hee*
express mail expresní zásilka ⓕ *eks-pres-nyee za-sil-kuh*
eye oko ⓝ *o-ko*

F

far daleko *duh-le-ko*
fast rychlý *rikh-lee*
father otec ⓜ *o-tets*
film (camera) film ⓜ *film*
finger prst ⓜ *prst*
first-aid kit lékárnička ⓕ *lair-kar-nyich-kuh*
first class první třída ⓕ *prv-nyee trzhee-duh*
fish ryba ⓕ *ri-buh*
food jídlo ⓝ *yeed-lo*
foot chodidlo ⓝ *kho-dyid-lo*
fork vidlička ⓕ *vid-lich-kuh*
free (of charge) bezplatný *bez-pluht-nee*
friend přítel/přítelkyně ⓜ/ⓕ
  przhee-tel/przhee-tel-ki-nye
fruit ovoce ⓝ *o-vo-tse*
full plný *pl-nee*
funny legrační *le-gruhch-nyee*

G

gift dar ⓜ *duhr*
girl dívka ⓕ *dyeef-kuh*
glass (drinking) sklenička ⓕ *skle-nyich-kuh*
glasses brýle ⓕ pl *bree-le*
go jít *yeet*
good dobrý *do-bree*
green zelený *ze-le-nee*
guide průvodce ⓜ *proo-vod-tse*

H

half polovina ⓕ *po-lo-vi-nuh*
hand ruka ⓕ *ru-kuh*
handbag kabelka ⓕ *kuh-bel-kuh*
happy šťastný *shtyast-nee*
have mít *meet*
he on *on*
head hlava ⓕ *hluh-vuh*
heart srdce ⓝ *srd-tse*

heat *horko* ⓝ hor-ko
heavy *těžký* tyezh-kee
help ∨ *pomoci* po-mo-tsi
here *tady* tuh-di
high *vysoký* vi-so-kee
highway *dálnice* ⓕ dal-nyi-tse
hike ∨ *trampovat* truhm-po-vuht
holiday *svátek* ⓜ sva-tek
homosexual *homosexuál* ⓜ ho-mo-sek-su-al
hospital *nemocnice* ⓕ ne-mots-nyi-tse
hot *horký* hor-kee
hotel *hotel* ⓜ ho-tel
hungry *hladový* hluh-do-vee
husband *manžel* ⓜ muhn-zhel

I

I *já* ya
identification (card) *osobní doklad* ⓝ
o-sob-nyee dok-luhd
ill *nemocný* ne-mots-nee
important *důležitý* doo-le-zhi-tee
included *včetně* fchet-nye
injury *zranění* ⓝ zruh-nye-nyee
insurance *pojištění* ⓝ po-yish-tye-nyee
Internet *internet* ⓜ in-ter-net
interpreter *tlumočník/tlumočnice* ⓜ/ⓕ
tlu-moch-nyeek/tlu-moch-nyi-tse

J

jewellery *šperky* ⓜ pl shper-ki
job *zaměstnání* ⓝ zuh-myest-na-nyee

K

key *klíč* ⓜ kleech
kilogram *kilogram* ⓜ ki-lo-gruhm
kitchen *kuchyň* ⓕ ku-khin'
knife *nůž* ⓜ noozh

L

laundry (place) *prádelna* ⓕ pra-del-nuh
lawyer *advokát/advokátka* ⓜ/ⓕ
uhd-vo-kat/uhd-vo-kat-kuh
left (direction) *levý* le-vee
left-luggage office *úschovna zavazadel* ⓕ
oos-khov-nuh zuh-vuh-zuh-del
leg *noha* ⓕ no-huh

lesbian *lesbička* ⓕ les-bich-kuh
less *menší* men-shee
letter (mail) *dopis* ⓜ do-pis
lift (elevator) *výtah* ⓜ vee-tah
light *světlo* svyet-lo
like ∨ *mít rád* meet rad
lock *zámek* ⓜ za-mek
long *dlouhý* dloh-hee
lost *ztracený* ztruh-tse-nee
lost-property office *ztráty a nálezy* ⓕ
ztra-ti uh na-le-zi
love ∨ *milovat* mi-lo-vuht
luggage *zavazadlo* ⓝ zuh-vuh-zuhd-lo
lunch *oběd* ⓜ o-byed

M

mail *pošta* ⓕ posh-tuh
man *muž* ⓜ muzh
map (of country) *mapa* ⓕ muh-puh
map (of town) *plán* ⓜ plan
market *trh* ⓜ trh
matches *zápalky* ⓕ pl za-puhl-ki
meat *maso* ⓝ muh-so
medicine *lék* ⓜ lairk
menu *jídelní lístek* ⓜ yee-del-nyee lees-tek
message *zpráva* ⓕ zpra-vuh
milk *mléko* ⓝ mlair-ko
minute *minuta* ⓕ mi-nu-tuh
mobile phone *mobil* ⓜ mo-bil
money *peníze* ⓜ pl pe-nyee-ze
month *měsíc* ⓜ mye-seets
morning *ráno* ⓝ ra-no
mother *matka* ⓕ muht-kuh
motorcycle *motorka* ⓕ mo-tor-kuh
motorway *dálnice* ⓕ dal-nyi-tse
mouth *ústa* ⓝ oos-tuh
music *hudba* ⓕ hud-buh

N

name *jméno* ⓝ ymair-no
napkin *ubrousek* ⓜ u-broh-sek
nappy *plenka* ⓕ plen-kuh
near *blízko* bleez-ko
neck *krk* ⓜ krk
new *nový* no-vee
news *zprávy* ⓕ pl zpra-vi
newspaper *noviny* ⓕ pl no-vi-ni
night *noc* ⓕ nots
no *ne* ne

noisy *hlučný* hluch-nee
nonsmoking *nekuřácký* ne-ku-rzhats-kee
north *sever* ⓜ se-ver
nose *nos* ⓜ nos
now *teď* teď
number *číslo* ⓝ chees-lo

O

oil (engine) *olej* ⓜ o-ley
old *starý* stuh-ree
one-way ticket *jednoduchá jízdenka* ⓕ
    yed-no-du-kha yeez-den-kuh
open a *otevřený* o-tev-rzhe-nee
outside *venku* ven-ku

P

package *balík* ⓜ buh-leek
paper *papír* ⓜ puh-peer
park (car) v *parkovat* puhr-ko-vuht
passport *pas* ⓜ puhs
pay *platit* pluh-tyit
pen *propiska* ⓕ pro-pis-kuh
petrol *benzín* ⓜ ben-zeen
pharmacy *lékárna* ⓕ lair-kar-nuh
phonecard *telefonní karta* ⓕ
    te-le-fo-nyee kuhr-tuh
photo *fotka* ⓕ fot-kuh
plate *talíř* ⓜ tuh-leerzh
police *policie* ⓕ po-li-tsi-ye
postcard *pohled* ⓜ po-hled
post office *pošta* ⓕ posh-tuh
pregnant *těhotná* tye-hot-na
price *cena* ⓕ tse-nuh

Q

quiet *tichý* tyi-khee

R

rain *déšť* ⓜ dairsht'
razor *břitva* ⓕ brzhit-vuh
receipt *stvrzenka* ⓕ stvr-zen-kuh
red *červený* cher-ve-nee
refund *vrácení peněz* ⓝ vruh-tse-nyee pe-nyez
registered mail *doporučená zásilka* ⓕ
    do-po-ru-che-na za-sil-kuh
rent v *pronajmout* pro-nai-moht

repair v *opravit* o-pruh-vit
reservation *rezervace* ⓕ re-zer-vuh-tse
restaurant *restaurace* ⓕ res-tow-ruh-tse
return v *vrátit se* vra-tyit se
return ticket *zpáteční jízdenka* ⓕ
    zpa-tech-nyee yeez-den-kuh
right (direction) *pravý* pruh-vee
road *silnice* ⓕ sil-nyi-tse
room *pokoj* ⓜ po-koy

S

safe a *bezpečný* bez-pech-nee
sanitary napkins *dámské vložky* ⓕ pl
    dams-kair vlozh-ki
seat *místo* ⓝ mees-to
send *poslat* pos-luht
service station *benzínová pumpa* ⓕ
    ben-zee-no-va pum-puh
sex *pohlaví* ⓝ po-hluh-vee
shampoo *šampon* ⓜ shuhm-pon
share (a dorm) *spolubývat* spo-lu-o-bee-vuht
shaving cream *pěna na holení* ⓕ
    pye-nuh nuh ho-le-nyee
she *ona* o-nuh
sheet (bed) *prostěradlo* ⓝ pros-tye-ruhd-lo
shirt *košile* ⓕ ko-shi-le
shoes *boty* ⓕ pl bo-ti
shop *obchod* ⓜ op-khod
short *krátký* krat-kee
shower *sprcha* ⓕ spr-khuh
single room *jednolůžkový pokoj* ⓝ
    yed-no-loozh-ko-vee po-koy
skin *kůže* ⓕ koo-zhe
skirt *sukně* ⓕ suk-nye
sleep v *spát* spat
slowly *pomalu* po-muh-lu
small *malý* muh-lee
smoke (cigarettes) v *kouřit* koh-rzhit
soap *mýdlo* ⓝ meed-lo
some *několik* nye-ko-lik
soon *brzy* br-zi
south *jih* ⓜ yih
souvenir shop *obchod se suvenýry* ⓜ
    op-khod se su-ve-nee-ri
speak *říci* rzhee-tsi
spoon *lžíce* ⓕ lzhee-tse
stamp *známka* ⓕ znam-kuh
station (train) *nádraží* ⓝ na-druh-zhee
stomach *žaludek* ⓜ zhuh-lu-dek

english–czech

stop v *zastavit* zuhs-tuh-vit
stop (bus) *zastávka* ① zuhs-taf-kuh
street *ulice* ① u-li-tse
student *student/studentka* ⓜ/①
   stu-dent/stu-dent-kuh
sun *slunce* ① slun-tse
sunscreen *opalovací krém* ⓜ o-puh-lo-vuh-tsee krairm
swim v *plavat* pluh-vuht

T

tampons *tampon* ⓜ tuhm-pon
taxi *taxík* ⓜ tuhk-seek
teaspoon *lžička* ① lzhich-kuh
teeth *zuby* pl zu-bi
telephone *telefon* ⓜ te-le-fon
television *televize* ① te-le-vi-ze
temperature (weather) *teplota* ① te-plo-tuh
tent *stan* ⓜ stuhn
that (one) *tamten* tuhm-ten
they *oni* o-nyi
thirsty *žíznivý* zheez-nyi-vee
this (one) *tenhle* ten-hle
throat *hrdlo* ⓝ hrd-lo
ticket *vstupenka* ① fstu-pen-kuh
time *čas* ⓜ chuhs
tired *unavený* u-nuh-ve-nee
tissues *kosmetické kapesníčky* ⓜ pl
   kos-me-tits-kair kuh-pes-neech-ki
today *dnes* dnes
toilet *toaleta* ① to-uh-le-tuh
tomorrow *zítra* zeet-ruh
tonight *dnes večer* dnes ve-cher
toothbrush *zubní kartáček* ⓜ zub-nyee kuhr-ta-chek
toothpaste *zubní pasta* ① zub-nyee puhs-tuh
torch (flashlight) *baterka* ① buh-ter-kuh
tour *okružní jízda* ① o-kruzh-nyee yeez-duh
tourist office *turistická informační kancelář* ①
   tu-ris-tits-ka in-for-muhch-nyee kuhn-tse-larzh
towel *ručník* ⓜ ruch-nyeek
train *vlak* ⓜ vluhk
translate *přeložit* przhe-lo-zhit
travel agency *cestovní kancelář* ①
   tses-tov-nyee kuhn-tse-larzh
travellers cheque *cestovní šek* ① tses-tov-nyee shek
trousers *kalhoty* ① pl kuhl-ho-ti
twin beds *dvoupostel* ① dvoh-pos-tel
tyre *pneumatika* ① pne-u-muh-ti-kuh

U

underwear *spodní prádlo* ⓝ spod-nyee prad-lo
urgent *naléhavý* nuh-lair-huh-vee

V

vacant *volný* vol-nee
vacation (from school) *prázdniny* ① prazd-nyi-ni
vacation (from work) *dovolená* ① do-vo-le-na
vegetable *zelenina* ① ze-le-nyi-nuh
vegetarian a *vegetariánský* ve-ge-tuh-ri-yans-kee

W

waiter/waitress *číšník/číšnice* ⓜ/①
   cheesh-nyeek/cheesh-nyi-tse
wallet *peněženka* ① pe-nye-zhen-ka
walk v *jít* yeet
warm a *teplý* tep-lee
wash (something) *umýt* u-meet
watch *hodinky* ① pl ho-dyin-ki
water *voda* ① vo-duh
we *my* mi
weekend *víkend* ⓜ vee-kend
west *západ* ⓜ za-puhd
wheelchair *invalidní vozík* ⓜ in-vuh-lid-nyee vo-zeek
when *kdy* gdi
where *kde* gde
white *bílý* bee-lee
who *kdo* gdo
why *proč* proch
wife *manželka* ① muhn-zhel-kuh
window *okno* ⓝ ok-no
wine *víno* ⓝ vee-no
with *s* s
without *bez* bez
woman *žena* ① zhe-nuh
write *psát* p-sat

Y

yellow *žlutý* zhlu-tee
yes *ano* uh-no
yesterday *včera* fche-ruh
you sg inf *ty* ti
you sg pol&pl *vy* vi

French

french alphabet

A a a	*B b* be	*C c* se	*D d* de	*E e* eu
F f ef	*G g* zhe	*H h* ash	*I i* i	*J j* zhi
K k ka	*L l* el	*M m* em	*N n* en	*O o* o
P p pe	*Q q* kew	*R r* er	*S s* es	*T t* te
U u ew	*V v* ve	*W w* dubl ve	*X x* iks	*Y y* i grek
Z z zed				

■ french

FRANÇAIS

FRENCH
français

about French

What do you think of when the word 'French' comes up? A *bon vivant*, drinking an *apéritif tête-à-tête* with a friend at a *café*, while studying the *à la carte* menu and making some witty *double entendres*? Are you getting *déjà vu* yet? Chances are you already know a few fragments of French (*français* fron·sey) – *bonjour, oui, au revoir, bon voyage* and so on. Even if you missed out on French lessons, though, that first sentence (forgive the stereotyping) is evidence that you probably know quite a few French words without realising it. And thanks to the Norman invasion of England in the 11th century, many common English words have a French origin – some estimate, in fact, that three-fifths of everyday English vocabulary arrived via French.

So, after centuries of contact with English, French offers English speakers a relatively smooth path to communicating in another language. The structure of a French sentence won't come as a surprise and the sounds of the language are generally common to English as well. The few sounds that do differ will be familiar to most through television and film examples of French speakers – the silent 'h' and the throaty 'r', for example. French is a distant cousin of English, but is most closely related to its Romance siblings, Italian and Spanish. These languages developed from the Latin spoken by the Romans during their conquests of the 1st century BC.

Almost 30 countries cite French as an official language (not always the only language, of course), in many cases due to France's colonisation of various countries in Africa, the Pacific and the Caribbean. It's the mother tongue of around 80 million people in places like Belgium, Switzerland, Luxembourg, Monaco, Canada and Senegal as well as France, and another 50 million speak it as a second language. French was the language of international diplomacy until the early 20th century, and is still an official language of a number of international organisations, including the Red Cross, the United Nations and the International Olympic Committee.

As well as the advantage of learning a language that's spoken all around the world, there are more subtle benefits to French. Being told of a wonderful vineyard off the tourist track, for example, or discovering that there's little truth in the cliché that the French are rude. And *regardez* the significant body of literature (the Nobel Prize for Literature has gone to French authors a dozen times), film and music ... You'll find the reasons to speak French just keep growing.

123

pronunciation

vowel sounds

Generally, French vowel sounds are short and don't glide into other vowels. Note that the ey in *café* is close to the English sound, but it's shorter and sharper.

symbol	english equivalent	french example	transliteration
a	**run**	*tasse*	tas
ai	**ai**sle	*travail*	tra·vai
air	**fair**	*faire*	fair
e	b**et**	*fesses*	fes
ee	s**ee**	*lit*	lee
eu	n**ur**se	*deux*	deu
ew	**ee** pronounced with rounded lips	*tu*	tew
ey	as in '**bet**', but longer	*musée*	moo·zey
o	p**o**t	*pomme*	pom
oo	m**oo**n	*chou*	shoo

There are also four nasal vowels in French. They're pronounced as if you're trying to force the sound out of your nose rather than your mouth. In French, nasal vowels cause the following nasal consonant sound to be omitted, but a 'hint' of what the implied consonant is can sometimes be heard. We've used nasal consonant sounds (m, n, ng) with the nasal vowel to help you produce the sound with more confidence. Since the four nasal sounds can be quite close, we've simplified it this way:

symbol	english equivalent	french example	transliteration
om/on/ong	like the 'o' in 'p**o**t', plus nasal conso- nant sound	*mouton*	moo·ton
um/un/ung	similar to the 'a' in 'b**a**t', plus nasal consonant sound	*magasin*	ma·ga·zun

consonant sounds

symbol	english equivalent	french example	transliteration
b	**bed**	*billet*	bee·yey
d	**dog**	*date*	dat
f	**fat**	*femme*	fam
g	**go**	*grand*	gron
k	**kit**	*carte*	kart
l	**lot**	*livre*	leev·re
m	**man**	*merci*	mair·see
n	**not**	*non*	non
ny	**canyon**	*signe*	see·nye
ng	**ring**	*cinquante*	sung·kont
p	**pet**	*parc*	park
r	**run** (throaty)	*rue*	rew
s	**sun**	*si*	see
sh	**shot**	*changer*	shon·zhey
t	**top**	*tout*	too
v	**very**	*verre*	vair
w	**win**	*oui*	wee
y	**yes**	*payer*	pe·yey
z	**zero**	*vous avez*	voo·za·vey
zh	**pleasure**	*je*	zhe

word stress

Syllables in French words are, for the most part, equally stressed. English speakers tend to stress the first syllable, so try adding a light stress on the final syllable to compensate. The rhythm of a French sentence is based on breaking the phrase into meaningful sections, then stressing the final syllable pronounced in each section. The stress at these points is characterised by a slight rise in intonation.

tools

language difficulties

Do you speak English?
Parlez-vous anglais?   par·ley·voo ong·gley

Do you understand?
Comprenez-vous?   kom·pre·ney·voo

I understand.
Je comprends.   zhe kom·pron

I don't understand.
Je ne comprends pas.   zhe ne kom·pron pa

What does (*beaucoup*) mean?
Que veut dire (beaucoup)?   ke veu deer (bo·koo)

How do you ...?	*Comment ...?*	ko·mon ...
pronounce this	*le prononcez-vous*	le pro·non·sey voo
write (*bonjour*)	*est-ce qu'on écrit (bonjour)*	es kon ey·kree (bon·zhoor)

Could you please ...?	*Pourriez-vous ..., s'il vous plaît?*	poo·ree·yey voo ... seel voo pley
repeat that	*répéter*	rey·pey·tey
speak more slowly	*parler plus lentement*	par·ley plew lon·te·mon
write it down	*l'écrire*	ley·kreer

essentials

Yes.	*Oui.*	wee
No.	*Non.*	non
Please.	*S'il vous plaît.*	seel voo pley
Thank you (very much).	*Merci (beaucoup).*	mair·see (bo·koo)
You're welcome.	*Je vous en prie.*	zhe voo zon·pree
Excuse me.	*Excusez-moi.*	ek·skew·zey·mwa
Sorry.	*Pardon.*	par·don

numbers

0	*zéro*	zey·ro	16	*seize*	sez
1	*un*	un	17	*dix-sept*	dee·set
2	*deux*	deu	18	*dix-huit*	dee·zweet
3	*trois*	trwa	19	*dix-neuf*	deez·neuf
4	*quatre*	ka·tre	20	*vingt*	vung
5	*cinq*	sungk	21	*vingt et un*	vung tey un
6	*six*	sees	22	*vingt-deux*	vung·deu
7	*sept*	set	30	*trente*	tront
8	*huit*	weet	40	*quarante*	ka·ront
9	*neuf*	neuf	50	*cinquante*	sung·kont
10	*dix*	dees	60	*soixante*	swa·sont
11	*onze*	onz	70	*soixante-dix*	swa·son·dees
12	*douze*	dooz	80	*quatre-vingts*	ka·tre·vung
13	*treize*	trez	90	*quatre-vingt-dix*	ka·tre·vung·dees
14	*quatorze*	ka·torz	100	*cent*	son
15	*quinze*	kunz	1000	*mille*	meel

time & dates

What time is it?	*Quelle heure est-il?*	kel eur ey·teel
It's one o'clock.	*Il est une heure.*	ee·ley ewn eu
It's (10) o'clock.	*Il est (dix) heures.*	ee·ley (deez) eu
Quarter past (one).	*Il est (une) heure et quart.*	ee·ley (ewn) eu ey kar
Half past (one).	*Il est (une) heure et demie.*	ee·ley (ewn) eu ey de·mee
Quarter to (one).	*Il est (une) heure moins le quart.*	ee·ley (ewn) eu mwun le kar
At what time ...?	*À quelle heure ...?*	a kel eu ...
At ...	*À ...*	a ...
in the morning	*du matin*	dew ma·tun
in the afternoon	*de l'après-midi*	de la·prey·mee·dee
in the evening	*du soir*	dew swar
Monday	*lundi*	lun·dee
Tuesday	*mardi*	mar·dee
Wednesday	*mercredi*	mair·kre·dee
Thursday	*jeudi*	zheu·dee
Friday	*vendredi*	von·dre·dee
Saturday	*samedi*	sam·dee
Sunday	*dimanche*	dee·monsh

January	*janvier*	zhon·vyey
February	*février*	feyv·ryey
March	*mars*	mars
April	*avril*	a·vreel
May	*mai*	mey
June	*juin*	zhwun
July	*juillet*	zhwee·yey
August	*août*	oot
September	*septembre*	sep·tom·bre
October	*octobre*	ok·to·bre
November	*novembre*	no·vom·bre
December	*décembre*	dey·som·bre

What date is it today?
C'est quel jour aujourd'hui? — sey kel zhoor o·zhoor·dwee

It's (18 October).
C'est le (dix-huit octobre). — sey le (dee·zwee tok·to·bre)

since (May)	*depuis (mai)*	de·pwee (mey)
until (June)	*jusqu'à (juin)*	zhoos·ka (zhwun)
today	*aujourd'hui*	o·zhoor·dwee
tonight	*ce soir*	se swar

last ...
night	*hier soir*	ee·yair swar
week	*la semaine dernière*	la se·men dair·nyair
month	*le mois dernier*	le mwa dair·nyey
year	*l'année dernière*	la·ney dair·nyair

next ...
week	*la semaine prochaine*	la se·men pro·shen
month	*le mois prochain*	le mwa pro·shen
year	*l'année prochaine*	la·ney pro·shen

yesterday/tomorrow ...
	hier/demain ...	ee·yair/de·mun ...
morning	*matin*	ma·tun
afternoon	*après-midi*	a·pre·mee·dee
evening	*soir*	swar

weather

What's the weather like?	*Quel temps fait-il?*	kel tom fey·teel
It's ...		
cloudy	*Le temps est couvert.*	le tom ey koo·vair
cold	*Il fait froid.*	eel fey frwa
hot	*Il fait chaud.*	eel fey sho
raining	*Il pleut.*	eel pleu
snowing	*Il neige.*	eel nezh
sunny	*Il fait beau.*	eel fey bo
warm	*Il fait chaud.*	eel fey sho
windy	*Il fait du vent.*	eel fey dew von
spring	*printemps* m	prun·tom
summer	*été* m	ey·tey
autumn	*automne* m	o·ton
winter	*hiver* m	ee·vair

border crossing

I'm here ...	*Je suis ici ...*	zhe swee zee·see ...
in transit	*de passage*	de pa·sazh
on business	*pour le travail*	poor le tra·vai
on holiday	*pour les vacances*	poor ley va·kons
I'm here for ...	*Je suis ici pour ...*	zhe swee zee·see poor ...
(10) days	*(dix) jours*	(dees) zhoor
(three) weeks	*(trois) semaines*	(trwa) se·men
(two) months	*(deux) mois*	(deu) mwa

I'm going to (Paris).
Je vais à (Paris). — zhe vey a (pa·ree)

I'm staying at the (Hotel Grand).
Je loge à (l'hotel Grand). — zhe lozh a (lo·tel gron)

I have nothing to declare.
Je n'ai rien à déclarer. — zhe ney ryun a dey·kla·rey

I have something to declare.
J'ai quelque chose à déclarer. — zhey kel·ke·shoz a dey·kla·rey

That's not mine.
Ce n'est pas à moi. — se ney pa a mwa

transport

tickets & luggage

Where can I buy a ticket?
Où peut-on acheter un billet?　　　oo pe·ton ash·tey um bee·yey

Do I need to book a seat?
Est-ce qu'il faut réserver une place?　es·keel fo rey·zer·vey ewn plas

One ... ticket	*Un billet ... (pour*	um bee·yey ... (poor
(to Bordeaux), please.	*Bordeaux), s'il vous plaît.*	bor·do) seel voo pley
one-way	*simple*	sum·ple
return	*aller et retour*	a·ley ey re·toor

I'd like to ... my	*Je voudrais ... mon*	zhe voo·drey ... mom
ticket, please.	*billet, s'il vous plaît.*	bee·yey seel voo pley
cancel	*annuler*	a·new·ley
change	*changer*	shon·zhey
collect	*retirer*	re·tee·rey
confirm	*confirmer*	kon·feer·mey

I'd like a ... seat,	*Je voudrais une place*	zhe voo·drey ewn plas
please.	*..., s'il vous plaît.*	... seel voo pley
(non)smoking	*non-fumeur*	non few·me
smoking	*fumeur*	few·me

How much is it?
C'est combien?　　　sey kom·byun

Is there air conditioning?
Est-qu'il y a la climatisation?　es·keel ya la klee·ma·tee·za·syon

Is there a toilet?
Est-qu'il y a des toilettes?　es·keel ya dey twa·let

How long does the trip take?
Le trajet dure combien de temps?　le tra·zhey dewr kom·byun de tom

Is it a direct route?
Est-ce que c'est direct?　es·ke sey dee·rekt

I'd like a luggage locker.
Je voudrais une　　　zhe voo·drey ewn
consigne automatique.　kon·see·nye o·to·ma·teek

My luggage	Mes bagages	mey ba-gazh
has been ...	ont été ...	on tey-tey ...
damaged	endommagés	on-do-ma-zhey
lost	perdus	per-dew
stolen	volés	vo-ley

getting around

Where does flight (008) arrive?
Où atteri le vol (008)? oo a-te-ree le vol (zey-ro zey-ro weet)

Where does flight (008) depart?
D'où décolle le vol (008)? doo dey-kol le vol (zey-ro zey-ro weet)

Where's (the) ...?	Où se trouve ...?	oo se troo-ve ...
arrivals hall	le hall d'arrivée	le hol da-ree-vey
departures hall	le hall des departs	le hol dey dey-par
duty-free shop	le magasin duty-free	le ma-ga-zun dyoo-tee free
gate (12)	porte (douze)	port (dooz)

Is this the ... to (Nice)?	Est ce ... pour (Nice)?	es se ... poor (nees)
boat	le bateau	le ba-to
bus	le bus	le bews
plane	l'avion	la-vyon
train	le train	le trun

What time's	Le ... bus passe	le ... bews pas
the ... bus?	à quelle heure?	a kel e
first	premier	pre-myey
last	dernier	dair-nyey
next	prochain	pro-shun

At what time does it arrive/leave?
A quelle heure est ce qu'il arrive/part? a kel eur es se keel a-ree-ve/par

How long will it be delayed?
De combien de temps est-il retardé? de kom-byun de tom es-teel re-tar-dey

What station is this?
C'est quelle gare? sey kel gar

What's the next station?
Quelle est la prochaine gare? kel ey la pro-shen gar

Does it stop at (Amboise)?
Est-ce qu'il s'arrête à (Amboise)? es-kil sa-ret a (om-bwaz)

Please tell me when we get to (Nantes).
Pouvez-vous me dire quand   poo·vey·voo me deer kon
nous arrivons à (Nantes)?   noo za·ree·von a (nont)

How long do we stop here?
Combien de temps on s'arrête ici?   kom·byun de tom on sa·ret ee·see

Is this seat available?
Est-ce que cette place est libre?   es·ke set plas ey lee·bre

That's my seat.
C'est ma place.   sey ma plas

I'd like a taxi ...	*Je voudrais un taxi ...*	zhe voo·drey un tak·see ...
at (9am)	*à (neuf heures*	a (neu veur
	du matin)	dew ma·tun)
now	*maintenant*	mun·te·non
tomorrow	*demain*	de·mun

Is this taxi available?
Vous êtes libre?   voo·zet lee·bre

How much is it to ...?
C'est combien pour aller à ...?   sey kom·byun poor a·ley a ...

Please put the meter on.
Mettez le compteur, s'il vous plaît.   me·tey le kon·teseel voo pley

Please take me to (this address).
Conduisez-moi à (cette adresse),   kon·dwee·zey mwa a (set a·dres)
s'il vous plaît.   seel voo pley

Please ...	*..., s'il vous plaît.*	... seel voo pley
slow down	*Roulez plus lentement*	roo·ley plew lont·mon
stop here	*Arrêtez-vous ici*	a·rey·tey voo ee·see
wait here	*Attendez ici*	a·ton·dey ee·see

car, motorbike & bicycle hire

I'd like to hire a ...	*Je voudrais louer ...*	zhe voo·drey loo·wey ...
bicycle	*un vélo*	un vey·lo
car	*une voiture*	ewn vwa·tewr
motorbike	*une moto*	ewn mo·to

with ...	*avec ...*	a·vek ...
a driver	*un chauffeur*	un sho·feur
air conditioning	*climatisation*	klee·ma·tee·za·syon

How much for ... hire?	*Quel est le tarif par ...?*	kel ey le ta·reef par ...
hourly	*heure*	eur
daily	*jour*	zhoor
weekly	*semaine*	se·men

air	*air* m	air
oil	*huile* f	weel
petrol	*essence* f	es·sons
tyres	*pneus* f pl	pneu

I need a mechanic.
J'ai besoin d'un mécanicien.   zhey be·zwun dun mey·ka·nee·syun

I've run out of petrol.
Je suis en panne d'essence.   zhe swee zon pan de·sons

I have a flat tyre.
Mon pneu est à plat.   mom pneu ey ta pla

directions

Where's the ...?	*Où est-ce qu'il y a ...?*	oo es·keel ya ...
bank	*la banque*	la bongk
city centre	*le centre-ville*	ler son·tre·veel
hotel	*l'hôtel*	lo·tel
market	*le marché*	le mar·shey
police station	*le commissariat*	le kom·mee·sar·ya
	de police	de po·lees
post office	*le bureau de poste*	le bew·ro de post
public toilet	*des toilettes*	dey twa·let
tourist office	*l'office de tourisme*	lo·fees de too·rees·me

Is this the road to (Toulouse)?
C'est la route pour (Toulouse)?   sey la root poor (too·looz)

Can you show me (on the map)?
Pouvez-vous m'indiquer (sur la carte)?   poo·vey·voo mun·dee·key (sewr la kart)

What's the address?
Quelle est l'adresse?   kel ey la·dres

How far is it?
C'est loin?   sey lwun

How do I get there?
Comment faire pour y aller?   ko·mon fair poor ee a·ley

Turn ...	Tournez ...	toor·ney ...
at the corner	au coin	o kwun
at the traffic lights	aux feux	o feu
left/right	à gauche/droite	a gosh/drwat

It's ...	C'est ...	sey ...
behind ...	derrière ...	dair·yair ...
far away	loin d'ici	lwun dee·see
here	ici	ee·see
in front of ...	devant ...	de·von ...
left	à gauche	a gosh
near (to ...)	près (de ...)	prey (de ...)
next to ...	à côté de ...	a ko·tey de ...
opposite ...	en face de ...	on fas de ...
right	à droite	a drwat
straight ahead	tout droit	too drwa
there	là	la

north	nord m	nor
south	sud m	sewd
east	est m	est
west	ouest m	west

by bus	en bus	om bews
by taxi	en taxi	on tak·see
by train	en train	on trun
on foot	à pied	a pyey

signs

Entrée/Sortie	on·trey/sor·tee	**Entrance/Exit**
Ouvert/Fermé	oo·vair/fair·mey	**Open/Closed**
Chambre Libre	shom·bre lee·bre	**Rooms Available**
Complet	kom·pley	**No Vacancies**
Renseignements	ron·sen·ye·mon	**Information**
Commissariat De Police	ko·mee·sar·ya de po·lees	**Police Station**
Interdit	in·teyr·dee	**Prohibited**
Toilettes	twa·let	**Toilets**
Hommes	om	**Men**
Femmes	fam	**Women**
Chaude/Froide	shod/frwad	**Hot/Cold**

134

accommodation

finding accommodation

Where's a …?	*Où est-ce qu'on peut trouver …?*	oo es·kon peu troo·vey …
camping ground	*un terrain de camping*	un tey·run de kom·peeng
guesthouse	*une pension*	ewn pon·see·on
hotel	*un hôtel*	un o·tel
youth hostel	*une auberge de jeunesse*	ewn o·bairzh de zhe·nes
Can you recommend somewhere …?	*Est-ce que vous pouvez recommander un logement …?*	es·ke voo poo·vey re·ko·mon·dey un lozh·mon …
cheap	*pas cher*	pa shair
good	*de bonne qualité*	de bon ka·lee·tey
nearby	*près d'ici*	prey dee·see

I'd like to book a room, please.
Je voudrais réserver   zhe voo·drey rey·zair·vey
une chambre, s'il vous plaît.   ewn shom·bre seel voo pley

I have a reservation.
J'ai une réservation.   zhey ewn rey·zair·va·syon

My name is …
Mon nom est …   mon nom ey …

Do you have a … room?	*Avez-vous une chambre …?*	a·vey·voo ewn shom·bre …
single	*à un lit*	a un lee
double	*avec un grand lit*	a·vek ung gron lee
twin	*avec des lits jumeaux*	a·vek dey lee zhew·mo
Can I pay by …?	*Est-ce qu'on peut payer avec …?*	es·kom peu pey·yey a·vek …
credit card	*une carte de crédit*	ewn kart de krey·dee
travellers cheque	*des chèques de voyage*	dey shek de vwa·yazh
How much is it per …?	*Quel est le prix par …?*	kel ey le pree par …
night	*nuit*	nwee
person	*personne*	pair·son

I'd like to stay for (two) nights.
Je voudrais rester pour (deux) nuits. zhe voo·drey res·tey poor (der) nwee

From (July 2) to (July 6).
Du (deux juillet) au (six juillet). dew (de zhwee·yey) o (see zhwee·yey)

Can I see it?
Est-ce que je peux la voir? es·ke zhe peu la vwar

Am I allowed to camp here?
Est-ce que je peux camper ici? es·ke zhe peu kom·pey ee·see

Where's the nearest camp site?
Où est le terrain de camping oo ey ler tey·run de kom·peeng
le plus proche? le plew prosh

requests & queries

When/Where is breakfast served?
Quand/Où le petit kon/oo le pe·tee
déjeuner est-il servi? dey·zhe·ney ey·teel sair·vee

Please wake me at (seven).
Réveillez-moi à (sept) rey·vey·yey·mwa a (set)
heures, s'il vous plaît. eur seel voo pley

Could I have my key, please?
Est-ce que je pourrais avoir es·ke zhe poo·rey a·vwar
la clé, s'il vous plaît? la kley seel voo pley

Can I get another (blanket)?
Est-ce que je peux avoir es·ke zhe pe a·vwar
une autre (couverture)? ewn o·tre (koo·vair·tewr)

Is there a/an ...?	*Avez-vous un ...?*	a·vey·voo un ...
elevator	*ascenseur*	a·son·seur
safe	*coffre-fort*	ko·fre·for

The room is too ...	*C'est trop ...*	sey tro ...
expensive	*cher*	shair
noisy	*bruyant*	brew·yon
small	*petit*	pe·tee

The ... doesn't work.	... ne fonctionne pas.	... ne fong·syon pa
air conditioning	La climatisation	klee·ma·tee·za·syon
fan	Le ventilateur	le von·tee·la·teur
toilet	Les toilettes	le twa·let

This ... isn't clean.	... n'est pas propre.	... ney pa pro·pre
pillow	Cet oreiller	set o·rey·yey
sheet	Ce drap	se drap
towel	Cette serviette	set sair·vee·et

checking out

What time is checkout?
Quand faut-il régler? — kon fo·teel rey·gley

Can I leave my luggage here?
Puis-je laisser mes bagages? — pweezh ley·sey mey ba·gazh

Could I have my ..., please?	Est-ce que je pourrais avoir ..., s'il vous plaît?	es·ke zhe poo·rey a·vwar ... seel voo pley
deposit	ma caution	ma ko·syon
passport	mon passeport	mon pas·por
valuables	mes biens précieux	mey byun prey·syeu

communications & banking

the internet

Where's the local Internet café?
Où est le cybercafé du coin? — oo ey le see·bair·ka·fey dew kwun

How much is it per hour?
C'est combien l'heure? — sey kom·byun leur

I'd like to ...	Je voudrais ...	zhe voo·drey ...
check my email	consulter mon courrier électronique	kon·sewl·tey mong koor·yey ey·lek·tro·neek
get Internet access	me connecter à l'internet	me ko·nek·tey a lun·tair·net
use a printer	utiliser une imprimante	ew·tee·lee·zey ewn um·pree·mont
use a scanner	utiliser un scanner	ew·tee·lee·zey un ska·nair

mobile/cell phone

I'd like a ...	Je voudrais ...	zhe voo-drey ...
mobile/cell phone for hire	louer un portable	loo-ey um por-ta-ble
SIM card for your network	une carte SIM pour le réseau	ewn kart seem poor le rey-zo

| What are the rates? | Quels sont les tarifs? | kel son ley ta-reef |

telephone

What's your phone number?
Quel est votre numéro de téléphone?
kel ey vo-tre new-mey-ro de tey-ley-fon

The number is ...
Le numéro est ...
le new-mey-ro ey ...

Where's the nearest public phone?
Où est le téléphone public le plus proche?
oo ey le tey-ley-fon pewb-leek le plew prosh

I'd like to buy a phone card.
Je voudrais acheter une carte téléphonique.
zhe voo-drey ash-tey ewn kart tey-ley-fo-neek

I want to ...	Je veux ...	zhe ve ...
call (Singapore)	téléphoner avec préavis (à Singapour)	tey-ley-fo-ney a-vek prey-a-vee (a sung-ga-poor)
make a local call	faire un appel local	fair un a-pel lo-kal
reverse the charges	téléphoner en PCV	tey-ley-fo-ney om pey-sey-vey

How much does ... cost?	Quel est le prix ...?	kel ey le pree ...
a (three)-minute call	d'une communication de (trois) minutes	dewn ko-mew-nee-ka-syon de (trwa) mee-newt
each extra minute	de chaque minute supplémentaire	de shak mee-newt sew-pley-mon-tair

It's (one euro) per (minute).
(Un euro) pour (une minute).
(un eu-ro) poor (ewn mee-newt)

post office

I want to send a ...	*Je voudrais envoyer ...*	zhe voo·drey on·vwa·yey ...
fax	*un fax*	un faks
letter	*une lettre*	ewn le·tre
parcel	*un colis*	ung ko·lee
postcard	*une carte postale*	ewn kart pos·tal
I want to buy a/an ...	*Je voudrais acheter ...*	zhe voo·drey ash·tey ...
envelope	*une enveloppe*	ewn on·vlop
stamp	*un timbre*	un tum·bre
Please send it (to Australia) by ...	*Envoyez-le (en Australie) ..., s'il vous plaît.*	on·vwa·yey·le (on os·tra·lee) ... seel voo pley
airmail	*par avion*	par a·vyon
express mail	*en exprès*	on neks·pres
registered mail	*en recommandé*	on re·ko·mon·dey
surface mail	*par voie de terre*	par vwa de tair

Is there any mail for me?
Y a-t-il du courrier pour moi? ya·teel dew koor·yey poor mwa

bank

Where's a/an ...?	*Où est ...?*	oo ey ...
ATM	*le guichet automatique*	le gee·shey o·to·ma·teek
foreign exchange office	*le bureau de change*	le bew·ro de shonzh
I'd like to ...	*Je voudrais ...*	zhe voo·drey ...
arrange a transfer	*faire un virement*	fair un veer·mon
cash a cheque	*encaisser un chèque*	ong·key·sey un shek
change a travellers cheque	*changer des chèques de voyage*	shon·zhey dey shek de vwa·yazh
change money	*changer de l'argent*	shon·zhey de lar·zhon
get a cash advance	*une avance de crédit*	ewn a·vons de krey·dee
withdraw money	*retirer de l'argent*	re·tee·rey de lar·zhon
What's the ...?	*Quel est ...?*	kel ey ...
charge for that	*le tarif*	le ta·reef
exchange rate	*le taux de change*	le to de shonzh

It's ...	C'est ...	sey ...
(12) euros	(douze) euros	(dooz) eu·ro
free	gratuit	gra·twee

What time does the bank open?
À quelle heure ouvre la banque? — a kel eur oo·vre la bongk

Has my money arrived yet?
Mon argent est-il arrivé? — mon ar·zhon ey·teel a·ree·vey

sightseeing

getting in

What time does it ...?	Quelle est l'heure ...?	kel ey leur ...
close	de fermeture	de fer·me·tewr
open	d'ouverture	doo·vair·tewr

What's the admission charge?
Quel est le prix d'admission? — kel ey le pree dad·mee·syon

Is there a discount for children/students?
Il y a une réduction pour les enfants/étudiants? — eel ya ewn rey·dewk·syon poor ley zon·fon/zey·tew·dyon

I'd like a ...	Je voudrais ...	zhe voo·drey ...
catalogue	un catalogue	ung ka·ta·log
guide	un guide	ung geed
local map	une carte de la région	ewn kart de la rey·zhyon

I'd like to see ...	J'aimerais voir ...	zhem·rey vwar ...
What's that?	Qu'est-ce que c'est?	kes·ke sey
Can I take photos?	Je peux prendre des photos?	zhe peu pron·dre dey fo·to

tours

When's the next ...?	C'est quand la prochaine ...?	sey kon la pro·shen ...
day trip	excursion d'une journée	eks·kewr·syon dewn zhoor·ney
tour	excursion	eks·kewr·syon

Is ... included?	Est-ce que ... est inclus/incluse? m/f	es·ke ... ey tung·klew/tung·klewz
accommodation	le logement m	le lozh·mon
the admission charge	l'admission f	lad·mee·syon
food	la nourriture f	la noo·ree·tewr
transport	le transport m	le trons·por

How long is the tour?
L'excursion dure combien de temps? leks·kewr·syon dewr kom·byun de tom

What time should we be back?
On doit rentrer pour quelle heure? on dwa ron·trey poor kel eur

sightseeing

castle	château m	sha·to
cathedral	cathédrale f	ka·tey·dral
church	église f	ey·gleez
main square	place centrale f	plas son·tral
monastery	monastère m	mo·na·stair
monument	monument m	mo·new·mon
museum	musée m	mew·zey
old city	vieille ville f	vyey veel
palace	palais m	pa·ley
ruins	ruines f pl	rween
stadium	stade m	stad
statues	statues f pl	sta·tew

shopping

enquiries

Where's a ...?	Où est ...?	oo es ...
bank	la banque	la bongk
bookshop	la librairie	la lee·brey·ree
camera shop	le magasin photo	le ma·ga·zun fo·to
department store	le grand magasin	le gron ma·ga·zun
grocery store	l'épicerie	ley·pee·sree
market	le marché	le mar·shey
newsagency	le marchand de journaux	le mar·shon de zhoor·no
supermarket	le supermarché	le sew·pair·mar·shey

Where can I buy (a padlock)?
Où puis-je acheter (un cadenas)?   oo pweezh ash·tey (un kad·na)

I'm looking for …
Je cherche …   zhe shairsh …

Can I look at it?
Est-ce que je peux le voir?   es·ke zhe peu le vwar

Do you have any others?
Vous en avez d'autres?   voo zon a·vey do·tre

Does it have a guarantee?
Est-ce qu'il y a une garantie?   es keel ya ewn ga·ron·tee

Can I have it sent overseas?
Pouvez-vous me l'envoyer   poo·vey·voo me lon·vwa·yey
à l'étranger?   a ley·tron·zhey

Can I have my … repaired?
Puis-je faire réparer …?   pwee·zhe fair rey·pa·rey …

It's faulty.
C'est défectueux.   sey dey·fek·tweu

I'd like …, please.   *Je voudrais …,*   zhe voo·drey …
     s'il vous plaît.   seel voo pley

     a bag   *un sac*   un sak
     a refund   *un remboursement*   un rom·boors·mon
     to return this   *rapporter ceci*   ra·por·tey se·see

paying

How much is it?
C'est combien?   sey kom·byun

Can you write down the price?
Pouvez-vous écrire le prix?   poo·vey·voo ey·kreer le pree

That's too expensive.
C'est trop cher.   sey tro shair

Can you lower the price?
Vous pouvez baisser le prix?   voo poo·vey bey·sey le pree

I'll give you (five) euros.
Je vous donnerai (cinq) euros.   zhe voo don·rey (sungk) eu·ro

There's a mistake in the bill.
Il y a une erreur dans la note.   eel ya ewn ey·reur don la not

Do you accept ...?	Est-ce que je peux payer avec ...?	es·ke zhe pe pey·yey a·vek ...
credit cards	une carte de crédit	ewn kart de krey·dee
debit cards	une carte de débit	ewn kart de dey·bee
travellers cheques	des chèques de voyages	dey shek de vwa·yazh

I'd like ..., please.	Je voudrais ..., s'il vous plaît.	zhe voo·drey ... seel voo pley
a receipt	un reçu	un re·sew
my change	ma monnaie	ma mo·ney

clothes & shoes

Can I try it on?	Puis-je l'essayer?	pwee·zhe ley·sey·yey
My size is (42).	Je fais du (quarante-deux).	zhe fey dew (ka·ront·deu)
It doesn't fit.	Ce n'est pas la bonne taille.	se ney pa la bon tai

small	petit	pe·tee
medium	moyen	mwa·yen
large	grand	gron

books & music

I'd like a ...	Je voudrais ...	zhe voo·drey ...
newspaper	un journal	un zhoor·nal
(in English)	(en anglais)	(on ong·gley)
pen	un stylo	un stee·lo

Is there an English-language bookshop?
Y a-t-il une librairie anglaise?   ya·teel ewn lee·brey·ree ong·gleyz

I'm looking for something by (Camus).
Je cherche quelque chose de (Camus).   zhe shairsh kel·ke shoz de (ka·mew)

Can I listen to this?
Je peux l'écouter ici?   zhe peu ley·koo·tey ee·see

photography

Can you ...?	Pouvez-vous ...?	poo·vey·voo ...
burn a CD from my memory card	copier un CD de ma carte memoire	ko·pyey un se·de de ma kart mey·mwar
develop this film	développer cette pellicule	dey·vlo·pey set pey·lee·kewl
load my film	charger ma pellicule	shar·zhey ma pey·lee·kewl

I need a/an ...	J'ai besoin d'une	zhey be·zwun dewn
film for this camera.	pellicule ... pour cet appareil.	pey·lee·kewl ... poor sey·ta·pa·rey
APS	APS	a·pey·es
B&W	en noir et blanc	on nwar ey·blong
colour	couleur	koo·leur
slide	diapositive	dya·po·zee·teev
(200) speed	rapidité (deux cent)	ra·pee·dee·tey (deu son)

When will it be ready?
Quand est-ce que cela sera prêt?   kon tes·ke se·la se·ra prey

meeting people

greetings, goodbyes & introductions

Hello.	Bonjour.	bon·zhoor
Hi.	Salut.	sa·lew
Good night.	Bonsoir.	bon·swar
Goodbye.	Au revoir.	o re·vwar
See you later.	À bientôt.	a byun·to

Mr	Monsieur	me·syeu
Mrs	Madame	ma·dam
Miss	Mademoiselle	mad·mwa·zel

How are you?	Comment allez-vous?	ko·mon ta·ley·voo
Fine, thanks. And you?	Bien, merci. Et vous?	byun mair·see ey voo
What's your name?	Comment vous appelez-vous?	ko·mon voo za·pley·voo
My name is ...	Je m'appelle ...	zhe ma·pel ...
I'm pleased to meet you.	Enchanté/Enchantée. m/f	on·shon·tey

This is my ...	*Voici mon/ma ...* m/f	vwa·see mon/ma ...
boyfriend	*petit ami*	pe·tee ta·mee
brother	*frère*	frair
daughter	*fille*	fee·ye
father	*père*	pair
friend	*ami/amie* m/f	a·mee
girlfriend	*petite amie*	pe·teet a·mee
husband	*mari*	ma·ree
mother	*mère*	mair
partner (intimate)	*partenaire*	par·te·nair
sister	*sœur*	seur
son	*fils*	fees
wife	*femme*	fam

Here's my ...	*Voici mon ...*	vwa·see mon ...
What's your ...?	*Quel est votre ...?* pol	kel ey vo·tre ...
	Quel est ton ...? inf	kel ey ton ...
address	*adresse*	a·dress
email address	*e-mail*	ey·mel
fax number	*numéro de fax*	new·mey·ro de faks
phone number	*numéro de*	new·mey·ro de
	téléphone	tey·ley·fon

occupations

What's your occupation?

Vous faites quoi comme métier? pol	voo fet kwa kom mey·tyey
Tu fais quoi comme métier? inf	tew fey kwa kom mey·tyey

I'm a/an ...	*Je suis un/une ...* m/f	zhe swee zun/zewn ...
artist	*artiste* m&f	ar·teest
businessperson	*homme/femme*	om/fem
	d'affaires m/f	da·fair
farmer	*agriculteur* m	a·gree·kewl·teur
	agricultrice f	a·gree·kewl·trees
manual worker	*ouvrier/ouvrière* m/f	oo·vree·yey/oo·vree·yair
office worker	*employé/employée*	om·plwa·yey
	de bureau m/f	de bew·ro
scientist	*scientifique* m&f	syon·tee·feek
student	*étudiant/étudiante* m/f	ey·tew·dyon/ey·tew·dyont
tradesperson	*ouvrier qualifié* m&f	oo·vree·yey ka·lee·fyey

background

Where are you from?	*Vous venez d'où?* pol	voo ve·ney doo
	Tu viens d'où? inf	tew vyun doo
I'm from ...	*Je viens ...*	zhe vyun ...
Australia	*d'Australie*	dos·tra·lee
Canada	*du Canada*	dew ka·na·da
England	*d'Angleterre*	dong·gle·tair
New Zealand	*de la Nouvelle-Zélande*	de la noo·vel·zey·lond
the USA	*des USA*	dey zew·es·a

Are you married?

Est-ce que vous êtes marié(e)? m/f pol	es·ke voo zet mar·yey
Est-ce que tu es marié(e)? m/f inf	es·ke tew ey mar·yey

I'm married.

Je suis marié/mariée. m/f	zhe swee mar·yey

I'm single.

Je suis célibataire. m&f	zhe swee sey·lee·ba·tair

age

How old ...?	*Quel âge ...?*	kel azh ...
are you	*avez-vous* pol	a·vey·voo
	as-tu inf	a·tew
is your daughter	*a votre fille* pol	a vo·tre fee·ye
is your son	*a votre fils* pol	a vo·tre fees
I'm ... years old.	*J'ai ... ans.*	zhey ... on
He/She is ... years old.	*Il/Elle a ... ans.*	eel/el a ... on

feelings

I'm (not) ...	*Je (ne) suis (pas)...*	zhe (ne) swee (pa) ...
Are you ...?	*Êtes-vous ...?* pol	et voo ...
	Es-tu ...? inf	ey·tew ...
happy	*heureux/heureuse* m/f	er·reu/er·reuz
sad	*triste* m&f	treest

I'm ...	J'ai ...	zhey ...
I'm not ...	Je n'ai pas ...	zhe ney pa ...
Are you ...?	Avez-vous ...? pol	a·vey voo ...
	As-tu ...? inf	a·tew ...
cold	froid/froide m/f	frwa/frwad
hot	chaud/chaude m/f	sho/shod
hungry	faim m&f	fum
thirsty	soif m&f	swaf

entertainment

going out

Where can I find ...?	Où sont les ...?	oo son ley ...
clubs	clubs	kleub
gay venues	boîtes gaies	bwat gey
pubs	pubs	peub
I feel like going to a/the ...	Je voudrais aller ...	zhe voo·drey a·ley ...
concert	à un concert	a ung kon·sair
movies	au cinéma	o see·ney·ma
party	à la fête	a la feyt
restaurant	au restaurant	o res·to·ron
theatre	au théâtre	o tey·a·tre

interests

Do you like ...?	Aimes-tu ...? inf	em·tew ...
I like ...	J'aime ...	zhem ...
I don't like ...	Je n'aime pas ...	zhe nem pa ...
art	l'art	lar
cooking	cuisiner	kwee·zee·ney
movies	le cinéma	le see·ney·ma
nightclubs	les boîtes	ley bwat
reading	lire	leer
shopping	faire des courses	fair dey koors
sport	le sport	le spor
travelling	voyager	vwa·ya·zhey

Do you like to ...?	Aimes-tu ...? inf	em·tew ...
dance	danser	don·sey
go to concerts	aller aux concerts	a·ley o kon·sair
listen to music	écouter de	ey·koo·tey de la
	la musique	mew·zeek

food & drink

finding a place to eat

Can you	Est-ce que vous pouvez	es·ke voo poo·vey
recommend a ...?	me conseiller ...?	me kon·sey·yey ...
bar	un bar	um bar
café	un café	ung ka·fey
restaurant	un restaurant	un res·to·ron
I'd like ..., please.	Je voudrais ...,	zhe voo·drey ...
	s'il vous plaît.	seel voo pley
a table for (five)	une table pour	ewn ta·ble poor
	(cinq) personnes	(sungk) pair·son
the (non)smoking	un endroit pour	un on·drwa poor
section	(non-)fumeurs	non·few·me

ordering food

breakfast	petit déjeuner m	pe·tee dey·zhe·ney
lunch	déjeuner m	dey·zhe·ney
dinner	dîner m	dee·ney
snack	casse-croûte m	kas·kroot

What would you recommend?
Qu'est-ce que vous conseillez?   kes·ke voo kon·sey·yey

I'd like (the) ...,	Je voudrais ...,	zhe voo·drey ...
please.	s'il vous plaît.	seel voo pley
bill	l'addition	la·dee·syon
drink list	la carte des boissons	la kart dey bwa·son
menu	la carte	la kart
that dish	ce plat	ser pla
wine list	la carte des vins	la kart dey vun

drinks

(cup of) coffee ...	*(un) café ...*	(ung) ka·fey ...
(cup of) tea ...	*(un) thé ...*	(un) tey ...
with milk	*au lait*	o ley
without sugar	*sans sucre*	son sew·kre
(orange) juice	*jus (d'orange)* m	zhew (do·ronzh)
soft drink	*boisson non-alcoolisée* f	bwa·son non·al·ko·lee·zey
... water	*eau ...*	o ...
hot	*chaude*	shod
sparkling mineral	*minérale gazeuse*	mee·ney·ral ga·zeuz
still mineral	*minérale non-gazeuse*	mee·ney·ral nong·ga·zeuz

in the bar

I'll have ...	*Je prends ...*	zhe pron ...
I'll buy you a drink.	*Je vous offre un verre.*	zhe voo zo·fre un vair
What would you like?	*Qu'est-ce que vous voulez?*	kes·ke voo voo·ley
Cheers!	*Santé!*	son·tey
brandy	*cognac* m	ko·nyak
champagne	*champagne* m	shom·pan·ye
cocktail	*cocktail* m	kok·tel
a shot of (whisky)	*un petit verre de (whisky)*	um pe·tee vair de (wees·kee)
a bottle of ... wine	*une bouteille de vin ...*	ewn boo·tey de vun ...
a glass of ... wine	*un verre de vin ...*	un vair de vun ...
red	*rouge*	roozh
sparkling	*mousseux*	moo·seu
white	*blanc*	blong
a ... of beer	*... de bière*	... de byair
glass	*un verre*	un vair
bottle	*une bouteille*	ewn boo·tey

self-catering

What's the local speciality?
Quelle est la spécialité locale?   kel ey la spey·sya·lee·tey lo·kal

What's that?
Qu'est-ce que c'est, ça?   kes·ke sey sa

How much is (a kilo of cheese)?
C'est combien (le kilo de fromage)?   sey kom·byun (le kee·lo de fro·mazh)

I'd like ...	*Je voudrais ...*	zhe voo·drey ...
(200) grams	*(deux cents) grammes*	(deu son) gram
(two) kilos	*(deux) kilos*	(deu) kee·lo
(three) pieces	*(trois) morceaux*	(trwa) mor·so
(six) slices	*(six) tranches*	(sees) tronsh

Less.	*Moins.*	mwun
Enough.	*Assez.*	a·sey
More.	*Plus.*	plew

special diets & allergies

Is there a vegetarian restaurant near here?
Y a-t-il un restaurant   ya·teel un res·to·ron
végétarien par ici?   vey·zhey·ta·ryun par ee·see

Do you have vegetarian food?
Vous faites les repas végétarien?   voo fet ley re·pa vey·zhey·ta·ryun

Could you prepare	*Pouvez-vous préparer*	poo·vey·voo prey·pa·rey
a meal without ...?	*un repas sans ...?*	un re·pa son ...
butter	*beurre*	beur
eggs	*œufs*	zeu
meat stock	*bouillon gras*	boo·yon gra

I'm allergic to ...	*Je suis allergique ...*	zhe swee za·lair·zheek ...
dairy produce	*aux produits laitiers*	o pro·dwee ley·tyey
gluten	*au gluten*	o glew·ten
MSG	*au glutamate*	o glew·ta·mat
	de sodium	de so·dyom
nuts	*au noix*	no nwa
seafood	*aux fruits de mer*	o frwee de mair

FRANÇAIS – food & drink

emergencies

basics

Help!	Au secours!	o skoor
Stop!	Arrêtez!	a·rey·tey
Go away!	Allez-vous-en!	a·ley·voo·zon
Thief!	Au voleur!	o vo·leur
Fire!	Au feu!	o feu
Watch out!	Faites attention!	fet a·ton·syon
Call …!	Appelez …!	a·pley …
a doctor	un médecin	un meyd·sun
an ambulance	une ambulance	ewn om·bew·lons
the police	la police	la po·lees

It's an emergency!
C'est urgent! — sey tewr·zhon

Could you help me, please?
Est-ce que vous pourriez — es·ke voo poo·ryey
m'aider, s'il vous plaît? — mey·dey seel voo pley

Could I use the telephone?
Est-ce que je pourrais utiliser — es·ke zhe poo·rey ew·tee·lee·zey
le téléphone? — le tey·ley·fon

I'm lost.
Je suis perdu/perdue. m/f — zhe swee pair·dew

Where are the toilets?
Où sont les toilettes? — oo son ley twa·let

police

Where's the police station?
Où est le commissariat de police? — oo ey le ko·mee·sar·ya de po·lees

I want to report an offence.
Je veux signaler un délit. — zhe veu see·nya·ley un dey·lee

I have insurance.
J'ai une assurance. — zhey ewn a·sew·rons

I've been assaulted.
J'ai été attaqué/attaquée. m/f — zhey ey·tey a·ta·key

I've been raped.
J'ai été violé/violée. m/f — zhey ey·tey vyo·ley

I've been robbed.
On m'a volé. — on ma vo·ley

I've lost my ...	*J'ai perdu ...*	zhey pair·dew ...
My ... was/were stolen.	*On m'a volé ...*	on ma vo·ley ...
backpack	*mon sac à dos*	mon sak a do
bags	*mes valises*	mey va·leez
credit card	*ma carte de crédit*	ma kart de krey·dee
handbag	*mon sac à main*	mon sak a mun
jewellery	*mes bijoux*	mey bee·zhoo
money	*mon argent*	mon ar·zhon
passport	*mon passeport*	mom pas·por
travellers cheques	*mes chèques de voyage*	mey shek de vwa·yazh
wallet	*mon portefeuille*	mom por·te·feu·ye
I want to contact my ...	*Je veux contacter mon ...*	zher veu kon·tak·tey mon ...
consulate	*consulat*	kon·sew·la
embassy	*ambassade*	om·ba·sad

health

medical needs

Where's the nearest ...?	*Où y a t-il ... par ici?*	oo ee a teel ... par ee·see
dentist	*un dentiste*	un don·teest
doctor	*un médecin*	un meyd·sun
hospital	*un hôpital*	u·no·pee·tal
(night) pharmacist	*une pharmacie (de nuit)*	ewn far·ma·see (de nwee)

I need a doctor (who speaks English).
J'ai besoin d'un médecin (qui parle anglais). — zhey be·zwun dun meyd·sun (kee parl ong·gley)

Could I see a female doctor?
Est-ce que je peux voir une femme médecin? — es·ke zhe peu vwar ewn fam meyd·sun

I've run out of my medication.
Je n'ai plus de médicaments. — zhe ney plew de mey·dee·ka·mon

symptoms, conditions & allergies

| I'm sick. | Je suis malade. | zhe swee ma·lad |
| It hurts here. | J'ai une douleur ici. | zhey ewn doo·leur ee·see |

I have (a) ...	J'ai ...	zhey ...
asthma	de l'asthme	de las·me
bronchitis	la bronchite	la bron·sheet
constipation	la constipation	la kon·stee·pa·syon
cough	la toux	la too
diarrhoea	la diarrhée	la dya·rey
fever	la fièvre	la fyev·re
headache	mal à la tête	mal a la tet
heart condition	maladie de cœur	ma·la·dee de keur
nausea	la nausée	la no·zey
pain	une douleur	ewn doo·leur
sore throat	mal à la gorge	mal a la gorzh
toothache	mal aux dents	mal o don

I'm allergic to ...	Je suis allergique ...	zhe swee za·lair·zheek ...
antibiotics	aux antibiotiques	o zon·tee·byo·teek
anti-inflammatories	aux antiinflammatoires	o zun·tee·un·fla·ma·twar
aspirin	à l'aspirine	a las·pee·reen
bees	aux abeilles	o za·bey·ye
codeine	à la codéine	a la ko·dey·een
penicillin	à la pénicilline	a la pey·nee·see·leen

antiseptic	antiseptique m	on·tee·sep·teek
bandage	pansement m	pons·mon
condoms	préservatifs m pl	prey·zair·va·teef
contraceptives	contraceptifs m pl	kon·tre·sep·teef
diarrhoea medicine	médecine pour la diarrhée f	med·seen poor la dya·ey
insect repellent	repulsif anti-insectes m	rey·pewl·seef on·tee·un·sekt
laxatives	laxatifs m pl	lak·sa·teef
painkillers	analgésiques m pl	a·nal·zhey·zeek
rehydration salts	sels de réhydratation m pl	seyl de rey·ee·dra·ta·syon
sleeping tablets	somnifères m pl	som·nee·fair

english–french dictionary

French nouns and adjectives in this dictionary have their gender indicated by ⓜ (masculine) or ⓕ (feminine). If it's a plural noun, you'll also see pl. Words are also marked as n (noun), a (adjective), v (verb), sg (singular), pl (plural), inf (informal) and pol (polite) where necessary.

A

accident *accident* ⓜ ak-see-don
accommodation *logement* ⓜ lozh-mon
adaptor *adaptateur* ⓜ a-dap-ta-teur
address *adresse* ⓕ a-dres
after *après* a-prey
air-conditioned *climatisé* kee-ma-tee-zey
airplane *avion* ⓜ a-vyon
airport *aéroport* ⓜ a-ey-ro-por
alcohol *alcool* ⓜ al-kol
all a *tout/toute* ⓜ/ⓕ too/toot
allergy *allergie* ⓕ a-lair-zhee
ambulance *ambulance* ⓕ om-bew-lons
and *et* ey
ankle *cheville* ⓕ she-vee-ye
arm *bras* ⓜ bra
ashtray *cendrier* ⓜ son-dree-yey
ATM *guichet automatique de banque* ⓜ gee-shey o-to-ma-teek de bonk

B

baby *bébé* ⓜ bey-bey
back (body) *dos* ⓜ do
backpack *sac à dos* ⓜ sak a do
bad *mauvais/mauvaise* ⓜ/ⓕ mo-vey/mo-veyz
bag *sac* ⓜ sak
baggage claim *retrait des bagages* ⓜ re-trey dey ba-gazh
bank *banque* ⓕ bonk
bar *bar* ⓜ bar
bathroom *salle de bain* ⓕ sal de bun
battery (car) *batterie* ⓕ bat-ree
battery (general) *pile* ⓕ peel
beautiful *beau/belle* ⓜ/ⓕ bo/bel
bed *lit* ⓜ lee
beer *bière* ⓕ byair
before *avant* a-von
behind *derrière* dair-yair
Belgium *Belgique* ⓕ bel-zheek
bicycle *vélo* ⓜ vey-lo

big *grand/grande* ⓜ/ⓕ gron/grond
bill *addition* ⓕ a-dee-syon
black *noir/noire* ⓜ/ⓕ nwar
blanket *couverture* ⓕ koo-vair-tewr
blood group *groupe sanguin* ⓜ groop song-gun
blue *bleu/bleue* ⓜ/ⓕ bler
book (make a reservation) v *réserver* rey-zair-vey
bottle *bouteille* ⓕ boo-tey
bottle opener *ouvre-bouteille* ⓜ oo-vre-boo-tey
boy *garçon* ⓜ gar-son
brakes (car) *freins* ⓜ frun
breakfast *petit déjeuner* ⓜ pe-tee dey-zheu-ney
broken (faulty) *défectueux/défectueuse* ⓜ/ⓕ dey-fek-tweu/dey-fek-tweuz
bus *(auto)bus* ⓜ (o-to)bews
business *affaires* ⓕ a-fair
buy *acheter* ash-tey

C

café *café* ⓜ ka-fey
camera *appareil photo* ⓜ a-pa-rey fo-to
camp site *terrain de camping* ⓜ tey-run de kom-peeng
cancel *annuler* a-new-ley
can opener *ouvre-boîte* ⓜ oo-vre-bwat
car *voiture* ⓕ vwa-tewr
cash *argent* ⓜ ar-zhon
cash (a cheque) v *encaisser* ong-key-sey
cell phone *téléphone portable* ⓜ tey-ley-fon por-ta-ble
centre *centre* ⓜ son-tre
change (money) v *échanger* ey-shon-zhey
cheap *bon marché* ⓜ & ⓕ bon mar-shey
check (bill) *addition* ⓕ la-dee-syon
check-in n *enregistrement* ⓜ on-re-zhee-stre-mon
chest *poitrine* ⓕ pwa-treen
child *enfant* ⓜ & ⓕ on-fon
cigarette *cigarette* ⓕ see-ga-ret
city *ville* ⓕ veel
clean a *propre* ⓜ & ⓕ pro-pre
closed *fermé/fermée* ⓜ/ⓕ fair-mey
coffee *café* ⓜ ka-fey
coins *pièces* ⓕ pyes
cold a *froid/froide* ⓜ/ⓕ frwa/frwad

collect call *appel en PCV* ⓜ a·pel on pey·sey·vey
come *venir* ve·neer
computer *ordinateur* ⓜ or·de·na·teur
condom *préservatif* ⓜ prey·zair·va·teef
contact lenses *verres de contact* ⓜ vair de kon·takt
cook v *cuire* kweer
cost *coût* ⓜ koo
credit card *carte de crédit* ⓕ kart de krey·dee
cup *tasse* ⓕ tas
currency exchange *taux de change* ⓜ to de shonzh
customs (immigration) *douane* ⓕ dwan

D

dangerous *dangereux/dangereuse* ⓜ/ⓕ
  don·zhreu/don·zhreuz
date (time) *date* ⓕ dat
day *date de naissance* ⓕ dat de ney·sons
delay *retard* ⓜ re·tard
dentist *dentiste* ⓜ don·teest
depart *partir* par·teer
diaper *couche* ⓕ koosh
dictionary *dictionnaire* ⓜ deek·syo·nair
dinner *dîner* ⓜ dee·ney
direct *direct/directe* ⓜ/ⓕ dee·rekt
dirty *sale* ⓜ&ⓕ sal
disabled *handicapé/handicapée* ⓜ/ⓕ on·dee·ka·pey
discount *remise* ⓕ re·meez
doctor *médecin* ⓜ meyd·sun
double bed *grand lit* ⓜ gron lee
double room *chambre pour deux personnes* ⓕ
  shom·bre poor de pair·son
drink *boisson* ⓕ bwa·son
drive v *conduire* kon·dweer
drivers licence *permis de conduire* ⓜ
  pair·mee de kon·dweer
drugs (illicit) *drogue* ⓕ drog
dummy (pacifier) *tétine* ⓕ tey·teen

E

ear *oreille* ⓕ o·rey
east *est* ⓜ est
eat *manger* mon·zhey
economy class *classe touriste* ⓕ klas too·reest
electricity *électricité* ⓕ ey·lek·tree·see·tey
elevator *ascenseur* ⓜ a·son·seur
email *e-mail* ⓜ ey·mel
embassy *ambassade* ⓕ om·ba·sad
emergency *cas urgent* ⓜ ka ewr·zhon

English (language) *anglais/anglaise* ⓜ/ⓕ
  ong·gley/ong·gleyz
entrance *entrée* ⓕ on·trey
evening *soir* ⓜ swar
exchange rate *taux de change* ⓜ to de shonzh
exit *sortie* ⓕ sor·tee
expensive *cher/chère* ⓜ/ⓕ shair
express mail *exprès* eks·pres
eye *œil* ⓜ eu·yee

F

far *lointain/lointaine* ⓜ/ⓕ lwun·tun/lwun·ten
fast *rapide* ⓜ&ⓕ ra·peed
father *père* ⓜ pair
film (camera) *pellicule* ⓕ pey·lee·kewl
finger *doigt* ⓜ dwa
first-aid kit *trousse à pharmacie* ⓕ troos a far·ma·see
first class *première classe* ⓕ pre·myair klas
fish *poisson* ⓜ pwa·son
food *nourriture* ⓕ noo·ree·tewr
foot *pied* ⓜ pyey
fork *fourchette* ⓕ foor·shet
France *France* frons
free (of charge) *gratuit/gratuite* ⓜ/ⓕ
  gra·twee/gra·tweet
French (language) *Français* fron·sey
friend *ami/amie* ⓜ/ⓕ a·mee
fruit *fruit* ⓜ frwee
full *plein/pleine* ⓜ/ⓕ plun/plen
funny *drôle* ⓜ&ⓕ drol

G

gift *cadeau* ⓜ ka·do
girl *fille* ⓕ fee·ye
glass (drinking) *verre* ⓜ vair
glasses *lunettes* ⓕ pl lew·net
go *aller* a·ley
good *bon/bonne* ⓜ/ⓕ bon
green *vert/verte* ⓜ/ⓕ vairt
guide n *guide* ⓜ geed

H

half *moitié* ⓕ mwa·tyey
hand *main* ⓕ mun
handbag *sac à main* ⓜ sak a mun
happy *heureux/heureuse* ⓜ/ⓕ eu·reu/eu·reuz
have *avoir* a·vwar

he *il* eel
head *tête* ① tet
heart *cœur* ⓜ keur
heat *chaleur* ① sha-leur
heavy *lourd/lourde* ⓜ/① loor/loord
help v *aider* ey-dey
here *ici* ee-see
high *haut/haute* ⓜ/① o/ot
highway *autoroute* ① o-to-root
hike v *faire la randonnée* fair la ron-do-ney
holiday *vacances* ① pl va-kons
homosexual n *homosexuel/homosexuelle* ⓜ/①
   o-mo-sek-swel
hospital *hôpital* ⓜ o-pee-tal
hot *chaud/chaude* ⓜ/① sho/shod
hotel *hôtel* ⓜ o-tel
(be) hungry *avoir faim* a-vwar fum
husband *mari* ⓜ ma-ree

I

I *je* zhe
identification (card) *carte d'identité* ①
   kart dee-don-tee-tey
ill *malade* ⓜ&① ma-lad
important *important/importante* ⓜ/①
   um-por-ton/um-por-tont
included *compris/comprise* ⓜ/①
   kom-pree/kom-preez
injury *blessure* ① bley-sewr
insurance *assurance* ① a-sew-rons
Internet *Internet* ⓜ un-tair-net
interpreter *interprète* ⓜ&① un-tair-pret

J

jewellery *bijoux* ⓜ pl bee-zhoo
job *travail* ⓜ tra-vai

K

key *clé* ① kley
kilogram *kilogramme* ⓜ kee-lo-gram
kitchen *cuisine* ① kwee zeen
knife *couteau* ⓜ koo-to

L

laundry (place) *blanchisserie* ① blon-shees-ree
lawyer *avocat/avocate* ⓜ/① a-vo-ka/a-vo-kat

left (direction) *à gauche* a gosh
left-luggage office *consigne* ① kon-see-nye
leg *jambe* ① zhomb
lesbian n *lesbienne* ① les-byen
less *moins* mwun
letter (mail) *lettre* ① ley-trer
lift (elevator) *ascenseur* ⓜ a-son-seur
light *lumière* ① lew-myair
like v *aimer* ey-mey
lock *serrure* ① sey-rewr
long *long/longue* ⓜ/① long(k)
lost *perdu/perdue* ⓜ/① pair-dew
lost-property office *bureau des objets trouvés* ⓜ
   bew-ro dey zob-zhey troo-vey
love v *aimer* ey-mey
luggage *bagages* ⓜ pl ba-gazh
lunch *déjeuner* ⓜ dey-zheu-ney

M

mail *courrier* ⓜ koo-ryey
man *homme* ⓜ om
map *carte* ① kart
market *marché* ⓜ mar-shey
matches *allumettes* ① pl a-lew-met
meat *viande* ① vyond
medicine *médecine* ① med-seen
menu *carte* kart
message *message* ⓜ mey-sazh
milk *lait* ① ley
minute *minute* ① mee-newt
mobile phone *téléphone portable* ⓜ
   tey-ley-fon por-ta-ble
money *argent* ⓜ ar-zhon
month *mois* ⓜ mwa
morning *matin* ⓜ ma-tun
mother *mère* ① mair
motorcycle *moto* ① mo-to
motorway *autoroute* ① o-to-root
mouth *bouche* ① boosh
music *musique* ① mew-zeek

N

name *nom* ⓜ nom
napkin *serviette* ① sair-vyet
nappy *couche* ① koosh
near *près de* prey de
neck *cou* ⓜ koo
new *nouveau/nouvelle* ⓜ/① noo-vo/noo-vel

news *les nouvelles* ley noo-vel

newspaper *journal* Ⓜ zhoor-nal

night *nuit* Ⓕ nwee

no *non* non

noisy *bruyant/bruyante* Ⓜ/Ⓕ brew-yon/brew-yont

nonsmoking *non-fumeur* non-few-meur

north *nord* Ⓜ nor

nose *nez* Ⓜ ney

now *maintenant* mun-te-non

number *numéro* Ⓜ new-mey-ro

O

oil (engine) *huile* Ⓕ weel

old *vieux/vieille* Ⓜ/Ⓕ vyeu/vyey

one-way ticket *billet simple* Ⓜ bee-yey sum-ple

open a *ouvert/ouverte* Ⓜ/Ⓕ oo-vair/oo-vairt

outside *dehors* de-or

P

package *paquet* Ⓜ pa-key

paper *papier* Ⓜ pa-pyey

park (car) v *garer (une voiture)* ga-rey (ewn vwa-tewr)

passport *passeport* Ⓜ pas-por

pay *payer* pey-yey

pen *stylo* Ⓜ stee-lo

petrol *essence* Ⓕ ey-sons

pharmacy *pharmacie* Ⓕ far-ma-see

phonecard *télécarte* Ⓕ tey-ley-kart

photo *photo* Ⓕ fo-to

plate *assiette* Ⓕ a-syet

police *police* Ⓕ po-lees

postcard *carte postale* Ⓕ kart pos-tal

post office *bureau de poste* Ⓜ bew-ro de post

pregnant *enceinte* on-sunt

price *prix* Ⓜ pree

Q

quiet *tranquille* Ⓜ&Ⓕ trong-keel

R

rain n *pluie* Ⓕ plwee

razor *rasoir* Ⓜ ra-zwar

receipt *reçu* Ⓜ re-sew

red *rouge* roozh

refund *remboursement* Ⓜ rom-boor-se-mon

registered mail *en recommandé* on re-ko-mon-dey

rent v *louer* loo-ey

repair v *réparer* rey-pa-rey

reservation *réservation* Ⓕ rey-zair-va-syon

restaurant *restaurant* Ⓜ res-to-ron

return v *revenir* rev-ner

return ticket *aller retour* Ⓜ a-ley re-toor

right (direction) *à droite* a drwat

road *route* Ⓕ root

room *chambre* Ⓕ shom-bre

S

safe a *sans danger* Ⓜ&Ⓕ son don-zhey

sanitary napkin *serviette hygiénique* Ⓕ sair-vyet ee-zhyey-neek

seat *place* Ⓕ plas

send *envoyer* on-vwa-yey

service station *station-service* Ⓕ sta-syon-sair-vees

sex *sexe* Ⓜ seks

shampoo *shampooing* Ⓜ shom-pwung

share (a dorm) *partager* par-ta-zhey

shaving cream *mousse à raser* Ⓕ moos a ra-zey

she *elle* el

sheet (bed) *drap* Ⓜ dra

shirt *chemise* Ⓕ she-meez

shoes *chaussures* Ⓕ pl sho-sewr

shop *magasin* Ⓜ ma-ga-zun

short *court/courte* Ⓜ/Ⓕ koor/koort

shower *douche* Ⓕ doosh

single room *chambre pour une personne* Ⓕ shom-bre poor ewn pair-son

skin *peau* Ⓕ po

skirt *jupe* Ⓕ zhewp

sleep v *dormir* dor-meer

slowly *lentement* lon-te-mon

small *petit/petite* Ⓜ/Ⓕ pe-tee/pe-teet

smoke (cigarettes) v *fumer* few-mey

soap *savon* Ⓜ sa-von

some *quelques* kel-ke

soon *bientôt* byun-to

south *sud* Ⓜ sewd

souvenir shop *magasin de souvenirs* Ⓜ ma-ga-zun de soov-neer

speak *parler* par-ley

spoon *cuillère* Ⓕ kwee-yair

stamp *timbre* Ⓜ tum-bre

stand-by ticket *billet stand-by* Ⓜ bee-yey stond-bai

station (train) *gare* Ⓕ gar

stomach *estomac* Ⓜ es-to-ma

stop v *arrêter* a-rey-tey

stop (bus) *arrêt* ⓜ a-rey
street *rue* ⓕ rew
student *étudiant/étudiante* ⓜ/ⓕ
 ey-tew-dyon/ey-tew-dyont
sun *soleil* ⓜ so-ley
sunscreen *écran solaire* ⓜ ey-kron so-lair
swim v *nager* na-zhey
Switzerland *Suisse* swees

T

tampons *tampons* ⓜ pl tom-pon
taxi *taxi* ⓜ tak-see
teaspoon *petite cuillère* ⓕ pe-teet kwee-yair
teeth *dents* ⓕ don
telephone n *téléphone* ⓜ tey-ley-fon
television *télé(vision)* ⓕ tey-ley(vee-zyon)
temperature (weather) *température* ⓕ
 tom-pey-ra-tewr
tent *tente* ⓕ tont
that (one) *cela* se-la
they *ils/elles* ⓜ/ⓕ eel/el
(be) thirsty *avoir soif* a-vwar swaf
this (one) *ceci* se-see
throat *gorge* ⓕ gorzh
ticket *billet* ⓜ bee-yey
time *temps* ⓜ tom
tired *fatigué/fatiguée* ⓜ/ⓕ fa-tee-gey
tissues *mouchoirs en papier* ⓜ pl
 moo-shwar om pa-pyey
today *aujourd'hui* o-zhoor-dwee
toilet *toilettes* ⓕ pl twa-let
tomorrow *demain* de-mun
tonight *ce soir* se swar
toothbrush *brosse à dents* ⓕ bros a don
toothpaste *dentifrice* ⓜ don-tee-frees
torch (flashlight) *lampe de poche* ⓕ lomp de posh
tour *voyage* ⓜ vwa-yazh
tourist office *office de tourisme* ⓜ
 o-fees de too-rees-me
towel *serviette* ⓕ sair-vyet
train *train* ⓜ trun
translate *traduire* tra-dweer
travel agency *agence de voyage* ⓕ
 a-zhons de vwa-yazh
travellers cheque *chèque de voyage* ⓜ
 shek de vwa-yazh
trousers *pantalon* ⓜ pon-ta-lon

twin beds *lits jumeaux* ⓜ pl dey lee zhew-mo
tyre *pneu* ⓜ pneu

U

underwear *sous-vêtements* ⓜ soo-vet-mon
urgent *urgent/urgente* ⓜ/ⓕ ewr-zhon/ewr-zhont

V

vacant *libre* ⓜ & ⓕ lee-bre
vacation *vacances* ⓕ pl va-kons
vegetable n *légume* ⓜ ley-gewm
vegetarian a *végétarien/végétarienne* ⓜ/ⓕ
 vey-zhey-ta-ryun/vey-zhey-ta-ryen
visa *visa* ⓕ vee-za

W

waiter *serveur/serveuse* ⓜ/ⓕ sair-veur/sair-veurz
walk v *marcher* mar-shey
wallet *portefeuille* ⓜ por-te-feu-ye
warm a *chaud/chaude* ⓜ/ⓕ sho/shod
wash (something) *laver* la-vey
watch *montre* ⓕ mon-tre
water *eau* ⓕ o
we *nous* noo
weekend *week-end* ⓜ week-end
west *ouest* ⓜ west
wheelchair *fauteuil roulant* ⓜ fo-teu-ye roo-lon
when *quand* kon
where *où* oo
white *blanc/blanche* ⓜ/ⓕ blong/blonsh
who *qui* kee
why *pourquoi* poor-kwa
wife *femme* ⓕ fam
window *fenêtre* ⓕ fe-ney-tre
wine *vin* ⓜ vun
with *avec* a-vek
without *sans* son
woman *femme* ⓕ fam
write *écrire* ey-kreer

Y

yellow *jaune* zhon
yes *oui* wee
yesterday *hier* ee-yair
you sg inf *tu* tew
you sg pol *vous* voo
you pl *vous* voo

German

german alphabet

A a a	*B b* be	*C c* tse	*D d* de	*E e* e
F f ef	*G g* ge	*H h* ha	*I i* i	*J j* yot
K k ka	*L l* el	*M m* em	*N n* en	*O o* o
P p pe	*Q q* ku	*R r* er	*S s* es	*T t* te
U u u	*V v* fau	*W w* ve	*X x* iks	*Y y* *ewp*·si·lon
Z z tset				

german

about German

Romantic, flowing, literary ... not usually how German (*Deutsch* doytsh) is described, but maybe it's time to reconsider. After all, this is the language that's played a major role in the history of Europe and remains one of the most widely spoken languages on the continent. It's taught throughout the world and chances are you're already familiar with a number of German words that have entered English – *kindergarten*, *kitsch* and *hamburger*, for example, are all of German origin.

German is spoken by around 100 million people, and is the official language of Germany, Austria and Liechtenstein, as well as one of the official languages of Belgium, Switzerland and Luxembourg. German didn't spread across the rest of the world with the same force as English, Spanish or French. Germany only became a unified nation in 1871 and never established itself as a colonial power. After the reunification of East and West Germany, however, German has become more important in global politics and economics. Its role in science has long been recognised and German literature lays claim to some of the most famous written works ever printed. Just think of the enormous influence of Goethe, Nietzsche, Freud and Einstein.

German is usually divided into two forms – Low German (*Plattdeutsch plat*-doytsh) and High German (*Hochdeutsch hohk*-doytsh). Low German is an umbrella term used for the dialects spoken in Northern Germany. High German is considered the standard form and is understood throughout German-speaking communities, from the Swiss Alps to the cosy cafés of Vienna; it's also the form used in this phrasebook.

Both German and English belong to the West Germanic language family, along with a number of other languages including Dutch and Yiddish. The primary reason why German and English have grown apart is that the Normans, on invading England in 1066, brought with them a large number of non-Germanic words. As well as the recognisable words, the grammar of German will also make sense to an English speaker. Even with a slight grasp of German grammar, you'll still manage to get your point across. On the other hand, German tends to join words together (while English uses a number of separate words) to express a single notion. You shouldn't be intimidated by this though – after a while you'll be able to tell parts of words and recognising 'the Football World Cup qualifying match' hidden within *Fussballweltmeisterschaftsqualifikationsspiel* won't be a problem at all!

pronunciation

vowel sounds

German vowels can be short or long, which influences the meaning of words. They're pronounced crisply and distinctly, so *Tee* (tea) is tey, not *tey*·ee.

symbol	english equivalent	german example	transliteration
a	run	*hat*	hat
aa	father	*habe*	*haa*·be
ai	aisle	*mein*	main
air	fair	*Bär*	bair
aw	saw	*Boot*	bawt
e	bet	*Männer*	*me*·ner
ee	see	*fliegen*	*flee*·gen
eu	nurse	*schön*	sheun
ew	ee pronounced with rounded lips	*zurück*	tsu·*rewk*
ey	as in 'bet', but longer	*leben*	*ley*·ben
i	hit	*mit*	mit
o	pot	*Koffer*	*ko*·fer
oo	zoo	*Schuhe*	*shoo*·e
ow	now	*Haus*	hows
oy	toy	*Leute, Häuser*	*loy*·te, *hoy*·zer
u	put	*unter*	*un*·ter

word stress

Almost all German words are pronounced with stress on the first syllable. While this is a handy rule of thumb, you can always rely on the coloured pronunciation guides, which show the stressed syllables in italics.

consonant sounds

All German consonant sounds exist in English except for the kh and r sounds. The kh sound is generally pronounced at the back of the throat, like the 'ch' in 'Bach' or the Scottish 'loch'. The r sound is pronounced at the back of the throat, almost like saying g, but with some friction, a bit like gargling.

symbol	english equivalent	german example	transliteration
b	**b**ed	*Bett*	bet
ch	**ch**eat	*Tschüss*	chews
d	**d**og	*dein*	dain
f	**f**at	*vier*	feer
g	**g**o	*gehen*	*gey*·en
h	**h**at	*helfen*	*hel*·fen
k	**k**it	*kein*	kain
kh	lo**ch**	*ich*	ikh
l	**l**ot	*laut*	lowt
m	**m**an	*Mann*	man
n	**n**ot	*nein*	nain
ng	ri**ng**	*singen*	*zing*·en
p	**p**et	*Preis*	prais
r	**r**un (throaty)	*Reise*	*rai*·ze
s	**s**un	*heiß*	hais
sh	**sh**ot	*schön*	sheun
t	**t**op	*Tag*	taak
ts	hi**ts**	*Zeit*	tsait
v	**v**ery	*wohnen*	*vaw*·nen
y	**y**es	*ja*	yaa
z	**z**ero	*sitzen*	*zi*·tsen
zh	plea**s**ure	*Garage*	ga·*raa*·zhe

tools

language difficulties

Do you speak English?
Sprechen Sie Englisch? — shpre·khen zee eng·lish

Do you understand?
Verstehen Sie? — fer·shtey·en zee

I (don't) understand.
Ich verstehe (nicht). — ikh fer·shtey·e (nikht)

What does (Kugel) mean?
Was bedeutet (Kugel)? — vas be·doy·tet (koo·gel)

How do you ...?	*Wie ...?*	vee ...
pronounce this	*spricht man dieses Wort aus*	shprikht man dee·zes vort ows
write (Schweiz)	*schreibt man (Schweiz)*	shraipt man (shvaits)

Could you please ...?	*Könnten Sie ...?*	keun·ten zee ...
repeat that	*das bitte wiederholen*	das bi·te vee·der·haw·len
speak more slowly	*bitte langsamer sprechen*	bi·te lang·za·mer shpre·khen
write it down	*das bitte aufschreiben*	das bi·te owf·shrai·ben

essentials

Yes.	*Ja.*	yaa
No.	*Nein.*	nain
Please.	*Bitte.*	bi·te
Thank you.	*Danke.*	dang·ke
Thank you very much.	*Vielen Dank.*	fee·len dangk
You're welcome.	*Bitte.*	bi·te
Excuse me.	*Entschuldigung.*	ent·shul·di·gung
Sorry.	*Entschuldigung.*	ent·shul·di·gung

numbers

0	*null*	nul	16	*sechzehn*	zeks·tseyn	
1	*eins*	ains	17	*siebzehn*	zeep·tseyn	
2	*zwei*	tsvai	18	*achtzehn*	akht·tseyn	
3	*drei*	drai	19	*neunzehn*	noyn·tseyn	
4	*vier*	feer	20	*zwanzig*	tsvan·tsikh	
5	*fünf*	fewnf	21	*einundzwanzig*	ain·unt·tsvan·tsikh	
6	*sechs*	zeks	22	*zweiundzwanzig*	tsvai·unt·tsvan·tsikh	
7	*sieben*	zee·ben	30	*dreißig*	drai·tsikh	
8	*acht*	akht	40	*vierzig*	feer·tsikh	
9	*neun*	noyn	50	*fünfzig*	fewnf·tsikh	
10	*zehn*	tseyn	60	*sechzig*	zekh·tsikh	
11	*elf*	elf	70	*siebzig*	zeep·tsikh	
12	*zwölf*	zveulf	80	*achtzig*	akht·tsikh	
13	*dreizehn*	drai·tseyn	90	*neunzig*	noyn·tsikh	
14	*vierzehn*	feer·tseyn	100	*hundert*	hun·dert	
15	*fünfzehn*	fewnf·tseyn	1000	*tausend*	tow·sent	

time & dates

What time is it?	*Wie spät ist es?*	vee shpeyt ist es
It's one o'clock.	*Es ist ein Uhr.*	es ist ain oor
It's (10) o'clock.	*Es ist (zehn) Uhr.*	es ist (tseyn) oor
Quarter past (one).	*Viertel nach (eins).*	fir·tel naakh (ains)
Half past (one).	*Halb (zwei).* (lit: half two)	halp (tsvai)
Quarter to (one).	*Viertel vor (eins).*	fir·tel fawr (ains)
At what time …?	*Um wie viel Uhr …?*	um vee feel oor …
At …	*Um …*	um …

am	*vormittags*	fawr·mi·taaks
pm (midday–6pm)	*nachmittags*	naakh·mi·taaks
pm (6pm–midnight)	*abends*	aa·bents

Monday	*Montag*	mawn·taak
Tuesday	*Dienstag*	deens·taak
Wednesday	*Mittwoch*	mit·vokh
Thursday	*Donnerstag*	do·ners·taak
Friday	*Freitag*	frai·taak
Saturday	*Samstag*	zams·taak
Sunday	*Sonntag*	zon·taak

January	Januar	yan·u·aar
February	Februar	fey·bru·aar
March	März	merts
April	April	a·pril
May	Mai	mai
June	Juni	yoo·ni
July	Juli	yoo·li
August	August	ow·gust
September	September	zep·tem·ber
October	Oktober	ok·taw·ber
November	November	no·vem·ber
December	Dezember	de·tsem·ber

What date is it today?
Der Wievielte ist heute? dair vee·feel·te ist *hoy*·te

It's (18 October).
Heute ist (der achtzehnte Oktober). *hoy*·te ist dair (*akh*·tseyn·te ok·*taw*·ber)

| since (May) | seit (Mai) | zait (mai) |
| until (June) | bis (Juni) | bis (yoo·ni) |

yesterday	gestern	ges·tern
today	heute	hoy·te
tonight	heute Abend	hoy·te aa·bent
tomorrow	morgen	mor·gen

last ...		
night	vergangene Nacht	fer·gang·e·ne nakht
week	letzte Woche	lets·te vo·khe
month	letzten Monat	lets·ten maw·nat
year	letztes Jahr	lets·tes yaar

next ...		
week	nächste Woche	neykhs·te vo·khe
month	nächsten Monat	neykhs·ten maw·nat
year	nächstes Jahr	neykhs·tes yaar

yesterday/	gestern/	ges·tern/
tomorrow ...	morgen ...	mor·gen ...
morning	Morgen	mor·gen
afternoon	Nachmittag	naakh·mi·taak
evening	Abend	aa·bent

weather

What's the weather like?	*Wie ist das Wetter?*	vee ist das *ve*·ter

It's ...		
cloudy	*Es ist wolkig.*	es ist *vol*·kikh
cold	*Es ist kalt.*	es ist kalt
hot	*Es ist heiß.*	es ist hais
raining	*Es regnet.*	es *reyg*·net
snowing	*Es schneit.*	es shnait
sunny	*Es ist sonnig.*	es ist *zo*·nikh
warm	*Es ist warm.*	es ist varm
windy	*Es ist windig.*	es ist *vin*·dikh

spring	*Frühling* m	*frew*·ling
summer	*Sommer* m	*zo*·mer
autumn	*Herbst* m	herpst
winter	*Winter* m	*vin*·ter

border crossing

I'm here ...	*Ich bin hier ...*	ikh bin heer ...
in transit	*auf der Durchreise*	owf dair *durkh*·rai·ze
on business	*auf Geschäftsreise*	owf ge·*shefts*·rai·ze
on holiday	*im Urlaub*	im *oor*·lowp

I'm here for ...	*Ich bin hier für ...*	ikh bin heer fewr ...
(10) days	*(zehn) Tage*	(tseyn) *taa*·ge
(three) weeks	*(drei) Wochen*	(drai) *vo*·khen
(two) months	*(zwei) Monate*	(tsvai) *maw*·na·te

I'm going to (Salzburg).
Ich gehe nach (Salzburg). ikh *gey*·e nakh *zalts*·boorg

I'm staying at the (Hotel Park).
Ich wohne im (Hotel Park). ikh *vaw*·ne im (ho·*tel* park)

I have nothing to declare.
Ich habe nichts zu verzollen. ikh *haa*·be nikhts tsoo fer·*tso*·len

I have something to declare.
Ich habe etwas zu verzollen. ikh *haa*·be *et*·vas tsoo fer·*tso*·len

That's (not) mine.
Das ist (nicht) meins. das ist (nikht) mains

transport

tickets & luggage

Where can I buy a ticket?
Wo kann ich eine Fahrkarte kaufen?   vaw kan ikh *ai*·ne *faar*·kar·te *kow*·fen

Do I need to book a seat?
Muss ich einen Platz   mus ikh *ai*·nen plats
reservieren lassen?   re·zer·*vee*·ren *la*·sen

One ...ticket to	*Einen ... nach*	*ai*·nen ... naakh
(Berlin), please.	*(Berlin), bitte.*	(ber·*leen*) *bi*·te
one-way	*einfache Fahrkarte*	*ain*·fa·khe *faar*·kar·te
return	*Rückfahrkarte*	*rewk*·faar·kar·te

I'd like to ...	*Ich möchte meine*	ikh *meukh*·te *mai*·ne
my ticket, please.	*Fahrkarte bitte ...*	*faar*·kar·te *bi*·te ...
cancel	*zurückgeben*	tsu·*rewk*·gey·ben
change	*ändern lassen*	*en*·dern *la*·sen
collect	*abholen*	ab·*ho*·len
confirm	*bestätigen lassen*	be·*shtey*·ti·gen *la*·sen

I'd like a ...	*Ich hätte gern*	ikh *he*·te gern
seat, please.	*einen ...*	*ai*·nen ...
nonsmoking	*Nichtraucherplatz*	*nikht*·row·kher·plats
smoking	*Raucherplatz*	*row*·kher·plats

How much is it?
Was kostet das?   vas *kos*·tet das

Is there air conditioning?
Gibt es eine Klimaanlage?   gipt es *ai*·ne *klee*·ma·an·*laa*·ge

Is there a toilet?
Gibt es eine Toilette?   gipt es *ai*·ne to·a·*le*·te

How long does the trip take?
Wie lange dauert die Fahrt?   vee *lang*·e *dow*·ert dee faart

Is it a direct route?
Ist es eine direkte Verbindung?   ist es *ai*·ne di·*rek*·te fer·*bin*·dung

I'd like a luggage locker.
Ich hätte gern ein Gepäckschließfach.   ikh *he*·te gern ain ge·*pek*·shlees·fakh

My luggage has been ...	Mein Gepäck ist ...	main ge·pek ist ...
damaged	beschädigt	be·shey·dikht
lost	verloren gegangen	fer·law·ren ge·gang·en
stolen	gestohlen worden	ge·shtaw·len vor·den

getting around

Where does flight (D4) arrive?
Wo ist die Ankunft des Fluges (D4)? vaw ist dee an·kunft des floo·ges (de feer)

Where does flight (D4) depart?
Wo ist die der Abflug des Fluges (D4)? vaw ist dair ab·flug des floo·ges (de feer)

Where's the ...?	Wo ist ...?	vaw ist ...
arrivalls hall	Ankunftshalle	an·kunfts·ha·le
departures hall	Abflughalle	ab·flug·ha·le

Is this the ...	Fährt ...	fairt ...
to (Hamburg)?	nach (Hamburg)?	nakh (ham·burg)
boat	das Boot	das bawt
bus	der Bus	dair bus
plane	das Flugzeug	das flook·tsoyk
train	der Zug	dair tsook

What time's the ... bus?	Wann fährt der ... Bus?	van fairt dair ... bus
first	erste	ers·te
last	letzte	lets·te
next	nächste	neykhs·te

At what time does it leave?
Wann fährt es ab? van fairt es ap

At what time does it arrive?
Wann kommt es an? van komt es an

How long will it be delayed?
Wie viel Verspätung wird es haben? vee feel fer·shpey·tung virt es haa·ben

What station/stop is this?
Welcher Bahnhof/Halt ist das? vel·kher baan·hawf/halt ist das

What's the next station/stop?
Welches ist der nächste Bahnhof/Halt? vel·khes ist dair neykhs·te baan·hawf/halt

Does it stop at (Freiburg)?
Hält es in (Freiburg)?   helt *es* in (*frai*·boorg)

Please tell me when we get to (Kiel).
Könnten Sie mir bitte sagen,   *keun*·ten zee meer *bi*·te *zaa*·gen
wann wir in (Kiel) ankommen?   van veer in (keel) *an*·ko·men

How long do we stop here?
Wie lange halten wir hier?   vee *lan*·ge *hal*·ten veer heer

Is this seat available?
Ist dieser Platz frei?   ist *dee*·zer plats frai

That's my seat.
Dieses ist mein Platz.   *dee*·zes ist main plats

I'd like a taxi ...   *Ich hätte gern*   ikh *he*·te gern
     ein Taxi für ...   ain *tak*·si fewr ...
     at (9am)   *(neun Uhr vormittags)*   (noyn oor *fawr*·mi·taaks)
     now   *sofort*   zo·fort
     tomorrow   *morgen*   *mor*·gen

Is this taxi available?
Ist dieses Taxi frei?   ist *dee*·zes *tak*·si frai

How much is it to ...?
Was kostet es bis ...?   vas *kos*·tet es bis ...

Please put the meter on.
Schalten Sie bitte den Taxameter ein.   *shal*·ten zee *bi*·te deyn tak·sa·*mey*·ter ain

Please take me to (this address).
Bitte bringen Sie mich zu   *bi*·te *bring*·en zee mikh tsoo
(dieser Adresse).   (*dee*·zer a·*dre*·se)

Please ...   *Bitte ...*   *bi*·te ...
     slow down   *fahren Sie langsamer*   *faa*·ren zee *lang*·za·mer
     stop here   *halten Sie hier*   *hal*·ten zee heer
     wait here   *warten Sie hier*   *var*·ten zee heer

car, motorbike & bicycle hire

I'd like to hire a ...	Ich möchte ... mieten.	ikh *meukh*·te ... *mee*·ten
bicycle	ein Fahrrad	ain *faar*·raat
car	ein Auto	ain *ow*·to
motorbike	ein Motorrad	ain *maw*·tor·raat

with ...	mit ...	mit ...
a driver	Fahrer	*faa*·rer
air conditioning	Klimaanlage	*klee*·ma·an·*laa*·ge

How much for ... hire?	Wie viel kostet es pro ...?	vee feel *kos*·tet es praw ...
hourly	Stunde	*shtun*·de
daily	Tag	taak
weekly	Woche	*vo*·khe

air	Luft f	luft
oil	Öl n	eul
petrol	Benzin n	ben·*tseen*
tyres	Reifen m pl	*rai*·fen

I need a mechanic.
Ich brauche einen Mechaniker.   ikh *brow*·khe *ai*·nen me·*khaa*·ni·ker

I've run out of petrol.
Ich habe kein Benzin mehr.   ikh *haa*·be kain ben·*tseen* mair

I have a flat tyre.
Ich habe eine Reifenpanne.   ikh *haa*·be *ai*·ne *rai*·fen·pa·ne

directions

Where's the ...?	Wo ist ...?	vaw ist ...
bank	die Bank	dee bangk
city centre	die Innenstadt	*i*·nen·shtat
hotel	das Hotel	das ho·*tel*
market	der Markt	dair markt
police station	das Polizeirevier	das po·li·*tsai*·re·veer
post office	das Postamt	das *post*·amt
public toilet	die öffentliche Toilette	dee *eu*·fent·li·khe to·a·*le*·te
tourist office	das Fremdenverkehrsbüro	das *frem*·den·fer·kairs·bew·raw

Is this the road to (Frankfurt)?
Führt diese Straße
nach (Frankfurt)?
fewrt *dee*·ze *shtraa*·se
naakh (*frank*·foort)

Can you show me (on the map)?
Können Sie es mir
(auf der Karte) zeigen?
keu·nen zee es meer
(owf dair *kar*·te) *tsai*·gen

What's the address?
Wie ist die Adresse?
vee ist dee a·*dre*·se

How far is it?
Wie weit ist es?
vee *vait* ist es

How do I get there?
Wie kann ich da hinkommen?
vee kan ikh daa *hin*·ko·men

Turn ...	*Biegen Sie ... ab.*	*bee*·gen zee ... ap
at the corner	*an der Ecke*	an dair *e*·ke
at the traffic lights	*bei der Ampel*	bai dair *am*·pel
left/right	*links/rechts*	lingks/rekhts

It's ...	*Es ist ...*	es ist ...
behind ...	*hinter ...*	*hin*·ter ...
far away	*weit weg*	vait vek
here	*hier*	heer
in front of ...	*vor ...*	fawr ...
left	*links*	lingks
near (to ...)	*nahe (zu ...)*	*naa*·e (zoo ...)
next to ...	*neben ...*	*ney*·ben ...
on the corner	*an der Ecke*	an dair *e*·ke
opposite ...	*gegenüber ...*	gey·gen·*ew*·ber ...
right	*rechts*	rekhts
straight ahead	*geradeaus*	ge·raa·de·*ows*
there	*dort*	dort

north	*Norden* m	*nor*·den
south	*Süden* m	*zew*·den
east	*Osten* m	*os*·ten
west	*Westen* m	*ves*·ten

by bus	*mit dem Bus*	mit deym *bus*
by taxi	*mit dem Taxi*	mit deym *tak*·si
by train	*mit dem Zug*	mit deym *tsook*
on foot	*zu Fuß*	tsoo *foos*

Eingang/Ausgang	*ain*·gang/*ows*·gang	**Entrance/Exit**
Offen/Geschlossen	*o*·fen/ge·*shlo*·sen	**Open/Closed**
Zimmer Frei	*tsi*·mer frai	**Rooms Available**
Ausgebucht	*ows*·ge·bukht	**No Vacancies**
Auskunft	*ows*·kunft	**Information**
Polizeirevier	po·li·*tsai*·re·veer	**Police Station**
Verboten	fer·*baw*·ten	**Prohibited**
Toiletten/WC	to·a·*le*·ten/vee·*tsee*	**Toilets**
Herren	*hair*·en	**Men**
Damen	*daa*·men	**Women**
Heiß/Kalt	hais/kalt	**Hot/Cold**

accommodation

finding accommodation

Where's a/an ...?	*Wo ist ...?*	vaw ist ...
camping ground	*ein Campingplatz*	ain *kem*·ping·plats
guesthouse	*eine Pension*	*ai*·ne paang·*zyawn*
hotel	*ein Hotel*	ain ho·*tel*
inn	*ein Gasthof*	ain *gast*·hawf
youth hostel	*eine Jugendherberge*	*ai*·ne *yoo*·gent·her·ber·ge

Can you recommend	*Können Sie etwas*	*keu*·nen zee et·vas
somewhere ...?	*... empfehlen?*	... emp·*fey*·len
cheap	*Billiges*	*bi*·li·ges
good	*Gutes*	*goo*·tes
luxurious	*Luxuriöses*	luk·su·ri·*eu*·ses
nearby	*in der Nähe*	in dair *ney*·e

I'd like to book a room, please.
Ich möchte bitte ein   ikh *meukh*·te *bi*·te ain
Zimmer reservieren.   *tsi*·mer re·zer·*vee*·ren

I have a reservation.
Ich habe eine Reservierung.   ikh *haa*·be *ai*·ne re·zer·*vee*·rung

My name's ...
Mein Name ist ...   main *naa*·me ist ...

accommodation – GERMAN

173

Do you have a . . . room?	*Haben Sie ein . . . ?*	*haa·ben zee ain . . .*
single	*Einzelzimmer*	*ain·tsel·tsi·mer*
double	*Doppelzimmer mit einem Doppelbett*	*do·pel·tsi·mer mit ai·nem do·pel·bet*
twin	*Doppelzimmer mit zwei Einzelbetten*	*do·pel·tsi·mer mit tsvai ain·tsel·be·ten*

Can I pay by . . . ?	*Nehmen Sie . . . ?*	*ney·men zee . . .*
credit card	*Kreditkarten*	*kre·deet·kar·ten*
travellers cheque	*Reiseschecks*	*rai·ze·sheks*

How much is it per . . . ?	*Wie viel kostet es pro . . . ?*	vee feel *kos·tet es praw . . .*
night	*Nacht*	*nakht*
person	*Person*	*per·zawn*

I'd like to stay for (two) nights.
Ich möchte für (zwei)   ikh *meukh·*te fewr (tsvai)
Nächte bleiben.   *nekh·*te *blai·*ben

From (July 2) to (July 6).
Vom (zweiten Juli) bis zum   vom (*tsvai·*ten *yoo·*li) bis tsum
(sechsten Juli).   (*zeks·*ten *yoo·*li)

Can I see it?
Kann ich es sehen?   kan ikh es *zey·*en

Am I allowed to camp here?
Kann ich hier zelten?   kan ikh heer *tsel·*ten

Is there a camp site nearby?
Gibt es in der Nähe einen Zeltplatz?   gipt es in dair *ney·*e *ai·*nen *tselt·*plats

requests & queries

When/Where is breakfast served?
Wann/Wo gibt es Frühstück?   van/vaw gipt es *frew·*shtewk

Please wake me at (seven).
Bitte wecken Sie mich   *bi·*te *ve·*ken zee mikh
um (sieben) Uhr.   um (*zee·*ben) oor

Could I have my key, please?
Könnte ich bitte meinen Schlüssel   *keun·*te ikh *bi·*te *mai·*nen *shlew·*sel
haben?   *haa·*ben

Can I get another (blanket)?
Kann ich noch (eine Decke) bekommen?   kan ikh nokh (*ai·*ne *de·*ke) be·*ko·*men

Is there a/an ...?	Haben Sie ...?	haa·ben zee ...
elevator	einen Aufzug	ai·nen owf·tsook
safe	einen Safe	ai·nen sayf

The room is too ...	Es ist zu ...	es ist tsoo ...
expensive	teuer	toy·er
noisy	laut	lowt
small	klein	klain

The ... doesn't work.	... funktioniert nicht.	... fungk·tsyo·neert nikht
air conditioning	Die Klimaanlage	dee klee·ma·an·laa·ge
fan	Der Ventilator	dair ven·ti·laa·tor
toilet	Die Toilette	dee to·a·le·te

This ... isn't clean.	Dieses ... ist nicht sauber.	dee·zes ... ist nikht zow·ber
pillow	Kopfkissen	kopf·ki·sen
sheet	Bettlaken	bet·laa·ken
towel	Handtuch	hant·tookh

checking out

What time is checkout?
Wann muss ich auschecken?
van mus ikh *ows*·che·ken

Can I leave my luggage here?
Kann ich meine Taschen hier lassen?
kan ikh *mai*·ne *ta*·shen heer *la*·sen

Could I have	Könnte ich bitte ...	keun·te ikh bi·te ...
my ..., please?	haben?	haa·ben
deposit	meine Anzahlung	mai·ne an·tsaa·lung
passport	meinen Pass	mai·nen pas
valuables	meine Wertsachen	mai·ne vert·za·khen

communications & banking

the internet

Where's the local Internet café?
Wo ist hier ein Internet-Café?
vaw ist heer ain *in*·ter·net·ka·fey

How much is it per hour?
Was kostet es pro Stunde?
vas *kos*·tet es praw *shtun*·de

I'd like to ...	Ich möchte ...	ikh *meukh*·te ...
check my email	meine E-Mails checken	*mai*·ne *ee*·mayls *che*·ken
get Internet access	Internetzugang haben	*in*·ter·net·tsoo·gang *haa*·ben
use a printer	einen Drucker benutzen	*ai*·nen *dru*·ker be·*nu*·tsen
use a scanner	einen Scanner benutzen	*ai*·nen *ske*·ner be·*nu*·tsen

mobile/cell phone

I'd like a ...	Ich hätte gern ...	ikh *he*·te gern ...
mobile/cell phone for hire	ein Miethandy	ain *meet*·hen·di
SIM card for your network	eine SIM-Karte für Ihr Netz	*ai*·ne *zim*·kar·te fewr eer nets

What are the rates?
Wie hoch sind die Gebühren?   vee hawkh zint dee ge·*bew*·ren

telephone

What's your phone number?
Wie ist Ihre Telefonnummer?   vee ist *ee*·re te·le·*fawn*·nu·mer

The number is ...
Die Nummer ist ...   dee *nu*·mer ist ...

Where's the nearest public phone?
Wo ist das nächste   vaw ist das *neykhs*·te
öffentliche Telefon?   *eu*·fent·li·khe te·le·*fawn*

I'd like to buy a phonecard.
Ich möchte eine   ikh *meukh*·te *ai*·ne
Telefonkarte kaufen.   te·le·*fawn*·kar·te *kow*·fen

I want to ...	Ich möchte ...	ikh *meukh*·te ...
call (Singapore)	(nach Singapur) telefonieren	(naakh *zing*·a·poor) te·le·fo·*nee*·ren
make a local call	ein Ortsgespräch machen	ain *awrts*·ge·shpreykh *ma*·khen
reverse the charges	ein R-Gespräch führen	ain *air*·ge·shpreykh *few*·ren

How much does ... cost?	*Wie viel kostet ...?*	vee feel kos·tet ...
a (three)-minute	*ein (drei)-minutiges*	ain (drai)·mi·noo·ti·ges
call	*Gespräch*	ge·shpreykh
each extra	*jede zusätzliche*	yey·de tsoo·zeyts·li·khe
minute	*Minute*	mi·noo·te

| It's (one euro) per (minute). | | |
| *(Ein Euro) für (eine Minute).* | | (ain oy·ro) fewr (ai·ne mi·noo·te) |

post office

I want to send a ...	*Ich möchte ... senden.*	ikh meukh·te ... zen·den
fax	*ein Fax*	ain faks
letter	*einen Brief*	ai·nen breef
parcel	*ein Paket*	ain pa·keyt
postcard	*eine Postkarte*	ai·ne post·kar·te

I want to buy a/an ...	*Ich möchte ... kaufen.*	ikh meukh·te ... kow·fen
envelope	*einen Umschlag*	ai·nen um·shlaak
stamp	*eine Briefmarke*	ai·ne breef·mar·ke

Please send it	*Bitte schicken Sie das*	bi·te shi·ken zee das
(to Australia) by ...	*(nach Australien) per ...*	(nakh ows·traa·li·en) per ...
airmail	*Luftpost*	luft·post
express mail	*Expresspost*	eks·pres·post
registered mail	*Einschreiben*	ain·shrai·ben
surface mail	*Landbeförderung*	lant·be·feur·de·rung

| Is there any mail for me? | *Ist Post für mich da?* | ist post fewr mikh da |

bank

Where's a/an ...?	*Wo ist ...?*	vaw ist ...
ATM	*der Geldautomat*	dair gelt·ow·to·maat
foreign exchange	*die Geldwechselstube*	dee gelt·vek·sel·shtoo·be
office		

I'd like to ...	Ich möchte ...	ikh *meukh*·te ...
Where can I ...?	Wo kann ich ...?	vaw kan ikh ...
arrange a transfer	einen Transfer tätigen	*ai*·nen trans·*fer* tey·ti·gen
cash a cheque	einen Scheck einlösen	*ai*·nen shek *ain*·leu·zen
change a travellers cheque	einen Reisescheck einlösen	*ai*·nen *rai*·ze·shek *ain*·leu·zen
change money	Geld umtauschen	gelt *um*·tow·shen
get a cash advance	eine Barauszahlung	*ai*·ne *baar*·ows·tsaa·lung
withdraw money	Geld abheben	gelt *ap*·hey·ben

What's the ...?	Wie ...?	vee ...
charge for that	hoch sind die Gebühren dafür	hawkh zint dee ge·*bew*·ren da·*fewr*
exchange rate	ist der Wechselkurs	ist dair *vek*·sel·kurs

It's ...	Das ...	das ...
(12) euros	kostet (zwölf) euro	*kos*·tet (zveulf) *oy*·ro
free	ist umsonst	ist um·*zonst*

What time does the bank open?
Wann macht die Bank auf? van makht dee bangk owf

Has my money arrived yet?
Ist mein Geld schon angekommen? ist main gelt shawn *an*·ge·ko·men

sightseeing

getting in

What time does it open/close?
Wann macht es auf/zu? van makht es owf/tsoo

What's the admission charge?
Was kostet der Eintritt? vas *kos*·tet dair *ain*·trit

Is there a discount for children/students?
Gibt es eine Ermäßigung für Kinder/Studenten? gipt es *ai*·ne er·*mey*·si·gung fewr *kin*·der/shtu·*den*·ten

I'd like a ...	Ich hätte gern ...	ikh *he*·te gern ...
catalogue	einen Katalog	*ai*·nen ka·ta·*lawg*
guide	einen Reiseführer	*ai*·nen *rai*·ze·few·rer
local map	eine Karte von hier	*ai*·ne *kar*·te fon heer

I'd like to see ...	Ich möchte ... sehen.	ikh *meukh*·te ... *zey*·en
What's that?	Was ist das?	vas ist das
Can I take a photo?	Kann ich fotografieren?	kan ikh fo·to·gra·*fee*·ren

tours

When's the next ...?	Wann ist der/die nächste ...? m/f	van ist dair/dee *neykhs*·te ...
day trip	Tagesausflug m	*taa*·ges·ows·flook
tour	Tour f	toor

Is ... included?	Ist ... inbegriffen?	ist ... *in*·be·gri·fen
accommodation	die Unterkunft	dee *un*·ter·kunft
the admission charge	der Eintritt	dair *ain*·trit
food	das Essen	das *e*·sen
transport	die Beförderung	dee be·*feur*·de·rung

How long is the tour?
Wie lange dauert die Führung?   vee *lang*·e *dow*·ert dee *few*·rung

What time should we be back?
Wann sollen wir zurück sein?   van *zo*·len veer tsu·*rewk* zain

sightseeing

castle	Burg f	burk
cathedral	Dom m	dawm
church	Kirche f	*kir*·khe
main square	Hauptplatz m	*howpt*·plats
monastery	Kloster n	*klaws*·ter
monument	Denkmal n	*dengk*·maal
museum	Museum n	mu·*zey*·um
old city	Altstadt f	*alt*·stat
palace	Schloss n	shlos
ruins	Ruinen f pl	ru·*ee*·nen
stadium	Stadion n	*shtaa*·di·on
statues	Statuen f pl	*shtaa*·tu·e

shopping

enquiries

Where's a ...?	Wo ist ...?	vaw ist ...
bank	die Bank	dee bangk
bookshop	die Buchhandlung	dee bookh·hand·lung
camera shop	das Fotogeschäft	das fo·to·ge·sheft
department store	das Warenhaus	das vaa·ren·hows
grocery store	der Lebensmittelladen	dair ley·bens·mi·tel·laa·den
market	der Markt	dair markt
newsagency	der Zeitungshändler	dair tsai·tungks·hen·dler
supermarket	der Supermarkt	dair zoo·per·markt

Where can I buy (a padlock)?
Wo kann ich (ein Vorhängeschloss) kaufen?
vaw kan ikh (ain fawr·heng·e·shlos) kow·fen

I'm looking for ...
Ich suche nach ...
ikh zoo·khe nakh ...

Can I look at it?
Können Sie es mir zeigen?
keu·nen zee es meer tsai·gen

Do you have any others?
Haben Sie noch andere?
haa·ben zee nokh an·de·re

Does it have a guarantee?
Gibt es darauf Garantie?
gipt es da·rowf ga·ran·tee

Can I have it sent overseas?
Kann ich es ins Ausland verschicken lassen?
kan ikh es ins ows·lant fer·shi·ken la·sen

Can I have my ... repaired?
Kann ich mein ... reparieren lassen?
kan ikh main ... re·pa·ree·ren la·sen

It's faulty.
Es ist fehlerhaft.
es ist fey·ler·haft

I'd like ..., please.	Ich möchte bitte ...	ikh *meukh*·te *bi*·te ...
a bag	eine Tüte	*ai*·ne *tew*·te
a refund	mein Geld	main gelt
	zurückhaben	tsu·*rewk*·haa·ben
to return this	dieses zurückgeben	*dee*·zes tsu·*rewk*·gey·ben

paying

How much is it?
Wie viel kostet das?   vee feel *kos*·tet das

Can you write down the price?
Können Sie den Preis aufschreiben?   *keu*·nen zee deyn prais *owf*·shrai·ben

That's too expensive.
Das ist zu teuer.   das ist tsoo *toy*·er

Can you lower the price?
Können Sie mit dem Preis   *keu*·nen zee mit dem prais
heruntergehen?   he·*run*·ter·gey·en

I'll give you (five) euros.
Ich gebe Ihnen (fünf) euro.   ikh *gey*·be *ee*·nen (fewnf) *oy*·ro

There's a mistake in the bill.
Da ist ein Fehler in der Rechnung.   daa ist ain *fey*·ler in dair *rekh*·nung

Do you accept ...?	Nehmen Sie ...?	*ney*·men zee ...
credit cards	Kreditkarten	kre·*deet*·kar·ten
debit cards	Debitkarten	*dey*·bit·kar·ten
travellers cheques	Reiseschecks	*rai*·ze·sheks

I'd like ..., please.	Ich möchte bitte ...	ikh *meukh*·te *bi*·te ...
a receipt	eine Quittung	*ai*·ne *kvi*·tung
my change	mein Wechselgeld	main *vek*·sel·gelt

clothes & shoes

Can I try it on?	Kann ich es anprobieren?	kan ikh es *an*·pro·bee·ren
My size is (40).	Ich habe Größe (vierzig).	ikh *haa*·be *greu*·se (*feer*·tsikh)
It doesn't fit.	Es passt nicht.	es past nikht

small	klein	klain
medium	mittelgroß	*mi*·tel·graws
large	groß	graws

books & music

I'd like a ...	Ich hätte gern ...	ikh *he*·te gern ...
newspaper	eine Zeitung	ai·ne *tsai*·tung
(in English)	(auf Englisch)	(owf *eng*·lish)
pen	einen Kugelschreiber	ai·nen *koo*·gel·shrai·ber

Is there an English-language bookshop?
Gibt es einen Buchladen   gipt es *ai*·nen *bookh*·laa·den
für englische Bücher?   fewr *eng*·li·she *bew*·kher

I'm looking for something by (Herman Hesse).
Ich suche nach etwas von   ikh *zoo*·khe nakh *et*·vas fon
(Herman Hesse).   (*her*·man *he*·se)

Can I listen to this?
Kann ich mir das anhören?   kan ikh meer das *an*·heu·ren

photography

Can you ...?	Können Sie ...?	keu·nen zee ...
burn a CD from	eine CD von meiner	ai·ne tse de von *mai*·ner
my memory card	Speicherkarte brennen	*shpai*·kher·*kar*·te *bre*·nen
develop this film	diesen Film entwickeln	*dee*·zen film ent·*vi*·keln
load my film	mir den Film einlegen	meer deyn film *ain*·ley·gen

I need a ... film	Ich brauche einen	ikh *brow*·khe *ai*·nen
for this camera.	... für diese Kamera.	... fewr *dee*·ze *ka*·me·ra
APS	APS-Film	aa·pey·*es*·film
B&W	Schwarzweißfilm	shvarts·*vais*·film
colour	Farbfilm	*farp*·film
slide	Diafilm	*dee*·a·film
(200) speed	(zweihundert)-	(*tsvai*·hun·dert)·
	ASA-Film	*aa*·za·film

When will it be ready?   *Wann ist er fertig?*   van ist air *fer*·tikh

meeting people

greetings, goodbyes & introductions

Hello. (Austria)	*Servus.*	*zer*·vus
Hello. (Germany)	*Guten Tag.*	*goo*·ten taak
Hello. (Switzerland)	*Grüezi.*	*grew*·e·tsi
Hi.	*Hallo.*	*ha*·lo
Good night.	*Gute Nacht.*	*goo*·te nakht
Goodbye.	*Auf Wiedersehen.*	owf *vee*·der·zey·en
Bye.	*Tschüss/Tschau.*	chews/chow
See you later.	*Bis später.*	bis *shpey*·ter

Mr	*Herr*	her
Mrs	*Frau*	frow
Miss	*Fräulein*	*froy*·lain

How are you?	*Wie geht es Ihnen?*	vee geyt es *ee*·nen
Fine. And you?	*Danke, gut. Und Ihnen?*	*dang*·ke goot unt *ee*·nen
What's your name?	*Wie ist Ihr Name?*	vee ist eer *naa*·me
My name is ...	*Mein Name ist ...*	main *naa*·me ist ...
I'm pleased to meet you.	*Angenehm.*	*an*·ge·neym

This is my ...	*Das ist mein/meine ...* m/f	das ist main/*mai*·ne ...
brother	*Bruder*	*broo*·der
daughter	*Tochter*	*tokh*·ter
father	*Vater*	*faa*·ter
friend	*Freund/Freundin* m/f	froynt/*froyn*·din
husband	*Mann*	man
mother	*Mutter*	*mu*·ter
partner (intimate)	*Partner/Partnerin* m/f	*part*·ner/*part*·ne·rin
sister	*Schwester*	*shves*·ter
son	*Sohn*	zawn
wife	*Frau*	frow

Here's my ...	*Hier ist meine ...*	heer ist *mai*·ne ...
What's your ...?	*Wie ist Ihre ...?*	vee ist *ee*·re ...
address	*Adresse*	a·*dre*·se
email address	*E-mail-Adresse*	*ee*·mayl·a·dre·se
fax number	*Faxnummer*	*faks*·nu·mer
phone number	*Telefonnummer*	te·le·*fawn*·nu·mer

occupations

What's your occupation?	Als was arbeiten Sie? pol	als vas *ar*·bai·ten zee
	Als was arbeitest du? inf	als vas *ar*·bai·test doo
I'm a/an ...	Ich bin ein/eine ... m/f	ikh bin ain/*ai*·ne ...
artist	Künstler/Künstlerin m/f	*kewnst*·ler/*kewnst*·le·rin
business person	Geschäftsmann m	ge·*shefts*·man
	Geschäftsfrau f	ge·*shefts*·frow
farmer	Bauer/Bäuerin m/f	*bow*·er/*boy*·e·rin
manual worker	Arbeiter/Arbeiterin m/f	*ar*·bai·ter/*ar*·bai·te·rin
office worker	Büroangestellte m&f	bew·*raw*·an·ge·shtel·te
scientist	Wissenschaftler m	*vi*·sen·shaft·ler
	Wissenschaftlerin f	*vi*·sen·shaft·le·rin
student	Student/Studentin m/f	shtu·*dent*/shtu·*den*·tin

background

Where are you from?	Woher kommen Sie? pol	vaw·hair *ko*·men zee
	Woher kommst du? inf	vaw·hair komst doo
I'm from ...	Ich komme aus ...	ikh *ko*·me ows ...
Australia	Australien	ows·*traa*·li·en
Canada	Kanada	*ka*·na·daa
England	England	*eng*·lant
New Zealand	Neuseeland	noy·*zey*·lant
the USA	den USA	deyn oo·es·*aa*
Are you married?	Sind Sie verheiratet? pol	zint zee fer·*hai*·ra·tet
	Bist du verheiratet? inf	bist doo fer·*hai*·ra·tet
I'm married.	Ich bin verheiratet.	ikh bin fer·*hai*·ra·tet
I'm single.	Ich bin ledig.	ikh bin *ley*·dikh

age

How old ...?	Wie alt ...?	vee alt ...
are you	sind Sie pol	zint zee
	bist du inf	bist doo
is your daughter	ist Ihre Tochter pol	ist *ee*·re tokh·ter
is your son	ist Ihr Sohn pol	ist eer zawn
I'm ... years old.	Ich bin ... Jahre alt.	ikh bin ... *yaa*·re alt
He/She is ... years old.	Er/Sie ist ... Jahre alt.	air/zee ist ... *yaa*·re alt

feelings

I'm (not) ... Are you ...?	Ich bin (nicht) ... Sind Sie ...? pol Bist du ...? inf	ikh bin (nikht) ... zint zee ... bist doo ...
happy	glücklich	glewk·likh
sad	traurig	trow·rikh

I'm (not) ... Are you ...?	Ich habe (kein) ... Haben Sie ...? pol Hast du ...? inf	ikh haa·be (kain) ... haa·ben zee ... hast doo ...
hungry	Hunger	hung·er
thirsty	Durst	durst

I'm (not) ... Are you ...?	Mir ist (nicht) ... Ist Ihnen/dir ...? pol/inf	meer ist (nikht) ... ist ee·nen/deer ...
cold	kalt	kalt
hot	heiß	hais

entertainment

going out

Where can I find ...?	Wo sind die ...?	vaw zint dee ...
clubs	Klubs	klups
gay venues	Schwulen- und Lesbenkneipen	shvoo·len unt les·ben·knai·pen
pubs	Kneipen	knai·pen

I feel like going to a/the ...	Ich hätte Lust, ... zu gehen.	ikh he·te lust ... tsoo gey·en
concert	zum Konzert	tsoom kon·tsert
movies	ins Kino	ins kee·no
party	zu eine Party	tsoo ai·ne par·ti
restaurant	in ein Restaurant	in ain res·to·rang
theatre	ins Theater	ins te·aa·ter

interests

Do you like ...?	*Magst du ...?* inf	maakst doo ...
I (don't) like ...	*Ich mag (keine/keinen) ...* m/f	ikh maak (*kai*·ne/*kai*·nen) ...
art	*Kunst* f	kunst
sport	*Sport* m	shport
I (don't) like ...	*Ich ... (nicht) gern.*	ikh ... (nikht) gern
cooking	*koche*	*ko*·khe
reading	*lese*	*ley*·ze
travelling	*reise*	*rai*·ze
Do you like to dance?	*Tanzt du gern?* inf	tantst doo gern
Do you like music?	*Hörst du gern Musik?* inf	heurst doo gern mu·*zeek*

food & drink

finding a place to eat

Can you recommend a ...?	*Können Sie ... empfehlen?*	*keu*·nen zee ... emp·*fey*·len
bar	*eine Kneipe*	*ai*·ne *knai*·pe
café	*ein Café*	ain ka·*fey*
restaurant	*ein Restaurant*	ain res·to·*rang*
I'd like ..., please.	*Ich hätte gern ..., bitte.*	ikh *he*·te gern ... *bi*·te
a table for (five)	*einen Tisch für (fünf) Personen*	*ai*·nen tish fewr (fewnf) per·*zaw*·nen
the (non)smoking section	*einen (Nicht-) rauchertisch*	*ai*·nen (*nikht*·) *row*·kher·tish

ordering food

breakfast	*Frühstück* n	*frew*·shtewk
lunch	*Mittagessen* n	*mi*·taak·e·sen
dinner	*Abendessen* n	*aa*·bent·e·sen
snack	*Snack* m	snek

What would you recommend?
Was empfehlen Sie?   vas emp·*fey*·len zee

I'd like (the) ..., please. *Bitte bringen Sie ...*   bi·te bring·en zee ...
    bill   *die Rechnung*   dee *rekh*·nung
    drink list   *die Getränkekarte*   dee ge·*treng*·ke·kar·te
    menu   *die Speisekarte*   dee *shpai*·ze·kar·te
    that dish   *dieses Gericht*   dee·zes ge·*rikht*

drinks

(cup of) coffee ...	*(eine Tasse) Kaffee ...*	(*ai*·ne *ta*·se) ka·*fey* ...
(cup of) tea ...	*(eine Tasse) Tee ...*	(*ai*·ne *ta*·se) tey ...
with milk	*mit Milch*	mit milkh
without sugar	*ohne Zucker*	*aw*·ne *tsu*·ker
(orange) juice	*(Orangen)Saft* m	(o·*rang*·zhen·)zaft
mineral water	*Mineralwasser* n	mi·ne·*raal*·va·ser
soft drink	*Softdrink* m	*soft*·dringk
(boiled) water	*(heißes) Wasser* n	(*hai*·ses) *va*·ser

in the bar

I'll have ...	*Ich hätte gern ...*	ikh *he*·te gern ...
I'll buy you a drink.	*Ich gebe dir einen aus.* inf	ikh *gey*·be deer *ai*·nen ows
What would you like?	*Was möchtest du?* inf	vas *meukh*·test doo
Cheers!	*Prost!*	prawst
brandy	*Weinbrand* m	*vain*·brant
cognac	*Kognak* m	*ko*·nyak
cocktail	*Cocktail* m	*kok*·tayl
a shot of (whisky)	*einen (Whisky)*	*ai*·nen (*vis*·ki)
a bottle of ...	*eine Flasche ...*	*ai*·ne *fla*·she ...
a glass of ...	*ein Glas ...*	ain glaas ...
red wine	*Rotwein*	*rawt*·vain
sparkling wine	*Sekt*	zekt
white wine	*Weißwein*	*vais*·vain
a ... of beer	*... Bier*	... beer
bottle	*eine Flasche*	*ai*·ne *fla*·she
glass	*ein Glas*	ain glaas

self-catering

What's the local speciality?
Was ist eine örtliche Spezialität? — vas ist *ai*·ne *eurt*·li·khe shpe·tsya·li·*teyt*

What's that?
Was ist das? — vas ist das

How much is (a kilo of cheese)?
Was kostet (ein Kilo Käse)? — vas *kos*·tet (ain *kee*·lo *key*·ze)

I'd like ...	*Ich möchte ...*	ikh *meukh*·te ...
(100) grams	*(hundert) Gramm*	(hun·dert) gram
(two) kilos	*(zwei) Kilo*	(tsvai) *kee*·lo
(three) pieces	*(drei) Stück*	(drai) shtewk
(six) slices	*(sechs) Scheiben*	(zeks) *shai*·ben

Less.	*Weniger.*	*vey*·ni·ger
Enough.	*Genug.*	ge·*nook*
More.	*Mehr.*	mair

special diets & allergies

Is there a vegetarian restaurant near here?
Gibt es ein vegetarisches Restaurant hier in der Nähe? — gipt es ain vege·*tar*·ish·shes res·to·*rang* heer in dair *ney*·e

Do you have vegetarian food?
Haben Sie vegetarisches Essen? — *haa*·ben zee ve·ge·*taa*·ri·shes *e*·sen

Could you prepare a meal without ...?	*Können Sie ein Gericht ohne ... zubereiten?*	*keu*·nen zee ain ge·*rikht aw*·ne ... *tsoo*·be·rai·ten
butter	*Butter*	*bu*·ter
eggs	*Eiern*	*ai*·ern
meat stock	*Fleischbrühe*	*flaish*·brew·e

I'm allergic to ...	*Ich bin allergisch gegen ...*	ikh bin a·*lair*·gish *gey*·gen ...
dairy produce	*Milchprodukte*	*milkh*·pro·duk·te
gluten	*Gluten*	*gloo*·ten
MSG	*Natrium-glutamat*	*naa*·tri·um·glu·ta·maat
nuts	*Nüsse*	*new*·se
seafood	*Meeresfrüchte*	*mair*·res·frewkh·te

emergencies

basics

Help!	*Hilfe!*	*hil*·fe
Stop!	*Halt!*	halt
Go away!	*Gehen Sie weg!*	*gey*·en zee vek
Thief!	*Dieb!*	deeb
Fire!	*Feuer!*	*foy*·er
Watch out!	*Vorsicht!*	for·*zikht*
Call ...!	*Rufen Sie ...!*	*roo*·fen zee ...
a doctor	*einen Arzt*	*ai*·nen artst
an ambulance	*einen Krankenwagen*	*ai*·nen *krang*·ken·vaa·gen
the police	*die Polizei*	dee po·li·*tsai*

It's an emergency!
Es ist ein Notfall!   es ist ain *nawt*·fal

Could you help me, please?
Könnten Sie mir bitte helfen?   *keun*·ten zee meer *bi*·te *hel*·fen

I have to use the telephone.
Ich muss das Telefon benutzen.   ikh mus das te·le·*fawn* be·*nu*·tsen

I'm lost.
Ich habe mich verirrt.   ikh *haa*·be mikh fer·*irt*

Where are the toilets?
Wo ist die Toilette?   vo ist dee to·a·*le*·te

police

Where's the police station?
Wo ist das Polizeirevier?   vaw ist das po·li·*tsai*·re·veer

I want to report an offence.
Ich möchte eine Straftat melden.   ikh *meukh*·te *ai*·ne *shtraaf*·taat *mel*·den

I have insurance.
Ich bin versichert.   ikh bin fer·*zi*·khert

I've been ...	*Ich bin ... worden.*	ikh bin ... *vor*·den
assaulted	*angegriffen*	*an*·ge·gri·fen
raped	*vergewaltigt*	fer·ge·*val*·tikht
robbed	*bestohlen*	be·*shtaw*·len

I've lost my...	Ich habe ... verloren.	ikh haa·be ... fer·law·ren
My ... was/	Man hat mir ...	man hat meer ...
were stolen.	gestohlen.	ge·shtaw·len
backpack	meinen Rucksack	mai·nen ruk·zak
bags	meine Reisetaschen	mai·ne rai·ze·ta·shen
credit card	meine Kreditkarte	mai·ne kre·deet·karte
handbag	meine Handtasche	mai·ne hant·ta·she
jewellery	meinen Schmuck	mai·nen shmuk
money	mein Geld	main gelt
passport	meinen Pass	mai·nen pas
travellers cheques	meine Reiseschecks	mai·ne rai·ze·sheks
wallet	meine Brieftasche	mai·ne breef·ta·she

I want to contact	Ich mochte mich mit	ikh meukh·te mikh mit
my ...	... in Verbindung setzen.	... in fer·bin·dung ze·tsen
consulate	meinem Konsulat	mai·nem kon·zu·laat
embassy	meiner Botschaft	mai·ner bawt·shaft

health

medical needs

Where's the	Wo ist der/die/das	vaw ist dair/dee/das
nearest ...?	nächste ...? m/f/n	neykhs·te ...
dentist	Zahnarzt m	tsaan·artst
doctor	Arzt m	artst
hospital	Krankenhaus n	krang·ken·hows
(night) pharmacist	(Nacht)Apotheke f	(nakht·)a·po·tey·ke

I need a doctor (who speaks English).
Ich brauche einen Arzt   ikh brow·khe ai·nen artst
(der Englisch spricht).   (dair eng·lish shprikht)

Could I see a female doctor?
Könnte ich von einer   keun·te ikh fon ai·ner
Ärztin behandelt werden?   erts·tin be·han·delt ver·den

I've run out of my medication.
Ich habe keine   ikh haa·be kai·ne
Medikamente mehr.   me·di·ka·men·te mair

symptoms, conditions & allergies

| I'm sick. | Ich bin krank. | ikh bin krangk |
| It hurts here. | Es tut hier weh. | es toot heer vey |

I have (a) ...	Ich habe ...	ikh haa·be ...
asthma	Asthma	ast·ma
bronchitis	Bronchitis	bron·khee·tis
constipation	Verstopfung	fer·shtop·fung
cough	Husten	hoos·ten
diarrhoea	Durchfall	durkh·fal
fever	Fieber	fee·ber
headache	Kopfschmerzen	kopf·shmer·tsen
heart condition	Herzbeschwerden	herts·be·shver·den
nausea	Übelkeit	ew·bel·kait
pain	Schmerzen	shmer·tsen
sore throat	Halsschmerzen	hals·shmer·tsen
toothache	Zahnschmerzen	tsaan·shmer·tsen

I'm allergic to ...	Ich bin allergisch gegen ...	ikh bin a·lair·gish gey·gen ...
antibiotics	Antibiotika	an·ti·bi·aw·ti·ka
anti-inflammatories	entzündungs-hemmende Mittel	en·tsewn·dungks·he·men·de mi·tel
aspirin	Aspirin	as·pi·reen
bees	Bienen	bee·nen
codeine	Kodein	ko·de·een
penicillin	Penizillin	pe·ni·tsi·leen

antiseptic	Antiseptikum n	an·ti·zep·ti·kum
bandage	Verband m	fer·bant
condoms	Kondom n	kon·dawm
contraceptives	Verhütungsmittel n	fer·hew·tungks·mi·tel
diarrhoea medicine	Mittel gegen Durchfall n	mi·tel gey·gen durkh·fal
insect repellent	Insektenschutzmittel n	in·zek·ten·shuts·mi·tel
laxatives	Abführmittel n	ap·fewr·mi·tel
painkillers	Schmerzmittel n	shmerts·mi·tel
rehydration salts	Kochsalzlösung n	kokh·zalts·leu·zung
sleeping tablets	Schlaftabletten f pl	shlaaf·ta·ble·ten

english–german dictionary

German nouns in this dictionary have their gender indicated by ⓜ (masculine), ⓕ (feminine) or ⓝ (neuter). If it's a plural noun, you'll also see pl. Words are also marked as n (noun), a (adjective), v (verb), sg (singular), pl (plural), inf (informal) and pol (polite) where necessary.

A

accident *Unfall* ⓜ un-fal
accommodation *Unterkunft* ⓕ un-ter-kunft
adaptor *Adapter* ⓜ a-dap-ter
address *Adresse* ⓕ a-dre-se
after *nach* naakh
air-conditioned *mit Klimaanlage* ⓕ
     mit klee-ma-an-laa-ge
airplane *Flugzeug* ⓝ flook-tsoyk
airport *Flughafen* ⓜ flook-haa-fen
alcohol *Alkohol* ⓜ al-ko-hawl
all a *alle* a-le
allergy *Allergie* ⓕ a-lair-gee
ambulance *Krankenwagen* ⓜ krang-ken-vaa-gen
and *und* unt
ankle *Knöchel* ⓜ kneu-khel
arm *Arm* ⓜ arm
ashtray *Aschenbecher* ⓜ a-shen-be-kher
ATM *Geldautomat* ⓜ gelt-ow-to-maat
Austria *Österreich* ⓝ eus-ter-raikh

B

baby *Baby* ⓝ bay-bi
back (body) *Rücken* ⓜ rew-ken
backpack *Rucksack* ⓜ ruk-zak
bad *schlecht* shlekht
bag *Tasche* ⓕ ta-she
baggage claim *Gepäckausgabe* ⓕ ge-pek-ows-gaa-be
bank *Bank* ⓕ bangk
bar *Lokal* ⓝ lo-kaal
bathroom *Badezimmer* ⓝ baa-de-tsi-mer
battery *Batterie* ⓕ ba-te-ree
beautiful *schön* sheun
bed *Bett* ⓝ bet
beer *Bier* ⓝ beer
before *vor* fawr
behind *hinter* hin-ter
Belgium ⓝ *Belgien* bel-gi-en

bicycle *Fahrrad* ⓝ faar-raat
big *groß* graws
bill *Rechnung* ⓕ rekh-nung
black *schwarz* shvarts
blanket *Decke* ⓕ de-ke
blood group *Blutgruppe* ⓕ bloot-gru-pe
blue *blau* blow
book (make a reservation) v *buchen* boo-khen
bottle *Flasche* ⓕ fla-she
bottle opener *Flaschenöffner* ⓜ fla-shen-euf-ner
boy *Junge* ⓜ yung-e
brakes (car) *Bremsen* ⓕ pl brem-zen
breakfast *Frühstück* ⓝ frew-shtewk
broken (faulty) *kaputt* ka-put
bus *Bus* ⓜ bus
business *Geschäft* ⓝ ge-sheft
buy *kaufen* kow-fen

C

café *Café* ⓝ ka-fey
camera *Kamera* ⓕ ka-me-ra
camp site *Zeltplatz* ⓜ tselt-plats
cancel *stornieren* shtor-nee-ren
can opener *Dosenöffner* ⓜ daw-zen-euf-ner
car *Auto* ⓝ ow-to
cash *Bargeld* ⓝ baar-gelt
cash (a cheque) v *(einen Scheck) einlösen*
     *(ai-*nen shek) ain-leu-zen
cell phone *Handy* ⓝ hen-di
centre *Zentrum* ⓝ tsen-trum
change (money) v *wechseln* vek-seln
cheap *billig* bi-likh
check (bill) *Rechnung* ⓕ rekh-nung
check-in *Abfertigungsschalter* ⓜ
     ap-fer-ti-gungks-shal-ter
chest *Brustkorb* ⓜ brust-korp
child *Kind* ⓝ kint
cigarette *Zigarette* ⓕ tsi-ga-re-te
city *Stadt* ⓕ shtat
clean a *sauber* zow-ber

closed *geschlossen* ge-*shlo*-sen
coffee *Kaffee* ⓜ *ka*-fey
coins *Münzen* ⓕ pl *mewn*-tsen
cold a *kalt* kalt
collect call *R-Gespräch* ⓝ air-ge-*shpreykh*
come *kommen* *ko*-men
computer *Computer* ⓜ kom-*pyoo*-ter
condom *Kondom* ⓝ kon-*dawm*
contact lenses *Kontaktlinsen* ⓕ pl kon-*takt*-lin-zen
cook v *kochen* *ko*-khen
cost *Preis* ⓜ prais
credit card *Kreditkarte* ⓕ kre-*deet*-kar-te
cup *Tasse* ⓕ *ta*-se
currency exchange *Geldwechsel* ⓜ *gelt*-vek-sel
customs (immigration) *Zoll* ⓜ tsol

D

dangerous *gefährlich* ge-*fair*-likh
date (time) *Datum* ⓝ *daa*-tum
day *Tag* ⓜ taak
delay n *Verspätung* ⓕ fer-*shpey*-tung
dentist *Zahnarzt/Zahnärztin* ⓜ/ⓕ *tsaan*-artst/*tsaan*-erts-tin
depart *abfahren* ap-*faa*-ren
diaper *Windel* ⓕ *vin*-del
dictionary *Wörterbuch* ⓝ *veur*-ter-bookh
dinner *Abendessen* ⓝ *aa*-bent-e-sen
direct *direkt* di-*rekt*
dirty *schmutzig* *shmu*-tsikh
disabled *behindert* be-*hin*-dert
discount n *Rabatt* ⓜ ra-*bat*
doctor *Arzt/Ärztin* ⓜ/ⓕ artst/*erts*-tin
double bed *Doppelbett* ⓝ *do*-pel-bet
double room *Doppelzimmer mit einem Doppelbett* ⓝ *do*-pel-tsi-mer mit *ai*-nem *do*-pel-bet
drink *Getränk* ⓝ ge-*trengk*
drive v *fahren* *faa*-ren
drivers licence *Führerschein* ⓜ *few*-rer-shain
drugs (illicit) *Droge* ⓕ *draw*-ge
dummy (pacifier) *Schnuller* ⓜ *shnu*-ler

E

ear *Ohr* ⓝ awr
east *Osten* ⓜ *os*-ten
eat *essen* *e*-sen
economy class *Touristenklasse* ⓕ tu-*ris*-ten-kla-se
electricity *Elektrizität* ⓕ e-lek-tri-tsi-*teyt*
elevator *Lift* ⓜ lift

email *E-Mail* *e*-mayl
embassy *Botschaft* ⓕ *bawt*-shaft
emergency *Notfall* ⓜ *nawt*-fal
English (language) *Englisch* ⓝ *eng*-lish
entrance *Eingang* ⓜ *ain*-gang
evening *Abend* ⓜ *aa*-bent
exchange rate *Wechselkurs* ⓜ *vek*-sel-kurs
exit *Ausgang* ⓜ *ows*-gang
expensive *teuer* *toy*-er
express mail *Expresspost* ⓕ eks-*pres*-post
eye *Auge* ⓝ *ow*-ge

F

far *weit* vait
fast *schnell* shnel
father *Vater* ⓜ *faa*-ter
film (camera) *Film* ⓜ film
finger *Finger* ⓜ *fing*-er
first-aid kit *Verbandskasten* ⓜ fer-*bants*-kas-ten
first class *erste Klasse* ⓕ *ers*-te *kla*-se
fish *Fisch* ⓜ fish
food *Essen* ⓝ *e*-sen
foot *Fuß* ⓜ foos
fork *Gabel* ⓕ *gaa*-bel
free (of charge) *gratis* *graa*-tis
friend *Freund/Freundin* ⓜ/ⓕ froynt/*froyn*-din
fruit *Frucht* ⓕ frukht
full *voll* fol
funny *lustig* *lus*-tikh

G

German (language) *Deutsch* ⓝ doytsh
Germany *Deutschland* ⓝ *doytsh*-lant
gift *Geschenk* ⓝ ge-*shengk*
girl *Mädchen* ⓝ *meyt*-khen
glass (drinking) *Glas* ⓝ glaas
glasses *Brille* ⓕ *bri*-le
go *gehen* *gey*-en
good *gut* goot
green *grün* grewn
guide *Führer* ⓜ *few*-rer

H

half *Hälfte* ⓕ *helf*-te
hand *Hand* ⓕ hant
handbag *Handtasche* ⓕ *hant*-ta-she
happy *glücklich* *glewk*-likh

have *haben* haa-ben
he *er* air
head *Kopf* ⓜ kopf
heart *Herz* ⓝ herts
heat n *Hitze* ⓕ hi-tse
heavy *schwer* shvair
help v *helfen* hel-fen
here *hier* heer
high *hoch* hawkh
highway *Autobahn* ⓕ ow-to-baan
hike v *wandern* van-dern
holiday *Urlaub* ⓜ oor-lowp
homosexual *homosexuell* haw-mo-zek-su-el
hospital *Krankenhaus* ⓝ krang-ken-hows
hot *heiß* hais
hotel *Hotel* ⓝ ho-tel
hungry *hungrig* hung-rikh
husband *Ehemann* ⓜ ey-e-man

I

I *ich* ikh
identification (card) *Personalausweis* ⓜ
  per-zo-naal-ows-vais
ill *krank* krangk
important *wichtig* vikh-tikh
included *inbegriffen* in-be-gri-fen
injury *Verletzung* ⓕ fer-let-tsung
insurance *Versicherung* ⓕ fer-zi-khe-rung
Internet *Internet* ⓝ in-ter-net
interpreter *Dolmetscher/Dolmetscherin* ⓜ/ⓕ
  dol-met-sher/dol-met-she-rin

J

jewellery *Schmuck* ⓜ shmuk
job *Arbeitsstelle* ⓕ ar-baits-shte-le

K

key *Schlüssel* ⓜ shlew-sel
kilogram *Kilogramm* ⓝ kee-lo-gram
kitchen *Küche* ⓕ kew-khe
knife *Messer* ⓝ me-ser

L

laundry (place) *Waschküche* ⓕ vash-kew-khe
lawyer *Rechtsanwalt/Rechtsanwältin* ⓜ/ⓕ
  rekhts-an-valt/rekhts-an-vel-tin

left (direction) *links* lingks
left-luggage office *Gepäckaufbewahrung* ⓕ
  ge-pek-owf-be-vaa-rung
leg *Bein* ⓝ bain
lesbian *Lesbierin* ⓕ les-bi-e-rin
less *weniger* vey-ni-ger
letter (mail) *Brief* ⓜ breef
lift (elevator) *Lift* ⓜ lift
light *Licht* ⓝ likht
like v *mögen* meu-gen
lock *Schloss* ⓝ shlos
long *lang* lang
lost *verloren* fer-law-ren
lost-property office *Fundbüro* ⓝ funt-bew-raw
love v *lieben* lee-ben
luggage *Gepäck* ⓝ ge-pek
lunch *Mittagessen* ⓝ mi-taak-e-sen

M

mail *Post* ⓕ post
man *Mann* ⓜ man
map *Karte* ⓕ kar-te
market *Markt* ⓜ markt
matches *Streichhölzer* ⓝ pl shtraikh-heul-tser
meat *Fleisch* ⓝ flaish
medicine *Medizin* ⓕ me-di-tseen
menu *Speisekarte* ⓕ shpai-ze-kar-te
message *Mitteilung* ⓕ mi-tai-lung
milk *Milch* ⓕ milkh
minute *Minute* ⓕ mi-noo-te
mobile phone *Handy* ⓝ hen-di
money *Geld* ⓝ gelt
month *Monat* ⓜ maw-nat
morning *Morgen* ⓜ mor-gen
mother *Mutter* ⓕ mu-ter
motorcycle *Motorrad* ⓝ maw-tor-raat
motorway *Autobahn* ⓕ ow-to-baan
mouth *Mund* ⓜ munt
music *Musik* ⓕ mu-zeek

N

name *Name* ⓜ naa-me
napkin *Serviette* ⓕ zer-vye-te
nappy *Windel* ⓕ vin-del
near *nahe* naa-e
neck *Hals* ⓜ hals
new *neu* noy
news *Nachrichten* ⓕ pl naakh-rikh-ten

newspaper *Zeitung* ① *tsai*-tung
night *Nacht* ① nakht
no *nein* nain
noisy *laut* lowt
nonsmoking *Nichtraucher* nikht-*row*-kher
north *Norden* ⓜ *nor*-den
nose *Nase* ① *naa*-ze
now *jetzt* yetst
number *Zahl* ① tsaal

O

oil (engine) *Öl* ⓝ eul
old *alt* alt
one-way ticket *einfache Fahrkarte* ①
    ain-fa-khe *faar*-kar-te
open a *offen* o-fen
outside *draußen* *drow*-sen

P

package *Paket* ⓝ pa-*keyt*
paper *Papier* ⓝ pa-*peer*
park (car) v *parken* *par*-ken
passport *(Reise)Pass* ⓜ *(rai*-ze-)pas
pay *bezahlen* be-*tsaa*-len
pen *Kugelschreiber* ⓜ *koo*-gel-shrai-ber
petrol *Benzin* ⓝ ben-*tseen*
pharmacy *Apotheke* ① a-po-*tey*-ke
phonecard *Telefonkarte* ① te-le-*fawn*-kar-te
photo *Foto* ⓝ *faw*-to
plate *Teller* ⓜ *te*-ler
police *Polizei* ① po-li-*tsai*
postcard *Postkarte* ① *post*-kar-te
post office *Postamt* ⓝ *post*-amt
pregnant *schwanger* *shvang*-er
price *Preis* ⓜ prais

Q

quiet *ruhig* *roo*-ikh

R

rain n *Regen* ⓜ *rey*-gen
razor *Rasierer* ⓜ ra-*zee*-rer
receipt *Quittung* ① *kvi*-tung
red *rot* rawt
refund *Rückzahlung* ① *rewk*-tsaa-lung
registered mail *Einschreiben* ⓝ *ain*-shrai-ben

rent v *mieten* *mee*-ten
repair v *reparieren* re-pa-*ree*-ren
reservation *Reservierung* ① re-zer-*vee*-rung
restaurant *Restaurant* ⓝ res-to-*raang*
return v *zurückkommen* tsu-*rewk*-ko-men
return ticket *Rückfahrkarte* ① *rewk*-faar-kar-te
right (direction) *rechts* rekhts
road *Straße* ① *shtraa*-se
room *Zimmer* ⓝ *tsi*-mer

S

safe a *sicher* *zi*-kher
sanitary napkin *Damenbinden* ① pl *daa*-men-bin-den
seat *Platz* ⓜ plats
send *senden* *zen*-den
service station *Tankstelle* ① tangk-shte-le
sex *Sex* ⓜ seks
shampoo *Shampoo* ⓝ *sham*-poo
share (a dorm) *teilen (mit)* *tai*-len (mit)
shaving cream *Rasiercreme* ① ra-*zeer*-kreym
she *sie* zee
sheet (bed) *Bettlaken* ⓝ *bet*-laa-ken
shirt *Hemd* ⓝ hemt
shoes *Schuhe* ⓝ pl *shoo*-e
shop n *Geschäft* ⓝ ge-*sheft*
short *kurz* kurts
shower *Dusche* ① *doo*-she
single room *Einzelzimmer* ⓝ *ain*-tsel-tsi-mer
skin *Haut* ① howt
skirt *Rock* ⓜ rok
sleep v *schlafen* *shlaa*-fen
slowly *langsam* *lang*-zaam
small *klein* klain
smoke (cigarettes) v *rauchen* *row*-khen
soap *Seife* ① *zai*-fe
some *einige* *ai*-ni-ge
soon *bald* balt
south *Süden* ⓜ *zew*-den
souvenir shop *Souvenirladen* ⓜ zu-ve-*neer*-laa-den
speak *sprechen* *shpre*-khen
spoon *Löffel* ⓜ *leu*-fel
stamp *Briefmarke* ① *breef*-mar-ke
stand-by ticket *Standby-Ticket* ⓝ stend-*bai*-ti-ket
station (train) *Bahnhof* ⓜ *baan*-hawf
stomach *Magen* ⓜ *maa*-gen
stop v *anhalten* *an*-hal-ten
stop (bus) *Bushaltestelle* ① *bus*-hal-te-shte-le
street *Straße* ① *shtraa*-se

student Student/Studentin ⓜ/ⓕ
shtu-*dent*/shtu-*den*-tin
sun Sonne ⓕ zo-ne
sunscreen Sonnencreme ⓕ zo-nen-kreym
swim v schwimmen shvi-men
Switzerland Schweiz ⓕ shvaits

T

tampons Tampons ⓜ pl tam-pons
taxi Taxi ⓝ tak-si
teaspoon Teelöffel ⓜ tey-leu-fel
teeth Zähne ⓜ pl tsey-ne
telephone Telefon ⓝ te-le-fawn
television Fernseher ⓜ fern-zey-er
temperature (weather) Temperatur ⓕ tem-pe-ra-toor
tent Zelt ⓝ tselt
that (one) jene yey-ne
they sie zee
thirsty durstig durs-tikh
this (one) diese dee-ze
throat Kehle ⓕ key-le
ticket (transport) Fahrkarte ⓕ faar-kar-te
ticket (sightseeing) Eintrittskarte ⓕ ain-trits-kar-te
time Zeit ⓕ tsait
tired müde mew-de
tissues Papiertaschentücher ⓝ pl
pa-*peer*-ta-shen-tew-kher
today heute hoy-te
toilet Toilette ⓕ to-a-*le*-te
tomorrow morgen mor-gen
tonight heute Abend hoy-te aa-bent
toothbrush Zahnbürste ⓕ tsaan-bewrs-te
toothpaste Zahnpasta ⓕ tsaan-pas-ta
torch (flashlight) Taschenlampe ⓕ ta-shen-lam-pe
tour Tour ⓕ toor
tourist office Fremdenverkehrsbüro ⓝ
frem-den-fer-kairs-bew-raw
towel Handtuch ⓝ hant-tookh
train Zug ⓜ tsook
translate übersetzen ew-ber-ze-tsen
travel agency Reisebüro ⓝ rai-ze-bew-raw
travellers cheque Reisescheck ⓜ rai-ze-shek
trousers Hose ⓕ haw-ze
twin beds zwei Einzelbetten ⓝ pl tsvai ain-tsel-be-ten
tyre Reifen ⓜ rai-fen

U

underwear Unterwäsche ⓕ un-ter-ve-she
urgent dringend dring-ent

V

vacant frei frai
vacation Ferien pl fair-i-en
vegetable Gemüse ⓝ ge-mew-ze
vegetarian a vegetarisch ve-ge-taa-rish
visa Visum ⓝ vee-zum

W

waiter Kellner/Kellnerin ⓜ/ⓕ kel-ner/kel-ne-rin
walk v gehen gey-en
wallet Brieftasche ⓕ breef-ta-she
warm a warm varm
wash (something) waschen va-shen
watch Uhr ⓕ oor
water Wasser ⓝ va-ser
we wir veer
weekend Wochenende ⓝ vo-khen-en-de
west Westen ⓝ ves-ten
wheelchair Rollstuhl ⓜ rol-shtool
when wann van
where wo vaw
white weiß vais
who wer vair
why warum va-rum
wife Ehefrau ⓕ ey-e-frow
window Fenster ⓝ fens-ter
wine Wein ⓜ vain
with mit mit
without ohne aw-ne
woman Frau ⓕ frow
write schreiben shrai-ben

Y

yellow gelb gelp
yes ja yaa
yesterday gestern ges-tern
you sg inf du doo
you sg pol Sie zee
you pl Sie zee

Greek

greek alphabet

Α α *al*·pha	Β β *vi*·ta	Γ γ *gha*·ma	Δ δ *dhel*·ta	Ε ε *ep*·si·lon
Ζ ζ *zi*·ta	Η η *i*·ta	Θ θ *thi*·ta	Ι ι *yio*·ta	Κ κ *ka*·pa
Λ λ *lam*·dha	Μ μ mi	Ν ν ni	Ξ ξ ksi	Ο ο *o*·mi·kron
Π π pi	Ρ ρ ro	Σ σ/ς* *sigh*·ma	Τ τ taf	Υ υ *ip*·si·lon
Φ φ fi	Χ χ hi	Ψ ψ psi	Ω ω *o*·*me*·gha	

* The letter Σ has two forms for the lower case – σ and ς. The second one is used at the end of words.

greek

ΕΛΛΗΝΙΚΑ

about Greek

Aristotle, Plato, Homer, Sappho and Herodotus can't all be wrong in their choice of language – if you've ever come across arcane concepts such as 'democracy', exotic disciplines like 'trigonometry' or a little-known neurosis termed 'the Oedipus complex', then you'll have some inkling of the widespread influence of Greek (Ελληνικά e·li·ni·ka). With just a little Modern Greek under your belt, you'll have a richer understanding of this language's impact on contemporary Western culture.

Modern Greek is a separate branch of the Indo-European language family, with Ancient Greek its only (extinct) relative. The first records of written Ancient Greek date from the 14th to the 12th centuries BC. By the 9th century BC, the Greeks had adapted the Phoenician alphabet to include vowels – the first alphabet to do so – and the script in use today came to its final form some time in the 5th century BC. The Greek script was the foundation for both the Cyrillic and the Latin alphabet.

Although written Greek has been remarkably stable over the millennia, the spoken language has evolved considerably. In the 5th century, the dialect spoken around Athens (known as 'Attic') became the dominant speech as a result of the city-state's cultural and political prestige. Attic gained even greater influence as the medium of administration for the vast empire of Alexander the Great, and remained the official language of the Eastern Roman Empire and the Orthodox Church after the demise of the Hellenistic world. Once the Ottoman Turks took Constantinople in 1453, the Attic dialect lost its official function. In the meantime, the common language, known as Koine (Κοινή ki·ni), continued to evolve, absorbing vocabulary from Turkish, Italian, Albanian and other Balkan languages.

When an independent Greece returned to the world stage in 1832, it needed to choose a national language. Purists advocated a slightly modernised version of Attic known as Καθαρεύουσα ka·tha·re·vu·sa (from the Greek word for 'clean'), which no longer resembled the spoken language. However, Koine had strong support as it was spoken and understood by the majority of Greeks, and in the end it gained official recognition, although it was banned during the military dictatorship (1967–74).

Today, Greek is the official language of Greece and a co-official language of Cyprus, and has over 13 million speakers worldwide. Start your Greek adventure with this chapter – and if you're having one of those days when you're dying to say 'It's all Greek to me!', remember that in your shoes, a Greek speaker would say: Αυτά για μένα είναι Κινέζικα af·ta yia me·na i·ne ki·ne·zi·ka (This is Chinese to me)!

pronunciation

vowel sounds

Greek vowels are pronounced separately even when they're written in sequence, eg ζώο *zo-o* (animal). You'll see though, in the table below, that some letter combinations correspond to a single sound – ουρά (queue) is pronounced u-*ra*. When a word ending in a vowel is followed by another word that starts with the same or a similar vowel sound, one vowel is usually omitted and the two words are pronounced as if they were one – Σε ευχαριστώ se ef-kha-ris-*to* becomes Σ' ευχαριστώ sef-kha-ris-*to* (Thank you). Note that the apostrophe (') is used in written Greek to show that two words are joined together.

symbol	english equivalent	greek example	transliteration
a	father	αλλά	a-*la*
e	bet	πλένομαι	*ple*-no-me
i	hit	πίσω, πόλη, υποφέρω, είδος, οικογένεια, υιός	*pi*-so, *po*-li, i-po-*fe*-ro, *i*-dhos, i-ko-ye-ni-a, i-*os*
ia	nostalgia	ζητιάνος	zi-*tia*-nos
io	ratio	πιο	pio
o	pot	πόνος, πίσω	*po*-nos, *pi*-so
u	put	ουρά	u-*ra*

word stress

Stress can fall on any of the last three syllables. In our pronunciation guides, the stressed syllable is always in italics, but in written Greek, the stressed syllable is always indicated by an accent over the vowel, eg καλά ka-*la* (good). If a vowel is represented by two letters, it's written on the second letter, eg ζητιάνος zi-*tia*-nos (beggar). If the accent is marked on the first of these two letters, they should be read separately, eg Μάιος *ma*-i-os (May). Where two vowels occur together but are not stressed, a diaeresis (¨) is used to indicate that they should be pronounced separately, eg λαϊκός la-i-*kos* (popular).

consonant sounds

Most Greek consonant sounds are also found in English – only the guttural gh and kh might need a bit of practice. Double consonants are only pronounced once – άλλος *a*-los (other). However, you'll notice that sometimes two Greek letters in combination form one single consonant sound – the combination of the letters μ and π makes the sound b, and the combination of the letters ν and τ makes the sound d.

symbol	english equivalent	greek example	transliteration
b	bed	μπαρ	bar
d	dog	ντομάτα	do-*ma*-ta
dh	that	δεν	dhen
dz	adds	τζάμι	dza-*mi*
f	fat	φως, αυτή	fos, af-*ti*
g	go	γκαρσόν	gar-*son*
gh	guttural sound, between 'goat' and 'loch'	γάτα	*gha*-ta
h	hat	χέρι	*he*-ri
k	kit	καλά	ka-*la*
kh	loch (guttural sound)	χαλί	kha-*li*
l	let	λάδι	*la*-dhi
m	man	μαζί	ma-*zi*
n	not	ναός	na-*os*
ng	ring	ελέγχω	e-*leng*-kho
p	pet	πάνω	*pa*-no
r	red (trilled)	ράβω	*ra*-vo
s	sun	στυλό	sti-*lo*
t	top	τι	ti
th	thin	θέα	*the*-a
ts	hats	τσέπη	*tse*-pi
v	very	βίζα, αύριο	*vi*-za, *av*-ri-o
y	yes	γέρος	*ye*-ros
z	zero	ζέστη	*ze*-sti

tools

language difficulties

Do you speak English?
Μιλάς Αγγλικά;   mi-*las* ang-gli-*ka*

Do you understand?
Καταλαβαίνεις;   ka-ta-la-*ve*-nis

I understand.
Καταλαβαίνω.   ka-ta-la-*ve*-no

I don't understand.
Δεν καταλαβαίνω.   dhen ka-ta-la-*ve*-no

What does (μώλος) mean?
Τι σημαίνει (μώλος);   ti si-*me*-ni (*mo*-los)

How do you ...?	Πως ...;	pos ...
pronounce this	προφέρεις αυτό	pro-*fe*-ris af-*to*
write (Madhuri)	γράφουν (Μαδουρή)	*ghra*-foun (ma-dhu-*ri*)

Could you	Θα μπορούσες	tha bo-*ru*-ses
please ...?	παρακαλώ να ...;	pa-ra-ka-*lo* na ...
repeat that	το επαναλάβεις	to e-pa-na-*la*-vis
speak more slowly	μιλάς πιο σιγά	mi-*las* pio si-*gha*
write it down	το γράψεις	to *ghrap*-sis

0	μηδέν	mi-*dhen*	15	δεκαπέντε	dhe-ka-*pe*-de
1	ένας/μία/ένα m/f/n	*e*-nas/*mi*-a/*e*-na	16	δεκαέξι	dhe-ka-*ek*-si
2	δύο	*dhi*-o	17	δεκαεφτά	dhe-ka-ef-*ta*
3	τρεις m&f	tris	18	δεκαοχτώ	dhe-ka-okh-*to*
	τρία n	*tri*-a	19	δεκαεννέα	dhe-ka-e-*ne*-a
4	τέσσερις m&f	*te*-se-ris	20	είκοσι	*i*-ko-si
	τέσσερα n	*te*-se-ra	21	είκοσι	*i*-ko-si
5	πέντε	*pe*-de		ένας/μία/	*e*-nas/*mi*-a/
6	έξι	*ek*-si		ένα m/f/n	*e*-na
7	εφτά	ef-*ta*	22	είκοσι δύο	*i*-ko-si *dhi*-o
8	οχτώ	okh-*to*	30	τριάντα	tri-*a*-da
9	εννέα	e-*ne*-a	40	σαράντα	sa-*ra*-da
10	δέκα	*dhe*-ka	50	πενήντα	pe-*ni*-da
11	έντεκα	*e*-de-ka	60	εξήντα	ek-*si*-da
12	δώδεκα	*dho*-dhe-ka	70	εβδομήντα	ev-dho-*mi*-da
13	δεκατρείς m&f	dhe-ka-*tris*	80	ογδόντα	ogh-*dho*-da
	δεκατρία n	dhe-ka-*tri*-a	90	ενενήντα	e-ne-*ni*-da
14	δεκατέσσερις m&f	dhe-ka-*te*-se-ris	100	εκατό	e-ka-*to*
	δεκατέσσερα n	dhe-ka-*te*-se-ra	1000	χίλια	*hi*-lia

time & dates

What time is it?	Τι ώρα είναι;	ti *o*-ra *i*-ne
It's one o'clock.	Είναι (μία) η ώρα.	*i*-ne (*mi*-a) i *o*-ra
It's (10) o'clock.	Είναι (δέκα) η ώρα.	*i*-ne (*dhe*-ka) i *o*-ra
Quarter past (10).	(Δέκα) και τέταρτο.	(*dhe*-ka) ke *te*-tar-to
Half past (10).	(Δέκα) και μισή.	(*dhe*-ka) ke mi-*si*
Quarter to (10).	(Δέκα) παρά τέταρτο.	(*dhe*-ka) pa-*ra* te-*tar*-to
At what time ...?	Τι ώρα ...;	ti *o*-ra ...
At ...	Στις ...	stis ...
Monday	Δευτέρα	dhef-*te*-ra
Tuesday	Τρίτη	*tri*-ti
Wednesday	Τετάρτη	te-*tar*-ti
Thursday	Πέμπτη	*pem*-ti
Friday	Παρασκευή	pa-ra-ske-*vi*
Saturday	Σάββατο	*sa*-va-to
Sunday	Κυριακή	ki-ria-*ki*

January	Ιανουάριος	i·a·nu·*a*·ri·os
February	Φεβρουάριος	fev·ru·*a*·ri·os
March	Μάρτιος	*mar*·ti·os
April	Απρίλιος	a·*pri*·li·os
May	Μάιος	*ma*·i·os
June	Ιούνιος	i·*u*·ni·os
July	Ιούλιος	i·*u*·li·os
August	Αύγουστος	*av*·ghu·stos
September	Σεπέμβριος	sep·*tem*·vri·os
October	Οκτώβριος	ok·*tov*·ri·os
November	Νοέμβριος	no·*em*·vri·os
December	Δεκέμβριος	dhe·*kem*·vri·os

What date is it today?

Τι ημερομηνία είναι σήμερα;   ti i·me·ro·mi·*ni*·a *i*·ne *si*·me·ra

It's (18 October).

Είναι (δεκαοχτώ Οκτωβρίου).   *i*·ne (dhe·ka·okh·*to* ok·tov·*ri*·u)

| since (May) | από (το Μάιο) | a·*po* (to *ma*·i·o) |
| until (June) | μέχρι (τον Ιούνιο) | *meh*·ri (ton i·u·ni·o) |

yesterday	χτες	khtes
today	σήμερα	*si*·me·ra
tonight	απόψε	a·*pop*·se
tomorrow	αύριο	*av*·ri·o

last ...
night	την περασμένη νύχτα	tin pe·raz·*me*·ni *nikh*·ta
week	την περασμένη εβδομάδα	tin pe·raz·*me*·ni ev·dho·*ma*·dha
month	τον περασμένο μήνα	ton pe·raz·*me*·no *mi*·na
year	τον περασμένο χρόνο	ton pe·raz·*me*·no *khro*·no

next ...
week	την επόμενη εβδομάδα	tin e·*po*·me·ni ev·dho·*ma*·dha
month	τον επόμενο μήνα	ton e·*po*·me·no *mi*·na
year	τον επόμενο χρόνο	ton e·*po*·me·no *khro*·no

yesterday/	χτες/	khtes/
tomorrow ...	αύριο το ...	*av*·ri·o to ...
morning	πρωί	pro·*i*
afternoon	απόγευμα	a·*po*·yev·ma
evening	βράδι	*vra*·dhi

204

weather

What's the weather like?	Πως είναι ο καιρός;	pos *i*-ne o ke-*ros*

It's ...

cloudy	Είναι συννεφιά.	*i*-ne si-ne-*fia*
cold	Κάνει κρύο.	*ka*-ni *kri*-o
hot	Κάνει πολλή ζέστη.	*ka*-ni po-*li* ze-sti
raining	Βρέχει.	*vre*-hi
snowing	Χιονίζει.	hio-*ni*-zi
sunny	Είναι λιακάδα.	*i*-ne lia-*ka*-dha
warm	Κάνει ζέστη.	*ka*-ni ze-sti
windy	Φυσάει.	fi-*sa*-i

spring	άνοιξη f	*a*-nik-si
summer	καλοκαίρι n	ka-lo-*ke*-ri
autumn	φθινόπωρο n	fthi-*no*-po-ro
winter	χειμώνας m	hi-*mo*-nas

border crossing

I'm here ...	Είμαι εδώ...	*i*-me e-*dho*...
in transit	τράνζιτ	*tran*-zit
on business	για δουλειά	yia dhu-*lia*
on holiday	σε διακοπές	se dhia-ko-*pes*

I'm here for (three) ...	Είμαι εδώ για (τρεις) ...	*i*-me e-*dho* yia (tris) ...
days	μέρες	*me*-res
weeks	εβδομάδες	ev-dho-*ma*-dhes
months	μήνες	*mi*-nes

I'm going to (Limassol).
Πηγαίνω στη (Λεμεσό).   pi-*ye*-no sti (le-me-*so*)

I'm staying at the (Xenia).
Μένω στο (Ξενία).   *me*-no sto (kse-*ni*-a)

I have nothing to declare.
Δεν έχω τίποτε να δηλώσω.   dhen *e*-kho *ti*-po-te na dhi-*lo*-so

I have something to declare.
Εχω κάτι να δηλώσω.   *e*-kho *ka*-ti na dhi-*lo*-so

That's (not) mine.
Αυτό (δεν) είναι δικό μου.   af-*to* (dhen) *i*-ne dhi-*ko* mu

transport

tickets & luggage

| Where can I buy a ticket? | Που αγοράζω εισιτήριο; | pu a·gho·*ra*·zo i·si·*ti*·ri·o |
| Do I need to book a seat? | Χρειάζεται να κλείσω θέση; | khri·*a*·ze·te na *kli*·so *the*·si |

One ... ticket	Ενα εισιτήριο ...	*e*·na i·si·*ti*·ri·o ...
to (Patras), please.	για την (Πάτρα), παρακαλώ.	yia tin (*pa*·tra) pa·ra·ka·*lo*
one-way	απλό	a·*plo*
return	με επιστροφή	me e·pi·stro·*fi*

I'd like to ... my	Θα ήθελα να ... το	tha *i*·the·la na ... to
ticket, please.	εισιτήριό μου, παρακαλώ.	i·si·*ti*·ri·o mu pa·ra·ka·*lo*
cancel	ακυρώσω	a·ki·*ro*·so
change	αλλάξω	a·*lak*·so
confirm	επικυρώσω	e·pi·ki·*ro*·so

I'd like a ... seat.	Θα ήθελα μια θέση ...	tha *i*·the·la mia *the*·si ...
nonsmoking	στους μη καπνίζοντες	stus mi kap·*ni*·zo·des
smoking	στους καπνίζοντες	stus kap·*ni*·zo·des

How much is it?
Πόσο κάνει;   *po*·so *ka*·ni

Is there air conditioning?
Υπάρχει έρκοντίσιον;   i·*par*·hi e·kon·*di*·si·on

Is there a toilet?
Υπάρχει τουαλέτα;   i·*par*·hi tu·a·*le*·ta

How long does the trip take?
Πόσο διαρκεί το ταξίδι;   *po*·so dhi·ar·*ki* to tak·*si*·dhi

Is it a direct route?
Πηγαίνει κατ'ευθείαν;   pi·*ye*·ni ka·tef·*thi*·an

Where can I find a luggage locker?
Που μπορώ να βρω τη φύλαξη   pu bo·*ro* na vro ti *fi*·lak·si
αντικειμένων;   a·di·ki·*me*·non

My luggage has	Οι αποσκευές	i a·pos·ke·*ves*
been ...	μου έχουν ...	mu e·*khun* ...
damaged	πάθει ζημιά	*pa*·thi zi·*mia*
lost	χαθεί	kha·*thi*
stolen	κλαπεί	kla·*pi*

getting around

Where does flight (10) arrive/depart?
Που προσγειώνεται/   pu pros·yi·o·ne·te/
απογειώνεται η πτήση (δέκα);   a·po·yi·o·ne·te i pti·si (dhe·ka)

Where's (the) ...?	Που είναι ...;	pu i·ne ...
arrivals hall	η αίθουσα των αφίξεων	i e·thu·sa tona·fik·se·on
departures hall	η αίθουσα των	i e·thu·sa ton
	ανα χωρήσεων	a·na kho·ri·se·on
duty-free shop	τα αφορολόγητα	ta a·fo·ro·lo·yi·ta
gate (nine)	η θύρα (εννέα)	i thi·ra (e·ne·a)

Is this the ...	Είναι αυτό το ...	i·ne af·to to ...
to (Athens)?	για την (Αθήνα);	yia tin (a·thi·na)
boat	πλοίο	pli·o
bus	λεωφορείο	le·o·fo·ri·o
ferry	φέρυ	fe·ri
plane	αεροπλάνο	a·e·ro·pla·no
train	τρένο	tre·no

What time's the	Πότε είναι το ...	po·te i·ne to ...
... (bus)?	(λεωφορείο);	(le·o·fo·ri·o)
first	πρώτο	pro·to
last	τελευταίο	te·lef·te·o
next	επόμενο	e·po·me·no

At what time does it arrive/depart?
Τι ώρα φτάνει/φεύγει;   ti o·ra fta·ni/fev·yi

What time does it get to (Thessaloniki)?
Τι ώρα φτάνει στη (Θεσσαλονίκη);   ti o·ra fta·ni sti (the·sa·lo·ni·ki)

How long will it be delayed?
Πόση ώρα θα καθυστερήσει;   po·si o·ra tha ka·thi·ste·ri·si

What station is this?
Ποιος σταθμός είναι αυτός;   pios stath·mos i·ne af·tos

What stop is this?
Ποια στάση είναι αυτή;   pia sta·si i·ne af·ti

What's the next station?
Ποιος είναι ο επόμενος σταθμός;   pios i·ne o e·po·me·nos stath·mos

What's the next stop?
Ποια είναι η επόμενη στάση;   pia i·ne i e·po·me·ni sta·si

Does it stop at (Iraklio)?
Σταματάει στο (Ηράκλειο);   sta·ma·*ta*·i sto (i·*ra*·kli·o)

Please tell me when we get to (Thessaloniki).
Παρακαλώ πέστε μου όταν   pa·ra·ka·*lo* pe·ste mu *o*·tan
φτάσουμε στη (Θεσσαλονίκη).   *fta*·su·me sti (the·sa·lo·*ni*·ki)

How long do we stop here?
Πόση ώρα θα σταματήσουμε εδώ;   *po*·si o·ra tha sta·ma·*ti*·su·me e·*dho*

Is this seat available?
Είναι αυτή η θέση ελεύθερη;   *i*·ne af·*ti* i *the*·si e·*lef*·the·ri

That's my seat.
Αυτή η θέση είναι δική μου.   af·*ti* i *the*·si *i*·ne dhi·*ki* mu

I'd like a taxi ...	Θα ήθελα ένα ταξί ...	tha *i*·the·la *e*·na tak·*si* ...
at (9am)	στις (εννέα	stis (e·*ne*·a
	πριν το μεσημέρι)	prin to me·si·*me*·ri)
now	τώρα	*to*·ra
tomorrow	αύριο	*av*·ri·o

Is this taxi available?
Είναι αυτό το ταξί ελεύθερο;   *i*·ne af·*to* to tak·*si* e·*lef*·the·ro

How much is it to ...?
Πόσο κάνει για ...;   *po*·so *ka*·ni yia ...

Please put the meter on.
Παρακαλώ βάλε το ταξίμετρο.   pa·ra·ka·*lo va*·le to tak·*si*·me·tro

Please take me to (this address).
Παρακαλώ πάρε με σε   pa·ra·ka·*lo pa*·re me se
(αυτή τη διεύθυνση).   (af·*ti* ti dhi·*ef*·thin·si)

Please ...	Παρακαλώ ...	pa·ra·ka·*lo* ...
slow down	πήγαινε πιο σιγά	*pi*·ye·ne pio si·*gha*
stop here	σταμάτα εδώ	sta·*ma*·ta e·*dho*
wait here	περίμενε εδώ	pe·*ri*·me·ne e·*dho*

car, motorbike & bicycle hire

I'd like to	Θα ήθελα να	tha *i*·the·la na
hire a ...	ενοικιάσω ένα ...	e·ni·ki·*a*·so *e*·na ...
bicycle	ποδήλατο	po·*dhi*·la·to
car	αυτοκίνητο	af·to·*ki*·ni·to
motorbike	μοτοσικλέτα	mo·to·si·*kle*·ta

with ...	με ...	me ...
a driver	οδηγό	o·dhi·*gho*
air conditioning	έρκοντίσιον	e·kon·*di*·si·on

How much for ... hire?	Πόσο νοικάζεται την ...;	*po*·so ni·*kia*·ze·te tin ...
hourly	ώρα	*o*·ra
daily	ημέρα	i·*me*·ra
weekly	εβδομάδα	ev·dho·*ma*·dha

air	αέρας m	a·*e*·ras
oil	λάδι αυτοκινήτου n	*la*·dhi af·to·ki·*ni*·tu
petrol	βενζίνα f	ven·*zi*·na
tyres	λάστιχα n	*la*·sti·kha

I need a mechanic.	Χρειάζομαι μηχανικό.	khri·*a*·zo·me mi·kha·ni·*ko*
I've run out of petrol.	Μου τελείωσε η βενζίνα.	mu te·*li*·o·se i ven·*zi*·na
I have a flat tyre.	Μ'έπιασε λάστιχο.	me·pia·se la·*sti*·kho

directions

Where's the ...?	Που είναι ...;	pu *i*·ne ...
bank	η τράπεζα	i *tra*·pe·za
city centre	το κέντρο της πόλης	to *ke*·dro tis *po*·lis
hotel	το ξενοδοχείο	to kse·no·dho·*hi*·o
market	η αγορά	i a·gho·*ra*
police station	ο αστυνομικός σταθμός	o a·sti·no·mi·*kos* stath·*mos*
post office	το ταχυδρομείο	to ta·hi·dhro·*mi*·o
public toilet	τα δημόσια αποχωρητήρια	ta dhi·*mo*·si·a a·po·kho·ri·*ti*·ria
tourist office	το τουριστικό γραφείο	to tu·ri·sti·*ko* ghra·*fi*·o

Is this the road to (Lamia)?
Είναι αυτός ο δρόμος για (τη Λαμία);
i·ne af·*tos* o *dhro*·mos yia (ti la·*mi*·a)

Can you show me (on the map)?
Μπορείς να μου δείξεις (στο χάρτη);
bo·*ris* na mu *dhik*·sis (sto *khar*·ti)

What's the address?
Ποια είναι η διεύθυνση;
pia *i*·ne i dhi·*ef*·thin·si

How far is it?
Πόσο μακριά είναι;
po·so ma·kri·*a i*·ne

How do I get there?
Πως πηγαίνω εκεί;
pos pi·*ye*·no e·*ki*

Turn ...	Στρίψε ...	*strip*·se ...
at the corner	στη γωνία	sti gho·*ni*·a
at the traffic lights	στα φανάρια	sta fa·*na*·ria
left/right	αριστερά/δεξιά	a·ris·te·*ra*/dhek·si·*a*

It's ...	Είναι ...	*i*·ne ...
behind ...	πίσω ...	*pi*·so ...
far away	μακριά	ma·kri·*a*
here	εδώ	e·*dho*
in front of ...	μπροστά από ...	bros·*ta* a·po ...
near ...	κοντά ...	ko·*da* ...
next to ...	δίπλα από ...	*dhip*·la a·*po* ...
on the corner	στη γωνία	sti gho·*ni*·a
opposite ...	απέναντι ...	a·*pe*·na·di ...
straight ahead	κατ'ευθείαν	ka·tef·*thi*·an
there	εκεί	e·*ki*

by bus	με λεωφορείο	me le·o·fo·*ri*·o
by boat	με πλοίο	me *pli*·o
by taxi	με ταξί	me tak·*si*
by train	με τρένο	me *tre*·no
on foot	με πόδια	me *po*·dhia

north	βόρια	*vo*·ri·a
south	νότια	*no*·ti·a
east	ανατολικά	a·na·to·li·*ka*
west	δυτικά	dhi·ti·*ka*

signs

Είσοδος/Έξοδος	*i*·so·dhos/*ek*·so·dhos	Entrance/Exit
Ανοικτός/Κλειστός	a·nik·*tos*/kli·*stos*	Open/Closed
Ελεύθερα Δωμάτια	e·*lef*·the·ra dho·*ma*·ti·a	Rooms Available
Πλήρες	*pli*·res	No Vacancies
Πληροφορίες	pli·ro·fo·*ri*·es	Information
Αστυνομικός Σταθμός	a·sti·no·mi·*kos* stath·*mos*	Police Station
Απαγορεύεται	a·pa·gho·*re*·ve·te	Prohibited
Τουαλέτες	tu·a·*le*·tes	Toilets
Ανδρών	an·*dhron*	Men
Γυναικών	yi·ne·*kon*	Women
Ζεστό/Κρύο	zes·*to*/khri·o	Hot/Cold

accommodation

finding accommodation

Where's a ...?	Που είναι ...;	pu *i*·ne ...
camping ground	χώρος για κάμπινγκ	*kho*·ros yia *kam*·ping
guesthouse	ξενώνας	kse·*no*·nas
hotel	ξενοδοχείο	kse·no·dho·*hi*·o
youth hostel	γιουθ χόστελ	yiuth *kho*·stel

Can you recommend somewhere ...?	Μπορείτε να συστήσετε κάπου ...;	bo·*ri*·te na si·*sti*·se·te *ka*·pu ...
cheap	φτηνό	fti·*no*
good	καλό	ka·*lo*
nearby	κοντινό	ko·di·*no*

I'd like to book a room, please.
Θα ήθελα να κλείσω ένα δωμάτιο, παρακαλώ.
tha *i*·the·la na *kli*·so *e*·na dho·*ma*·ti·o pa·ra·ka·*lo*

I have a reservation.
Εχω κάνει κάποια κράτηση.
e·kho *ka*·ni *ka*·pia *kra*·ti·si

My name's ...
Με λένε ...
me *le*·ne ...

Do you have a ... room?	Εχετε ένα ... δωμάτιο;	*e*·he·te *e*·na ... dho·*ma*·ti·o
single	μονό	mo·*no*
double	διπλό	dhi·*plo*
twin	δίκλινο	*dhi*·kli·no

How much is it per ...?	Πόσο είναι για κάθε ...;	*po*·so *i*·ne yia *ka*·the ...
night	νύχτα	*nikh*·ta
person	άτομο	*a*·to·mo

Can I pay ...?	Μπορώ να πληρώσω με ...;	bo·*ro* na pli·*ro*·so me ...
by credit card	πιστωτική κάρτα	pi·sto·ti·*ki kar*·ta
with a travellers cheque	ταξιδιωτική επιταγή	tak·si·dhio·ti·*ki* e·pi·ta·*yi*

For (three) nights/weeks.

Για (τρεις) νύχτες/εβδομάδες.   yia (tris) *nikh*·tes/ev·dho·*ma*·dhes

From (2 July) to (6 July).

Από (τις δύο Ιουλίου)   a·*po* (tis *dhi*·o i·u·*li*·u)
μέχρι (τις έξι Ιουλίου).   *me*·khri (tis *ek*·si i·u·*li*·u)

Can I see it?

Μπορώ να το δω;   bo·*ro* na to dho

Am I allowed to camp here?

Μπορώ να κατασκηνώσω εδώ;   bo·*ro* na ka·ta·ski·*no*·so e·*dho*

Where can I find a camp site?

Που μπορώ να βρω το   pu bo·*ro* na vro to
χώρο του κάμπινγκ;   *kho*·ro tu *kam*·ping

requests & queries

When/Where is breakfast served?

Πότε/Που σερβίρεται το πρόγευμα;   *po*·te/pu ser·*vi*·re·te to *pro*·yev·ma

Please wake me at (seven).

Παρακαλώ ξύπνησέ με στις (εφτά).   pa·ra·ka·*lo* *ksip*·ni·*se* me stis (ef·*ta*)

Could I have my key, please?

Μπορώ να έχω το κλειδί μου   bo·*ro* na *e*·kho to kli·*dhi* mu
παρακαλώ;   pa·ra·ka·*lo*

Can I get another (blanket)?

Μπορώ να έχω και άλλη (κουβέρτα);   bo·*ro* na *e*·kho ke *a*·li (ku·*ver*·ta)

This (towel) isn't clean.

Αυτή (η πετσέτα) δεν είναι καθαρό.   af·*ti* (i pet·*se*·ta) dhen *i*·ne ka·tha·*ri*

Is there a/an ...?	Εχετε ...;	*e*·he·te ...
elevator	ασανσέρ	a·san·*ser*
safe	χρηματοκιβώτιο	khri·ma·to·ki·*vo*·ti·o

The room is too ...	Είναι πάρα πολύ ...	*i*·ne *pa*·ra po·*li* ...
expensive	ακριβό	a·kri·*vo*
noisy	θορυβώδες	tho·ri·*vo*·dhes
small	μικρό	mi·*kro*

The ... doesn't work.	... δεν λειτουργεί.	... dhen li·tur·*ghi*
air conditioning	Το έρκοντίσιον	to er·kon·*di*·si·on
fan	Ο ανεμιστήρας	o a·ne·mi·*sti*·ras
toilet	Η τουαλέτα	i tu·a·*le*·ta

checking out

What time is checkout?

Τι ώρα είναι η αναχώρηση;   ti o·ra i·ne i a·na·kho·ri·si

Can I leave my luggage here?

Μπορώ να αφήσω τις βαλίτσες μου εδώ;   bo·ro na a·fi·so tis va·lit·ses mu e·dho

Could I have my ..., please?	Μπορώ να έχω ... μου παρακλώ;	bo·ro na e·kho ... mu pa·ra·ka·lo
deposit	την προκαταβολή	tin pro·ka·ta·vo·li
passport	το διαβατήριό	to dhia·va·ti·rio
valuables	τα κοσμήματά	ta koz·mi·ma·ta

communications & banking

the internet

Where's the local Internet cafe?

Που είναι το τοπικό   pu i·ne to to·pi·ko
καφενείο με διαδίκτυο;   ka·fe·ni·o me dhi·a·dhik·ti·o

How much is it per hour?

Πόσο κοστίζει κάθε ώρα;   po·so ko·sti·zi ka·the o·ra

I'd like to ...	θα ήθελα να ...	tha i·the·la na ...
check my email	ελέγξω την ηλεκτρονική αλληλογραφία μου	e·leng·so tin i·lek·tro·ni·ki a·li·lo·ghra·fi·a mu
get Internet access	έχω πρόσβαση στο διαδίκτυο	e·kho pros·va·si sto dhi·a·dhik·ti·o
use a printer	χρησιμοποιήσω έναν εκτυπωτή	khri·si·mo·pi·i·so e·nan ek·ti·po·ti
use a scanner	χρησιμοποιήσω ένα σκάνερ	khri·si·mo·pi·i·so e·na ska·ner

mobile/cell phone

I'd like a …	Θα ήθελα …	tha *i*-the-la …
mobile/cell phone for hire	να νοικιάσω ένα κινητό τηλέφωνο	na ni-*kia*-so e-na ki-ni-*to* ti-*le*-fo-no
SIM card for	μια κάρτα SIM	mia *kar*-ta sim
your network	για το δίκτυό σας	yia to *dhik*-tio sas

| What are the rates? | Ποιες είναι οι τιμές; | pies *i*-ne i ti-*mes* |

telephone

What's your phone number?
Τι αριθμό τηλεφώνου έχεις;
ti a-rith-*mo* ti-le-*fo*-nu *e*-his

The number is …
Ο αριθμός είναι …
o a-rith-*mos i*-ne …

Where's the nearest public phone?
Που είναι το πιο κοντινό
δημόσιο τηλέφωνο;
pu *i*-ne to pio ko-di-*no*
dhi-*mo*-si-o ti-*le*-fo-no

I'd like to buy a phonecard.
Θέλω να αγοράσω μια
τηλεφωνική κάρτα.
the-lo na a-gho-*ra*-so mia
ti-le-fo-ni-*ki kar*-ta

I want to …	Θέλω να …	*the*-lo na …
call (Singapore)	τηλεφωνήσω (στη Σιγγαπούρη)	ti-le-fo-*ni*-so (sti sing-ga-*pu*-ri)
make a local call	κάνω ένα τοπικό τηλέφωνο	*ka*-no e-na to-pi-*ko* ti-*le*-fo-no
reverse the charges	αντιστρέψω τα έξοδα	a-di-*strep*-so ta *ek*-so-dha

How much does … cost?	Πόσο κοστίζει …;	*po*-so ko-*sti*-zi …
a (three)- minute call	ένα τηλεφώνημα (τριών) λεπτών	*e*-na ti-le-*fo*-ni-ma (tri-*on*) lep-*ton*
each extra minute	κάθε έξτρα λεπτό	*ka*-the *eks*-tra lep-*to*

It's (40c) per (30) seconds.
(Σαράντα λεπτα) για (τριάντα)
δευτερόλεπτα.
(sa-*ra*-da lep-*ta*) yia (tri-*a*-da)
dhef-te-*ro*-lep-ta

post office

I want to send a ...	Θέλω να στείλω ...	*the*·lo na *sti*·lo ...
fax	ένα φαξ	*e*·na faks
letter	ένα γράμμα	*e*·na *ghra*·ma
parcel	ένα δέμα	*e*·na *dhe*·ma
postcard	μια κάρτα	mia *kar*·ta

I want to buy	Θέλω να αγοράσω	*the*·lo na a·gho·*ra*·so
a/an ...	ένα ...	*e*·na ...
envelope	φάκελο	*fa*·ke·lo
stamp	γραμματόσημο	ghra·ma·*to*·si·mo

Please send it	Παρακαλώ στείλτε το	pa·ra·ka·*lo stil*·te to
(to Australia) by ...	... (στην Αυστραλία).	... (stin af·stra·*li*·a)
airmail	αεροπορικώς	a·e·ro·po·ri·*kos*
express mail	εξπρές	eks·*pres*
registered mail	συστημένο	si·sti·*me*·no
surface mail	δια ξηράς	dhia ksi·*ras*

Is there any mail for me?
Υπάρχουν γράμματα για μένα; i·*par*·khun *ghra*·ma·ta yia *me*·na

bank

Where's a/an ...?	Που είναι ...;	pu *i*·ne ...
ATM	μια αυτόματη	mia af·*to*·ma·ti
	μηχανή χρημάτων	mi·kha·*ni* khri·*ma*·ton
foreign exchange	ένα γραφείο	*e*·na ghra·*fi*·o
office	αλλαγής χρημάτων	a·la·*yis* khri·*ma*·ton

I'd like to ...	Θα ήθελα να ...	tha *i*·the·la na ...
Where can I ...?	Που μπορώ να ...;	pu bo·*ro* na ...
arrange a transfer	τακτοποιήσω	tak·to·pi·*i*·so
	μια μεταβίβαση	mia me·ta·*vi*·va·si
cash a cheque	εξαργυρώσω	ek·sar·yi·*ro*·so
	μια επιταγή	mia e·pi·ta·*yi*
change a travellers	αλλάξω μια	a·*lak*·so mia
cheque	ταξιδιωτική επιταγή	tak·si·dhio·ti·*ki* e·pi·ta·*yi*
change money	αλλάξω χρήματα	a·*lak*·so *khri*·ma·ta
get a cash advance	κάνω μια ανάληψη	*ka*·no mia a·*na*·lip·si
	σε μετρητά	se me·tri·*ta*
withdraw money	αποσύρω χρήματα	a·po·*si*·ro *khri*·ma·ta

What's the ...?	Ποια είναι ... ;	pia *i*·ne ...
charge for that	η χρέωση για αυτό	i *khre*·o·si yia af·*to*
exchange rate	η τιμή συναλλάγματος	i ti·*mi* si·na·*lagh*·ma·tos

It's (12) ...	Κάνει (δώδεκα) ...	*ka*·ni (*dho*·dhe·ka) ...
Cyprus pounds	λίρες Κύπρου	*li*·res *ki*·pru
euros	ευρώ	ev·*ro*

It's free.
Είναι δωρεάν.　　　　　　　　　*i*·ne dho·re·*an*

What time does the bank open?
Τι ώρα ανοίγει η τράπεζα;　　　ti *o*·ra a·*ni*·yi i *tra*·pe·za

Has my money arrived yet?
Εχουν φτάσει τα χρήματά μου;　*e*·khun *fta*·si ta *khri*·ma·*ta* mu

sightseeing

getting in

What time does it open/close?
Τι ώρα ανοίγει/κλείνει;　　　　ti *o*·ra a·*ni*·yi/*kli*·ni

What's the admission charge?
Πόσο κοστίζει η είσοδος;　　　po·so ko·*sti*·zi i *i*·so·dhos

Is there a discount for students/children?
Υπάρχει έκπτωση για　　　　　i·*par*·hi *ek*·pto·si yia
σπουδαστές/παιδιά;　　　　　　spu·dha·*stes*/pe·*dhia*

I'd like a ...	Θα ήθελα ...	tha *i*·the·la ...
catalogue	ένα κατάλογο	e·na ka·*ta*·lo·gho
guide	έναν οδηγό	e·nan o·dhi·*gho*
local map	ένα τοπικό χάρτη	e·na to·pi·*ko* khar·ti

I'd like to see ...	Θα ήθελα να δω ...	tha *i*·the·la na dho ...
What's that?	Τι είναι εκείνο;	ti *i*·ne e·*ki*·no
Can I take a photo?	Μπορώ να πάρω μια	bo·ro na *pa*·ro mia
	φωτογραφία;	fo·to·ghra·*fi*·a

tours

When's the next tour?
Πότε είναι η επόμενη περιήγηση;   *po·te i·ne i e·po·me·ni pe·ri·i·yi·si*

When's the next ...?   Πότε είναι το επόμενο ...;   *po·te i·ne to e·po·me·no ...*
   boat trip   ταξίδι με τη βάρκα   tak·si·dhi me ti *var·*ka
   day trip   ημερήσιο ταξίδι   i·me·ri·si·o tak·si·dhi

Is ... included?   Συμπεριλαμβάνεται ...;   si·be·ri·lam·va·ne·te ...
   accommodation   κατάλυμα   ka·ta·li·ma
   the admission charge   τιμή εισόδου   ti·mi i·so·dhu
   food   φαγητό   fa·yi·to
   transport   μεταφορά   me·ta·fo·ra

How long is the tour?
Πόση ώρα διαρκεί η περιήγηση;   *po·si o·ra dhi·ar·ki i pe·ri·i·yi·si*

What time should we be back?
Τι ώρα πρέπει να επιστρέψουμε;   *ti o·ra pre·pi na e·pi·strep·su·me*

sightseeing

amphitheatre	αμφιθέατρο n	am·fi·*the·*a·tro
castle	κάστρο n	*ka·*stro
cathedral	μητρόπολη f	mi·*tro·*po·li
church	εκκλησία f	e·kli·si·a
fresco	φρέσκο n	*fres·*ko
labyrinth	λαβύρινθος m	la·*vi·*rin·thos
main square	κεντρική πλατεία f	ken·dhri·*ki* pla·*ti·*a
monastery	μοναστήρι n	mo·na·*sti·*ri
monument	μνημείο n	mni·*mi·*o
mosaic	μωσαϊκό n	mo·sa·i·*ko*
museum	μουσείο n	mu·*si·*o
old city	αρχαία πόλη	ar·*khe·*a po·li
palace	παλάτι n	pa·*la·*ti
ruins	ερρίπια n pl	e·*ri·*pi·a
sculpture	γλυπτική f	ghlip·ti·*ki*
stadium	στάδιο n	*sta·*dhi·o
statue	άγαλμα n	*a·*ghal·ma
temple	ναός m	na·*os*

shopping

enquiries

Where's a ...?	Που είναι ...;	pu *i*·ne ...
bank	μια τράπεζα	mia *tra*·pe·za
bookshop	ένα βιβλιοπωλείο	e·na viv·li·o·po·*li*·o
camera shop	ένα κατάστημα φωτογραφικών ειδών	e·na ka·*ta*·sti·ma fo·to·ghra·fi·*kon* i·*dhon*
department store	ένα κατάστημα	e·na ka·*ta*·sti·ma
grocery store	ένα οπωροπωλείο	e·na o·po·ro·po·*li*·o
kiosk	ένα περίπτερο	e·na pe·*rip*·te·ro
market	μια αγορά	mia a·gho·*ra*
newsagency	το εφημεριδοπωλείο	to e·fi·me·ri·dho·po·*li*·o
supermarket	ένα σούπερμάρκετ	e·na *su*·per·*mar*·ket

Where can I buy (a padlock)?
Που μπορώ να αγοράσω
(μια κλειδαριά);
pu bo·*ro* na a·gho·*ra*·so
(mia kli·dha·*ria*)

I'd like to buy ...
Θα ήθελα να αγοράσω ...
tha *i*·the·la na a·gho·*ra*·so ...

Can I look at it?
Μπορώ να το κοιτάξω;
bo·*ro* na to ki·*tak*·so

Do you have any others?
Εχετε άλλα;
e·he·te *a*·la

Does it have a guarantee?
Εχει εγγύηση;
e·hi e·*gi*·i·si

Can I have it sent overseas?
Μπορείς να το στείλεις
στο εξωτερικό;
bo·*ris* na to *sti*·lis
sto ek·so·te·ri·*ko*

Can I have ... repaired?
Μπορώ να επισκευάσω εδώ ...;
bo·*ro* na e·pi·ske·*va*·so e·*dho* ...

Can I have a bag, please?
Μπορώ να έχω μια τσάντα, παρακαλώ;
bo·*ro* na *e*·kho mia *tsa*·da pa·ra·ka·*lo*

It's faulty.
Είναι ελαττωματικό.
i·ne e·la·to·ma·ti·*ko*

I'd like ..., please.
Θα ήθελα ..., παρακαλώ.
tha *i*·the·la ... pa·ra·ka·*lo*
| a refund | επιστροφή χρημάτων | e·pi·stro·*fi* khri·*ma*·ton |
| to return this | να επιστρέψω αυτό | na e·pi·*strep*·so af·*to* |

paying

How much is it?
Πόσο κάνει;

po·so ka·ni

Can you write down the price?
Μπορείς να γράψεις την τιμή;

bo·ris na ghrap·sis tin ti·mi

That's too expensive.
Είναι πάρα πολύ ακριβό.

i·ne pa·ra po·li a·kri·vo

Can you lower the price?
Μπορείς να κατεβάσεις την τιμή;

bo·ris na ka·te·va·sis tin ti·mi

I'll give you (five) euros.
Θα σου δώσω (πέντε) ευρώ.

tha su dho·so (pe·de) ev·ro

I'll give you (five) Cyprus pounds.
Θα σου δώσω (πέντε) λίρες Κύπρου.

tha su dho·so (pe·de) li·res ki·pru

There's a mistake in the bill.
Υπάρχει κάποιο λάθος
στο λογαριασμό.

i·par·hi ka·pio la·thos
sto lo·gha·riaz·mo

Do you accept ...?   Δέχεστε ...;   dhe·he·ste ...
   credit cards   πιστωτικές κάρτες   pi·sto·ti·kes kar·tes
   debit cards   χρεωτικές κάρτες   khre·o·ti·kes kar·tes
   travellers cheques ταξιδιωτικές   tak·si·dhio·ti·kes
                       επιταγές   e·pi·ta·yes

I'd like my change, please.
Θα ήθελα τα ρέστα μου, παρακαλώ.

tha i·the·la ta re·sta mu pa·ra·ka·lo

Can I have a receipt, please?
Μπορώ να έχω μια
απόδειξη, παρακαλώ;

bo·ro na e·kho mia
a·po·dhik·si pa·ra·ka·lo

clothes & shoes

Can I try it on?   Μπορώ να το προβάρω;   bo·ro na to pro·va·ro
My size is (40).   Το νούμερό μου είναι   to nu·me·ro mu i·ne
            (σαράντα).   (sa·ra·da)
It doesn't fit.   Δε μου κάνει.   dhe mu ka·ni

small   μικρό   mi·kro
medium   μεσαίο   me·se·o
large   μεγάλο   me·gha·lo

books & music

I'd like a ...	Θα ήθελα ...	tha i·the·la ...
newspaper	μια εφημερίδα	mia e·fi·me·ri·dha
(in English)	(στα Αγγλικά)	(sta ang·gli·ka)
pen	ένα στυλό	e·na sti·lo

Is there an English-language bookshop?
Υπάρχει ένα βιβλιοπωλείο   i·par·hi e·na viv·li·o·po·li·o
Αγγλικής γλώσσας;   ang·gli·kis ghlo·sas

I'm looking for something by (Anna Vissi).
Ψάχνω για κάτι (της Άννας Βίση).   psakh·no yia ka·ti (tis a·nas vi·si)

Can I listen to this?
Μπορώ να το ακούσω;   bo·ro na to a·ku·so

photography

Can you ...?	Μπορείς να ...;	bo·ris na ...
develop this	εμφανίσεις αυτό	em·fa·ni·sis af·to
film	το φιλμ	to film
load my film	βάλεις το φιλμ	va·lis to film
	στη μηχανή μου	sti mi·kha·ni mu
transfer photos	μεταφέρεις	me·ta·fe·ris
from my	φωτογραφίες από	fo·to·ghra·fi·es a·po
camera to CD	την φωτογραφική	ti fo·to·ghra·fi·ki
	μου μηχανή στο CD	mu mi·kha·ni sto si·di

I need a/an ... film	Χρειάζομαι φιλμ ...	khri·a·zo·me film ...
for this camera.	για αυτή τη μηχανή.	yia af·ti ti mi·kha·ni
APS	APS	e·i·pi·es
B&W	μαυρόασπρο	mav·ro·a·spro
colour	έγχρωμο	eng·khro·mo
slide	σλάιντ	sla·id
(200) speed	ταχύτητα (διακοσίων)	ta·hi·ti·ta (dhia·ko·si·on)

When will it be ready?   Πότε θα είναι έτοιμο;   po·te tha i·ne e·ti·mo

meeting people

greetings, goodbyes & introductions

Hello/Hi.	Γεια σου.	yia su
Good night.	Καληνύχτα.	ka·li·*nikh*·ta
Goodbye/Bye.	Αντίο.	a·*di*·o
Mr	Κύριε	*ki*·ri·e
Mrs	Κυρία	ki·*ri*·a
Miss	Δις	dhes·pi·*nis*
How are you?	Τι κάνεις;	ti *ka*·nis
Fine. And you?	Καλά. Εσύ;	ka·*la* e·*si*
What's your name?	Πως σε λένε;	pos se *le*·ne
My name is ...	Με λένε ...	me *le*·ne ...
I'm pleased to meet you.	Χαίρω πολύ.	*he*·ro po·*li*

This is my ...	Από εδώ ... μου.	a·*po* e·*dho* ... mu
boyfriend	ο φίλος	o *fi*·los
brother	ο αδερφός	o a·dher·*fos*
daughter	η κόρη	i *ko*·ri
father	ο πατέρας	o pa·*te*·ras
friend	ο φίλος/η φίλη m/f	o *fi*·los/i *fi*·li
girlfriend	η φιλενάδα	i fi·le·*na*·dha
husband	ο σύζυγός	o *si*·zi·ghos
mother	η μητέρα	i mi·*te*·ra
partner (intimate)	ο/η σύντροφός m/f	o/i *si*·dro·*fos*
sister	η αδερφή	i a·dher·*fi*
son	ο γιος	o yios
wife	η σύζυγός	i *si*·zi·ghos

Here's my ...	Εδώ είναι ... μου.	e·*dho* i·ne ... mu
What's your ...?	Ποιο είναι ... σου;	pio *i*·ne ... su
email address	το ημέιλ	to i·*me*·il
fax number	το φαξ	to faks
phone number	το τηλέφωνό	to ti·*le*·fo·*no*

Here's my address.
Εδώ είναι η διεύθυνσή μου.   e·*dho* i·ne i dhi·*ef*·thin·*si* mu

What's your address?
Ποια είναι η δική σου διεύθυνση;   pia *i*·ne i dhi·*ki* su dhi·*ef*·thin·si

occupations

What's your occupation?	Τι δουλειά κάνεις;	ti dhu-*lia ka*-nis
I'm a/an ...	Είμαι/Δουλεύω ...	*i*-me/dhou-*lev*-o ...
businessperson	επιχειρηματίας m&f	e-pi-hi-ri-ma-*ti*-as
farmer	γεωργός m&f	ye-or-*ghos*
manual worker	εργάτης/εργάτρια m/f	er-*gha*-tis/er-*gha*-tri-a
office worker	σε γραφείο	se ghra-*phi*-o
scientist	επιστήμονας m&f	e-pi-*sti*-mo-nas
tradesperson	έμπορος m&f	*e*-bo-ros

background

Where are you from?	Από που είσαι;	a-*po* pu *i*-se
I'm from ...	Είμαι από ...	*i*-me a-*po* ...
Australia	την Αυστραλία	tin af-stra-*li*-a
Canada	τον Καναδά	ton ka-na-*dha*
England	την Αγγλία	tin ang-*gli*-a
New Zealand	την Νέα Ζηλανδία	tin *ne*-a zi-lan-*dhi*-a
the USA	την Αμερική	tin A-me-ri-*ki*
Are you married?	Είσαι παντρεμένος/ παντρεμένη; m/f	*i*-se pa-dre-*me*-nos/ pa-dre-*me*-ni
I'm married.	Είμαι παντρεμένος/ παντρεμένη. m/f	*i*-me pa-dre-*me*-nos/ pa-dre-*me*-ni
I'm single.	Είμαι ανύπαντρος/ ανύπαντρη. m/f	*i*-me a-*ni*-pa-dros/ a-*ni*-pa-dri

age

How old ...?	Πόσο χρονών ...;	*po*-so khro-*non* ...
are you	είσαι	*i*-se
is your daughter	είναι η κόρη σου	*i*-ne i *ko*-ri su
is your son	είναι ο γιος σου	*i*-ne o yios su
I'm ... years old.	Είμαι ... χρονών.	*i*-me ... khro-*non*
He/She is ... years old.	Αυτός/αυτή είναι ... χρονών.	af-*tos*/af-*ti i*-ne ... khro-*non*

feelings

I'm (not) ...	(Δεν) Είμαι ...	(dhen) *i*-me ...
Are you ...?	Είσαι ...;	*i*-se ...
happy	ευτυχισμένος m	ef-ti-hiz-*me*-nos
	ευτυχισμένη f	ef-ti-hiz-*me*-ni
hot	ζεστός/ζεστή m/f	ze-*stos*/ze-*sti*
hungry	πεινασμένος m	pi-naz-*me*-nos
	πεινασμένη f	pi-naz-*me*-ni
sad	στενοχωρημένος m	ste-no-kho-ri-*me*-nos
	στενοχωρημένη f	ste-no-kho-ri-*me*-ni
thirsty	διψασμένος m	dhip-saz-*me*-nos
	διψασμένη f	dhip-saz-*me*-ni

entertainment

going out

Where can I find ...?	Που μπορώ να βρω ...;	pu bo-*ro* na vro ...
clubs	κλαμπ	klab
gay venues	Χώρους συνάντησης	*kho*-rus si-*na*-di-sis
	για γκέη	yia *ge*-i
pubs	μπυραρίες	bi-ra-*ri*-es
I feel like going	Εχω όρεξη να	*e*-kho *o*-rek-si na
to a/the ...	πάω σε ...	*pa*-o se ...
concert	κονσέρτο	kon-*ser*-to
the movies	φιλμ	film
party	πάρτυ	*par*-ti
restaurant	εστιατόριο	e-sti-a-*to*-ri-o
theatre	θέατρο	*the*-a-tro

interests

Do you like ...?	Σου αρέσει ...;	su a-*re*-si ...
I (don't) like ...	(Δεν) μου αρέσει ...	(dhen) mu a-*re*-si ...
cooking	η μαγειρική	i ma-yi-ri-*ki*
reading	το διάβασμα	to *dhia*-vaz-ma

Do you like ...?	Σου αρέσουν ...;	su a·*re*·sun ...
I (don't) like ...	(Δεν) μου αρέσουν τα ...	(dhen) mu a·*re*·sun ta ...
art	καλλιτεχνικά	ka·li·tekh·ni·*ka*
movies	φιλμ	film
nightclubs	νάιτ κλαμπ	*na*·it klab
sport	σπορ	spor

Do you like to ...?	Σου αρέσει να ...;	sou a·*re*·si na ...
dance	χορεύεις	kho·*re*·vis
go to concerts	πηγαίνεις σε κονσέρτα	pi·*ye*·nis se kon·*ser*·ta
listen to music	ακούς μουσική	a·*kus* mu·si·*ki*

food & drink

finding a place to eat

Can you	Μπορείς να	bo·*ris* na
recommend a ...?	συστήσεις ...;	si·*sti*·sis ...
bar	ένα μπαρ	*e*·na bar
café	μία καφετέρια	*mi*·a ka·fe·*te*·ria
restaurant	ένα εστιατόριο	e·sti·a·*to*·ri·o

I'd like ..., please.	Θα ήθελα ..., παρακαλώ.	tha *i*·thela ... pa·ra·ka·*lo*
a table for (five)	ένα τραπέζι για (πέντε)	*e*·na tra·*pe*·zi yia (*pe*·de)
the (non)smoking	στους (μη)	stus (mi)
section	καπνίζοντες	kap·*ni*·zo·des

ordering food

breakfast	πρόγευμα n	*pro*·yev·ma
lunch	γεύμα n	*yev*·mà
dinner	δείπνο n	*dhip*·no
snack	μεζεδάκι n	me·ze·*dha*·ki

What would you recommend?
Τι θα συνιστούσες;   ti tha si·ni·*stu*·ses

I'd like (a/the) ..., please.	Θα ήθελα ..., παρακαλώ.	tha i·the·la ... pa·ra·ka·lo
bill	το λογαριασμό	to lo·gha·riaz·mo
drink list	τον κατάλογο με τα ποτά	ton ka·ta·lo·gho me ta po·ta
menu	το μενού	to me·nu
that dish	εκείνο το φαγητό	e·ki·no to fa·yi·to

drinks

(cup of) coffee ...	(ένα φλυτζάνι) καφέ ...	(e·na fli·dza·ni) ka·fe ...
(cup of) tea ...	(ένα φλυτζάνι) τσάι ...	(e·na fli·dza·ni) tsa·i ...
with milk	με γάλα	me gha·la
without sugar	χωρίς ζάχαρη	kho·ris za·kha·ri
(orange) juice	χυμός (πορτοκάλι) m	hi·mos (por·to·ka·li)
soft drink	αναψυκτικό n	a·nap·sik·ti·ko
... water	... νερό	... ne·ro
hot	ζεστό	ze·sto
(sparkling) mineral	(γαζόζα) μεταλλικό	(gha·zo·za) me·ta·li·ko

in the bar

I'll have ...	Θα πάρω ...	tha pa·ro ...
I'll buy you a drink.	Θα σε κεράσω εγώ.	tha se ke·ra·so e·gho
What would you like?	Τι θα ήθελες;	ti tha i·the·les
Cheers!	Εις υγείαν!	is i·yi·an

brandy	μπράντι n	bran·di
champagne	σαμπάνια f	sam·pa·nia
a glass/bottle of	ένα ποτήρι/μπουκάλι	e·na po·ti·ri/bu·ka·li
beer	μπύρα	bi·ra
ouzo	ούζο n	u·zo
a shot of (whisky)	ένα (ουίσκι)	e·na (u·i·ski)

a glass/bottle of ... wine	ένα ποτήρι/μπουκάλι ... κρασί	e·na po·ti·ri/bu·ka·li ... kra·si
red	κόκκινο	ko·ki·no
sparkling	σαμπάνια	sam·pa·nia
white	άσπρο	a·spro

self-catering

What's the local speciality?

Ποιες είναι οι τοπικές λιχουδιές;   pies *i*·ne i to·pi·*kes* li·khu·*dhies*

What's that?

Τι είναι εκείνο;   ti *i*·ne e·*ki*·no

How much is (a kilo of cheese)?

Πόσο κάνει (ένα κιλό τυρί);   *po*·so *ka*·ni (*e*·na ki·*lo* ti·*ri*)

I'd like ...	Θα ήθελα ...	tha *i*·the·la ...
(100) grams	(εκατό) γραμμάρια	(e·ka·*to*) ghra·*ma*·ria
(two) kilos	(δύο) κιλά	(*dhi*·o) ki·*la*
(three) pieces	(τρία) κομμάτια	(*tri*·a) ko·*ma*·tia
(six) slices	(έξι) φέτες	(*ek*·si) *fe*·tes

Less.	Πιο λίγο.	pio *li*·gho
Enough.	Αρκετά.	ar·ke·*ta*
More.	Πιο πολύ.	pio po·*li*

special diets & allergies

Is there a vegetarian restaurant near here?

Υπάρχει ένα εστιατόριο χορτοφάγων   i·*par*·hi *e*·na e·sti·a·*to*·ri·o hor·to·*fa*·ghon
εδώ κοντά;   e·*dho* ko·*da*

Do you have vegetarian food?

Εχετε φαγητό για χορτοφάγους;   e·he·te fa·yi·*to* yia khor·to·*fa*·ghus

I don't eat ...	Δεν τρώγω ...	dhen *tro*·gho ...
butter	βούτυρο	*vu*·ti·ro
eggs	αβγά	av·*gha*
meat stock	ζουμί από κρέας	zu·*mi* a·*po* kre·as

I'm allergic to ...	Είμαι αλλεργικός/	*i*·me a·ler·yi·*kos*
	αλλεργική ... m/f	a·ler·yi·*ki* ...
dairy produce	στα γαλακτικά	sta gha·lak·ti·*ka*
gluten	στη γλουτένη	sti ghlu·*te*·ni
MSG	στο MSG	sto em es dzi
nuts	στους ξηρούς καρπούς	stus ksi·*rus* kar·*pus*
seafood	στα θαλασσινά	sta tha·la·si·*na*

emergencies

basics

Help!	Βοήθεια!	vo·*i*·thia
Stop!	Σταμάτα!	sta·*ma*·ta
Go away!	Φύγε!	*fi*·ye
Thief!	Κλέφτης!	*klef*·tis
Fire!	Φωτιά!	fo·*tia*
Watch out!	Πρόσεχε!	*pro*·se·he

Call ...!	Κάλεσε ...!	*ka*·le·se ...
an ambulance	το ασθενοφόρο	to as·the·no·*fo*·ro
the doctor	ένα γιατρό	*e*·na yia·*tro*
the police	την αστυνομία	tin a·sti·no·*mi*·a

It's an emergency.
Είναι μια έκτακτη ανάγκη.   *i*·ne mia *ek*·tak·ti a·*na*·gi

Could you help me, please?
Μπορείς να βοηθήσεις, παρακαλώ;   bo·*ris* na vo·i·*thi*·sis pa·ra·ka·*lo*

Can I make a phone call?
Μπορώ να κάνω ένα τηλεφώνημα;   bo·*ro* na *ka*·no *e*·na ti·le·*fo*·ni·ma

I'm lost.
Έχω χαθεί.   *e*·kho kha·*thi*

Where are the toilets?
Που είναι η τουαλέτα;   pu *i*·ne i tu·a·*le*·ta

police

Where's the police station?
Που είναι ο αστυνομικός σταθμός;   pu *i*·ne o a·sti·no·mi·*kos* stath·*mos*

I want to report an offence.
Θέλω να αναφέρω μια παρανομία.   *the*·lo na a·na·*fe*·ro mia pa·ra·no·*mi*·a

I have insurance.
Έχω ασφάλεια.   *e*·kho as·*fa*·li·a

I've been ...	Με έχουν ...	me *e*·khun ...
assaulted	κακοποιήσει	ka·ko·pi·*i*·si
raped	βιάσει	vi·*a*·si
robbed	ληστέψει	li·*step*·si

I've lost my ...	Έχασα ... μου.	*e*·kha·sa ... mu
My ... was/were stolen.	Έκλεψαν ... μου.	*e*·klep·san ... mu
backpack	το σακίδιό	to sa·*ki*·dhio
bags	τις βαλίτσες	tis va·lits·*es*
credit card	την πιστωτική κάρτα	tin pi·sto·ti·*ki kar*·ta
handbag	την τσάντα	tin *tsa*·da
jewellery	τα κοσμήματά	ta koz·*mi*·ma·*ta*
money	τα χρήματά	ta khri·ma·*ta*
passport	το διαβατήριό	to dhia·va·*ti*·rio
travellers cheques	τις ταξιδιωτικές επιταγές	tis tak·si·dhio·ti·*kes* e·pi·ta·*yes*
wallet	το πορτοφόλι	to por·to·*fo*·li
I want to contact my ...	Θέλω να έρθω σε επαφή με ... μου.	*the*·lo na *er*·tho se e·pa·*fi* me ... mu
consulate	τηνπρεσβεία	tin prez·*vi*·a
embassy	το προξενείο	to pro·ksee·*ni*·o

health

medical needs

Where's the nearest ...?	Που είναι ο πιο κοντινός ...;	pu *i*·ne o pio ko·di·*nos* ...
dentist	οδοντίατρος	o·dho·*di*·a·tros
doctor	γιατρός	yia·*tros*

Where's the nearest ...?	Που είναι το πιο κοντινό ...;	pu *i*·ne to pio ko·di·*no* ...
hospital	νοσοκομείο	no·so·ko·*mi*·o
(night) pharmacy	(νυχτερινό) φαρμακείο	(nikh·te·ri·*no*) far·ma·*ki*·o

I need a doctor (who speaks English).
Χρειάζομαι ένα γιατρό (που να μιλάει αγγλικά).
khri·*a*·zo·me *e*·na yia·*tro* (pu na mi·*la*·i ang·gli·*ka*)

Could I see a female doctor?
Μπορώ να δω μια γυναίκα γιατρό;
bo·*ro* na dho mia yi·*ne*·ka yia·*tro*

I've run out of my medication.
Μου έχουν τελειώσει τα φάρμακά μου.
mu *e*·khun te·li·*o*·si ta *far*·ma·ka mu

symptoms, conditions & allergies

I'm sick.	Είμαι άρρωστος/άρρωστη m/f	i·me a·ro·stos/a·ro·sti
It hurts here.	Πονάει εδώ.	po·na·i e·dho
I have (a/an) ...	Εχω ...	e·kho ...

asthma	άσθμα n	as·thma
bronchitis	βρογχίτιδα f	vro·hi·ti·dha
constipation	δυσκοιλιότητα f	dhis·ki·li·o·ti·ta
cough	βήχα m	vi·kha
diarrhoea	διάρροια f	dhi·a·ri·a
fever	πυρετό m	pi·re·to
headache	πονοκέφαλο m	po·no·ke·fa·lo
heart condition	καρδιακή	kar·dhi·a·ki
	κατάσταση f	ka·ta·sta·si
nausea	ναυτία f	naf·ti·a
pain	πόνο m	po·no
sore throat	πονόλαιμο m	po·no·le·mo
toothache	πονόδοντο	po·no·dho·do

I'm allergic to ...	Είμαι αλλεργικός/	i·me a·ler·yi·kos
	αλλεργική ... m/f	a·ler·yi·ki ...
antibiotics	στα αντιβιοτικά	sta a·di·vi·o·ti·ka
anti-inflammatories	στα αντιφλεγμονώδη	sta a·di·flegh·mo·no·dhi
aspirin	στην ασπιρίνη	stin as·pi·ri·ni
bees	στις μέλισσες	stis me·li·ses
codeine	στην κωδεΐνη	stin ko·dhe·i·ni
penicillin	στην πενικιλλίνη	stin pe·ni·ki·li·ni

antiseptic	αντισηπτικό n	a·di·sip·ti·ko
bandage	επίδεσμος m	e·pi·dhez·mos
condoms	προφυλακτικά n	pro·fi·lak·ti·ka
contraceptives	αντισυλληπτικά n pl	a·di·si·lip·ti·ka
diarrhoea medicine	φάρμακο διάροιας	far·ma·ko dhiar·ghias
insect repellent	εντομοαπωθητικό n	e·do·mo·a·po·thi·ti·ko
laxatives	καθαρτικό n	ka·thar·ti·ko
painkillers	παυσίπονα	paf·si·po·na
rehydration salts	ενυδρωτικά άλατα n pl	en·i·dhro·ti·ka a·la·ta
sleeping tablets	υπνωτικά χάπια n pl	ip·no·ti·ka kha·pia

english–greek dictionary

Greek nouns in this dictionary have their gender indicated by ⓜ (masculine), ⓕ (feminine) or ⓝ (neuter). If it's a plural noun you'll also see pl. Adjectives are given in the masculine form only. Words are also marked as n (noun), a (adjective), v (verb), sg (singular), pl (plural), inf (informal) and pol (polite) where necessary.

A

accident ατύχημα ⓝ a-*ti*-hi-ma
accommodation κατάλυμα ⓝ ka-*ta*-li-ma
adaptor μετασχηματιστής ⓜ me-ta-shi-ma-ti-*stis*
address διεύθυνση ⓕ dhi-*ef*-thin-si
aeroplane αεροπλάνο ⓝ a-e-ro-*pla*-no
after μετά me-*ta*
air-conditioned με έρκοντίσιον me er-kon-*di*-si-on
airport αεροδρόμιο ⓝ a-e-ro-*dhro*-mi-o
alcohol αλκοόλ ⓝ al-ko-*ol*
all όλοι ⓝ o-li
allergy αλλεργία ⓕ a-ler-*yi*-a
ambulance νοσοκομειακό ⓝ no-so-ko-mi-a-*ko*
and και ke
ankle αστράγαλος ⓜ a-*stra*-gha-los
arm χέρι ⓝ *he*-ri
ashtray σταχτοθήκη ⓕ stakh-to-*thi*-ki
ATM αυτόματη μηχανή χρημάτων ⓕ af-*to*-ma-ti mi-kha-*ni* khri-*ma*-ton

B

baby μωρό ⓝ mo-*ro*
back (body) πλάτη ⓕ *pla*-ti
backpack σακίδιο ⓝ sa-*ki*-dhi-o
bad κακός ka-*kos*
bag σάκος ⓜ *sa*-kos
baggage claim παραλαβή αποσκευών ⓕ pa-ra-la-*vi* a-po-ske-*von*
bank τράπεζα ⓕ *tra*-pe-za
bar μπαρ ⓜ bar
bathroom μπάνιο ⓝ *ba*-nio
battery μπαταρία ⓕ ba-ta-*ri*-a
beautiful όμορφος *o*-mor-fos
bed κρεβάτι ⓝ kre-*va*-ti
beer μπύρα ⓕ *bi*-ra
before πριν prin
behind πίσω *pi*-so
bicycle ποδήλατο ⓝ po-*dhi*-la-to
big μεγάλος me-*gha*-los

bill λογαριασμός ⓜ lo-gha-riaz-*mos*
black a μαύρος *mav*-ros
blanket κουβέρτα ⓕ ku-*ver*-ta
blood group ομάδα αίματος ⓕ o-*ma*-dha e-ma-tos
blue a μπλε ble
boat βάρκα ⓕ *var*-ka
book (make a reservation) v κλείσω θέση *kli*-so *the*-si
bottle μπουκάλι ⓝ bu-*ka*-li
bottle opener ανοιχτήρι ⓝ a-nikh-*ti*-ri
boy αγόρι ⓝ a-*gho*-ri
brakes (car) φρένα ⓝ pl *fre*-na
breakfast πρωινό ⓝ pro-i-no
broken (faulty) ελαττωματικός e-la-to-ma-ti-*kos*
bus λεωφορείο ⓝ le-o-fo-*ri*-o
business επιχείρηση ⓕ e-pi-*hi*-ri-si
buy αγοράζω a-gho-*ra*-zo

C

café καφετέρια ⓝ ka-fe-*te*-ria
camera φωτογραφική μηχανή ⓕ fo-to-ghra-fi-*ki* mi-kha-*ni*
camp site χώρος για κάμπινγκ ⓜ *kho*-ros yia *kam*-ping
cancel ακυρώνω a-ki-*ro*-no
can opener ανοιχτήρι ⓝ a-nikh-*ti*-ri
car αυτοκίνητο ⓝ af-to-*ki*-ni-to
cash μετρητά ⓝ pl me-tri-*ta*
cash (a cheque) v εξαργυρώνω ek-sar-yi-*ro*-no
cell phone κινητό ⓝ ki-ni-*to*
centre κέντρο ⓝ *ke*-dro
change (money) v αλλάζω a-*la*-zo
cheap φτηνός fti-*nos*
check (bill) λογαριασμός ⓜ lo-gha-riaz-*mos*
check-in ρεσεψιόν ⓕ re-sep-*sion*
chest στήθος ⓝ *sti*-thos
child παιδί ⓝ pe-*dhi*
cigarette τσιγάρο ⓝ tsi-*gha*-ro
city πόλη ⓕ *po*-li
clean a καθαρός ka-tha-*ros*
closed κλεισμένος kliz-me-nos
coffee καφές ⓜ ka-*fes*
coins κέρματα ⓝ pl *ker*-ma-ta
cold a κρυωμένος kri-o-me-nos

collect call κλήση με αντιστροφή της επιβάρυνσης ①
kli-si me a-dis-tro-*fi* tis e-pi-*va*-rin-sis
come έρχομαι er-kho-me
computer κομπιούτερ ⑩ kom-*piu*-ter
condom προφυλακτικό ⑩ pro-fi-lak-ti-*ko*
contact lenses φακοί επαφής ⑩ pl fa-*ki* e-pa-*fis*
cook v μαγειρεύω ma-yi-*re*-vo
cost τιμή ① ti-*mi*
credit card πιστωτική κάρτα ① pi-sto-ti-*ki kar*-ta
cup φλυτζάνι ⑩ fli-*dza*-ni
currency exchange τιμή συναλλάγματος ①
ti-*mi* si-na-*lagh*-ma-tos
customs (immigration) τελωνείο ⑩ te-lo-*ni*-o
Cypriot (nationality) Κύπριος/Κύπρια ⑩/①
ki-pri-os/*ki*-pri-a
Cypriot a κυπριακός/κυπριακή ⑩/①
ki-pri-a-*kos*/ki-pri-a-*ki*
Cyprus Κύπρος ① *ki*-pros

D

dangerous επικίνδυνος e-pi-*kin*-dhi-nos
date (time) ημερομηνία ① i-me-ro-mi-*ni*-a
day ημέρα ① i-*me*-ra
delay καθυστέρηση ① ka-thi-*ste*-ri-si
dentist οδοντίατρος ⑩&① o-dho-*di*-a-tros
depart αναχωρώ a-na-kho-*ro*
diaper πάνα ① *pa*-na
dictionary λεξικό ⑩ lek-si-*ko*
dinner δείπνο ⑩ *dhip*-no
direct άμεσος *a*-me-sos
dirty βρόμικος *vro*-mi-kos
disabled ανάπηρος a-*na*-pi-ros
discount έκπτωση ① *ek*-pto-si
doctor γιατρός ⑩&① yia-*tros*
double bed διπλό κρεβάτι ⑩ dhi-*plo* kre-*va*-ti
double room διπλό δωμάτιο ⑩ dhi-*plo* dho-*ma*-ti-o
drink ποτό ⑩ po-*to*
drive v οδηγώ o-dhi-*gho*
drivers licence άδεια οδήγησης ① *a*-dhi-a o-*dhi*-yi-sis
drugs (illicit) ναρκωτικό ⑩ nar-ko-ti-*ko*
dummy (pacifier) πιπίλα ① pi-*pi*-la

E

ear αφτί ⑩ af-*ti*
east ανατολή ① a-na-to-*li*
eat τρώγω tro-*gho*
economy class τουριστική θέση ① tu-ri-sti-*ki the*-si
electricity ηλεκτρισμός ⑩ i-lek-triz-*mos*

elevator ασανσέρ ⑩ a-san-*ser*
email ημέιλ ⑩ i-*me*-il
embassy πρεσβεία ① pre-*zvi*-a
emergency έκτακτη ανάγκη ① *ek*-tak-ti a-*na*-gi
English (language) Αγγλικά ⑩ ang-gli-*ka*
entrance είσοδος ① *i*-so-dhos
evening βράδι ⑩ *vra*-dhi
exchange rate τιμή συναλλάγματος ①
ti-*mi* si-na-*lagh*-ma-tos
exit έξοδος ① *ek*-so-dhos
expensive ακριβός a-kri-*vos*
express mail επείγον ταχυδρομείο ⑩
e-*pi*-ghon ta-hi-dhro-*mi*-o
eye μάτι ⑩ *ma*-ti

F

far μακριά ma-kri-*a*
fast γρήγορος *ghri*-gho-ros
father πατέρας ⑩ pa-*te*-ras
film (camera) φιλμ ⑩ film
finger δάκτυλο ⑩ *dhak*-ti-lo
first-aid kit κυτίο πρώτων βοηθειών ⑩
ki-*ti*-o *pro*-ton vo-i-thi-*on*
first class πρώτη τάξη ① *pro*-ti tak-si
fish ψάρι ⑩ *psa*-ri
food φαγητό ⑩ fa-yi-*to*
foot πόδι ⑩ *po*-dhi
fork πιρούνι ⑩ pi-*ru*-ni
free (of charge) δωρεάν dho-re-*an*
friend φίλος/φίλη ⑩/① *fi*-los/*fi*-li
fruit φρούτα ⑩ pl *fru*-ta
full γεμάτο ye-*ma*-to
funny αστείος a-*sti*-os

G

gift δώρο ⑩ *dho*-ro
girl κορίτσι ⑩ ko-*rit*-si
glass (drinking) ποτήρι ⑩ po-*ti*-ri
glasses γιαλιά ⑩ yia-*lia*
go πηγαίνω pi-*ye*-no
good καλός ka-*los*
Greece Ελλάδα ① e-*la*-dha
Greek (language) Ελληνικά ⑩ e-li-ni-*ka*
Greek (nationality) Έλληνες ⑩ pl *e*-li-nes
green πράσινος *pra*-si-nos
guide οδηγός ⑩&① o-dhi-*ghos*

H

half μισό ⓝ mi·so
hand χέρι ⓝ he·ri
handbag τσάντα ⓕ tsa·da
happy ευτυχισμένος ef·ti·hiz·me·nos
have έχω e·kho
he αυτός ⓜ af·tos
head κεφάλι ⓝ ke·fa·li
heart καρδιά ⓕ kar·dhia
heat ζέστη ⓕ ze·sti
heavy βαρύς va·ris
help v βοηθώ vo·i·tho
here εδώ e·dho
high ψηλός psi·los
highway δημόσιος δρόμος ⓜ dhi·mo·si·os dhro·mos
hike v πεζοπορώ pe·zo·po·ro
holiday διακοπές ⓕ dhia·ko·pes
homosexual ομοφυλόφιλος ⓜ o·mo·fi·lo·fi·los
hospital νοσοκομείο ⓝ no·so·ko·mi·o
hot ζεστός ze·stos
hotel ξενοδοχείο ⓝ kse·no·dho·hi·o
hungry πεινασμένος pi·naz·me·nos
husband σύζυγος ⓜ si·zi·ghos

I

I εγώ e·gho
identification (card) ταυτότητα ⓕ taf·to·ti·ta
ill άρρωστος a·ro·stos
important σπουδαίος spu·dhe·os
included συμπεριλαμβανομένου si·be·ri·lam·va·no·me·nu
injury πληγή ⓕ pli·yi
insurance ασφάλεια ⓕ as·fa·li·a
Internet διαδίκτυο ⓝ dhi·a·dhik·ti·o
interpreter διερμηνέας ⓜ&ⓕ dhi·er·mi·ne·as

J

jewellery κοσμήματα ⓝ pl koz·mi·ma·ta
job δουλειά ⓕ dhu·lia

K

key κλειδί ⓝ kli·dhi
kilogram χιλιόγραμμο ⓝ hi·lio·gra·mo
kitchen κουζίνα ⓕ ku·zi·na
knife μαχαίρι ⓝ ma·he·ri

L

laundry (place) πλυντήριο ⓝ pli·di·ri·o
lawyer δικηγόρος ⓜ&ⓕ dhi·ki·gho·ros
left (direction) αριστερός ⓜ a·ri·ste·ros
left-luggage office γραφείο φύλαξη αποσκεών ⓝ gra·fi·o fi·lak·si a·po·ske·von
leg πόδι ⓝ po·dhi
lesbian λεσβία ⓕ les·vi·a
less λιγότερο li·gho·te·ro
letter (mail) γράμμα ⓝ ghra·ma
lift (elevator) ασανσέρ ⓝ a·san·ser
light φως ⓝ fos
like v μου αρέσει mu a·re·si
lock κλειδαριά ⓕ kli·dha·ria
long μακρύς ma·kris
lost χαμένος kha·me·nos
lost-property office γραφείο απωλεσθέντων αντικειμένων ⓝ gra·fi·o a·po·les·the·don a·di·ki·me·non
love v αγαπώ a·gha·po
luggage αποσκευές ⓕ pl a·po·ske·ves
lunch μεσημεριανό φαγητό ⓝ me·si·me·ria·no fa·yi·to

M

mail (letters) αλληλογραφία ⓕ a·li·lo·ghra·fi·a
mail (postal system) ταχυδρομείο ⓝ ta·hi·dhro·mi·o
man άντρας ⓜ a·dras
map χάρτης ⓜ khar·tis
market αγορά ⓕ a·gho·ra
matches σπίρτα ⓝ pl spir·ta
meat κρέας ⓝ kre·as
medicine φάρμακο ⓝ far·ma·ko
menu μενού ⓝ me·nu
message μήνυμα ⓝ mi·ni·ma
milk γάλα ⓝ gha·la
minute λεπτό ⓝ lep·to
mobile phone κινητό ⓝ ki·ni·to
money χρήματα ⓝ khri·ma·ta
month μήνας ⓜ mi·nas
morning πρωί ⓝ pro·i
mother μητέρα ⓕ mi·te·ra
motorcycle μοτοσυκλέτα ⓕ mo·to·si·kle·ta
motorway αυτοκινητόδρομος ⓜ af·to·ki·ni·to·dhro·mos
mouth στόμα ⓝ sto·ma
music μουσική ⓕ mu·si·ki

N

name όνομα ⓝ o·no·ma
napkin πετσετάκι ⓝ pet·se·ta·ki
nappy πάνα ⓕ pa·na

near κοντά ko-*da*
neck λαιμός ⓜ le-*mos*
new νέος *ne*-os
news νέα ⓝ *ne*-a
newspaper εφημερίδα ⓕ e-fi-me-*ri*-dha
night νύχτα ⓕ *nikh*-ta
no όχι o-hi
noisy a θορυβώδης tho-ri-*vo*-dhis
nonsmoking μη καπνίζοντες mi kap-*ni*-zo-des
north βοράς ⓜ vo-*ras*
nose μύτη ⓕ *mi*-ti
now τώρα *to*-ra
number αριθμός ⓜ a-rith-*mos*

O

oil (engine) λάδι αυτοκινήτου ⓝ *la*-dhi af-to-ki-*ni*-tu
old παλιός pa-*lios*
one-way ticket απλό εισιτήριο ⓝ a-*plo* i-si-*ti*-ri-o
open a ανοιχτός a-nikh-*tos*
outside έξω *ek*-so

P

package πακέτο ⓝ pa-*ke*-to
paper χαρτί ⓝ khar-*ti*
park (car) ν παρκάρω par-*ka*-ro
passport διαβατήριο ⓝ dhia-va-*ti*-ri-o
pay ν πληρώνω pli-*ro*-no
pen στυλό ⓝ sti-*lo*
petrol πετρέλαιο ⓝ pe-*tre*-le-o
pharmacy φαρμακείο ⓝ far-ma-*ki*-o
phonecard τηλεκάρτα ⓕ ti-le-*kar*-ta
photo φωτογραφία ⓕ fo-to-gra-*fi*-a
plate πιάτο ⓝ *pia*-to
police αστυνομία ⓕ a-sti-no-*mi*-a
postcard κάρτα ⓕ *kar*-ta
post office ταχυδρομείο ⓝ ta-hi-dhro-*mi*-o
pregnant έγκυος *e*-gi-os
price τιμή ⓕ ti-*mi*

Q

quiet ήσυχος *i*-si-khos

R

rain βροχή vro-*hi*
razor ξυριστική μηχανή ⓕ ksi-ri-sti-*ki* mi-kha-*ni*
receipt απόδειξη ⓕ a-*po*-dhik-si

red κόκκινο *ko*-ki-no
refund ⓝ επιστροφή χρημάτων ⓕ e-pi-stro-*fi* khri-*ma*-ton
registered mail συστημένο sis-ti-*me*-no
rent ν ενοικιάζω e-ni-ki-*a*-zo
repair ν επισκευάζω e-pi-ske-*va*-zo
reservation κράτηση ⓕ *kra*-ti-si
restaurant εστιατόριο ⓝ e-sti-a-*to*-ri-o
return ν επιστρέφω e-pi-*stre*-fo
return ticket εισιτήριο μετ' επιστροφής ⓝ i-si-*ti*-ri-o me-te-pis-tro-*fis*
right (direction) δεξιός dhek-si-*os*
road δρόμος ⓜ *dhro*-mos
room δωμάτιο ⓝ dho-*ma*-ti-o

S

safe a ασφαλής as-fa-*lis*
sanitary napkin πετσετάκι υγείας ⓝ pet-se-*ta*-ki i-*yi*-as
seat θέση ⓕ *the*-si
send στέλνω *stel*-no
service station βενζινάδικο ⓝ ven-zi-*na*-dhi-ko
sex σεξ ⓝ seks
shampoo σαμπουάν ⓝ sam-pu-*an*
share (a dorm) μοιράζομαι mi-*ra*-zo-me
shaving cream κρέμα ξυρίσματος ⓕ *kre*-ma ksi-*riz*-ma-tos
she αυτή af-*ti*
sheet (bed) σεντόνι ⓝ se-*do*-ni
shirt πουκάμισο ⓝ pu-*ka*-mi-so
shoes παπούτσια ⓝ pl pa-*put*-si-a
shop μαγαζί ⓝ ma-gha-*zi*
short κοντός ko-*dos*
shower ντους ⓝ duz
single room μονό δωμάτιο ⓝ mo-*no* dho-*ma*-tio
skin δέρμα ⓝ *dher*-ma
skirt φούστα ⓕ *fu*-sta
sleep ν κοιμάμαι ki-*ma*-me
slowly αργά ar-*gha*
small μικρός mi-*kros*
smoke (cigarettes) ν καπνίζω kap-*ni*-zo
soap σαπούνι ⓝ sa-*pu*-ni
some μερικοί me-ri-*ki*
soon σύντομα *si*-do-ma
south νότος ⓜ *no*-tos
souvenir shop κατάστημα για σουβενίρ ka-*ta*-sti-ma yia su-ve-*nir*
speak μιλάω mi-*la*-o
spoon κουτάλι ⓝ ku-*ta*-li
stamp γραμματόσημο ⓝ ghra-ma-*to*-si-mo

233

stand-by ticket εισιτήριο σταντ μπάι ⊙
i-si-*ti*-ri-o stand *ba*-i
station (train) σταθμός ⓜ stath-*mos*
stomach στομάχι ⓝ sto-*ma*-hi
stop v σταματάω sta-ma-*ta*-o
stop (bus) στάση ⓕ *sta*-si
street οδός ⓕ o-*dhos*
student σπουδαστής/σπουδάστρια ⓜ/ⓕ
spu-dha-*stis*/spu-*dha*-stri-a
sun ήλιος ⓜ *i*-li-os
sunscreen αντιηλιακό ⓝ a-di-i-li-a-*ko*
swim v κολυμπώ ko-li-*bo*

T

tampon ταμπόν ⓝ ta-*bon*
taxi ταξί ⓝ tak-*si*
teaspoon κουτάλι τσαγιού ⓝ ku-*ta*-li tsa-*yiu*
teeth δόντια ⓝ *dho*-dia
telephone τηλέφωνο ⓝ ti-*le*-fo-no
television τηλεόραση ⓕ ti-le-o-ra-si
temperature (weather) θερμοκρασία ⓕ
ther-mo-kra-*si*-a
tent τέντα ⓕ *te*-da
that (one) εκείνο e-*ki*-no
they αυτοί af-*ti*
thirsty διψασμένος dhip-saz-*me*-nos
this (one) αυτός af-*tos*
throat λαιμός ⓜ le-*mos*
ticket εισιτήριο ⓝ i-si-*ti*-ri-o
time ώρα ⓕ *o*-ra
tired κουρασμένος ku-raz-*me*-nos
tissues χαρτομάντηλα ⓝ pl khar-to-*ma*-di-la
today σήμερα *si*-me-ra
toilet τουαλέτα ⓕ tu-a-*le*-ta
tomorrow αύριο *av*-ri-o
tonight απόψε a-*pop*-se
toothbrush οδοντόβουρτσα ⓕ o-dho-*do*-vur-tsa
toothpaste οδοντόπαστα ⓕ o-dho-*do*-pa-sta
torch (flashlight) φακός ⓜ fa-*kos*
tour περιήγηση ⓕ pe-ri-*i*-yi-si
tourist office τουριστικό γραφείο ⓝ
tu-ri-sti-*ko* ghra-*fi*-o
towel πετσέτα ⓕ pet-*se*-ta
train τρένο ⓝ *tre*-no
translate v μεταφράζω me-ta-*fra*-zo
travel agency ταξιδιωτικό γραφείο ⓝ
tak-si-dhi-o-ti-*ko* ghra-*fi*-o
travellers cheque ταξιδιωτική επιταγή ⓕ
tak-si-dhi-o-ti-*ki* e-pi-ta-*yi*

trousers παντελόνι ⓝ pa-de-*lo*-ni
twin beds δίκλινο δωμάτιο ⓝ *dhi*-kli-no dho-*ma*-ti-o
tyre λάστιχο ⓝ *la*-sti-kho

U

underwear εσώρουχα ⓝ pl e-*so*-ru-kha
urgent επείγον e-*pi*-ghon

V

vacant ελεύθερος e-*lef*-the-ros
vacation διακοπές ⓕ dhia-ko-*pes*
vegetable λαχανικά ⓝ pl la-kha-ni-*ka*
vegetarian n χορτοφάγος ⓜ&ⓕ khor-to-*fa*-ghos
visa βίζα ⓕ *vi*-za

W

waiter γκαρσόν ⓝ gar-*son*
walk v περπατάω per-pa-*ta*-o
wallet πορτοφόλι ⓝ por-to-*fo*-li
warm a ζεστός ze-*stos*
wash (something) v πλένω *ple*-no
watch ρολόι ⓝ ro-*lo*-i
water νερό ⓝ ne-*ro*
we εμείς e-*mis*
weekend Σαββατοκύριακο ⓝ sa-va-to-*ki*-ria-ko
west δύση ⓕ *dhi*-si
wheelchair αναπηρική καρέκλα ⓕ
a-na-pi-ri-*ki* ka-*re*-kla
when όταν o-tan
where πού pu
white άσπρος *as*-pros
who ποιος pios
why γιατί yia-*ti*
wife σύζυγος ⓕ *si*-zi-ghos
window παράθυρο ⓝ pa-*ra*-thi-ro
wine κρασί ⓝ kra-*si*
with με me
without χωρίς kho-*ris*
woman γυναίκα ⓕ yi-*ne*-ka
write v γράφω *ghra*-fo

Y

yellow a κίτρινος *ki*-tri-nos
yes ναι ne
yesterday χτες khtes
you sg inf εσύ e-*si*
you sg pol & pl εσείς e-*sis*

Hungarian

hungarian alphabet

A a o	*Á á* a	*B b* bey	*C c* tsey	*Cs cs* chey	*D d* dey	*Dz dz* dzey	*Dzs dzs* jey
E e e	*É é* ey	*F f* ef	*G g* gey	*Gy gy* dyey	*H h* ha	*I i* i	*Í í* ee
J j yey	*K k* ka	*L l* el	*Ly ly* ey	*M m* em	*N n* en	*Ny ny* en'	*O o* aw
Ó ó āw	*Ö ö* eu	*Ő ő* ēū	*P p* pey	*Q q* ku	*R r* er	*S s* esh	*Sz sz* es
T t tey	*Ty ty* tyey	*U u* u	*Ú ú* ū	*Ü ü* ew	*Ű ű* ēw	*V v* vey	*W w* du·plo·vey
X x iks	*Y y* ip·sil·awn	*Z z* zey	*Zs zs* zhey				

■ hungarian

MAGYAR

about Hungarian

Hungarian (*magyar mo·*dyor) is a unique language. Though distantly related to Finnish, it has no significant similarities to any other language in the world. If you have some background in European languages you'll be surprised at just how different Hungarian is. English actually has more in common with Russian and Sinhala (from Sri Lanka) than it does with Hungarian – even though words like *goulash*, *paprika* and *vampire* came to English from this language.

So how did such an unusual language end up in the heart of the European continent? The answer lies somewhere beyond the Ural mountains in western Siberia, where the nomadic ancestors of today's Hungarian speakers began a slow migration west about 2000 years ago. At some point in the journey the group began to split. One group turned towards Finland, while the other continued towards the Carpathian Basin, arriving in the late 9th century. Calling themselves Magyars (derived from the Finno-Ugric words for 'speak' and 'man') they cultivated and developed the occupied lands. By AD 1000 the Kingdom of Hungary was officially established. Along the way Hungarian acquired words from languages like Latin, Persian, Turkish and Bulgarian, yet overall changed remarkably little.

With more than 14.5 million speakers worldwide, Hungarian is nowadays the official language of Hungary and a minority language in the parts of Eastern Europe which belonged to the Austro-Hungarian Empire before WWI – Slovakia, Croatia, the northern Serbian province of Vojvodina and parts of Austria, Romania and the Ukraine.

Hungarian is a language rich in grammar and expression. These characteristics can be both alluring and intimidating. Word order in Hungarian is fairly free, and it has been argued that this stimulates creative or experimental thinking. Some believe that the flexibility of the tongue, combined with Hungary's linguistic isolation, has encouraged the culture's strong tradition of poetry and literature. For the same reason, however, the language is resistant to translation and much of the nation's literary heritage is still unavailable to English speakers. Another theory holds that Hungary's extraordinary number of great scientists is also attributable to the language's versatile nature. Still, Hungarian needn't be intimidating and you won't need to look very far to discover the beauty of the language. You may even find yourself unlocking the poet or scientist within!

pronunciation

The Hungarian language may seem daunting with its long words and many accent marks, but it's surprisingly easy to pronounce. Like English, Hungarian isn't always written the way it's pronounced, but just stick to the coloured phonetic guides that accompany each phrase or word and you can't go wrong.

vowel sounds

Hungarian vowels sounds are similar to those found in the English words listed in the table below. The symbol ¯ over a vowel, like ā, means you say it as a long vowel sound.

symbol	english equivalent	hungarian example	transliteration
a	father	*hátizsák*	*ha*·ti·zhak
aw	law (but short)	*kor*	kawr
e	bet	*zsebkés*	*zheb*·keysh
ee	see	*cím*	tseem
eu	her	*zöld*	zeuld
ew	ee pronounced with rounded lips	*csütörtök*	*chew*·teur·teuk
ey	hey	*én*	eyn
i	bit	*rizs*	rizh
o	pot	*gazda*	*goz*·do
oy	toy	*megfojt,* *komoly*	meg·*foyt,* *kaw*·moy
u	put	*utas*	*u*·tosh

word stress

Accent marks over vowels don't influence word stress, which always falls on the first syllable of the word. The stressed syllables in our coloured pronunciation guides are always in italics.

consonant sounds

Always pronounce y like the 'y' in 'yes'. We've also used the ' symbol to show this y sound when it's attached to n, d, and t and at the end of a syllable. You'll also see double consonants like bb, dd or tt — draw them out a little longer than you would in English.

symbol	english equivalent	hungarian example	transliteration
b	**bed**	*bajusz*	*bo*·yus
ch	**ch**eat	*család*	*cho*·lad
d	**dog**	*dervis*	*der*·vish
dy	**d**uring	*magyar*	*mo*·dyor
f	**fat**	*farok*	*fo*·rawk
g	**go**	*gallér, igen*	*gol*·leyr, *i*·gen
h	**hat**	*hát*	hat
j	**j**oke	*dzsem, hogy*	jem, hawj
k	**k**it	*kacsa*	*ko*·cho
l	**lot**	*lakat*	*lo*·kot
m	**man**	*most*	mawsht
n	**not**	*nem*	nem
p	**pet**	*pamut*	*po*·mut
r	**r**un (rolled)	*piros*	*pi*·rawsh
s	**s**un	*kolbász*	*kawl*·bas
sh	**sh**ot	*tojást*	*taw*·yasht
t	**top**	*tag*	tog
ty	**t**utor	*kártya*	*kar*·tyo
ts	ha**ts**	*koncert*	*kawn*·tsert
v	**very**	*vajon*	*vo*·yawn
y	**yes**	*hajó, melyik*	*ho*·yàw, *me*·yik
z	**z**ero	*zab*	zob
zh	plea**s**ure	*zsemle*	*zhem*·le
'	a slight y sound	*poggyász, hány*	*pawd'*·dyas, han'

tools

language difficulties

Do you speak English?
Beszél/Beszélsz angolul? pol/inf · be·seyl/be·seyls on·gaw·lul

Do you understand?
Érti/Érted? pol/inf · eyr·ti/eyr·ted

I (don't) understand.
(Nem) Értem. · (nem) eyr·tem

What does (lángos) mean?
Mit jelent az, hogy (lángos)? · mit ye·lent oz hawj (lan·gawsh)

How do you ...?	*Hogyan ...?*	haw·dyon ...
pronounce this	*mondja ki ezt*	mawnd·yo ki ezt
write (útlevél)	*írja azt, hogy (útlevél)*	eer·yo ozt hawj (üt·le·veyl)

Could you please ...?	..., *kérem.*	... key·rem
repeat that	*Megismételné ezt*	meg·ish·mey·tel·ney ezt
speak more slowly	*Tudna lassabban beszélni*	tud·no losh·shob·bon be·seyl·ni
write it down	*Leírná*	le·eer·na

numbers

0	*nulla*	nul·lo	16	*tizenhat*	ti·zen·hot
1	*egy*	ej	17	*tizenhét*	ti·zen·heyt
2	*kettő*	ket·tēū	18	*tizennyolc*	ti·zen·nyawlts
3	*három*	ha·rawm	19	*tizenkilenc*	ti·zen·ki·lents
4	*négy*	neyj	20	*húsz*	hūs
5	*öt*	eut	21	*huszonegy*	hu·sawn·ej
6	*hat*	hot	22	*huszonkettő*	hu·sawn·ket·tēū
7	*hét*	heyt	30	*harminc*	hor·mints
8	*nyolc*	nyawlts	40	*negyven*	nej·ven
9	*kilenc*	ki·lents	50	*ötven*	eut·ven
10	*tíz*	teez	60	*hatvan*	hot·von
11	*tizenegy*	ti·zen·ej	70	*hetven*	het·ven
12	*tizenkettő*	ti·zen·ket·tēū	80	*nyolcvan*	nyawlts·von
13	*tizenhárom*	ti·zen·ha·rawm	90	*kilencven*	ki·lents·ven
14	*tizennégy*	ti·zen·neyj	100	*száz*	saz
15	*tizenöt*	ti·zen·eut	1000	*ezer*	e·zer

time & dates

What time is it?	*Hány óra?*	han' āw·ra
It's one o'clock.	*(Egy) óra van.*	(ej) āw·ra von
It's (10) o'clock.	*(Tíz) óra van.*	(teez) āw·ra von
Quarter past (10).	*Negyed (tizenegy).*	ne·dyed (ti·zen·ej)
Half past (10).	*Fél (tizenegy).*	feyl (ti·zen·ej)
Quarter to (11).	*Háromnegyed (tizenegy).*	ha·rawm·ne·dyed (ti·zen·ej)
At what time ...?	*Hány órakor ...?*	han' āw·ro·kawr ...
At ...	*... kor.*	...kawr
am (morning)	*délelőtt*	deyl·e·lēūtt
pm (afternoon)	*délután*	deyl·u·tan
pm (evening)	*este*	esh·te
Monday	*hétfő*	heyt·fēū
Tuesday	*kedd*	kedd
Wednesday	*szerda*	ser·do
Thursday	*csütörtök*	chew·teur·teuk
Friday	*péntek*	peyn·tek
Saturday	*szombat*	sawm·bot
Sunday	*vasárnap*	vo·shar·nop

January	*január*	*yo*·nu·ar
February	*február*	*feb*·ru·ar
March	*március*	*mar*·tsi·ush
April	*április*	*ap*·ri·lish
May	*május*	*ma*·yush
June	*június*	*yū*·ni·ush
July	*július*	*yū*·li·ush
August	*augusztus*	*o*·u·gus·tush
September	*szeptember*	*sep*·tem·ber
October	*október*	*awk*·tāw·ber
November	*november*	*naw*·vem·ber
December	*december*	*de*·tsem·ber

What date is it today?

Hányadika van ma?	*ha*·nyo·di·ko von mo

It's (18 October).

(Október tizennyolcadika) van.	*(awk*·tāw·ber *ti*·zen·nyawl·tso·di·ko) von

since (May)	*(május) óta*	*(ma*·yush) *āw*·to
until (June)	*(június)ig*	*(yū*·ni·ush)·ig
yesterday	*tegnap*	*teg*·nop
last night	*tegnap éjjel*	*hawl*·nop *ey*·yel
today	*ma*	mo
tonight	*ma este*	mo *esh*·te
tomorrow	*holnap*	*hawl*·nop
last/next ...	*a múlt/a jövő ...*	o mült/o *yeu*·vēū ...
week	*héten*	*hey*·ten
month	*hónapban*	*hāw*·nop·bon
year	*évben*	*eyv*·hen
yesterday/tomorrow ...	*tegnap/holnap ...*	*teg*·nop/*hawl*·nop ...
morning	*reggel*	*reg*·gel
afternoon	*délután*	*deyl*·u·tan
evening	*este*	*esh*·te

weather

What's the weather like?	*Milyen az idő?*	*mi*-yen oz *i*-dēū

It's ...

cloudy	*Az idő felhős.*	oz *i*-dēū *fel*-hēūsh
cold	*Az idő hideg.*	oz *i*-dēū *hi*-deg
hot	*Az idő nagyon meleg.*	oz *i*-dēū *no*-dyawn *me*-leg
raining	*Esik az eső.*	*e*-shik oz *e*-shēū
snowing	*Esik a hó.*	*e*-shik o hāw
sunny	*Az idő napos.*	oz *i*-dēū *no*-pawsh
warm	*Az idő meleg.*	oz *i*-dēū *me*-leg
windy	*Az idő szeles.*	oz *i*-dēū *se*-lesh

spring	*tavasz*	*to*-vos
summer	*nyár*	nyar
autumn	*ősz*	ēūs
winter	*tél*	teyl

border crossing

I'm ...	*... vagyok.*	*... vo*-dyawk
in transit	*Átutazóban*	*at*-u-to-zāw-bon
on business	*Üzleti úton*	*ewz*-le-ti *ū*-tawn
on holiday	*Szabadságon*	*so*-bod-sha-gawn

I'm here for ...	*... vagyok itt.*	*... vo*-dyawk itt
(10) days	*(Tíz) napig*	(teez) *no*-pig
(two) months	*(Két) hónapig*	(keyt) *hāw*-no-pig
(three) weeks	*(Három) hétig*	(*ha*-rawm) *hey*-tig

I'm going to (Szeged).
(Szeged)re megyek. — (*se*-ged)-re *me*-dyek

I'm staying at (the Gellért Hotel).
A (Gellért)ben fogok lakni. — o (*gel*-leyrt)-ben *faw*-gawk *lok*-ni

I have nothing to declare.
Nincs elvámolnivalóm. — ninch *el*-va-mawl-ni-vo-lāwm

I have something to declare.
Van valami elvámolnivalóm. — von *vo*-lo-mi *el*-va-mawl-ni-vo-lāwm

That's (not) mine.
Az (nem) az enyém. — oz (nem) oz *e*-nyeym

transport

tickets & luggage

Where can I buy a ticket?
Hol kapok jegyet? — hawl *ko*·pawk *ye*·dyet

Do I need to book a seat?
Kell helyjegyet váltanom? — kell *he*·ye·dyet *val*·ta·nawm

One ... ticket	*Egy ... jegy*	ej ... yej
to (Eger), please.	*(Eger)be.*	(*e*·ger)·be
one-way	*csak oda*	chok *aw*·do
return	*oda-vissza*	*aw*·do·*vis*·so

I'd like to ... my	*Szeretném ...*	se·ret·neym ...
ticket, please.	*a jegyemet.*	o *ye*·dye·met
cancel	*törölni*	*teu*·reul·ni
change	*megváltoztatni*	*meg*·val·tawz·tot·ni
collect	*átvenni*	*at*·ven·ni
confirm	*megerősíteni*	*meg*·e·rëü·shee·te·ni

I'd like a ... seat,	*... helyet*	... *he*·yet
please.	*szeretnék.*	se·ret·neyk
nonsmoking	*Nemdohányzó*	nem·daw·han'·zãw
smoking	*Dohányzó*	daw·han'·zãw

How much is it?
Mennyibe kerül? — men'·nyi·be *ke*·rewl

Is there air conditioning?
Van légkondicionálás? — von *leyg*·kawn·di·tsi·aw·na·lash

Is there a toilet?
Van vécé? — von *vey*·tsey

How long does the trip take?
Mennyi ideig tart az út? — men'·nyi *i*·de·ig tort oz üt

Is it a direct route?
Ez közvetlen járat? — ez *keuz*·vet·len *ya*·rot

My luggage has been ...	*A poggyászom ...*	o *pawd'*·dya·sawm ...
damaged	*megsérült*	*meg*·shey·rewlt
lost	*elveszett*	*el*·ve·sett

My luggage has been stolen.
Ellopták a poggyászomat.   el·lawp·tak o pawd'·dya·saw·mot

Where can I find a luggage locker?
Hol találok egy poggyász-   hawl to·la·lawk ej pawd'·dyas·
megőrző automatát?   meg·ēūr·zēū o·u·taw·mo·tat

getting around

Where does flight (BA15) arrive?
Hova érkezik a (BA tizenötös)   haw·vo eyr·ke·zik a (bey o ti·zen·eu·teush)
számú járat?   sa·mū ya·rot

Where does flight (BA26) depart?
Honnan indul a (BA huszonhatos)   hawn·non in·dul a (bey o hu·sawn·ho·tawsh)
számú járat?   sa·mū ya·rot

Where's (the) ...?	*Hol van ...?*	hawl von ...
arrivals hall	*az érkezési csarnok*	oz eyr·ke·zey·shi chor·nawk
departures hall	*az indulási csarnok*	oz in·du·la·shi chor·nawk
duty-free shop	*a vámmentes üzlet*	o vam·men·tesh ewz·let
gate (five)	*az (ötös) kapu*	oz (eu·teush) ko·pu

Which ... goes	*Melyik ... megy*	me·yik ... mej
to (Budapest)?	*(Budapest)re?*	(bu·do·pesht)·re
boat	*hajó*	ho·yāw
bus	*busz*	bus
plane	*repülőgép*	re·pew·lēū·geyp
train	*vonat*	vaw·not

What time's the	*Mikor megy ... (busz)?*	mi·kawr mej ... (bus)
... (bus)?		
first	*az első*	oz el·shēū
last	*az utolsó*	oz u·tawl·shāw
next	*a következő*	o keu·vet·ke·zēū

At what time does it arrive/leave?
Mikor érkezik/indul?   mi·kawr eyr·ke·zik/in·dul

How long will it be delayed?
Mennyit késik?   men'·nyit key·shik

What station/stop is this?
Ez milyen állomás/megálló?   ez mi·yen al·law·mash/meg·al·lāw

What's the next station/stop?
Mi a következő állomás/megálló?   mi o *keu*-vet-ke-zēū *al*-law-mash/*meg*-al-lāw

Does it stop at (Visegrád)?
Megáll (Visegrád)on?   *meg*-all (*vi*-she-grad)-on

Please tell me when we get to (Eger).
Kérem, szóljon, amikor   *key*-rem *sāwl*-yawn *o*-mi-kawr
(Eger)be érünk.   (e-ger)-be *ey*-rewnk

How long do we stop here?
Mennyi ideig állunk itt?   men'-nyi *i*-de-ig *al*-lunk itt

Is this seat available?
Szabad ez a hely?   *so*-bod ez o *he*-y

That's my seat.
Az az én helyem.   oz oz eyn *he*-yem

I'd like a taxi ...	Szeretnék egy taxit ...	*se*-ret-neyk ej *tok*-sit ...
at (9am)	(reggel kilenc)re	(*reg*-gel *ki*-lents)-re
now	most	mawsht
tomorrow	holnapra	*hawl*-nop-ro

Is this taxi available?
Szabad ez a taxi?   *so*-bod ez o *tok*-si

How much is it to ...?
Mennyibe kerül ...ba?   men'-nyi-be *ke*-rewl ...-bo

Please put the meter on.
Kérem, kapcsolja be az órát.   *key*-rem *kop*-chawl-yo be oz *āw*-rat

Please take me to (this address).
Kérem, vigyen el (erre a címre).   *kay*-rem *vi*-dyen el (*er*-re o *tseem*-re)

Please ...	Kérem, ...	*key*-rem ...
slow down	lassítson	*losh*-sheet-shawn
stop here	álljon meg itt	*all*-yawn meg itt
here	várjon itt	*var*-yawn itt

car, motorbike & bicycle hire

I'd like to hire a ...	Szeretnék egy ... bérelni.	*se*-ret-neyk ej ... *bey*-rel-ni
bicycle	biciklit	*bi*-tsik-lit
car	autót	*o*-u-tāwt
motorbike	motort	*maw*-tawrt

with a driver	sofőrrel	shaw-fēūr-rel
with air conditioning	lég-kondicionálóval	leyg-kawn-di-tsi-aw-na-lāw-vol
with antifreeze	fagyállóval	fod'-al-lāw-vol
with snow chains	hólánccal	hāw-lant'-tsol

How much	Mennyibe kerül	men'-nyi-be ke-rewl
for ... hire?	a kölcsönzés ...?	o keul-cheun-zeysh ...
hourly	óránként	āw-ran-keynt
daily	egy napra	ej nop-ro
weekly	egy hétre	ej heyt-re

air	levegő	le-ve-gēū
oil	olaj	aw-lo-y
petrol	benzin	ben-zin
tyres	gumi	gu-mi

I need a mechanic.
*Szükségem van egy
autószerelőre.*
sewk-shey-gem von ej
o-u-tāw-se-re-lēū-re

I've run out of petrol.
Kifogyott a benzinem.
ki-faw-dyawtt o ben-zi-nem

I have a flat tyre.
Defektem van.
de-fek-tem von

directions

Where's the ...?	Hol van a ...?	hawl von o ...
bank	bank	bonk
city centre	városközpont	va-rawsh-keuz-pawnt
hotel	szálloda	sal-law-do
market	piac	pi-ots
police station	rendőrség	rend-ēūr-sheyg
post office	postahivatal	pawsh-to-hi-vo-tol
public toilet	nyilvános vécé	nyil-va-nawsh vey-tsey
tourist office	turistairoda	tu-rish-to-i-raw-do

Is this the road to (Sopron)?
Ez az út vezet (Sopron)ba?
ez oz üt ve-zet (shawp-rawn)-bo

Can you show me (on the map)?
*Meg tudja mutatni nekem
(a térképen)?*
meg tud'-yo mu-tot-ni ne-kem
(o teyr-key-pen)

What's the address?
Mi a cím?   mi o tseem

How far is it?
Milyen messze van?   *mi*·yen *mes*·se von

How do I get there?
Hogyan jutok oda?   *haw*·dyon *yu*·tawk *aw*·do

Turn ...	*Forduljon ...*	*fawr*·dul·yawn ...
at the corner	*a saroknál*	o *sho*·rawk·nal
at the traffic	*a közlekedési*	o *keuz*·le·ke·dey·shi
lights	*lámpánál*	*lam*·pa·nal
left/right	*balra/jobbra*	*bol*·ro/*yawbb*·ro

It's ...	*... van.*	*... von*
behind ...	*... mögött*	*... meu*·geutt
far away	*Messze*	*mes*·se
here	*Itt*	itt
in front of ...	*... előtt*	*... e*·lēütt
left	*Balra*	*bol*·ro
near ...	*... közelében*	*... keu*·ze·ley·ben
next to ...	*... mellett*	*... mel*·lett
on the corner	*A sarkon*	o *shor*·kawn
opposite ...	*... val szemben*	*... vol sem*·ben
right	*Jobbra*	*yawbb*·ro
straight ahead	*Egyenesen előttünk*	*e*·dye·ne·shen *e*·lēüt·tewnk
there	*Ott*	ott

by bus	*busszal*	*bus*·sol
by taxi	*taxival*	*tok*·si·vol
by train	*vonattal*	*vaw*·not·tol
on foot	*gyalog*	*dyo*·lawg

north	*észak*	*ey*·sok
south	*dél*	deyl
east	*kelet*	*ke*·let
west	*nyugat*	*nyu*·got

Bejárat/Kijárat	be·ya·rot/ki·ya·rot	Entrance/Exit
Nyitva/Zárva	nyit·vo/zar·vo	Open/Closed
Van Üres Szoba	von ew·resh saw·bo	Rooms Available
Minden Szoba Foglalt	min·den saw·bo fawg·lolt	No Vacancies
Információ	in·fawr·ma·tsi·āw	Information
Rendőrség	rend·ēűr·sheyg	Police Station
Tilos	ti·lawsh	Prohibited
Mosdó	mawsh·dāw	Toilets
Férfiak	feyr·fi·ok	Men
Nők	nēūk	Women
Meleg/Hideg	me·leg/hi·deg	Hot/Cold

accommodation

finding accommodation

Where's a ...?	Hol van egy ...?	hawl von ej ...
camping ground	kemping	kem·ping
guesthouse	panzió	pon·zi·āw
hotel	szálloda	sal·law·do
youth hostel	ifjúsági szálló	if·yū·sha·gi sal·lāw

Can you recommend somewhere ...?	Tud ajánlani egy ... helyet?	tud o·yan·lo·ni ej ... he·yet
cheap	olcsó	awl·chāw
good	jó	yāw
nearby	közeli	keu·ze·li

I'd like to book a room, please.	Szeretnék egy szobát foglalni.	se·ret·neyk ej saw·bat fawg·lol·ni
I have a reservation.	Van foglalásom.	von fawg·lo·la·shawm
My name's ...	A nevem ...	o ne·vem ...

Do you have a ... room?	Van Önnek kiadó egy ... szobája?	von eun·nek ki·o·dāw ed' ... saw·ba·yo
single	egyágyas	ej·a·dyosh
double	dupla ágyas	dup·lo·a·dyosh
twin	kétágyas	keyt·a·dyosh

How much is it per ...?	Mennyibe kerül egy ...?	men'·nyi·be ke·rewl ej ...
night	éjszakára	ey·so·ka·ro
person	főre	fēū·re

Can I pay by ...?	Fizethetek ...?	fi·zet·he·tek ...
credit card	hitelkártyával	hi·tel·kar·tya·vol
travellers cheque	utazási csekkel	u·to·za·shi chek·kel

I'd like to stay for (three) nights.
(Három) éjszakára. (ha·rawm) ey·so·ka·ro

From (July 2) to (July 6).
(Július kettő)től (július hat)ig. (yū·li·ush ket·tēū)·tēūl (yū·li·ush hot)·ig

Can I see it?
Megnézhetem? meg·neyz·he·tem

Am I allowed to camp here?
Táborozhatok itt? ta·baw·rawz·ho·tawk itt

Where can I find the camping ground?
Hol találom a kempinget? hawl to·la·lawm o kem·pin·get

requests & queries

When/Where is breakfast served?
Mikor/Hol van a reggeli? mi·kawr/hawl von o reg·ge·li

Please wake me at (seven).
Kérem, ébresszen fel (hét)kor. key·rem eyb·res·sen fel (heyt)·kawr

Could I have my key, please?
Megkaphatnám a kulcsomat, kérem? meg·kop·hot·nam o kul·chaw·mot key·rem

Can I get another (blanket)?
Kaphatok egy másik (takaró)t? kop·ho·tawk ej ma·shik (to·ko·rāw)t

Is there a/an ...?	Van Önöknél ...?	von eu·neuk·neyl ...
elevator	lift	lift
safe	széf	seyf

The room is too ...	Túl ...	tül ...
expensive	drága	dra·go
noisy	zajos	zo·yawsh
small	kicsi	ki·chi

The ... doesn't work.	A ... nem működik.	o ... nem *mēw*·keu·dik
air conditioning	légkondicionáló	*leyg*·kawn·di·tsi·aw·na·lāw
fan	ventilátor	*ven*·ti·la·tawr
toilet	vécé	*vey*·tsey

This ... isn't clean.	Ez a ... nem tiszta.	ez o ... nem *tis*·to
sheet	lepedő	*le*·pe·dēū
towel	törülköző	*teu*·rewl·keu·zēū

checking out

What time is checkout?
Mikor kell kijelentkezni?   *mi*·kawr kell *ki*·ye·lent·kez·ni

Can I leave my luggage here?
Itt hagyhatom a csomagjaimat?   itt *hoj*·ho·tawm o *chaw*·mog·yo·i·mot

Could I have my ..., please?	Visszakaphatnám ..., kérem?	*vis*·so·kop·hot·nam ... *key*·rem
deposit	a letétemet	o *le*·tey·te·met
passport	az útlevelemet	oz *üt*·le·ve·le·met
valuables	az értékeimet	oz *eyr*·tey·ke·i·met

communications & banking

the internet

Where's the local Internet café?
Hol van a legközelebbi internet kávézó?   hawl von o *leg*·keu·ze·leb·bi *in*·ter·net *ka*·vey·zāw

How much is it per hour?
Mennyibe kerül óránként?   *men*·nyi·be *ke*·rewl *āw*·ran·keynt

I'd like to check my email.
Szeretném megnézni az e-mailjeimet.   *se*·ret·neym *meg*·neyz·ni oz *ee*·meyl·ye·i·met

I'd like to ...	Szeretnék ...	*se*·ret·neyk ...
get Internet access	rámenni az internetre	*ra*·men·ni oz *in*·ter·net·re
use a printer	használni egy nyomtatót	*hos*·nal·ni ej *nyawm*·to·tāwt
use a scanner	használni egy szkennert	*hos*·nal·ni ej *sken*·nert

mobile/cell phone

I'd like a ...	*Szeretnék egy ...*	*se·ret·neyk ej ...*
mobile/cell phone	*mobiltelefont*	*maw·bil·te·le·fawnt*
for hire	*bérelni*	*bey·rel·ni*
SIM card	*SIM-kártyát*	*sim·kar·tyat*
for your network	*ennek a hálózatnak*	*en·nek o ha·lāw·zot·nok*
What are the rates?	*Milyen díjak vannak?*	*mi·yen dee·yok von·nok*

telephone

What's your phone number?
Mi a telefonszáma/   mi o *te*·le·*fawn*·sa·ma/
telefonszámod? pol/inf   *te*·le·fawn·sa·mawd

The number is ...
A szám ...   o sam ...

Where's the nearest public phone?
Hol a legközelebbi   hawl o *leg*·keu·ze·leb·bi
nyilvános telefon?   *nyil*·va·nawsh *te*·le·fawn

I'd like to buy a phonecard.
Szeretnék telefonkártyát venni.   se·ret·neyk *te*·le·fawn·kar·tyat *ven*·ni

I want to make a reverse-charge call.
'R' beszélgetést szeretnék kérni.   er·be·seyl·ge·teysht se·ret·neyk *keyr*·ni

I want to ...	*Szeretnék ...*	*se·ret·neyk ...*
call (Singapore)	*(Szingapúr)ba*	*(sin*·go·pūr)·bo
	telefonálni	*te*·le·faw·nal·ni
make a local call	*helyi telefon-*	*he*·yi *te*·le·fawn·
	beszélgetést	be·seyl·ge·teysht
	folytatni	*faw*·y·tot·ni
How much	*Mennyibe*	*men'*·nyi·be
does ... cost?	*kerül ...?*	*ke*·rewl ...
a (three)-minute	*egy (három)perces*	ej *(ha*·rawm)·per·tsesh
call	*beszélgetés*	be·seyl·ge·teysh
each extra minute	*minden további perc*	*min*·den *taw*·vab·bi perts

(30) forints per (30) seconds.
(Harminc) másodpercenként   *(hor*·mints) ma·shawd·per·tsen·keynt
(harminc) forint.   *(hor*·mints) *faw*·rint

252

post office

I want to send a ...	... szeretnék küldeni.	... se·ret·neyk kewl·de·ni
fax	Faxot	fok·sawt
letter	Levelet	le·ve·let
parcel	Csomagot	chaw·mo·gawt
postcard	Képeslapot	key·pesh·lo·pawt
I want to buy a/an ...	... szeretnék venni.	... se·ret·neyk ven·ni
envelope	Borítékot	baw·ree·tey·kawt
stamp	Bélyeget	bey·ye·get
Please send it to (Australia) by ...	Kérem, küldje ... (Ausztráliá)ba.	key·rem kewld·ye ... (o·ust·ra·li·a)·bo
airmail	légipostán	ley·gi·pawsh·tan
express mail	expresszel	eks·press·zel
registered mail	ajánlottan	o·yan·law·tton
surface mail	simán	shi·man
Is there any mail for me?	Van levelem?	von le·ve·lem

bank

Where's a/an ...?	Hol van egy ...?	hawl von ej ...
ATM	bankautomata	bonk·o·u·taw·mo·to
foreign exchange office	valutaváltó	vo·lu·to·val·taw
	ügynökség	ewj·neuk·sheyg
I'd like to ...	Szeretnék ...	se·ret·neyk ...
Where can I ...?	Hol tudok ...?	hawl tu·dawk ...
arrange a transfer	pénzt átutalni	peynzt at·u·tol·ni
cash a cheque	beváltani egy csekket	be·val·to·ni ej chek·ket
change a travellers cheque	beváltani egy utazási csekket	be·val·to·ni ej u·to·za·shi chek·ket
change money	pénzt váltani	peynzt val·to·ni
get a cash advance	készpénzelőleget felvenni	keys·peynz·e·leü·le·get fel·ven·ni
withdraw money	pénzt kivenni	peynzt ki·ven·ni

What's the ...?	Mennyi ...?	men'·nyi ...
charge for that	a díj	o dee·y
exchange rate	a valutaárfolyam	o vo·lu·to·ar·faw·yom

It's (100) euros.	(Száz) euró.	(saz) e·u·raw
It's (500) forints.	(Ötszáz) forint.	(eut·saz) faw·rint
It's free.	Ingyen van.	in·dyen von

What time does the bank open?
Mikor nyit a bank? — mi·kawr nyit o bonk

Has my money arrived yet?
Megérkezett már a pénzem? — meg·eyr·ke·zett mar o peyn·zem

sightseeing

getting in

What time does it open/close?
Mikor nyit/zár? — mi·kawr nyit/zar

What's the admission charge?
Mennyibe kerül a belépőjegy? — men'·nyi·be ke·rewl o be·ley·pēū·yej

Is there a discount for students/children?
Van kedvezmény diákok/ — von ked·vez·meyn' di·a·kawk/
gyerekek számára? — dye·re·kek sa·ma·ro

I'd like a ...	Szeretnék egy ...	se·ret·neyk ej ...
catalogue	katalógust	ko·to·lāw·gusht
guide	idegenvezetőt	i·de·gen·ve·ze·tēūt
local map	itteni térképet	it·te·ni teyr·key·pet

I'd like to see ...	Szeretnék látni ...	se·ret·neyk lat·ni ...
What's that?	Az mi?	oz mi
Can I take a photo?	Fényképezhetek?	feyn'·key·pez·he·tek

tours

When's the	Mikor van a	mi·kawr von o
next ...?	következő ...?	keu·vet·ke·zēū ...
day trip	egynapos kirándulás	ej·no·pawsh ki·ran·du·lash
tour	túra	tū·ro

sightseeing

castle	*vár*	var
cathedral	*székesegyház*	sey·kesh·ej·haz
church	*templom*	temp·lawm
main square	*fő tér*	fēū ter
monastery	*kolostor*	kaw·lawsh·tawr
monument	*emlékmű*	em·leyk·mēw
museum	*múzeum*	mū·ze·um
old city	*óváros*	āw·va·rawsh
palace	*palota*	po·law·to
ruins	*romok*	raw·mawk
stadium	*stadion*	shto·di·awn
statues	*szobrok*	saw·brawk

Is ... included?	*Benne van az árban ...?*	ben·ne von oz ar·bon ...
accommodation	*a szállás*	o sal·lash
the admission charge	*a belépőjegy*	o be·ley·pēū·yej
food	*az ennivaló*	oz en·ni·vo·lāw
transport	*a közlekedés*	o keuz·le·ke·deysh

How long is the tour?
Mennyi ideig tart a túra? men'·nyi i·de·ig tort o tū·ra

What time should we be back?
Mikorra érünk vissza? mi·kawr·ro ey·rewnk vis·so

shopping

enquiries

Where's a ...?	*Hol van egy ...?*	hawl von ej ...
bank	*bank*	bonk
bookshop	*könyvesbolt*	keun'·vesh·bawlt
camera shop	*fényképezőgép-bolt*	feyn'·key·pe·zēū·geyp·bawlt
department store	*áruház*	a·ru·haz
grocery store	*élelmiszerbolt*	ey·lel·mi·ser·bawlt
market	*piac*	pi·ots
newsagency	*újságárus*	ū·y·shag·a·rush
supermarket	*élelmiszeráruház*	ey·lel·mi·ser·a·ru·haz

Where can I buy (a padlock)?
Hol tudok venni (egy lakatot)? — hawl *tu*·dawk *ven*·ni (ej *lo*·ko·tawt)

I'm looking for ...
Keresem a ... — *ke*·re·shem o ...

Can I look at it?
Megnézhetem? — *meg*·neyz·he·tem

Do you have any others?
Van másmilyen is? — von *mash*·mi·yen ish

Does it have a guarantee?
Van rajta garancia? — von *ro*·y·to go·*ron*·tsi·o

Can I have it sent overseas?
El lehet küldetni külföldre? — el *le*·het *kewl*·det·ni *kewl*·feuld·re

Can I have my ... repaired?
Megjavíttathatnám itt ...? — *meg*·yo·veet·tot·hot·nam itt ...

It's faulty.
Hibás. — *hi*·bash

I'd like ..., please.	*..., kérem.*	*... key*·rem
a bag	*Kaphatnék egy zacskót*	*kop*·hot·neyk ej *zoch*·käwt
a refund	*Vissza szeretném*	*vis*·so se·*ret*·neym
	kapni a pénzemet	*kop*·ni o *peyn*·ze·met
to return this	*Szeretném*	se·*ret*·neym
	visszaadni ezt	*vis*·so·od·ni ezt

paying

How much is it?
Mennyibe kerül? — men'·nyi·be *ke*·rewl

Could you write down the price?
Le tudná írni az árat? — le *tud*·na *eer*·ni oz *a*·rot

That's too expensive.
Ez túl drága. — ez tül *dra*·go

Do you have something cheaper?
Van valami olcsóbb? — von *vo*·lo·mi *awl*·chāwbb

I'll give you (500 forints).
Adok Önnek (ötszáz forintot). — *o*·dawk *eun*·nek (*eut*·saz *faw*·rin·tawt)

There's a mistake in the bill.
Valami nem stimmel a számlával. — *vo*·lo·mi nem *shtim*·mel o *sam*·la·vol

Do you accept ...?	Elfogadnak ...?	el·faw·god·nok ...
credit cards	hitelkártyát	hi·tel·kar·tyat
debit cards	bankkártyát	bonk·kar·tyat
travellers cheques	utazási csekket	u·to·za·shi chek·ket

I'd like ..., please.	..., kérem.	... key·rem
a receipt	Kaphatnék egy nyugtát	kop·hot·neyk ej nyug·tat
my change	Szeretném megkapni	se·ret·neym meg·kop·ni
	a visszajáró pénzt	o vis·so·ya·rāw peynzt

clothes & shoes

Can I try it on?	Felpróbálhatom?	fel·prāw·bal·ho·tawm
My size is (40).	A méretem	o mey·re·tem
	(negyvenes).	(nej·ve·nesh)
It doesn't fit.	Nem jó.	nem yāw

small	kicsi	ki·chi
medium	közepes	keu·ze·pesh
large	nagy	noj

books & music

I'd like a ...	Szeretnék egy ...	se·ret·neyk ej ...
newspaper	(angol)	(on·gawl)
(in English)	újságot	ūy·sha·gawt
pen	tollat	tawl·lot

Is there an English-language bookshop?
| Van valahol egy angol | von vo·lo·hawl ej on·gawl |
| nyelvű könyvesbolt? | nyel·vēw keun·vesh·bawlt |

I'm looking for something by (Zsuzsa Koncz).
| (Koncz Zsuzsá)tól | (konts zhu·zha)·tāwl |
| keresek valamit. | ke·re·shek vo·lo·mit |

Can I listen to this?
| Meghallgathatom ezt? | meg·holl·got·ho·tawm ezt |

photography

Can you transfer photos from my camera to CD?
Át tudják vinni a képeket   at tud·yak vin·ni o key·pe·ket
a fényképezőgépemről CD-re?   o feyn'·key·pe·zēū·gey·pem·rēūl tsey·dey·re

Can you develop this film?
Elő tudják hívni ezt a filmet?   e·lēū tud·yak heev·ni ezt o fil·met

Can you load my film?
Bele tudják tenni a filmet   be·le tud·yak ten·ni o fil·met
a gépembe?   o gey·pem·be

I need a ... film for this camera.	... filmet szeretnék.	... fil·met se·ret·neyk
B&W	Fekete-fehér	fe·ke·te·fe·heyr
colour	Színes	see·nesh
slide	Dia	di·o
(200) speed	(Kétszáz)as	(keyt·saz)·osh
	fényérzékenységű	feyn'·eyr·zey·ken'·shey·gēw

When will it be ready?   *Mikor lesz kész?*   mi·kawr les keys

meeting people

greetings, goodbyes & introductions

Hello.	Szervusz/Szervusztok. sg/pl	ser·vus/ser·vus·tawk
Hi.	Szia/Sziasztok. sg/pl	si·o/si·os·tawk
Good night.	Jó éjszakát.	yāw ey·y·so·kat
Goodbye.	Viszlát.	vis·lat
Bye.	Szia/Sziasztok. sg/pl	si·o/si·os·tawk

Mr	Úr	ür
Mrs	Asszony	os·sawn'
Miss	Kisasszony	kish·os·sawn'

How are you?	Hogy van/vagy? pol/inf	hawj von/voj
Fine. And you?	Jól. És Ön/te? pol/inf	yāwl eysh eun/te
What's your name?	Mi a neve/neved? pol/inf	mi o ne·ve/ne·ved
My name is ...	A nevem ...	o ne·vem ...
I'm pleased to meet you.	Örvendek.	eur·ven·dek

This is my ...	*Ez ...*	ez ...
boyfriend	*a barátom*	o bo·ra·tawm
brother (older)	*a bátyám*	o ba·tyam
brother (younger)	*az öcsém*	oz eu·cheym
daughter	*a lányom*	o la·nyawm
father	*az apám*	oz o·pam
friend	*a barátom/barátnőm* m/f	o bo·ra·tawm/bo·rat·nēūm
girlfriend	*a barátnőm*	o bo·rat·nēūm
husband	*a férjem*	o feyr·yem
mother	*az anyám*	oz o·nyam
partner (intimate)	*a barátom/barátnőm* m/f	o bo·ra·tawm/bo·rat·nēūm
sister (older)	*a nővérem*	o nēū·vey·rem
sister (younger)	*a húgom*	o hū·gawm
son	*a fiam*	o fi·om
wife	*a feleségem*	o fe·le·shey·gem

Here's my ...	*Itt van ...*	itt von ...
address	*a címem*	o tsee·mem
email address	*az e-mail címem*	oz ee·meyl tsee·mem
fax number	*a faxszámom*	o foks·sa·mawm
phone number	*a telefonszámom*	o te·le·fawn·sa·mawm

What's your ...?	*Mi ...?*	mi ...
address	*a címe*	o tsee·me
email address	*az e-mail címe*	oz ee·meyl tsee·me
fax number	*a faxszáma*	o foks·sa·ma
phone number	*a telefonszáma*	o te·le·fawn·sa·ma

occupations

What's your occupation?	*Mi a foglalkozása/ foglalkozásod?* pol/inf	mi o fawg·lol·kaw·za·sho/ fawg·lol·kaw·za·shawd
I'm a/an ...	*... vagyok.*	... vo·dyawk
artist	*Művész*	mēw·veys
businessperson	*Üzletember* m	ewz·let·em·ber
	Üzletasszony f	ewz·let·os·sawn'
farmer	*Gazda*	goz·do
office worker	*Irodai dolgozó*	i·raw·do·i dawl·gaw·zāw
scientist	*Természettudós*	ter·mey·set·tu·dāwsh
student	*Diák*	di·ak
tradesperson	*Kereskedő*	ke·resh·ke·dēū

background

Where are you from?	*Ön honnan jön?* pol	eun *hawn*-non yeun
	Te honnan jössz? inf	te *hawn*-non yeuss
I'm from ...	*Én ... jövök.*	eyn ... *yeu*-veuk
Australia	*Ausztráliából*	o-ust-ra-li-a-bāwl
Canada	*Kanadából*	ko-no-da-bāwl
England	*Angliából*	ong-li-a-bāwl
New Zealand	*Új-Zélandból*	ū-y-zey-lond-bāwl
the USA	*USAból*	u-sho-bāwl
Are you married? m	*Nős?*	nēush
Are you married? f	*Férjnél van?*	feyr-y-neyl von
I'm ...	*... vagyok.*	... vo-dyawk
married	*Nős/Férjnél* m/f	nēush/feyr-y-neyl
single	*Egyedülálló*	e-dye-dewl-al-lāw

age

How old are you?	*Hány éves?* pol	han' ey-vesh
	Hány éves vagy? inf	han' ey-vesh voj
How old are your children?	*Hány évesek a gyerekei/gyerekeid?* pol/inf	han' ey-ve-shek o dye-re-ke-i/dye-re-ke-id
I'm ... years old.	*... éves vagyok.*	... ey-vesh vo-dyawk
He/She is ... years old.	*... éves.*	... ey-vesh

feelings

Are you ...?	*... vagy?*	... voj
happy	*Boldog*	bawl-dawg
hungry	*Éhes*	ey-hesh
sad	*Szomorú*	saw-maw-rū
thirsty	*Szomjas*	sawm-yosh
I'm ...	*... vagyok.*	... vo-dyawk
I'm not ...	*Nem vagyok ...*	nem vo-dyawk ...
happy	*boldog*	bawl-dawg
hungry	*éhes*	ey-hesh
sad	*szomorú*	saw-maw-rū
thirsty	*szomjas*	sawm-yosh

Are you cold?	Fázik/Fázol? pol/inf	fa·zik/fa·zawl
I'm (not) cold.	(Nem) Fázom.	(nem) fa·zawm
Are you hot?	Melege/Meleged van? pol/inf	me·le·ge/me·le·ged von
I'm hot.	Melegem van.	me·le·gem von
I'm not hot.	Nincs melegem.	ninch me·le·gem

entertainment

going out

Where can I find ...?	Hol találok ...?	hawl to·la·lawk ...
clubs	klubokat	klu·baw·kot
gay venues	meleg	me·leg
	szórakozóhelyeket	sāw·ro·kaw·zāw·he·ye·ket
pubs	pubokat	po·baw·kot

I feel like going	Szeretnék	se·ret·neyk
to a/the ...	elmenni egy ...	el·men·ni ej ...
concert	koncertre	kawn·tsert·re
movies	moziba	maw·zi·bo
party	partira	por·ti·ro
restaurant	étterembe	eyt·te·rem·be
theatre	színházba	seen·haz·bo

interests

Do you like ...?	Szereted ...?	se·re·ted ...
I (don't) like ...	(Nem) Szeretem ...	(nem) se·re·tem ...
art	a művészetet	o mēw·vey·se·tet
movies	a filmeket	o fil·me·ket
sport	a sportot	o shpawr·tawt

Do you like ...?	Szeretsz ...?	se·rets ...
I (don't) like ...	(Nem) Szeretek ...	(nem) se·re·tek ...
cooking	főzni	fēūz·ni
nightclubs	diszkóba járni	dis·kāw·bo yar·ni
reading	olvasni	awl·vosh·ni
shopping	vásárolni	va·sha·rawl·ni
travelling	utazni	u·toz·ni

Do you ...?		
dance	*Táncolsz?*	*tan*·tsawls
go to concerts	*Jársz koncertre?*	yars *kawn*-tsert·re
listen to music	*Hallgatsz zenét?*	*holl*·gots ze·neyt

food & drink

finding a place to eat

Can you recommend	*Tud/Tudsz ajánlani*	tud/tuds o·yan·lo·ni
a ...?	*egy ...?* pol/inf	ej ...
bar	*bárt*	bart
café	*kávézót*	ka·vey·zawt
restaurant	*éttermet*	eyt·ter·met
I'd like ...	*Szeretnék ...*	se·ret·neyk ...
a table for (five)	*egy asztalt (öt)*	ej os·tolt (eut)
	személyre	se·mey·re
the (non)smoking	*a (nem)dohányzó*	o (nem)·daw·han'·zāw
section	*részben ülni*	reys·ben ewl·ni

ordering food

breakfast	*reggeli*	*reg*·ge·li
lunch	*ebéd*	e·beyd
dinner	*vacsora*	*vo*·chaw·ro
snack	*snack*	snekk
today's special	*napi ajánlat*	*no*·pi oy·an·lot

How long is the wait?
Mennyi ideig kell várni?   men'·nyi i·de·ig kell *vaar*·ni

What would you recommend?
Mit ajánlana?   mit o·yan·lo·no

I'd like (the) ...	... *szeretném.*	... se·ret·neym
bill	*A számlát*	o *sam*·lat
drink list	*Az itallapot*	oz i·tol·lo·pawt
menu	*Az étlapot*	oz eyt·lo·pawt
that dish	*Azt az ételt*	ozt oz ey·telt

drinks

(cup of) coffee ...	(csésze) kávé ...	(chey·se) ka·vey ...
(cup of) tea ...	(csésze) tea ...	(chey·se) te·o ...
with milk	tejjel	ey·yel
without sugar	cukor nélkül	tsu·kawr neyl·kewl
... mineral water	... ásványvíz	... ash·van'·veez
sparkling	szénsavas	seyn·sho·vosh
still	szénsavmentes	seyn·shov·men·tesh
orange juice	narancslé	no·ronch·ley
soft drink	üdítőital	ew·dee·tēū·i·tal
(boiled) water	(forralt) víz	(fawr·rolt) veez

in the bar

I'll have ...	... kérek.	... key·rek
I'll buy you a drink.	Fizetek neked egy italt.	fi·ze·tek ne·ked ej i·tolt
What would you like?	Mit kérsz?	mit keyrs
Cheers! (to one person)	Egészségedre!	e·geys·shey·ged·re
Cheers! (to more than one person)	Egészségetekre!	e·geys·shey·ge·tek·re
brandy	brandy	bren·di
champagne	pezsgő	pezh·gēū
cocktail	koktél	kawk·teyl
a bottle/glass of (beer)	egy üveg/pohár (sör)	ej ew·veg/paw·har (sheur)
a shot of (whisky)	egy kupica (whisky)	ej ku·pi·tso (vis·ki)
a bottle/glass of ... wine	egy üveg/pohár ... bor	ej ew·veg/paw·har ... bawr
red	vörös	veu·reush
sparkling	pezsgő	pezh·gēū
white	fehér	fe·heyr

self-catering

What's the local speciality?
Mi az itteni specialitás?   mi oz *it*·te·ni *shpe*·tsi·o·li·tash

What's that?
Az mi?   oz mi

How much is (a kilo of cheese)?
Mennyibe kerül (egy kiló sajt)?   men'·nyi·be ke·rewl (ej *ki*·läw shoyt)

I'd like ...	*Kérek ...*	*key*·rek ...
200 grams	*húsz dekát*	hüs *de*·kat
a kilo	*egy kilót*	ej *ki*·läwt
a piece	*egy darabot*	ej *do*·ro·bawt
a slice	*egy szeletet*	ej *se*·le·tet

Less.	*Kevésbé.*	ke·veysh·bey
Enough.	*Elég.*	e·leyg
More.	*Több.*	teubb

special diets & allergies

Is there a vegetarian restaurant near here?
Van a közelben   von o *keu*·zel·ben
vegetáriánus étterem?   ve·ge·ta·ri·a·nush *eyt*·te·rem

Do you have vegetarian food?
Vannak Önöknél   von·nok *eu*·neuk·neyl
vegetáriánus ételek?   ve·ge·ta·ri·a·nush *ey*·te·lek

Could you prepare	*Tudna készíteni*	tud·no *key*·see·te·ni
a meal without ...?	*egy ételt ... nélkül?*	ej *ey*·telt ... *neyl*·kewl
butter	*vaj*	vo·y
eggs	*tojás*	*taw*·yash
meat stock	*húsleveskocka*	*hüsh*·le·vesh·kawts·ko

I'm allergic to ...	*Allergiás vagyok a ...*	*ol*·ler·gi·ash *vo*·dyawk o ...
dairy produce	*tejtermékekre*	*te*·y·ter·mey·kek·re
gluten	*sikérre*	*shi*·keyr·re
MSG	*monoszódium*	*maw*·naw·säw·di·um
	glutamátra	*glu*·to·mat·ro
nuts	*diófélékre*	*di*·äw·fey·leyk·re
seafood	*tenger gyümölcseire*	*ten*·ger *yew*·meul·che·i·re

emergencies

basics

Help!	Segítség!	*she*·geet·sheyg
Stop!	Álljon meg!	*all*·yawn meg
Go away!	Menjen innen!	*men*·yen *in*·nen
Thief!	Tolvaj!	*tawl*·voy
Fire!	Tűz!	tēwz
Watch out!	Vigyázzon!	*vi*·dyaz·zawn

Call a doctor!	Hívjon orvost!	*heev*·yawn *awr*·vawsht
Call an ambulance!	Hívja a mentőket!	*heev*·yo o men·tēū·ket
Call the police!	Hívja a rendőrséget!	*heev*·yo o rend·ēūr·shey·get

It's an emergency!
Sürgős esetről van szó.   *shewr*·gēūsh *e*·shet·rēūl von sāw

Could you help me, please?
Tudna segíteni?   *tud*·no she·gee·te·ni

Can I use your phone?
Használhatom a telefonját?   *hos*·nal·ho·tawm o *te*·le·fawn·yat

I'm lost.
Eltévedtem.   *el*·tey·ved·tem

Where are the toilets?
Hol a vécé?   hawl o *vey*·tsey

police

Where's the police station?
Hol a rendőrség?   hawl o rend·ēūr·sheyg

I want to report an offence.
Bűncselekményt szeretnék   *bēwn*·che·lek·meynyt se·ret·neyk
bejelenteni.   be·ye·len·te·ni

I have insurance.
Van biztosításom.   von *biz*·taw·shee·ta·shawm

I've been ...

assaulted	Megtámadtak.	*meg*·ta·mod·tok
raped	Megerőszakoltak.	*meg*·e·rēū·so·kawl·tok
robbed	Kiraboltak.	*ki*·ro·bawl·tok

I've lost my ...	Elvesztettem ...	el·ves·tet·tem ...
My ... was/were stolen.	Ellopták ...	el·lawp·tak ...
backpack	a hátizsákomat	o ha·ti·zha·kaw·mot
bags	a csomagjaimat	o chaw·mog·yo·i·mot
credit card	a hitelkártyámat	o hi·tel·kar·tya·mot
handbag	a kézitáskámat	o key·zi·tash·ka·mot
jewellery	az ékszereimet	oz eyk·se·re·i·met
money	a pénzemet	o peyn·ze·met
passport	az útlevelemet	oz üt·le·ve·le·met
travellers cheques	az utazási csekkjeimet	oz u·to·za·shi chekk·ye·i·met
wallet	a tárcámat	o tar·tsa·mot

I want to contact my embassy/consulate.
Kapcsolatba akarok lépni a követségemmel/ konzulátusommal.
kop·chaw·lot·bo o·ko·rawk leyp·ni o keu·vet·shey·gem·mel/ kawn·zu·la·tu·shawm·mol

health

medical needs

Where's the nearest ...?	Hol a legközelebbi ...?	hawl o leg·keu·ze·leb·bi ...
dentist	fogorvos	fawg·awr·vawsh
doctor	orvos	awr·vawsh
hospital	kórház	kāwr·haz
(night) pharmacist	(éjszaka nyitvatartó) gyógyszertár	(ey·so·ko nyit·vo·tor·tāw) dyāwj·ser·tar

I need a doctor (who speaks English).
(Angolul beszélő) Orvosra van szükségem.
(on·gaw·lul be·sey·lēü) awr·vawsh·ro von sewk·shey·gem

Could I see a female doctor?
Beszélhetnék egy orvosnővel?
be·seyl·het·neyk ej awr·vawsh·nēü·vel

I've run out of my medication.
Elfogyott az orvosságom.
el·faw·dyawtt oz awr·vawsh·sha·gawm

symptoms, conditions & allergies

| I'm sick. | Rosszul vagyok. | raws·sul vo·dyawk |
| It hurts here. | Itt fáj. | itt fa·y |

I have a ...

cough	Köhögök.	keu·heu·geuk
headache	Fáj a fejem.	fa·y o fe·yem
sore throat	Fáj o torkom.	fa·y o tawr·kawm
toothache	Fáj a fogam.	fa·y o faw·gom

I have (a) ... | ... van. | ... von |

asthma	Asztmám	ost·mam
bronchitis	Hörghurutom	heurg·hu·rut·awm
constipation	Székrekedésem	seyk·re·ke·dey·shem
diarrhoea	Hasmenésem	hosh·me·ney·shem
fever	Lázam	la·zom
heart condition	Szívbetegségem	seev·be·teg·sheyg·em
nausea	Hányingerem	han'·in·ge·rem
pain	Fájdalmam	fay·dol·mom

I'm allergic to ... | Allergiás vagyok ... | ol·ler·gi·ash vo·dyawk ... |

antibiotics	az antibiotikumokra	oz on·ti·bi·aw·ti·ku·mawk·ro
anti-inflammatories	a gyulladásgátlókra	o dyul·lo·dash·gat·lawk·ro
aspirin	az aszpirinre	oz os·pi·rin·re
bees	a méhekre	o mey·hek·re
codeine	a kodeinre	o ko·de·in·re
penicillin	a penicillinre	o pe·ni·tsil·lin·re

antiseptic n	fertőzésgátló	fer·tēū·zeysh·gat·law
bandage	kötés	keu·teysh
condoms	óvszer	āwv·ser
contraceptives	fogamzásgátló	faw·gom·zash·gat·law
diarrhoea medicine	hasmenés gyógyszer	hosh·men·eysh dyãwd'·ser
insect repellent	rovarirtó	raw·vor·ir·tāw
laxatives	hashajtó	hosh·ho·y·tāw
painkillers	fájdalomcsillapító	fa·y·do·lawm·chil·lo·pee·tāw
rehydration salts	folyadékpótló sók	faw·yo·deyk·pāwt·law shāwk
sleeping tablets	altató	ol·to·tāw

english–hungarian dictionary

In this dictionary, words are marked as n (noun), a (adjective), v (verb), sg (singular), pl (plural), inf (informal) or pol (polite) where necessary.

A

accident *baleset* bol-e-shet
accommodation *szállás* sal-lash
adaptor *adapter* o-dop-ter
address n *cím* tseem
after *után* u-tan
air-conditioned *légkondicionált*
  leyg-kawn-di-tsi-aw-nalt
airplane *repülőgép* re-pew-leü-geyp
airport *repülőtér* re-pew-leü-teyr
alcohol *alkohol* ol-kaw-hawl
all *minden* min-den
allergy *allergia* ol-ler-gi-o
ambulance *mentő* men-teü
and *és* eysh
ankle *boka* baw-ko
arm *kar* kor
ashtray *hamutartó* ho-mu-tor-tāw
ATM *bankautomata* bonk-o-u-taw-mo-to

B

baby *baba* bo-bo
back (body) *hát* hat
backpack *hátizsák* ha-ti-zhak
bad *rossz* rawss
bag *táska* tash-ko
baggage claim *poggyászkiadó* pawd'-dyas-ki-o-dāw
bank *bank* bonk
bar *bár* bar
bathroom *fürdőszoba* fewr-dēü-saw-bo
battery *elem* e-lem
beautiful *szép* seyp
bed *ágy* aj
beer *sör* sheur
before *előtt* e-lēütt
behind *mögött* meu-geutt
bicycle *bicikli* bi-tsik-li
big *nagy* noj
bill *számla* sam-lo
black *fekete* fe-ke-te

blanket *takaró* to-ko-rāw
blood group *vércsoport* veyr-chaw-pawrt
blue *kék* keyk
boat (big) *hajó* ho-yāw
boat (small) *csónak* chāw-nok
book (make a reservation) v *lefoglal* le-fawg-lol
bottle *üveg* ew-veg
bottle opener *sörnyitó* sheur-nyi-tāw
boy *fiú* fi-ū
brake (car) *fék* feyk
breakfast *reggeli* reg-ge-li
broken (faulty) *hibás* hi-bash
bus *busz* bus
business *üzlet* ewz-let
buy *vesz* ves

C

café *kávézó* ka-vey-zāw
camera *fényképezőgép* feyn'-key-pe-zēü-geyp
camp site *táborhely* ta-bawr-he-y
cancel *töröl* teu-reul
can opener *konzervnyitó* kawn-zerv-nyi-tāw
car *autó* o-u-tāw
cash n *készpénz* keys-peynz
cash (a cheque) v *bevált csekket* be-valt chek-ket
cell phone *mobil telefon* maw-bil te-le-fawn
centre n *központ* keuz-pawnt
change (money) v *pénzt vált* peynzt valt
cheap *olcsó* awl-chāw
check (bill) *számla* sam-lo
check-in n *bejelentkezés* be-ye-lent-ke-zeysh
chest *mellkas* mell-kosh
child *gyerek* dye-rek
cigarette *cigaretta* tsi-go-ret-to
city *város* va-rawsh
clean a *tiszta* tis-to
closed *zárva* zar-vo
coffee *kávé* ka-vey
coins *pénzérmék* peynz-eyr-meyk
cold a *hideg* hi-deg
collect call *'R' beszélgetés* er-be-seyl-ge-teysh
come *jön* yeun

computer *számítógép* sa-mee-tāw-geyp
condom *óvszer* āwv-ser
contact lenses *kontaktlencse* kawn-tokt-len-che
cook v *főz* fēūz
cost n *ár* ar
credit card *hitelkártya* hi-tel-kar-tyo
cup *csésze* chey-se
currency exchange *valutaátváltás* vo-lu-to-at-val-tash
customs (immigration) *vám* vam

D

dangerous *veszélyes* ve-sey-yesh
date (time) *dátum* da-tum
day *nap* nop
delay n *késés* key-sheysh
dentist *fogorvos* fawg-awr-vawsh
depart *elutazik* el-u-to-zik
diaper *pelenka* pe-len-ko
dictionary *szótár* sāw-tar
dinner *vacsora* vo-chaw-ro
direct *közvetlen* keuz-vet-len
dirty *piszkos* pis-kawsh
disabled *mozgássérült* mawz-gash-shey-rewlt
discount n *árengedmény* ar-en-ged-meyn'
doctor *orvos* awr-vawsh
double bed *dupla ágy* dup-lo aj
double room *dupladgyas szoba* dup-lo-a-dyosh saw-bo
drink n *ital* i-tol
drive v *vezet* ve-zet
drivers licence *jogosítvány* yaw-gaw-sheet-van'
drug (illicit) *kábítószerek* ka-bee-tāw-se-rek
dummy (pacifier) *cumi* tsu-mi

E

ear *fül* fewl
east *kelet* ke-let
eat *eszik* e-sik
economy class *turistaosztály* tu-rish-to-aws-ta-y
electricity *villany* vil-lon'
elevator *lift* lift
email *e-mail* ee-meyl
embassy *nagykövetség* noj-keu-vet-sheyg
emergency *vészhelyzet* veys-he-y-zet
English (language) *angol* on-gawl
entrance *bejárat* be-ya-rot
evening *este* esh-te
exchange rate *átváltási árfolyam* at-val-ta-shi ar-faw-yom

exit n *kijárat* ki-ya-rot
expensive *drága* dra-go
express mail *expressz posta* eks-press pawsh-to
eye *szem* sem

F

far *messze* mes-se
fast *gyors* dyawrsh
father *apa* o-po
film (camera) *film* film
finger *ujj* u-y
first-aid kit *elsősegély-láda* el-shēū-she-gey-la-do
first class *első osztály* el-shēū aws-ta-y
fish n *hal* hol
food *ennivaló* en-ni-vo-lāw
foot *lábfej* lab-fe-y
fork *villa* vil-lo
free (of charge) *ingyenes* in-dye-nesh
friend (female) *barátnő* bo-rat-nēū
friend (male) *barát* bo-rat
fruit *gyümölcs* dyew-meulch
full *tele* te-le
funny *mulatságos* mu-lot-sha-gawsh

G

gift *ajándék* o-yan-deyk
girl *lány* lan'
glass (drinking) *üveg* ew-veg
glasses *szemüveg* sem-ew-veg
go *megy* mej
good *jó* yāw
green *zöld* zeuld
guide n *idegenvezető* i-de-gen-ve-ze-tēū

H

half n *fél* feyl
hand *kéz* keyz
handbag *kézitáska* key-zi-tash-ko
happy *boldog* bawl-dawg
have *van neki* von ne-ki
he *ő* ēū
head *fej* fe-y
heart *szív* seev
heat n *forróság* fawr-rāw-shag
heavy *nehéz* ne-heyz
help v *segít* she-geet
here *itt* itt

high *magas* mo-gosh
highway *országút* awr-sag-üt
hike v *kirándul* ki-ran-dul
holiday *szabadság* so-bod-shag
homosexual n *homoszexuális* haw-maw-sek-su-a-lish
hospital *kórház* kawr-haz
hot *forró* fawr-rāw
hotel *szálloda* sal-law-do
Hungarian (language) *magyar* mo-dyor
Hungary *Magyarország* mo-dyor-awr-sag
hungry *éhes* ey-hesh
husband *férj* feyr-y

I

I *én* eyn
identification (card) *személyi igazolvány*
    se-mey-yi i-go-zawl-van'
ill *beteg* be-teg
important *fontos* fawn-tawsh
included *beleértve* be-le-eyrt-ve
injury *sérülés* shey-rew-leysh
insurance *biztosítás* biz-taw-shee-tash
Internet *Internet* in-ter-net
interpreter *tolmács* tawl-mach

J

jewellery *ékszerek* eyk-se-rek
job *állás* al-lash

K

key *kulcs* kulch
kilogram *kilogramm* ki-lāw-gromm
kitchen *konyha* kawn'-ho
knife *kés* keysh

L

laundry (place) *mosoda* maw-shaw-do
lawyer *jogász* yaw-gas
left (direction) *balra* bol-ro
left-luggage office *csomagmegőrző*
    chaw-mog-meg-ēūr-zēū
leg *láb* lab
lesbian n *leszbikus* les-bi-kush
less *kevésbé* ke-veysh-bey
letter (mail) *levél* le-veyl
lift (elevator) *lift* lift

light n *fény* feyn'
like v *szeret* se-ret
lock n *zár* zar
long *hosszú* haws-sü
lost *elveszett* el-ve-sett
lost-property office *talált tárgyak hivatala*
    to-lalt tar-dyok hi-vo-to-lo
love v *szeret* se-ret
luggage *poggyász* pawd'-dyas
lunch *ebéd* e-beyd

M

mail n *posta* pawsh-to
man *férfi* feyr-fi
map *térkép* teyr-keyp
market *piac* pi-ots
matches *gyufa* dyu-fo
meat *hús* hüsh
medicine *orvosság* awr-vawsh-shag
menu *étlap* eyt-lop
message *üzenet* ew-ze-net
milk *tej* te-y
minute *perc* perts
mobile phone *mobil telefon* maw-bil te-le-fawn
money *pénz* peynz
month *hónap* hāw-nop
morning *reggel* reg-gel
mother *anya* o-nyo
motorcycle *motorbicikli* maw-tawr-bi-tsik-li
motorway *autópálya* o-u-tāw-pa-yo
mouth *száj* sa-y
music *zene* ze-ne

N

name *keresztnév* ke-rest-neyv
napkin *szalvéta* sol-vey-to
nappy *pelenka* pe-len-ko
near *közelében* keu-ze-ley-ben
neck *nyak* nyok
new *új* ü-y
news *hírek* hee-rek
newspaper *újság* ü-y-shag
night *éjszaka* ey-so-ko
no *nem* nem
noisy *zajos* zo-yawsh
nonsmoking *nemdohányzó* nem-daw-han'-zāw
north *észak* ey-sok
nose *orr* awrr
now *most* mawsht
number *szám* sam

O

oil (engine) *olaj* aw-lo-y
old (person/thing) *öreg/régi* eu-reg/rey-gi
one-way ticket *csak oda jegy* chok aw-do yej
open a *nyitva* nyit-vo
outside *kint* kint

P

package *csomag* chaw-mog
paper *papír* po-peer
park (a car) v *parkol* por-kawl
passport *útlevél* üt-le-veyl
pay *fizet* fi-zet
pen *golyóstoll* gaw-yäwsh-tawll
petrol *benzin* ben-zin
pharmacy *gyógyszertár* dyäwj-ser-tar
phonecard *telefonkártya* te-le-fawn-kar-tyo
photo *fénykép* feyn'-keyp
plate *tányér* ta-nyeyr
police *rendőrség* rend-ëür-sheyg
postcard *levelezőlap* le-ve-le-zëü-lop
post office *postahivatal* pawsh-to-hi-vo-tol
pregnant *terhes* ter-hesh
price *ár* ar

Q

quiet *csendes* chen-desh

R

rain n *eső* e-shëü
razor *borotva* baw-rawt-vo
receipt n *nyugta* nyug-to
red *piros* pi-rawsh
refund n *visszatérítés* vis-so-tey-ree-teysh
registered mail *ajánlott levél* o-yan-lawtt le-veyl
rent v *bérel* bey-rel
repair v *megjavít* meg-yo-veet
reservation *foglalás* fawg-lo-lash
restaurant *étterem* eyt-te-rem
return v *visszatér* vis-so-teyr
return ticket *oda-vissza jegy* aw-do-vis-so yej
right (direction) *jobbra* yawbb-ro
road *út* üt
room *szoba* saw-bo

S

safe a *biztonságos* biz-tawn-sha-gawsh
sanitary napkin *egészségügyi törlőkendő* e-geys-sheyg-ew-dyi teur-lëü-ken-dëü
seat *ülés* ew-leysh
send *küld* kewld
service station *benzinkút* ben-zin-küt
sex *szex* seks
shampoo *sampon* shom-pawn
share (a dorm) *ben/ban lakik* -ben/-ban lo-kik
shaving cream *borotvakrém* baw-rawt-vo-kreym
she *ő* ëü
sheet (bed) *lepedő* le-pe-dëü
shirt *ing* ing
shoes *cipők* tsi-pëük
shop n *üzlet* ewz-let
short *alacsony* o-lo-chawn'
shower *zuhany* zu-hon'
single room *egyágyas szoba* ej-a-dyosh saw-bo
skin *bőr* bëür
skirt *szoknya* sawk-nyo
sleep v *alszik* ol-sik
slowly *lassan* losh-shon
small *kicsi* ki-chi
smoke (cigarettes) v *dohányzik* daw-han'-zik
soap *szappan* sop-pon
some *néhány* ney-han'
soon *hamarosan* ho-mo-raw-shon
south *dél* deyl
souvenir shop *ajándékbolt* o-yan-deyk-bawlt
speak *beszél* be-seyl
spoon *kanál* ko-nal
stamp n *bélyeg* bey-yeg
stand-by ticket *készenléti jegy* key-sen-ley-ti yej
station (train) *állomás* al-law-mash
stomach *gyomor* dyaw-mawr
stop v *abbahagy* ob-bo-hoj
stop (bus) n *megálló* meg-al-läw
street *utca* ut-tso
student *diák* di-ak
sun *nap* nop
sunscreen *napolaj* nop-aw-lo-y
swim v *úszik* ü-sik

T

tampons *tampon* tom-pawn
taxi *taxi* tok-si
teaspoon *teáskanál* te-ash-ko-nal
teeth *fogak* faw-gok
telephone n *telefon* te-le-fawn

television *televízió* te-le-vee-zi-äw
temperature (weather) *hőmérséklet*
  hēü-meyr-sheyk-let
tent *sátor* sha-tawr
that (one) *az* oz
they *ők* ëük
thirsty *szomjas* sawm-yosh
this (one) *ez* ez
throat *torok* taw-rawk
ticket *jegy* yej
time *idő* i-dēü
tired *fáradt* fa-rott
tissues *szövetek* seu-ve-tek
today *ma* mo
toilet *vécé* vey-tsey
tomorrow *holnap* hawl-nop
tonight *ma este* mo esh-te
toothbrush *fogkefe* fawg-ke-fe
toothpaste *fogkrém* fawg-kreym
torch (flashlight) *zseblámpa* zheb-lam-po
tour n *túra* tū-ro
tourist office *turistairoda* tu-rish-to-i-raw-do
towel *törülköző* teu-rewl-keu-zēü
train *vonat* vaw-not
translate *fordít* fawr-deet
travel agency *utazási iroda* u-to-za-shi i-raw-do
travellers cheque *utazási csekk* u-to-za-shi chekk
trousers *nadrág* nod-rag
twin beds *két ágy* keyt aj
tyre *autógumi* o-u-tāw-gu-mi

U

underwear *alsónemű* ol-shāw-ne-mēw
urgent *sürgős* shewr-gēüsh

V

vacant *üres* ew-resh
vacation *vakáció* vo-ka-tsi-āw

vegetable n *zöldség* zeuld-sheyg
vegetarian a *vegetáriánus* ve-ge-ta-ri-a-nush
visa *vízum* vee-zum

W

waiter *pincér* pin-tseyr
walk v *sétál* shey-tal
wallet *tárcá* tar-tsa-mot
warm a *meleg* me-leg
wash (something) *megmos* meg-mawsh
watch n *óra* āw-ro
water *víz* veez
we *mi* mi
weekend *hétvége* heyt-vey-ge
west *nyugat* nyu-got
wheelchair *rokkantkocsi* rawk-kont-kaw-chi
when *mikor* mi-kawr
where *hol* hawl
white *fehér* fe-heyr
who *ki* ki
why *miért* mi-eyrt
wife *feleség* fe-le-sheyg
window *ablak* ob-lok
wine *bor* bawr
with *-val/-vel* -vol/-vel
without *nélkül* neyl-kewl
woman *nő* nēü
write *ír* eer

Y

yellow *sárga* shar-go
yes *igen* i-gen
yesterday *tegnap* teg-nop
you sg inf *te* te
you pl inf *ti* ti
you sg pol *Ön* eun
you pl pol *Önök* eu-neuk

Italian

italian alphabet

A a a	*B b* bee	*C c* chee	*D d* dee	*E e* e
F f e·fe	*G g* jee	*H h* a·ka	*I i* ee	*L l* e·le
M m e·me	*N n* e·ne	*O o* o	*P p* pee	*Q q* koo
R r e·re	*S s* e·se	*T t* tee	*U u* oo	*V v* voo
Z z tse·ta				

italian

ITALIANO

ITALIAN
italiano

about Italian

All you need for *la dolce vita* is to be able to tell your *Moschino* from your *macchiato* and your *Fellini* from your *fettuccine*. Happily, you'll find Italian (*italiano* ee·ta·*lya*·no) an easy language to start speaking as well as a beautiful one to listen to. When even a simple sentence sounds like an aria it can be difficult to resist striking up a conversation – and thanks to widespread migration and the huge popularity of Italian culture and cuisine, you're probably familiar with words like *ciao*, *pasta* and *bella* already.

There are also many similarities between Italian and English which smooth the way for language learners. Italian is a Romance language – a descendent of Latin, the language of the Romans (as are French, Spanish, Portuguese and Romanian), and English has been heavily influenced by Latin, particularly via contact with French.

Up until the 19th century, Italy was a collection of autonomous states, rather than a nation-state. As a result, Italian has many regional dialects, including Sardinian and Sicilian. Some dialects are so different from standard Italian as to be considered distinct languages in their own right. It wasn't until the 19th century that the Tuscan dialect – the language of Dante, Boccaccio and Petrarch – became the standard language of the nation, and the official language of schools, media and administration. 'Standard Italian' is the variety that will take you from the top of the boot to the very toe – all the language in this phrasebook is in standard Italian.

The majority of the approximately 65 million people who speak Italian live, of course, in Italy. However, the language also has official status in San Marino, Vatican City, parts of Switzerland, Slovenia and the Istrian peninsula of Croatia. Italian was the official language of Malta during the period of the Knights of St John (1530–1798) and afterwards shared that status with English during the British rule. Only in 1934 was Italian withdrawn and substituted with the native Maltese language. Today, Maltese people are generally fluent in Italian. It might surprise you to learn that Italian is also spoken in the African nation of Eritrea, which was a colony of Italy from 1880 until 1941. Most Eritreans nowadays speak Italian only as a second language. Italian is widely used in Albania, Monaco and France, and spoken by large communities of immigrants worldwide. This chapter is designed to help you on your adventures in the Italian-speaking world – so, as the Italians would say, *In bocca al lupo!* een bo·ka·*loo*·po (lit: in the mouth of the wolf) – good luck!

about ITALIAN

275

pronunciation

vowel sounds

Italian vowel sounds are generally shorter than those in English. They also tend not to run together to form vowel sound combinations (diphthongs), though it can often sound as if they do to English speakers.

symbol	english equivalent	italian example	transliteration
a	father	*pane*	*pa*·ne
ai	aisle	*mai*	mai
ay	say	*vorrei*	vo·*ray*
e	bet	*letto*	*le*·to
ee	see	*vino*	vee·no
o	pot	*molo*	*mo*·lo
oo	zoo	*frutta*	*froo*·ta
oy	toy	*poi*	poy
ow	how	*ciao, autobus*	chow, *ow*·to·boos

word stress

In Italian, you generally emphasise the second-last syllable of a word. When a written word has an accent marked on a vowel, though, the stress is on that syllable. The stressed syllable is always italicised in our pronunciation guides. The characteristic sing-song quality of an Italian sentence is created by pronouncing the syllables evenly and rhythmically, then swinging down on the last word.

consonant sounds

In addition to the sounds described on the next page, Italian consonants can also have a stronger, more emphatic pronunciation. The actual sounds are basically the same, though meaning can be altered between a normal consonant sound and this double consonant sound. The phonetic guides in this book don't distinguish between the two forms. Refer to the written Italian beside each phonetic guide as the cue –

if the word is written with a double consonant, use the stronger form. Even if you never distinguish them, you'll always be understood in context. Here are some examples where this 'double consonant' effect can make a difference:

| *sonno* | *son*·no | **sleep** | *sono* | *so*·no | **I am** |
| *pappa* | *pap*·pa | **baby food** | *papa* | *pa*·pa | **pope** |

symbol	english equivalent	italian example	transliteration
b	**bed**	*bello*	*be*·lo
ch	**cheat**	*centro*	*chen*·tro
d	**dog**	*denaro*	*de·na·ro*
dz	**adds**	*mezzo, zaino*	*me*·dzo, *dzai*·no
f	**fat**	*fare*	*fa*·re
g	**go**	*gomma*	*go*·ma
j	**joke**	*cugino*	ku·*jee*·no
k	**kit**	*cambio, quanto*	*kam*·byo, *kwan*·to
l	**lot**	*linea*	*lee*·ne·a
ly	**million**	*figlia*	*fee*·**lya**
m	**man**	*madre*	*ma*·dre
n	**not**	*numero*	*noo*·me·ro
ny	**canyon**	*bagno*	*ba*·nyo
p	**pet**	*pronto*	*pron*·to
r	**red** (stronger and rolled)	*ristorante*	ree·sto·*ran*·te
s	**sun**	*sera*	*se*·ra
sh	**shot**	*sciare*	*shya*·re
t	**top**	*teatro*	te·*a*·tro
ts	**hits**	*grazie, sicurezza*	*gra*·tsye, see·koo·*re*·tsa
v	**very**	*viaggio*	*vya*·jo
w	**win**	*uomo*	*wo*·mo
y	**yes**	*italiano*	ee·ta·*lya*·no
z	**zero**	*casa*	*ka*·za

tools

language difficulties

Do you speak English?
Parla inglese?   *par*·la een·*gle*·ze

Do you understand?
Capisce?   ka·*pee*·she

I (don't) understand.
(Non) capisco.   (non) ka·*pee*·sko

What does (*giorno*) mean?
Che cosa vuol dire (giorno)?   ke *ko*·za vwol *dee*·re (*jor*·no)

How do you ...?	*Come si ...?*	*ko*·me see ...
pronounce this	*pronuncia questo*	pro·*noon*·cha *kwe*·sto
write (*arrivederci*)	*scrive (arrivederci)*	*skree*·ve (a·ree·ve·*der*·chee)

Could you please ...?	*Può ... per favore?*	pwo ... per fa·*vo*·re
repeat that	*ripeterlo*	ree·*pe*·ter·lo
speak more	*parlare più*	par·*la*·re pyoo
slowly	*lentamente*	len·ta·*men*·te
write it down	*scriverlo*	*skree*·ver·lo

essentials

Yes.	*Sì.*	see
No.	*No.*	no
Please.	*Per favore.*	per fa·*vo*·re
Thank you (very much).	*Grazie (mille).*	*gra*·tsye (*mee*·le)
You're welcome.	*Prego.*	*pre*·go
Excuse me.	*Mi scusi.* pol	mee *skoo*·zee
	Scusami. inf	*skoo*·za·mee
Sorry.	*Mi dispiace.*	mee dees·*pya*·che

numbers

0	zero	dze·ro	16	sedici	se·dee·chee	
1	uno	oo·no	17	diciassette	dee·cha·se·te	
2	due	doo·e	18	diciotto	dee·cho·to	
3	tre	tre	19	diciannove	dee·cha·no·ve	
4	quattro	kwa·tro	20	venti	ven·tee	
5	cinque	cheen·kwe	21	ventuno	ven·too·no	
6	sei	say	22	ventidue	ven·tee·doo·e	
7	sette	se·te	30	trenta	tren·ta	
8	otto	o·to	40	quaranta	kwa·ran·ta	
9	nove	no·ve	50	cinquanta	cheen·kwan·ta	
10	dieci	dye·chee	60	sessanta	se·san·ta	
11	undici	oon·dee·chee	70	settanta	se·tan·ta	
12	dodici	do·dee·chee	80	ottanta	o·tan·ta	
13	tredici	tre·dee·chee	90	novanta	no·van·ta	
14	quattordici	kwa·tor·dee·chee	100	cento	chen·to	
15	quindici	kween·dee·chee	1000	mille	mee·le	

time & dates

What time is it?	Che ora è?	ke o·ra e
It's one o'clock.	È l'una.	e loo·na
It's (two) o'clock.	Sono le (due).	so·no le (doo·e)
Quarter past (one).	(L'una) e un quarto.	(loo·na) e oon kwar·to
Half past (one).	(L'una) e mezza.	(loo·na) e me·dza
Quarter to (eight).	(Le otto) meno un quarto.	(le o·to) me·no oon kwar·to
At what time ...?	A che ora ...?	a ke o·ra ...
At ...	Alle ...	a·le ...
am	di mattina	dee ma·tee·na
pm	di pomeriggio	dee po·me·ree·jo
Monday	lunedì	loo·ne·dee
Tuesday	martedì	mar·te·dee
Wednesday	mercoledì	mer·ko·le·dee
Thursday	giovedì	jo·ve·dee
Friday	venerdì	ve·ner·dee
Saturday	sabato	sa·ba·to
Sunday	domenica	do·me·nee·ka

January	*gennaio*	je·*na*·yo
February	*febbraio*	fe·*bra*·yo
March	*marzo*	*mar*·tso
April	*aprile*	a·*pree*·le
May	*maggio*	*ma*·jo
June	*giugno*	*joo*·nyo
July	*luglio*	*loo*·lyo
August	*agosto*	a·*gos*·to
September	*settembre*	se·*tem*·bre
October	*ottobre*	o·*to*·bre
November	*novembre*	no·*vem*·bre
December	*dicembre*	dee·*chem*·bre

What date is it today?
   Che giorno è oggi? ke *jor*·no e *o*·jee

It's (15 December).
   È (il quindici) dicembre. e (eel *kween*·dee·chee) dee·*chem*·bre

| since (May) | *da (maggio)* | da (*ma*·jo) |
| until (June) | *fino a (giugno)* | *fee*·no a (*joo*·nyo) |

yesterday	*ieri*	*ye*·ree
today	*oggi*	*o*·jee
tonight	*stasera*	sta·*se*·ra
tomorrow	*domani*	do·*ma*·nee

last ...		
night	*ieri notte*	*ye*·ree *no*·te
week	*la settimana scorsa*	la se·tee·*ma*·na *skor*·sa
month	*il mese scorso*	eel *me*·ze *skor*·so
year	*l'anno scorso*	*la*·no *skor*·so

next ...		
week	*la settimana prossima*	la se·tee·*ma*·na *pro*·see·ma
month	*il mese prossimo*	eel *me*·ze *pro*·see·mo
year	*l'anno prossimo*	*la*·no *pro*·see·mo

yesterday/tomorrow ...	*ieri/domani ...*	*ye*·ree/do·*ma*·nee ...
morning	*mattina*	ma·*tee*·na
afternoon	*pomeriggio*	po·me·*ree*·jo
evening	*sera*	*se*·ra

weather

What's the weather like?	*Che tempo fa?*	ke *tem*·po fa

It's ...
cloudy	*È nuvoloso.*	e noo·vo·*lo*·zo
cold	*Fa freddo.*	fa *fre*·do
hot	*Fa caldo.*	fa *kal*·do
raining	*Piove.*	*pyo*·ve
snowing	*Nevica.*	ne·*vee*·ka
sunny	*È soleggiato.*	e so·le·*ja*·to
warm	*Fa bel tempo.*	fa bel *tem*·po
windy	*Tira vento.*	*tee*·ra *ven*·to

spring	*primavera* f	pree·ma·*ve*·ra
summer	*estate* f	es·*ta*·te
autumn	*autunno* m	ow·*too*·no
winter	*inverno* m	een·*ver*·no

border crossing

I'm here ...	*Sono qui ...*	*so*·no kwee ...
in transit	*in transito*	een *tran*·see·to
on business	*per affari*	per a·*fa*·ree
on holiday	*in vacanza*	een va·*kan*·tsa

I'm here for ...	*Sono qui per ...*	*so*·no kwee per ...
(10) days	*(dieci) giorni*	(*dye*·chee) *jor*·nee
(three) weeks	*(tre) settimane*	(tre) se·tee·*ma*·ne
(two) months	*(due) mesi*	(*doo*·e) *me*·zee

I'm going to (Perugia).
Vado a (Perugia).   *va*·do a (pe·*roo*·ja)

I'm staying at the (Minerva Hotel).
Alloggio al (Minerva).   a·*lo*·jo al (mee·*ner*·va)

I have nothing to declare.
Non ho niente da dichiarare.   non o *nyen*·te da dee·kya·*ra*·re

I have something to declare.
Ho delle cose da dichiarare.   o *de*·le *ko*·ze da dee·kya·*ra*·re

That's (not) mine. m/f
(Non) è mio/mia. m/f   (non) e *mee*·o/*mee*·a

transport

tickets & luggage

Where can I buy a ticket?
Dove posso comprare un biglietto?   do·ve po·so kom·pra·re oon bee·lye·to

Do I need to book a seat?
Bisogna prenotare un posto?   bee·zo·nya pre·no·ta·re oon pos·to

One ... ticket (to Rome), please.	*Un biglietto ... (per Roma), per favore.*	oon bee·lye·to ... (per ro·ma) per fa·vo·re
one-way	*di sola andata*	dee so·la an·da·ta
return	*di andata e ritorno*	dee an·da·ta e ree·tor·no

I'd like to ... my ticket, please.	*Vorrei ... il mio biglietto, per favore.*	vo·ray ... eel mee·o bee·lye·to per fa·vo·re
cancel	*cancellare*	kan·che·la·re
change	*cambiare*	kam·bya·re
collect	*ritirare*	ree·tee·ra·re
confirm	*confermare*	kon·fer·ma·re

I'd like a ... seat, please.	*Vorrei un posto ..., per favore.*	vo·ray oon pos·to ... per fa·vo·re
nonsmoking	*per non fumatori*	per non foo·ma·to·ree
smoking	*per fumatori*	per foo·ma·to·ree

How much is it?
Quant'è?   kwan·te

Is there air conditioning?
C'è l'aria condizionata?   che la·rya kon·dee·tsyo·na·ta

Is there a toilet?
C'è un gabinetto?   che oon ga·bee·ne·to

How long does the trip take?
Quanto ci vuole?   kwan·to chee vwo·le

Is it a direct route?
È un itinerario diretto?   e oo·nee·tee·ne·ra·ryo dee·re·to

I'd like a luggage locker.
Vorrei un armadietto per il bagaglio.   vo·ray oon ar·ma·dye·to per eel ba·ga·lyo

My luggage	Il mio bagaglio	eel *mee*·o ba·*ga*·lyo
has been ...	è stato ...	e *sta*·to ...
damaged	danneggiato	da·ne·*ja*·to
lost	perso	*per*·so
stolen	rubato	roo·*ba*·to

getting around

Where does flight (004) arrive?
Dove arriva il volo (004)?   *do*·ve a·*ree*·va eel *vo*·lo (*dze*·ro *dze*·ro *kwa*·tro)

Where does flight (004) depart?
Da dove parte il volo (004)?   da *do*·ve *par*·te eel *vo*·lo (*dze*·ro *dze*·ro *kwa*·tro)

Where's the ...?	Dove sono ...?	*do*·ve *so*·no ...
arrivalls hall	gli arrivi	lyee a·*ree*·vee
departures hall	le partenze	le par·*ten*·dze

Is this the ...	È questo/questa ...	e *kwes*·to/*kwes*·ta ...
to (Venice)?	per (Venezia)? m/f	per (ve·*ne*·tsya)
boat	la nave f	la *na*·ve
bus	l'autobus m	*low*·to·boos
plane	l'aereo m	la·*e*·re·o
train	il treno m	eel *tre*·no

What time's	A che ora passa	a ke *o*·ra *pa*·sa
the ... bus?	... autobus?	... *ow*·to·boos
first	il primo	eel *pree*·mo
last	l'ultimo	*lool*·tee·mo
next	il prossimo	eel *pro*·see·mo

At what time does it arrive/leave?
A che ora arriva/parte?   a ke *o*·ra a·*ree*·va/*par*·te

How long will it be delayed?
Di quanto ritarderà?   dee *kwan*·to ree·tar·de·*ra*

What station/stop is this?
Che stazione/fermata è questa?   ke sta·*tsyo*·ne/fer·*ma*·ta e *kwe*·sta

What's the next station/stop?
Qual'è la prossima stazione/fermata?   kwa·*le* la *pro*·see·ma sta·*tsyo*·ne/fer·*ma*·ta

Does it stop at (Milan)?
Si ferma a (Milano)?   see *fer*·ma a (mee·*la*·no)

Please tell me when we get to (Taranto).
Mi dica per favore quando   mee *dee*·ka per fa·*vo*·re *kwan*·do
arriviamo a (Taranto).   a·ree·*vya*·mo a (ta·*ran*·to)

How long do we stop here?
Per quanto tempo ci fermiamo qui?   per *kwan*·to *tem*·po chee fer·*mya*·mo kwee

Is this seat available?
È libero questo posto?   e *lee*·be·ro *kwe*·sto *pos*·to

That's my seat.
Quel posto è mio.   kwel *pos*·to e *mee*·o

I'd like a taxi …	*Vorrei un tassì …*	vo·*ray* oon ta·*see* …
at (9am)	*alle (nove*	*a*·le (*no*·ve
	di mattina)	dee ma·*tee*·na)
now	*adesso*	a·*de*·so
tomorrow	*domani*	do·*ma*·nee

Is this taxi available?
È libero questo tassì?   e *lee*·be·ro *kwe*·sto ta·*see*

How much is it to …?
Quant'è per …?   kwan·*te* per …

Please put the meter on.
Usi il tassametro, per favore.   *oo*·zee eel ta·sa·*me*·tro per fa·*vo*·re

Please take me to (this address).
Mi porti a (questo indirizzo),   mee *por*·tee a (*kwe*·sto een·dee·*ree*·tso)
per piacere.   per pya·*che*·re

Please …	*…, per favore.*	… per fa·*vo*·re
slow down	*Rallenti*	ra·*len*·tee
stop here	*Si fermi qui*	see *fer*·mee kwee
wait here	*Mi aspetti qui*	mee as·*pe*·tee kwee

car, motorbike & bicycle hire

I'd like to hire a/an …	*Vorrei noleggiare …*	vo·*ray* no·le·*ja*·re …
bicycle	*una bicicletta*	*oo*·na bee·chee·*kle*·ta
car	*una macchina*	*oo*·na *ma*·kee·na
motorbike	*una moto*	*oo*·na *mo*·to

with …	*con …*	kon …
a driver	*un'autista*	oo·now·*tee*·sta
air conditioning	*aria condizionata*	*a*·rya kon·dee·tsyo·*na*·ta

How much for ... hire?	Quanto costa ...?	kwan·to kos·ta ...
hourly	all'ora	a·lo·ra
daily	al giorno	al jor·no
weekly	alla settimana	a·la se·tee·ma·na

air	aria f	a·rya
oil	olio m	o·lyo
petrol	benzina f	ben·dzee·na
tyres	gomme f pl	go·me

I need a mechanic.
Ho bisogno di un meccanico. o bee·zo·nyo dee oon me·ka·nee·ko

I've run out of petrol.
Ho esaurito la benzina. o e·zow·ree·to la ben·dzee·na

I have a flat tyre.
Ho una gomma bucata. o oo·na go·ma boo·ka·ta

directions

Where's the ...?	Dov'è ...?	do·ve ...
bank	la banca	la ban·ka
city centre	il centro città	eel chen·tro chee·ta
hotel	l'albergo	lal·ber·go
market	il mercato	eel mer·ka·to
police station	il posto di polizia	eel pos·to dee po·lee·tsee·a
post office	l'ufficio postale	loo·fee·cho pos·ta·le
public toilet	il gabinetto	eel ga·bee·ne·to
	pubblico	poo·blee·ko
tourist office	l'ufficio del turismo	loo·fee·cho del too·reez·mo

Is this the road to (Milan)?
Questa strada porta a (Milano)? kwe·sta stra·da por·ta a (mee·la·no)

Can you show me (on the map)?
Può mostrarmi (sulla pianta)? pwo mos·trar·mee (soo·la pyan·ta)

What's the address?
Qual'è l'indirizzo? kwa·le leen·dee·ree·tso

How far is it?
Quant'è distante? kwan·te dees·tan·te

How do I get there?
Come ci si arriva? ko·me chee see a·ree·va

Turn ...	Giri ...	jee·ree ...
at the corner	all'angolo	a·*lan*·go·lo
at the traffic lights	al semaforo	al se·*ma*·fo·ro
left/right	a sinistra/destra	a see·*nee*·stra/*de*·stra

It's ...	È ...	e ...
behind ...	dietro ...	*dye*·tro ...
far away	lontano	lon·*ta*·no
here	qui	kwee
in front of ...	davanti a ...	da·*van*·tee a ...
left	a sinistra	a see·*nee*·stra
near (to ...)	vicino (a ...)	vee·*chee*·no (a ...)
next to ...	accanto a ...	a·*kan*·to a ...
on the corner	all'angolo	a·*lan*·go·lo
opposite ...	di fronte a ...	dee *fron*·te a ...
right	a destra	a *de*·stra
straight ahead	sempre diritto	*sem*·pre dee·*ree*·to
there	là	la

by bus	con l'autobus	kon *low*·to·boos
by taxi	con il tassì	ko·neel ta·*see*
by train	con il treno	ko·neel *tre*·no
on foot	a piedi	a *pye*·dee

north	nord m	nord
south	sud m	sood
east	est m	est
west	ovest m	*o*·vest

signs

Entrata/Uscita	en·*tra*·ta/oo·*shee*·ta	**Entrance/Exit**
Aperto/Chiuso	a·*per*·to/*kyoo*·zo	**Open/Closed**
Camere Libere	*ka*·me·re *lee*·be·re	**Rooms Available**
Completo	kom·*ple*·to	**No Vacancies**
Informazioni	een·for·ma·*tsyo*·nee	**Information**
Posto di Polizia	*pos*·to dee po·lee·*tsee*·a	**Police Station**
Proibito	pro·ee·*bee*·to	**Prohibited**
Gabinetti	ga·bee·*ne*·tee	**Toilets**
Uomini	*wo*·mee·nee	**Men**
Donne	*do*·ne	**Women**
Caldo/Freddo	*kal*·do/*fre*·do	**Hot/Cold**

accommodation

finding accommodation

Where's a/an ...?	Dov'è ...?	do·ve ...
camping ground	un campeggio	oon kam·pe·jo
guesthouse	una pensione	oo·na pen·syo·ne
inn	una locanda	oo·na lo·kan·da
hotel	un albergo	oo·nal·ber·go
youth hostel	un ostello della	oo·nos·te·lo de·la
	gioventù	jo·ven·too

Can you recommend	Può consigliare	pwo kon·see·lya·re
somewhere ...?	qualche posto ...?	kwal·ke pos·to ...
cheap	economico	e·ko·no·mee·ko
good	buono	bwo·no
nearby	vicino	vee·chee·no

I'd like to book a room, please.
Vorrei prenotare una camera,
per favore.

vo·ray pre·no·ta·re oo·na ka·me·ra
per fa·vo·re

I have a reservation.
Ho una prenotazione.

o oo·na pre·no·ta·tsyo·ne

My name's ...
Mi chiamo ...

mee kya·mo ...

Do you have	Avete una	a·ve·te oo·na
a ... room?	camera ...?	ka·me·ra ...
single	singola	seen·go·la
double	doppia con letto	do·pya kon le·to
	matrimoniale	ma·tree·mo·nya·le
twin	doppia a due letti	do·pya a doo·e le·tee

How much is it per ...?	Quanto costa per ...?	kwan·to kos·ta per ...
night	una notte	oo·na no·te
person	persona	per·so·na

Can I pay by ...?	Posso pagare con ...?	po·so pa·ga·re kon ...
credit card	la carta di credito	la kar·ta dee kre·dee·to
travellers	un assegno	oo·na·se·nyo
cheque	di viaggio	dee vee·a·jo

I'd like to stay for (two) nights.
Vorrei rimanere (due) notti.   vo·*ray* ree·ma·*ne*·re (*doo*·e) *no*·tee

From (July 2) to (July 6).
Dal (due luglio) al (sei luglio).   dal (*doo*·e *loo*·lyo) al (say *loo*·lyo)

Can I see it?
Posso vederla?   *po*·so ve·*der*·la

Am I allowed to camp here?
Si può campeggiare qui?   see pwo kam·pe·*ja*·re kwee

Is there a camp site nearby?
C'è un campeggio qui vicino?   che oon kam·*pe*·jo kwee vee·*chee*·no

requests & queries

When's breakfast served?
A che ora è la prima colazione?   a ke *o*·ra e la *pree*·ma ko·la·*tsyo*·ne

Where's breakfast served?
Dove si prende la prima colazione?   *do*·ve see *pren*·de la *pree*·ma ko·la·*tsyo*·ne

Please wake me at (seven).
Mi svegli alle (sette), per favore.   mee *sve*·lyee *a*·le (*se*·te) per fa·*vo*·re

Could I have my key, please?
Posso avere la chiave, per favore?   *po*·so a·*ve*·re la *kya*·ve per fa·*vo*·re

Can I get another (blanket)?
Può darmi un altra (coperta)?   pwo *dar*·mee oo·*nal*·tra (ko·*per*·ta)

This (sheet) isn't clean.
Questo (lenzuolo) non è pulito.   *kwe*·sto (len·*tzwo*·lo) non e poo·*lee*·to

Is there a/an ...?	*C'è ...?*	che ...
elevator	*un ascensore*	oo·na·shen·*so*·re
safe	*una cassaforte*	*oo*·na ka·sa·*for*·te

The room is too ...	*La camera è troppo ...*	la *ka*·me·ra e *tro*·po ...
expensive	*cara*	*ka*·ra
noisy	*rumorosa*	roo·mo·*ro*·za
small	*piccola*	*pee*·ko·la

The ... doesn't work.	*... non funziona.*	... non foon·*tsyo*·na
air conditioning	*L'aria condizionata*	*la*·rya kon·dee·tsyo·*na*·ta
fan	*Il ventilatore*	eel ven·tee·la·*to*·re
toilet	*Il gabinetto*	eel ga·bee·*ne*·to

checking out

What time is checkout?
A che ora si deve lasciar a ke o·*ra* see *de*·ve la·*shar*
libera la camera? lee·be·ra la *ka*·me·ra

Can I leave my luggage here?
Posso lasciare ili mio bagaglio qui? po·so la·*sha*·re eel *mee*·o ba·*ga*·lyo kwee

Could I have my ..., please?	*Posso avere ...,*	po·so a·*ve*·re ...
	per favore?	per fa·*vo*·re
deposit	*la caparra*	la ka·*pa*·ra
passport	*il mio passaporto*	eel *mee*·o pa·sa·*por*·to
valuables	*i miei oggetti*	ee myay o·*je*·tee
	di valore	dee va·*lo*·re

communications & banking

the internet

Where's the local Internet café?
Dove si trova l'Internet point? *do*·ve see *tro*·va leen·ter·net poynt

How much is it per hour?
Quanto costa all'ora? kwan·to *kos*·ta a·*lo*·ra

I'd like to ...	*Vorrei ...*	vo·*ray* ...
check my email	*controllare le mie email*	kon·tro·*la*·re le *mee*·e e·mayl
get Internet access	*usare Internet*	oo·*za*·re een·ter·net
use a printer	*usare una stampante*	oo·*za*·re *oo*·na stam·*pan*·te
use a scanner	*scandire*	skan·*dee*·re

mobile/cell phone

I'd like a ...	*Vorrei ...*	vo·*ray* ...
mobile/cell phone	*un cellulare da*	oon che·loo·*la*·re da
for hire	*noleggiare*	no·le·*ja*·re
SIM card for your	*un SIM card per*	oon seem kard per
network	*la rete telefonica*	la *re*·te te·le·*fo*·nee·ka

What are the rates? *Quali sono le tariffe?* kwa·lee *so*·no le ta·*ree*·fe

telephone

What's your phone number?
Qual'è il Suo/tuo numero — kwa-*le* eel *soo*-o/*too*-o *noo*-me-ro
di telefono? pol/inf — dee te-*le*-fo-no

The number is ...
Il numero è ... — eel *noo*-me-ro e ...

Where's the nearest public phone?
Dov'è il telefono pubblico — do-*ve* eel te-*le*-fo-no *poo*-blee-ko
più vicino? — pyoo vee-*chee*-no

I'd like to buy a phonecard.
Vorrei comprare una — vo-*ray* kom-*pra*-re *oo*-na
scheda telefonica. — *ske*-da te-le-*fo*-nee-ka

I want to ...	*Vorrei ...*	vo-*ray* ...
call (Singapore)	*fare una chiamata a (Singapore)*	*fa*-re *oo*-na kya-*ma*-ta a (seen-ga-*po*-re)
make a local call	*fare una chiamata locale*	*fa*-re *oo*-na kya-*ma*-ta lo-*ka*-le
reverse the charges	*fare una chiamata a carico del destinatario*	*fa*-re *oo*-na kya-*ma*-ta a ka-ree-ko del des-tee-na-*ta*-ryo

How much does ... cost?	*Quanto costa ...?*	kwan-to kos-ta ...
a (three)-minute call	*una telefonata di (tre) minuti*	*oo*-na te-le-fo-*na*-ta dee (tre) mee-*noo*-tee
each extra minute	*ogni minuto in più*	*o*-nyee mee-*noo*-to een pyoo

It's (one euro) per (minute).
(Un euro) per (un minuto). — (oon e-*oo*-ro) per (oon mee-*noo*-to)

post office

I want to send a ...	*Vorrei mandare ...*	vo-*ray* man-*da*-re ...
fax	*un fax*	oon faks
letter	*una lettera*	*oo*-na *le*-te-ra
parcel	*un pacchetto*	oon pa-*ke*-to
postcard	*una cartolina*	*oo*-na kar-to-*lee*-na

I want to buy ...	*Vorrei comprare ...*	vo-*ray* kom-*pra*-re ...
an envelope	*una busta*	*oo*-na *boo*-sta
stamps	*dei francobolli*	day fran-ko-*bo*-lee

Please send it (to Australia) by ...	Lo mandi ... (in Australia), per favore.	lo *man*·dee ... (een ow·*stra*·lya) per fa·*vo*·re
airmail	via aerea	*vee*·a a·e·re·a
express mail	posta prioritaria	*pos*·ta pryo·ree·*ta*·rya
registered mail	posta raccomandata	*pos*·ta ra·ko·man·*da*·ta
surface mail	posta ordinaria	*pos*·ta or·dee·*na*·rya
Is there any mail for me?	C'è posta per me?	che *pos*·ta per me

bank

Where's a/an ...?	Dov'è ... più vicino?	do·*ve* ... pyoo vee·*chee*·no
ATM	il Bancomat	eel *ban*·ko·mat
foreign exchange office	il cambio	eel *kam*·byo

I'd like to ...	Vorrei ...	vo·*ray* ...
Where can I ...?	Dove posso ...?	*do*·ve *po*·so ...
arrange a transfer	trasferire soldi	tras·fe·*ree*·re *sol*·dee
cash a cheque	riscuotere un assegno	ree·*skwo*·te·re oo·na·*se*·nyo
change a travellers cheque	cambiare un assegno di viaggio	kam·*bya*·re oo·na·*se*·nyo dee vee·*a*·jo
change money	cambiare denaro	kam·*bya*·re de·*na*·ro
get a cash advance	prelevare con carta di credito	pre·le·*va*·re kon *kar*·ta dee *kre*·dee·to
withdraw money	fare un prelievo	*fa*·re oon pre·*lye*·vo

What's the ...?	Quant'è ...?	kwan·*te* ...
commission	la commissione	la ko·mee·*syo*·ne
exchange rate	il cambio	eel *kam*·byo

It's ...	È ...	e ...
(12) euros	(dodici) euro	(*do*·dee·chee) e·*oo*·ro
free	gratuito	gra·too·*ee*·to

What's the charge for that?
Quanto costa? kwan·to *kos*·ta

What time does the bank open?
A che ora apre la banca? a ke *o*·ra *a*·pre la *ban*·ka

Has my money arrived yet?
È arrivato il mio denaro? e a·ree·*va*·to eel *mee*·o de·*na*·ro

sightseeing

getting in

What time does it open/close?
A che ora apre/chiude?
a ke *o*-ra *a*-pre/*kyoo*-de

What's the admission charge?
Quant'è il prezzo d'ingresso?
kwan-*te* eel *pre*-tso deen-*gre*-so

Is there a discount for children/students?
C'è uno sconto per
bambini/studenti?
che *oo*-no *skon*-to per
bam-*bee*-nee/stoo-*den*-tee

I'd like a ...	*Vorrei ...*	vo-*ray* ...
catalogue	*un catalogo*	oon ka-*ta*-lo-go
guide	*una guida*	*oo*-na *gwee*-da
local map	*una cartina*	*oo*-na kar-*tee*-na
	della zona	de-la *dzo*-na

I'd like to see ...	*Vorrei vedere ...*	vo-*ray* ve-*de*-re ...
What's that?	*Cos'è?*	ko-*ze*
Can I take a photo?	*Posso fare una foto?*	*po*-so *fa*-re *oo*-na *fo*-to

tours

When's the	*A che ora parte la*	a ke *o*-ra *par*-te la
next ...?	*prossima ...?*	*pro*-see-ma ...
day trip	*escursione*	es-koor-*syo*-ne
	in giornata	een jor-*na*-ta
tour	*gita turistica*	*jee*-ta too-ree-*stee*-ka

Is ... included?	*È incluso ...?*	e een-*kloo*-zo ...
accommodation	*l'alloggio*	la-*lo*-jo
the admission charge	*il prezzo d'ingresso*	eel *pre*-tso deen-*gre*-so
food	*il vitto*	eel *vee*-to
transport	*il trasporto*	eel tras-*por*-to

How long is the tour?
Quanto dura la gita?
kwan-to *doo*-ra la *jee*-ta

What time should we be back?
A che ora dovremmo ritornare?
a ke *o*-ra dov-*re*-mo ree-tor-*na*-re

castle	castello m	kas-*te*-lo
cathedral	duomo m	*dwo*-mo
church	chiesa f	*kye*-za
main square	piazza principale f	*pya*-tsa preen-chee-*pa*-le
monastery	monastero m	mo-nas-*te*-ro
monument	monumento m	mo-noo-*men*-to
museum	museo m	moo-*ze*-o
old city	centro storico m	*chen*-tro *sto*-ree-ko
palace	palazzo m	pa-*la*-tso
ruins	rovine f pl	ro-*vee*-ne
stadium	stadio m	*sta*-dyo
statues	statue f pl	*sta*-too-e

shopping

enquiries

Where's a ... ?	Dov'è ... ?	do-*ve* ...
bank	la banca	la *ban*-ka
bookshop	la libreria	la lee-bre-*ree*-a
camera shop	il fotografo	eel fo-*to*-gra-fo
department store	il grande magazzino	eel *gran*-de ma-ga-*dzee*-no
grocery store	la drogheria	la dro-ge-*ree*-a
market	il mercato	eel mer-*ka*-to
newsagency	l'edicola	le-*dee*-ko-la
supermarket	il supermercato	eel soo-per-mer-*ka*-to

Where can I buy (a padlock)?
Dove posso comprare (un lucchetto)?   do-ve po-so kom-*pra*-re (oon loo-*ke*-to)

I'm looking for ...
Sto cercando ...   sto cher-*kan*-do ...

Can I look at it?
Posso dare un'occhiata? — po·so da·re oo·no·kya·ta

Do you have any others?
Ne avete altri? — ne a·ve·te al·tree

Does it have a guarantee?
Ha la garanzia? — a la ga·ran·tsee·a

Can I have it sent overseas?
Può spedirlo all'estero? — pwo spe·deer·lo a·les·te·ro

Can I have my ... repaired?
Posso far aggiustare ... qui? — po·so far a·joo·sta·re ... kwee

It's faulty.
È difettoso. — e dee·fe·to·zo

I'd like (a) ..., please.	*Vorrei ..., per favore.*	vo·ray ... per fa·vo·re
bag	un sacchetto	oon sa·ke·to
refund	un rimborso	oon reem·bor·so
to return this	restituire questo	res·tee·twee·re kwe·sto

paying

How much is it?
Quant'è? — kwan·te

Can you write down the price?
Può scrivere il prezzo? — pwo skree·ve·re eel pre·tso

That's too expensive.
È troppo caro. — e tro·po ka·ro

Can you lower the price?
Può farmi lo sconto? — pwo far·mee lo skon·to

I'll give you (five) euros.
Le offro (cinque) euro. — le o·fro (cheen·kwe) e·oo·ro

There's a mistake in the bill.
C'è un errore nel conto. — che oon e·ro·re nel kon·to

Do you accept ...?	*Accettate ...?*	a·che·ta·te ...
credit cards	la carta di credito	la kar·ta dee kre·dee·to
debit cards	la carta di debito	la kar·ta dee de·bee·to
travellers cheques	gli assegni di viaggio	lyee a·se·nyee dee vee·a·jo

I'd like ..., please.	Vorrei ..., per favore.	vo·ray ... per fa·vo·re
a receipt	una ricevuta	oo·na ree·che·voo·ta
my change	il mio resto	eel mee·o res·to

clothes & shoes

Can I try it on?	Potrei provarmelo?	po·tray pro·var·me·lo
My size is (40).	Sono una taglia (quaranta).	so·no oo·na ta·lya (kwa·ran·ta)
It doesn't fit.	Non va bene.	non va be·ne
small	piccola	pee·ko·la
medium	media	me·dya
large	forte	for·te

books & music

I'd like a ...	Vorrei ...	vo·ray ...
newspaper	un giornale	oon jor·na·le
(in English)	(in inglese)	(een een·gle·ze)
pen	una penna	oo·na pe·na

Is there an English-language bookshop?

| C'è una libreria specializzata in lingua inglese? | che oo·na lee·bre·ree·a spe·cha·lee·dza·ta een leen·gwa een·gle·ze |

I'm looking for something by (Alberto Moravia).

| Sto cercando qualcosa di (Alberto Moravia). | sto cher·kan·do kwal·ko·za dee (al·ber·to mo·ra·vee·a) |

Can I listen to this?

| Potrei ascoltarlo? | po·tray as·kol·tar·lo |

photography

Can you ...?	Potrebbe ...?	po·tre·be ...
burn a CD from	masterizzare un	mas·te·ree·tsa·re oon
my memory card	CD dalla mia	chee dee da·la mee·a
	memory card	me·mo·ree kard
develop this	sviluppare	svee·loo·pa·re
film	questo rullino	kwe·sto roo·lee·no
load my film	inserire il	een·se·ree·re eel
	mio rullino	mee·o roo·lee·no

I need a/an … film for this camera.	Vorrei un rullino … per questa macchina fotografica.	vo-*ray* oon roo-*lee*-no … per *kwe*-sta ma-*kee*-na fo-to-*gra*-fee-ka
APS	da APS	da a-pee-*e*-se
B&W	in bianco e nero	een *byan*-ko e *ne*-ro
colour	a colori	a *ko*-lo-ree
slide	per diapositive	per dee-a-po-zee-*tee*-ve
(200) speed	da (duecento) ASA	da (*doo*-e *chen*-to) *a*-za
When will it be ready?	Quando sarà pronto?	*kwan*-do sa-*ra pron*-to

meeting people

greetings, goodbyes & introductions

Hello.	Buongiorno.	bwon-*jor*-no
Hi.	Ciao.	chow
Good night.	Buonanotte.	bwo-na-*no*-te
Goodbye.	Arrivederci.	a-ree-ve-*der*-chee
Bye.	Ciao.	chow
See you later.	A più tardi.	a pyoo *tar*-dee

Mr	Signore	see-*nyo*-re
Mrs	Signora	see-*nyo*-ra
Miss	Signorina	see-nyo-*ree*-na

How are you?	Come sta? pol	*ko*-me sta
	Come stai? inf	*ko*-me stai
Fine. And you?	Bene. E Lei? pol	*be*-ne e lay
	Bene. E tu? inf	*be*-ne e too
What's your name?	Come si chiama? pol	*ko*-me see *kya*-ma
	Come ti chiami? inf	*ko*-me tee *kya*-mee
My name is …	Mi chiamo …	mee *kya*-mo …
I'm pleased to meet you.	Piacere.	pya-*che*-re

This is my ...	Le/Ti presento ... pol/inf	le/tee pre·zen·to ...
boyfriend	mio ragazzo	mee·o ra·ga·tso
brother	mio fratello	mee·o fra·te·lo
daughter	mia figlia	mee·a fee·lya
father	mio padre	mee·o pa·dre
friend	il mio amico m	eel mee·o a·mee·ko
	la mia amica f	la mee·a a·mee·ka
girlfriend	mia ragazza	mee·a ra·ga·tsa
husband	mio marito	mee·o ma·ree·to
mother	mia madre	mee·a ma·dre
partner (intimate)	il mio compagno m	eel mee·o kom·pa·nyo
	la mia compagna f	la mee·a kom·pa·nya
sister	mia sorella	mee·a so·re·la
son	mio figlio	mee·o fee·lyo
wife	mia moglie	mee·a mo·lye

Here's my ...	Ecco il mio ...	e·ko eel mee·o ...
What's your ...?	Qual'è il	kwa·le eel
	Suo/tuo ...? pol/inf	soo·o/too·o ...
address	indirizzo	een·dee·ree·tso
email address	indirizzo di email	een·dee·ree·tso dee e·mayl
fax number	numero di fax	noo·me·ro dee faks
phone number	numero di telefono	noo·me·ro dee te·le·fo·no

occupations

What's your occupation?	Che lavoro fa/fai? pol/inf	ke la·vo·ro fa/fai

I'm a/an ...	Sono ...	so·no ...
artist	artista m&f	ar·tees·ta
business person	uomo/donna	wo·mo/do·na
	d'affari m/f	da·fa·ree
farmer	agricoltore m	a·gree·kol·to·re
	agricoltrice f	a·gree·kol·tree·che
manual worker	manovale m&f	ma·no·va·le
office worker	impiegato/a m/f	eem·pye·ga·to/a
scientist	scienziato/a m/f	shen·tsee·a·to/a
student	studente m	stoo·den·te
	studentessa f	stoo·den·te·sa
tradesperson	operaio/a m/f	o·pe·ra·yo/a

background

Where are you from?	*Da dove viene/vieni?* pol/inf	da *do*·ve vye·ne/*vye*·nee
I'm from ...	*Vengo ...*	*ven*·go ...
Australia	*dall'Australia*	dal·ow·*stra*·lya
Canada	*dal Canada*	dal *ka*·na·da
England	*dall'Inghilterra*	da·leen·geel·*te*·ra
New Zealand	*dalla Nuova Zelanda*	*da*·la nwo·va ze·*lan*·da
the USA	*dagli Stati Uniti*	*da*·lyee sta·tee oo·*nee*·tee
Are you married?	*È sposato/a?* m/f pol	e spo·*za*·to/a
	Sei sposato/a? m/f inf	say spo·*za*·to/a
I'm married.	*Sono sposato/a.* m/f	*so*·no spo·*za*·to/a
I'm single.	*Sono celibe/nubile.* m/f	*che*·lee·be/*noo*·bee·le

age

How old ...?	*Quanti anni ...?*	*kwan*·tee *a*·nee ...
are you	*ha/hai* pol/inf	a/ai
is your daughter	*ha Sua/tua*	a *soo*·a/*too*·a
	figlia pol/inf	*fee*·lya
is your son	*ha Suo/tuo*	a *soo*·o/*too*·o
	figlio pol/inf	*fee*·lyo
I'm ... years old.	*Ho ... anni.*	o ... *a*·nee
He/She is ... years old.	*Ha ... anni.*	a ... *a*·nee

feelings

I'm (not) ...	*(Non) Ho ...*	(non) o ...
Are you ...?	*Ha/Hai ...?* pol/inf	a/ai ...
cold	*freddo*	*fre*·do
hot	*caldo*	*kal*·do
hungry	*fame*	*fa*·me
thirsty	*sete*	*se*·te
I'm (not) ...	*(Non) Sono ...*	(non) *so*·no ...
Are you ...?	*È/Sei ...?* pol/inf	e/say ...
happy	*felice*	fe·*lee*·che
sad	*triste*	*tree*·ste

entertainment

going out

Where can I find ...?	*Dove sono ...?*	do·ve so·no ...
clubs	*dei clubs*	day kloob
gay venues	*dei locali gay*	day lo·ka·lee ge
pubs	*dei pub*	day pab
I feel like going to a/the ...	*Ho voglia d'andare ...*	o vo·lya dan·da·re ...
concert	*a un concerto*	a oon kon·cher·to
movies	*al cinema*	al chee·nee·ma
party	*a una festa*	a oo·na fes·ta
restaurant	*in un ristorante*	een oon rees·to·ran·te
theatre	*a teatro*	a te·a·tro

interests

Do you like ...?	*Ti piace/ piacciono ...?* sg/pl	tee pya·che/ pya·cho·no ...
I (don't) like ...	*(Non) Mi piace/ piacciono ...* sg/pl	(non) mee pya·che/ pya·cho·no ...
art	*l'arte* sg	lar·te
cooking	*cucinare* sg	koo·chee·na·re
movies	*i film* pl	ee feelm
nightclubs	*le discoteche* pl	le dees·ko·te·ke
reading	*leggere* sg	le·je·re
shopping	*lo shopping* sg	lo sho·ping
sport	*lo sport* sg	lo sport
travelling	*viaggiare* sg	vee·a·ja·re
Do you like to ...?	*Ti piace ...?*	tee pya·che ...
dance	*ballare*	ba·la·re
go to concerts	*andare ai concerti*	an·da·re ai kon·cher·tee
listen to music	*ascoltare la musica*	as·kol·ta·re la moo·zee·ka

food & drink

finding a place to eat

Can you recommend a ...?	Potrebbe consigliare un ...?	po·*tre*·be kon·see·*lya*·re oon ...
bar	locale	lo·*ka*·le
café	bar	bar
restaurant	ristorante	rees·to·*ran*·te
I'd like ..., please.	Vorrei ..., per favore.	vo·*ray* ... per fa·*vo*·re
a table for	un tavolo per	oon *ta*·vo·lo per
(four)	(quattro)	(*kwa*·tro)
the (non)smoking section	(non) fumatori	(non) foo·ma·*to*·ree

ordering food

breakfast	prima colazione f	*pree*·ma ko·la·*tsyo*·ne
lunch	pranzo m	*pran*·dzo
dinner	cena f	*che*·na
snack	spuntino m	spoon·*tee*·no

What would you recommend?
Cosa mi consiglia?   *ko*·za mee kon·*see*·lya

I'd like (the) ..., please.	Vorrei ..., per favore.	vo·*ray* ... per fa·*vo*·re
bill	il conto	eel *kon*·to
drink list	la lista delle bevande	la *lee*·sta *de*·le be·*van*·de
menu	il menù	eel me·*noo*
that dish	questo piatto	*kwe*·sto *pya*·to

drinks

(cup of) coffee ...	(un) caffè ...	(oon) ka·fe ...
(cup of) tea ...	(un) tè ...	(oon) te ...
with milk	con latte	kon la·te
without sugar	senza zucchero	sen·tsa tsoo·ke·ro
orange juice (bottled)	succo d'arancia m	soo·ko da·ran·cha
orange juice (fresh)	spremuta d'arancia f	spre·moo·ta da·ran·cha
soft drink	bibita f	bee·bee·ta
... water	acqua ...	a·kwa ...
boiled	bollita	bo·lee·ta
mineral	minerale	mee·ne·ra·le
sparkling mineral	frizzante	free·tsan·te
still mineral	naturale	na·too·ra·le

in the bar

I'll have ...	Prendo ...	pren·do ...
I'll buy you a drink.	Ti offro da bere. inf	tee of·ro da be·re
What would you like?	Cosa prendi?	ko·za pren·dee
Cheers!	Salute!	sa·loo·te
brandy	cognac m	ko·nyak
champagne	champagne m	sham·pa·nye
cocktail	cocktail m	kok·tayl
a shot of (whisky)	un sorso di (whisky)	oon sor·so dee (wee·skee)
a ... of beer	... di birra	... dee bee·ra
bottle	una bottiglia	oo·na bo·tee·lya
glass	un bicchiere	oon bee·kye·re
a bottle of ...	una bottiglia di	oo·na bo·tee·lya dee
wine	vino ...	vee·no ...
a glass of ...	un bicchiere di	oon bee·kye·re dee
wine	vino ...	vee·no ...
red	rosso	ro·so
sparkling	spumante	spoo·man·te
white	bianco	byan·ko

self-catering

What's the local speciality?
Qual'è la specialità   kwa-*le* la spe-cha-lee-*ta*
di questa regione?   dee *kwe*-sta re-*jo*-ne

What's that?
Cos'è?   ko-*ze*

How much is (a kilo of cheese)?
Quanto costa (un chilo   *kwan*-to *kos*-ta (oon *kee*-lo
di formaggio)?   dee for-*ma*-jo)

I'd like ...	*Vorrei ...*	vo-*ray* ...
100 grams	*un etto*	oo-*ne*-to
(two) kilos	*(due) chili*	(*doo*-e) *kee*-lee
(three) pieces	*(tre) pezzi*	(tre) *pe*-tsee
(six) slices	*(sei) fette*	(say) *fe*-te
Less.	*Meno.*	*me*-no
Enough.	*Basta.*	*bas*-ta
More.	*Più.*	pyoo

special diets & allergies

Is there a vegetarian restaurant near here?
C'è un ristorante vegetariano   che oon rees-to-*ran*-te ve-je-ta-*rya*-no
qui vicino?   kwee vee-*chee*-no

Do you have vegetarian food?
Avete piatti vegetariani?   a-*ve*-te *pya*-tee ve-je-ta-*rya*-nee

Could you prepare	*Potreste preparare*	po-*tres*-te pre-pa-*ra*-re
a meal without ...?	*un pasto senza ...?*	oon *pas*-to *sen*-tsa ...
butter	*burro*	*boo*-ro
eggs	*uova*	*wo*-va
meat stock	*brodo di carne*	*bro*-do dee *kar*-ne
I'm allergic to ...	*Sono allergico/a ...* m/f	*so*-no a-*ler*-jee-ko/a ...
dairy produce	*ui latticini*	ai la-tee-*chee*-nee
gluten	*al glutine*	al *gloo*-tee-ne
MSG	*al glutammato*	al glu-ta-*ma*-to
	monosodico	mo-no-*so*-dee-ko
nuts	*alle noci*	*a*-le *no*-chee
seafood	*ai frutti di mare*	ai *froo*-tee dee *ma*-re

emergencies

basics

Help!	*Aiuto!*	ai·*yoo*·to
Stop!	*Fermi!*	*fer*·mee
Go away!	*Vai via!*	vai *vee*·a
Thief!	*Ladro!*	*la*·dro
Fire!	*Al fuoco!*	al *fwo*·ko
Watch out!	*Attenzione!*	a·ten·*tsyo*·ne
Call …!	*Chiami …!*	*kya*·mee …
a doctor	*un medico*	oon *me*·dee·ko
an ambulance	*un'ambulanza*	o·nam·boo·*lan*·tsa
the police	*la polizia*	la po·lee·*tsee*·a

It's an emergency!
È un'emergenza! e oo·ne·mer·*jen*·tsa

Could you help me, please?
Mi può aiutare, per favore? mee pwo ai·yoo·*ta*·re per fa·*vo*·re

I have to use the telephone.
Devo fare una telefonata. *de*·vo *fa*·re *oo*·na te·le·fo·*na*·ta

I'm lost.
Mi sono perso/a. m/f mee *so*·no *per*·so/a

Where are the toilets?
Dove sono i gabinetti? *do*·ve *so*·no ee ga·bee·*ne*·tee

police

Where's the police station?
Dov'è il posto di polizia? do·*ve* eel *pos*·to dee po·lee·*tsee*·a

I want to report an offence.
Voglio fare una denuncia. *vo*·lyo *fa*·re *oo*·na de·*noon*·cha

I have insurance.
Ho l'assicurazione. o la·see·koo·ra·*tsyo*·ne

I've been …	*Sono stato/a …* m/f	*so*·no *sta*·to/a …
assaulted	*aggredito/a* m/f	a·gre·*dee*·to/a
raped	*violentato/a* m/f	vyo·len·*ta*·to/a
robbed	*derubato/a* m/f	roo·*ba*·to/a

I've lost my ...	Ho perso ...	o *per*·so ...
My ... was/were stolen.	Mi hanno rubato ...	mee *a*·no roo·*ba*·to ...
backpack	il mio zaino	eel *mee*·o *dzai*·no
bags	i miei bagagli	ee mee·*ay* ba·*ga*·lyee
credit card	la mia carta di credito	la *mee*·a *kar*·ta dee *kre*·dee·to
handbag	la mia borsa	la *mee*·a *bor*·sa
jewellery	i miei gioielli	ee mee·*ay* jo·*ye*·lee
money	i miei soldi	ee mee·*ay* *sol*·dee
passport	il mio passaporte	eel *mee*·o pa·sa·*por*·te
travellers cheques	i miei assegni di viaggio	ee mee·*ay* a·*se*·nyee dee vee·*a*·jo
wallet	portafoglio	por·ta·*fo*·lyo
I want to contact my ...	Vorrei contattare ...	vo·*ray* kon·ta·*ta*·re ...
consulate	il mio consolato	eel *mee*·o kon·so·*la*·to
embassy	la mia ambasciata	la *mee*·a am·ba·*sha*·ta

health

medical needs

Where's the nearest ...?	Dov'è ... più vicino/a? m/f	do·*ve* ... pyoo vee·*chee*·no/a
dentist	il dentista m	eel den·*tee*·sta
doctor	il medico m	eel *me*·dee·ko
hospital	l'ospedale m	los·pe·*da*·le
(night) pharmacist	la farmacia (di turno) f	la far·ma·*chee*·a (dee *toor*·no)

I need a doctor (who speaks English).
Ho bisogno di un medico (che parli inglese).
o bee·*zo*·nyo dee oon *me*·dee·ko (ke *par*·lee een·*gle*·ze)

Could I see a female doctor?
Posso vedere una dottoressa?
po·so ve·*de*·re *oo*·na do·to·*re*·sa

I've run out of my medication.
Ho finito la mia medicina.
o fee·*nee*·to la *mee*·a me·dee·*chee*·na

symptoms, conditions & allergies

I'm sick.	Mi sento male.	mee sen·to ma·le
It hurts here.	Mi fa male qui.	mee fa ma·le kwee

I have (a) ...	Ho ...	o ...
asthma	asma	as·ma
bronchitis	la bronchite	la bron·kee·te
constipation	la stitichezza	la stee·tee·ke·tsa
cough	la tosse	la to·se
diarrhoea	la diarrea	la dee·a·re·a
fever	la febbre	la fe·bre
headache	mal di testa	mal dee tes·ta
heart condition	un problema cardiaco	oon pro·ble·ma kar·dee·a·ko
nausea	la nausea	la now·ze·a
pain	un dolore	oon do·lo·re
sore throat	mal di gola	mal dee go·la
toothache	mal di denti	mal dee den·tee

I'm allergic to ...	Sono allergico/a ... m/f	so·no a·ler·jee·ko/a ...
antibiotics	agli	a·lyee
	antibiotici	an·tee·bee·o·tee·chee
anti-inflammatories	agli	a·lyee
	antinfiammatori	an·teen·fya·ma·to·ree
aspirin	all'aspirina	a·las·pee·ree·na
bees	alle api	a·le a·pee
codeine	alla codeina	a·la ko·de·ee·na
penicillin	alla penicillina	a·la pe·nee·chee·lee·na

antiseptic	antisettico m	an·tee·se·tee·ko
bandage	fascia f	fa·sha
condoms	preservativi m pl	pre·zer·va·tee·vee
contraceptives	contraccettivi m pl	kon·tra·che·tee·vee
diarrhoea medicine	antidissenterico m	an·tee·dee·sen·te·ree·ko
insect repellent	repellente per	re·pe·len·te per
	gli insetti m	lyee een·se·tee
laxatives	lassativi m pl	la·sa·tee·vee
painkillers	analgesico m	a·nal·je·zee·ko
rehydration salts	sali minerali m pl	sa·lee mee·ne·ra·lee
sleeping tablets	sonniferi m pl	so·nee·fe·ree

english–italian dictionary

Italian nouns in this dictionary, and adjectives affected by gender, have their gender indicated by ⓜ (masculine) or ⓕ (feminine). If it's a plural noun, you'll also see pl. Words are also marked as n (noun), a (adjective), v (verb), sg (singular), pl (plural), inf (informal) and pol (polite) where necessary.

A

accident *incidente* ⓜ een-chee-*den*-te
accommodation *alloggio* ⓜ a-*lo*-jo
adaptor *presa multipla* ⓕ *pre*-sa *mool*-tee-pla
address *indirizzo* ⓜ een-dee-*ree*-tso
after *dopo* do-po
air-conditioned *ad aria condizionata*
  ad *a*-rya kon-dee-*tsyo*-na-ta
airplane *aereo* ⓜ a-e-*re*-o
airport *aeroporto* ⓜ a-e-ro-*por*-to
alcohol *alcol* ⓜ *al*-kol
all a *tutto/a* *too*-to/a
allergy *allergia* ⓕ a-ler-*jee*-a
ambulance *ambulanza* ⓕ am-boo-*lan*-tsa
and e e
ankle *caviglia* ⓕ ka-*vee*-lya
arm *braccio* ⓜ *bra*-cho
ashtray *portacenere* ⓜ por-ta-*che*-ne-re
ATM *Bancomat* ⓜ *ban*-ko-mat

B

baby *bimbo/a* ⓜ/ⓕ *beem*-bo/a
back (body) *schiena* ⓕ *skye*-na
backpack *zaino* ⓜ *dzai*-no
bad *cattivo/a* ⓜ/ⓕ ka-*tee*-vo/a
bag *borsa* ⓕ *bor*-sa
baggage claim *ritiro bagagli* ⓜ *ree*-tee-ro ba-*ga*-lyee
bank *banca* ⓕ *ban*-ka
bar *locale* ⓜ lo-*ka*-le
bathroom *bagno* ⓜ *ba*-nyo
battery *pila* ⓕ *pee*-la
beautiful *bello/a* ⓜ/ⓕ *be*-lo/a
bed *letto* ⓜ *le*-to
beer *birra* ⓕ *bee*-ra
before *prima* *pree*-ma
behind *dietro* *dye*-tro
bicycle *bicicletta* ⓕ bee-chee-*kle*-ta
big *grande* *gran*-de
bill *conto* ⓜ *kon*-to

black *nero/a* ⓜ/ⓕ *ne*-ro/a
blanket *coperta* ⓕ ko-*per*-ta
blood group *gruppo sanguigno* ⓜ *groo*-po san-*gwee*-nyo
blue *azzurro/a* ⓜ/ⓕ a-*dzoo*-ro/a
boat *barca* ⓕ *bar*-ka
book (make a reservation) v *prenotare* pre-no-*ta*-re
bottle *bottiglia* ⓕ bo-*tee*-lya
bottle opener *apribottiglie* a a-pree-bo-*tee*-lye
boy *ragazzo* ⓜ ra-*ga*-tso
brakes (car) *freno* ⓜ *fre*-no
breakfast *(prima) colazione* ⓕ *(pree*-ma) ko-la-*tsyo*-ne
broken (faulty) *rotto/a* ⓜ/ⓕ *ro*-to/a
bus *autobus* ⓜ *ow*-to-boos
business *affari* ⓜ pl a-*fa*-ree
buy *comprare* kom-*pra*-re

C

café *bar* ⓜ bar
camera *macchina fotografica* ⓕ
  ma-kee-na fo-to-*gra*-fee-ka
camp site *campeggio* ⓜ kam-*pe*-jo
can opener *apriscatole* ⓜ a-pree-*ska*-to-le
car *macchina* ⓕ *ma*-kee-na
cash *soldi* ⓜ pl *sol*-dee
cash (a cheque) v *riscuotere un assegno*
  ree-*skwo*-te-re oon a-se-nyo
cell phone *telefono cellulare* ⓜ te-*le*-fo-no che-loo-*la*-re
centre *centro* ⓜ *chen*-tro
change (money) v *cambiare* kam-*bya*-re
cheap *economico/a* ⓜ/ⓕ e-ko-no-*mee*-ko/a
check (bill) *conto* ⓜ *kon*-to
check-in *registrazione* ⓕ re-jee-stra-*tsyo*-ne
chest *petto* ⓜ *pe*-to
child *bambino/a* ⓜ/ⓕ bam-*bee*-no/a
cigarette *sigaretta* ⓕ see-ga-*re*-ta
city *città* ⓕ chee-*ta*
clean a *pulito/a* ⓜ/ⓕ poo-*lee*-to/a
closed *chiuso/a* ⓜ/ⓕ *kyoo*-zo/a
coffee *caffè* ⓜ ka-*fe*
coins *monete* ⓕ pl mo-*ne*-te

cold a *freddo/a* ⓜ/ⓕ *fre-*do/a
collect call *chiamata a carico del destinatario* ⓕ
　kya-*ma-*ta a *ka-*ree-ko del des-tee-na-*ta-*ryo
come *venire* ve-*nee-*re
computer *computer* ⓜ kom-*pyoo-*ter
condom *preservativo* ⓜ pre-zer-va-*tee-*vo
contact lenses *lenti a contatto* ⓕ pl *len-*tee a kon-*ta-*to
cook v *cucinare* koo-chee-*na-*re
cost *prezzo* ⓜ *pre-*tso
credit card *carta di credito* ⓕ *kar-*ta dee *kre-*de-to
cup *tazza* ⓕ *ta-*tsa
currency exchange *cambio valuta* ⓜ *kam-*byo va-*loo-*ta
customs (immigration) *dogana* ⓕ do-*ga-*na

D

dangerous *pericoloso/a* ⓜ/ⓕ pe-ree-ko-*lo-*zo/a
date (time) *data* ⓕ *da-*ta
day *giorno* ⓜ *jor-*no
delay *ritardo* ⓜ ree-*tar-*do
dentist *dentista* ⓜ/ⓕ den-*tee-*sta
depart *partire* par-*tee-*re
diaper *pannolino* ⓜ pa-no-*lee-*no
dictionary *vocabolario* ⓜ vo-ka-bo-*la-*ryo
dinner *cena* ⓕ *che-*na
direct *diretto/a* ⓜ/ⓕ dee-*re-*to/a
dirty *sporco/a* ⓜ/ⓕ *spor-*ko/a
disabled *disabile* dee-za-*bee-*le
discount *sconto* ⓜ *skon-*to
doctor *medico* ⓜ *me-*dee-ko
double bed *letto matrimoniale* ⓜ *le-*to ma-tree-mo-*nya-*le
double room *camera doppia* ⓕ *ka-*mer-a *do-*pya
drink *bevanda* ⓕ be-*van-*da
drive v *guidare* gwee-*da-*re
drivers licence *patente di guida* ⓕ pa-*ten-*te dee *gwee-*da
drugs (illicit) *droga* ⓕ *dro-*ga
dummy (pacifier) *ciuccotto* ⓜ choo-*cho-*to

E

ear *orecchio* ⓜ o-*re-*kyo
east *est* ⓜ est
eat *mangiare* man-*ja-*re
economy class *classe turistica* ⓕ *kla-*se too-*ree-*stee-ka
electricity *elettricità* ⓕ e-le-tree-chee-*ta*
elevator *ascensore* ⓜ a-shen-*so-*re
email *email* ⓜ e-mayl
embassy *ambasciata* ⓕ am-ba-*sha-*ta
emergency *emergenza* ⓕ e-mer-*jen-*tsa
English (language) *inglese* een-*gle-*ze

entrance *entrata* ⓕ en-*tra-*ta
evening *sera* ⓕ *se-*ra
exchange rate *tasso di cambio* ⓜ *ta-*so dee *kam-*byo
exit *uscita* ⓕ *ta-*so dee *kam-*byo
expensive *caro/a* ⓜ/ⓕ *ka-*ro/a
express mail *posta prioritaria* ⓕ *pos-*ta pree-o-ree-*ta-*rya
eye *occhio* ⓜ *o-*kyo

F

far *lontano/a* ⓜ/ⓕ lon-*ta-*no/a
fast *veloce* ve-*lo-*che
father *padre* ⓜ *pa-*dre
film (camera) *rullino* ⓜ roo-*lee-*no
finger *dito* ⓜ *dee-*to
first-aid kit *valigetta del pronto soccorso* ⓕ
　va-lee-je-ta del *pron-*to so-*kor-*so
first class *prima classe* ⓕ *pree-*ma *kla-*se
fish n *pesce* ⓜ *pe-*she
food *cibo* ⓜ *chee-*bo
foot *piede* ⓜ *pye-*de
fork *forchetta* ⓕ for-*ke-*ta
free (of charge) *gratuito/a* ⓜ/ⓕ gra-*too-*ee-to/a
friend *amico/a* ⓜ/ⓕ a-*mee-*ko/a
fruit *frutta* ⓕ *froo-*ta
full *pieno/a* ⓜ/ⓕ *pye-*no/a
funny *divertente* dee-ver-*ten-*te

G

gift *regalo* ⓜ re-*ga-*lo
girl *ragazza* ⓕ ra-*ga-*tsa
glass (drinking) *bicchiere* ⓜ bee-*kye-*re
glasses *occhiali* ⓜ pl o-*kya-*lee
go *andare* an-*da-*re
good *buono/a* ⓜ/ⓕ *bwo-*no/a
green *verde* *ver-*de
guide n *guida* ⓕ *gwee-*da

H

half *mezzo* ⓜ *me-*dzo
hand *mano* ⓕ *ma-*no
handbag *borsetta* ⓕ bor-*se-*ta
happy *felice* ⓜ/ⓕ fe-*lee-*che
have *avere* a-*ve-*re
he *lui* loo-ee
head *testa* ⓕ *tes-*ta
heart *cuore* ⓜ *kwo-*re
heat n *caldo* ⓜ *kal-*do

heavy *pesante* pe-*zan*-te
help v *aiutare* a-yoo-*ta*-re
here *qui* kwee
high *alto/a* ⓜ/ⓕ *al*-to/a
highway *autostrada* ⓕ ow-to-*stra*-da
hike v *fare un'escursione a piedi*
  fa-re oon es-koor-*syo*-ne a *pye*-de
holiday *vacanze* ⓕ pl va-*kan*-tse
homosexual n *omosessuale* ⓜ&ⓕ o-mo-se-*swa*-le
hospital *ospedale* ⓜ os-pe-*da*-le
hot *caldo/a* ⓜ/ⓕ *kal*-do/a
hotel *albergo* ⓜ al-*ber*-go
hungry *affamato/a* ⓜ/ⓕ a-fa-*ma*-to
husband *marito* ⓜ ma-*ree*-to

I

I *io* ee-o
identification (card) *carta d'identità* ⓕ
  kar-ta dee-den-tee-*ta*
ill *malato/a* ⓜ/ⓕ ma-*la*-to/a
important *importante* eem-por-*tan*-te
included *compreso/a* ⓜ/ⓕ kom-*pre*-zo/a
injury *ferita* ⓕ fe-*ree*-ta
insurance *assicurazione* ⓕ a-see-koo-ra-*tsyo*-ne
Internet *Internet* ⓜ een-ter-net
interpreter *interprete* ⓜ/ⓕ een-*ter*-pre-te
Italy *Italia* ⓕ ee-*ta*-lya
Italian (language) *italiano* ⓜ ee-ta-*lya*-no

J

jewellery *gioielli* ⓜ pl jo-*ye*-lee
job *lavoro* ⓜ la-*vo*-ro

K

key *chiave* ⓕ *kya*-ve
kilogram *chilo* ⓜ *kee*-lo
kitchen *cucina* ⓕ koo-*chee*-na
knife *coltello* ⓜ kol-*te*-lo

L

laundry (place) *lavanderia* ⓕ la-van-de-*ree*-a
lawyer *avvocato/a* ⓜ/ⓕ a-vo-*ka*-to/a
left (direction) *sinistra* see-*nee*-stra
left-luggage office *deposito bagagli* ⓜ
  de-po-zee-to ba-*ga*-lyee
leg *gamba* ⓕ *gam*-ba

lesbian n *lesbica* ⓕ *lez*-bee-ka
less *(di) meno* (dee) *me*-no
letter (mail) *lettera* ⓕ *le*-te-ra
lift (elevator) *ascensore* ⓜ a-shen-*so*-re
light *luce* ⓕ *loo*-che
like v *piacere* pya-*che*-re
lock *serratura* ⓕ se-ra-*too*-ra
long *lungo/a* ⓜ/ⓕ *loon*-go/a
lost *perso/a* ⓜ/ⓕ *per*-so/a
lost-property office *ufficio oggetti smarriti* ⓜ
  oo-*fee*-cho o-*je*-tee sma-*ree*-tee
love v *amare* a-*ma*-re
luggage *bagaglio* ⓜ ba-*ga*-lyo
lunch *pranzo* ⓜ *pran*-dzo

M

mail *posta* ⓕ *pos*-ta
man *uomo* ⓜ *wo*-mo
map *pianta* ⓕ *pyan*-ta
market *mercato* ⓜ mer-*ka*-to
matches *fiammiferi* ⓜ pl fya-*mee*-fe-ree
meat *carne* ⓕ *kar*-ne
medicine *medicina* ⓕ me-dee-*chee*-na
menu *menu* ⓜ me-*noo*
message *messaggio* ⓜ me-*sa*-jo
milk *latte* ⓕ *la*-te
minute *minuto* ⓜ mee-*noo*-to
mobile phone *telefono cellulare* ⓜ te-*le*-fo-no che-loo-*la*-re
money *denaro* ⓜ de-*na*-ro
month *mese* ⓜ *me*-ze
morning *mattina* ⓕ ma-*tee*-na
mother *madre* ⓕ *ma*-dre
motorcycle *moto* ⓕ *mo*-to
motorway *autostrada* ⓕ ow-to-*stra*-da
mouth *bocca* ⓕ *bo*-ka
music *musica* ⓕ *moo*-zee-ka

N

name *nome* ⓜ *no*-me
napkin *tovagliolo* ⓜ to-va-*lyo*-lo
nappy *pannolino* ⓜ pa-no-*lee*-no
near *vicino (a)* vee-*chee*-no (a)
neck *collo* ⓜ *ko*-lo
new *nuovo/a* ⓜ/ⓕ *nwo*-vo/a
news *notizie* ⓕ pl no-*tee*-tsye
newspaper *giornale* ⓜ jor-*na*-le
night *notte* ⓕ *no*-te
no *no* no

noisy *rumoroso/a* ⓜ/ⓕ roo-mo-ro-zo/a
nonsmoking *non fumatore* non foo-ma-ta-re
north *nord* ⓜ nord
nose *naso* ⓜ na-zo
now *adesso* a-de-so
number *numero* ⓜ noo-me-ro

O

oil (engine) *olio* ⓜ o-lyo
old *vecchio/a* ⓜ/ⓕ ve-kyo/a
one-way ticket *biglietto di solo andata*
bee-lye-to dee so-lo an-da-ta
open a *aperto/a* ⓜ/ⓕ a-per-to/a
outside *fuori* fwo-ree

P

package *pacchetto* ⓜ pa-ke-to
paper *carta* ⓕ kar-ta
park (car) v *parcheggiare* par-ke-ja-re
passport *passaporto* ⓜ pa-sa-por-to
pay *pagare* pa-ga-re
pen *penna (a sfera)* ⓕ pe-na (a sfe-ra)
petrol *benzina* ⓕ ben-dzee-na
pharmacy *farmacia* ⓕ far-ma-chee-a
phonecard *scheda telefonica* ⓕ ske-da te-le-fo-nee-ka
photo *foto* ⓕ fo-to
plate *piatto* ⓜ pya-to
police *polizia* ⓕ po-lee-tsee-a
postcard *cartolina* ⓕ kar-to-lee-na
post office *ufficio postale* ⓜ oo-fee-cho pos-ta-le
pregnant *incinta* een-cheen-ta
price *prezzo* ⓜ pre-tso

Q

quiet *tranquillo/a* ⓜ/ⓕ tran-kwee-lo/a

R

rain n *pioggia* ⓜ pyo-ja
razor *rasoio* ⓜ ra-zo-yo
receipt *ricevuta* ⓕ ree-che-voo-ta
red *rosso/a* ⓜ/ⓕ ro-so/a
refund *rimborso* ⓜ reem-bor-so
registered mail *posta raccomandata* ⓕ
pos-ta ra-ko-man-da-ta
rent v *prendere in affitto* pren-de-re een a-fee-to
repair v *riparare* ree-pa-ra-re

reservation *prenotazione* ⓕ pre-no-ta-tsyo-ne
restaurant *ristorante* ⓜ rees-to-ran-te
return v *ritornare* ree-tor-na-re
return ticket *biglietto di andata e ritorno*
bee-lye-to dee an-da-ta e ree-tor-no
right (direction) *destra* de-stra
road *strada* ⓕ stra-da
room *camera* ⓕ ka-me-ra

S

safe a *sicuro/a* ⓜ/ⓕ see-koo-ro/a
sanitary napkins *assorbenti igienici* ⓜ pl
as-or-ben-tee ee-je-nee-chee
seat *posto* ⓜ pos-to
send *mandare* man-da-re
service station *stazione di servizio* ⓕ
sta-tsyo-ne dee ser-vee-tsyo
sex *sesso* ⓜ se-so
shampoo *shampoo* ⓜ sham-poo
share (a dorm) *condividere* kon-dee-vee-de-re
shaving cream *crema da barba* ⓕ kre-ma da bar-ba
she *lei* lay
sheet (bed) *lenzuolo* ⓜ len-tswo-lo
shirt *camicia* ⓕ ka-mee-cha
shoes *scarpe* ⓕ pl skar-pe
shop *negozio* ⓜ ne-go-tsyo
short *corto/a* ⓜ/ⓕ kor-to/a
shower *doccia* ⓕ do-cha
single room *camera singola* ⓕ ka-me-ra seen-go-la
skin *pelle* ⓕ pe-le
skirt *gonna* ⓕ go-na
sleep v *dormire* dor-mee-re
slowly *lentamente* len-ta-men-te
small *piccola/a* ⓜ/ⓕ pee-ko-lo/a
smoke (cigarettes) v *fumare* foo-ma-re
soap *sapone* ⓜ sa-po-ne
some *alcuni/e* ⓜ/ⓕ pl al-koo-nee/al-koo-ne
soon *fra poco* fra po-ko
south *sud* ⓜ sood
souvenir shop *negozio di souvenir* ⓜ
ne-go-tsyo dee soo-ve-neer
speak *parlare* par-la-re
spoon *cucchiaio* ⓜ koo-kya-yo
stamp *francobollo* ⓜ fran-ko-bo-lo
stand-by ticket *in lista d'attesa* een lee-sta da-te-za
station (train) *stazione* ⓕ sta-tsyo-ne
stomach *stomaco* ⓜ sto-ma-ko
stop v *fermare* fer-ma-re
stop (bus) *fermata* ⓕ fer-ma-ta

street *strada* ① *stra*-da
student *studente/studentessa* ⓜ/①
    stoo-*den*-te/stoo-den-*te*-sa
sun *sole* ① *so*-le
sunscreen *crema solare* ① *kre*-ma so-*la*-re
swim v *nuotare* nwo-*ta*-re
Switzerland *Svizzera* ① svee-*tse*-ra

T

tampons *assorbenti interni* ⓜ pl
    a-sor-*ben*-tee een-*ter*-nee
taxi *tassì* ① ta-*see*
teaspoon *cucchiaino* ① koo-kya-ee-*no*
teeth *denti* ⓜ pl *den*-tee
telephone *telefono* ⓜ te-*le*-fo-no
television *televisione* ① te-le-vee-*zyo*-ne
temperature (weather) *temperatura* ①
    tem-pe-ra-*too*-ra
tent *tenda* ① *ten*-da
that (one) *quello/a* ⓜ/① *kwe*-lo/a
they *loro* *lo*-ro
thirsty *assetato/a* ⓜ/① a-se-*ta*-to
this (one) *questo/a* ⓜ/① *kwe*-sto/a
throat *gola* ① *go*-la
ticket *biglietto* ⓜ bee-*lye*-to
time *tempo* ⓜ *tem*-po
tired *stanco/a* ⓜ/① *stan*-ko/a
tissues *fazzolettini di carta* ⓜ pl
    fa-tso-le-*tee*-nee dee *kar*-ta
today *oggi* o-jee
toilet *gabinetto* ⓜ ga-bee-*ne*-to
tomorrow *domani* do-*ma*-nee
tonight *stasera* sta-se-ra
toothbrush *spazzolino da denti* ⓜ
    spa-tso-*lee*-no da *den*-tee
toothpaste *dentifricio* ⓜ den-tee-*free*-cho
torch (flashlight) *torcia elettrica* ① *tor*-cha e-*le*-tree-ka
tour *gita* ① *jee*-ta
tourist office *ufficio del turismo* ⓜ
    oo-*fee*-cho del too-*reez*-mo
towel *asciugamano* ⓜ a-shoo-ga-*ma*-no
train *treno* ⓜ *tre*-no
translate *tradurre* tra-*doo*-re
travel agency *agenzia di viaggio* ①
    a-jen-*tsee*-a dee vee-*a*-jo
travellers cheque *assegno di viaggio* ⓜ
    a-*se*-nyo dee vee-*a*-jo
trousers *pantaloni* ⓜ pl pan-ta-*lo*-nee

twin beds *due letti* *doo*-e le-tee
tyre *gomma* ① *go*-ma

U

underwear *biancheria intima* ① byan-ke-*ree*-a *een*-tee-ma
urgent *urgente* ⓜ/① oor-*jen*-te

V

vacant *libero/a* ⓜ/① *lee*-be-ro/a
vacation *vacanza* ① va-*kan*-tsa
vegetable *verdura* ① ver-*doo*-ra
vegetarian a *vegetariano/a* ⓜ/① ve-je-ta-*rya*-no/a
visa *visto* ⓜ *vee*-sto

W

waiter *cameriere/a* ⓜ/① ka-mer-*ye*-re/a
walk v *camminare* ka-mee-*na*-re
wallet *portafoglio* ⓜ por-ta-*fo*-lyo
warm a *tiepido/a* ⓜ/① *tye*-pee-do/a
wash (something) *lavare* la-*va*-re
watch *orologio* o-ro-*lo*-jo
water *acqua* ① *a*-kwa
we *noi* noy
weekend *fine settimana* ⓜ *fee*-ne se-tee-*ma*-na
west *ovest* ⓜ o-vest
wheelchair *sedia a rotelle* ① *se*-dya a ro-*te*-le
when *quando* *kwan*-do
where *dove* *do*-ve
white *bianco/a* ⓜ/① *byan*-ko/a
who *chi* kee
why *perché* per-*ke*
wife *moglie* ① *mo*-lye
window *finestra* ① fee-*nes*-tra
wine *vino* ⓜ *vee*-no
with *con* kon
without *senza* *sen*-tsa
woman *donna* ① *do*-na
write *scrivere* *skree*-ve-re

Y

yellow *giallo/a* ⓜ/① *ja*-lo/a
yes *sì* see
yesterday *ieri* *ye*-ree
you sg inf *tu* too
you sg pol *Lei* lay
you pl *voi* voy

Polish

polish alphabet

A a a	*Ą ą* om/on	*B b* be	*C c* tse	*Ć ć* che	*D d* de
E e e	*Ę ę* em/en	*F f* ef	*G g* gye	*H h* kha	*I i* ee
J j yot	*K k* ka	*L l* el	*Ł ł* ew	*M m* em	*N n* en
Ń ń en'	*O o* o	*Ó ó* oo	*P p* pe	*R r* er	*S s* es
Ś ś esh	*T t* te	*U u* oo	*W w* woo	*Y y* i	*Z z* zet
Ź ź zhet	*Ż ż* zhyet				

■ polish

POLSKI

POLISH
polski

about Polish

Ask most English speakers what they know about Polish (*polski pol*-skee), the language which donated the words *horde, mazurka* and *vodka* to English, and they will most likely dismiss it as an unpronounceable language. Who could pronounce an apparently vowel-less word like *szczyt* shchit (peak), for example? To be put off by this unfairly gained reputation, however, would be to miss out on a rich and rewarding language. The mother tongue of Copernicus, Chopin, Marie Curie and Pope John Paul II has a fascinating and turbulent past and symbolises the resilience of the Polish people in the face of domination and adversity.

The Polish tribes who occupied the basins of the Oder and Vistula rivers in the 6th century spoke a range of West Slavic dialects, which over time evolved into Polish. The closest living relatives of Polish are Czech and Slovak which also belong to the wider West Slavic family of languages. The language reached the apex of its influence during the era of the Polish Lithuanian Commonwealth (1569–1795). The Commonwealth covered a swath of territory from what are now Poland and Lithuania through Belarus, Ukraine and Latvia and part of Western Russia. Polish became a lingua franca throughout much of Central and Eastern Europe at this time due to the political, cultural, scientific and military might of this power.

When Poland was wiped off the map of Europe from 1795 to 1918 after three successive partitions in the second half of the 18th century (when it was carved up between Russia, Austria and Prussia), the language suffered attempts at both Germanisation and Russification. Later, after WWII, Poland became a satellite state of the Soviet Union and the language came under the renewed influence of Russian. Polish showed impressive resistance in the face of this oppression. The language not only survived these onslaughts but enriched itself by borrowing many words from both Russian and German. The works of Poland's greatest literary figures who wrote in exile – the Romantic poet Adam Mickiewicz and, during Communist rule, the Nobel Prize winner Czesław Miłosz – are testament to this fact.

Today, Poland is linguistically one of the most homogenous countries in Europe – over 95% of the population speaks Polish as their first language. There are significant Polish-speaking minorities in the western border areas of Ukraine, Belarus and in southern Lithuania, with smaller populations in other neighbouring countries.

pronunciation

vowel sounds

Polish vowels are generally prounounced short, giving them a 'clipped' quality.

symbol	english equivalent	polish example	transliteration
a	run	*tak*	tak
ai	aisle	*tutaj*	*too*·tai
e	bet	*bez*	bes
ee	see	*wino*	*vee*·no
ey	hey	*kolejka*	ko·*ley*·ka
i	bit	*czy*	chi
o	pot	*woda*	*vo*·da
oo	zoo	*zakupy, mój*	za·*koo*·pi, mooy
ow	how	*migdał*	meeg·*dow*
oy	toy	*ojciec*	*oy*·chets

Polish also has nasal vowels, pronounced as though you're trying to force the air out of your nose rather than your mouth. Nasal vowels are indicated in written Polish by the letters *ą* and *ę*. Depending upon the letters that follow these vowels, they're pronounced with either an 'm' or an 'n' sound following the vowel.

symbol	english equivalent	polish example	transliteration
em	like the 'e' in 'get' plus	*wstęp*	fstemp
en	nasal consonant sound	*mięso*	*myen*·so
om	like the 'o' in 'not' plus	*kąpiel*	*kom*·pyel
on	nasal consonant sound	*wąsy*	*von*·si

word stress

In Polish, stress almost always falls on the second-last syllable. In our coloured pronunciation guides, the stressed syllable is italicised.

consonant sounds

Most Polish consonant sounds are also found in English, with the exception of the kh sound (pronounced as in the Scottish word *loch*) and the rolled r sound.

symbol	english equivalent	polish example	transliteration
b	bed	*babka*	*bap*·ka
ch	cheat	*cień, czas, ćma*	chen', chas, chma
d	dog	*drobne*	*drob*·ne
f	fat	*fala*	*fa*·la
g	go	*garnek*	*gar*·nek
j	joke	*dzieci*	*je*·chee
k	kit	*kac*	kats
kh	loch	*chata, hałas*	*kha*·ta, *kha*·was
l	lot	*lato*	*la*·to
m	man	*malarz*	*ma*·lash
n	not	*nagle*	*na*·gle
p	pet	*palec*	*pa*·lets
r	run (rolled)	*róg*	roog
s	sun	*samolot*	*sa*·mo·lot
sh	shot	*siedem, śnieg, szlak*	*shye*·dem, shnyek, shlak
t	top	*targ*	tark
v	very	*widok*	*vee*·dok
w	win	*złoto*	*zwo*·to
y	yes	*zajęty*	za·*yen*·ti
z	zero	*zachód*	*za*·khoot
zh	pleasure	*zima, żart, rzeźba*	*zhee*·ma, zhart, *zhezh*·ba
'	a slight y sound	*kwiecień*	*kfye*·chen'

tools

language difficulties

Do you speak English?
*Czy pan/pani mówi
po angielsku?* m/f pol

chi pan/*pa*-nee *moo*-vee
po an-*gyel*-skoo

Do you understand?
Czy pan/pani rozumie? m/f pol

chi pan/*pa*-nee ro-*zoo*-mye

I (don't) understand.
(Nie) Rozumiem.

(nye) ro-*zoo*-myem

What does (*nieczynne*) mean?
Co to znaczy (nieczynne)?

tso to *zna*-chi (nye-*chi*-ne)

How do you ...?
  pronounce this
  write (*pierogi*)

Jak się ...?
to wymawia
pisze (pierogi)

yak shye ...
to vi-*mav*-ya
pee-she (pye-*ro*-gee)

Could you please ...?
  repeat that
  speak more
   slowly
  write it down

Proszę ...
to powtórzyć
mówić trochę
wolniej
to napisać

pro-she ...
to pov-*too*-zhich
moo-veech tro-khe
vol-nyey
to na-*pee*-sach

essentials

Yes.	*Tak.*	tak
No.	*Nie.*	nye
Please.	*Proszę.*	*pro*-she
Thank you (very much).	*Dziękuję (bardzo).*	jyen-*koo*-ye (*bar*-dzo)
You're welcome.	*Proszę.*	*pro*-she
Excuse me.	*Przepraszam.*	pshe-*pra*-sham
Sorry.	*Przepraszam.*	pshe-*pra*-sham

numbers

0	zero	ze·ro		15	piętnaście	pyent·nash·chye
1	jeden m	ye·den		16	szesnaście	shes·nash·chye
	jedna f	yed·na		17	siedemnaście	shye·dem·nash·chye
	jedno n	yed·no		18	osiemnaście	o·shem·nash·chye
2	dwa m	dva		19	dziewiętnaście	jye·vyet·nash·chye
	dwie f	dvye		20	dwadzieścia	dva·jyesh·chya
	dwoje n	dvo·ye		21	dwadzieścia	dva·jyesh·chya
3	trzy	tshi			jeden	ye·den
4	cztery	chte·ri		22	dwadzieścia	dva·jyesh·chya
5	pięć	pyench			dwa	dva
6	sześć	sheshch		30	trzydzieści	tshi·jyesh·chee
7	siedem	shye·dem		40	czterdzieści	chter·jyesh·chee
8	osiem	o·shyem		50	pięćdziesiąt	pyen·jye·shont
9	dziewięć	jye·vyench		60	sześćdziesiąt	shesh·jye·shont
10	dziesięć	jye·shench		70	siedemdziesiąt	shye·dem·jye·shont
11	jedenaście	ye·de·nash·chye		80	osiemdziesiąt	o·shem·jye·shont
12	dwanaście	dva·nash·chye		90	dziewięćdziesiąt	jye·vyen·jye·shont
13	trzynaście	tshi·nash·chye		100	sto	sto
14	czternaście	chter·nash·chye		1000	tysiąc	ti·shonts

time & dates

What time is it?	Która jest godzina?	ktoo·ra yest go·jee·na
It's one o'clock.	Pierwsza.	pyerf·sha
It's (10) o'clock.	Jest (dziesiąta).	yest (jye·shon·ta)
Quarter past (10).	Piętnaście po (dziesiątej).	pyent·nash·chye po (jye·shon·tey)
Half past (10).	Wpół do (jedenastej).	fpoow do (ye·de·nas·tey)
Quarter to (11).	Za piętnaście (jedenasta).	za pyent·nash·chye (ye·de·nas·ta)
At what time ...?	O której godzinie ...?	o ktoo·rey go·jee·nye ...
At ...	O ...	o ...
in the morning	rano	ra·no
in the afternoon	po południu	po po·wood·nyoo
in the evening (6pm–10pm)	wieczorem	vye·cho·rem
at night (11pm–3am)	w nocy	v no·tsi

Monday	*poniedziałek*	po·nye·*jya*·wek
Tuesday	*wtorek*	*fto*·rek
Wednesday	*środa*	*shro*·da
Thursday	*czwartek*	*chfar*·tek
Friday	*piątek*	*pyon*·tek
Saturday	*sobota*	so·*bo*·ta
Sunday	*niedziela*	nye·*jye*·la
January	*styczeń*	*sti*·chen'
February	*luty*	*loo*·ti
March	*marzec*	*ma*·zhets
April	*kwiecień*	*kfye*·chyen'
May	*maj*	mai
June	*czerwiec*	*cher*·vyets
July	*lipiec*	*lee*·pyets
August	*sierpień*	*shyer*·pyen'
September	*wrzesień*	*vzhe*·shyen'
October	*październik*	pazh·*jyer*·neek
November	*listopad*	*lees*·to·pat
December	*grudzień*	*groo*·jyen'

What date is it today?	*Którego jest dzisiaj?*	ktoo·*re*·go yest *jee*·shai
It's (18 October).	*Jest (osiemnastego*	yest (o·shem·nas·*te*·go
	października).	pazh·jyer·*nee*·ka)
last night	*wczoraj wieczorem*	*fcho*·rai vye·*cho*·rem
last/next ...	*w zeszłym/przyszłym ...*	v *zesh*·wim/*pshish*·wim ...
week	*tygodniu*	ti·*god*·nyoo
month	*miesiącu*	mye·*shon*·tsoo
year	*roku*	*ro*·koo
yesterday/	*wczoraj/*	*fcho*·rai/
tomorrow ...	*jutro ...*	*yoo*·tro ...
morning	*rano*	*ra*·no
afternoon	*po południu*	po po·*wood*·nyoo
evening	*wieczorem*	vye·*cho*·rem

weather

What's the weather like?	Jaka jest pogoda?	ya·ka yest po·go·da
It's ...		
cloudy	Jest pochmurnie.	yest pokh·moor·nye
cold	Jest zimno.	yest zheem·no
hot	Jest gorąco.	yest go·ron·tso
raining	Pada deszcz.	pa·da deshch
snowing	Pada śnieg.	pa·da shnyeg
sunny	Jest słonecznie.	yest swo·nech·nye
warm	Jest ciepło.	yest chyep·wo
windy	Jest wietrznie.	yest vyetzh·nye
spring	wiosna f	vyos·na
summer	lato n	la·to
autumn	jesień f	ye·shyen'
winter	zima f	zhee·ma

border crossing

I'm ...	Jestem ...	yes·tem ...
in transit	w tranzycie	v tran·zi·chye
on business	służbowo	swoozh·bo·vo
on holiday	na wakacjach	na va·kats·yakh
I'm here for ...	Będę tu przez ...	ben·de too pshes ...
(10) days	(dziesięć) dni	(jye·shench) dnee
(three) weeks	(trzy) tygodnie	(tshi) ti·god·nye
(two) months	(dwa) miesiące	(dva) mye·shon·tse

I'm going to (Kraków).
Jadę do (Krakowa).   ya·de do (kra·ko·va)

I'm staying at the (Pod Różą Hotel).
Zatrzymuję się w (hotelu 'pod Różą').   za·tshi·moo·ye shye v (ho·te·loo pod roo·zhom)

I have nothing to declare.
Nie mam nic do zgłoszenia.   nye mam neets do zgwo·she·nya

I have something to declare.
Mam coś do zgłoszenia.   mam tsosh do zgwo·she·nya

That's (not) mine.
To (nie) jest moje.   to (nye) yest mo·ye

transport

tickets & luggage

Where can I buy a ticket?
Gdzie mogę kupić bilet?   gjye *mo*·ge *koo*·peech *bee*·let

Do I need to book a seat?
Czy muszę rezerwować?   chi *moo*·she re·zer·*vo*·vach

One ... ticket (to Katowice), please.	*Proszę bilet ... (do Katowic).*	*pro*·she *bee*·let ... do (ka·*to*·veets)
one-way	*w jedną stronę*	v *yed*·nom *stro*·ne
return	*powrotny*	po·*vro*·tni

I'd like to ... my ticket, please.	*Chcę ... mój bilet.*	khtse ... mooy *bee*·let
cancel	*odwołać*	od·*vo*·wach
change	*zmienić*	zmye·neech
collect	*odebrać*	o·*de*·brach
confirm	*potwierdzić*	po·*tvyer*·jyeech

I'd like a ... seat, please.	*Proszę miejsce ...*	*pro*·she *myeys*·tse ...
nonsmoking	*dla niepalących*	dla nye·pa·*lon*·tsikh
smoking	*dla palących*	dla pa·*lon*·tsikh

How much is it?
Ile kosztuje?   *ee*·le kosh·*too*·ye

Is there air conditioning?
Czy jest tam klimatyzacja?   chi yest tam klee·ma·ti·*za*·tsya

Is there a toilet?
Czy jest tam toaleta?   chi yest tam to·a·*le*·ta

How long does the trip take?
Ile trwa podróż?   *ee*·le trfa po·*droosh*

Is it a direct route?
Czy to jest bezpośrednie połączenie?   chi to yest bes·po·*shred*·nye po·won·*che*·nye

Where can I find a luggage locker?
Gdzie jest schowek na bagaż?   gjye yest *skho*·vek na ba·gazh

My luggage	Mój bagaż	mooy ba·gazh
has been ...	został ...	zos·tow ...
damaged	uszkodzony	oosh·ko·dzo·ni
lost	zagubiony	za·goo·byo·ni
stolen	skradziony	skra·jyo·ni

getting around

Where does flight (LO125) arrive/depart?
Skąd przylatuje/odlatuje   skont pshi·la·too·ye/od·la·too·ye
lot (LO125)?   lot (el o sto dva·jyesh·chya pyench)

Where's (the) ...?	Gdzie jest ...?	gjye yest ...
arrivals hall	hala przylotów	kha·la pshi·lo·toof
departures hall	hala odlotów	kha·la od·lo·toof
duty-free shop	sklep wolnocłowy	sklep vol·no·tswo·vi
gate (five)	wejście	veysh·chye
	(numer pięć)	(noo·mer pyench)

Is this the ...	Czy to jest ...	chi to yest ...
to (Wrocław)?	do (Wrocławia)?	do (vrots·wa·vya)
bus	autobus	ow·to·boos
plane	samolot	sa·mo·lot
train	pociąg	po·chonk

When's the ... bus?	Kiedy jest ... autobus?	kye·di yest ... ow·to·boos
first	pierwszy	pyerf·shi
last	ostatni	os·tat·nee
next	następny	nas·temp·ni

At what time does it arrive/leave?
O której godzinie przyjeżdża/   o ktoo·rey go·jee·nye pshi·yezh·ja/
odjeżdża?   ot·yezh·ja

How long will it be delayed?
Jakie będzie opóźnienie?   ya·kye ben·jye o·poozh·nye·nye

What's the next station?
Jaka jest następna stacja?   ya·ka yest nas·temp·na sta·tsya

What's the next stop?
Jaki jest następny przystanek?   ya·kee yest nas·tem·pni pshi·sta·nek

Does it stop at (Kalisz)?
Czy on się zatrzymuje w (Kaliszu)?   chi on shye za·tshi·*moo*·ye f (ka·*lee*·shoo)

Please tell me when we get to (Krynica).
Proszę mi powiedzieć gdy   pro·she mee po·*vye*·jyech gdi
dojedziemy do (Krynicy).   do·ye·*jye*·mi do (kri·*nee*·tsi)

How long do we stop here?
Na jak długo się tu zatrzymamy?   na yak *dwoo*·go shye too za·tshi·*ma*·mi

Is this seat available?
Czy to miejsce jest wolne?   chi to *myeys*·tse yest *vol*·ne

That's my seat.
To jest moje miejsce.   to yest *mo*·ye *myeys*·tse

I'd like a taxi . . .	*Chcę zamówić*	khtse za·*moo*·veech
	taksówę na . . .	tak·*soof*·ke na . . .
now	*teraz*	*te*·ras
tomorrow	*jutro*	*yoo*·tro
at (9am)	*(dziewiątą rano)*	(jye·*vyon*·tom *ra*·no)

Is this taxi available?
Czy ta taksówka jest wolna?   chi ta tak·*soof*·ka yest *vol*·na

How much is it to (Szczecin)?
Ile kosztuje do (Szczecina)?   ee·le kosh·*too*·ye (do shche·*chee*·na)

Please put the meter on.
Proszę włączyć taksometr.   pro·she vwon·chich tak·*so*·metr

Please take me to (this address).
Proszę mnie zawieźć pod (ten adres).   pro·she mnye za·*vyeshch* pod (ten *ad*·res)

Please . . .	*Proszę . . .*	*pro*·she . . .
slow down	*zwolnić*	*zvol*·neech
stop here	*się tu zatrzymać*	shye too za·*tshi*·mach
wait here	*tu zaczekać*	too za·*che*·kach

car, motorbike & bicycle hire

I'd like to hire a . . .	*Chcę wypożyczyć . . .*	khtse vi·po·*zhi*·chich . . .
bicycle	*rower*	*ro*·ver
car	*samochód*	sa·*mo*·khoot
motorbike	*motocykl*	mo·*to*·tsikl

with ...	z ...	z ...
air conditioning	*klimatyzacją*	klee·ma·ti·za·tsyom
a driver	*kierowcą*	kye·*rof*·tsom
antifreeze	*płynem nie zamarzającym*	*pwi*·nem nye za·mar·za·*yon*·tsim
snow chains	*łańcuchami śnieżnymi*	wan'·tsoo·*kha*·mee shnezh·*ni*·mee

How much for ... hire?	*Ile kosztuje wypożyczenie na ...?*	ee·le kosh·*too*·ye vi·po·zhi·*che*·nye na ...
hourly	*godzinę*	go·*jee*·ne
daily	*dzień*	jyen'
weekly	*tydzień*	ti·jyen'

air	*powietrze* n	po·*vye*·tshe
oil	*olej* m	*o*·ley
petrol	*benzyna* f	ben·*zi*·na
tyre	*opona* f	o·*po*·na

I need a mechanic.
Potrzebuję mechanika. po·tshe·*boo*·ye me·kha·*nee*·ka

I've run out of petrol.
Zabrakło mi benzyny. za·*bra*·kwo mee ben·*zi*·ni

I have a flat tyre.
Złapałem/Złapałam gumę. m/f zwa·*pa*·wem/zwa·*pa*·wam *goo*·me

directions

Where's the ...?	*Gdzie jest ...?*	gjye yest ...
bank	*bank*	bank
city centre	*centrum miasta*	*tsen*·troom *myas*·ta
hotel	*hotel*	*ho*·tel
market	*targ*	tark
police station	*komisariat policji*	ko·mee·*sar*·yat po·*leets*·yee
post office	*urząd pocztowy*	*oo*·zhond poch·*to*·vi
public toilet	*toaleta publiczna*	to·a·*le*·ta poo·*bleech*·na
tourist office	*biuro turystyczne*	*byoo*·ro too·ris·*tich*·ne

Is this the road to (Malbork)?
Czy to jest droga do (Malborka)? chi to yest *dro*·ga do (mal·*bor*·ka)

Can you show me (on the map)?
Czy może pan/pani
mi pokazać (na mapie)? m/f
chi *mo·*zhe pan/*pa·*nee
mee po·*ka·*zach (na *ma·*pye)

What's the address?
Jaki jest adres?
*ya·*kee yest *ad·*res

How far is it?
Jak daleko to jest?
yak da·*le·*ko to yest

How do I get there?
Jak tam mogę się dostać?
yak tam *mo·*ge shye *dos·*tach

Turn ...	*Proszę skręcić ...*	*pro·*she skren·cheech ...
at the corner	*na rogu*	na *ro·*goo
at the traffic lights	*na światłach*	na *shfyat·*wakh
left/right	*w lewo/prawo*	v *le·*vo/*pra·*vo
It's ...	*To jest ...*	to yest ...
behind ...	*za ...*	za ...
far away	*daleko*	da·*le·*ko
here	*tu*	too
in front of ...	*przed ...*	pshet ...
left	*po lewej*	po *le·*vey
near	*blisko*	*blees·*ko
next to ...	*obok ...*	*o·*bok ...
on the corner	*na rogu*	na *ro·*goo
opposite ...	*naprzeciwko ...*	nap·she·*cheef·*ko ...
right	*po prawej*	po *pra·*vey
straight ahead	*na wprost*	na fprost
there	*tam*	tam
by bus	*autobusem*	ow·to·*boo·*sem
by taxi	*taksówką*	tak·*soof·*kom
by train	*pociągiem*	po·*chon·*gyem
on foot	*pieszo*	*pye·*sho
north	*północ*	*poow·*nots
south	*południe*	po·*wood·*nye
east	*wschód*	fskhoot
west	*zachód*	*za·*khoot

Wjazd/Wyjazd	vyazd/*vi*-yazd	**Entrance/Exit**
Otwarte/Zamknięte	ot-*far*-te/zamk-*nyen*-te	**Open/Closed**
Wolne pokoje	*vol*-ne po-*ko*-ye	**Rooms Available**
Brak wolnych miejsc	brak *vol*-nikh myeysts	**No Vacancies**
Informacja	een-for-*ma*-tsya	**Information**
Komisariat policji	ko-mee-*sar*-yat po-*lee*-tsyee	**Police Station**
Zabroniony	za-bro-*nyo*-ni	**Prohibited**
Toalety	to-a-*le*-ti	**Toilets**
Męskie	*mens*-kye	**Men**
Damskie	*dams*-kye	**Women**
Zimna/Gorąca	*zheem*-na/go-*ron*-tsa	**Hot/Cold**

accommodation

finding accommodation

Where's a ...?	*Gdzie jest ...?*	*gjye yest ...*
camping ground	*kamping*	*kam*-peeng
guesthouse	*pokoje gościnne*	po-*ko*-ye gosh-*chee*-ne
hotel	*hotel*	*ho*-tel
youth hostel	*schronisko*	skhro-*nees*-ko
	młodzieżowe	mwo-jye-*zho*-ve

Can you recommend	*Czy może pan/pani*	chi *mo*-zhe pan/*pa*-nee
somewhere ...?	*polecić coś ...?* m/f	po-*le*-cheech tsosh ...
cheap	*taniego*	ta-*nye*-go
good	*dobrego*	do-*bre*-go
nearby	*coś w pobliżu*	tsosh f po-*blee*-zhoo

I'd like to book a room, please.
  Chcę zarezerwować pokój.   khtse za-re-zer-*vo*-vach *po*-kooy

I have a reservation.
  Mam rezerwację.   mam re-zer-*va*-tsye

My name's ...
  Nazywam się ...   na-*zi*-vam shye ...

Do you have a ... room?	Czy jest pokój ...?	chi yest po·kooy ...
single	jednoosobowy	yed·no·o·so·bo·vi
double	z podwójnym łóżkiem	z pod·vooy·nim woozh·kyem
twin	z dwoma łóżkami	z dvo·ma wozh·ka·mee

How much is it per ...?	Ile kosztuje za ...?	ee·le kosh·too·ye za ...
night	noc	nots
person	osobę	o·so·be

Can I pay ...?	Czy mogę zapłacić ...?	chi mo·ge za·pwa·cheech ...
by credit card	kartą kredytową	kar·tom kre·di·to·vom
with a travellers cheque	czekami podróżnymi	che·ka·mee po·droozh·ni·mee

For (three) nights/weeks.
Na (trzy) noce/tygodnie.　　na (tshi) no·tse/ti·god·nye

From (2 July) to (6 July).
Od (drugiego lipca) do (szóstego lipca).　　od (droo·gye·go leep·tsa) do (shoos·te·go leep·tsa)

Can I see it?
Czy mogę go zobaczyć?　　chi mo·ge go zo·ba·chich

Am I allowed to I camp here?
Czy mogę się tutaj rozbić?　　chi mo·ge shye too·tai roz·beech

Where can I find the camping ground?
Gdzie jest pole kampingowe?　　gjye yest po·le kam·peen·go·ve

requests & queries

When's breakfast served?
O której jest śniadanie?　　o ktoo·rey yest shnya·da·nye

Where's breakfast served?
Gdzie jest śniadanie?　　gjye yest shnya·da·nye

Please wake me at (seven).
Proszę obudzić mnie o (siódmej).　　pro·she o·boo·jeech mnye o (shyood·mey)

Could I have my key, please?
Czy mogę prosić o klucz?　　chi mo·ge pro·sheech o klooch

Can I get another (blanket)?
Czy mogę prosić o jeszcze jeden (koc)?　　chi mo·ge pro·sheech o yesh·che ye·den (kots)

Is there an elevator/a safe?
   Czy jest winda/sejf?   chi yest *veen*·da/seyf

This (towel) isn't clean.
   Ten (ręcznik) nie jest czysty.   ten (*rench*·neek) nye yest *chis*·ti

It's too ...	*Jest zbyt ...*	yest zbit ...
expensive	*drogi*	*dro*·gee
noisy	*głośny*	*gwosh*·ni
small	*mały*	*ma*·wi

The ... doesn't work.	*... nie działa.*	... nye *jya*·wa
air conditioner	*Klimatyzator*	klee·ma·ti·*za*·tor
fan	*Wentylator*	ven·ti·*la*·tor
toilet	*Ubikacja*	oo·bee·*kats*·ya

checking out

What time is checkout?
   O której godzinie   o *ktoo*·rey go·*jye*·nye
   muszę się wymeldować?   *moo*·she shye vi·mel·*do*·vach

Can I leave my luggage here?
   Czy mogę tu zostawić   chi *mo*·ge too zo·*sta*·veech
   moje bagaże?   *mo*·ye ba·*ga*·zhe

Could I have	*Czy mogę prosić*	chi *mo*·ge *pro*·sheech
my ..., please?	*o mój/moje ...?* sg/pl	o mooy/*mo*·ye ...
deposit	*depozyt* sg	de·*po*·zit
passport	*paszport* sg	*pash*·port
valuables	*kosztowności* pl	kosh·tov·*nosh*·chee

communications & banking

the internet

Where's the local Internet café?
   Gdzie jest kawiarnia internetowa?   gjye yest ka·*vyar*·nya een·ter·ne·*to*·va

How much is it per hour?
   Ile kosztuje za godzinę?   *ee*·le kosh·*too*·ye za go·*jee*·ne

I'd like to ...	Chciałem/Chciałam ... m/f	khchow-em/khchow-am ...
check my email	sprawdzić mój email	sprav-jeech mooy ee-mayl
get Internet access	podłączyć się do internetu	pod-won-chich shye do een-ter-ne-too
use a printer	użyć drukarki	oo-zhich droo-kar-kee
use a scanner	użyć skaner	oo-zhich ska-ner

mobile/cell phone

I'd like a ...	Chciałem/Chciałam ... m/f	khchow-em/khchow-am ...
mobile/cell phone for hire	wypożyczyć telefon komórkowy	vi-po-zhi-chich te-le-fon ko-moor-ko-vi
SIM card for your network	kartę SIM na waszą sieć	kar-te seem na va-shom shyech
What are the rates?	Jakie są stawki za rozmowy?	ya-kye som staf-kee za roz-mo-vi

telephone

What's your phone number?
Jaki jest pana/pani numer telefonu? m/f pol
ya-kee yest pa-na/pa-nee noo-mer te-le-fo-noo

The number is ...
Numer jest ...
noo-mer yest ...

Where's the nearest public phone?
Gdzie jest najbliższy telefon?
gjye yest nai-bleezh-shi te-le-fon

I'd like to buy a chip phonecard.
Chciałem/Chciałam kupić czipową kartę telefoniczną. m/f
khchow-em/khchow-am koo-peech chee-po-vom kar-te te-le-fo-neech-nom

I want to ...	Chciałem/Chciałam ... m/f	khchow-em/khchow-am ...
call (Singapore)	zadzwonić do (Singapuru)	zad-zvo-neech do (seen-ga-poo-roo)
make a local call	zadzwonić pod lokalny numer	zad-zvo-neech pod lo-kal-ni noo-mer
reverse the charges	zamówić rozmowę na koszt odbiorcy	za-moo-veech roz-mo-ve na kosht od-byor-tsi

How much does ... cost?	Ile kosztuje ...?	ee·le kosh·too·ye ...
a (three)-minute call	rozmowa (trzy) minutowa	roz·mo·va (tshi) mee·noo·to·va
each extra minute	każda dodatkowa minuta	kazh·da do·dat·ko·va mee·noo·ta
(Two złotys) per (30) seconds.	(Dwa złote) za (trzydzieści) sekund.	(dva zwo·te) za (tshi·jyesh·chee) se·koond

post office

I want to send a ...	Chciałem/Chciałam wysłać ... m/f	khchow·em/khchow·am vis·wach ...
fax	faks	faks
letter	list	leest
parcel	paczkę	pach·ke
postcard	pocztówkę	poch·toof·ke
I want to buy a/an ...	Chciałem/Chciałam kupić ... m/f	khchow·em/khchow·am koo·peech ...
envelope	kopertę	ko·per·te
stamp	znaczek	zna·chek
Please send it (to Australia) by ...	Proszę wysłać to ... (do Australii).	pro·she vis·wach to ... (do aus·tra·lyee)
airmail	pocztą lotniczą	poch·tom lot·nee·chom
express mail	pocztą ekspresową	poch·tom eks·pre·so·vom
registered mail	pocztą poleconą	poch·tom po·le·tso·nom
surface mail	pocztą lądową	poch·tom lon·do·vom
Is there any mail for me?	Czy jest dla mnie jakaś korespondencja?	chi yest dla mnye ya·kash ko·res·pon·den·tsya

bank

Where's a/an ...?	Gdzie jest ...?	gjye yest ...
ATM	bankomat	ban·ko·mat
foreign exchange office	kantor walut	kan·tor va·loot

I'd like to ...	Chciałem/Chciałam ... m/f	khchow·em/khchow·am ...
Where can I ...?	Gdzie mogę ...?	gjye mo·ge ...
cash a cheque	wymienić czek	vi·mye·neech chek
	na gotówkę	na go·toof·ke
change a travellers cheque	wymienić czek podróżny	vi·mye·neech chek po·droozh·ni
change money	wymienić pieniądze	vi·mye·neech pye·nyon·dze
get a cash advance	dostać zaliczkę na moją kartę kredytową	dos·tach za·leech·ke na mo·yom kar·te kre·di·to·vom
withdraw money	wypłacić pieniądze	vi·pwa·cheech pye·nyon·dze

What's the ...?	Jaki/Jaka jest ...? m/f	ya·kee/ya·ka yest ...
charge for that	prowizja f	pro·veez·ya
exchange rate	kurs wymiany m	koors vi·mya·ni

It's (12) złotys.
To kosztuje (dwanaście) złotych.   to kosh·too·ye (dva·nash·chye) zwo·tikh

It's free.
Jest bezpłatny.   yest bes·pwat·ni

What time does the bank open?
W jakich godzinach   v ya·keekh go·jee·nakh
jest bank otwarty?   yest bank ot·far·ti

Has my money arrived yet?
Czy doszły już moje pieniądze?   chi dosh·wi yoosh mo·ye pye·nyon·dze

sightseeing

getting in

What time does it open/close?
O której godzinie jest   o ktoo·rey go·jee·nye yest
otwarte/zamknięte?   ot·far·te/zam·knyen·te

What's the admission charge?
Ile kosztuje wstęp?   ee·le kosh·too·ye fstemp

Is there a discount for students/children?
    Czy jest zniżka dla   chi yest *zneezh*·ka dla
    studentów/dzieci?   stoo·*den*·toof/jye·chee

I'd like to see ...
    Chciałem/Chciałam obejrzeć ... m/f   khchow·em/khchow·am o·*bey*·zhech ...

What's that?
    Co to jest?   tso to yest

Can I take a photo?
    Czy mogę zrobić zdjęcie?   chi *mo*·ge *zro*·beech *zdyen*·chye

I'd like a ...   *Chciałem/Chciałam ...* m/f   khchow·em/khchow·am ...
    catalogue   *broszurę*   bro·*shoo*·re
    guide   *przewodnik*   pshe·*vod*·neek
    local map   *mapę okolic*   *ma*·pe o·*ko*·leets

tours

When's the next ...?   *Kiedy jest następna ...?*   kye·di yest nas·*temp*·na ...
    day trip   *wycieczka*   vi·*chyech*·ka
          jednodniowa pl   yed·no·*dnyo*·va
    tour   *tura*   *too*·ra

Is ... included?   *Czy ... wliczone/a?* n&pl/f   chi ... vlee·*cho*·ne/na
    accommodation   *noclegi są* pl   nots·*le*·gee som
    the admission charge   *opłata za wstęp jest* f   o·*pwa*·ta za fstemp yest
    food   *wyżywienie jest* n   vi·zhi·*vye*·nye yest

Is transport included?
    Czy transport jest wliczony?   chi *trans*·port yest vlee·*cho*·ne

How long is the tour?
    Jak długo trwa wycieczka?   yak *dwoo*·go trfa vi·*chyech*·ka

What time should we be back?
    O której godzinie   o *ktoo*·rey go·*jee*·nye
    powinniśmy wrócić?   po·vee·*neesh*·mi *vroo*·cheech

sightseeing

castle	*zamek* m	*za*·mek
cathedral	*katedra* f	ka·*te*·dra
church	*kościół* m	*kosh*·chyoow'
main square	*rynek główny* m	*ri*·nek *gwoov*·ni
monastery	*klasztor* m	*klash*·tor
monument	*pomnik* m	*pom*·neek
museum	*muzeum* n	moo·*ze*·oom
old city	*stare miasto* n	*sta*·re *myas*·to
palace	*pałac* m	*pa*·wats
ruins	*ruiny* f pl	roo·*ee*·ni
stadium	*stadion* m	*sta*·dyon
statue	*pomnik* m	*pom*·neek

shopping

enquiries

Where's a ...?	*Gdzie jest ...?*	gjye yest ...
bank	*bank*	bank
bookshop	*księgarnia*	kshyen·*gar*·nya
camera shop	*sklep fotograficzny*	sklep fo·to·gra·*feech*·ni
department store	*dom towarowy*	dom to·va·*ro*·vi
grocery store	*sklep spożywczy*	sklep spo·*zhiv*·chi
market	*targ*	tark
newsagency	*kiosk*	kyosk
supermarket	*supermarket*	soo·per·*mar*·ket

Where can I buy (a padlock)?
Gdzie mogę kupić (kłódkę)?   gjye *mo*·ge koo·peech (*kwoot*·ke)

I'm looking for ...
Szukam ...   *shoo*·kam

Can I look at it?
Czy mogę to zobaczyć?   chi *mo*·ge to zo·*ba*·chich

Do you have any others?
Czy są jakieś inne?   chi som *ya*·kyesh *ee*·ne

Does it have a guarantee?
Czy to ma gwarancję?   chi to ma gva·*ran*·tsye

Can I have it sent overseas?
Czy mogę to wysłać za granicę?   chi *mo*·ge to *vis*·wach za gra·*nee*·tse

Can I have my ... repaired?
Czy mogę tu oddać ... do naprawy?   chi *mo*·ge too *ot*·dach ... do na·*pra*·vi

It's faulty.
To jest wadliwe.   to yest vad·*lee*·ve

I'd like to return this, please.
Chciałem/Chciałam to zwrócić. m/f   *khchow*·em/*khchow*·am to *zvroo*·cheech

I'd like a ..., please.	*Proszę o ...*	pro·she o ...
bag	*torbę*	*tor*·be
refund	*zwrot pieniędzy*	zvrot pye·*nyen*·dzi

paying

How much is it?
Ile to kosztuje?   ee·le to kosh·*too*·ye

Can you write down the price?
Proszę napisać cenę.   pro·she na·*pee*·sach *tse*·ne

That's too expensive.
To jest za drogie.   to yest za *dro*·gye

What's your final price?
Jaka jest pana/pani   *ya*·ka yest *pa*·na/*pa*·nee
ostateczna cena? m/f   os·ta·*tech*·na *tse*·na

I'll give you (10 złotys).
Dam panu/pani (dziesięć złotych). m/f   dam *pa*·noo/*pa*·nee (*jye*·shench *zwo*·tikh)

There's a mistake in the bill.
Na czeku jest pomyłka.   na *che*·koo yest po·*miw*·ka

Do you accept ...?	*Czy mogę zapłacić ...?*	chi *mo*·ge za·*pwa*·cheech ...
credit cards	*kartą kredytową*	*kar*·tom kre·di·*to*·vom
debit cards	*kartą debetową*	*kar*·tom de·be·*to*·vom
travellers cheques	*czekami podróżnymi*	che·*ka*·mee pod·roozh·*ni*·mee

I'd like ..., please.	*Proszę o ...*	pro·she o ...
a receipt	*rachunek*	ra·*khoo*·nek
my change	*moją resztę*	*mo*·yom *resh*·te

clothes & shoes

Can I try it on?	*Czy mogę przymierzyć?*	chi *mo*·ge pshi·*mye*·zhich
My size is (40).	*Noszę rozmiar (czterdzieści).*	*no*·she *roz*·myar (chter·*jyesh*·chee)
It doesn't fit.	*Nie pasuje.*	nye pa·*soo*·ye
large/medium/small	*L/M/S*	el·ke/em·ke/es·ke

books & music

I'd like a ...	*Chciałem/Chciałam ... m/f*	khchow·em/khchow·am ...
newspaper	*gazetę (w języku*	ga·*ze*·te (v yen·*zi*·koo
(in English)	*angielskim)*	an·*gyel*·skeem)
pen	*długopis*	dwoo·*go*·pees

Is there an English-language bookshop?
Czy jest tu księgarnia angielska? chi yest too kshyen·*gar*·nya an·*gyel*·ska

I'm looking for something by (Górecki).
Szukam czegoś (Góreckiego). *shoo*·kam *che*·gosh (goo·rets·*kye*·go)

Can I listen to this?
Czy mogę tego posłuchać? chi *mo*·ge *te*·go pos·*woo*·khach

photography

Can you ...?	*Czy może pan/pani ...? m/f*	chi *mo*·zhe pan/*pa*·nee ...
develop this film	*wywołać ten film*	vi·*vo*·wach ten film
load my film	*założyć film*	za·*wo*·zhich film
transfer photos	*skopiować zdjęcia*	sko·*pyo*·vach *zdyen*·chya
from my camera	*z mojego aparatu*	z mo·*ye*·go a·pa·*ra*·too
to CD	*na płytę kompaktową*	na *pwi*·te kom·pak·*to*·vom

I need a/an ... film	*Potrzebuję film ...*	po·tshe·*boo*·ye film ...
for this camera.	*do tego aparatu.*	do *te*·go a·pa·*ra*·too ...
APS	*APS*	a pe es
B&W	*panchromatyczny*	pan·khro·ma·*tich*·ni
colour	*kolorowy*	ko·lo·*ro*·vi
slide	*do slajdów*	do slai·doof
(200) speed	*(dwieście) ASA*	(dvyesh·chye) *a*·sa

When will it be ready? *Na kiedy będzie gotowe?* na *kye*·di *ben*·jye go·*to*·ve

meeting people

greetings, goodbyes & introductions

Hello/Hi.	Cześć.	cheshch
Good night.	Dobranoc.	do·bra·nots
Goodbye.	Do widzenia.	do vee·dze·nya
Bye.	Pa.	pa
See you later.	Do zobaczenia.	do zo·ba·che·nya
Mr/Mrs/Miss	Pan/Pani/Panna	pan/pa·nee/pa·na
How are you?	Jak pan/pani	yak pan/pa·nee
	się miewa? m/f pol	shye mye·va
	Jak się masz? inf	yak shye mash
Fine. And you?	Dobrze. A pan/pani? m/f pol	dob·zhe a pan/pa·nee
	Dobrze. A ty? inf	dob·zhe a ti
What's your name?	Jak się pan/pani	yak shye pan/pa·nee
	nazywa? m/f pol	na·zi·va
	Jakie się nazywasz? inf	yak shye na·zi·vash …
My name is …	Nazywam się …	na·zi·vam shye …
I'm pleased to	Miło mi pana/panią	mee·wo mee pa·na/pa·nyom
meet you.	poznać. m/f pol	po·znach
	Miło mi ciebie poznać. inf	mee·wo mee chye·bye po·znach
This is my …	To jest mój/moja … m/f	to yest mooy/mo·ya …
boyfriend	chłopak	khwo·pak
brother	brat	brat
daughter	córka	tsoor·ka
father	ojciec	oy·chyets
friend	przyjaciel m	pzhi·ya·chyel
	przyjaciółka f	pzhi·ya·chyoow·ka
girlfriend	dziewczyna	jyev·chi·na
husband	mąż	monzh
mother	matka	mat·ka
partner (intimate)	partner/partnerka m/f	part·ner/part·ner·ka
sister	siostra	shyos·tra
son	syn	sin
wife	żona	zho·na

Here's my ...	Tu jest mój ...	too yest mooy ...
What's your ...?	Jaki jest pana/	ya·kee yest pa·na/
	pani ...? m/f pol	pa·nee ...
(email) address	adres (emailowy)	ad·res (e·mai·lo·vi)
fax number	numer faksu	noo·mer fak·soo
phone number	numer telefonu	noo·mer te·le·fo·noo

occupations

What's your occupation?	Jaki jest pana/pani zawód? m/f pol	ya·kee yest pa·na/pa·nee za·vood
I'm a/an ...	Jestem ...	yes·tem ...
artist	artystą/artystką m/f	ar·tis·tom/ar·tist·kom
farmer	rolnikiem m&f	rol·nee·kyem
manual worker	pracownikiem fizycznym m&f	pra·tsov·nee·kyem fee·zich·nim
office worker	pracownikiem biurowym m&f	pra·tsov·nee·kyem byoo·ro·vim
scientist	naukowcem m&f	now·kov·tsem
tradesperson	rzemieślnikiem m&f	zhe·mye·shlnee·kyem

background

Where are you from?	Skąd pan/pani jest? m/f pol	skont pan/pa·nee yest
I'm from ...	Jestem z ...	yes·tem z ...
Australia	Australii	ow·stra·lyee
Canada	Kanady	ka·na·di
England	Anglii	ang·lee
New Zealand	Nowej Zelandii	no·vey ze·lan·dyee
the USA	USA	oo es a

Are you married? (to a man)
Czy jest pan żonaty? pol   chi yest pan zho·na·ti

Are you married? (to a woman)
Czy jest pani zamężna? pol   chi yest pa·nee za·menzh·na

I'm married.
Jestem żonaty/zamężna. m/f   yes·tem zho·na·ti/za·menzh·na

I'm single.
Jestem nieżonaty/niezamężna. m/f   nye·zho·na·ti/nye·za·menzh·na

age

How old is your ...?	Ile lat ma pana/ pani ...? m/f pol	ee·le lat ma pa·na/ pa·nee ...
daughter	córka	tsoor·ka
son	syn	sin
How old are you?	Ile pan/pani ma lat? m/f pol	ee·le pan/pa·nee ma lat
	Ile masz lat? inf	ee·le mash lat
I'm ... years old.	Mam ... lat.	mam ... lat
He/She is ... years old.	On/Ona ma ... lat.	on/o·na ma ... lat

feelings

I'm (not) ...	(Nie) Jestem ...	(nye) yes·tem ...
Are you ...?	Czy jest pan/pani ...? m/f pol	chi yest pan/pa·nee ...
cold	zmarznięty/a m/f	zmar·znyen·ti/a
happy	szczęśliwy/a m/f	shchen·shlee·vi/a
hungry	głodny/a m/f	gwod·ni/a
sad	smutny/a m/f	smoot·ni/a
thirsty	spragniony/a m/f	sprag·nyo·ni/a

entertainment

going out

Where can I find ...?	Gdzie mogę znaleźć ...?	gjye mo·ge zna·lezhch ...
clubs	kluby nocne	kloo·bi nots·ne
gay venues	kluby dla gejów	kloo·bi dla ge·yoof
pubs	puby	pa·bi
I feel like going to a/the ...	Mam ochotę pójść ...	mam o·kho·te pooyshch ...
concert	na koncert	na kon·tsert
movies	na film	na feelm
party	na imprezę	na eem·pre·ze
restaurant	do restauracji	do res·tow·ra·tsyee
theatre	na sztukę	na shtoo·ke

interests

Do you like ...?	Czy lubisz ...? inf	chi loo·beesh ...
I like ...	Lubię ...	loo·bye ...
cooking	gotować	go·to·vach
movies	oglądać filmy	o·glon·dach feel·mi
reading	czytać	chi·tach
sport	sport	sport
travelling	podróżować	po·droo·zho·vach

| Do you like art? | Czy lubisz sztukę? inf | chi loo·beesh shtoo·ke |
| I like art. | Lubię sztukę. | loo·bye shtoo·ke |

Do you ...?	Czy ...? inf	chi ...
dance	tańczysz	tan'·chish
go to concerts	chodzisz na koncerty	kho·jeesh na kon·tser·ti
listen to music	słuchasz muzyki	swoo·khash moo·zi·kee

food & drink

finding a place to eat

Can you	Czy może pan/pani	chi mo·zhe pan/pa·nee
recommend a ...?	polecić ...? m/f	po·le·cheech ...
bar	bar	bar
café	kawiarnię	ka·vyar·nye
restaurant	restaurację	res·tow·rats·ye

I'd like ..., please.	Proszę ...	pro·she ...
a table for (five)	o stolik na (pięć) osób	o sto·leek na (pyench) o·soob
the (non)smoking section	dla (nie)palących	dla (nye·)pa·lon·tsikh

ordering food

breakfast	śniadanie n	shnya·da·nye
lunch	obiad m	o·byad
dinner	kolacja f	ko·la·tsya
snack	przekąska f	pshe·kons·ka

What would you recommend?

Co by pan polecił? m		tso bi pan po-*le*-cheew
Co by pani poleciła? f		tso bi *pa*-nee po-le-*chee*-wa

I'd like (the) ..., please.	*Proszę ...*	*pro*-she ...
bill	*o rachunek*	o ra-*khoo*-nek
drink list	*o spis napojów*	o spees na-*po*-yoof
menu	*o jadłospis*	o ya-*dwo*-spees
that dish	*to danie*	to *da*-nye

drinks

(cup of) coffee ...	*(filiżanka) kawy ...*	(fee-lee-*zhan*-ka) *ka*-vi ...
(cup of) tea ...	*(filiżanka) herbaty ...*	(fee-lee-*zhan*-ka) her-*ba*-ti ...
with milk	*z mlekiem*	z *mle*-kyem
without sugar	*bez cukru*	bez *tsoo*-kroo
(orange) juice	*sok (pomarańczowy)* m	sok (po-ma-ran'-*cho*-vi)
soft drink	*napój* m	*na*-pooy
... water	*woda ...*	*vo*-da ...
hot	*gorąca*	go-*ron*-tsa
mineral	*mineralna*	mee-ne-*ral*-na

in the bar

I'll have ...	*Proszę ...*	*pro*-she ...
I'll buy you a drink.	*Kupię ci drinka.* inf	*koo*-pye chee *dreen*-ka
What would you like?	*Co zamówić dla ciebie?* inf	tso za-*moo*-veech dla *chye*-bye
Cheers!	*Na zdrowie!*	na *zdro*-vye

brandy	*brandy* m	*bren*-di
champagne	*szampan* m	*sham*-pan
a shot of (vodka)	*kieliszek (wódki)*	kye-*lee*-shek (*vood*-kee)
a bottle/glass of beer	*butelka/szklanka piwa*	boo-*tel*-ka/*shklan*-ka *pee*-va
a bottle/glass	*butelka/kieliszek*	boo-*tel*-ka/kye-*lee*-shek
of ... wine	*wina ...*	*vee*-na...
red	*czerwonego*	cher-vo-*ne*-go
sparkling	*musującego*	moo-soo-yon-*tse*-go
white	*białego*	bya-*we*-go

self-catering

What's the local speciality?
Co jest miejscową   tso yest myeys·*tso*·vom
specjalnością?   spe·tsyal·*nosh*·chyom

What's that?
Co to jest?   tso to yest

How much (is a kilo of cheese)?
Ile kosztuje (kilogram sera)?   ee·le kosh·*too*·ye (kee·*lo*·gram se·ra)

I'd like ...	*Proszę ...*	*pro·*she ...
200 grams	*dwadzieścia deko*	dva·*jyesh*·chya de·ko
(two) kilos	*(dwa) kilo*	(dva) *kee*·lo
(three) pieces	*(trzy) kawałki*	(tshi) ka·*vow*·kee
(six) slices	*(sześć) plasterków*	(sheshch) plas·*ter*·koof

Less.	*Mniej.*	mney
Enough.	*Wystarczy.*	vis·*tar*·chi
More.	*Więcej.*	*vyen*·tsey

special diets & allergies

Is there a vegetarian restaurant near here?
Czy jest tu gdzieś restauracja   chi yest too gjyesh res·tow·*ra*·tsya
wegetariańska?   ve·ge·ta·*ryan*'·ska

Do you have vegetarian food?
Czy jest żywność wegetariańska?   chi yest *zhiv*·noshch ve·ge·tar·*yan*'·ska

Could you prepare	*Czy można przygotować*	chi *mo*·zhna pshi·go·to·*vach*
a meal without ...?	*jedzenie bez ...?*	ye·*dze*·nye bes ...
butter	*masła*	*mas*·wa
eggs	*jajek*	*yai*·ek
meat stock	*wywaru mięsnego*	vi·*va*·roo myens·*ne*·go

I'm allergic to ...	*Mam uczulenie na ...*	mam oo·choo·*le*·nye na ...
dairy produce	*produkty mleczne*	pro·*dook*·ti mlech·ne
gluten	*gluten*	*gloo*·ten
MSG	*glutaminian sodu*	gloo·ta·*mee*·nyan so·doo
nuts	*orzechy*	o·*zhe*·khi
seafood	*owoce morza*	o·*vo*·tse mo·zha

emergencies

basics

Help!	*Na pomoc!*	na po·mots
Stop!	*Stój!*	stooy
Go away!	*Odejdź!*	o·deyj
Thief!	*Złodziej!*	zwo·jyey
Fire!	*Pożar!*	po·zhar
Watch out!	*Uważaj!*	oo·va·zhai
Call ...!	*Zadzwoń po ...!*	zad·zvon' po ...
a doctor	*lekarza*	le·ka·zha
an ambulance	*karetkę*	ka·ret·ke
the police	*policję*	po·lee·tsye

It's an emergency.
To nagły wypadek. — to nag·wi vi·pa·dek

Could you help me, please?
Czy może pan/pani mi pomóc? m/f — chi mo·zhe pan/pa·nee mee po·moots

Can I use the telephone?
Czy mogę użyć telefon? — chi mo·ge oo·zhich te·le·fon

I'm lost.
Zgubiłem/Zgubiłam się. m/f — zgoo·bee·wem/zgoo·bee·wam shye

Where are the toilets?
Gdzie są toalety? — gjye som to·a·le·ti

police

Where's the police station?
Gdzie jest posterunek policji? — gje yest pos·te·roo·nek po·lee·tsyee

I want to report an offence.
Chciałem/Chciałam zgłosić przestępstwo. m/f — khchow·em/khchow·am zgwo·sheech pshe·stemps·tfo

I have insurance.
Mam ubezpieczenie. — mam oo·bes·pye·che·nye

I've been ...	Zostałem/Zostałam ... m/f	zo-stow-em/zo-stow-am ...
assaulted	napadnięty/a m/f	na-pad-nyen-ti/a
raped	zgwałcony/a m/f	zgvow-tso-ni/a
robbed	okradziony/a m/f	o-kra-jyo-ni/a

I've lost my ...	Zgubiłem/Zgubiłam ... m/f	zgoo-bee-wem/zgoo-bee-wam ...
backpack	plecak	ple-tsak
bag	torbę	tor-be
credit card	kartę kredytową	kar-te kre-di-to-vom
handbag	torebkę	to-rep-ke
jewellery	biżuterię	bee-zhoo-ter-ye
money	pieniądze	pye-nyon-dze
passport	paszport	pash-port
wallet	portfel	port-fel

I want to contact my ...	Chcę się skontaktować z ...	khtse shye skon-tak-to-vach z ...
consulate	moim konsulatem	mo-yeem kon-soo-la-tem
embassy	moją ambasadą	mo-yom am-ba-sa-dom

health

medical needs

Where's the nearest ...?	Gdzie jest najbliższy/a ...? m/f	gjye yest nai-bleezh-shi/a ...
dentist	dentysta m	den-tis-ta
doctor	lekarz m	le-kash
hospital	szpital m	shpee-tal
(night) pharmacist	apteka (nocna) f	ap-te-ka (nots-na)

I need a doctor (who speaks English).
Szukam lekarza (który mówi po angielsku).
shoo-kam le-ka-zha (ktoo-ri moo-vee po an-gyel-skoo)

Could I see a female doctor?
Czy mogę się widzieć z lekarzem kobietą?
chi mo-ge shye vee-jyech z le-ka-zhem ko-bye-tom

I've run out of my medication.
Skończyły mi się lekarstwa.
skon-chi-wi mee shye le-kars-tfa

symptoms, conditions & allergies

I'm sick.	Jestem chory/a. m/f	yes·tem kho·ri/a
It hurts here.	Tutaj boli.	too·tai bo·lee
I have (a) ...	Mam ...	mam ...

asthma	astma f	ast·ma
constipation	zatwardzenie n	zat·far·dze·nye
cough	kaszel m	ka·shel
diarrhoea	rozwolnienie n	roz·vol·nye·nye
fever	gorączka f	go·ronch·ka
headache	ból głowy m	bool gwo·vi
heart condition	stan serca m	stan ser·tsa
nausea	mdłości f pl	mdwosh·chee
pain	ból m	bool
sore throat	ból gardła m	bool gar·dwa
toothache	ból zęba m	bool zem·ba

I'm allergic to ...	Mam alergię na ...	mam a·ler·gye na ...
antibiotics	antybiotyki	an·ti·byo·ti·kee
anti-inflammatories	leki przeciwzapalne	le·kee pshe·cheef·za·pal·ne
aspirin	aspirynę	as·pee·ri·ne
bees	pszczoły	pshcho·wi
codeine	kodeinę	ko·de·ee·ne
penicillin	penicylinę	pe·nee·tsi·lee·ne

antiseptic	środki odkażające m pl	shrod·kee od·ka·zha·yon·tse
bandage	bandaż m	ban·dash
condoms	kondom m pl	kon·dom
contraceptives	środki	shrod·kee
	antykoncepcyjne m pl	an·ti·kon·tsep·tsiy·ne
diarrhoea medicine	rozwolnienie	ros·vol·nye·nye
insect repellent	środek na owady m	shro·dek na o·va·di
laxatives	środek	shro·dek
	przeczyszczający m	pshe·chish·cha·yon·tsi
painkillers	środki	shrod·kee
	przeciwbólowe m pl	pshe·cheef·boo·lo·ve
rehydration salts	sole fizjologiczne f pl	so·le fee·zyo·lo·geech·ne
sleeping tablets	pigułki nasenne f pl	pee·goow·kee na·se·ne

english–polish dictionary

Polish nouns in this dictionary have their gender indicated by ⓜ (masculine), ⓕ (feminine) or ⓝ (neuter). If it's a plural noun, you'll also see pl. Adjectives are given in the masculine form only. Words are also marked as a (adjective), v (verb), sg (singular), pl (plural), inf (informal) or pol (polite) where necessary.

A

accident *wypadek* ⓜ vi-*pa*-dek
accommodation *nocleg* ⓜ *nots*-leg
adaptor *zasilacz* ⓜ za-*shee*-lach
address *adres* ⓜ *a*-dres
after *po • za* po • za
air conditioning *klimatyzacja* ⓕ klee-ma-ti-*za*-tsya
airplane *samolot* ⓜ sa-*mo*-lot
airport *lotnisko* ⓝ lot-*nees*-ko
alcohol *alkohol* ⓜ al-*ko*-khol
all *wszystko* fshist-ko
allergy *alergia* ⓕ a-*ler*-gya
ambulance *karetka pogotowia* ⓕ ka-*ret*-ka po-go-*to*-vya
and *i* ee
ankle *kostka* ⓕ *kost*-ka
arm *ręka* ⓕ *ren*-ka
ashtray *popielniczka* ⓕ po-pyel-*neech*-ka
ATM *bankomat* ⓜ ban-*ko*-mat

B

baby *niemowlę* ⓝ nye-*mov*-le
back (body) *plecy* pl *ple*-tsi
backpack *plecak* ⓜ *ple*-tsak
bad *zły* zwi
bag *torba* ⓕ *tor*-ba
baggage claim *odbiór bagażu* ⓜ *od*-byoor ba-*ga*-zhoo
bank *bank* ⓜ bank
bar *bar* ⓜ bar
bathroom *łazienka* ⓕ wa-*zhyen*-ka
battery *bateria* ⓕ ba-*te*-rya
beautiful *piękny* *pyen*-kni
bed *łóżko* ⓝ *woozh*-ko
beer *piwo* ⓝ *pee*-vo
before *przed* pshet
behind *za* za
bicycle *rower* ⓜ *ro*-ver
big *duży* *doo*-zhi
bill *rachunek* ⓜ ra-*khoo*-nek
black *czarny* *char*-ni
blanket *koc* ⓜ kots

blood group *grupa krwi* ⓕ *groo*-pa krfee
blue *niebieski* nye-*byes*-kee
boat *łódź* ⓕ wooj
book (make a reservation) v *rezerwować* re-zer-*vo*-vach
bottle *butelka* ⓕ boo-*tel*-ka
bottle opener *otwieracz do butelek* ⓜ ot-*fye*-rach do boo-*te*-lek
boy *chłopiec* ⓜ *khwo*-pyets
brakes (car) *hamulce* pl ha-*mool*-tse
breakfast *śniadanie* ⓝ shnya-*da*-nye
broken (faulty) *połamany* po-wa-*ma*-ni
bus *autobus* ⓜ *ow*-to-boos
business *firma* ⓕ *feer*-ma
buy *kupować* koo-*po*-vach

C

café *kawiarnia* ⓕ ka-*vyar*-nya
camera *aparat* ⓜ a-*pa*-rat
camp site *kamping* ⓜ *kam*-peeng
cancel *unieważniać* oo-nye-*vazh*-nyach
can opener *otwieracz do konserw* ⓜ ot-*fye*-rach do *kon*-serf
car *samochód* ⓜ sa-*mo*-khoot
cash *gotówka* ⓕ go-*toof*-ka
cash (a cheque) v *zrealizować czek* zre-a-lee-*zo*-vach chek
cell phone *telefon komórkowy* ⓜ te-*le*-fon ko-moor-*ko*-vi
centre *środek* ⓜ *shro*-dek
change (money) v *rozmieniać* roz-*mye*-nyach
cheap *tani* *ta*-nee
check (bill) *sprawdzenie* ⓝ sprav-*dze*-nye
check-in *zameldowanie* ⓝ za-mel-do-*va*-nye
chest *klatka piersiowa* ⓕ *klat*-ka pyer-*shyo*-va
child *dziecko* ⓝ *jye*-tsko
cigarette *papieros* ⓜ pa-*pye*-ros
city *miasto* ⓝ *myas*-to
clean a *czysty* *chis*-ti
closed *zamknięty* zam-*knyen*-ti
coffee *kawa* ⓕ *ka*-va
coins *monety* ⓕ pl mo-*ne*-ti
cold a *zimny* *zheem*-ni

collect call *rozmowa opłacona przez odbierającego* ⓕ
roz·*mo*·va o·*pwa*·tso·na pshes od·bye·ra·yon·*tse*·go
come (by vehicle) *przyjść* pshiyshch
come (on foot) *przychodzić* pshi·*kho*·jeech
computer *komputer* ⓜ kom·*poo*·ter
condom *kondom* ⓜ *kon*·dom
contact lenses *soczewki kontaktowe* ⓕ pl
so·*chef*·kee kon·tak·*to*·ve
cook v *gotować* go·*to*·vach
cost *koszt* ⓜ kosht
credit card *karta kredytowa* ⓕ *kar*·ta kre·di·*to*·va
cup *filiżanka* ⓕ fee·lee·*zhan*·ka
currency exchange *kantor* ⓜ *kan*·tor
customs (immigration) *urząd celny* ⓜ
oo·zhont *tsel*·ni

D

dangerous *niebezpieczny* nye·bes·*pyech*·ni
date (time) *data* ⓕ *da*·ta
day *dzień* ⓜ jyen´
delay *opóźnienie* ⓝ o·poozh·*nye*·nye
dentist *dentysta* ⓜ den·*tis*·ta
depart *odjeżdżać* od·*yezh*·jach
diaper *pieluszka* ⓕ pye·*loosh*·ka
dictionary *słownik* ⓜ *swov*·neek
dinner *kolacja* ⓕ ko·*la*·tsya
direct *bezpośredni* bes·po·*shred*·nee
dirty *brudny* *brood*·ni
disabled *niepełnosprawny* nye·pew·no·*sprav*·ni
discount *zniżka* ⓕ *zneesh*·ka
doctor *lekarz* ⓜ *le*·kash
double bed *łóżko małżeńskie* ⓝ
woozh·ko mow·*zhen´*·skye
double room *pokój dwuosobowy* ⓜ
po·kooy dvoo·o·so·*bo*·vi
drink *napój* ⓜ *na*·pooy
drive v *kierować* kye·*ro*·vach
drivers licence *prawo jazdy* ⓝ *pra*·vo *yaz*·di
drugs (illicit) *narkotyki* ⓝ pl nar·ko·*ti*·kee
dummy (pacifier) *smoczek* ⓜ *smo*·chek

E

ear *ucho* ⓝ *oo*·kho
east *wschód* ⓜ vskhood
eat *jeść* yeshch
economy class *klasa oszczędnościowa* ⓕ
kla·sa osh·chend·nosh·*chyo*·va
electricity *elektryczność* ⓕ e·lek·*trich*·noshch
elevator *winda* ⓕ *veen*·da
email *email* ⓜ *e*·mail

embassy *ambasada* ⓕ am·ba·*sa*·da
emergency *nagły przypadek* ⓜ *nag*·wi pshi·*pa*·dek
English (language) *angielski* an·*gyel*·skee
entrance *wejście* ⓝ *veysh*·chye
evening *wieczór* ⓜ *vye*·choor
exchange rate *kurs wymiany* ⓜ koors vi·*mya*·ni
exit *wyjście* ⓝ *viysh*·chye
expensive *drogi* *dro*·gee
express mail *list ekspresowy* ⓜ leest eks·pre·*so*·vi
eye *oko* ⓝ *o*·ko

F

far *daleki* da·*le*·kee
fast *szybki* *shib*·kee
father *ojciec* ⓜ *oy*·chyets
film (camera) *film* ⓜ feelm
finger *palec* ⓜ *pa*·lets
first-aid kit *apteczka pierwszej pomocy* ⓕ
ap·*tech*·ka *pyerf*·shey po·*mo*·tsi
first class *pierwsza klasa* ⓕ *pyerf*·sha *kla*·sa
fish *ryba* ⓕ *ri*·ba
food *żywność* ⓕ *zhiv*·noshch
foot *stopa* ⓕ *sto*·pa
fork *widelec* ⓜ vee·*de*·lets
free (of charge) *bezpłatny* bes·*pwat*·ni
friend *przyjaciel/przyjaciółka* ⓜ / ⓕ
pshi·ya·*chyel*/pshi·ya·*choow*·ka
fruit *owoc* ⓜ *o*·vots
full *pełny* *pew*·ni
funny *zabawny* za·*bav*·ni

G

gift *prezent* ⓜ *pre*·zent
girl *dziewczyna* ⓕ jyev·*chi*·na
glass (drinking) *szklanka* ⓕ *shklan*·ka
glasses *okulary* pl o·koo·*la*·ri
go (by vehicle) *jechać* *ye*·khach
go (on foot) *iść* eeshch
good *dobry* *do*·bri
green *zielony* zhye·*lo*·ni
guide *przewodnik* ⓜ pshe·*vod*·neek

H

half *połówka* ⓕ po·*woof*·ka
hand *ręka* ⓕ *ren*·ka
handbag *torebka* ⓕ to·*rep*·ka
happy *szczęśliwy* shchen·*shlee*·vi
have *mieć* myech
he *on* on

head *głowa* ⓕ gwo-va
heart *serce* ⓝ ser-tse
heat *upał* ⓜ oo-pow
heavy *ciężki* ⓜ chyensh-kee
help v *pomagać* po-ma-gach
here *tutaj* too-tai
high *wysoki* vi-so-kee
highway *szosa* ⓕ sho-sa
hike v *wędrować* ven-dro-vach
holiday *święto* ⓝ shvyen-to
homosexual n *homoseksualista* ⓜ
ho-mo-sek-soo-a-lees-ta
hospital *szpital* ⓜ shpee-tal
hot *gorący* go-ron-tsi
hotel *hotel* ⓜ ho-tel
hungry *głodny* gwo-dni
husband *mąż* ⓜ monzh

I

I *ja* ya
identification (card) *dowód tożsamości* ⓜ
do-vood tozh-sa-mosh-chee
ill *chory* kho-ri
important *ważny* vazh-ni
included *wliczony* vlee-cho-ni
injury *rana* ⓕ ra-na
insurance *ubezpieczenie* ⓝ oo-bes-pye-che-nye
Internet *internet* ⓜ een-ter-net
interpreter *tłumacz/tłumaczka* ⓜ / ⓕ
twoo-mach/twoo-mach-ka

J

jewellery *biżuteria* ⓕ bee-zhoo-ter-ya
job *praca* ⓕ pra-tsa

K

key *klucz* ⓜ klooch
kilogram *kilogram* ⓜ kee-lo-gram
kitchen *kuchnia* ⓕ kookh-nya
knife *nóż* ⓜ noosh

L

laundry (place) *pralnia* ⓕ pral-nya
lawyer *prawnik* ⓜ prav-neek
left (direction) *lewy* ⓝ le-vi
left-luggage office *przechowalnia bagażu* ⓕ
pshe-kho-val-nya ba-ga-zhoo

leg *noga* ⓕ no-ga
lesbian n *lesbijka* ⓕ les-beey-ka
less *mniej* mnyey
letter (mail) *list* ⓜ leest
lift (elevator) *winda* ⓕ veen-da
light *światło* ⓝ shvyat-wo
like v *lubić* loo-beech
lock *zamek* ⓜ za-mek
long *długi* dwoo-gee
lost *zgubiony* zgoo-byo-ni
lost-property office *biuro rzeczy znalezionych* ⓝ
byoo-ro zhe-chi zna-le-zhyo-nikh
love v *kochać* ko-khach
luggage *bagaż* ⓜ ba-gash
lunch *lunch* ⓜ lanch

M

mail (letters) *list* ⓜ leest
mail (postal system) *poczta* ⓕ poch-ta
man *mężczyzna* ⓜ menzh-chiz-na
map (of country) *mapa* ⓕ ma-pa
map (of town) *plan* ⓜ plan
market *rynek* ⓜ ri-nek
matches *zapałki* ⓜ pl za-pow-kee
meat *mięso* ⓝ myen-so
medicine *lekarstwo* ⓝ le-karst-fo
menu *jadłospis* ⓜ ya-dwo-spees
message *wiadomość* ⓕ vya-do-moshch
milk *mleko* ⓝ mle-ko
minute *minuta* ⓕ mee-noo-ta
mobile phone *telefon komórkowy* ⓜ
te-le-fon ko-moor-ko-vi
money *pieniądze* ⓜ pl pye-nyon-dze
month *miesiąc* ⓜ mye-shonts
morning *rano* ⓝ ra-no
mother *matka* ⓕ mat-ka
motorcycle *motor* ⓜ mo-tor
motorway *autostrada* ⓕ ow-to-stra-da
mouth *usta* pl oos-ta
music *muzyka* ⓕ moo-zi-ka

N

name *imię* ⓝ ee-mye
napkin *serwetka* ⓕ ser vet ka
nappy *pieluszka* ⓕ pye-loosh-ka
near *bliski* blees-kee
neck *szyja* ⓕ shi-ya
new *nowy* no-vi
news *wiadomości* ⓕ pl vya-do-mosh-chee
newspaper *gazeta* ⓕ ga-ze-ta
night *noc* ⓕ nots

no *nie* nye
noisy *hałaśliwy* ha-wa-*shlee*-vi
nonsmoking *niepalący* nye-pa-*lon*-tsi
north *północ* ① poow-nots
nose *nos* ⓜ nos
now *teraz* te-ras
number *numer* ⓜ *noo*-mer

O

oil (engine) *olej* ⓜ o-ley
old *stary* sta-ri
one-way ticket *bilet w jedną stronę* ⓜ
    bee-let v yed-nom *stro*-ne
open a *otwarty* ot-*far*-ti
outside *na zewnątrz* na *zev*-nontsh

P

package *paczka* ① *pach*-ka
paper *papier* ⓜ *pa*-pyer
park (car) v *parkować* par-*ko*-vach
passport *paszport* ⓜ *pash*-port
pay *płacić* *pwa*-cheech
pen *długopis* ⓜ dwoo-*go*-pees
petrol *benzyna* ① ben-*zi*-na
pharmacy *apteka* ① ap-*te*-ka
phonecard *karta telefoniczna* ① *kar*-ta te-le-fo-*neech*-na
photo *zdjęcie* ⓝ *zdyen*-chye
plate *talerz* ⓜ *ta*-lesh
Poland *Polska* ① *pol*-ska
police *policja* ① po-*lee*-tsya
Polish (language) *polski* ⓜ *pol*-skee
postcard *pocztówka* ① poch-*toof*-ka
post office *urząd pocztowy* ⓜ *oo*-zhond poch-*to*-vi
pregnant *w ciąży* v *chyon*-zhi
price *cena* ① *tse*-na

Q

quiet *cichy* chee-khi

R

rain *deszcz* ⓜ deshch
razor *brzytwa* ① *bzhit*-fa
receipt *rachunek* ① ra-*khoo*-nek
red *czerwony* cher-*vo*-ni
refund *zwrot pieniędzy* ⓜ zvrot pye-*nyen*-dzi
registered mail *list polecony* ⓜ leest po-le-*tso*-ni
rent v *wynająć* vi-*na*-yonch

repair v *naprawić* na-*pra*-veech
reservation *rezerwacja* ① re-zer-*va*-tsya
restaurant *restauracja* ① res-tow-*ra*-tsya
return v *wracać* vra-tsach
return ticket *bilet powrotny* ⓜ *bee*-let po-*vro*-tni
right (direction) *prawoskrętny* pra-vo-*skrent*-ni
road *droga* ① *dro*-ga
room *pokój* ⓜ *po*-kooy

S

safe a *bezpieczny* bes-*pyech*-ni
sanitary napkin *podpaski higieniczne* ① pl
    pod-*pas*-kee hee-gye-*neech*-ne
seat *miejsce* ⓝ *myeys*-tse
send *wysyłać* vi-*si*-wach
service station *stacja obsługi* ① *sta*-tsya ob-*swoo*-gee
sex *seks* ⓜ seks
shampoo *szampon* ⓜ *sham*-pon
share (a dorm) v *mieszkać z kimś* myesh-kach z keemsh
shaving cream *krem do golenia* ⓜ krem do go-*le*-nya
she *ona* o-na
sheet (bed) *prześcieradło* ⓝ pshesh-chye-*ra*-dwo
shirt *koszula* ① ko-*shoo*-la
shoes *buty* ⓜ pl *boo*-ti
shop *sklep* ⓜ sklep
short *krótki* kroot-kee
shower *prysznic* ⓜ *prish*-neets
single room *pokój jednoosobowy* ⓜ
    po-kooy ye-dno-o-so-*bo*-vi
skin *skóra* ① *skoo*-ra
skirt *spódnica* ① spood-*nee*-tsa
sleep v *spać* spach
slowly *powoli* po-*vo*-lee
small *mały* ma-wi
smoke (cigarettes) v *palić* pa-leech
soap *mydło* ⓝ *mid*-wo
some *kilka* keel-ka
soon *wkrótce* fkroot-tse
south *południe* ⓝ po-*wood*-nye
souvenir shop *sklep z pamiątkami* ⓜ
    sklep z pa-*myont*-ka-mi
speak *mówić* moo-veech
spoon *łyżka* ① *wish*-ka
stamp *znaczek* ⓜ *zna*-chek
stand-by ticket *bilet z listy rezerwowej* ⓜ
    bee-let z *lees*-ti re-zer-*vo*-vey
station (train) *stacja* ① *sta*-tsya
stomach *żołądek* ⓜ zho-*won*-dek
stop v *przestać* pshes-tach
stop (bus) *przystanek* ⓜ pshis-*ta*-nek
street *ulica* ① oo-*lee*-tsa
student *student* ⓜ *stoo*-dent

sun *słońce* ⋒ swon'-tse
sunscreen *krem przeciwsłoneczny* ⋒ krem pshe-cheef-swo-*nech*-ni
swim v *pływać* pwi-vach

T

tampon *tampon* ⋒ tam-pon
taxi *taksówka* ⨍ tak-*soof*-ka
teaspoon *łyżeczka* ⨍ wi-*zhech*-ka
teeth *zęby* ⋒ pl zem-bi
telephone *telefon* ⋒ te-*le*-fon
television *telewizja* ⨍ te-le-*veez*-ya
temperature (weather) *temperatura* ⨍ tem-pe-ra-*too*-ra
tent *namiot* ⋒ *na*-myot
that (one) *który* ktoo-ri
they *oni* o-nee
thirsty *spragniony* sprag-*nyo*-ni
this (one) *ten* ⋒ ten
throat *gardło* gard-wo
ticket *bilet* ⋒ *bee*-let
time *czas* ⋒ chas
tired *zmęczony* zmen-*cho*-ni
tissues *chusteczki* ⨍ pl khoos-*tech*-kee
today *dzisiaj* jee-shyai
toilet *toaleta* ⨍ to-a-*le*-ta
tomorrow *jutro* yoo-tro
tonight *dzisiaj wieczorem* jee-shyai vye-*cho*-rem
toothbrush *szczotka do zębów* ⨍ shchot-ka do zem-boof
toothpaste *pasta do zębów* ⨍ *pas*-ta do zem-boof
torch (flashlight) *latarka* ⨍ la-*tar*-ka
tour *wycieczka* ⨍ vi-*chech*-ka
tourist office *biuro turystyczne* ⋒ byoo-ro too-ris-*tich*-ne
towel *ręcznik* ⋒ rench-neek
train *pociąg* ⋒ po-chyonk
translate *przetłumaczyć* pshe-twoo-*ma*-chich
travel agency *biuro podróży* ⋒ byoo-ro po-*droo*-zhi
travellers cheques *czeki podróżne* ⋒ pl che-kee po-*droozh*-ne
trousers *spodnie* pl spo-dnye
twin beds *dwa łóżka* ⋒ pl dva *woosh*-ka
tyre *opona* ⨍ o-*po*-na

U

underwear *bielizna* ⨍ bye-*leez*-na
urgent *pilny* peel-ni

V

vacant *wolny* vol-ni
vacation *wakacje* pl va-*ka*-tsye
vegetable *warzywo* ⋒ va-*zhi*-vo
vegetarian a *wegetariański* ve-ge-tar-*yan*-skee
visa *wiza* ⨍ *vee*-za

W

waiter *kelner* ⋒ *kel*-ner
walk v *spacerować* spa-tse-*ro*-vach
wallet *portfel* ⋒ port-fel
warm a *ciepły* chyep-wi
Warsaw *Warszawa* ⨍ var-*sha*-va
wash (something) *prać* prach
watch *zegarek* ⋒ ze-*ga*-rek
water *woda* ⨍ *vo*-da
we *my* mi
weekend *weekend* ⋒ *wee*-kend
west *zachód* ⋒ za-khood
wheelchair *wózek inwalidzki* ⋒ voo-zek een-va-*leets*-kee
when *kiedy* kye-di
where *gdzie* gjye
white *biały* bya-wi
who *kto* kto
why *dlaczego* dla-*che*-go
wife *żona* ⨍ zho-na
window *okno* ⋒ ok-no
wine *wino* ⋒ *vee*-no
with *z* z
without *bez* bes
woman *kobieta* ⨍ ko-*bye*-ta
write *pisać* pee-sach

Y

yellow *żółty* zhoow-ti
yes *tak* tak
yesterday *wczoraj* fcho-rai
you sg inf *ty* ti
you sg pol *pan/pani* ⋒/⨍ pan/*pa*-nee
you pl inf *wy* vi
you pl pol *panowie/panie* ⋒/⨍ pa-no-vye/*pa*-nye
you pl pol *państwo* ⋒&⨍ pan'-stfo

Portuguese

portuguese alphabet

A a aa	B b be	C c se	D d de	E e e
F f e·fe	G g je	H h a-*gaah*	I i ee	J j *jo*·ta
K k *ka*·pa	L l e·le	M m e·me	N n e·ne	O o o
P p pe	Q q ke	R r e·rre	S s e·se	T t te
U u oo	V v ve	W w *da*·blyoo	X x sheesh	Y y *eeps*·lon
Z z ze				

portuguese

about Portuguese

Portuguese (*português* poor·too·*gesh*), the language which produced words such as *albino*, *brocade* and *molasses*, comes from the Romance language family and is closely related to Spanish, French and Italian. Descended from the colloquial Latin spoken by Roman soldiers, it's now used by over 200 million people worldwide.

Linguists believe that before the Roman invasion of the Iberian Peninsula in 218 BC, the locals of modern-day Portugal spoke a Celtic language. That local language was supplanted by the vernacular form of Latin (sometimes called 'Romance') spoken by the occupying forces under the Romans' 500-year rule of the province of Lusitania (present-day Portugal and Spanish Galicia). During this period, Portuguese also absorbed elements of the languages of invading Germanic tribes. The greatest influence on today's Portuguese, however, was a result of the Moorish invasion of the peninsula in AD 711. Arabic was imposed as the official language of the region until the expulsion of the Moors in 1249, and although Romance was still spoken by the masses, the Moorish language left its mark on the vocabulary. From the 16th century on, there were only minor changes to the language, mostly influences from France and Spain. The earliest written documents were composed in the 12th century, and the Portuguese used in 1572 by Luís de Camões (author of the first great Portuguese classic, *Os Lusíadas*) was already identifiable as the language of José Saramago's Nobel Prize-winning works in the 20th century.

The global distribution of the Portuguese language began during the period know as *Os Descobrimentos* (the Discoveries), the golden era of Portugal's colonial expansion into Africa, Asia and South America. In the 15th and 16th centuries, the peninsular nation was a world power and had enormous economic, cultural and political influence. The empire's reach can be seen today in the number of countries besides Portugal where Portuguese still has the status of an official language – Brazil, Madeira and the Azores in the Atlantic Ocean off Europe, Cape Verde, São Tomé and Príncipe, Guinea-Bissau, Angola and Mozambique (all in Africa), and Macau and East Timor in Asia.

While there are differences between European Portuguese and that spoken elsewhere, you shouldn't have many problems being understood throughout the Portuguese-speaking world. As the Portuguese say, *Quem não arrisca, não petisca* keng nowng a·*rreesh*·ka, nowng pe·*teesh*·ka (If you don't take a risk, you won't eat delicacies).

pronunciation

vowel sounds

The vowel sounds in Portuguese are quite similar to those found in English. Most vowel sounds in Portuguese also have a nasal version with an effect similar to the silent '-ng' ending in English, as in *amanhã* aa·ma·*nyang* (tomorrow), for example. The letter 'n' or 'm' at the end of a syllable or a tilde (~) in written Portuguese indicate that the vowel is nasal.

symbol	english equivalent	portuguese example	transliteration
a	run	*maçã*	ma·*sang*
aa	father	*tomate*	too·*maa*·te
ai	aisle	*pai*	pai
ay	say	*lei*	lay
e	bet	*cedo*	*se*·doo
ee	see	*fino*	*fee*·noo
o	pot	*sobre*	*so*·bre
oh	oh	*couve*	*koh*·ve
oo	book	*gato*	*ga*·too
ow	how	*Austrália*	ow·*shtraa*·lya
oy	toy	*noite*	*noy*·te

word stress

In Portuguese, stress generally falls on the second-to-last syllable of a word, though there are exceptions. If a written vowel has a circumflex (ˆ) or an acute (ˊ) or grave (ˋ) accent marked on it, this cancels the general rule and the stress falls on that syllable. When a word ends in a written *i*, *im*, *l*, *r*, *u*, *um* or *z*, or is pronounced with a nasalised vowel, the stress falls on the last syllable. Don't worry too much about it when using phrases from this book though — the stressed syllable is always italicised in our coloured pronunciation guides.

consonant sounds

Most of the consonant sounds in Portuguese are also found in English, and even *r* (rr) will be familiar to many people (it's similar to the French 'r'). Note that the letter *ç* ('c' with a cedilla) is pronounced as s rather than k.

symbol	english equivalent	portuguese example	transliteration
b	bed	*beber*	be·*ber*
d	dog	*dedo*	*de*·doo
f	fat	*faca*	*faa*·ka
g	go	*gasolina*	ga·zoo·*lee*·na
k	kit	*cama*	*ka*·ma
l	lot	*lixo*	*lee*·shoo
ly	million	*muralhas*	moo·*raa*·lyash
m	man	*macaco*	ma·*kaa*·koo
n	not	*nada*	*naa*·da
ng	ring (indicates the nasalisation of the preceding vowel)	*ambos,* *uns,* *amanhã*	*ang*·boosh, *oong*sh, aa·ma·*nyang*
ny	canyon	*linha*	*lee*·nya
p	pet	*padre*	*paa*·dre
r	like 'tt' in 'butter' said fast	*hora*	*o*·ra
rr	run (throaty)	*relva*	*rrel*·va
s	sun	*criança*	kree·*ang*·sa
sh	shot	*chave*	*shaa*·ve
t	top	*tacho*	*taa*·shoo
v	very	*vago*	*vaa*·goo
w	win	*água*	*aa*·gwa
y	yes	*edifício*	ee·dee·*fee*·syoo
z	zero	*camisa*	ka·*mee*·za
zh	pleasure	*cerveja*	serr·ve·*zha*

tools

language difficulties

Do you speak English?
Fala inglês? faa·la eeng·glesh

Do you understand?
Entende? eng·teng·de

I (don't) understand.
(Não) Entendo. (nowng) eng·teng·doo

What does (bem-vindo) mean?
O que quer dizer (bem-vindo)? oo ke ker dee·zer (beng·veeng·doo)

How do you ...? *Como é que se ...?* ko·moo e ke se ...
  pronounce this *pronuncia isto* proo·noong·see·a esh·too
  write (ajuda) *escreve (ajuda)* shkre·ve (a·zhoo·da)

Could you please ...? *Podia ..., por favor?* poo·dee·a ... poor fa·vor
  repeat that *repetir isto* rre·pe·teer eesh·too
  speak more slowly *falar mais devagar* fa·laar maish de·va·gaar
  write it down *escrever isso* shkre·ver ee·soo

essentials

Yes.	*Sim.*	seeng
No.	*Não.*	nowng
Please.	*Por favor.*	poor fa·vor
Thank you	*(Muito)*	(mweeng·too)
(very much).	*Obrigado/a.* m/f	o·bree·gaa·doo/a
You're welcome.	*De nada.*	de naa·da
Excuse me.	*Faz favor!*	faash fa·vor
Sorry.	*Desculpe.*	desh·kool·pe

numbers

0	*zero*	ze·roo	16	*dezasseis*	de·za·saysh
1	*um*	oong	17	*dezassete*	de·za·se·te
2	*dois*	doysh	18	*dezoito*	de·zoy·too
3	*três*	tresh	19	*dezanove*	de·za·no·ve
4	*quatro*	kwaa·troo	20	*vinte*	veeng·te
5	*cinco*	seeng·koo	21	*vinte e um*	veeng·te e oong
6	*seis*	saysh	22	*vinte e dois*	veeng·te e doysh
7	*sete*	se·te	30	*trinta*	treeng·ta
8	*oito*	oy·too	40	*quarenta*	kwa·reng·ta
9	*nove*	no·ve	50	*cinquenta*	seeng·kweng·ta
10	*dez*	desh	60	*sessenta*	se·seng·ta
11	*onze*	ong·ze	70	*setenta*	se·teng·ta
12	*doze*	do·ze	80	*oitenta*	oy·teng·ta
13	*treze*	tre·ze	90	*noventa*	no·veng·ta
14	*catorze*	ka·tor·ze	100	*cem*	seng
15	*quinze*	keeng·ze	1000	*mil*	meel

time & dates

What time is it?	*Que horas são?*	kee o·rash sowng
It's one o'clock.	*É uma hora.*	e oo·ma o·ra
It's (10) o'clock.	*São (dez) horas.*	sowng (desh) o·rash
Quarter past (10).	*(Dez) e quinze.*	(desh) e keeng·ze
Half past (10).	*(Dez) e meia.*	(desh) e may·a
Quarter to (10).	*Quinze para as (dez).*	keeng·ze pa·ra ash (desh)
At what time ...?	*A que horas ...?*	a ke o·rash ...
At ...	*Às ...*	ash ...

in the morning	*da manhã*	da ma·nyang
in the afternoon	*da tarde*	da taar·de
in the evening	*da noite*	da noy·te

Monday	*segunda-feira*	se·goong·da·fay·ra
Tuesday	*terça-feira*	ter·sa·fay·ra
Wednesday	*quarta-feira*	kwaar·ta·fay·ra
Thursday	*quinta-feira*	keeng·ta·fay·ra
Friday	*sexta-feira*	saysh·ta·fay·ra
Saturday	*sábado*	saa·ba·doo
Sunday	*domingo*	doo·meeng·goo

January	*Janeiro*	zha·*nay*·roo
February	*Fevereiro*	fe·*vray*·roo
March	*Março*	maar·soo
April	*Abril*	a·*breel*
May	*Maio*	maa·yoo
June	*Junho*	zhoo·nyoo
July	*Julho*	zhoo·lyoo
August	*Agosto*	a·*gosh*·too
September	*Setembro*	se·*teng*·broo
October	*Outubro*	oh·*too*·broo
November	*Novembro*	no·*veng*·broo
December	*Dezembro*	de·*zeng*·broo

What date is it today?
Qual é a data de hoje? — kwaal e a *daa*·ta de *o*·zhe

It's (18 October).
Hoje é dia (dezoito de Outubro). — *o*·zhe e *dee*·a (de·*zoy*·too de oh·*too*·broo)

| since (May) | *desde (Maio)* | *desh*·de (*maa*·yoo) |
| until (June) | *até (Junho)* | a·*te* (zhoo·nyoo) |

last ...
night	*a noite passada*	a *noy*·te pa·*saa*·da
week	*a semana passada*	a se·*ma*·na pa·*saa*·da
month	*o mês passado*	oo mesh pa·*saa*·doo
year	*o ano passado*	oo *a*·noo pa·*saa*·doo

next ...
week	*na próxima semana*	na *pro*·see·ma se·*ma*·na
month	*no próximo mês*	noo *pro*·see·moo mesh
year	*no próximo ano*	noo *pro*·see·moo *a*·noo

yesterday/tomorrow ...	*ontem/amanhã ...*	ong·teng/aa·ma·*nyang* ...
morning	*de manhã*	de ma·*nyang*
afternoon	*à tarde*	aa *taar*·de
evening	*à noite*	aa *noy*·te

weather

What's the weather like?	Como está o tempo?	ko-moo shtaa oo teng-poo
It's ...	Está ...	shtaa ...
cloudy	enublado	e-noo-blaa-doo
cold	frio	free-oo
hot	muito quente	mweeng-too keng-te
raining	a chover	a shoo-ver
snowing	a nevar	a ne-vaar
sunny	sol	sol
warm	quente	keng-te
windy	ventoso	veng-to-zoo
spring	primavera f	pree-ma-ve-ra
summer	verão m	ve-rowng
autumn	outono m	oh-to-noo
winter	inverno m	eeng-ver-noo

border crossing

I'm here ...	Estou ...	shtoh ...
in transit	em trânsito	eng trang-zee-too
on business	em negócios	eng ne-go-syoosh
on holiday	de férias	de fe-ree-ash
I'm here for ...	Vou ficar por ...	voh fee-kaar poor ...
(10) days	(dez) dias	(desh) dee-ash
(three) weeks	(três) semanas	(tresh) se-ma-nash
(two) months	(dois) meses	(doysh) me-zesh

I'm going to (Elvas).
Vou para (Elvas).   voh pa-ra (el-vash)

I'm staying at the (Hotel Lisbon).
Estou no (Hotel Lisboa).   shtoh noo (o-tel leezh-bo-a)

I have nothing to declare.
Não tenho nada a declarar.   nowng ta-nyoo naa-da a de-kla-raar

I have something to declare.
Tenho algo a declarar.   ta-nyoo al-goo a de-kla-raar

That's (not) mine.
Isto (não) é meu.   eesh-too (nowng) e me-oo

transport

tickets & luggage

Where can I buy a ticket?
Onde é que eu compro o bilhete? ong·de e ke e·oo kong·proo oo bee·lye·te

Do I need to book a seat?
Preciso de fazer reserva? pre·see·zoo de fa·zer rre·zer·va

One ... ticket (to Braga), please.	*Um bilhete de ... (para Braga), por favor.*	oong bee·lye·te de ... (pra brag·ga) poor fa·vor
one-way	*ida*	ee·da
return	*ida e volta*	ee·da ee vol·ta

I'd like to ... my ticket, please.	*Queria ... o bilhete, por favor.*	ke·ree·a ... oo bee·lye·te poor fa·vor
cancel	*cancelar*	kang·se·laar
change	*trocar*	troo·kaar
collect	*cobrar*	koo·braar
confirm	*confirmar*	kong·feer·maar

I'd like a ... seat, please.	*Queria um lugar ... por favor.*	ke·ree·a oong loo·gaar ... poor fa·vor
nonsmoking	*de não fumadores*	de nowng foo·ma·do·resh
smoking	*para fumadores*	pra foo·ma·do·resh

How much is it?
Quanto é? kwang·too e

Is there air conditioning?
Tem ar condicionado? teng aar kong·dee·syoo·naa·doo

Is there a toilet?
Tem casa de banho? teng kaa·za de ba·nyoo

How long does the trip take?
Quanto tempo é que leva a viagem? kwang·too teng·poo e ke le·va a vee·aa·zheng

Is it a direct route?
É uma rota directa? e oo·ma rro·ta dee·re·ta

I'd like a luggage locker.
Queria o depósito de bagagens. ke·ree·a oo de·po·zee·too de ba·gaa·zhengsh

My luggage has been ...	A minha bagagem ...	a *mee*-nya ba-*gaa*-zheng ...
damaged	foi danificada	foy da-nee-fee-*kaa*-da
lost	perdeu-se	per-*de*-oo-se
stolen	foi roubada	foy rroh-*baa*-da

getting around

Where does flight (TP 615) arrive/depart?

De onde pára/parte o voo (TP 615)?
de *ong*-de *paa*-ra/*paar*-te oo *vo*-oo (te pe saysh-*seng*-toosh e *keeng*-ze)

Where's (the) ...?	Onde é ...?	*ong*-de e ...
arrivals hall	a porta de chegada	a *por*-ta de she-*gaa*-da
departures hall	a porta de partida	a *por*-ta de par-*tee*-da
duty-free shop	a loja duty-free	a *lo*-zha *doo*-tee-free
gate (12)	a porta (doze)	a *por*-ta (*do*-ze)

Is this the ... to (Lisbon)?	Este é o ... para (Lisboa)?	*esh*-te e oo ... pra (leezh-*bo*-a)
boat	barco	*baar*-koo
bus	autocarro	ow-to-*kaa*-rroo
plane	avião	a-vee-*owng*
train	comboio	kong-*boy*-oo

What time's the ... bus?	Quando é que sai o ... autocarro?	*kwang*-doo e ke sai oo ... ow-to-*kaa*-rroo
first	primeiro	pree-*may*-roo
last	último	*ool*-tee-moo
next	próximo	*pro*-see-moo

At what time does it arrive/leave?

A que horas chega/sai?
a ke *o*-rash *she*-ga/sai

How long will it be delayed?

Quanto tempo é que vai chegar atrasado?
kwang-too *teng*-poo e ke vai she-*gaar* a-tra-*zaa*-doo

What station/stop is this?

Qual estação/paragem é este?
kwaal shta-*sowng*/pa-*raa*-zheng e *esh*-te

What's the next station/stop?

Qual é a próxima estação/ paragem?
kwaal e a *pro*-see-ma shta-*sowng*/ pa-*raa*-zheng

Does it stop at (Amarante)?
 Pára em (Amarante)?   paa·ra eng (a·ma·rang·te)

Please tell me when we get to (Évora).
 Por favor avise-me quando   poor fa·vor a·vee·ze·me kwang·doo
 chegarmos a (Évora).   she·gaar·moosh a (e·voo·ra)

How long do we stop here?
 Quanto tempo vamos   kwang·too teng·poo va·moosh
 ficar parados aqui?   fee·kaar pa·raa·doosh a·kee

Is this seat available?
 Este lugar está vago?   esh·te loo·gaar shtaa va·goo

That's my seat.
 Este é o meu lugar.   esh·te e oo me·oo loo·gaar

I'd like a taxi …	*Queria chamar*	ke·ree·a sha·maar
	um táxi …	oong taak·see …
at (9am)	*para as (nove*	pra ash (no·ve
	da manhã)	da ma·nyang)
now	*agora*	a·go·ra
tomorrow	*amanhã*	aa·ma·nyang

Is this taxi available?
 Este táxi está livre?   esh·te taak·see shtaa lee·vre

How much is it to …?
 Quanto custa até ao …?   kwang·too koosh·ta a·te ow …

Please put the meter on.
 Por favor, ligue o taxímetro.   poor fa·vor lee·ge oo taak·see·me·troo

Please take me to (this address).
 Leve-me para (este endereço),   le·ve·me pa·ra (esh·te eng·de·re·soo)
 por favor.   poor fa·vor

Please …	*Por favor …*	poor fa·vor …
slow down	*vá mais devagar*	vaa maish de·va·gaar
stop here	*pare aqui*	paa·re a·kee
wait here	*espere aqui*	shpe·re a·kee

car, motorbike & bicycle hire

I'd like to hire a ...	*Queria alugar ...*	ke·*ree*·a a·loo·*gaar* ...
bicycle	*uma bicicleta*	*oo*·ma bee·see·*kle*·ta
car	*um carro*	oong *kaa*·rro
motorbike	*uma mota*	*oo*·ma *mo*·ta

with ...	*com ...*	kong ...
a driver	*motorista*	moo·too·*reesh*·ta
air conditioning	*ar condicionado*	aar kong·dee·syoo·*naa*·doo

How much	*Quanto custa para*	*kwang*·too *koosh*·ta *pa*·ra
for ... hire?	*alugar por ...?*	a·loo·*gaar* poor ...
hourly	*hora*	*o*·ra
daily	*dia*	*dee*·a
weekly	*semana*	se·*ma*·na

air	*ar* m	aar
oil	*óleo* m	*o*·le·oo
petrol	*gasolina* f	ga·zoo·*lee*·na
tyres	*pneus* m pl	pe·*ne*·oosh

I need a mechanic.
Preciso de um mecânico.   pre·*see*·zoo de oong me·*kaa*·nee·koo

I've run out of petrol.
Estou sem gasolina.   shtoh seng ga·zoo·*lee*·na

I have a flat tyre.
Tenho um furo no pneu.   ta·nyoo oong *foo*·roo noo pe·*ne*·oo

directions

Where's the ...?	*Onde é ...?*	*ong*·de e ...
bank	*o banco*	oo *bang*·koo
city centre	*o centro da cidade*	oo *seng*·troo da see·*daa*·de
hotel	*o hotel*	oo o·*tel*
market	*o mercado*	oo mer·*kaa*·doo
police station	*a esquadra da polícia*	a *shkwaa*·dra da poo·*lee*·sya
post office	*o correio*	oo koo·*rray*·oo
public toilet	*a casa de banho pública*	a *kaa*·za de *ba*·nyoo *poo*·blee·ka
tourist office	*o escritório de turismo*	oo shkree·*to*·ryoo de too·*reezh*·moo

Is this the road to (Sintra)?
Esta é a estrada para (Sintra)? — esh-ta e a shtraa-da pa-ra (seeng-tra)

Can you show me (on the map)?
Pode-me mostrar (no mapa)? — po-de-me moosh-traar (noo maa-pa)

How far is it?
A que distância fica? — a ke deesh-tang-sya fee-ka

How do I get there?
Como é que eu chego lá? — ko-moo e ke e-oo she-goo laa

Turn ...	*Vire ...*	vee-re ...
at the corner	*na esquina*	na shkee-na
at the traffic lights	*nos semáforos*	noosh se-maa-foo-roosh
left	*à esquerda*	aa shker-da
right	*à direita*	aa dee-ray-ta

It's ...	*É ...*	e ...
behind ...	*atrás de ...*	a-traash de ...
far away	*longe*	long-zhe
here	*aqui*	a-kee
in front of ...	*em frente de ...*	eng freng-te de ...
left	*à esquerda*	aa shker-da
near (to ...)	*perto (de ...)*	per-too (de ...)
next to ...	*ao lado de ...*	ow laa-doo de ...
on the corner	*na esquina*	na shkee-na
opposite ...	*do lado oposto ...*	doo laa-doo oo-posh-too ...
right	*à direita*	aa dee-ray-ta
straight ahead	*em frente*	eng freng-te
there	*lá*	laa

by bus	*de autocarro*	de ow-to-kaa-rroo
by taxi	*de táxi*	de taak-see
by train	*de comboio*	de kong-boy-oo
on foot	*a pé*	a pe

north	*norte*	nor-te
south	*sul*	sool
east	*leste*	lesh-te
west	*oeste*	o-esh-te

signs

Entrada/Saída	eng-*traa*-da/sa-*ee*-da	**Entrance/Exit**
Aberto/Fechado	a-*ber*-too/fe-*shaa*-doo	**Open/Closed**
Há Vaga	aa *vaa*-ga	**Rooms Available**
Não Há Vaga	nowng aa *vaa*-ga	**No Vacancies**
Informação	eeng-for-ma-*sowng*	**Information**
Esquadra da Polícia	shkwaa-dra da poo-*lee*-sya	**Police Station**
Proibido	pro-ee-*bee*-doo	**Prohibited**
Casa de Banho	*kaa*-za de ba-nyoo	**Toilets**
Homens	o-mengsh	**Men**
Mulheres	moo-*lye*-resh	**Women**
Quente/Frio	keng-te/*free*-oo	**Hot/Cold**

accommodation

finding accommodation

Where's a ...?	*Onde é que há ...?*	ong-de e ke aa ...
camping ground	*um parque de campismo*	oong *paar*-ke de kang-*peezh*-moo
guesthouse	*uma casa de hóspedes*	oo-ma *kaa*-za de *osh*-pe-desh
hotel	*um hotel*	oong o-*tel*
youth hostel	*uma pousada de juventude*	oo-ma poh-*zaa*-da de zhoo-veng-*too*-de

Can you recommend somewhere ...?	*Pode recomendar algum lugar ...?*	po-de rre-koo-meng-*daar* aal-*goong* loo-*gaar* ...
cheap	*barato*	ba-*raa*-too
good	*bom*	bong
nearby	*perto daqui*	*per*-too da-*kee*

I'd like to book a room, please.
Eu queria fazer uma reserva, por favor.
e-oo ke-*ree*-a fa-*zer* oo-ma rre-*zer*-va poor fa-*vor*

I have a reservation.
Eu tenho uma reserva.
e-oo *ta*-nyoo oo-ma rre-*zer*-va

My name's ...
O meu nome é ...
oo *me*-oo *no*-me e ...

Do you have a ... room?	*Tem um quarto ...?*	teng oong *kwaar*·too ...
single	*de solteiro*	de sol·*tay*·roo
double	*de casal*	de ka·*zaal*
twin	*duplo*	*doo*·ploo

How much is it per ...?	*Quanto custa por ...?*	*kwang*·too *koosh*·ta poor ...
night	*noite*	*noy*·te
person	*pessoa*	pe·*so*·a

Can I pay by ...?	*Posso pagar com ...?*	*po*·soo pa·*gaar* kong ...
credit card	*cartão de crédito*	kar·*towng* de *kre*·dee·too
travellers cheque	*traveller cheque*	*tra*·ve·ler shek

I'd like to stay for (three) nights.
Para (três) noites. — pa·ra (tresh) *noy*·tesh

From (2 July) to (6 July).
*De (dois de julho) até
(seis de julho).* — de (doysh de *zhoo*·lyoo) a·te
(saysh de *zhoo*·lyoo)

Can I see it?
Posso ver? — *po*·soo ver

Am I allowed to camp here?
Posso acampar aqui? — *po*·soo a·kang·*paar* a·*kee*

Where can I find a camping ground?
Onde é o parque de campismo? — *ong*·de e oo *par*·ke de kang·*peesh*·moo

requests & queries

When/Where is breakfast served?
*Quando/Onde é que servem
o pequeno almoço?* — *kwang*·doo/*ong*·de e ke *ser*·veng
oo pe·*ke*·noo aal·*mo*·soo

Please wake me at (seven).
Por favor acorde-me às (sete). — poor fa·*vor* aa·*kor*·de·me aash (*se*·te)

Could I have my key, please?
*Pode-me dar a minha chave,
por favor?* — *po*·de·me daar a *mee*·nya *shaa*·ve
poor fa·*vor*

Can I get another (blanket)?
Pode-me dar mais um (cobertor)? — *po*·de·me daar maish oong (koo·ber·*tor*)

Is there a/an ...?	Tem ...?	teng ...
elevator	elevador	e·le·va·dor
safe	cofre	ko·fre

The room is too ...	É demasiado ...	e·de·ma·zee·aa·doo ...
expensive	caro	kaa·roo
noisy	barulhento	ba·roo·lyeng·too
small	pequeno	pe·ke·noo

The ... doesn't work.	... não funciona.	... nowng foong·see·o·na
air conditioner	O ar condicionado	oo aar kong·dee·syoo·naa·doo
fan	A ventoínha	a veng·too·ee·na
toilet	A sanita	a sa·nee·ta

This ... isn't clean.	Esta ... está suja.	esh·ta ... shtaa soo·zha
pillow	almofada	aal·moo·faa·da
towel	toalha	twaa·lya

| This sheet isn't clean. | Este lençol está sujo. | esh·te leng·sol shtaa soo·zho |

checking out

What time is checkout?
A que horas é a partida? — a ke o·rash e a par·tee·da

Can I leave my luggage here?
Posso deixar as minhas — po·soo day·shaar ash mee·nyash
malas aqui? — maa·lash a·kee

Could I have	Pode-me devolver	po·de·me de·vol·ver
my ..., please?	..., por favor?	... poor fa·vor
deposit	o depósito	oo de·po·zee·too
passport	o passaporte	oo paa·sa·por·te
valuables	os objectos	oosh o·be·zhe·toosh
	de valor	de va·lor

communications & banking

the internet

Where's the local Internet café?
Onde fica um café da internet nas redondezas?
ong·de fee·ka oong ka·fe da eeng·ter·net nash rre·dong·de·zash

How much is it per hour?
Quanto custa por hora?
kwang·too koosh·ta pooro·ra

I'd like to ... *Queria ...* ke·ree·a ...
  check my email *ler o meu email* ler oo me·oo ee·mayl
  get Internet access *ter acesso à internet* ter a·se·soo aa eeng·ter·net
  use a printer *usar uma impressora* oo·zaar oo·ma eeng·pre·so·ra
  use a scanner *usar um digitalizador* oo·zaar oong dee·zhee·ta·lee·za·dor

mobile/cell phone

I'd like a ... *Queria ...* ke·ree·a ...
  mobile/cell phone for hire *alugar um telemóvel* a·loo·gaar oong te·le·mo·vel
  SIM card for your network *cartão SIM para a sua rede* kar·towng seeng pa·ra a soo·a rre·de

What are the rates? *Qual é o valor cobrado?* kwaal e oo va·lor koo·braa·doo

telephone

What's your phone number?
Qual é o seu número de telefone?
kwaal e oo se·oo noo·me·roo de te·le·fo·ne

The number is ...
O número é ...
oo noo·me·roo e ...

Where's the nearest public phone?
Onde fica o telefone público mais perto?
ong·de fee·ka o te·le·fo·ne poo·blee·koo maish per·too

I'd like to buy a phonecard.
Quero comprar um cartão telefónico.
ke·roo kong·praar oong kar·towng te·le·fo·nee·koo

I want to ...	Quero ...	ke·roo ...
call (Singapore)	telefonar (para Singapura)	te·le·foo·naar (pa·ra seeng·ga·poo·ra)
make a local call	fazer uma chamada local	fa·zer oo·ma sha·maa·da loo·kaal
reverse the charges	fazer uma chamada a cobrar	fa·zer oo·ma sha·maa·da a koo·braar

How much does ... cost?	Quanto custa ...?	kwang·too koosh·ta ...
a (three)-minute call	uma ligação de (três) minutos	oo·ma lee·ga·sowng de (tresh) mee·noo·toosh
each extra minute	cada minuto extra	kaa·da mee·noo·too aysh·tra

It's (30c) per (30) seconds.
(Trinta cêntimos) por (trinta) segundos.
(treeng·ta seng·tee·moosh) poor (treeng·ta) se·goong·doosh

post office

I want to send a ...	Quero enviar ...	ke·roo eng·vee·aar ...
fax	um fax	oong faks
letter	uma carta	oo·ma kaar·ta
parcel	uma encomenda	oo·ma eng·koo·meng·da
postcard	um postal	oong poosh·taal

I want to buy a/an ...	Quero comprar um ...	ke·roo kong·praar oong ...
envelope	envelope	eng·ve·lo·pe
stamp	selo	se·loo

Please send it (to Australia) by ...	Por favor envie isto (para Australia) por ...	poor fa·vor eng·vee·e eesh·too (pa·ra owsh·traa·lya) poor ...
airmail	via aérea	vee·a a·e·ree·a
express mail	correio azul	koo·rray·oo a·zool
registered mail	registado/a m/f	rre·zheesh·taa·doo/a
surface mail	via terrestre	vee·a te·rresh·tre

Is there any mail for me?
Há alguma correspondência para mim?
aa aal·goo·ma koo·rresh·pong·deng·sya pa·ra meeng

bank

Where's a/an ...?	Onde é que há ...?	*ong*-de e ke aa ...
ATM	um caixa automático	oong *kai*-sha ow-too-*maa*-tee-koo
foreign exchange office	um câmbio	oong *kang*-byoo

I'd like to ...	Queria ...	ke-*ree*-a ...
Where can I ...?	Onde é que posso ...?	*ong*-de e ke *po*-soo ...
arrange a transfer	fazer uma transferencia	faa-*zer oo*-ma trans-fe-*reng*-sya
cash a cheque	trocar um cheque	troo-*kaar* oong *she*-ke
change a travellers cheque	trocar traveller cheque	troo-*kaar* tra-ve-ler shek
change money	trocar dinheiro	troo-*kaar* dee-*nyay*-roo
get a cash advance	fazer um levantamento adiantado	fa-*zer* oong le-vang-ta-*meng*-too a-dee-ang-*taa*-doo
withdraw money	levantar dinheiro	le-vang-*taar* dee-*nyay*-roo

What's the ...?	Qual é ...?	kwaal e ...
commission	a comissão	a koo-mee-*sowng*
charge for that	o imposto	oo eeng-*posh*-too
exchange rate	o câmbio do dia	oo *kang*-byoo doo *dee*-a

It's ...	É ...	e ...
(12) euros	(doze) euros	(*do*-ze) e-*oo*-roosh
free	gratuito	gra-*twee*-too

What time does the bank open?
A que horas é que abre o banco? a ke *o*-rash e ke *aa*-bre oo *bang*-koo

Has my money arrived yet?
O meu dinheiro já chegou? oo *me*-oo dee-*nyay*-roo zhaa she-*goh*

sightseeing

getting in

What time does it open/close?
A que horas abre/fecha?
a ke o·rash *aa*·bre/*fe*·sha

What's the admission charge?
Qual é o preço de entrada?
kwaal e oo *pre*·soo de eng·*traa*·da

Is there a discount for children/students?
Tem desconto para crianças/
estudantes?
teng desh·*kong*·too *pa*·ra kree·*ang*·sash/
shtoo·*dang*·tesh

I'd like a ...	*Queria um ...*	ke·*ree*·a oong ...
catalogue	*catálogo*	ka·*taa*·loo·goo
guide	*guia*	*gee*·a
local map	*mapa local*	*maa*·pa loo·*kaal*

I'd like to see ...
Eu gostava de ver ...
e·oo goosh·*taa*·va de ver ...

What's that?
O que é aquilo?
oo ke e a·*kee*·loo

Can I take a photo?
Posso tirar uma
fotografia?
po·soo tee·*raar* oo·ma
foo·too·gra·*fee*·a

tours

When's the next ...?
Quando é ...?
kwang·doo e ...

   day trip
o próximo passeio
oo *pro*·see·moo pa·*say*·oo

   tour
a próxima excursão
a *pro*·see·ma shkoor·*sowng*

Is ... included?
Inclui ...?
eeng·*kloo*·ee ...

   accommodation
hospedagem
osh·pe·*daa*·zheng

   the admission charge
preço de entrada
pre·soo de eng·*traa*·da

   food
comida
koo·*mee*·da

   transport
transporte
trangsh·*por*·te

How long is the tour?
Quanto tempo dura
a excursão?
kwang·too teng·poo *doo*·ra
a shkoor·*sowng*

What time should we be back?
A que hora é que devemos
estar de volta?
a ke *o*·ra e ke de·*ve*·moosh
shtaar de *vol*·ta

castle	*castelo* m	kash·*te*·loo
cathedral	*catedral* f	ka·te·*draal*
church	*igreja* f	ee·*gre*·zha
main square	*praça principal* f	*praa*·sa preeng·see·*paal*
monastery	*mosteiro* m	moosh·*tay*·roo
monument	*monumento* m	moo·noo·*meng*·too
museum	*museu* m	moo·*ze*·oo
old city	*cidade antiga* f	see·*daa*·de ang·*tee*·ga
palace	*palácio* m	pa·*laa*·syoo
ruins	*ruínas* f pl	rroo·*ee*·nash
stadium	*estádio* m	*shtaa*·dyoo
statues	*estátuas* f pl	shtaa·*too*·ash

shopping

enquiries

Where's a ...?	*Onde é ...?*	*ong*·de e ...
bank	*o banco*	oo *bang*·koo
bookshop	*a livraria*	a lee·vra·*ree*·a
department store	*loja de departamentos*	*lo*·zha de de·par·ta·*meng*·toosh
grocery store	*a mercearia*	a mer·see·a·*ree*·a
market	*o mercado*	oo mer·*kaa*·doo
newsagency	*o quiosque*	oo kee·*osh*·ke
supermarket	*o supermercado*	oo soo·per·mer·*kaa*·doo

Where can I buy (a padlock)?
Onde é que posso comprar (um cadeado)?
ong·de e ke *po*·soo kong·*praar* (oong ka·de·*aa*·doo)

I'm looking for ...
Estou à procura de ...
shtoh aa proo·*koo*·ra de ...

Can I look at it?
Posso ver?
po·soo ver

Do you have any others?
Tem outros?
teng *oh*·troosh

Does it have a guarantee?
   Tem garantia?   teng ga·rang·*tee*·a

Can I have it sent overseas?
   Podem enviar para o   po·deng eng·vee·*aar* pa·ra oo
   estrangeiro?   shtrang·*zhay*·roo

Can I have my ... repaired?
   Vocês consertam ...?   vo·*sesh* kong·*ser*·tang ...

It's faulty.
   Tem defeito.   teng de·*fay*·too

I'd like ..., please.	*Queria ..., por favor.*	ke·*ree*·a ... poor fa·*vor*
a bag	*um saco*	oong *saa*·koo
a refund	*ser reembolsado/a* m/f	ser rre·eng·bol·*saa*·doo/a
to return this	*devolver isto*	de·vol·*ver* eesh·too

paying

How much is it?
   Quanto custa?   kwang·too *koosh*·ta

Can you write down the price?
   Pode escrever o preço?   po·de shkre·*ver* oo *pre*·soo

That's too expensive.
   Está muito caro.   shtaa *mweeng*·too *kaa*·roo

What's your lowest price?
   Qual é o seu último preço? kwaal e oo se·oo *ool*·tee·moo *pre*·soo

I'll give you (five) euros.
   Dou-lhe (cinco) euros.   doh·lye (*seeng*·koo) e·oo·roosh

There's a mistake in the bill.
   Há um erro na conta.   aa oong e·rroo na *kong*·ta

Do you accept ...?	*Aceitam ...?*	a·*say*·tang ...
credit cards	*cartão de crédito*	kar·*towng* de kre·dee·too
debit cards	*multibanco*	mool·tee·*bang*·koo
travellers cheques	*travellers cheques*	tra·ve·ler *she*·kesh

I'd like ..., please.	*Queria ..., por favor.*	ke·*ree*·a ... poor fa·*vor*
a receipt	*um recibo*	oong rre·*see*·boo
my change	*o troco*	oo *tro*·koo

clothes & shoes

Can I try it on?	*Posso experimentar?*	po·soo shpree·meng·*taar*
My size is (40).	*O meu número é (quarenta).*	oo *me*·oo *noo*·me·roo e (kwa·*reng*·ta)
It doesn't fit.	*Não serve.*	nowng *ser*·ve
small	*pequeno/pequena* m/f	pe·*ke*·noo/pe·*ke*·na
medium	*meio/meia* m/f	*may*·oo/*may*·a
large	*grande* m&f	*grang*·de

books & music

I'd like a ...	*Queria comprar ...*	ke·*ree*·a kong·*praar* ...
newspaper (in English)	*um jornal (em inglês)*	oong zhor·*naal* (eng eeng·*glesh*)
pen	*uma caneta*	*oo*·ma ka·*ne*·ta

Is there an English-language bookshop?
Há uma livraria de língua inglesa?
aa *oo*·ma lee·vra·*ree*·a de *leeng*·gwa eeng·*gle*·za

I'm looking for something by (Fernando Pessoa).
Estou à procura de qualquer coisa do (Fernando Pessoa).
shtoh aa proo·*koo*·ra de kwaal·*ker koy*·za doo (fer·*nang*·doo pe·*so*·a)

Can I listen to this?
Posso ouvir?
po·soo oh·*veer*

photography

I need a/an ... film for this camera.	*Preciso de filme ... para esta máquina.*	pre·*see*·zoo de *feel*·me ... *pa*·ra *esh*·ta *maa*·kee·na
APS	*sistema APS*	seesh·*te*·ma aa pe *e*·se
B&W	*a preto e branco*	a *pre*·too e *brang*·koo
colour	*a cores*	a *ko*·resh
slide	*de diapositivos*	de dee·a·po·zee·*tee*·voosh
(200) ASA	*de (duzentos) ASA*	de (doo·*zeng*·toosh) *aa*·za
When will it be ready?	*Quando fica pronto?*	kwang·doo *fee*·ka *prong*·too

Can you ...?	Pode ...?	po-de ...
develop this film	revelar este filme	rre-ve-*laar* esh-te *feel*-me
load my film	carregar o filme	kaa-rre-*gaar* oo *feel*-me
transfer photos	transferir as	trangsh-fe-*reer* ash
from my camera	fotografias	foo-too-gra-*fee*-ash
to CD	da minha máquina	da *mee*-nya *maa*-kee-na
	para um CD	*pa*-ra oong se-*de*

meeting people

greetings, goodbyes & introductions

Hello/Hi.	Olá.	o-*laa*
Good night.	Boa noite.	bo-a *noy*-te
Goodbye/Bye.	Adeus.	a-de-*oosh*
See you later.	Até logo.	a-*te* lo-goo

Mr	Senhor	se-*nyor*
Mrs	Senhora	se-*nyo*-ra
Ms	Senhorita	se-nyo-*ree*-ta

How are you?	Como está?	*ko*-moo shtaa
Fine. And you?	Bem. E você?	beng e vo-*se*
What's your name?	Qual é o seu nome?	kwaal e oo se-oo *no*-me
My name is ...	O meu nome é ...	oo me-oo *no*-me e ...
I'm pleased to	Prazer em conhecê-lo/	pra-*zer* eng koo-nye-*se*-lo/
meet you.	conhecê-la. m/f	koo-nye-*se*-la

This is my ...	Este é o meu ... m	*esh*-te e oo *me*-oo ...
	Esta é a minha ... f	*esh*-ta e a *mee*-nya ...
brother	irmão	eer-*mowng*
daughter	filha	*fee*-lya
father	pai	pai
friend	amigo/a m/f	a-*mee*-goo/a
husband	marido	ma-*ree*-doo
mother	mãe	maing
partner (intimate)	companheiro/a m/f	kong-pa-*nyay*-roo/a
sister	irmã	eer-*mang*
son	filho	*fee*-lyoo
wife	esposa	*shpo*-za

Here's my ...	*Aqui está o meu ...*	a·*kee* shtaa oo *me*·oo ...
What's your ...?	*Qual é o seu ...?*	kwaal e oo *se*·oo ...
address	*endereço*	eng·de·*re*·soo
email address	*email*	ee·*mayl*
fax number	*número de fax*	*noo*·me·roo de faaks
phone number	*número de telefone*	*noo*·me·roo de te·le·*fo*·ne

occupations

What's your occupation?		
Qual é a sua profissão?		kwaal e a *soo*·a proo·fee·*sowng*
I'm a/an ...	*Sou ...*	soh ...
artist	*artista* m&f	ar·*teesh*·ta
business person	*homem/mulher de*	o·meng/moo·*lyer* de
	negócios m/f	ne·*go*·syoosh
farmer	*agricultor* m&f	a·gree·kool·*tor*
manual worker	*trabalhador* m	tra·ba·lya·*dor*
	trabalhadora f	tra·ba·lya·*do*·ra
office worker	*empregado/a*	eng·pre·*gaa*·doo/a
	de escritório m/f	de shkree·*to*·ryoo
scientist	*cientista* m&f	see·eng·*teesh*·ta
student	*estudante* m&f	shtoo·*dang*·te
tradesperson	*comerciante* m&f	koo·mer·see·*aang*·te

background

Where are you from?	*De onde é?*	dong·de e
I'm from ...	*Eu sou ...*	e·oo soh ...
Australia	*da Austrália*	da owsh·*traa*·lya
Canada	*do Canadá*	doo ka·na·*daa*
England	*da Inglaterra*	da eeng·gla·*te*·rra
New Zealand	*da Nova Zelândia*	da *no*·va ze·*lang*·dya
the USA	*dos Estados*	doosh *shtaa*·doosh
	Unidos	oo·*nee*·doosh
Are you married?	*É casado/a?* m/f	e ka·*zaa*·doo/a
I'm ...	*Eu sou ...*	e·oo soh ...
married	*casado/a* m/f	ka·*zaa*·doo/a
single	*solteiro/a* m/f	sol·*tay*·roo/a

age

How old ...?	Quantos anos ...?	kwang·toosh a·noosh ...
are you	tem	teng
is your daughter	tem a sua filha	teng a soo·a fee·lya
is your son	tem o seu filho	teng oo se·oo fee·lyoo
I'm ... years old.	Tenho ... anos.	ta·nyoo ... a·noosh
He/She is ... years old.	Ele/Ela tem ... anos.	e·le/e·la teng ... a·noosh

feelings

I'm (not) ...	(Não) Estou ...	(nowng) shtoh ...
Are you ...?	Está ...	shtaa ...
cold	com frio	kong free·oo
happy	feliz	fe·leesh
hot	com calor	kong ka·lor
hungry	com fome	kong fo·me
OK	bem	beng
sad	triste	treesh·te
thirsty	com sede	kong se·de
tired	cansado/a m/f	kang·saa·doo/a

entertainment

going out

Where can I find ...?	Onde é que há ...?	ong·de e ke aa ...
clubs	discotecas	deesh·koo·te·kash
gay/lesbian	lugares de	loo·gaa·resh de
venues	gays/lésbicas	gaysh/lezh·bee·kash
pubs	bares	ba·resh
I feel like	Está-me a	shtaa·me a
going to a ...	apetecer ir a ...	a·pe·te·ser eer a ...
concert	um concerto	oong kong·ser·too
movies	um filme	oong feel·me
party	uma festa	oo·ma fesh·ta
restaurant	um restaurante	oong rresh·tow·rang·te
theatre	uma peça de teatro	oo·ma pe·sa de tee·aa·troo

interests

Do you like ...?	Gosta de ...?	gosh·ta de ...
I (don't) like ...	Eu (não) gosto de ...	e·oo (nowng) gosh·too de ...
art	arte	aar·te
cooking	cozinhar	koo·zee·nyaar
movies	ver filmes	ver feel·mesh
reading	ler	ler
sport	fazer desporto	fa·zer desh·por·too
travelling	viajar	vee·a·zhaar
Do you like to ...?	Costuma ...?	koosh·too·ma ...
dance	ir dançar	eer dang·saar
go to concerts	ir a concertos	eer a kong·ser·toosh
listen to music	ouvir música	oh·veer moo·zee·ka

food & drink

finding a place to eat

Can you	Pode-me	po·de·me
recommend a ...?	recomendar um ...?	rre·koo·meng·daar oong ...
bar	bar	bar
café	café	ka·fe
restaurant	restaurante	rresh·tow·rang·te
I'd like ..., please.	Queria uma ..., por favor.	ke·ree·a oo·ma ... poor fa·vor
a table for (five)	mesa para (cinco)	me·za pa·ra (seeng·koo)
the (non)smoking	mesa de (não)	me·za de (nowng)
section	fumador	foo·ma·dor

ordering food

breakfast	pequeno almoço m	pe·ke·noo aal·mo·soo
lunch	almoço m	aal·mo·soo
dinner	jantar m	zhang·taar
snack	lanche m	lang·she

What would you recommend?
O que é que recomenda?   oo ke e ke rre·koo·meng·da

I'd like (the) ..., please.	Queria ..., por favor.	ke-ree-a ...poor fa-vor
bill	a conta	a kong-ta
drink list	a lista das bebidas	a leesh-ta dash be-bee-dash
menu	um menu	oong me-noo
that dish	aquele prato	a-ke-le praa-too

drinks

(cup of) coffee ...	(chávena de) café ...	(shaa-ve-na de) ka-fe ...
(cup of) tea ...	(chávena de) chá ...	(shaa-ve-na de) shaa ...
with milk	com leite	kong lay-te
without sugar	sem açúcar	seng a-soo-kar
(orange) juice	sumo (de laranja) m	soo-moo (de la-rang-zha)
soft drink	refrigerante m	rre-free-zhe-rang-te
... water	água ...	aa-gwa ...
hot	quente	keng-te
(sparkling) mineral	mineral (com gás)	mee-ne-raal (kong gaash)

in the bar

I'll have ...	Eu queria ...	e-oo ke-ree-a ...
I'll buy you a drink.	Eu pago-lhe uma bebida.	e-oo paa-goo-lye oo-ma be-bee-da
What would you like?	O que é que quer?	oo ke e ke ker
Cheers!	À nossa!	aa no-sa
brandy	brandy f	brang-dee
cocktail	cocktail m	kok-tayl
a shot of (whisky)	um copinho de (uísque)	oong koo-pee-nyoo de (oo-eesh-kee)
a ... of beer	... de cerveja	... de ser-ve-zha
bottle	uma garrafa	oo-ma ga-rraa-fa
glass	um copo	oong ko-poo
a bottle of ... wine	uma garrafa de vinho ...	oo-ma ga-rraa-fa de vee-nyoo ...
a glass of ... wine	um copo de vinho ...	oong ko-poo de vee-nyoo ...
red	tinto	teeng-too
sparkling	espumante	shpoo-mang-te
white	branco	brang-koo

self-catering

What's the local speciality?
Qual é a especialidade local?   kwaal e a shpe·see·a·lee·*daa*·de loo·*kaal*

What's that?
O que é aquilo?   oo ke e a·*kee*·loo

How much is (a kilo of cheese)?
Quanto é (um quilo de queijo)?   *kwang*·too e (oong *kee*·loo de *kay*·zhoo)

I'd like ...	*Eu queria ...*	e·oo ke·*ree*·a ...
(200) grams	*(duzentos) gramas*	(doo·*zeng*·toosh) *graa*·mash
(two) kilos	*(dois) quilos*	(doysh) *kee*·loosh
(three) pieces	*(três) peças*	(tresh) *pe*·sash
(six) slices	*(seis) fatias*	(saysh) fa·*tee*·ash

Less.	*Menos.*	*me*·noosh
Enough.	*Chega.*	*she*·ga
More.	*Mais.*	maish

special diets & allergies

Is there a vegetarian restaurant near here?
Há algum restaurante   aa aal·*goong* rresh·tow·*rang*·te
vegetariano perto daqui?   ve·zhe·ta·ree·*aa*·noo per·too da·*kee*

Do you have vegetarian food?
Tem comida vegetariana?   teng koo·*mee*·da ve·zhe·ta·ree·*aa*·na

Could you prepare	*Pode preparar*	*po*·de pre·pa·*raar*
a meal without ...?	*sem ...?*	seng ...
butter	*manteiga*	mang·*tay*·ga
eggs	*ovos*	*o*·voosh
meat stock	*caldo de carne*	*kaal*·doo de *kaar*·ne

I'm allergic to ...	*Eu sou alérgico/a*	e·oo soh a·*ler*·zhee·koo/a
	a ... m/f	a ...
dairy produce	*produtos lácteos*	pro·*doo*·toosh *laak*·tee·oosh
gluten	*glúten*	*gloo*·teng
MSG	*MSG*	e·me·e·se·*zhe*
nuts	*oleaginosas*	o·lee·a·zhee·*no*·zash
seafood	*marisco*	ma·*reesh*·koo

emergencies

basics

English	Portuguese	Pronunciation
Help!	*Socorro!*	soo·*ko*·rroo
Stop!	*Stop!*	stop
Go away!	*Vá-se embora!*	*vaa*·se eng·*bo*·ra
Thief!	*Ladrão!*	la·*drowng*
Fire!	*Fogo!*	*fo*·goo
Watch out!	*Cuidado!*	kwee·*daa*·doo
Call ...!	*Chame ...!*	*shaa*·me ...
a doctor	*um médico*	oong *me*·dee·koo
an ambulance	*uma ambulância*	*oo*·ma ang·boo·*lang*·sya
the police	*a polícia*	a poo·*lee*·sya

It's an emergency.
É uma emergência. — e *oo*·ma ee·mer·*zheng*·sya

Could you help me, please?
Pode ajudar, por favor? — *po*·de a·zhoo·*daar* poor fa·*vor*

Can I use the telephone?
Posso usar o seu telefone? — *po*·soo oo·*zaar* oo *se*·oo te·le·*fo*·ne

I'm lost.
Estou perdido/a. m/f — shtoh per·*dee*·doo/a

Where are the toilets?
Onde é a casa de banho? — *ong*·de e a *kaa*·za de *ba*·nyoo

police

Where's the police station?
Onde é a esquadra da polícia? — *ong*·de e a *shkwaa*·dra da poo·*lee*·sya

I want to report an offence.
Eu quero denunciar um crime. — *e*·oo *ke*·roo de·noong·see·*aar* oong *kree*·me

I have insurance.
Eu estou coberto/a pelo seguro. m/f — *e*·oo shtoh koo·*ber*·too/a *pe*·loo se·*goo*·roo

I've been assaulted. *Eu fui agredido/a.* m/f — *e*·oo fwee a·gre·*dee*·doo/a
I've been raped. *Eu fui violado/a.* m/f — *e*·oo fwee vee·oo·*laa*·doo/a
I've been robbed. *Eu fui roubado/a.* m/f — *e*·oo fwee rroh·*baa*·doo/a

I've lost my ...	Eu perdi ...	e-oo per-dee
My ... was/were stolen.	Roubaram ...	rroh-baa-rang ...
backpack	a minha mochila	a meeng-nya moo-shee-la
bags	os meus sacos	oosh me-oosh saa-koosh
credit card	o meu cartão de crédito	oo me-oo kar-towng de kre-dee-too
handbag	a minha bolsa	a mee-nya bol-sa
jewellery	as minhas jóias	ash mee-nyash zhoy-ash
money	o meu dinheiro	oo me-oo dee-nyay-roo
passport	o meu passaporte	oo me-oo paa-sa-por-te
travellers cheques	os meus travellers cheques	oosh me-oosh tra-ve-ler she-kesh
wallet	a minha carteira	a mee-nya kar-tay-ra
I want to contact my ...	Eu quero contactar com ...	e-oo ke-roo kong-tak-taar kong ...
consulate	o meu consulado	oo me-oo kong-soo-laa-doo
embassy	a minha embaixada	a mee-nya eng-bai-shaa-da

health

medical needs

Where's the nearest ...?	Qual é ... mais perto?	kwaal e ... maish per-too
dentist	o dentista	oo deng-teesh-ta
doctor	o médico m	oo me-dee-koo
	a médica f	a me-dee-ka
hospital	o hospital	oo osh-pee-taal
(night) pharmacist	a farmácia (de serviço)	a far-maa-sya (de ser-vee-soo)

I need a doctor (who speaks English).
Eu preciso de um médico (que fale inglês).
e-oo pre-see-zoo de oong me-dee-koo (que faa-le eeng-glesh)

Could I see a female doctor?
Posso ser vista por uma médica?
po-soo ser veesh-ta poor oo-ma me-dee-ka

I've run out of my medication.
Os meus medicamentos acabaram.
oosh me-oosh me-dee-ka-meng-toosh a-ka-baa-rowng

symptoms, conditions & allergies

| I'm sick. | Estou doente. | shtoh doo-*eng*-te |
| It hurts here. | Dói-me aqui. | doy-me a-*kee* |

I have (a) ...	Eu tenho ...	e-oo ta-nyoo ...
asthma	asma	*ash*-ma
bronchitis	bronquite	brong-*kee*-te
constipation	prisão de ventre	pree-*zowng* de *veng*-tre
cough	tosse	*to*-se
diarrhoea	diarreia	dee-a-*rray*-a
fever	febre	*fe*-bre
headache	dor de cabeça	dor de ka-*be*-sa
heart condition	problemas cardíacos	proo-*ble*-mash kar-*dee*-a-koosh
nausea	náusea	*now*-zee-a
pain	dor	dor
sore throat	dores de garganta	*do*-resh de gar-*gang*-ta
toothache	uma dor de dentes	*oo*-ma dor de *deng*-tesh

I'm allergic to ...	Eu sou alérgico/a a ... m/f	e-oo soh a-*ler*-zhee-koo/a a ...
antibiotics	antibióticos	ang-tee-bee-*o*-tee-koosh
anti-inflammatories	anti-inflamatórios	ang-tee-eeng-fla-ma-*to*-ryoosh
aspirin	aspirina	ash-pee-*ree*-na
bees	abelhas	a-*be*-lyash
codeine	codeína	ko-de-*ee*-na
penicillin	penicilina	pe-nee-see-*lee*-na

antiseptic	antiséptico m	ang-tee-*se*-tee-koo
bandage	ligadura f	lee-ga-*doo*-ra
condoms	preservativos m pl	pre-zer-va-*tee*-voosh
contraceptives	contraceptivos m pl	kong-tra-se-*tee*-voosh
diarrhoea medicine	remédio para diarreia m	re-*me*-dyo *pa*-ra dee-a-*rray*-a
insect repellent	repelente m	rre-pe-*leng*-te
laxatives	laxantes m pl	la-*shang*-tesh
painkillers	comprimidos para as dores m pl	kong-pree-*mee*-doosh *pa*-ra ash *do*-resh
rehydration salts	sais rehidratantes m pl	saish rre-ee-dra-*tang*-tesh
sleeping tablets	pílulas para dormir f pl	*pee*-loo-laash *pa*-ra door-*meer*

english–portuguese dictionary

Portuguese nouns and adjectives in this dictionary have their gender indicated with ⓜ (masculine) and ⓕ (feminine). If it's a plural noun, you'll also see pl. Words are also marked as v (verb), n (noun), a (adjective), pl (plural), sg (singular), inf (informal) and pol (polite) where necessary.

A

accident *acidente* ⓜ a·see·*deng*·te
accommodation *hospedagem* ⓕ osh·pe·*daa*·zheng
adaptor *adaptador* ⓜ a·da·pe·ta·*dor*
address *endereço* ⓜ eng·de·*re*·soo
after *depois* de·*poysh*
air conditioned *com ar condicionado*
    kong aar kong·dee·syoo·*naa*·doo
airplane *avião* ⓜ a·vee·*owng*
airport *aeroporto* ⓜ a·e·ro·*por*·too
alcohol *alcool* ⓜ al·ko·ol
all a *todo/a* ⓜ/ⓕ *to*·doo/a
allergy *alergia* ⓕ a·ler·*zhee*·a
ambulance *ambulância* ⓕ ang·boo·*lang*·sya
and e e
ankle *tornozelo* ⓜ toor·noo·*ze*·loo
arm *braço* ⓜ *braa*·soo
ashtray *cinzeiro* ⓜ seeng·*zay*·roo
ATM *caixa automática* ⓕ *kai*·sha ow·too·*maa*·tee·koo

B

baby *bebé* ⓜ&ⓕ be·*be*
back (body) *costas* ⓕ pl *kosh*·tash
backpack *mochila* ⓕ moo·*shee*·la
bad *mau/má* ⓜ/ⓕ *ma*·oo/maa
bag *saco* ⓜ *saa*·koo
baggage claim *balcão de bagagens* ⓜ
    bal·*kowng* de ba·*gaa*·zhengsh
bank *banco* ⓜ *bang*·koo
bar *bar* ⓜ baar
bathroom *casa de banho* ⓕ *kaa*·za de *ba*·nyoo
battery *pilha* ⓕ *pee*·lya
beautiful *bonito/a* ⓜ/ⓕ boo·*nee*·too/a
bed *cama* ⓕ *ka*·ma
beer *cerveja* ⓕ ser·*ve*·zha
before *antes* *ang*·tesh
behind *atrás* a·*traash*
bicycle *bicicleta* ⓕ bee·see·*kle*·ta
big *grande* ⓜ&ⓕ *grang*·de

bill *conta* ⓕ *kong*·ta
black *preto/a* ⓜ/ⓕ *pre*·too/a
blanket *cobertor* ⓜ koo·ber·*tor*
blood group *grupo sanguíneo* ⓜ
    groo·poo sang·*gwee*·nee·oo
blue *azul* a·*zool*
boat *barco* ⓜ *baar*·koo
book (make a reservation) v *reservar* rre·zer·*vaar*
bottle *garrafa* ⓕ ga·*rraa*·fa
bottle opener *saca-rolhas* ⓕ *saa*·ka·*rro*·lyash
boy *menino* ⓜ me·*nee*·noo
brake (car) *travão* ⓜ tra·*vowng*
breakfast *pequeno almoço* ⓜ pe·*ke*·noo aal·*mo*·soo
broken (faulty) *defeituoso/a* ⓜ/ⓕ de·fay·too·o·*zoo*/a
bus *autocarro* ⓜ ow·to·*kaa*·roo
business *negócios* ⓜ pl ne·*go*·syoosh
buy *comprar* kong·*praar*

C

café *café* ⓜ ka·*fe*
camera *máquina fotográfica* ⓕ
    maa·kee·na foo·too·*graa*·fee·ka
camp site *parque de campismo* ⓜ
    paar·ke de kang·*peezh*·moo
cancel *cancelar* kang·se·*laar*
can opener *abre latas* ⓜ *aa*·bre *laa*·tash
car *carro* ⓜ *kaa*·rroo
cash *dinheiro* ⓜ dee·*nyay*·roo
cash (a cheque) v *levantar (um cheque)*
    le·vang·*taar* (oong *she*·ke)
cell phone *telemóvel* ⓜ te·le·*mo*·vel
centre *centro* ⓜ *seng*·troo
change (money) v *trocar* troo·*kaar*
cheap *barato/a* ⓜ/ⓕ ba·*raa*·too/a
check (bill) *conta* ⓕ *kong*·ta
check-in *check-in* ⓜ shek·*eeng*
chest *peito* ⓜ *pay*·too
child *criança* ⓜ&ⓕ kree·*ang*·sa
cigarette *cigarro* ⓜ see·*gaa*·rroo
city *cidade* ⓕ see·*daa*·de
clean a *limpa/o* ⓜ/ⓕ *leeng*·poo/a

closed *fechado/a* ⓜ/ⓕ fe-*shaa*-doo/a

coffee *café* ⓜ ka-*fe*

coins *moedas* ⓕ pl moo-e-dash

cold a *frio/a* ⓜ/ⓕ *free*-oo/a

collect call *ligação a cobrar* ⓕ lee-ga-*sowng* a ko-*braar*

come *vir* veer

computer *computador* ⓜ kong-poo-ta-*dor*

condom *preservativo* ⓜ pre-zer-va-*tee*-voo

contact lenses *lentes de contacto* ⓕ pl
  leng-tesh de kong-*taak*-too

cook v *cozinhar* koo-zee-*nyaar*

cost *preço* ⓜ *pre*-soo

credit card *cartão de crédito* ⓜ kar-*towng* de *kre*-dee-too

cup *chávena* ⓕ *shaa*-ve-na

currency exchange *câmbio* ⓜ *kang*-byoo

customs (immigration) *alfândega* ⓕ aal-*fang*-de-ga

D

dangerous *perigoso/a* ⓜ/ⓕ pe-ree-*go*-zoo/a

date (time) *data* ⓕ *daa*-ta

day *dia* ⓜ *dee*-a

delay n *atraso* ⓜ a-*traa*-zoo

dentist *dentista* ⓜ&ⓕ deng-*teesh*-ta

depart *partir* par-*teer*

diaper *fralda* ⓕ *fraal*-da

dictionary *dicionário* ⓜ dee-syoo-*naa*-ryoo

dinner *jantar* ⓜ zhang-*taar*

direct *directo/a* ⓜ/ⓕ dee-*re*-too/a

dirty *sujo/a* ⓜ/ⓕ *soo*-zhoo/a

disabled *deficiente* de-fee-see-*eng*-te

discount *desconto* ⓜ desh-*kong*-too

doctor *médico/a* ⓜ/ⓕ *me*-dee-koo/a

double bed *cama de casal* ⓕ *ka*-ma de ka-*zaal*

double room *quarto de casal* ⓜ *kwaar*-too de ka-*zaal*

drink *bebida* ⓕ be-*bee*-da

drive v *conduzir* kong-doo-*zeer*

drivers licence *carta de condução* ⓕ
  kaar-ta de kong-doo-*sowng*

drugs (illicit) *droga* ⓕ *dro*-ga

dummy (pacifier) *chupeta* ⓕ shoo-*pe*-ta

E

ear *orelha* ⓕ o-*re*-lya

east *leste* *lesh*-te

eat *comer* koo-*mer*

economy class *classe económica* ⓕ
  klaa-se ee-koo-no-*mee*-ka

electricity *electricidade* ⓕ ee-le-tree-see-*daa*-de

elevator *elevador* ⓜ ee-le-va-*dor*

email *email* ⓜ ee-*mayl*

embassy *embaixada* ⓕ eng-bai-*shaa*-da

emergency *emergência* ⓕ ee-mer-*zheng*-sya

English (language) *inglês* ⓜ eeng-*glesh*

entrance *entrada* ⓕ eng-*traa*-da

evening *noite* ⓕ *noy*-te

exchange rate *taxa de câmbio* ⓕ *taa*-sha de *kang*-byoo

exit *saída* ⓕ saa-*ee*-da

expensive *caro/a* ⓜ/ⓕ *kaa*-roo/a

express mail *correio azul* ⓜ koo-*rray*-oo a-*zool*

eye *olho* ⓜ *o*-lyoo

F

far *longe* *long*-zhe

fast *rápido/a* ⓜ/ⓕ *rraa*-pee-doo/a

father *pai* ⓜ pai

film (camera) *filme* ⓜ *feel*-me

finger *dedo* ⓜ *de*-doo

first-aid kit *estojo de primeiros socorros* ⓜ
  shto-zhoo de pree-*may*-roosh so-*ko*-rroosh

first class *primeira classe* ⓕ pree-*may*-ra *klaa*-se

fish *peixe* ⓜ *pay*-she

food *comida* ⓕ koo-*mee*-da

foot *pé* ⓜ pe

fork *garfo* ⓜ *gaar*-foo

free (of charge) a *grátis* *graa*-teesh

friend *amigo/a* ⓜ/ⓕ a-*mee*-goo/a

fruit *fruta* ⓕ *froo*-ta

full *cheio/a* ⓜ/ⓕ *shay*-oo/a

funny *engraçado/a* ⓜ/ⓕ eng-gra-*saa*-doo/a

G

gift *presente* ⓜ pre-*zeng*-te

girl *menina* ⓕ me-*nee*-na

glass (drinking) *copo* ⓜ *ko*-poo

glasses *óculos* ⓜ pl o-koo-loosh

go *ir* eer

good *bom/boa* ⓜ/ⓕ bong/*bo*-a

green *verde* *ver*-de

guide n *guia* ⓜ *gee*-a

H

half *metade* ⓕ me-*taa*-de

hand *mão* ⓕ mowng

handbag *mala de mão* ⓕ *maa*-la de mowng

happy *feliz* ⓜ&ⓕ fe-*leesh*

D

have *ter* ter
he *ele* e·le
head *cabeça* ① ka·*be*·sa
heart *coração* ⓜ koo·ra·*sowng*
heat *calor* ka·*lor*
heavy *pesado/a* ⓜ/① pe·*zaa*·doo/a
help v *ajudar* a·zhoo·*daar*
here *aqui* a·*kee*
high *alto/a* ⓜ/① *aal*·too/a
highway *autoestrada* ① ow·to·*shtraa*·da
hike v *caminhar* ka·mee·*nyaar*
holiday *feriado* ⓜ fe·ree·*aa*·doo
homosexual n&a *homosexual* ⓜ&①
    o·mo·sek·soo·*aal*
hospital *hospital* ⓜ osh·pee·*taal*
hot *quente* keng·te
hotel *hotel* ⓜ o·*tel*
hungry *faminto/a* ⓜ/① fa·*meeng*·too/a
husband *marido* ⓜ ma·*ree*·doo

I

I *eu* e·oo
identification (card) *bilhete de identidade* ⓜ
    bee·*lye*·te de e·deeng·tee·*daa*·de
ill *doente* ⓜ&① doo·*eng*·te
important *importante* ⓜ&① eeng·por·*tang*·te
included *incluído/a* ⓜ/① eeng·kloo·*ee*·doo/a
injury *ferimento* ⓜ fe·ree·*meng*·too
insurance *seguro* ⓜ se·*goo*·roo
Internet *internet* ⓜ eeng·ter·*net*
interpreter *intérprete* ⓜ&① eeng·*ter*·pre·te

J

jewellery *ourivesaria* ① oh·ree·ve·za·*ree*·a
job *emprego* ⓜ eng·*pre*·goo

K

key *chave* ① *shaa*·ve
kilogram *quilograma* ⓜ kee·loo·*graa*·ma
kitchen *cozinha* ① koo·*zee*·nya
knife *faca* ① *faa*·ka

L

laundry (place) *lavandaria* ① la·vang·da·*ree*·a
lawyer *advogado/a* ⓜ/① a·de·voo·*gaa*·doo/a
left (direction) *esquerda* ① *shker*·da

left-luggage office *perdidos e achados* ⓜ pl
    per·*dee*·doosh ee aa·*shaa*·doosh
leg *perna* ① *per*·na
lesbian n&a *lésbica* ① *lezh*·bee·ka
less *menos* me·*noosh*
letter (mail) *carta* ① *kaar*·ta
lift (elevator) *elevador* ⓜ ee·le·va·*dor*
light *luz* ① loosh
like v *gostar* goosh·*taar*
lock *tranca* ① *trang*·ka
long *longo/a* ⓜ/① *long*·goo/a
lost *perdido/a* ⓜ/① per·*dee*·doo/a
lost-property office *gabinete de perdidos e achados* ⓜ
    gaa·bee·*ne*·te de per·*dee*·doosh ee a·*shaa*·doosh
love v *amar* a·*maar*
luggage *bagagem* ① ba·*gaa*·zheng
lunch *almoço* ⓜ aal·*mo*·soo

M

mail *correio* ⓜ koo·*rray*·oo
man *homem* ⓜ *o*·meng
map *mapa* ⓜ *maa*·pa
market *mercado* ⓜ mer·*kaa*·doo
matches *fósforos* ⓜ pl fosh·*foo*·roosh
meat *carne* ① *kaar*·ne
medicine *medicamentos* ⓜ pl me·dee·ka·*meng*·toosh
menu *ementa* ① ee·*meng*·ta
message *mensagem* ① meng·*saa*·zheng
milk *leite* ① *lay*·te
minute *minuto* ⓜ mee·*noo*·too
mobile phone *telemóvel* ⓜ te·le·*mo*·vel
money *dinheiro* ⓜ dee·*nyay*·roo
month *mês* ⓜ mesh
morning *manhã* ① ma·*nyang*
mother *mãe* ① maing
motorcycle *mota* ① *mo*·ta
motorway *autoestrada* ① ow·to·*shtraa*·da
mouth *boca* ① *bo*·ka
music *música* ① *moo*·zee·ka

N

name *nome* ⓜ *no*·me
napkin *guardanapo* ⓜ gwar·da·*naa*·poo
nappy *fralda* ① *fraal*·da
near *perto* *per*·too
neck *pescoço* ⓜ pesh·*ko*·soo
new *novo/a* ⓜ/① *no*·voo/a
news *notícias* ① pl noo·*tee*·syash

newspaper *jornal* Ⓜ zhor-*naal*
night *noite* Ⓕ *noy*-te
no *não* nowng
noisy *barulhento/a* Ⓜ/Ⓕ ba-roo-*lyeng*-too/a
nonsmoking *não-fumador* nowng-foo-ma-*dor*
north *norte* nor-te
nose *nariz* Ⓕ na-*reesh*
now *agora* a-*go*-ra
number *número* Ⓜ *noo*-me-roo

O

oil (engine) *petróleo* Ⓜ pe-*tro*-lyoo
old *velho/a* Ⓜ/Ⓕ *ve*-lyoo/a
one-way ticket *bilhete de ida* Ⓜ bee-*lye*-te de *ee*-da
open a *aberto/a* Ⓜ/Ⓕ a-*ber*-too/a
outside *fora* *fo*-ra

P

package *embrulho* Ⓜ eng-*broo*-lyoo
paper *papel* Ⓜ pa-*pel*
park (car) v *estacionar* shta-syoo-*naar*
passport *passaporte* Ⓜ paa-sa-*por*-te
pay *pagar* pa-*gaar*
pen *caneta* Ⓕ ka-*ne*-ta
petrol *gasolina* Ⓕ ga-zoo-*lee*-na
pharmacy *farmácia* Ⓕ far-*maa*-sya
phonecard *cartão telefónico* Ⓜ kar-*towng* te-le-fo-nee-koo
photo *fotografia* Ⓕ foo-too-gra-*fee*-a
plate *prato* Ⓜ *praa*-too
police *polícia* Ⓕ poo-*lee*-sya
Portugal *Portugal* Ⓜ poor-too-*gaal*
Portuguese (language) *português* poor-too-*gesh*
postcard *postal* Ⓜ poosh-*taal*
post office *correio* Ⓜ koo-*rray*-oo
pregnant *grávida* Ⓕ *graa*-vee-da
price *preço* Ⓜ *pre*-soo

Q

quiet *calado/a* Ⓜ/Ⓕ ka-*laa*-doo/a

R

rain *chuva* Ⓕ *shoo*-va
razor *gilete* Ⓕ zhee-*le*-te
receipt *recibo* Ⓜ rre-*see*-boo
red *vermelho/a* Ⓜ/Ⓕ ver-me-*lyoo*/a

refund *reembolso* Ⓜ rre-eng-*bol*-soo
registered mail *correio registado* Ⓜ koo-*rray*-oo re-zhee-*shtaa*-doo
rent v *alugar* a-loo-*gaar*
repair v *consertar* kong-ser-*taar*
reservation *reserva* Ⓕ rre-*zer*-va
restaurant *restaurante* Ⓜ rresh-tow-*rang*-te
return v *voltar* vol-*taar*
return ticket *bilhete de ida e volta* Ⓜ bee-*lye*-te de ee-da ee *vol*-ta
right (direction) *direita* Ⓕ dee-*ray*-ta
road *estrada* Ⓕ *shtraa*-da
room *quarto* Ⓜ *kwaar*-too

S

safe a *seguro/a* Ⓜ/Ⓕ se-*goo*-roo/a
sanitary napkin *penso higiénico* Ⓜ *peng*-soo ee-zhee-*e*-nee-koo
seat *assento* Ⓜ a-*seng*-too
send *enviar* eng-vee-*aar*
service station *posto de gasolina* Ⓜ *posh*-too de ga-zoo-*lee*-na
sex *sexo* Ⓜ *sek*-soo
shampoo *champô* Ⓜ shang-*poo*
share (a dorm) *partilhar* par-tee-*lyaar*
shaving cream *creme de barbear* Ⓜ *kre*-me de bar-bee-*aar*
she *ela* *e*-la
sheet (bed) *lençol* Ⓜ leng-*sol*
shirt *camisa* Ⓕ ka-*mee*-za
shoes *sapatos* Ⓜ pl sa-*paa*-toosh
shop n *loja* Ⓕ *lo*-zha
short *curto/a* Ⓜ/Ⓕ *koor*-too/a
shower n *chuveiro* Ⓜ shoo-*vay*-roo
single room *quarto de solteiro* Ⓜ *kwaar*-too de sol-*tay*-roo
skin *pele* Ⓕ *pe*-le
skirt *saia* Ⓕ *sai*-a
sleep v *dormir* door-*meer*
slowly *vagarosamente* va-ga-ro-za-*meng*-te
small *pequeno/a* Ⓜ/Ⓕ pe-*ke*-noo/a
smoke (cigarettes) v *fumar* foo-*maar*
soap *sabonete* Ⓜ sa-boo-*ne*-te
some *uns/umas* Ⓜ/Ⓕ pl oongsh/*oo*-mash
soon *em breve* eng *bre*-ve
south *sul* sool
souvenir shop *loja de lembranças* Ⓕ *lo*-zha de leng-*brang*-sash
speak *falar* fa-*laar*

spoon *colher* ⓕ koo-*lyer*

stamp *selo* ⓜ *se*-loo

stand-by ticket *bilhete sem garantia* ⓜ bee-*lye*-te seng ga-rang-*tee*-a

station (train) *estação* ⓕ shta-*sowng*

stomach *estômago* ⓜ *shto*-ma-goo

stop ∨ *parar* pa-*raar*

stop (bus) *paragem* ⓕ pa-*raa*-zheng

street *rua* ⓕ *rroo*-a

student *estudante* ⓜ & ⓕ shtoo-*dang*-te

sun *sol* ⓜ sol

sunscreen *protecção anti-solar* ⓕ proo-te-*sowng* ang-tee-soo-*laar*

swim ∨ *nadar* na-*daar*

T

tampons *tampões* ⓜ pl tang-*powngsh*

taxi *táxi* ⓜ *taak*-see

teaspoon *colher de chá* ⓕ koo-*lyer* de shaa

teeth *dentes* ⓜ pl *deng*-tesh

telephone *telefone* ⓕ te-le-*fo*-ne

television *televisão* ⓕ te-le-vee-*zowng*

temperature (weather) *temperatura* ⓕ teng-pe-ra-*too*-ra

tent *tenda* ⓕ *teng*-da

that (one) *aquele/a* ⓜ/ⓕ a-*ke*-le/a

they *eles/elas* ⓜ/ⓕ *e*-lesh/*e*-lash

thirsty *sedento/a* ⓜ/ⓕ se-*deng*-too/a

this (one) *este/a* ⓜ/ⓕ *esh*-te/a

throat *garganta* ⓕ gar-*gang*-ta

ticket *bilhete* ⓜ bee-*lye*-te

time *tempo* ⓜ *teng*-poo

tired *cansado/a* ⓜ/ⓕ kang-*saa*-doo/a

tissues *lenços de papel* ⓜ pl *leng*-soosh de pa-*pel*

today *hoje* o-*zhe*

toilet *casa de banho* ⓕ *kaa*-za de *ba*-nyoo

tomorrow *amanhã* aa-ma-*nyang*

tonight *hoje à noite* o-zhe aa *noy*-te

toothbrush *escova de dentes* ⓕ *shko*-va de *deng*-tesh

toothpaste *pasta de dentes* ⓕ *paash*-ta de *deng*-tesh

torch (flashlight) *lanterna eléctrica* ⓕ lang-*ter*-na e-*le*-tree-ka

tour n *excursão* ⓕ shkoor-*sowng*

tourist office *escritório de turismo* ⓜ shkree-*to*-ryoo de too-*reezh*-moo

towel *toalha* ⓕ *twaa*-lya

train *comboio* ⓜ kong-*boy*-oo

translate *traduzir* tra-doo-*zeer*

travel agency *agência de viagens* ⓕ a-*zheng*-sya de vee-*aa*-zhengsh

travellers cheque *travellers cheque* ⓜ *tra*-ve-ler shek

trousers *calças* ⓕ pl *kaal*-sash

twin beds *camas gémeas* ⓕ pl *ka*-mash *zhe*-me-ash

tyre *pneu* ⓜ pe-ne-oo

U

underwear *roupa interior* ⓕ *rroh*-pa eeng-te-ree-*or*

urgent *urgente* ⓜ & ⓕ oor-*zheng*-te

V

vacant *vago/a* ⓜ/ⓕ *vaa*-goo/a

vacation *férias* ⓕ pl *fe*-ree-ash

vegetable *legume* ⓜ le-*goo*-me

vegetarian a *vegetariano/a* ⓜ/ⓕ ve-zhe-ta-ree-*a*-noo/a

visa *visto* ⓜ *veesh*-too

W

waiter *criado/a de mesa* ⓜ/ⓕ kree-*aa*-doo/a de *me*-za

walk ∨ *caminhar* ka-mee-*nyaar*

wallet *carteira* ⓕ kar-*tay*-ra

warm a *morno/a* ⓜ/ⓕ *mor*-noo/a

wash (something) *lavar* la-*vaar*

watch *relógio* ⓜ rre-*lo*-zhyoo

water *água* ⓕ *aa*-gwa

we *nós* nosh

weekend *fim-de-semana* ⓜ feeng-de-se-*ma*-na

west *oeste* o-*esh*-te

wheelchair *cadeira de rodas* ⓕ ka-*day*-ra de *rro*-dash

when *quando* kwang-doo

where *onde* *ong*-de

white *branco/a* ⓜ/ⓕ *brang*-koo/a

who *quem* keng

why *porquê* poor-*ke*

wife *esposa* ⓕ *shpo*-za

window *janela* ⓕ zha-*ne*-la

wine *vinho* ⓜ *vee*-nyoo

with *com* kong

without *sem* seng

woman *mulher* ⓕ moo-*lyer*

write *escrever* shkre-*ver*

Y

yellow *amarelo/a* ⓜ/ⓕ a-ma-*re*-loo/a

yes *sim* seeng

yesterday *ontem* ong-teng

you inf sg/pl *tu/vocês* too/vo-*sesh*

you pol sg/pl *você/vós* vo-se/vosh

Romanian

romanian alphabet

A a a	*Ă ă* uh	*Â â* ew	*B b* be	*C c* che
D d de	*E e* e	*F f* ef	*G g* je	*H h* hash
I i ee	*Î î* ew	*J j* zhe	*K k* ka	*L l* el
M m em	*N n* en	*O o* o	*P p* pe	*R r* er
S s es	*Ş ş* shew	*T t* te	*Ţ ţ* tsew	*U u* oo
V v ve	*X x* eeks	*Y y* ee grek	*Z z* zed	

romanian

about Romanian

Romanian (*limba română leem*·ba ro·*mew*·nuh), 'a Latin island in a Slav sea', holds the intriguing status of being the only member of the Romance language family in Eastern Europe. As a descendant of Latin, it shares a common heritage with French, Italian, Spanish and Portuguese – but its evolution took a separate path, mainly due to its geographical isolation from Rome and the influence of Catholicism. The Slavic invasion of the Balkans and the historical circumstances which placed Romanians in the Orthodox cultural sphere added to Romanian's distinguishing characteristics. Greek, Turkish and Hungarian touches spiced up the mixture even more.

It's generally believed that the base for modern Romanian was the language of the Dacians, who in ancient times inhabited the Danubian lands near the Black Sea. After Dacia became a province of the Roman Empire in AD 106, its Romanisation was so thorough that most of vocabulary and grammar of Romanian today is of Latin origin. However, with the withdrawal of the Romans from the area by AD 275, their linguistic influence ceased, leaving behind in Romanian many aspects of Latin that no longer exist in other Romance languages (such as noun cases). The void was filled with the arrival of the Slavs in the Balkans in the 6th century. The interaction with Bulgarian and Serbian (reflected in many loanwords) was intensified from the 13th century, through the shared Byzantine culture and the influence of Old Church Slavonic, the liturgical language of the Orthodox Church until the 18th century.

The oldest written record in Romanian is a letter from 1521 to the mayor of Braşov, written in the Cyrillic alphabet. The Roman alphabet first came into use in the 17th century, along with Hungarian spelling conventions, but it only replaced the earlier script in the mid-19th century. It was gradually adapted to the sounds of Romanian with the creation of some additional letters and was officially recognised in 1859. During the Soviet rule, a Russian version of the Cyrillic alphabet was used in Moldova, but the Roman alphabet was reintroduced in 1989.

Today, Romanian is the official language of Romania and Moldova (where it's called Moldovan – *limba moldovenească leem*·ba mol·do·ve·ne·*as*·kuh), with about 24 million speakers, including the Romanian-speaking minorities in Hungary, Serbia and Ukraine. Considering the Latin origin of much of the English vocabulary and the phonetic nature of the Romanian alphabet, communicating in Romanian with this phrasebook should be *floare la ureche* flo·*a*·re la oo·*re*·ke (lit: 'flower at your ear') – a piece of cake!

pronunciation

vowel sounds

Romanian vowels form vowel combinations with adjacent vowels. At the beginning of a word, *e* and *i* are pronounced as if there were a faint y sound preceding them. At the end of a word, a single *i* is usually almost silent (and represented in our pronunciation guides with an apostrophe), while *ii* is pronounced as ee.

symbol	english equivalent	romanian example	transliteration
a	father	*pat*	pat
ai	aisle	*mai*	mai
e	bet	*sete*	se·te
ee	see	*bine*	bee·ne
ew	ee pronounced with rounded lips	*frîne*	frew·ne
i	bit	*ochi*	o·ki
o	pot	*opt*	opt
oh	oh	*cadou*	ka·doh
oo	zoo	*bun*	boon
ow	how	*restaurant*	res·tow·rant
oy	toy	*noi*	noy
uh	ago	*casă*	ka·suh
'	very short, unstressed i	*cinci*	cheench'

word stress

There's no general rule for stress in Romanian. It falls on different syllables in different words, and just has to be learned. You'll be fine if you just follow our coloured pronunciation guides, in which the stressed syllable is always in italics.

consonant sounds

Romanian consonant sounds all have equivalents in English. Note that the sounds w and y generally act as semi-vowels.

symbol	english equivalent	romanian example	transliteration
b	**bed**	*bilet*	bee-*let*
ch	**cheat**	*rece*	re-*che*
d	**dog**	*verde*	*ver*-de
f	**fat**	*frate*	*fra*-te
g	**go**	*negru*	*ne*-groo
h	**hat**	*hartă*	*har*-tuh
j	**joke**	*gest*	jest
k	**kit**	*cald*	kald
l	**lot**	*lapte*	*lap*-te
m	**man**	*maro*	ma-*ro*
n	**not**	*inel*	ee-*nel*
p	**pet**	*opus*	o-*poos*
r	**run**	*aprozar*	a-pro-*zar*
s	**sun**	*săpun*	suh-*poon*
sh	**shot**	*şah*	shah
t	**top**	*trist*	treest
ts	**hats**	*soţ*	sots
v	**very**	*vin*	veen
w	**win**	*două*	*do*-wuh
y	**yes**	*iată*	*yaa*-tuh
z	**zero**	*zero*	*ze*-ro
zh	**pleasure**	*dejun*	de-*zhoon*

tools

language difficulties

Do you speak English?
Vorbiţi engleza?
vor-*beets'* en-*gle*-za

Do you understand?
Înţelegeţi?
ewn-tse-*le*-gets'

I (don't) understand.
Eu (nu) înţeleg.
ye-oo (noo) ewn-tse-*leg*

What does (*azi*) mean?
Ce înseamnă (azi)?
che ewn-se-*am*-nuh (*a*-zi)

How do you ...?	*Cum ...?*	koom ...
pronounce this	*se pronunţă asta*	se pro-*noon*-tsuh *as*-ta
write (*mulţumesc*)	*se scrie*	se *skree*-ye
	(mulţumesc)	(mool-tsoo-*mesk*)

Could you please ...?	*Aţi putea ...?*	uhts' poo-te-*a* ...
repeat that	*repeta*	re-pe-*ta*
speak more slowly	*vorbi mai rar*	vor-*bee* mai rar
write it down	*scrie*	*skree*-ye

numbers

0	zero	ze·ro		17	şapte-	shap·te·	
1	unu	oo·noo			sprezece	spre·ze·che	
2	doi	doy		18	optsprezece	opt·spre·ze·che	
3	trei	trey		19	nouă-	no·wuh·	
4	patru	pa·troo			sprezece	spre·ze·che	
5	cinci	cheench'		20	douăzeci	do·wuh·ze·chi	
6	şase	sha·se		21	douăzeci	do·wuh·ze·chi	
7	şapte	shap·te			şi unu	shee oo·noo	
8	opt	opt		22	douăzeci	do·wuh·ze·chi	
9	nouă	no·wuh			şi doi	shee doy	
10	zece	ze·che		30	treizeci	trey·ze·chi	
11	unsprezece	oon·spre·ze·che		40	patruzeci	pa·troo·ze·chi	
12	doisprezece	doy·spre·ze·che		50	cincizeci	cheench·ze·chi	
13	treisprezece	trey·spre·ze·che		60	şaizeci	shai·ze·chi	
14	paisprezece	pai·spre·ze·che		70	şaptezeci	shap·te·ze·chi	
15	cinci-	cheench'·		80	optzeci	opt·ze·chi	
	sprezece	spre·ze·che		90	nouăzeci	no·wuh·ze·chi	
16	şai-	shai·		100	o sută	o soo·tuh	
	sprezece	spre·ze·che		1000	o mie	o mee·e	

time & dates

What time is it?	Cât e ceasul?	kewt ye che·a·sool
It's one o'clock.	E ora unu.	ye o·ra oo·noo
It's (two) o'clock.	E ora (două).	ye o·ra (do·wuh)
Quarter past (one).	(Unu) şi un sfert.	(oo·noo) shee oon sfert
Half past (one).	(Unu) şi	(oo·noo) shee
	jumătate.	zhoo·muh·ta·te
Quarter to (eight).	(Opt) fără un sfert.	(opt) fuh·ruh oon sfert
At what time ...?	La ce oră ...?	la che o·ruh ...
At ...	La ora ...	la o·ra ...
am	dimineaţa	dee·mee·ne·a·tsa
pm (afternoon)	după masa	doo·puh ma·sa
pm (evening)	seara	se·a·ra

Monday	*luni*	*loo*-ni
Tuesday	*marţi*	*muhr*-tsi
Wednesday	*miercuri*	*myer*-koo-ri
Thursday	*joi*	zhoy
Friday	*vineri*	*vee*-ne-ri
Saturday	*sâmbătă*	*sewm*-buh-tuh
Sunday	*duminică*	doo-*mee*-nee-kuh

January	*ianuarie*	ya-*nwa*-rye
February	*februarie*	fe-*brwa*-rye
March	*martie*	*mar*-tye
April	*aprilie*	a-*pree*-lye
May	*mai*	mai
June	*iunie*	*yoo*-nye
July	*iulie*	*yoo*-lye
August	*august*	*ow*-goost
September	*septembrie*	sep-*tem*-brye
October	*octombrie*	ok-*tom*-brye
November	*noiembrie*	no-*yem*-brye
December	*decembrie*	de-*chem*-brye

What date is it today?
Ce dată este astăzi?   che *da*-tuh *yes*-te as-*tuh*-zi

It's (15 December).
E (cincisprezece decembrie).   ye (*cheench*-spre-ze-che de-*chem*-brye)

| since (May) | *din (mai)* | deen (mai) |
| until (June) | *până în (iunie)* | *pew*-nuh ewn (*yoo*-nye) |

last ...	... *trecut/trecută* m/f	... tre-*koot*/tre-*koo*-tuh
next ...	... *viitor/viitoare* m/f	... vee-ee-*tor*/vee-ee-to-*a*-re
night	*noaptea* f	*no*-ap-te-a
week	*săptămâna* f	suhp-tuh-*mew*-na
month	*luna* f	*loo*-na
year	*anul* m	*a*-nool

yesterday/tomorrow ...	*ieri/mâine* ...	*ye*-ri/mew-*ee*-ne ...
morning	*dimineaţă*	dee-mee-ne-*a*-tsuh
afternoon	*după amiază*	*doo*-puh a-*mya*-zuh
evening	*seară*	se-*a*-ruh

weather

What's the weather like?	*Cum e afară?*	koom ye a·*fa*·ruh
It's...	*E ...*	ye ...
cloudy	*înnorat*	ew·no·*rat*
cold	*frig*	freeg
hot	*foarte cald*	fo·*ar*·te kald
sunny	*soare*	so·*a*·re
warm	*cald*	kald
It's snowing.	*Ninge.*	neen·je
It's raining.	*Plouă.*	plo·wuh
It's windy.	*Bate vântul.*	ba·te vewn·tool
spring	*primăvară* f	pree·muh·*va*·ruh
summer	*vară* f	va·ruh
autumn	*toamnă* f	to·*am*·nuh
winter	*iarnă* f	yar·nuh

border crossing

I'm here ...	*Sunt aici ...*	soont a·*eech* ...
on business	*cu afaceri*	koo a·*fa*·che·ri
on holiday	*în vacanţă*	ewn va·*kan*·tsuh
I'm here for ...	*Sunt aici pentru ...*	soont a·*eech* pen·troo ...
(10) days	*(zece) zile*	(ze·che) zee·le
(two) months	*(două) luni*	(do·wuh) loo·ni
(three) weeks	*(trei) săptămâni*	(trey) suhp·tuh·mew·ni

I'm going to (Braşov).
Mă duc la (Braşov).
muh dook la (bra·*shov*)

I'm staying at the (Park Hotel).
Stau la (Hotel Park).
stow la (ho·*tel* park)

I have nothing to declare.
Nu am nimic de declarat.
noo am nee·*meek* de de·kla·*rat*

I have something to declare.
Am ceva de declarat.
am che·*va* de de·kla·*rat*

That's (not) mine.
Acesta (nu) e al meu.
a·*ches*·ta (noo) ye al me·oo

transport

tickets & luggage

Where can I buy a ticket?
   Unde pot cumpăra un bilet?   *oon*-de pot koom-puh-*ra* oon bee-*let*

Do I need to book a seat?
   Trebuie să rezerv locul?   tre-boo-ye suh re-*zerv* lo-*kool*

One ... ticket	*Un bilet ...*	oon bee-*let* ...
(to Cluj), please.	*(până la Cluj), vă rog.*	(*pew*-nuh la kloozh) vuh rog
one-way	*dus*	doos
return	*dus-întors*	doos ewn-*tors*

I'd like to ...	*Aş dori să-mi ...*	ash do-*ree* suhm' ...
my ticket, please.	*biletul, vă rog.*	bee-*le*-tool vuh rog
cancel	*anulez*	a-noo-*lez*
change	*schimb*	skeemb
collect	*jau*	yow
confirm	*confirm*	kon-*feerm*

I'd like a ... seat,	*Aş dori un loc la ...,*	ash do-*ree* oon lok la ...
please.	*vă rog.*	vuh rog
nonsmoking	*nefumători*	ne-foo-muh-*to*-ri
smoking	*fumători*	foo-muh-*to*-ri

How much is it?
   Cât costă?   kewt *kos*-tuh

Is there air conditioning?
   Are aer condiţionat?   *a*-re *a*-er kon-dee-tsyo-*nat*

Is there a toilet?
   Are toaletă?   *a*-re to-a-*le*-tuh

How long does the trip take?
   Cât durează călătoria?   kewt doo-re-*a*-zuh kuh-luh-to-*ree*-a

Is it a direct route?
   E o rută directă?   ye o *roo*-tuh dee-*rek*-tuh

I'd like a luggage locker.
   Aş dori un dulap de încuiat   ash do-*ree* oon doo-*lap* de ewn-koo-*yat*
   bagajul.   ba-*ga*-zhool

My luggage has been ...	*Bagajul meu a fost ...*	ba·*ga*·zhool *me*·oo a fost ...
damaged	*deteriorat*	de·te·*ryo*·rat
lost	*pierdut*	pyer·*doot*
stolen	*furat*	foo·*rat*

getting around

Where does flight (7) arrive/depart?
Unde soseşte/pleacă   *oon*·de so·*sesh*·te/ple·*a*·kuh
cursa (7)?   *koor*·sa (*shap*·te)

Where's (the) ...?	*Unde este ...?*	*oon*·de *yes*·te ...
arrivals hall	*sala pentru sosiri*	*sa*·la *pen*·troo so·*see*·ri
departures hall	*sala pentru plecări*	*sa*·la *pen*·troo ple·*kuh*·ri
duty-free shop	*magazinul*	ma·ga·*zee*·nool
	duty-free	*dyoo*·tee·free
gate (12)	*poarta de îmbarcare*	po·*ar*·ta de ewm·bar·*ka*·re
	(doisprezece)	(*doy*·spre·ze·che)

Is this the ... to (Cluj)?	*Acesta e ... de (Cluj)?*	a·*ches*·ta ye ... de (kloozh)
boat	*vaporul*	va·*po*·rool
bus	*autobuzul*	ow·to·*boo*·zool
plane	*avionul*	a·*vyo*·nool
train	*trenul*	*tre*·nool

What time's the	*Când este ...*	kewnd *yes*·te ...
... bus?	*autobuz?*	ow·to·*booz*
first	*primul*	*pree*·mool
last	*ultimul*	*ool*·tee·mool
next	*următorul*	oor·muh·*to*·rool

At what time does it arrive/leave?
La ce oră soseşte/pleacă?   la che *o*·ruh so·*sesh*·te/ple·*a*·kuh

How long will it be delayed?
Cât întârzie?   kewt ewn·*tewr*·zye

What station/stop is this?
Ce gară/staţie e aceasta?   che *ga*·ruh/*sta*·tsye ye a·che·*as*·ta

What's the next station/stop?
Care este următoarea   *ca*·re *yes*·te oor·muh·to·*a*·re·a
gară/staţie?   *ga*·ruh/*sta*·tsye

Does it stop at (Galaţi)?
Opreşte la (Galaţi)?   o-*presh*-te la (ga-*la*-tsi)

Please tell me when we get to (Iaşi).
Vă rog, când ajungem la (Iaşi)?   vuh rog kewnd a-*zhoon*-jem la (*ya*-shi)

How long do we stop here?
Cât stăm aici?   kewt stuhm a-*eech*

Is this seat available?
E liber locul?   ye *lee*-ber lo-*kool*

That's my seat.
Acesta e locul meu.   a-*ches*-ta ye lo-*kool* me-oo

I'd like a taxi ...	*Aş dori un taxi ...*	ash do-*ree* oon tak-*see* ...
at (9am)	*la ora (nouă dimineaţa)*	la *o*-ra (*no*-wuh dee-mee-*ne*-a-tsa)
now	*acum*	a-*koom*
tomorrow	*mâine*	mew-ee-ne

Is this taxi available?
E liber taxiul?   ye *lee*-ber tak-*see*-ool

How much is it to ...?
Cât costă până la ...?   kewt kos-tuh *pew*-nuh la ...

Please put the meter on.
Vă rog, daţi drumul la aparat.   vuh rog dats' *droo*-mool la a-pa-*rat*

Please take me to (this address).
Vă rog, duceţi-mă la (această adresă).   vuh rog doo-*chets*'-muh la (a-che-*as*-tuh a-*dre*-suh)

Please ...	*Vă rog, ...*	vuh rog ...
slow down	*încetiniţi*	ewn-che-tee-*neets*'
stop here	*opriţi aici*	o-*preets* a-*eech*
wait here	*aşteptaţi aici*	ash-tep-*tats*' a-*eech*

car, motorbike & bicycle hire

I'd like to hire a ...	*Aş dori să închiriez o ...*	ash do-*ree* suh ewn-kee-*ryez* o ...
bicycle	*bicicletă*	bee-chee-*kle*-tuh
car	*maşină*	ma-*shee*-nuh
motorbike	*motocicletă*	mo-to-chee-*kle*-tuh

with ...	cu ...	koo ...
a driver	şofer	sho-*fer*
air conditioning	aer condiţionat	*a*-er kon-dee-tsyo-*nat*
antifreeze	antigel	an-tee-*jel*
snow chains	lanţuri pentru zăpadă	lan-*tsoo*-ri pen-troo zuh-*pa*-duh

How much for ... hire?	Cât costă chiria pe ...?	kewt *kos*-tuh kee-*ree*-a pe ...
hourly	oră	*o*-ruh
daily	zi	zee
weekly	săptămână	suhp-tuh-*mew*-nuh

air	aer n	*a*-er
oil	ulei n	oo-*ley*
petrol	benzină f	ben-*zee*-nuh
tyres	cauciucuri n pl	kow-*choo*-koo-ri

I need a mechanic.
Am nevoie de un mecanic. am ne-*vo*-ye de oon me-*ka*-neek

I've run out of petrol.
Am rămas fără benzină. am ruh-*mas* fuh-ruh ben-*zee*-nuh

I have a flat tyre.
Am un cauciuc dezumflat. am oon kow-*chook* de-zoom-*flat*

directions

Where's the ...?	Unde este ...?	*oon*-de *yes*-te ...
bank	banca	*ban*-ka
city centre	centrul oraşului	*chen*-trool o-*ra*-shoo-looy
hotel	hotelul	ho-*te*-lool
market	piaţa	*pya*-tsa
police station	secţia de poliţie	*sek*-tsya de po-*lee*-tsye
post office	poşta	*posh*-ta
public toilet	toaleta publică	to-a-*le*-ta *poo*-blee-kuh
tourist office	biroul de informaţii turistice	bee-*ro*-ool de een-for-*ma*-tsee too-*rees*-tee-che

Is this the road to (Arad)?
Acesta e drumul spre (Arad)?   a·*ches*·ta ye *droo*·mool spre (a·*rad*)

Can you show me (on the map)?
Puteţi să-mi arătaţi   poo·*te*·tsi *suh*·mi a·ruh·*tats'*
(pe hartă)?   (pe *har*·tuh)

What's the address?
Care este adresa?   ka·re *yes*·te a·*dre*·sa

How far is it?
Cît e de departe?   kewt ye de de·*par*·te

How do I get there?
Cum ajung acolo?   koom a·*zhoong* a·*ko*·lo

Turn ...	*Viraţi la ...*	vee·*rats'* la ...
at the corner	*colţ*	kolts
at the traffic lights	*semafor*	se·ma·*for*
left/right	*stînga/dreapta*	stewn·*ga*/dre·*ap*·ta

It's ...	*Este ...*	*yes*·te ...
behind ...	*în spatele ...*	ewn *spa*·te·le ...
far away	*departe*	de·*par*·te
here	*aici*	a·*eech*
in front of ...	*în faţa ...*	ewn *fa*·tsa ...
left	*la stânga*	la stewn·*ga*
near (to ...)	*aproape (de ...)*	a·pro·*a*·pe (de ...)
next to ...	*lângă ...*	*lewn*·guh ...
on the corner	*pe colţ*	pe kolts
opposite ...	*vis-à-vis de ...*	vee·za·*vee* de ...
right	*la dreapta*	la dre·*ap*·ta
straight ahead	*tot înainte*	tot ew·na·*een*·te
there	*acolo*	a·*ko*·lo

by bus	*cu autobuzul*	koo ow·to·*boo*·zool
by taxi	*cu taxiul*	koo tak·*see*·ool
by train	*cu trenul*	koo *tre*·nool
on foot	*pe jos*	pe zhos

north	*nord*	nord
south	*sud*	sood
east	*est*	est
west	*vest*	vest

signs

Intrare	een-*tra*-re	**Entrance**
Ieşire	ye-*shee*-re	**Exit**
Deschis	des-*kees*	**Open**
Închis	ewn-*kees*	**Closed**
Camere libere	ka-me-re *lee*-be-re	**Rooms Available**
Ocupat	o-koo-*pat*	**No Vacancies**
Informaţii	een-for-*ma*-tsee	**Information**
Secţie de poliţie	sek-tsye de po-*lee*-tsye	**Police Station**
Interzis	een-ter-*zees*	**Prohibited**
Toalete	to-a-*le*-te	**Toilets**
Bărbaţi	buhr-*ba*-tsi	**Men**
Femei	fe-*mey*	**Women**
Cald/Rece	kald/*re*-che	**Hot/Cold**

accommodation

finding accommodation

Where's a ...?	*Unde se află ...?*	oon-de se *a*-fluh ...
camping ground	*un teren de camping*	oon te-*ren* de *kem*-peeng
guesthouse	*o pensiune*	o pen-*syoo*-ne
hotel	*un hotel*	oon ho-*tel*
youth hostel	*un hostel*	oon *hos*-tel

Can you recommend	*Puteţi recomanda*	poo-*te*-tsi re-ko-man-*da*
somewhere ...?	*ceva ...?*	che-*va* ...
cheap	*ieftin*	*yef*-teen
good	*bun*	boon
nearby	*în apropiere*	ewn a-pro-*pye*-re

I'd like to book a room, please.
Aş dori să rezerv o cameră, vă rog.   ash do-*ree* suh re-*zerv* o *ka*-me-ruh vuh rog

I have a reservation.
Am o rezervaţie.   am o re-zer-*va*-tsye

My name's ...
Numele meu este ...   noo-me-le *me*-oo *yes*-te ...

Do you have a ... room?	Aveţi o cameră ...?	a·vets' o ka·me·ruh ...
single	de o persoană	de o per·so·a·nuh
double	dublă	doo·bluh
twin	dublă cu două	doo·bluh koo do·wuh
	paturi separate	pa·too·ri se·pa·ra·te

How much is it per ...?	Cît costă ...?	kewt kos·tuh ...
night	pe noapte	pe no·ap·te
person	de persoană	de per·so·a·nuh

Can I pay ...?	Pot plăti ...?	pot pluh·tee ...
by credit card	cu carte de credit	koo kar·te de kre·deet
with a travellers	cu un cec de	koo oon chek de
cheque	călătorie	kuh·luh·to·ree·e

I'd like to stay for (two) nights.
Aş dori să stau (două) nopţi.   ash doo·ree suh stow (do·wuh) nop·tsi

From (2 July) to (6 July).
Din (doi iulie) până în   deen (doy yoo·lye) pew·nuh ewn
(şase iulie).   (sha·se yoo·lye)

Can I see it?
Pot să văd?   pot suh vuhd

Am I allowed to camp here?
Pot să-mi pun cortul aici?   pot suhm' poon kor·tool a·eech

Is there a camp site nearby?
Există un loc de camping   eg·zees·tuh oon lok de kem·peeng
prin apropiere?   preen a·pro·pye·re

requests & queries

When/Where is breakfast served?
Când/Unde se serveşte   kewnd/oon·de se ser·vesh·te
micul dejun?   mee·kool de·zhoon

Please wake me at (seven).
Vă rog treziţi-mă la (şapte).   vuh rog tre·zee·tsee·muh la (shap·te)

Could I have my key, please?
    Puteţi să-mi daţi o cheie?   poo-*tets'* suhm' dats' o *ke*-ye

Can I get another (blanket)?
    Puteţi să-mi daţi încă   poo-*tets'* suhm' dats' *ewn*-kuh
    (o pătură)?   (o *puh*-too-ruh)

Is there a/an ...?	*Există ...?*	eg-*zees*-tuh ...
elevator	*lift*	leeft
safe	*seif*	seyf

The room is too ...	*Camera e prea ...*	*ka*-me-ra ye pre-*a* ...
expensive	*scumpă*	*skoom*-puh
noisy	*gălăgioasă*	guh-luhj-yo-*a*-suh
small	*mică*	*mee*-kuh

The ... doesn't work.	*Nu funcţionează ...*	noo foonk-tsyo-ne-*a*-zuh ...
air conditioning	*aerul condiţionat*	*a*-e-rool kon-dee-tsyo-*nat*
fan	*ventilatorul*	ven-tee-la-*to*-rool
toilet	*toaleta*	to-a-*le*-ta

This ... isn't clean.	*Acest ... nu este curat.*	a-*chest* ... noo *yes*-te koo-*rat*
sheet	*cearceaf*	che-ar-che-*af*
towel	*prosop*	pro-*sop*

This pillow isn't clean.
    Această pernă   a-che-*as*-tuh *per*-nuh
    nu este curată.   noo *yes*-te koo-*ra*-tuh

checking out

What time is checkout?
    La ce oră trebuie   la che *o*-ruh tre-*boo*-ye
    eliberată camera?   e-lee-be-*ra*-tuh *ka*-me-ra

Can I leave my luggage here?
    Pot să-mi las bagajul aici?   pot suhm' las ba-*ga*-zhool a-*eech*

Could I have my ..., please?	*Vă rog, îmi puteţi înapoia ...?*	vuh rog ewm' poo-*tets'* ew-na-po-*ya* ...
deposit	*aconto-ul*	a-*kon*-to-ool
passport	*paşaportul*	pa-sha-*por*-tool
valuables	*obiectele de valoare*	o-*byek*-te-le de va-lo-*a*-re

communications & banking

the internet

Where's the local Internet café?
Unde se află un internet
café în apropiere?
oon·de se a·fluh oon een·ter·net
ka·fe ewn a·pro·pye·re

How much is it per hour?
Cât costă pe oră?
kewt kos·tuh pe o·ruh

I'd like to ...	*Aş dori ...*	ash do·ree ...
check my email	*să-mi verific*	suhm' ve·ree·feek
	e-mailul	ee·meyl·ool
get Internet access	*să accesez*	suh ak·che·sez
	internetul	een·ter·ne·tool
use a printer	*să folosesc o*	suh fo·lo·sesk o
	imprimantă	eem·pree·man·tuh
use a scanner	*să folosesc un scanner*	suh fo·lo·sesk oon ske·ner

mobile/cell phone

I'd like a ...	*Aş dori ...*	ash do·ree ...
mobile/cell phone	*să închiriez*	suh ewn·kee·ryez
for hire	*un telefon mobil*	oon te·le·fon mo·beel
SIM card for your	*un SIM card pentru*	oon seem kard pen·troo
network	*reţeaua locală*	re·tse·a·wa lo·ka·luh

What are the rates?
Care este tariful?
ka·re yes·te ta·ree·fool

telephone

What's your phone number?
Ce număr de telefon aveţi?
che noo·muhr de te·le·fon a·vets'

Where's the nearest public phone?
Unde se află cel mai apropiat
telefon public?
oon·de se a·fluh chel mai a·pro·pyat
te·le·fon poo·bleek

I'd like to buy a phonecard.
Aş dori să cumpăr o cartelă
de telefon.
ash do·ree suh koom·puhr o kar·te·luh
de te·le·fon

I want to ...	Aş dori ...	ash do·ree ...
call (Singapore)	să telefonez la (Singapore)	suh te·le·fo·nez la (seen·ga·po·re)
make a local call	să dau un telefon local	suh dow oon te·le·fon lo·kal
reverse the charges	o convorbire cu taxă inversă	o kon·vor·bee·re koo tak·suh een·ver·suh

How much does ... cost?	Cât costă ...?	kewt kos·tuh ...
a (three)-minute call	o convorbire de (trei) minute	o kon·vor·bee·re de (trey) mee·noo·te
each extra minute	fiecare minut suplimentar	fye·ka·re mee·noot soo·plee·men·tar

| (10) lei per minute. | (Zece) lei pe minut. | (ze·che) ley pe mee·noot |

post office

I want to send a ...	Aş dori să trimit ...	ash do·ree suh tree·meet ...
letter	o scrisoare	o skree·so·a·re
parcel	un colet	oon ko·let
postcard	o carte poştală	o kar·te posh·ta·luh

I want to buy a/an ...	Aş dori să cumpăr un ...	ash do·ree suh koom·puhr oon ...
envelope	plic	pleek
stamp	timbru	teem·broo

Please send it (to Australia) by ...	Vă rog, expediaţi-l (în Australia) ...	vuh rog ek·spe·dya·tseel (ewn ows·tra·lya) ...
airmail	cu avionul	koo a·vyo·nool
express mail	expres	eks·pres
registered mail	recomandat	re·ko·man·dat
surface mail	cu vaporul	koo va·po·rool

| Is there any mail for me? | Am primit scrisori? | am pree·meet skree·so·ri |

bank

Where's a/an ...?	Unde se află un ...?	oon·de se a·fluh oon ...
ATM	bancomat	ban·ko·mat
foreign exchange office	birou de schimb valutar	bee·roh de skeemb va·loo·tar

I'd like to ...	Aş dori să ...	ash do·ree suh ...
Where can I ...?	Unde aş putea ...?	oon·de ash poo·te·a ...
arrange a transfer	efectua un transfer	e·fek·twa oon trans·fer
cash a cheque	încasa un cec	ewn·ka·sa oon chek
change a travellers cheque	schimba un cec de călătorie	skeem·ba oon chek de kuh·luh·to·ree·e
change money	schimba bani	skeem·ba ba·ni
get a cash advance	obţine un imprumut financiar	ob·tsee·ne oon ewm·proo·moot fee·nan·chyar
withdraw money	retrage bani	re·tra·je ba·ni

What's the ...?	Care este ...?	ka·re yes·te ...
charge for that	taxa pentru	tak·sa pen·troo
commission	comision	ko·mee·syon
exchange rate	rata de schimb	ra·ta de skeemb

It's ...	Este ...	yes·te ...
(12) euros	(doisprezece) euro	(doy·spre·ze·che) e·oo·ro
(20) lei	(douăzeci) lei	(do·wuh·ze·chi) ley
free	gratis	gra·tees

What time does the bank open?
La ce oră se deschide banca? — la che o·ruh se des·kee·de ban·ka

Has my money arrived yet?
Mi-au sosit banii? — myow so·seet ba·nee

sightseeing

getting in

What time does it open/close?
La ce oră se deschide/închide? — la che o·ruh se des·kee·de/ewn·kee·de

What's the admission charge?
Cât costă intrarea? — kewt kos·tuh een·tra·re·a

Is there a discount for students/children?
Există reducere pentru studenţi/copii? — eg·zees·tuh re·doo·che·re pen·troo stoo·den·tsi/ko·pee

I'd like a ...	Aş dori ...	ash do·ree ...
catalogue	un catalog	oon ka·ta·*log*
guide	un ghid	oon geed
local map	o hartă a	o *har*·tuh a
	localităţii	lo·ka·lee·*tuh*·tsee

I'd like to see ...	Aş dori să văd ...	ash do·*ree* suh vuhd ...
What's that?	Ce-i asta?	chey *as*·ta
Can I take a photo?	Pot să fac o fotografie?	pot suh fak o fo·to·gra·*fye*

tours

When's the next ...?	Când este ...?	kewnd *yes*·te ...
day trip	următoarea	oor·muh·to·*a*·re·a
	excursie de zi	eks·*koor*·sye de zee
tour	următorul tur	oor·muh·*to*·rool toor

Is ... included?	Sunt incluse ...?	soont een·*kloo*·se ...
accommodation	cazarea	ka·*za*·re·a
the admission charge	taxa de intrare	*tak*·sa de een·*tra*·re
food	mâncarea	mewn·*ka*·re·a
transport	transportul	trans·*por*·tool

How long is the tour?
Cît durează turul?   kewt doo·re·*a*·zuh *too*·rool

What time should we be back?
La ce oră e întoarcerea?   la che o·ruh ye ewn·to·*ar*·che·re·a

sightseeing

castle	castel n	kas·*tel*
cathedral	catedrală f	ka·te·*dra*·luh
church	biserică f	bee·se·ree·kuh
main square	piaţa centrală f	*pya*·tsa chen·*tra*·luh
monastery	mănăstire f	muh·nuhs·*tee*·re
monument	monument n	mo·noo·*ment*
museum	muzeu n	moo·ze·oo
old city	oraşul vechi n	o·*ra*·shool *ve*·ki
palace	palat n	pa·*lat*
ruins	ruine f pl	roo·ee·ne
statue	statuie f	sta·*too*·ye

shopping

enquiries

Where's a ... ?	*Unde se află ...?*	oon·de se a·fluh ...
bank	*o bancă*	o ban·kuh
bookshop	*o librărie*	o lee·bruh·ree·e
camera shop	*un magazin foto*	oon ma·ga·zeen fo·to
grocery store	*un magazin*	oon ma·ga·zeen
	alimentar	a·lee·men·tar
department store	*un magazin*	oon ma·ga·zeen
	universal	oo·nee·ver·sal
market	*o piață*	o pya·tsuh
newsagency	*un stand de ziare*	oon stand de zee·a·re
supermarket	*un supermarket*	oon soo·per·mar·ket

Where can I buy (a padlock)?
Unde pot cumpăra (un lacăt)? oon·de pot koom·puh·ra (oon la·kuht)

I'm looking for ...
Caut ... kowt ...

Can I look at it?
Pot să mă uit? pot suh muh ooyt

Do you have any others?
Mai aveți și altele? mai a·vets' shee al·te·le

Does it have a guarantee?
E cu garanție? ye koo ga·ran·tsee·e

Can I have it sent overseas?
Îl puteți expedia peste hotare? ewl poo·tets' eks·pe·dya pes·te ho·ta·re

Can I have my ... repaired?
Îmi puteți repara ...? ewm' poo·tets' re·pa·ra ...

It's faulty.
E defect. ye de·fekt

I'd like ..., please.	*Vă rog, aș dori ...*	vuh rog ash do·ree ...
a bag	*o geantă*	o je·an·tuh
a refund	*o rambursare*	o ram·boor·sa·re
to return this	*să returnez asta*	suh re·toor·nez as·ta

paying

How much is it?
Cât costă? — kewt *kos*·tuh

Can you write down the price?
Puteți scrie prețul? — poo·tets' *skree*·e *pre*·tsool

That's too expensive.
E prea scump. — ye pre·*a* skoomp

What's your lowest price?
Care e prețul cel mai redus? — *ka*·re ye *pre*·tsool chel mai re·*doos*

I'll give you (five) euros.
Vă dau (cinci) euro. — vuh dow (cheench') *e*·oo·ro

I'll give you (50) lei.
Vă dau (cincizeci) lei. — vuh dow (cheench·ze·chi) ley

There's a mistake in the bill.
Chitanța conține o greșeală. — kee·*tan*·tsa kon·*tsee*·ne o gre·she·*a*·luh

Do you accept ...?	*Acceptați ...?*	ak·chep·tats' ...
credit cards	*cărți de credit*	*kuhr*·tsi de *kre*·deet
debit cards	*cărți de debit*	*kuhr*·tsi de *de*·beet
travellers cheques	*cecuri de* *călătorie*	*che*·koo·ri de kuh·luh·to·*ree*·e

I'd like ..., please.	*Vă rog, dați-mi ...*	vuh rog *da*·tsee·mi ...
a receipt	*chitanța*	kee·*tan*·tsa
my change	*restul*	*res*·tool

clothes & shoes

Can I try it on?
Pot să probez? — pot suh pro·*bez*

My size is (40).
Port numărul (patruzeci). — port *noo*·muh·rool (*pa*·troo·ze·chi)

It doesn't fit.
Nu mi se potrivește. — noo mee se po·tree·*vesh*·te

small	*mic*	meek
medium	*mijlociu*	meezh·lo·*chyoo*
large	*mare*	*ma*·re

books & music

I'd like a ...	Aş dori ...	ash do·ree ...
newspaper	un ziar	oon zee·ar
(in English)	(în engleză)	(ewn en·gle·zuh)
pen	un pix	oon peeks

Is there an English-language bookshop?
Există o librărie cu cărţi — eg·zees·tuh o lee·bruh·ree·e koo kuhr·tsi
în limba engleză? — ewn leem·ba en·gle·zuh

I'm looking for something by (Enescu/Caragiale).
Caut ceva de (Enescu/Caragiale). — kowt che·va de (e·nes·koo/ka·raj·ya·le)

Can I listen to this?
Pot asculta asta? — pot as·kool·ta as·ta

photography

Can you ...?	Îmi puteţi ...?	ewm' poo·tets' ...
burn a CD from	imprima un	eem·pree·ma oon
my memory card	CD după	see·dee doo·puh
	cardul de memorie	kar·dool de me·mo·ree·e
develop this film	developa acest film	de·ve·lo·pa a·chest feelm
load my film	încărca filmul	ewn·kuhr·ka feel·mool
	în aparat	ewn a·pa·rat
I need a/an ... film	Am nevoie de un film ...	am ne·vo·ye de oon feelm ...
for this camera.	pentru acest aparat.	pen·troo a·chest a·pa·rat
APS	APS	a·pe·se
B&W	alb-negru	alb·ne·groo
colour	color	ko·lor
slide	diapozitiv	dee·a·po·zee·teev
(200) speed	de (două sute) ASA	de (do·wuh soo·te) a·sa

When will it be ready? *Când va fi gata?* — kewnd va fee ga·ta

meeting people

greetings, goodbyes & introductions

Hello/Hi.	*Bună ziua/Bună.*	*boo*-nuh *zee*-wa/*boo*-nuh
Good night.	*Noapte bună.*	no-*ap*-te *boo*-nuh
Goodbye/Bye.	*La revedere/Pa.*	la re-ve-*de*-re/pa
Mr/Mrs	*Domnul/Doamna*	*dom*-nool/do-*am*-na
Miss	*Domnişoara*	dom-nee-sho-*a*-ra
How are you?	*Ce mai faceţi?*	che mai *fa*-chets'
Fine. And you?	*Bine.*	*bee*-ne
	Dumneavoastră?	doom-ne-a-vo-*as*-truh
What's your name?	*Cum vă numiţi?*	koom vuh noo-*meets'*
My name is ...	*Numele meu este ...*	*noo*-me-le *me*-oo *yes*-te ...
I'm pleased to	*Încântat/*	ewn-kewn-*tat*/
meet you.	*Încântată*	ewn-kewn-*ta*-tuh
	de cunoştinţă. m/f	de koo-nosh-*teen*-tsuh
This is my ...	*Vă prezint ...*	vuh pre-*zeent* ...
boyfriend	*prietenul meu*	pree-*e*-te-nool *me*-oo
brother	*fratele meu*	*fra*-te-le *me*-oo
daughter	*fiica mea*	fee-ee-ka *me*-a
father	*tatăl meu*	*ta*-tuhl *me*-oo
friend	*un prieten* m	oon pree-*e*-ten
	o prietenă f	o pree-*e*-te-nuh
girlfriend	*prietena mea*	pree-*e*-te-na *me*-a
husband	*soţul meu*	*so*-tsool *me*-oo
mother	*mama mea*	*ma*-ma *me*-a
partner (intimate)	*partenerul meu* m	par-te-*ne*-rool *me*-oo
	partenera mea f	par-te-*ne*-ra *me*-a
sister	*sora mea*	*so*-ra *me*-a
son	*fiul meu*	fee-*ool me*-oo
wife	*soţia mea*	so-*tsee*-a *me*-a
Here's my ...	*Acesta/Aceasta este*	a-*ches*-ta/a-*che*-as-ta *yes*-te
	... meu/mea. m/f	... *me*-oo/*me*-a
What's your ...?	*Care e ...?*	*ka*-re ye ...
(email) address	*adresa ta (de e-mail)*	a-*dre*-sa ta (de *ee*-meyl)
phone number	*numărul tău*	*noo*-muh-rool *tuh*-oo
	de telefon	de te-le-*fon*

occupations

What's your occupation?	*Ce meserie aveţi?*	che me·se·ree·e a·vets'
I'm a/an ...	*Sunt ...*	soont ...
artist	*artist* m&f	ar·*teest*
businessperson	*om de afaceri* m&f	om de a·*fa*·che·ri
farmer	*fermier* m&f	fer·*myer*
office worker	*funcţionar* m	foonk·tsyo·*nar*
	funcţionară f	foonk·tsyo·*na*·ruh
scientist	*om de ştiinţă* m&f	om de *shteen*·tsuh
student	*student/studentă* m/f	stoo·*dent*/stoo·*den*·tuh
tradesperson	*comerciant* m&f	ko·mer·*chyant*

background

Where are you from?	*De unde sunteţi?*	de oon·de soon·tets'
I'm from ...	*Sunt din ...*	soont deen ...
Australia	*Australia*	ows·*tra*·lya
Canada	*Canada*	ka·*na*·da
England	*Anglia*	*ang*·lya
New Zealand	*Noua Zeelandă*	*no*·wa ze·e·*lan*·duh
the USA	*Statele Unite*	*sta*·te·le oo·*nee*·te
Are you married?	*Sunteţi căsătorit/ căsătorită?* m/f	soon·tets' kuh·suh·to·*reet*/ kuh·suh·to·*ree*·tuh
I'm ...	*Sunt ...*	soont ...
married	*căsătorit* m	kuh·suh·to·*reet*
	căsătorită f	kuh·suh·to·*ree*·tuh
single	*necăsătorit* m	ne·kuh·suh·to·*reet*
	necăsătorită f	ne·kuh·suh·to·*ree*·tuh

age

How old ...?	*Ce vârstă ...?*	che vewr·stuh ...
are you	*aveţi*	a·*vets'*
is your daughter	*are fiica*	*a*·re fee·ee·ka
	dumneavoastră	doom·ne·a·vo·*as*·truh
is your son	*are fiul*	*a*·re fee·*ool*
	dumneavoastră	doom·ne·a·vo·*as*·truh

I'm ... years old.
  Am ... ani.   am ... *a*·ni

He/She is ... years old.
  El/Ea are ... ani.   yel/ya *a*·re ... *a*·ni

feelings

I'm (not) ...	*(Nu) Îmi este ...*	(noo) *ew*·mi *yes*·te ...
Are you ...?	*Vă este ...?*	vuh *yes*·te ...
cold	*frig*	freeg
hot	*cald*	kald
hungry	*foame*	fo·*a*·me
thirsty	*sete*	*se*·te
I'm (not) ...	*(Nu) Sunt ...*	(noo) soont ...
Are you ...?	*Sunteți ...?*	*soon*·tets' ...
happy	*fericit* m	fe·ree·*cheet*
	fericită f	fe·ree·*chee*·tuh
OK	*bine* m&f	*bee*·ne
sad	*trist/tristă* m/f	treest/*trees*·tuh
tired	*obosit/obosită* m/f	o·bo·*seet*/o·bo·*see*·tuh

entertainment

going out

Where can I find ...?	*Unde pot găsi ...?*	*oon*·de pot guh·*see* ...
clubs	*cluburi*	*kloo*·boo·ri
gay venues	*cluburi gay*	*kloo*·boo·ri gey
pubs	*localuri*	lo·*ka*·loo·ri
I feel like going to a/the ...	*Aș merge la ...*	ash *mer*·je la ...
concert	*un concert*	oon kon·*chert*
movies	*un film*	oon feelm
party	*o petrecere*	o pe·*tre*·che·re
restaurant	*un restaurant*	oon res·tow·*rant*
theatre	*un teatru*	oon te·*a*·troo

interests

Do you like ...?	*Vă place ...?*	vuh *pla*·che ...
I (don't) like ...	*Mie (nu) îmi place ...*	*mee*·e (noo) *ew*·mi *pla*·che ...
art	*arta*	*ar*·ta
cooking	*bucătăria*	boo·kuh·tuh·*ree*·a
movies	*cinema-ul*	chee·ne·*ma*·ool
reading	*lectura*	lek·*too*·ra
shopping	*la cumpărături*	la koom·puh·ruh·*too*·ri
sport	*sportul*	*spor*·tool
travelling	*să călătoresc*	suh kuh·luh·to·*resk*
Do you like to ...?	*Vă place ...?*	vuh *pla*·che ...
dance	*dansul*	*dan*·sool
go to concerts	*mersul la concerte*	*mer*·sool la kon·*cher*·te
listen to music	*să ascultați muzică*	as·kool·*tats'* *moo*·zee·kuh

food & drink

finding a place to eat

Can you recommend a ...?	*Îmi puteți recomanda ...?*	ew·mi poo·*tets'* re·ko·man·*da* ...
bar	*un bar*	oon bar
café	*o cafenea*	o ka·fe·ne·*a*
restaurant	*un restaurant*	oon res·tow·*rant*
I'd like ..., please.	*Vă rog, aș dori ...*	vuh rog ash do·*ree* ...
a table for (four) persoane	*o masă de (patru) persoane*	o *ma*·suh de (*pa*·troo) per·so·*a*·ne
the (non)smoking section	*la (ne)fumători*	la (*ne*·)foo·muh·*to*·ri

ordering food

breakfast	*micul dejun* n	*mee*·kool de·*zhoon*
lunch	*dejun* n	de·*zhoon*
dinner	*cină* f	*chee*·nuh
snack	*gustare* f	*goos*·ta·re

What would you recommend?
Ce recomandaţi?   che re·ko·man·dats'

I'd like (the) ..., please.	*Vă rog, aş dori ...*	vuh rog ash do·ree ...
bill	*nota de plată*	*no*·ta de *pla*·tuh
drink list	*lista de băuturi*	*lees*·ta de buh·oo·*too*·ri
menu	*meniul*	me·*nee*·ool
that dish	*acel fel de mâncare*	a·*chel* fel de mewn·*ka*·re

drinks

(cup of) coffee ...	*(o ceaşcă de) cafea ...*	(o che·*ash*·kuh de) ka·fe·*a* ...
(cup of) tea ...	*(o cană de) ceai ...*	(o *ka*·nuh de) che·*ai* ...
with milk	*cu lapte*	koo *lap*·te
without sugar	*fără zahăr*	*fuh*·ruh *za*·huhr
(orange) juice	*suc (de portocale)* n	sook (de por·to·*ka*·le)
soft drink	*băutură*	buh·oo·*too*·ruh
	nealcoolică f	ne·al·ko·o·*lee*·kuh
(boiled/mineral)	*apă (fiartă/*	*a*·puh (*fyar*·tuh/
water	*minerală)* f	mee·ne·*ra*·luh)

in the bar

I'll have ...	*Aş dori ...*	ash do·*ree* ...
I'll buy you a drink.	*Vă ofer o băutură.*	vuh o·*fer* o buh·oo·*too*·ruh
What would you like?	*Ce v-ar plăcea?*	che var *pluh*·che·a
Cheers!	*Noroc!*	no·*rok*
brandy	*ţuică* f	*tsooy*·kuh
cocktail	*cocteil* n	*kok*·teyl
a shot of (whisky)	*un (whisky) mic*	oon (*wee*·skee) meek
a ... of beer	*... de bere*	... de *be*·re
bottle	*o sticlă*	o *stee*·kluh
glass	*un pahar*	oon pa·*har*
a bottle of ... wine	*o sticlă de vin ...*	o *stee*·kluh de veen ...
a glass of ... wine	*un pahar de vin ...*	oon pa·*har* de veen ...
red	*roşu*	*ro*·shoo
sparkling	*spumos*	spoo·*mos*
white	*alb*	alb

self-catering

What's the local speciality?
Care e specialitatea locală?   ka·re ye spe·chya·lee·ta·te·a lo·ka·luh

What's that?
Ce-i aia?   chey a·ya

How much is (a kilo of cheese)?
Cât costă (kilogramul de brânză)?   kewt kos·tuh (kee·lo·gra·mool de brewn·zuh)

I'd like ...	*Aş dori ...*	ash do·ree ...
(100) grams	*(o sută) de grame*	(o soo·tuh) de gra·me
(two) kilos	*(două) kile*	(do·wuh) kee·le
(three) pieces	*(trei) bucăţi*	(trey) boo·kuh·tsi
(six) slices	*(şase) felii*	(sha·se) fe·lee

Less.	*Mai puţin.*	mai poo·tseen
Enough.	*Destul.*	des·tool
More.	*Mai mult.*	mai moolt

special diets & allergies

Is there a vegetarian restaurant near here?
Există pe aici un restaurant vegetarian?   eg·zees·tuh pe a·eech oon res·tow·rant ve·je·ta·ryan

Do you have vegetarian food?
Aveţi mâncare vegetariană?   a·ve·tsi mewn·ka·re ve·je·ta·rya·nuh

Could you prepare	*Puteţi servi ceva*	poo·tets' ser·vee che·va
a meal without ...?	*fără ...?*	fuh·ruh ...
butter	*unt*	oont
eggs	*ouă*	o·wuh
meat stock	*zeamă de carne*	ze·a·muh de kar·ne

I'm allergic to ...	*Am alergie la ...*	am a·ler·jee·ye la ...
dairy produce	*produse lactate*	pro·doo·se lak·ta·te
gluten	*gluten*	gloo·ten
MSG	*MSG (monosodiu glutamat)*	em·es·je (mo·no·so·dyoo gloo·ta·mat)
nuts	*nuci şi alune*	noo·chi shee a·loo·ne
seafood	*peşte şi fructe de mare*	pesh·te shee frook·te de ma·re

emergencies

basics

Help!	Ajutor!	a·zhoo·tor
Stop!	Stop!	stop
Go away!	Pleacă!	ple·a·kuh
Thief!	Hoţii!	ho·tsee
Fire!	Foc!	fok
Watch out!	Atenţie!	a·ten·tsye
Call ...!	Chemaţi ...!	ke·mats' ...
a doctor	un doctor	oon dok·tor
an ambulance	o ambulanţă	o am·boo·lan·tsuh
the police	poliţia	po·lee·tsya

It's an emergency!
E un caz de urgenţă! — ye oon kaz de oor·jen·tsuh

Could you help me, please?
Ajutaţi-mă, vă rog! — a·zhoo·ta·tsee·muh vuh rog

I have to use the telephone.
Trebuie să dau un telefon. — tre·boo·ye suh dow oon te·le·fon

I'm lost.
M-am rătăcit. — mam ruh·tuh·cheet

Where are the toilets?
Unde este o toaletă? — oon·de yes·te o to·a·le·tuh

police

Where's the police station?
Unde e secţia de poliţie? — oon·de ye sek·tsya de po·lee·tsye

I want to report an offence.
Vreau să raportez o contravenţie. — vre·ow suh ra·por·tez o kon·tra·ven·tsye

I have insurance.
Am asigurare. — am a·see·goo·ra·re

I've been ...	Am fost ...	am fost ...
assaulted	atacat/atacată m/f	a·ta·kat/a·ta·ka·tuh
raped	violat/violată m/f	vee·o·lat/vee·o·la·tuh
robbed	jefuit/jefuită m/f	zhe·foo·eet/zhe·foo·ee·tuh

I've lost my ...	Mi-am pierdut ...	myam pyer·doot ...
My ... was/were	Mi s-a/s-au	mee sa/sow
stolen.	furat ... sg/pl	foo·rat ...
bags	valizele pl	va·lee·ze·le
credit card	cartea de credit sg	kar·te·a de kre·deet
handbag	geanta sg	je·an·ta
jewellery	bijuteriile pl	bee·zhoo·te·ree·ee·le
passport	pașaportul sg	pa·sha·por·tool
travellers	cecurile de	che·koo·ree·le de
cheques	călătorie pl	kuh·luh·to·ree·e
wallet	portofelul sg	por·to·fe·lool

I want to contact my consulate/embassy.
Aș dori să contactez — ash do·ree suh kon·tak·tez
consulatul/ambasada. — kon·soo·la·tool/am·ba·sa·da

health

medical needs

Where's the	Unde se află cel mai	oon·de se a·fluh chel mai
nearest ...?	apropiat ...?	a·pro·pyat ...
dentist	dentist	den·teest
doctor	doctor	dok·tor
hospital	spital	spee·tal

Where's the nearest (night) pharmacist?
Unde se află cea mai — oon·de se a·fluh che·a mai
apropiată farmacie — a·pro·pya·tuh far·ma·chee·e
(cu program non-stop)? — (koo pro·gram non stop)

I need a doctor (who speaks English).
Am nevoie de un doctor — am ne·vo·ye de oon dok·tor
(care să vorbească engleza). — (ka·re suh vor·be·as·kuh en·gle·za)

Could I see a female doctor?
Pot fi consultată de o — pot fee kon·sool·ta·tuh de o
doctoriță? — dok·to·ree·tsuh

I've run out of my medication.
Mi s-a terminat doctoria — mee sa ter·mee·nat dok·to·ree·a
prescrisă. — pre·skree·suh

symptoms, conditions & allergies

| I'm sick. | Mă simt rău. | muh seemt *ruh*·oo |
| It hurts here. | Mă doare aici. | muh do·*a*·re a·*eech* |

I have (a) ...	Sufăr de ...	soo·fuhr de ...
asthma	astm	astm
bronchitis	bronşită	bron·*shee*·tuh
constipation	constipaţie	kon·stee·*pa*·tsye
cough	tuse	*too*·se
diarrhoea	diaree	dee·a·*re*·e
fever	febră	*fe*·bruh
headache	durere de cap	doo·*re*·re de kap
heart condition	inimă	*ee*·nee·muh
nausea	greaţă	gre·*a*·tsuh
pain	dureri	doo·*re*·ri
sore throat	durere în gât	doo·*re*·re ewn gewt
toothache	durere de dinţi	doo·*re*·re de *deen*·tsi

I'm allergic to ...	Am alergie la ...	am a·ler·*jee*·ye la ...
antibiotics	antibiotice	an·tee·byo·*tee*·che
anti-inflammatories	anti-inflamatorii	an·tee·een·fla·ma·*to*·ree
aspirin	aspirină	as·pee·*ree*·nuh
bees	albine	al·*bee*·ne
codeine	codeină	ko·de·*ee*·nuh
penicillin	penicilină	pe·nee·chee·*lee*·nuh

antiseptic	antiseptic n	an·tee·*sep*·teek
bandage	bandaj n	ban·*dazh*
condoms	prezervative n pl	pre·zer·va·*tee*·ve
contraceptives	contraceptive n pl	kon·tra·chep·*tee*·ve
diarrhoea medicine	medicament	me·dee·ka·*ment*
	împotriva	ewm·po·*tree*·va
	diareei n	dee·a·*re*·ey
insect repellent	loţiune	lo·*tsyoo*·ne
	împotriva	ewm·po·*tree*·va
	insectelor f	een·*sek*·te·lor
laxatives	laxative n pl	lak·sa·*tee*·ve
painkillers	analgezice n pl	a·nal·*je*·zee·che
rehydration salts	săruri rehidratante f pl	suh·roo·ri re·hee·dra·*tan*·te
sleeping tablets	somnifere n pl	som·nee·*fe*·re

english–romanian dictionary

Romanian nouns in this dictionary have their gender indicated by ⓜ (masculine), ⓕ (feminine) or ⓝ (neuter). If it's a plural noun, you'll also see pl. Note that neuter nouns take feminine adjectives in the plural and masculine adjectives in the singular. Words are also marked as a (adjective), v (verb), sg (singular), pl (plural), inf (informal) or pol (polite) where necessary.

A

accident *accident* ⓝ ak-*chee*-dent
accommodation *cazare* ⓕ ka-za-re
adaptor *adaptor* ⓐ a-dap-*tor*
address *adresă* ⓕ a-*dre*-suh
after *după* doo-puh
air-conditioned *cu aer condiţionat*
  koo a-er kon-dee-tsyo-*nat*
airplane *avion* ⓝ a-*vyon*
airport *aeroport* ⓝ a-e-ro-*port*
alcohol *alcool* ⓝ al-ko-*ol*
all *tot/toată* ⓜ/ⓕ tot/to-a-tă
allergy *alergie* ⓕ a-ler-*jee*-e
ambulance *ambulanţă* ⓕ am-boo-*lan*-tsuh
and *şi* shee
ankle *glezna* ⓕ *glez*-na
arm *braţ* ⓝ brats
ashtray *scrumieră* ⓕ skroo-*mye*-ruh
ATM *bancomat* ⓝ ban-ko-*mat*

B

baby *bebeluş* ⓜ be-be-*loosh*
back (body) *spatele* ⓜ *spa*-te-le
backpack *rucsac* ⓝ rook-sak
bad *rău/rea* ⓜ/ⓕ ruh-oo/re-a
bag *geantă* ⓕ *je-an*-tuh
baggage claim *bandă de bagaje* ⓕ
  ban-duh de ba-*ga*-zhe
bank *bancă* ⓕ *ban*-kuh
bar *bar* ⓝ bar
bathroom *baie* ⓕ *ba*-ye
battery *baterie* ⓕ ba-te-*ree*-e
beautiful *frumos/frumoasă* ⓜ/ⓕ
  froo-*mos*/froo-mo-a-suh
bed *pat* ⓝ pat
beer *bere* ⓕ *be*-re
before *înainte* ew-na-*een*-te
behind *înapoi* ew-na-*poy*
bicycle *bicicletă* ⓕ bee-chee-*kle*-tuh
big *mare* ⓜ&ⓕ *ma*-re
bill *plată* ⓕ *pla*-tuh
black *negru/neagră* ⓜ/ⓕ *ne*-groo/ne-a-gruh
blanket *pătură* ⓕ *puh*-too-ruh

blood group *grupa sanguină* ⓕ
  groo-pa san-*gooy*-nuh
blue *albastru/albastră* ⓜ/ⓕ
  al-*bas*-troo/al-bas-truh
boat *barcă* ⓕ *bar*-kuh
book (make a reservation) v *rezerva* re-zer-*va*
bottle *sticlă* ⓕ *stee*-kluh
bottle opener *tirbuşon* ⓝ teer-boo-*shon*
boy *băiat* ⓜ buh-*yat*
brakes (car) *frâne* ⓕ pl *frew*-ne
breakfast *micul dejun* ⓜ *mee*-kool de-*zhoon*
broken (faulty) *defect/defectă* ⓜ/ⓕ
  de-*fekt*/de-fek-tuh
bus *autobuz* ⓝ ow-to-*booz*
business *afacere* ⓕ a-*fa*-che-re
buy v *cumpăra* koom-puh-*ra*

C

café *cafenea* ⓕ ka-fe-ne-a
camera *aparat foto* ⓝ a-pa-*rat* fo-to
camp site *loc de camping* ⓝ lok de *kem*-peeng
cancel v *anula* a-noo-*la*
can opener *deschizător de conserve* ⓝ
  des-kee-zuh-tor de kon-*ser*-ve
car *maşină* ⓕ ma-*shee*-nuh
cash *bani cash* ⓜ pl *ba*-ni kesh
cash (a cheque) v *încasa (un cec)*
  ewn-ka-sa (oon check)
cell phone *celular* ⓝ che-loo-*lar*
centre *centru* ⓝ *chen*-troo
change (money) v *schimba (bani)* skeem-*ba* (*ba*-ni)
cheap *ieftin/ieftină* ⓜ/ⓕ *yef*-teen/*yef*-tee-nuh
check (bill) *nota de plată* ⓕ *no*-ta de *pla*-tuh
chest *cufăr* ⓝ *koo*-fuhr
child *copil* ⓜ ko-*peel*
cigarette *ţigaretă* ⓕ tsee-ga-*re*-tuh
city *oraş* ⓝ o-*rash*
clean *curat/curată* ⓜ/ⓕ koo-*rat*/koo-ra-tuh
closed *închis/închisă* ⓜ/ⓕ
  ewn-kees/ewn-kee-suh
coffee *cafea* ⓕ ka-fe-a
coins *monezi* ⓕ pl mo-ne-zi
cold a *rece* ⓜ&ⓕ *re*-che

collect call *telefon cu taxă inversă* ⓝ
te-le-*fon* koo *tak*-suh een-ver-suh
come *veni* ve-nee
computer *calculator* ⓝ kal-koo-*la*-tor
condom *prezervativ* ⓝ pre-zer-va-*teev*
contact lenses *lentile de contact* ① pl
len-*tee*-le de kon-*takt*
cook v *găti* guh-tee
cost *cost* ⓝ kost
credit card *carte de credit* ① *kar*-te de *kre*-deet
cup *cană* ① *ka*-nuh
currency exchange *schimb valutar* ⓝ
skeemb va-loo-*tar*
customs (immigration) *vamă* ① *va*-muh

D

dangerous *periculos/periculoasă* ⓜ/①
pe-ree-koo-*los*/pe-ree-koo-lo-*a*-suh
date (time) *data* ① *da*-ta
day *ziua* ① *zee*-wa
delay *întârziere* ① ewn-*tewr*-zye-re
dentist *dentist* ⓜ den-*teest*
depart *pleca* ple-*ka*
diaper *scutec* ⓝ *skoo*-tek
dictionary *dicționar* ⓝ deek-tsyo-*nar*
dinner *cină* ① *chee*-nuh
direct *direct/directă* ⓜ/① dee-*rekt*/dee-*rek*-tuh
dirty *murdar/murdară* ⓜ/① moor-*dar*/moor-*da*-ruh
disabled *invalid/invalidă* ⓜ/①
een-va-*leed*/een-va-*lee*-duh
discount *reducere* ① re-*doo*-che-re
doctor *doctor* ⓜ *dok*-tor
double bed *pat dublu* ⓝ pat *doo*-bloo
double room *cameră dublă* ① *ka*-me-ruh *doo*-bluh
drink *băutură* ① buh-oo-*too*-ruh
drive v *conduce* kon-*doo*-che
drivers licence *carnet de conducere* ⓝ
kar-*net* de kon-*doo*-che-re
drugs (illicit) *droguri* ⓝ pl *dro*-goo-ri
dummy (pacifier) *suzetă* ① soo-*ze*-tuh

E

ear *ureche* ① oo-*re*-ke
east *est* est
eat v *mânca* mewn-*ka*
economy class *clasa economy* ① *kla*-sa e-*ko*-no-mee
electricity *electricitate* ① e-lek-tree-chee-*ta*-te
elevator *lift* ⓝ leeft
email *e-mail* ⓝ *ee*-meyl
embassy *ambasadă* ① am-ba-*sa*-duh
emergency *urgență* ① oor-*jen*-tsuh
English (language) *engleza* ① en-*gle*-za
entrance *intrare* ① een-*tra*-re

evening *seară* ① se-*a*-ruh
exchange rate *rata de schimb* ① *ra*-ta de skeemb
exit *ieșire* ① ye-*shee*-re
expensive *scump/scumpă* ⓜ/① skoomp/*skoom*-puh
express mail *poștă expres* ① *posh*-tuh eks-*pres*
eye *ochi* ⓝ *o*-ki

F

far *departe* de-*par*-te
fast *repede* re-pe-de
father *tată* ⓜ *ta*-tuh
film (camera) *film* ⓝ feelm
finger *deget* ⓝ *de*-jet
first-aid kit *trusă de prim ajutor* ①
troo-suh de preem a-*zhoo*-tor
first class *clasa întâi* ① *kla*-sa ewn-*tew*-ee
fish *pește* ⓝ *pesh*-te
food *mâncare* ⓝ mewn-*ka*-re
foot *picior* ⓝ pee-*chyor*
fork *furculiță* ① foor-koo-*lee*-tsuh
free (of charge) *gratis* *gra*-tees
friend *prieten/prietenă* ⓜ/① pree-*e*-ten/pree-*e*-te-nuh
fruit *fructe* ⓝ pl *frook*-te
full *plin/plină* ⓜ/① pleen/*plee*-nuh
funny *nostim/nostimă* ⓜ/① *nos*-teem/*nos*-tee-muh

G

gift *cadou* ⓝ ka-*doh*
girl *fată* ① *fa*-tuh
glass (drinking) *pahar* ⓝ pa-*har*
glasses *ochelari* ⓜ pl o-ke-*la*-ri
go *merge* mer-je
good *bun/bună* ⓜ/① boon/*boo*-nuh
green *verde* ⓜ&① *ver*-de
guide *ghid* ⓝ geed

H

half *jumătate* ① zhoo-muh-*ta*-te
hand *mână* ① *mew*-nuh
handbag *poșetă* ① po-*she*-tuh
happy *bucuros/bucuroasă* ⓜ/①
boo-koo-*ros*/boo-koo-ro-*a*-suh
have *avea* a-ve-*a*
he *el* yel
head *cap* ⓝ kap
heart *inimă* ① *ee*-nee-muh
heat *căldură* ① kuhl-*doo*-ruh
heavy *greu/grea* ⓜ/① *gre*-oo/gre-*a*
help v *ajuta* a-zhoo-*ta*
here *aici* a-*eech'*

high *înalt/înaltă* ⓜ/ⓕ ew-*nalt*/ew-*nal*-tuh
highway *şosea* ⓕ sho-se-*a*
hike v *merge pe jos* mer-je pe zhos
holiday *vacanţă* ⓕ va-*kan*-tsuh
homosexual *homosexual* ⓜ ho-mo-sek-*swal*
hospital *spital* ⓜ spee-*tal*
hot *fierbinte* ⓜ/ⓕ fyer-*been*-te
hotel *hotel* ⓜ ho-*tel*
hungry *înfometat/înfometată* ⓜ/ⓕ
 ewn-fo-me-*tat*/ewn-fo-me-*ta*-tuh
husband *soţ* ⓜ sots

I

I *eu* ye-*oo*
identification (card) *buletin de identitate* ⓜ
 boo-le-*teen* de ee-den-tee-*ta*-te
ill *bolnav/bolnavă* ⓜ/ⓕ bol-*nav*/bol-*na*-vuh
important *important/importantă* ⓜ/ⓕ
 eem-por-*tant*/eem-por-*tan*-tuh
included *inclus/inclusă* ⓜ/ⓕ een-*kloos*/een-*kloo*-suh
injury *rană* ⓕ *ra*-nuh
insurance *asigurare* ⓕ a-see-goo-*ra*-re
Internet *internet* ⓜ een-ter-*net*
interpreter *interpret* ⓜ een-ter-*pret*

J

jewellery *bijuterii* ⓕ pl bee-zhoo-te-*ree*
job *serviciu* ⓜ ser-*vee*-chyoo

K

key *cheie* ⓕ *ke*-ye
kilogram *kilogram* ⓜ kee-lo-*gram*
kitchen *bucătărie* ⓕ boo-kuh-tuh-*ree*-e
knife *cuţit* ⓜ koo-*tseet*

L

laundry (place) *spălătorie* ⓕ spuh-luh-to-*ree*-e
lawyer *avocat* ⓜ a-vo-*kat*
left (direction) *la stânga* la *stewn*-ga
left-luggage office *birou pentru păstrarea bagajelor*
 ⓜ bee-*roh* pen-troo puhs-*tra*-re-a ba-*ga*-zhe-lor
leg *picior* ⓜ pee-*chyor*
lesbian *lesbiană* ⓕ les-*bya*-nuh
less *mai puţin* mai poo-*tseen*
letter (mail) *scrisoare* ⓕ skree-so-*a*-re
lift (elevator) *lift* ⓜ leeft
light *lumină* ⓕ loo-*mee*-nuh

like v *place* pla-che
lock *lacăt* ⓜ *la*-kuht
long *lung/lungă* ⓜ/ⓕ loong/*loon*-guh
lost *pierdut/pierdută* ⓜ/ⓕ pyer-*doot*/pyer-*doo*-tuh
lost-property office *birou bagaje pierdute* ⓜ
 bee-*roh* ba-ga-zhe pyer-*doo*-te
love v *iubi* yoo-*bee*
luggage *bagaje* ⓜ pl ba-*ga*-zhe
lunch *dejun* ⓜ de-*zhoon*

M

mail *poştă* ⓕ *posh*-tuh
man *bărbat* ⓜ buhr-*bat*
map *hartă* ⓕ *har*-tuh
market *piaţă* ⓕ *pya*-tsuh
matches *chibrituri* ⓜ pl kee-*bree*-too-ri
meat *carne* ⓕ *kar*-ne
medicine *doctorie* ⓕ dok-to-*ree*-e
menu *meniu* ⓜ me-*nyoo*
message *mesaj* ⓜ me-*sazh*
milk *lapte* ⓜ *lap*-te
minute *minut* ⓜ mee-*noot*
mobile phone *telefon mobil* ⓜ te-le-*fon* mo-*beel*
Moldova *Moldova* mol-*do*-va
money *bani* ⓜ pl ba-ni
month *lună* ⓕ *loo*-nuh
morning *dimineaţă* ⓕ dee-mee-ne-*a*-tsuh
mother *mamă* ⓕ *ma*-muh
motorcycle *motocicletă* ⓕ mo-to-chee-*kle*-tuh
motorway *autostradă* ⓕ ow-to-*stra*-duh
mouth *gură* ⓕ *goo*-ruh
music *muzică* ⓕ *moo*-zee-kuh

N

name *nume* ⓜ *noo*-me
napkin *şerveţel* ⓜ sher-ve-*tsel*
nappy *scutec* ⓜ *skoo*-tek
near *aproape* a-pro-*a*-pe
neck *gâtul* ⓜ *gew*-tool
new *nou/nouă* ⓜ/ⓕ noh/no-*wuh*
news *ştiri* ⓜ pl *shtee*-ri
newspaper *ziar* ⓜ zee-*ar*
night *noapte* ⓕ no-*ap*-te
no *nu* noo
noisy *zgomotos/zgomotoasă* ⓜ/ⓕ
 zgo-mo-*tos*/zgo-mo-to-*a*-suh
nonsmoking section *la nefumători* la ne-foo-muh-*to*-ri
north *nord* nord
nose *nas* ⓜ nas
now *acum* a-*koom*
number *număr* ⓜ *noo*-muhr

O

oil (engine) *ulei de motor* ⓝ oo-ley de mo-tor
old *vechi/veche* ⓜ/ⓕ ve-ki/ve-ke
one-way ticket *bilet dus* ⓝ bee-let doos
open a *deschis/deschisă* ⓜ/ⓕ des-kees/des-kee-suh
outside *afară* a-fa-ruh

P

package *pachet* ⓝ pa-ket
paper *hârtie* ⓕ hewr-tee-e
park (car) v *parca* par-ka
passport *pașaport* ⓝ pa-sha-port
pay v *plăti* pluh-tee
pen *pix* ⓝ peeks
petrol *benzină* ⓕ ben-zee-nuh
pharmacy *farmacie* ⓕ far-ma-chee-e
phonecard *cartelă de telefon* ⓕ kar-te-luh de te-le-fon
photo *fotografie* ⓕ fo-to-gra-fee-e
plate *farfurie* ⓕ far-foo-ree-e
police *poliție* ⓕ po-lee-tsye
postcard *carte poștală* ⓕ kar-te posh-ta-luh
post office *oficiu poștal* ⓝ o-fee-chyoo posh-tal
pregnant *însărcinată* ⓕ ewn-suhr-chee-na-tuh
price *preț* ⓝ prets

Q

quiet *liniștit/liniștită* ⓜ/ⓕ lee-neesh-teet/lee-neesh-tee-tuh

R

rain *ploaie* ⓕ plo-a-ye
razor *aparat de ras* ⓝ a-pa-rat de ras
receipt *chitanță* ⓕ kee-tan-tsuh
red *roșu/roșie* ⓜ/ⓕ ro-shoo/ro-shee-e
refund *rambursare* ⓕ ram-boor-sa-re
registered mail *poștă înregistrată* ⓕ posh-tuh ewn-re-jees-tra-tuh
rent v *închiria* ewn-kee-rya
repair v *repara* re-pa-ra
reservation *rezervație* ⓕ re-zer-va-tsye
restaurant *restaurant* ⓝ res-tow-rant
return v *se întoarce* se ewn-to-ar-che
return ticket *bilet dus-întors* ⓝ bee-let doos-ewn-tors
right (direction) *la dreapta* la dre-ap-ta
road *șosea* ⓕ sho-se-a
Romania *România* ro-mew-nee-a

Romanian (language) *limba română* leem-ba ro-mew-nuh
Romanian a *românesc/românească* ⓜ/ⓕ ro-mew-nesk/ro-mew-ne-as-kuh
room *cameră* ⓕ ka-me-ruh

S

safe a *protejat/protejată* ⓜ/ⓕ pro-te-zhat/pro-te-zha-tuh
sanitary napkin *absorbante* ⓝ ab-sor-ban-te
seat *loc* ⓝ lok
send v *trimite* tree-mee-te
service station *stație de benzină* ⓕ sta-tsye de ben-zee-nuh
sex *sex* ⓝ seks
shampoo *șampon* ⓝ sham-pon
share (a dorm) *împărți* ewm-puhr-tsee
shaving cream *cremă de ras* ⓕ kre-muh de ras
she *ea* ya
sheet (bed) *cearceaf* ⓝ che-ar-che-af
shirt *cămașă* ⓕ kuh-ma-shuh
shoes *pantofi* ⓜ pl pan-to-fi
shop *magazin* ⓝ ma-ga-zeen
short *scurt/scurtă* ⓜ/ⓕ skoort/skoor-tuh
shower *duș* ⓝ doosh
single room *cameră de o persoană* ⓕ ka-me-ruh de o per-so-a-nuh
skin *piele* ⓕ pye-le
skirt *fustă* ⓕ foos-tuh
sleep v *dormi* dor-mee
slowly *încet* ewn-chet
small *mic/mică* ⓜ/ⓕ meek/mee-kuh
smoke (cigarettes) v *fuma* foo-ma
soap *săpun* ⓝ suh-poon
some *niște* ⓜ&ⓕ neesh-te
soon *curând* koo-rewnd
south *sud* sood
souvenir shop *magazin de suveniruri* ⓝ ma-ga-zeen de soo-ve-nee-roo-ri
speak *vorbi* vor-bee
spoon *lingură* ⓕ leen-goo-ruh
stamp *timbru* ⓝ teem-broo
stand-by ticket *bilet neconfirmat* ⓝ bee-let ne-kon-feer-mat
station (train) *gară* ⓕ ga-ruh
stomach *stomac* ⓝ sto-mak
stop v *opri* o-pree
stop (bus) *stație de autobuz* ⓕ sta-tsye de ow-to-booz
street *stradă* ⓕ stra-duh

student *student/studentă* ⓜ/ⓕ
  stoo-*dent*/stoo-*den*-tuh
sun *soare* ⓕ so-*a*-re
sunscreen *loţiune contra soarelui* ⓕ
  lo-*tsyoo*-ne *kon*-tra so-*a*-re-looy
swim v *înota* ew-no-*ta*

T

tampons *tampoane* ⓝ pl tam-po-*a*-ne
taxi *taxi* ⓝ *tak*-see
teaspoon *linguriţă* ⓕ leen-goo-*ree*-tsa
teeth *dinţi* ⓝ pl *deen*-tsi
telephone *telefon* ⓝ te-le-*fon*
television (set) *televizor* ⓝ te-le-vee-*zor*
temperature (weather) *temperatură* ⓕ
  tem-pe-ra-*too*-ruh
tent *cort* ⓝ kort
that (one) *acela/aceea* ⓜ/ⓕ a-*che*-la/a-*che*-ya
they *ei/ele* yey/ye-le
thirsty *însetat/însetată* ⓜ/ⓕ ewn-se-*tat*/ewn-se-*ta*-tuh
this (one) *acesta/aceasta* ⓜ/ⓕ a-*ches*-ta/a-*che*-as-ta
throat *în gât* ⓝ ewn gewt
ticket *bilet* ⓝ bee-*let*
time *ora* ⓕ *o*-ra
tired *obosit/obosită* ⓜ/ⓕ o-bo-*seet*/o-bo-*see*-tuh
tissues *şerveţele* ⓝ pl sher-ve-*tse*-le
today *azi* a-*zi*
toilet *toaletă* ⓕ to-a-*le*-tuh
tomorrow *mâine* mew-ee-ne
tonight *diseară* dee-se-a-ruh
toothbrush *periuţă de dinţi* ⓕ
  pe-*ree*-oo-tsuh de *deen*-tsi
toothpaste *pastă de dinţi* ⓕ *pas*-tuh de *deen*-tsi
torch (flashlight) *lanternă* ⓕ lan-*ter*-nuh
tour *tur* ⓝ toor
tourist office *birou de informaţii turistice* ⓝ
  bi-*roh* de in-for-*ma*-tsee too-rees-tee-che
towel *prosop* ⓝ pro-*sop*
train *tren* ⓝ tren
translate *traduce* tra-*doo*-che
travel agency *agenţie de voiaj* ⓕ
  a-jen-*tsee*-e de vo-*yazh*
travellers cheque *cecuri de călătorie* ⓝ pl
  che-*koo*-ri de kuh-luh-to-*ree*-e
trousers *pantaloni* ⓝ pan-ta-*lo*-ni
twin beds *cameră cu două paturi separate* ⓕ
  ka-me-ruh koo do-*wuh* pa-*too*-ri se-pa-*ra*-te
tyre *cauciuc* ⓝ kow-*chook*

U

underwear *lenjerie de corp* ⓕ len-zhe-*ree*-e de korp
urgent *urgent/urgentă* ⓜ/ⓕ oor-*jent*/oor-*jen*-tuh

V

vacant *liber/liberă* ⓜ/ⓕ *lee*-ber/*lee*-be-ruh
vacation *vacanţă* ⓕ va-*kan*-tsuh
vegetable *legumă* ⓕ le-*goo*-muh
vegetarian a *vegetarian/vegetariana* ⓜ/ⓕ
  ve-je-ta-*ryan*/ve-je-ta-*rya*-nuh
visa *viză* ⓕ *vee*-zuh

W

waiter *chelner* ⓜ *kel*-ner
walk v *merge pe jos* mer-je pe zhos
wallet *portofel* ⓝ por-to-*fel*
warm a *cald/caldă* ⓜ/ⓕ kald/*kal*-duh
wash (something) v *spăla* spuh-*la*
watch *ceas* ⓝ che-*as*
water *apă* ⓕ *a*-puh
we *noi* noy
weekend *weekend* ⓝ wee-*kend*
west *vest* vest
wheelchair *scaun cu rotile* ⓝ skown koo ro-*tee*-le
when *când* kewnd
where *unde* oon-de
white *alb/albă* ⓜ/ⓕ alb/*al*-buh
who *cine* chee-ne
why *de ce* de che
wife *nevastă* ⓕ ne-*vas*-tuh
window *fereastră* ⓕ fe-re-*as*-truh
wine *vin* ⓝ veen
with *cu* koo
without *fără* fuh-ruh
woman *femeie* ⓕ fe-*me*-ye
write v *scrie* skree-ye

Y

yellow *galben/galbenă* ⓜ/ⓕ *gal*-ben/*gal*-be-nuh
yes *da* da
yesterday *ieri* ye-ri
you sg inf *tu* too
you pl inf *voi* voy
you sg&pl pol *dumneavoastră* doom-ne-a-vo-*as*-truh

Russian

russian alphabet

А а a	**Б б** be	**В в** ve	**Г г** ge	**Д д** de
Е е ye	**Ё ё** yo	**Ж ж** zhe	**З з** ze	**И и** ee
Й й ee-*krat*-ka-ye	**К к** ka	**Л л** el	**М м** em	**Н н** en
О о o	**П п** pe	**Р р** er	**С с** es	**Т т** te
У у u	**Ф ф** ef	**Х х** kha	**Ц ц** tse	**Ч ч** che
Ш ш sha	**Щ щ** shcha	**Ъ ъ** *tvyor*-di znak	**Ы ы** ih	**Ь ь** *myakh*-ki znak
Э э e	**Ю ю** yu	**Я я** ya		

■ **russian**

about Russian

Words such as *apparatchik*, *tsar* and *vodka* come from Russian (русский *rus*·kee) – the language which unites the largest nation in the world, the 'riddle wrapped in a mystery inside an enigma' spread over two continents and 11 time zones. The official language of the Russian Federation, Russian is also used as a second language in the former republics of the USSR and is widely spoken throughout Eastern Europe. With a total of more than 270 million speakers, it's the fifth most spoken language in the world.

Russian belongs to the East Slavic group of languages, together with Belarusian and Ukrainian. These languages were initially considered so similar that they were classified as one language – Old Russian. Russian was recognised as a distinct, modern language in the 10th century, when the Cyrillic alphabet was adopted along with Orthodox Christianity by way of Old Church Slavonic. This South Slavic language was used principally in religious literature, while written secular texts were much closer to the spoken East Slavic language. For centuries these two forms of Old Russian coexisted, and it was a third, 'middle' style which emerged in the 18th century as the basis of modern Russian. Pushkin, the nation's first great poet, was essentially writing in the Russian of today when he published *Eugene Onegin* in 1831. The alphabet was radically simplified at two major turning points in Russian history – as part of Peter the Great's reforms at the turn of the 17th century, and after the October Revolution in 1917.

For a language spoken across such a vast geographical area, Russian is surprisingly uniform, and the regional differences don't get in the way of communication. The language was standardised by the centralised education system in the USSR, which spread literacy and enforced 'literary' Russian. In practical terms, Russian is divided into the northern and the southern dialects; Moscow's dialect has some features of both. From the 16th century onward Muscovite Russian was the standard tongue, even after Peter the Great's court had moved to St Petersburg.

Some admirers of Russian literature have claimed that the русская душа *rus*·ka·ya du·*sha* (Russian soul) of Dostoevsky, Chekhov and Tolstoy simply can't be understood, or at least fully appreciated, in translation. All exaggeration aside, the Russian language boasts a rich vocabulary and highly colourful expressions. This linguistic flamboyance has thankfully resisted the influence of dour communist style and the 'socrealist' literature of the 20th century, as you'll soon find out on your travels!

pronunciation

Russian is often considered difficult to learn because of its script, but this is merely prejudice – some Cyrillic letters look and sound the same as their English peers, and the others aren't difficult to learn. Contrary to popular caricatures of the 'harsh' Russian accent, the language has a pleasant, soft sound characterised by several 'lisping' consonants. Most of the sounds in Russian are also found in English, and those that are unfamiliar aren't difficult to master. Use the coloured pronunciation guides to become familiar with them, and then read from the Cyrillic alphabet when you feel more confident.

There are remarkably few variations in modern Russian pronunciation and vocabulary. This phrasebook is written in standard Russian as it's spoken around Moscow, and you're sure to be understood by Russian speakers everywhere.

vowel sounds

symbol	english equivalent	russian example	transliteration
a	father	да	da
ai	aisle	май	mai
e	bet	это	e·ta
ee	see	мир	meer
ey	hey	бассейн	bas·yeyn
i	bit	мыло	mi·la
o	pot	дом	dom
oy	toy	сырой	si·roy
u	put	ужин	u·zheen

word stress

Russian stress is free (it can fall on any syllable) and mobile (it can change in different forms of the same word). Each word has only one stressed syllable, which you'll need to learn as you go. In the meantime, follow our pronunciation guides, which have the stressed syllable marked in italics.

consonant sounds

Most Russian consonants are similar to English sounds, so they won't cause you too much difficulty. The 'soft' sign ь and the 'hard' sign ъ don't have a sound of their own, but show in writing whether the consonant before them is pronounced 'soft' (with a slight y sound after it) or 'hard' (as it's written). In our pronunciation guides, the soft sign is represented with an apostrophe (') – as in бедность *byed*·nast' – but the hard sign isn't included as it's very rarely used.

symbol	english equivalent	russian example	transliteration
b	bed	брат	brat
ch	cheat	чай	chai
d	dog	вода	va-*da*
f	fat	кофе	*ko*·fee
g	go	город	*go*·rat
k	kit	сок	sok
kh	loch	смех	smyekh
l	lot	лифт	leeft
m	man	место	*mye*·sta
n	not	нога	na-*ga*
p	pet	письмо	pees-*mo*
r	run (rolled)	река	ree-*ka*
s	sun	снег	snyek
sh	shot	душа	du-*sha*
t	top	так	tak
ts	hats	отец	at-*yets*
v	very	врач	vrach
y	yes	мой	moy
z	zoo	звук	zvuk
zh	pleasure	жизнь	zhizn'
'	a slight y sound	власть	vlast'

tools

language difficulties

Do you speak English?
Вы говорите по-английски?
vi ga-va-*reet*-ye pa-an-*glee*-skee

Do you understand?
Вы понимаете?
vi pa-nee-*ma*-eet-ye

I (don't) understand.
Я (не) понимаю.
ya (nye) pa-nee-*ma*-yu

What does (пуп) mean?
Что обозначает слово (пуп)?
shto a-baz-na-*cha*-eet *slo*-va (pup)

How do you say ... in Russian?
Как будет ... по-русски?
kak *bu*-deet ... pa-*ru*-skee

How do you ...?   Как ...?   kak ...
  pronounce this   это произносится   *e*-ta pra-eez-*no*-seet-sa
  write (Путин)   пишется (Путин)   *pee*-shit-sa (*pu*-teen)

Could you please ...?   ..., пожалуйста.   ... pa-*zhal*-sta
  repeat that   Повторите   paf-ta-*reet*-ye
  speak more   Говорите   ga-va-*reet*-ye
   slowly   помедленее   pa-meed-leen-*ye*-ye
  write it down   Запишите   za-pee-*shit*-ye

essentials

Yes.	Да.	da
No.	Нет.	nyet
Please.	Пожалуйста.	pa-*zhal*-sta
Thank you	Спасибо	spa-*see*-ba
(very much).	(большое).	(bal'-*sho*-ye)
You're welcome.	Пожалуйста.	pa-*zhal*-sta
Excuse me.	Извините, пожалуйста.	eez-vee-*neet*-ye pa-*zhal*-sta
Sorry.	Извините, пожалуйста.	eez-vee-*neet*-ye pa-*zhal*-sta

numbers

0	ноль	nol'	15	пятнадцать	peet·nat·sat'
1	один m	a·deen	16	шестнадцать	shist·nat·sat'
	одна f	ad·na	17	семнадцать	seem·nat·sat'
	одно n	ad·no	18	восемнадцать	va·seem·nat·sat'
2	два m&n	dva	19	девятнадцать	dee·veet·nat·sat'
	две f	dvye	20	двадцать	dvat·sat'
3	три	tree	21	двадцать	dvat·sat'
4	четыре	chee·ti·ree		один	a·deen
5	пять	pyat'	22	двадцать два	dvat·sat' dva
6	шесть	shest'	30	тридцать	treet·sat'
7	семь	syem'	40	сорок	so·rak
8	восемь	vo·seem'	50	пятьдесят	pee·dees·yat
9	девять	dye·veet'	60	шестдесят	shis·dees·yat
10	десять	dye·seet'	70	семьдесят	syem'·dee·seet
11	одиннадцать	a·dee·nat·sat'	80	восемьдесят	vo·seem'·dee·seet
12	двенадцать	dvee·nat·sat'	90	девяносто	dee·vee·no·sta
13	тринадцать	tree·nat·sat'	100	сто	sto
14	четырнадцать	chee·tir·nat·sat'	1000	тысяча	ti·see·cha

time & dates

What time is it?	Который час?	ka·to·ri chas
It's one o'clock.	Час.	chas
It's (two/three/four) o'clock.	(Два/Три/Четыре) часа.	(dva/tree/chee·ti·ree) chee·sa
It's (10) o'clock.	(Десять) часов.	(dye·veet') chee·sof
Quarter past (10).	(Десять) пятнадцать.	(dye·seet') peet·nat·sat'
Half past (10).	(Десять) тридцать.	(dye·seet') treet·sat'
Twenty to (11).	(Десять) сорок. (lit: ten forty)	(dye·seet') so·rak
At what time ...?	В котором часу ...?	f ka·to·ram chee·su ...
At ...	В ... часов.	v ... chee·sof
in the morning	утра	ut·ra
in the afternoon	дня	dnya
in the evening	вечера	vye·chee·ra

Monday	понедельник	pa·nee·*dyel'*·neek
Tuesday	вторник	*ftor*·neek
Wednesday	среда	sree·*da*
Thursday	четверг	cheet·*vyerk*
Friday	пятница	*pyat*·neet·sa
Saturday	суббота	su·*bo*·ta
Sunday	воскресенье	vas·krees·*yen'*·ye
January	январь	yeen·*var'*
February	февраль	feev·*ral'*
March	март	mart
April	апрель	ap·*ryel'*
May	май	mai
June	июнь	ee·*yun'*
July	июль	ee·*yul'*
August	август	*av*·gust
September	сентябрь	seent·*yabr'*
October	октябрь	akt·*yabr'*
November	ноябрь	na·*yabr'*
December	декабрь	dee·*kabr'*
What date is it today?	Какое сегодня число?	ka·*ko*·ye see·*vod*·nya chees·*lo*
It's (1 May).	(Первое мая).	(*pyer*·va·ye *ma*·ya)
since (May)	с (мая)	s (*ma*·ya)
until (June)	до (июня)	da (ee·*yun*·ya)
last ...		
night	вчера вечером	fchee·*ra* vye·chee·ram
week	на прошлой неделе	na *prosh*·ley need·*yel*·ye
month	в прошлом месяце	f *prosh*·lam *mye*·seet·se
year	в прошлом году	f *prosh*·lam ga·du
next ...		
week	на следующей	na *slye*·du·yu·shee
	неделе	need·*yel*·ye
month	в следующем месяце	f *slye*·du·yu·sheem *mye*·seet·se
year	в следующем году	f *slye*·du·yu·sheem ga·*doo*
yesterday/tomorrow ...	вчера/завтра ...	fchee·*ra*/*zaf*·tra ...
morning	утром	*ut*·ram
afternoon	днём	dnyom
evening	вечером	*vye*·chee·ram

weather

What's the weather like?	Какая погода?	ka·*ka*·ya pa·*go*·da
It's ...		
cloudy	Облачно.	*ob*·lach·na
cold	Холодно.	*kho*·lad·na
hot	Жарко.	*zhar*·ka
raining	Идёт дождь.	eed·*yot* dozhd'
snowing	Идёт снег.	eed·*yot* snyek
sunny	Солнечно.	*sol*·neech·na
warm	Тепло.	tee·*plo*
windy	Ветрено.	*vye*·tree·na
spring	весна f	vees·*na*
summer	лето n	*lye*·ta
autumn	осень f	*o*·seen'
winter	зима f	zee·*ma*

border crossing

I'm here ...	Я здесь ...	ya zdyes' ...
for study	учусь	u·*chus'*
on business	по бизнесу	pa *beez*·nee·su
on holiday	в отпуске	v *ot*·pus·kye
I'm here for ...	Я здесь ...	ya zdyes' ...
(10) days	(десять) дней	(*dye*·seet') dnyey
(three) weeks	(три) недели	(tree) need·*ye*·lee
(two) months	(два) месяца	(dva) *mye*·seet·sa

I'm going to (Akademgorodok).
Я еду в (Академгородок).　ya *ye*·du v (a·ka·deem·ga·ra·*dok*)

I'm staying at (the Kosmos).
Я останавливаюсь в (Космосе).　ya as·ta·*nav*·lee·va·yus' v (*kos*·mas·ye)

I have nothing to declare.
Мне нечего декларировать.　mnye *nye*·chee·va dee·kla·*ree*·ra·vat'

I have something to declare.
Мне нужно что-то задекларировать.　mnye *nuzh*·na *shto*·ta za·dee·kla·*ree*·ra·vat'

That's (not) mine.
Это (не) моё.　*e*·ta (nye) ma·*yo*

transport

tickets & luggage

Where can I buy a ticket?
Где можно купить билет?
gdye mozh·na ku·peet' beel·yet

Do I need to book a seat?
Мне нужно зарезервировать
место?
mnye nuzh·na za·re·zer·vee·ra·vat'
myes·ta

One ... ticket (to Novgorod), please.	Билет ... (на Новгород).	beel·yet ... (na nov·ga·rat)
one-way	в один конец	v a·deen kan·yets
return	в оба конца	v o·ba kant·sa

I'd like to ... my ticket, please.	Я бы хотел/хотела ... билет, пожалуйста. m/f	ya bi khat·yel/khat·ye·la ... beel·yet pa·zhal·sta
cancel	отменить	at·mee·neet'
change	поменять	pa·meen·yat'
collect	забрать	zab·rat'
confirm	подтвердить	pat·veer·deet'

I'd like a (non)smoking seat, please.
Я бы хотел/хотела место в
отделении для (не)курящих,
пожалуйста. m/f
ya bi khat·yel/khat·ye·la mye·sta v
a·deel·ye·nee·ee dlya (nee·)kur·ya·sheekh
pa·zhal·sta

How much is it?
Сколько стоит?
skol'·ka sto·eet

Is there air conditioning?
Есть кондиционер?
yest' kan·deet·si·an·yer

Is there a toilet?
Есть туалет?
yest' tu·al·yet

How long does the trip take?
Сколько времени
уйдёт на эту поездку?
skol'·ka vrye·mee·nee
uyd·yot na e·tu pa·yest·ku

Is it a direct route?
Это прямой рейс?
e·ta pree·moy ryeys

Where's the luggage locker?
Где камера-автомат?
gdye ka·mee·ra·af·ta·mat

My luggage	**Мой багаж ...**	moy ba-*gash* ...
has been ...		
damaged	повредили	pa-vree-*dee*-lee
lost	пропал	pra-*pal*
stolen	украли	u-*kra*-lee

getting around

Where does flight (M2) arrive?
Куда прибывает самолёт (M2)?   ku-*da* pree-bi-*va*-et sa-ma-*lyot* (em dva)

Where does flight (M2) depart?
Откуда отправляется
самолёт (M2)?   at-*ku*-da at-prav-*lya*-eet-sa
sa-ma-*lyot* (em dva)

Which gate for (Omsk)?
Какой выход на посадку до (Омска)?   ka-*koy* vi-khat na pa-*sat*-ku da (*om*-ska)

Where's (the) ...?	**Где ...?**	gdye ...
arrivals hall	зал прибытий	zal pree-*bi*-tee-ye
departures hall	зал отправлений	zal at-prav-*lye*-nee
duty-free shop	товары без пошлины	ta-*va*-ri byes *posh*-lee-ni
gate (three)	выход на посадку (три)	*vi*-khat na pa-*sat*-ku (tree)

Is this the ...	**Этот ... идёт**	*e*-tat ... eed-*yot*
to (Moscow)?	**в (Москву)?**	v (mask-*vu*)
boat	параход	pa-ra-*khot*
bus	автобус	af-*to*-bus
plane	самолёт	sa-mal-*yot*
train	поезд	*po*-yeest

What time's	**Когда будет**	kag-*da bu*-deet
the ... bus?	**... автобус?**	... af-*to*-bus
first	первый	*pyer*-vi
last	последний	pas-*lyed*-nee
next	следующий	*slye*-du-yu-shee

At what time does it arrive/leave?
Когда он прибывает/
отправляется?   kag-*da* on pree-bi-*va*-et/
at-prav-*lya*-eet-sa

How long will it be delayed?
На сколько он опаздывает?   na *skol'*-ka on a-*paz*-di-va-yet

What station/stop is this?

Какая эта станция/остановка? — ka·*ka*·ya e·ta *stant*·si·ya/a·sta·*nof*·ka

What's the next station/stop?

Какая следующая — ka·*ka*·ya *slye*·du·yu·sha·ya
станция/остановка? — *stant*·si·ya/a·sta·*nof*·ka

Does it stop at (Solntsevo)?

Поезд останавливается — *po*·yeest a·sta·*nav*·lee·va·yeet·sa
в (Солнцево)? — v (*sont*·see·va)

Please tell me when we get to (Magadan).

Объявите, пожалуйста, когда — ab·yee·*veet*·ye pa·*zhal*·sta kag·*da*
мы подъедем к (Магадану). — mi pad·*ye*·deem k (ma·ga·da·*nu*)

How long do we stop here?

Сколько времени поезд — *skol'*·ka *vrye*·mee·nee *po*·eest
стоит на этой станции? — sta·*eet* na *e*·tay *stant*·see

Is this seat available?

Это место занято? — e·ta *mye*·sta *za*·nee·ta

That's my seat.

Это моё место. — e·ta ma·*yo mye*·sta

I'd like a taxi ... — Мне нужно такси ... — mnye *nuzh*·na tak·*see* ...
  at (9am) — в (девять часов утра) — v (*dye*·veet' chee·*sof* u·*tra*)
  now — сейчас — see·*chas*
  tomorrow — завтра — *zaf*·tra

Is this taxi available?

Свободен? — sva·*bo*·deen

How much is it to ...?

Сколько стоит доехать до ...? — *skol'*·ka *sto*·eet da·*ye*·khat' da ...

Please put the meter on.

Включите счётчик, пожалуйста! — fklyu·*cheet*·ye *shot*·cheek pa·*zhal*·sta

Please take me to (this address).

До (этого адреса) не довезёте? — da (e·ta·va u·*dree*·sa) nye da·veez·*yot*·ye

Please ... — ..., пожалуйста! — ... pa·*zhal*·sta
  slow down — Не так быстро — nee tak *bi*·stra
  stop here — Остановитесь здесь — a·sta·na·*veet*·yes' zdyes'
  wait here — Подождите здесь — pa·dazh·*deet*·ye zdyes'

car, motorbike & bicycle hire

I'd like to hire a …	Я бы хотел/хотела	ya bi khat-*yel*/khat-*ye*-la
	взять … на прокат. m/f	vzyat' … na pra-*kat*
bicycle	велосипед	vee-la-seep-*yet*
car	машину	ma-*shi*-nu
motorbike	мотоцикл	ma-tat-*sikl*

with …	с …	s …
a driver	шофёром	shaf-*yo*-ram
air conditioning	кондиционером	kan-deet-si-an-*ye*-ram
antifreeze	антифриз	an-tee-*freez*
snow chains	снеговые цепи	snye-*go*-vi-ye tse-pee

How much for … hire?	Сколько стоит … прокат?	*skol'*ka sto-eet … pra-*kat*
hourly	часовой	cha-sa-*voy*
daily	однодневный	ad-nad-*nyev*-ni
weekly	недельный	need-*yel'*-ni

air	воздух m	*voz*-dukh
oil	масло n	*mas*-la
petrol	бензин m	been-*zeen*
tyre	шина f	*shi*-na

I need a mechanic.
Мне нужен автомеханик. — mnye *nu*-zhin af-ta-mee-*kha*-neek

I've run out of petrol.
У меня кончился бензин. — u meen-*ya* kon-cheel-sa been-*zeen*

I have a flat tyre.
У меня лопнула шина. — u meen-*ya* lop-*nu*-la *shi*-na

directions

Where's the …?	Где (здесь) …?	gdye (zdyes') …
bank	банк	bank
city centre	центр города	tsentr *go*-ra-da
hotel	гостиница	ga-*stee*-neet-sa
market	рынок	*ri*-nak
police station	полицейский участок	pa-leet-*sey*-skee u-*cha*-stak
post office	почта	*poch*-ta
public toilet	общественный туалет	ap-*shest*-vee-ni tu-al-*yet*

Is this the road to (Kursk)?
Эта дорога ведёт в (Курск)?   *e*·ta da·*ro*·ga veed·*yot* f (kursk)

Can you show me (on the map)?
Покажите мне,   pa·ka·*zhi*·tye mnye
пожалуйста (на карте).   pa·*zhal*·sta (na *kart*·ye)

What's the address?
Какой адрес?   ka·*koy a*·drees

Is it nearby/far away?
Близко/Далеко?   *blees*·ka/da·lee·*ko*

How do I get there?
Как туда попасть?   kak tu·*da* pa·*past'*

Turn ...	Поверните ...	pa·veer·*neet*·ye ...
at the corner	за угол	*za*·u·gal
at the traffic lights	на светофоре	na svee·ta·*for*·ye
left/right	налево/направо	nal·*ye*·va/na·*pra*·va

It's ...		
behind ...	За ...	za ...
far away	Далеко.	da·lee·*ko*
here	Здесь.	zdyes'
in front of ...	Перед ...	*pye*·reet ...
left	Налево.	nal·*ye*·va
near ...	Около ...	*o*·ka·la ...
next to ...	Рядом с ...	*rya*·dam s ...
on the corner	На углу.	na u·*glu*
opposite ...	Напротив ...	na·*pro*·teef ...
straight ahead	Прямо.	*prya*·ma
right	Направо.	na·*pra*·va
there	Там.	tam

by bus	автобусом	af·*to*·bu·sam
by taxi	на такси	na tak·*see*
by train	электричкой	e·leek·*treech*·key
on foot	пешком	peesh·*kom*

north	север	*sye*·veer
south	юг	yuk
east	восток	va·*stok*
west	запад	*za*·pat

ВЪЕЗД/ВЫЕЗД	vyest/*vi*-yest	**Entrance/Exit**
ОТКРЫТО/ЗАКРЫТО	at-*kri*-ta/za-*kri*-ta	**Open/Closed**
СВОБОДНЫЕ МЕСТА	sva-*bod*-ni-ye mee-*sta*	**Rooms Available**
МЕСТ НЕТ	myest nyet	**No Vacancies**
ИНФОРМАЦИЯ	een-far-*mat*-si-ya	**Information**
ОТДЕЛЕНИЕ МИЛИЦИИ	a-deel-*ye*-nee-ye mee-*leet*-si	**Police Station**
ЗАПРЕЩЕНО	za-pree-shee-*no*	**Prohibited**
ТУАЛЕТ	tu-al-*yet*	**Toilets**
МУЖСКОЙ (М)	mush-*skoy*	**Men**
ЖЕНСКИЙ (Ж)	zhen-ski	**Women**
ГОРЯЧИЙ/ХОЛОДНЫЙ	ga-*rya*-chi/kha-*lod*-ni	**Hot/Cold**

accommodation

finding accommodation

Where's a ...?	Где ...?	gdye ...
camping ground	кемпинг	*kyem*-peeng
guesthouse	пансионат	pan-see-a-*nat*
hotel	гостиница	ga-*stee*-neet-sa
youth hostel	общежитие	ap-shee-*zhi*-tee-ye
Can you	Вы можете	vi *mo*-zhit-ye
recommend	порекомендовать	pa-ree-ka-meen-da-*vat'*
somewhere ...?	что-нибудь ...?	*shto*-nee-bud' ...
cheap	дешёвое	dee-*sho*-va-ye
good	хорошее	kha-*ro*-she-ye
luxurious	роскошное	ras-*kosh*-na-ye
nearby	близко отсюда	*blees*-ka at-*syu*-da

I'd like to book a room, please.

Я бы хотел/хотела   ya bi khat-*yel*/khat-*ye*-la
забронировать номер. m/f   za-bra-*nee*-ra-vat' *no*-meer

I have a reservation.

Я заказал/заказала номер. m/f   ya za-ka-*zal*/za-ka-*za*-la *no*-meer

My surname is ...

Моя фамилия ...   ma-*ya* fa-*mee*-lee-ya ...

Do you have a … room?	У вас есть …?	u vas yest' …
single	одноместный	ad·nam·yes·ni
	номер	no·meer
double	номер с двуспальней	no·meer z dvu·spaln·yey
	кроватью	kra·vat·yu
twin	двухместный	dvukh·myes·ni
	номер	no·meer
How much is it per/for …?	Сколько стоит за …?	skol'·ka sto·eet za …
night	ночь	noch'
two people	двоих	dva·eekh
Can I pay …?	Можно расплатиться …?	mozh·na ras·pla·teet'·sa …
by credit card	кредитной карточкой	kree·deet·nay kar·tach·kay
with a travellers cheque	дорожным чеком	da·rozh·nim che·kam

For (three) nights.
(Трое) суток.   (tro·ye) su·tak

From (5 July) to (8 July).
С (пятого июля)   s (pya·ta·va ee·yul·ya)
по (восьмое июля).   pa (vas'·mo·ye ee·yul·ya)

Can I see it?
Можно посмотреть?   mozh·na pas·mat·ryet'

Am I allowed to camp here?
Можно устроить стоянку здесь?   mozh·na u·stro·eet' sta·yan·ku zdyes'

Where can I find a camp site?
Где кемпинг?   gdye kyem·peenk

requests & queries

When/Where is breakfast served?
Когда/Где завтрак?   kag·da/gdye zaf·trak

Please wake me at (seven).
Позвоните мне,   paz·va·neet·ye mnye
пожалуйста, в (семь) часов.   pa·zhal·sta v (syem') chee·sof

Could I have my key, please?

Дайте, пожалуйста ключ · *dayt·ye pa·zhal·sta klyuch*
от моего номера. · *at ma·yee·vo no·mee·ra*

Can I get another (blanket)?

Дайте, пожалуйста ещё (одеяло). · *dayt·ye pa·zhal·sta yee·sho (a·dee·ya·la)*

Is there an elevator/a safe?

У вас есть лифт/сейф? · *u vas yest' leeft/syeyf*

The room is too ...	В комнате очень ...	f *kom*·nat·ye *o*·cheen' ...
cold	холодно	*kho*·lad·na
noisy	шумно	*shum*·na
small	тесно	*tyes*·na

The ... doesn't work.	... не работает.	... nye ra·*bo*·ta·yeet
air conditioner	Кондиционер	kan·*deet*·si·an·*yer*
heater	Отопление	a·tap·*lye*·nee·ye
toilet	Туалет	tu·al·*yet*

This ... isn't clean.	Эта ... грязная.	*e*·ta ... *gryaz*·na·ya
pillow	подушка	pa·*dush*·ka
sheet	простыня	pra·stin·*ya*

This towel isn't clean. · Это полотенце грязное. · *e*·ta pa·lat·*yent*·se *gryaz*·no·ye

checking out

What time is checkout?

Когда нужно освободить номер? · kag·*da nuzh*·na as·va·ba·*deet' no*·meer

Can I leave my bags here?

Здесь можно оставлять багаж? · zdyes' *mozh*·na a·stav·*lyat'* ba·*gash*

Could I have my ..., please?	Дайте, пожалуйста ...	*dayt*·ye pa·*zhal*·sta ...
deposit	мой аванс	moy a·*vans*
passport	мой паспорт	moy *pas*·part
valuables	мои ценности	ma·*ee tse*·nas·tee

communications & banking

the internet

Where's the local Internet café?
Где здесь интернет-кафе?   gdye zdyes' een·ter·net·ka·fe

How much is it per hour?
Сколько стоит час?   *skol'*·ka *sto*·eet chas

I'd like to ...	Я бы хотел/	ya bi khat·*yel*/
	хотела ... m/f	khat·*ye*·la ...
check my email	проверить	prav·*ye*·reet'
	свой и-мэйл	svoy ee·*meyl*
get Internet	подключиться	pat·klyu·*cheet'*·sa
access	к интернету	k een·ter·*ne*·tu
use a printer	воспользоваться	vas·*pol'*·za·vat'·sa
	принтером	een·ter·*ne*·tam
use a scanner	воспользоваться	vas·*pol'*·za·vat'·sa
	сканером	*skan*·ye·ram

mobile/cell phone

I'd like a ...	Я бы хотел/	ya bi khat·*yel*/
	хотела ... m/f	khat·*ye*·la ...
mobile/cell	взять мобильный	vzyat' ma·*beel*'·ni
phone for hire	телефон напрокат	tee·lee·*fon* nap·ra·*kat*
SIM card for your	СИМ-карту	*seem*·kar·tu
network	для вашей сети	dlya *va*·shey se·*tee*

What are the rates?   Какие тарифы?   ka·*kee*·ye ta·*ree*·fi

telephone

What's your phone number?
Можно ваш номер телефона?   *mozh*·na vash *no*·meer tee·lee·*fo*·na

The number is ...
Телефон ...   tee·lee·*fon* ...

Where's the nearest public phone?
Где ближайший   gdye blee·*zhey*·shee
телефон-автомат?   tee·lee·*fon*·af·ta·*mat*

I want to ...	Я бы хотел/	ya bi khat·*yel*/
	хотела ... m/f	khat·*ye*·la ...
call (Singapore)	позвонить	paz·va·*neet'*
	(в Сингапур)	(v seen·ga·*por*)
make a local call	сделать местный	*sdye*·lat' *myest*·ni
	звонок	zva·*nok*
reverse the charges	позвонить с оплатой	paz·va·*neet'* s a·*pla*·tey
	вызываемого	vi·zi·*va*·yee·ma·va

How much does each minute cost?
Сколько стоит минута?   skol'·ka *sto*·eet mee·nu·ta

(Five) roubles per (30) seconds.
(Пять) рублей за (тридцать) секунд.   (pyat') *rub*·lyey za (*treet·sat'*) see·*kunt*

I'd like to buy a phonecard.
Я бы хотел/хотела купить   ya bi khat·*yel*/khat·*ye*·la ku·*peet'*
телефонную карточку. m/f   tee·lee·fo·nu·yu *kar*·tach·ku

post office

I want to send a ...	Я хочу послать ...	ya kha·*chu* pas·*lat'* ...
fax	факс	faks
letter	письмо	pees'·*mo*
parcel	посылку	pa·*sil*·ku
postcard	открытку	at·*krit*·ku

I want to buy ...	Я хочу купить ...	yak ha·*chu* ku·*peet'* ...
an envelope	конверт	kan·*vyert*
a stamp	марку	*mar*·ku

Please send it	Пошлите, пожалуйста,	pash·*leet'*·ye pa·*zhal*·sta
(to Australia) by ...	... в (Австралию).	... v (af·*stra*·lee·yu)
airmail	авиа почтой	*a*·vee·a *poch*·tay
express mail	экспресс почтой	eeks·*pres* *poch*·tay
registered mail	заказной почтой	za·kaz·*noy* *poch*·tay
surface mail	обычной почтой	a·*bich*·nay *poch*·tay

Is there any mail for me?   Есть почта для меня?   yest' *poch*·ta dlya meen·*ya*

Where's a/an ...?	Где ...?	gdye ...
ATM	банкомат	ban·ka·mat
foreign exchange office	обмен валюты	ab·myen val·yu·ti

Where can I ...?	Где можно ...?	gdye mozh·na ...
I'd like to ...	Я бы хотел/ хотела ... m/f	ya bi khat·yel/ khat·ye·la ...
arrange a transfer	сделать денежный перевод	sdye·lat' dye·neezh·ni pee·ree·vod
cash a cheque	обменять чек	ab·meen·yat' chek
change a travellers cheque	обменять дорожный чек	ab·meen·yat' da·rozh·ni chek
change money	поменять деньги	pa·meen·yat' dyen'·gee
get a cash advance	снять деньги по кредитной карточке	snyat' dyen'·gee pa kree·deet·ney kar·tach·kye
withdraw money	снять деньги	snyat' dyen'·gee

What's the charge for that?
Сколько нужно заплатить? — skol'·ka nuzh·na za·pla·teet'

What's the exchange rate?
Какой курс? — ka·koy kurs

It's (12) roubles.
Это будет (двенадцать) рублей. — e·ta bu·deet (dvee·nat·sat') rub·lyey

It's free.
Это будет бесплатно. — e·ta bu·deet bees·plat·na

What time does the bank open?
Когда открывается банк? — kag·da at·kri·va·yeet·sa bank

Has my money arrived yet?
Мои деньги уже пришли? — moy dyen'·gee u·zhe preesh·lee

sightseeing

getting in

What time does it open/close?
Когда открывается/
закрывается?

kag·*da* at·kri·*va*·yeet·sa/
za·kri·*va*·yeet·sa

What's the admission charge?
Сколько стоит входной билет?

skol'·ka *sto*·eet fkhad·*noy* beel·*yet*

Is there a discount for students/children?
Есть скидка для студентов/детей?

yest' *skeet*·ka dlya stud·*yen*·taf/deet·*yey*

I'd like a ...	Я бы хотел/	ya bi khat·*yel*/
	хотела ... m/f	khat·*ye*·la ...
catalogue	каталог	ka·ta·*lok*
guide	гида	*gee*·da
local map	карту города	*kar*·tu *go*·ra·da

I'd like to see ...	Я бы хотел/хотела	ya bi khat·*yel*/khat·*ye*·la
	посетить ... m/f	pa·see·*teet'* ...
What's that?	Что это?	shto *e*·ta
Can I take a photo?	Можно	*mozh*·na
	сфотографировать?	sfa·ta·gra·*fee*·ra·vat'

tours

When's the next tour?
Когда следующая экскурсия?

kag·*da* slye·du·yu·sha·ya eks·*kur*·see·ya

How long is the tour?
Как долго продолжается
экскурсия?

kag *dol*·ga pra·dal·*zha*·yeet·sa
eks·*kur*·see·ya

What time should we be back?
Когда мы возвращаемся?

kag·*da* mi vaz·vra·*sha*·yeem·sa

Is ... included?	Цена включает ...?	tse·*na* fklyu·*cha*·yeet ...
accommodation	помещение	pa·mee·*she*·nee·ye
the admission charge	входной билет	fkhad·*noy* beel·*yet*
food	обед	ab·*yet*
transport	транспорт	*tran*·spart

sightseeing

castle	замок m	za·mak
cathedral	собор m	sa·bor
church	церковь f	tser·kaf
main square	главная площадь f	glav·na·ya plo·shat'
monastery	монастырь m	ma·na·stir
monument	памятник m	pam·yeet·neek
museum	музей m	muz·yey
old city	старый город m	sta·ri go·rat
palace	дворец m	dvar·yets
ruins	развалины f pl	raz·va·lee·ni
stadium	стадион m	sta·dee·on
statue	статуя f	sta·tu·ya

shopping

enquiries

Where's a ...?	Где ...?	gdye ...
bank	банк	bank
bookshop	книжный магазин	kneezh·ni ma·ga·zeen
camera shop	фотографический магазин	fo·to·gra·fee·chee·skee ma·ga·zeen
department store	универмаг	u·nee·veer·mak
grocery store	гастроном	gast·ra·nom
market	рынок	ri·nak
newsagency	газетный киоск	gaz·yet·ni kee·osk
supermarket	универсам	u·nee·veer·sam

Where can I buy ...?
Где можно купить ...?　　　　gdye mozh·na ku·peet' ...

Can I look at it?
Покажите, пожалуйста.　　　　pa·ka·zhit·ye pa·zhal·sta

Do you have any others?
У вас есть другие?　　　　u vas yest' dru·gee·ye

Does it have a guarantee?
Есть гарантия?　　　　yest' ga·ran·tee·ya

Can I have it sent overseas?
Вы можете переслать — vi *mo*-zhit-ye pee-rees-*lat'*
это за границу? — *e*-ta za gra-*neet*-su

Can you repair this?
Вы можете это починить? — vi *mo*-zhit-ye *e*-ta pa-chee-*neet'*

It's faulty.
Это бракованно. — *e*-ta z bra-*ko*-va-na

I'd like ... | Я бы хотел/ | ya bi khat-*yel*/
 | хотела ... m/f | khat-*ye*-la ...
 a bag | пакет | pak-*yet*
 a refund | получить | pa-lu-*cheet'*
 | обратно деньги | ab-*rat*-na dyen'-gee
 to return this | это возвратить | *e*-ta vaz-vra-*teet'*

paying

How much is it?
Сколько стоит? — *skol'*-ka *sto*-eet

Can you write down the price?
Запишите, пожалуйста, цену. — za-pee-*shit*-ye pa-*zhal*-sta *tse*-nu

That's too expensive.
Это очень дорого. — *e*-ta *o*-cheen' *do*-ra-ga

Can you lower the price?
Вы можете снизить цену? — vi *mo*-zhit-ye snee-zeet' *tse*-nu

I'll give you (100) roubles.
Я вам дам (сто) рублей. — ya vam dam (sto) rub-*lyey*

There's a mistake in the bill.
Меня обсчитали. — meen-*ya* ap-shee-*ta*-lee

Do you accept ...? | Вы принимаете | vi pri-ni-*ma*-it-ye
 | оплату ...? | a-*pla*-tu ...
 credit cards | кредитной карточкой | kri-*dit*-ney *kar*-tach-key
 debit cards | дебитной карточкой | *dye*-bit-ney *kar*-tach-key
 travellers cheques | дорожным чеком | da-*rozh*-nihm *che*-kam

I'd like ... | Я бы хотел/ | ya bi khat-*yel*/
 | хотела ... m/f | khat-*ye*-la ...
 a receipt | квитанцию | kvee-*tant*-si-yu
 my change | сдачу | *zda*-chu

clothes & shoes

Can I try it on?	Можно это примерить?	*mozh*·na *e*·ta preem·*ye*·reet'
My size is (40).	Мой размер (сорок).	moy raz·*myer* (*so*·rak)
It doesn't fit.	Это не подходит.	*e*·ta nye pat·*kho*·deet
small	маленький	ma·*leen*'·kee
medium	средний	*sryed*·nee
large	большой	bal'·*shoy*

books & music

I'd like a ...	Я бы хотел/	ya bi khat·*yel*/
	хотела ... m/f	khat·*ye*·la ...
newspaper	газету	gaz·*ye*·tu
(in English)	(на английском)	(na an·*glee*·skam)
pen	ручку	*ruch*·ku

Is there an English-language bookshop?
Есть магазин английской книги?   yest' ma·ga·*zeen* an·*glee*·skey *knee*·gee

Can I listen to this?
Можно послушать?   *mozh*·na pas·*lu*·shat'

photography

Can you ...?	Вы можете ...?	vi *mo*·zhit·ye ...
develop this film	проявить эту плёнку	pra·yee·*veet'* e·tu *plyon*·ku
load this film	вложить эту плёнку	vla·*zhit'* e·tu *plyon*·ku
transfer photos	перебросить	pee·ree·*bro*·seet'
from my camera	снимки с камеры	*sneem*·kee s *kam*·ye·ri
to CD	на компакт-диск	na kam·*pakt*·deesk
I need a ... film	Мне нужна ... плёнка	mnye nuzh·*na* ... *plyon*·ka
for this camera.	на эту камеру.	na e·tu *kam*·ye·ru
B&W	чёрно-белая	chor·nab·*ye*·la·ya
colour	цветная	tsvet·*na*·ya
slide	слайд-овая	*slaid*·a·va·ya
(high) speed	(высоко-)	(vi·sa·*ko*·)
	чувствительная	chus·*vee*·teel'·na·ya

When will it be ready?   Когда она будет готова?   kag·*da* a·*na* bu·deet ga·*to*·va

meeting people

greetings, goodbyes & introductions

Hello.	Здравствуйте.	*zdrast*·vuyt·ye
Hi.	Привет.	preev·*yet*
Goodbye/Bye.	До свидания/Пока.	da svee·*dan*·ya/pa·*ka*
See you later.	До скорой встречи.	da *sko*·rey fstrye·chee
Mr	господин	ga·spa·*deen*
Mrs/Miss	госпожа	ga·spa·*zha*
How are you?	Как дела?	kag dyee·*la*
Fine, thanks.	Спасибо, хорошо.	spa·*see*·ba kha·ra·*sho*
And you?	А у вас?	a u vas
What's your name?	Как вас зовут?	kak vaz za·*vut*
My name is ...	Меня зовут ...	meen·*ya* za·*vut* ...
I'm pleased to meet you.	Очень приятно.	*o*·cheen' pree·*yat*·na
This is my ...	Это ...	*e*·ta ...
boyfriend	мой парень	moy *pa*·reen
brother	мой брат	moy brat
daughter	моя дочка	ma·*ya doch*·ka
father	мой отец	moy at·*yets*
friend	мой друг m	moy druk
	моя подруга f	ma·ya pa·*dru*·ga
girlfriend	моя девушка	ma·ya dye·vush·ka
husband	мой муж	moy mush
mother	моя мать	ma·*ya* mat'
partner	мой парень m	moy *pa*·reen
(intimate)	моя девушка f	ma·ya dye·vush·ka
sister	моя сестра	ma·*ya* seest·*ra*
son	мой сын	moy sin
wife	моя жена	ma·*ya* zhi·*na*
Here's my ...	Вот мой ...	vot moy ...
What's your ...?	Можно ваш ...?	*mozh*·na vash ...
address	адрес	*a*·drees
email address	и-мейл	ee·*meyl*
fax number	номер факса	*no*·meer *fak*·sa
phone number	номер телефона	*no*·meer tee·lee·*fo*·na

occupations

What's your occupation?	Кем вы работаете?	kyem vi ra·bo·ta·yeet·ye
I'm a/an ...	Я ...	ya ...
artist	художник m	khu·dozh·neek
	художница f	khu·dozh·neet·sa
businessperson	бизнесмен	beez·nees·myen
farmer	фермер	fyer·meer
office worker	служащий m	slu·zha·shee
	служащая f	slu·zha·shee·ya
scientist	учёный/учёная m/f	u·cho·ni/u·cho·na·ya
student	студент m	stud·yent
	студентка f	stud·yent·ka
tradesperson	ремесленник	reem·yes·lee·neek

background

Where are you from?	Вы откуда?	vi at·ku·da
I'm from ...	Я из ...	ya eez ...
Australia	Австралии	af·stra·lee·ee
Canada	Канады	ka·na·di
England	Англии	an·glee·ee
New Zealand	Новой Зеландии	no·voy zee·lan·dee·ee
the USA	США	se·sha·a
Are you married?	Вы женаты? m	vi zhi·na·ti
	Вы замужем? f	vi za·mu·zhim
I'm married.	Я женат/замужем. m/f	ya zhi·nat/za·mu·zhim
I'm single.	Я холост/холоста. m/f	ya kho·last/kha·la·sta

age

How old ...?	Сколько ... лет?	skol'·ka ... lyet
are you	вам	vam
is your daughter	вашей дочке	va·shey doch·kye
is your son	вашему сыну	va·shi·mu si·nu
I'm ... years old.	Мне ... лет.	mnye ... lyet
He/She is ... years old.	Ему/Ей ... лет.	ye·mu/yey ... lyet

feelings

I'm (not) ...	Я (не) ...	ya (nye) ...
cold	замёрз m	zam-*yors*
	замёрзла f	zam-*yorz*-la
happy	счастлив m	shas-*leef*
	счастлива f	shas-*lee*-va
hot	умираю от жары	u-mee-*ra*-yu ad zha-*ri*
hungry	голоден m	*go*-la-deen
	голодна f	ga-lad-*na*
sad	грущу	gru-*shu*
thirsty	хочу пить	kha-*chu* peet'

What about you?	А вы?	a vih

entertainment

going out

Where can I find ...?	Где находятся ...?	gdye na-*kho*-deet-sa ...
clubs	клубы	*klu*-bi
gay venues	гей-клубы	gyey-*klu*-bi
pubs	пивные	peev-*ni*-ye

I feel like	Мне хочется	mnye *kho*-cheet-sa
going to a/the ...	пойти ...	pey-*tee* ...
concert	на концерт	na kant-*sert*
movies	в кино	v kee-*no*
party	на тусовку	na tu-*sof*-ku
restaurant	в ресторан	v ree-sta-*ran*
theatre	в театр	f tee-*atr*

interests

Do you like ...?	Вам нравится ...?	vam *nra*-veet-sa ...
I (don't) like ...	Мне (не) нравится ...	mnye (nye) *nra*-veet-sa ...
art	искусство	ees-*kust*-va
cooking	готовить	ga-*to*-veet'
movies	кино	kee-*no*
reading	читать	chee-*tat'*
sport	спорт	sport
travelling	путешествовать	pu-tee-*shest*-va-vat'

451

Do you like to ...?	Вы ...?	vi ...
dance	танцуете	tant·su·eet·ye
go to concerts	ходите на	kho·deet·ye na
	концерты	kant·ser·ti
listen to music	слушаете музыку	slu·sha·yeet·ye mu·zi·ku

food & drink

finding a place to eat

Can you	Вы можете	vi mo·zhit·ye
recommend a ...?	порекомендовать ...?	pa·ree·ka·meen·da·vat' ...
bar	бар	bar
café	кафе	ka·fe
restaurant	ресторан	ree·sta·ran

I'd like ...,	Я бы хотел/	ya bi khat·yel/
please.	хотела ... m/f	khat·ye·la ...
a table for (three)	столик на (троих)	sto·leek na (tra·eekh)
the nonsmoking	некурящий	nye·kur·yash·chee
section		
the smoking section	курящий	kur·yash·chee

ordering food

breakfast	завтрак m	zaf·trak
lunch	обед m	ab·yet
dinner	ужин m	u·zhin
snack	закуска f	za·kus·ka

| What would you | Что вы | shto vi |
| recommend? | рекомендуете? | ree·ka·meen·du·eet·ye |

I'd like (the) ...,	Я бы хотел/	ya bi khat·yel/
please.	хотела ... m/f	khat·ye·la ...
bill	счёт	shot
drink list	карту вин	kar·tu veen
menu	меню	meen·yu
that dish	это блюдо	e·ta blyu·da

drinks

cup of coffee/tea ...	чашка кофе/чаю ...	chash·ka kof·ye/cha·yu ...
with milk	с молоком	s ma·la·kom
without sugar	без сахару	byez sa·kha·ru
... water	... вода	... va·da
boiled	кипячёная	kee·pee·cho·na·ya
(sparkling) mineral	(шипучая)	(shi·pu·cha·ya)
	минеральная	mee·nee·ral'·na·ya
(orange) juice	(апельсиновый) сок m	(a·peel'·see·na·vi) sok
soft drink	безалкогольный	bye·zal·ka·gol'·ni
	напиток m	na·pee·tak

in the bar

I'll have ...	..., пожалуйста.	... pa·zhal·sta
I'll buy you a drink.	Я угощаю.	ya u·ga·sha·yu
What would you like?	Что вы хотите?	shto vi kha·tee·tye
Cheers!	Пей до дна!	pyey da dna
champagne	шампанское n	sham·pan·ska·ye
cocktail	коктейль m	kak·teyl
vodka	водка f	vot·ka
whisky	виски m	vees·kee
a ... of beer	... пива	... pee·va
bottle	бутылка	bu·til·ka
glass	стакан	sta·kan
a bottle/glass	бутылка/рюмка	bu·til·ka/ryum·ka
of ... wine	... вина	... vee·na
red	красного	kras·na·va
sparkling	шипучего	shi·pu·chee·va
white	белого	bye·la·va

self-catering

What's the local speciality?
Что типично местное? — shto tee·*peech*·na *myes*·na·ye

What's that?
Что это? — shto e·ta

How much (is a kilo of cheese)?
Сколько стоит (кило сыра)? — *skol'*·ka *sto*·eet (kee·*lo si*·ra)

I'd like ...	Дайте ...	*deyt*·ye ...
(200) grams	(двести) грамм	(*dvye*·stee) gram
(two) kilos	(два) кило	(dva) kee·*lo*
(three) pieces	(три) куска	(tree) kus·*ka*
(six) slices	(шесть) ломтика	(shest') *lom*·tee·ka

Less.	Меньше.	*myen'*·shi
Enough.	Достаточно.	da·*sta*·tach·na
More.	Немного.	neem·*no*·ga

special diets & allergies

Is there a vegetarian restaurant nearby?
Здесь есть вегетарианский ресторан? — zdyes' yest' vee·gee·ta·ree·*an*·skee ree·sta·*ran*

Do you have vegetarian food?
У вас есть овощные блюда? — u vas yest' a·vashch·*ni*·ye *blyu*·da

Could you	Вы могли бы	vi ma·*glee* bi
prepare a meal	приготовить	pree·ga·*to*·veet'
without ...?	блюдо без ...?	*blu*·da byez ...
butter	масла	*mas*·la
eggs	яиц	*ya*·eets
meat stock	мясного бульона	myas·*no*·va bu·*lo*·na

I'm allergic to ...	У меня аллергия на ...	u meen·*ya* a·leer·*gee*·ya na ...
dairy produce	молочные продукты	ma·*loch*·ni·ye pra·*duk*·ti
gluten	клейковину	klyey·ka·*vee*·nu
MSG	МНГ	em·en·*ge*
nuts	орехи	ar·*ye*·khee
seafood	морепродукты	mor·ye·pra·*duk*·ti

emergencies

basics

Help!	Помогите!	pa·ma·*gee*·tye
Stop!	Прекратите!	pree·kra·*tee*·tye
Go away!	Идите отсюда!	ee·*deet*·ye at·*syu*·da
Thief!	Вор!	vor
Fire!	Пожар!	pa·*zhar*
Watch out!	Осторожно!	a·sta·*rozh*·na

Call ...!	Вызовите ...!	*vi*·za·*veet*·ye ...
a doctor	врача	vra·*cha*
an ambulance	скорую помощь	*sko*·ru·yu *po*·mash'
the police	милицию	*vi*·za·*veet*·ye mee·*leet*·si·yu

It's an emergency.
Это срочно!   e·ta *sroch*·na

Could you help me, please?
Помогите, пожалуйста!   pa·ma·*geet*·ye pa·*zhal*·sta

Can I use your phone?
Можно воспользоваться телефоном?   *mozh*·na vas·*pol*'·za·vat'·sa tee·lee·*fo*·nam

Where are the toilets?
Где здесь туалет?   gdye zdyes' tu·al·*yet*

I'm lost.
Я потерялся/потерялась. m/f   ya pa·teer·*yal*·sa/pa·teer·*ya*·las'

police

Where's the police station?
Где милицейский участок?   gdye mee·leet·*sey*·skee u·*cha*·stak

I want to report an offence.
Я хочу заявить в милицию.   ya kha·*chu* za·ya·*veet*' v mee·*leet*·si·yu

I have insurance.
У меня есть страховка.   u meen·*ya* yest' stra·*khof*·ka

I've been ...	Меня ...	meen·*ya* ...
assaulted	побили	pa·*bee*·lee
raped	изнасиловали	eez·na·*see*·la·va·lee
robbed	ограбили	a·*gra*·bee·lee

I've lost my ...	Я потерял/	ya pa-teer-*yal*/
	потеряла ... m/f	pa-teer-*ya*-la ...
My ... was/were stolen.	У меня украли ...	u meen-*ya* u-*kra*-lee ...
backpack	рюкзак	ryug-*zak*
bags	багаж	ba-*gash*
credit card	кредитную	kree-*deet*-nu-yu
	карточку	*kar*-tach-ku
handbag	сумку	*sum*-ku
jewellery	драгоценности	dra-gat-*se*-na-stee
money	деньги	*dyen'*-gee
passport	паспорт	*pas*-part
travellers cheques	дорожные	da-*rozh*-ni-ye
	чеки	*che*-kee
wallet	бумажник	bu-*mazh*-neek
I want to contact	Я хочу обратиться	ya kha-*chu* a-bra-*teet'*-sa
my ...	в своё ...	f sva-*yo* ...
consulate	консульство	kan-sulst-*vo*
embassy	посольство	pa-*solst*-va

health

medical needs

Where's the nearest ...?	Где здесь ...?	gdye zdyes' ...
dentist	зубной врач	zub-*noy* vrach
doctor	врач	vrach
hospital	больница	*bal'*-neet-sa
(night) pharmacist	(ночная) аптека	(nach-*na*-ya) ap-*tye*-ka

I need a doctor (who speaks English).

Мне нужен врач,
(говорящий на
английском языке).

mnye *nu*-zhin vrach
(ga-var-*ya*-shee na
an-*glee*-skam ya-zik-*ye*)

Could I see a female doctor?

Можно записаться на
приём к женщине-врачу?

mozh-na za-pee-*sat'*-sa na
pree-*yom* k *zhen*-sheen-ye-vra-*chu*

I've run out of my medication.

У меня кончилось лекарство.

u meen-*ya* *kon*-chee-las' lee-*karst*-va

symptoms, conditions & allergies

I'm sick.	Я болею.	ya bal·ye·yu
It hurts here.	Здесь болит.	zdyes' ba·leet
I have (a) ...	У меня ...	u meen·ya ...
asthma	астма f	ast·ma
bronchitis	бронхит m	bran·kheet
constipation	запор m	za·por
cough	кашель m	ka·shel'
diarrhoea	понос m	pa·nos
fever	температура f	teem·pee·ra·tu·ra
headache	головная боль f	ga·lav·na·ya bol'
heart condition	болезнь сердца f	bal·yezn' syerd·tsa
nausea	тошнота f	tash·na·ta
pain	боль f	bol'
sore throat	болит горло n	ba·leet gor·la
toothache	зубная боль f	zub·na·ya bol
I'm allergic to ...	У меня аллергия на ...	u meen·ya a·leer·gee·ya na ...
antibiotics	антибиотики	an·tee·bee·o·tee·kee
anti-inflammatories	противо-воспалительные препараты	pra·tee·va·va·spa·leet·il'·ni·ye pree·pa·ra·ti
aspirin	аспирин	a·spee·reen
bees	пчелиный укус	pchee·lee·ni u·kus
codeine	кодеин	kad·ye·een
penicillin	пеницилин	pee·neet·si·leen
antiseptic	антисептик m	an·tees·yep·teek
bandage	бинт m	beent
condoms	презерватив m	pree·zeer·va·teef
contraceptives	противозачаточные средства n pl	pra·tee·va·za·cha·tach·ni·ye sryets·tva
diarrhoea medicine	лекарство от поноса n	li·karst·va at pa·no·sa
insect repellent	средство от насекомых n	sryets·tva at na·see·ko·mikh
laxative	слабительное n	sla·bee·teel'·na·ye
painkillers	болеутоляющие n pl	bo·lee·u·tal·ya·yu·shee·ye
rehydration salts	нюхательная соль m	nyu·kha·teel'·na·ya sol'
sleeping tablets	снотворные таблетки f pl	snat·vor·ni·ye tab·lyet·kee

english–russian dictionary

Russian nouns in this dictionary have their gender indicated by ⓜ masculine, ⓕ feminine or ⓝ neuter. If it's a plural noun you'll also see pl. Adjectives are given in the masculine form only. Words are also marked as a (adjective), v (verb), sg (singular), pl (plural), inf (informal) or pol (polite) where necessary.

A

accident авария ⓕ a-*va*-ree-ya
accommodation помещение ⓝ pa-mee-*she*-ee-ye
adaptor адаптер ⓜ a-*dap*-teer
address адрес ⓜ *a*-drees
after после *pos*-lye
air conditioning кондиционирование ⓝ kan-deet-si-a-*nee*-ra-va-nee-ye
airplane самолёт ⓜ sa-mal-*yot*
airport аэропорт ⓜ a-e-ra-*port*
alcohol алкоголь ⓜ al-ka-*gol'*
all все fsye
allergy аллергия ⓕ al-*yer*-gee-ya
ambulance скорая помощь ⓕ *sko*-ra-ya *po*-mash
and и ee
ankle лодыжка ⓕ la-*dish*-ka
arm рука ⓕ ru-*ka*
ashtray пепельница ⓕ *pye*-peel'-neet-sa
ATM банкомат ⓜ ban-ka-*mat*

B

baby ребёнок ⓜ reeb-*yo*-nak
back (body) спина ⓕ spee-*na*
backpack рюкзак ⓜ ryug-*zak*
bad плохой pla-*khoy*
bag мешок ⓜ mee-*shok*
baggage claim выдача багажа ⓕ *vi*-da-cha ba-*ga*-zha
bank банк ⓜ bank
bar бар ⓜ bar
bathroom ванная ⓕ *va*-na-ya
battery батарея ⓕ ba-tar-*ye*-ya
beautiful красивый kra-*see*-vi
bed кровать ⓕ kra-*vat'*
beer пиво ⓝ *pee*-va
before до do
behind за za
bicycle велосипед ⓜ vee-la-seep-*yet*
big большой bal'-*shoy*
bill счёт ⓜ shot
black чёрный *chor*-ni
blanket одеяло ⓝ a-dee-*ya*-la
blood group группа крови ⓕ *gru*-pa *kro*-vee

blue (dark) синий *see*-nee
blue (light) голубой ga-lu-*boy*
boat лодка ⓕ *lot*-ka
book (make a reservation) v заказать za-ka-*zat'*
bottle бутылка ⓕ bu-*til*-ka
bottle opener (beer) открывалка ⓕ at-kri-*val*-ka
bottle opener (wine) штопор ⓜ *shto*-par
boy мальчик ⓜ *mal'*-cheek
brakes (car) тормоза ⓜ pl tar-ma-*za*
breakfast завтрак ⓜ *zaf*-trak
broken (faulty) ошибочный a-*shi*-bach-ni
bus автобус ⓜ af-*to*-bus
business бизнес ⓜ *beez*-nees
buy купить ku-*peet'*

C

café кафе ⓝ ka-*fe*
camera фотоаппарат ⓜ fo-to-a-pa-*rat*
camp site кемпинг ⓜ *kyem*-peenk
cancel отменить at-mee-*neet'*
can opener открывашка ⓕ at-kri-*vash*-ka
car машина ⓕ ma-*shi*-na
cash наличные ⓝ pl na-*leech*-ni-ye
cash (a cheque) v обменять ab-meen-*yat'*
cell phone мобильный телефон ⓜ ma-*beel'*-ni tee-lee-*fon*
centre центр ⓜ tsentr
change (money) v обменять ab-meen-*yat'*
cheap дешёвый dee-*sho*-vi
check (bill) счёт ⓜ shot
check-in регистрация ⓕ ree-geest-*rat*-si-ya
chest грудная клетка ⓕ grud-*na*-ya *klyet*-ka
child ребёнок ⓜ reeb-*yo*-nak
cigarette сигарета ⓕ see-gar-*ye*-ta
city город ⓜ *go*-rat
clean a чистый *chee*-sti
closed закрытый za-*kri*-ti
coffee кофе ⓜ *kof*-ye
coins монеты ⓕ pl man-*ye*-ti
cold a холодный kha-*lod*-ni
collect call звонок по коллекту ⓜ zva-*nok* pa kal-*yek*-tu
come прийти pree-*tee*
computer компьютер ⓜ kam-*pyu*-teer

condom презерватив ⓜ pree-zeer-va-*teef*
contact lenses контактные линзы ⓘ pl
kan-*takt*-ni-ye *leen*-zi
cook v готовить ga-*to*-veet'
cost цена ⓘ tse-*na*
credit card кредитная карточка ⓘ
kri-*deet*-na-ya *kar*-tach-ka
cup чашка ⓘ *chash*-ka
currency exchange обмен валюты ⓜ
ab-*myen* val-*yu*-ti
customs (immigration) таможня ⓘ ta-*mozh*-nya

D

dangerous опасный a-*pas*-ni
date (time) число ⓝ chees-*lo*
day день ⓜ dyen'
delay задержка ⓘ zad-*yersh*-ka
dentist зубной врач ⓜ zub-*noy* vrach
depart отправиться at-*pra*-veet'-sa
diaper подгузник ⓜ pad-*guz*-neek
dictionary словарь ⓜ sla-*var*'
dinner ужин ⓜ *u*-zhin
direct прямой pree-*moy*
dirty грязный *gryaz*-ni
disabled инвалид ⓜ een-va-*leet*
discount скидка ⓘ *skeet*-ka
doctor врач ⓜ vrach
double bed двуспальная кровать ⓘ
dvu-*spal*'-na-ya kra-*vat*'
double room номер на двоих ⓜ *no*-meer na
dva-*eekh*
drink напиток ⓜ na-*pee*-tak
drive v водить машину va-*deet*' ma-*shi*-nu
drivers licence водительские права ⓝ pl
va-*dee*-teel'-skee-ye pra-*va*
drugs (illicit) наркотики ⓜ pl nar-*ko*-tee-kee
dummy (pacifier) соска ⓘ *sos*-ka

E

ear ухо ⓝ *u*-kha
east восток ⓜ va-*stok*
eat есть yest'
economy class пассажирский класс ⓜ
pa-sa-*zhir*-skee klas
electricity электричество ⓝ e-leek-*tree*-cheest-va
elevator лифт ⓜ leeft
email и-мейл ⓜ ee-*meyl*
embassy посольство ⓝ pa-*solst*-va
emergency авария ⓘ a-*va*-ree-ya
English (language) английский an-*glee*-skee
entrance вход ⓜ fkhot

evening вечер ⓜ *vye*-cheer
exchange rate обменный курс ⓜ ab-*mye*-nì kurs
exit выход ⓜ *vi*-khat
expensive дорогой da-ra-*goy*
express mail экспресс почта ⓘ eks-*pres poch*-ta
eyes глаза ⓝ pl gla-*za*

F

far далеко da-lee-*ko*
fast быстрый *bist*-ri
father отец ⓜ at-*yets*
film (camera) плёнка ⓘ *plyon*-ka
finger палец ⓜ *pa*-leets
first-aid kit санитарная сумка ⓘ
sa-nee-*tar*-na-ya *sum*-ka
first class в первом классе f *pyer*-vam *klas*-ye
fish рыба ⓘ *ri*-ba
food еда ⓘ yee-*da*
foot нога ⓘ na-*ga*
fork вилка ⓘ *veel*-ka
free (of charge) бесплатный bees-*plat*-ni
friend друг/подруга ⓜ/ⓘ druk/pa-*dru*-ga
fruit фрукты ⓜ pl *fruk*-ti
full полный *pol*-ni
funny смешной smeesh-*noy*

G

gift подарок ⓜ pa-*da*-rak
girl (teenage) девушка ⓘ *dye*-vush-ka
girl (pre-teen) девочка ⓘ *dye*-vach-ka
glass (drinking) стакан ⓜ sta-*kan*
glasses очки ⓝ pl ach-*kee*
go (on foot) идти ee-*tee*
go (by vehicle) ехать ye-*khat*'
good хороший kha-*ro*-shi
green зелёный zeel'-*yo*-ni
guide гид ⓜ geet

H

half половина ⓘ pa-la-*vee*-na
hand рука ⓘ ru-*ka*
handbag сумочка ⓘ *su*-mach-ka
happy счастливый shees-*lee*-vi
have y ... есть u ... yest'
he он on
head голова ⓘ ga-la-*va*
heart сердце ⓝ *syerd*-tsi
heat жара ⓘ zha-*ra*
heavy тяжёлый tya-*zho*-li
help v помочь pa-*moch*'

here здесь zdyes'
high высокий vi-*so*-kee
highway шоссе ⓝ sha-*se*
hike v ходить пешком kha-*deet'* peesh-*kom*
holiday каникулы ⓕ pl ka-*nee*-ku-li
homosexual гомосексуалист ⓜ
go-mo-seek-su-a-*leest*
hospital больница ⓕ bol'-*neet*-sa
hot жаркий *zhar*-kee
hotel гостиница ⓕ ga-*stee*-neet-sa
hungry голоден *go*-la-deen
husband муж ⓜ mush

I

I я ya
identification (card) идентификационная карта ⓕ
eed-yen-tee-fee-kat-si-o-na-ya *kar*-ta
ill болен *bo*-leen
important важный *vazh*-ni
included включая fklyu-*cha*-ya
injury травма ⓕ *trav*-ma
insurance страхование ⓝ stra-kha-*va*-nee-ye
Internet интернет ⓜ een-ter-*net*
interpreter переводчик ⓜ pee-ree-*vot*-cheek

J

jewellery ювелирные изделия ⓝ pl
yu-vi-*leer*-ni-ye eez-*dye*-lee-ya
job работа ⓕ ra-*bo*-ta

K

key ключ ⓜ klyuch
kilogram килограмм ⓜ kee-la-*gram*
kitchen кухня ⓕ *kukh*-nya
knife нож ⓜ nosh

L

laundry (place) прачечная ⓕ *pra*-cheech-na-ya
lawyer адвокат ⓜ ad-va-*kat*
left (direction) левый *lye*-vi
left-luggage office камера хранения ⓕ
ka-mee-ra khran-*ye*-nee-ya
leg нога ⓕ na-*ga*
lesbian лесбиянка ⓕ lees-bee-*an*-ka
less меньше *myen'*-she
letter (mail) письмо ⓝ pees'-*mo*
lift (elevator) лифт ⓜ leeft
light свет ⓜ svyet

like v любить lyu-*beet'*
lock замок ⓜ za-*mok*
long длинный *dlee*-ni
lost пропавший pra-*paf*-shi
lost-property office бюро находок ⓝ
byu-ro na-*kho*-dak
love v любить lyu-*beet'*
luggage багаж ⓜ ba-*gash*
lunch обед ⓜ ab-*yet*

M

mail почта ⓕ *poch*-ta
man мужчина ⓜ mush-*chee*-na
map карта ⓕ *kar*-ta
market рынок ⓜ *ri*-nak
matches спички ⓕ pl *speech*-kee
meat мясо ⓝ *mya*-sa
medicine лекарство ⓝ lee-*karst*-va
menu меню ⓝ meen-*yu*
message записка ⓕ za-*pees*-ka
milk молоко ⓝ ma-la-*ko*
minute минута ⓕ mee-*nu*-ta
mobile phone мобильный телефон ⓜ
ma-*beel'*-ni tee-lee-*fon*
money деньги ⓕ pl *dyen'*-gee
month месяц ⓜ *mye*-seets
morning утро ⓝ *u*-tra
mother мать ⓕ mat'
motorcycle мотоцикл ⓜ ma-tat-*sikl*
motorway шоссе ⓝ sha-*se*
mouth рот ⓜ rot
music музыка ⓕ *mu*-zi-ka

N

name (personal) имя ⓝ *eem*-ya
name (of object) название ⓝ na-*zva*-nee-ye
napkin салфетка ⓕ salf-*yet*-ka
nappy подгузник ⓜ pad-*guz*-neek
near близко *blees*-ka
neck шея ⓕ *she*-ya
new новый *no*-vi
news новости ⓕ pl *no*-va-stee
newspaper газета ⓕ gaz-*ye*-ta
night ночь ⓕ noch'
no нет nyet
noisy шумный *shum*-ni
nonsmoking некурящий nee-kur-*ya*-shee
north север ⓜ *sye*-veer
nose нос ⓜ nos
now сейчас see-*chas*
number номер ⓜ *no*-meer

O

oil (engine) масло ⑩ *mas*-la
old старый *sta*-ri ⑩
one-way ticket билет в один конец ⑩
  beel-yet v a-*deen* kan-*yets*
open a открытый at-*kri*-ti
outside снаружи sna-*ru*-zhi

P

package посылка ① pa-*sil*-ka
paper бумага ① bu-*ma*-ga
park (a car) v поставить (машину)
  pa-*sta*-veet' (ma-*shi*-nu)
passport паспорт ⑩ *pas*-part
pay заплатить za-pla-*teet'*
pen ручка ① *ruch*-ka
petrol бензин ⑩ been-*zeen*
pharmacy аптека ① apt-*ye*-ka
phonecard телефонная карточка ①
  tee-lee-*fo*-na-ya *kar*-tach-ka
photo снимок ⑩ *snee*-mak
plate тарелка ① tar-*yel*-ka
police милиция ① mee-*leet*-si-ya
postcard открытка ① at-*krit*-ka
post office почта ① *poch*-ta
pregnant беременная beer-*ye*-mee-na-ya
price цена ① tse-*na*

Q

quiet тихий *ti*-khee

R

rain дождь ⑩ dozht'
razor бритва ① *breet*-va
receipt квитанция ① kvee-*tan*-tsi-ya
red красный *kras*-ni
refund возвращение денег ⑩
  vaz-vra-*she*-nee-ye dye-neek
registered mail заказной ① za-kaz-*noy*
rent v арендовать a-reen-da-*vat'*
repair v починить pa-chee-*neet'*
reservation заказ ⑩ za-*kas*
restaurant ресторан ⑩ rees-ta-*ran*
return v вернуться veer-*nut'*-sa
return ticket обратный билет ⑩ a-*brat*-ni beel-*yet*
right (direction) правый *pra*-vi
road дорога ① da-*ro*-ga
room (hotel) номер ⑩ *no*-meer
room (house) комната ① *kom*-na-ta
Russia Россия ① ra-*see*-ya

Russian (language) русский ⑩ *rus*-kee
Russian a русский/русская ⑩/① *rus*-kee/*rus*-ka-ya

S

safe a безопасный beez-a-*pas*-ni
sanitary napkin гигиеническая салфетка ①
  gee-gee-ee-*nee*-chee-ska-ya salf-*yet*-ka
seat место ⑩ *myes*-ta
send послать pas-*lat'*
service station заправочная станция ①
  za-*pra*-vach-na-ya *stant*-si-ya
sex секс ⑩ syeks
shampoo шампунь ⑩ sham-*pun'*
share (a dorm) жить в одной комнате
  zhit' v ad-*noy* *kom*-nat-ye
shaving cream крем для бритья ⑩
  kryem dlya breet'-*ya*
she она a-*na*
sheet (bed) простыня ① pra-*stin*-ya
shirt рубашка ① ru-*bash*-ka
shoes туфли ① pl *tuf*-lee
shop магазин ⑩ ma-ga-*zeen*
short короткий ka-*rot*-kee
shower душ ⑩ dush
single room одноместный номер ⑩
  ad-na-*mes*-ni *no*-meer
skin кожа ① *ko*-zha
skirt юбка ① *yup*-ka
sleep v спать spat'
slowly медленно *myed*-lee-na
small маленький *ma*-leen'-kee
smoke (cigarettes) v курить ku-*reet'*
soap мыло ⑩ *mi*-la
some несколько nye-*skal'*-ka
soon скоро *sko*-ra
south юг ⑩ yuk
souvenir shop сувенирный магазин ⑩
  su-vee-*neer*-ni ma-ga-*zeen*
speak говорить ga-va-*reet'*
spoon ложка ① *losh*-ka
stamp марка ① *mar*-ka
stand-by ticket стенд-бай билет ⑩
  styend-bai beel-*yet*
station (train) станция ① *stant*-see-ya
stomach желудок ⑩ zhi-*lu*-dak
stop v перестать pee-ree-*stat'*
stop (bus) остановка ① a-sta-*nof*-ka
street улица ① u-lee-tsa
student студент/студентка ⑩/①
  stud-*yent*/stud-*yent*-ka
sun солнце ⑩ *solnt*-se
sunscreen солнцезащитный крем ⑩
  sont-se-za-*sheet*-ni kryem
swim v плавать *pla*-vat'

T

tampons тампон ⓜ tam-*pon*
taxi такси ⓜ tak-*see*
teaspoon чайная ложка ⓕ *chey*-na-ya *losh*-ka
teeth зубы ⓜ pl *zu*-bi
telephone телефон ⓜ tee-lee-*fon*
television телевизор ⓜ tee-lee-*vee*-zar
temperature (weather) температура ⓕ
    teem-pee-ra-*tu*-ra
tent палатка ⓕ pa-*lat*-ka
that (one) то to
they они a-*nee*
thirsty (be) хочется пить *kho*-cheet-sa peet'
this (one) это e-ta
throat горло ⓝ *gor*-la
ticket билет ⓜ beel-*yet*
time время ⓝ *vryem*-ya
tired устал u-*stal*
tissues салфетки ⓕ pl salf-*yet*-kee
today сегодня see-*vod*-nya
toilet туалет ⓜ tu-al-*yet*
tomorrow завтра *zaf*-tra
tonight сегодня вечером see-*vod*-nya *vye*-chee-ram
toothbrush зубная щётка ⓕ zub-*na*-ya *shot*-ka
toothpaste зубная паста ⓕ zub-*na*-ya *pa*-sta
torch (flashlight) фонарик ⓜ fa-*na*-reek
tour экскурсия ⓕ eks-*kur*-see-ya
tourist office туристическое бюро ⓝ
    tu-rees-*tee*-chee-ska-ye byu-*ro*
towel полотенце ⓝ pa-lat-*yent*-se
train поезд ⓜ *po*-eest
translate перевести pee-ree-vee-*stee*
travel agency бюро путешествий ⓝ
    byu-*ro* pu-tee-*shest*-vee
travellers cheque дорожный чек ⓜ
    da-*rozh*-ni chek
trousers брюки ⓜ pl *bryu*-kee
twin beds две односпальные кровати
    dvye ad-na-*spal*-ni-ye kra-*va*-tee
tyre шина ⓕ *shi*-na

U

underwear бельё ⓝ beel-*yo*
urgent срочный *sroch*-ni

V

vacant свободный sva-*bod*-ni
vacation каникулы ⓕ pl ka-*nee*-ku-li
vegetable овощ ⓜ *o*-vash
vegetarian вегетарианец/вегетарианка ⓜ/ⓕ
    vee-gee-ta-ree-*a*-neets/vee-gee-ta-ree-*an*-ka
visa виза ⓕ *vee*-za

W

waiter официант/официантка ⓜ/ⓕ
    a-feet-si-*ant*/a-feet-si-*ant*-ka
walk v гулять gul-*yat'*
wallet кошелёк ⓜ ka-she-*lyok*
warm a тёплый *tyop*-li
wash (something) выстирать *vi*-stee-rat'
watch часы ⓜ pl chee-*si*
water вода ⓕ va-*da*
we мы mi
weekend выходные ⓜ pl vi-khad-*ni*-ye
west запад ⓜ *za*-pat
wheelchair инвалидная коляска ⓕ
    een-va-*leed*-na-ya kal-*yas*-ka
when когда kag-*da*
where где gdye
white белый *bye*-li
who кто kto
why почему pa-chee-*mu*
wife жена ⓕ zhi-*na*
window окно ⓝ ak-*no*
wine вино ⓝ vee-*no*
with с s
without без byez
woman женщина ⓕ *zhen*-shee-na
write написать na-pee-*sat'*

Y

yellow жёлтый *zhol*-ti
yes да da
yesterday вчера fchee-*ra*
you sg inf ты ti
you sg pol & pl вы vi

Spanish

spanish alphabet

A a a	*B b* be	*C c* the	*Ch ch* che	*D d* de
E e e	*F f* e·fe	*G g* khe	*H h* a·che	*I i* ee
J j kho·ta	*K k* ka	*L l* e·le	*LL ll* e·lye	*M m* e·me
N n e·ne	*Ñ ñ* e·nye	*O o* o	*P p* pe	*Q q* koo
R r e·re	*S s* e·se	*T t* te	*U u* oo	*V v* oo·ve
W w oo·ve do·vle	*X x* e·kees	*Y y* ee·grye·ga	*Z z* the·ta	

spanish

about Spanish

The lively and picturesque language of Cervantes' *Don Quijote* and Almodóvar's movies, Spanish (*español* es·pa·*nyol*), or Castilian (*castellano* kas·te·*lya*·no), as it's also called in Spain, has over 390 million speakers worldwide. Outside Spain, it's the language of most of Latin America and the West Indies and is also spoken in the Philippines and Guam, in some areas of the African coast and in the US.

Spanish belongs to the Romance group of languages – the descendents of Latin – together with French, Italian, Portuguese and Romanian. It's derived from Vulgar Latin, which Roman soldiers and merchants brought to the Iberian Peninsula during the period of Roman conquest (3rd to 1st century BC). By 19 BC Spain had become totally Romanised and Latin became the language of the peninsula in the four centuries that followed. Thanks to the Arabic invasion in AD 711 and the Arabs' continuing presence in Spain during the next eight centuries, Spanish has also been strongly influenced by Arabic, although mostly in the vocabulary. Today's Castilian is spoken in the north, centre and south of Spain. Completing the colourful linguistic profile of the country, Basque (*euskera* e·*oos*·ke·ra), Catalan (*catalán* ka·ta·*lan*) and Galician (*gallego* ga·*lye*·go) are also official languages in Spain, though Castilian covers by far the largest territory.

Besides the shared vocabulary of Latin origin that English and Spanish have in common, there's also a large corpus of words from the indigenous American languages that have entered English via Spanish. After Columbus' discovery of the New World in 1492, America's indigenous languages had a considerable impact on Spanish, especially in words to do with flora, fauna and topography (such as *tobacco*, *chocolate*, *coyote*, *canyon*, to name only a few).

Even if you're not familiar with the sound of Spanish through, say, the voices of José Carreras or Julio Iglesias, you'll be easily seduced by this melodic language and have fun trying to roll your *rr*'s like the locals. You may have heard the popular legend about one of the Spanish kings having a slight speech impediment which prompted all of Spain to mimic his lisp. Unfortunately, this charming explanation of the lisping 's' is only a myth – it's actually due to the way Spanish evolved from Latin and has nothing to do with lisping monarchs at all. So, when you hear someone say *gracias* gra·thyas, they're no more lisping than when you say 'thank you' in English.

pronunciation

vowel sounds

Vowels are pronounced short and fairly closed. The sound remains level, and each vowel is pronounced as an individual unit. There are, however, a number of cases where two vowel sounds become very closely combined (so-called diphthongs).

symbol	english equivalent	spanish example	transliteration
a	run	*agua*	*a*·gwa
ai	aisle	*bailar*	bai·*lar*
ay	say	*seis*	says
e	bet	*número*	*noo*·me·ro
ee	see	*día*	*dee*·a
o	pot	*ojo*	*o*·kho
oo	zoo	*gusto*	*goo*·sto
ow	how	*autobús*	ow·to·*boos*
oy	toy	*hoy*	oy

word stress

Spanish words have stress, which means you emphasise one syllable of a word over another. Here's a rule of thumb: when a written word ends in *n*, *s* or a vowel, the stress falls on the second-last syllable. Otherwise, the final syllable is stressed. If you see an accent mark over a syllable, it cancels out this rule and you just stress that syllable instead. You needn't worry about this though, as the stressed syllables are always italicised in our pronunciation guides .

consonant sounds

Remember that in Spanish the letter *h* is never pronounced. The Spanish *v* sounds more like a *b*, said with the lips pressed together. When ending a word, *d* is pronounced soft, like a *th*, or it's so slight it doesn't get pronounced at all. Finally, try to roll your *r*'s, especially at the start of a word and in words with *rr*.

symbol	english equivalent	spanish example	transliteration
b	**b**ed	*barco*	*bar*·ko
ch	**ch**eat	*chica*	*chee*·ka
d	**d**og	*dinero*	dee·*ne*·ro
f	**f**at	*fiesta*	*fye*·sta
g	**g**o	*gato*	*ga*·to
k	**k**it	*cabeza, queso*	ka·*be*·tha, *ke*·so
kh	lo**ch** (harsh and guttural)	*jardín, gente*	khar·*deen*, *khen*·te
l	**l**ot	*lago*	*la*·go
ly	mi**lli**on	*llamada*	lya·*ma*·da
m	**m**an	*mañana*	ma·*nya*·na
n	**n**ot	*nuevo*	*nwe*·vo
ny	ca**ny**on	*señora*	se·*nyo*·ra
p	**p**et	*padre*	*pa*·dre
r	like 'tt' in 'bu**tt**er' said fast	*hora*	*o*·ra
rr	**r**un (but stronger and rolled)	*ritmo, burro*	*rreet*·mo, *boo*·rro
s	**s**un	*semana*	se·*ma*·na
t	**t**op	*tienda*	*tyen*·da
th	**th**in	*Barcelona, manzana*	bar·*the·lo*·na, man·*tha*·na
v	soft 'b', between 'v' and 'b'	*abrir*	a·*vreer*
w	**w**in	*guardia*	*gwar*·dya
y	**y**es	*viaje*	*vya*·khe

tools

language difficulties

Do you speak English?
¿Habla inglés?   *ab*·la een·*gles*

Do you understand?
¿Me entiende?   me en·*tyen*·de

I (don't) understand.
(No) Entiendo.   (no) een·*tyen*·do

What does (*cuenta*) mean?
¿Qué significa (cuenta)?   ke seeg·nee·*fee*·ka (*kwen*·ta)

How do you ...?	*¿Cómo se ...?*	*ko*·mo se ...
pronounce this	*pronuncia esta*	pro·*noon*·thya *es*·ta
word	*palabra*	pa·*lab*·ra
write (*ciudad*)	*escribe (ciudad)*	es·*kree*·be (thee·oo·*da*)

Could you	*¿Puede ...,*	*pwe*·de ...
please ...?	*por favor?*	por fa·*vor*
repeat that	*repetir*	rre·pe·*teer*
speak more slowly	*hablar más despacio*	ab·*lar* mas des·*pa*·thyo
write it down	*escribirlo*	es·kree·*beer*·lo

essentials

Yes.	*Sí.*	see
No.	*No.*	no
Please.	*Por favor.*	por fa·*vor*
Thank you (very much).	*(Muchas) Gracias.*	(*moo*·chas) *gra*·thyas
You're welcome.	*De nada.*	de *na*·da
Excuse me.	*Perdón/Discúlpeme.*	per·*don*/dees·*kool*·pe·me
Sorry.	*Lo siento.*	lo *syen*·to

numbers

0	cero	*the*·ro	16	dieciséis	dye·thee·*seys*
1	uno	*oo*·no	17	diecisiete	dye·thee·*sye*·te
2	dos	dos	18	dieciocho	dye·thee·*o*·cho
3	tres	tres	19	diecinueve	dye·thee·*nwe*·ve
4	cuatro	*kwa*·tro	20	veinte	*veyn*·te
5	cinco	*theen*·ko	21	veintiuno	veyn·tee·*oo*·no
6	seis	seys	22	veintidós	veyn·tee·*dos*
7	siete	*sye*·te	30	treinta	*treyn*·ta
8	ocho	*o*·cho	40	cuarenta	kwa·*ren*·ta
9	nueve	*nwe*·ve	50	cincuenta	theen·*kwen*·ta
10	diez	dyeth	60	sesenta	se·*sen*·ta
11	once	*on*·the	70	setenta	se·*ten*·ta
12	doce	*do*·the	80	ochenta	o·*chen*·ta
13	trece	*tre*·the	90	noventa	no·*ven*·ta
14	catorce	ka·*tor*·the	100	cien	thyen
15	quince	*keen*·the	1000	mil	mil

time & dates

What time is it?	¿Qué hora es?	ke *o*·ra es
It's one o'clock.	Es la una.	es la *oo*·na
It's (10) o'clock.	Son (las diez).	son (las dyeth)
Quarter past (one).	Es (la una) y cuarto.	es (la *oo*·na) ee *kwar*·to
Half past (one).	Es (la una) y media.	es (la *oo*·na) ee *me*·dya
Quarter to (one).	Es (la una) menos cuarto.	es (la *oo*·na) *me*·nos *kwar*·to
At what time ...?	¿A qué hora ...?	a ke *o*·ra ...
At ...	A las ...	a las ...
am	de la mañana	de la ma·*nya*·na
pm	de la tarde	de la *tar*·de
Monday	lunes	*loo*·nes
Tuesday	martes	*mar*·tes
Wednesday	miércoles	*myer*·ko·les
Thursday	jueves	*khwe*·ves
Friday	viernes	*vyer*·nes
Saturday	sábado	*sa*·ba·do
Sunday	domingo	do·*meen*·go

January	enero	e·*ne*·ro
February	febrero	fe·*bre*·ro
March	marzo	*mar*·tho
April	abril	a·*breel*
May	mayo	*ma*·yo
June	junio	khoo·nyo
July	julio	khoo·lyo
August	agosto	a·*gos*·to
September	septiembre	sep·*tyem*·bre
October	octubre	ok·*too*·bre
November	noviembre	no·*vyem*·bre
December	diciembre	dee·*thyem*·bre

What date is it today?
¿Qué día es hoy?   ke *dee*·a es oy

It's (18 October).
Es (el dieciocho de octubre).   es (el dye·thee·o·cho de ok·*too*·bre)

| since (May) | desde (mayo) | *des*·de (*ma*·yo) |
| until (June) | hasta (junio) | *as*·ta (khoo·nyo) |

last ...		
night	anoche	a·*no*·che
week	la semana pasada	la se·*ma*·na pa·*sa*·da
month	el mes pasado	el mes pa·*sa*·do
year	el año pasado	el *a*·nyo pa·*sa*·do

next ...	... que viene	... ke *vye*·ne
week	la semana	la se·*ma*·na
month	el mes	el mes
year	el año	el *a*·nyo

yesterday/tomorrow ...	ayer/mañana por la ...	a·*yer*/ma·*nya*·na por la ...
morning	mañana	ma·*nya*·na
afternoon	tarde	*tar*·de
evening	noche	*no*·che

weather

What's the weather like?	¿Qué tiempo hace?	ke *tyem*·po *a*·the
It's ...		
cloudy	Está nublado.	es·*ta* noo·*bla*·do
cold	Hace frío.	*a*·the *free*·o
hot	Hace calor.	*a*·the ka·*lor*
raining	Está lloviendo.	es·*ta* lyo·*vyen*·do
snowing	Está nevando.	es·*ta* ne·*van*·do
sunny	Hace sol.	*a*·the sol
warm	Hace calor.	*a*·the ka·*lor*
windy	Hace viento.	*a*·the *vyen*·to
spring	primavera f	pree·ma·*ve*·ra
summer	verano m	ve·*ra*·no
autumn	otoño m	o·*to*·nyo
winter	invierno m	een·*vyer*·no

border crossing

I'm here ...	Estoy aquí ...	es·*toy* a·*kee* ...
in transit	en tránsito	en *tran*·see·to
on business	de negocios	de ne·*go*·thyos
on holiday	de vacaciones	de va·ka·*thyo*·nes
I'm here for ...	Estoy aquí por ...	es·*toy* a·*kee* por ...
(10) days	(diez) días	(dyeth) *dee*·as
(three) weeks	(tres) semanas	(tres) se·*ma*·nas
(two) months	(dos) meses	(dos) *me*·ses

I'm going to (Salamanca).
Voy a (Salamanca).   voy a (sa·la·*man*·ka)

I'm staying at the (Flores Hotel).
Me estoy alojando en (hotel Flores).   me es·*toy* a·lo·*khan*·do en (o·*tel* flo·res)

I have nothing to declare.
No tengo nada que declarar.   no *ten*·go *na*·da ke dek·la·*rar*

I have something to declare.
Quisiera declarar algo.   kee·*sye*·ra dek·la·*rar* al·go

That's (not) mine.
Eso (no) es mío.   eso (no) es *mee*·o

transport

tickets & luggage

Where can I buy a ticket?
¿Dónde puedo comprar un billete? don·de *pwe*·do kom·*prar* oon bee·*lye*·te

Do I need to book a seat?
¿Tengo que reservar? *ten*·go ke rre·ser·*var*

One ... ticket to (Barcelona), please.	*Un billete ... a (Barcelona), por favor.*	oon bee·*lye*·te ... a (bar·the·*lo*·na) por fa·*vor*
one-way	*sencillo*	sen·*thee*·lyo a
return	*de ida y vuelta*	de *ee*·da ee *vwel*·ta

I'd like to ...	*Me gustaría ...*	me goos·ta·*ree*·a ...
my ticket.	*mi billete.*	mee bee·*lye*·te
cancel	*cancelar*	kan·the·*lar*
change	*cambiar*	kam·*byar*
confirm	*confirmar*	kon·feer·*mar*

I'd like a ... seat.	*Quisiera un asiento ...*	kee·*sye*·ra oon a·*syen*·to ...
nonsmoking	*de no fumadores*	de no foo·ma·*do*·res
smoking	*de fumadores*	de foo·ma·*do*·res

How much is it?
¿Cuánto cuesta? *kwan*·to *kwes*·ta

Is there air conditioning?
¿Hay aire acondicionado? ai *ai*·re a·kon·dee·thyo·*na*·do

Is there a toilet?
¿Hay servicios? ai ser·*vee*·thyos

How long does the trip take?
¿Cuánto se tarda? *kwan*·to se *tar*·da

Is it a direct route?
¿Es un viaje directo? es oon *vya*·khe dee·*rek*·to

I'd like a luggage locker.
Quisiera un casillero de consigna. kee·*sye*·ra oon ka·see·*lye*·ro de kon·*seeg*·na

My luggage	Mis maletas	mees ma·le·tas
has been ...	han sido ...	an see·do ...
damaged	dañadas	da·nya·das
lost	perdidas	per·dee·das
stolen	robadas	rro·ba·das

getting around

Where does flight (G10) arrive/depart?
¿Dónde llega/sale el vuelo (G10)? don·de lye·ga/sa·le el vwe·lo (khe dyeth)

Where's the ...?	¿Dónde está...?	don·de es·ta ...
arrivals hall	el hall de partidas	el hol de par·tee·das
departures hall	el hall de llegadas	el hol de lye·ga·das
duty-free shop	la tienda libre de	la tyen·da lee·bre de
	impuestos	eem·pwe·stos
gate (12)	la puerta (doce)	la pwer·ta (do·the)

Is this the ...	¿Es el ... para	es el ... pa·ra
to (Valencia)?	(Valencia)?	(va·len·thya)
boat	barco	bar·ko
bus	autobús	ow·to·boos
plane	avión	a·vyon
train	tren	tren

What time's	¿A qué hora es el	a ke o·ra es el
the ... bus?	... autobús?	... ow·to·boos
first	primer	pree·mer
last	último	ool·tee·mo
next	próximo	prok·see·mo

At what time does it arrive/leave?
¿A qué hora llega/sale? a ke o·ra lye·ga/sa·le

How long will it be delayed?
¿Cuánto tiempo se retrasará? kwan·to tyem·po se rre·tra·sa·ra

What station/stop is this?
¿Cuál es esta estación/parada? kwal es es·ta es·ta·thyon/pa·ra·da

What's the next station/stop?
¿Cuál es la próxima kwal es la prok·see·ma
estación/parada? es·ta·thyon/pa·ra·da

Does it stop at (Aranjuez)?
¿Para en (Aranjuez)?   pa·ra en (a·*ran*·khweth)

Please tell me when we get to (Seville).
¿Puede avisarme   *pwe*·de a·vee·*sar*·me
cuando lleguemos a (Sevilla)?   kwan·do lye·*ge*·mos a (se·*vee*·lya)

How long do we stop here?
¿Cuánto tiempo vamos a parar aquí? kwan·to *tyem*·po va·mos a pa·*rar* a·*kee*

Is this seat available?
¿Está libre este asiento?   es·*ta* lee·bre *es*·te a·*syen*·to

That's my seat.
Ése es mi asiento.   *e*·se es mee a·*syen*·to

I'd like a taxi ...   Quisiera un taxi ...   kee·*sye*·ra oon *tak*·see ...
  at (9am)   a (las nueve   a (las *nwe*·ve
                        de la mañana)   de la ma·*nya*·na)
  now   ahora   a·*o*·ra
  tomorrow   mañana   ma·*nya*·na

Is this taxi available?
¿Está libre este taxi?   es·*ta* lee·bre *es*·te *tak*·see

How much is it to ...?
¿Cuánto cuesta ir a ...?   kwan·to *kwes*·ta eer a ...

Please put the meter on.
Por favor, ponga el taxímetro.   por fa·*vor* pon·ga el tak·*see*·me·tro

Please take me to (this address).
Por favor, lléveme a (esta dirección). por fa·*vor* lye·ve·me a (es·ta dee·rek·*thyon*)

Please ...   Por favor ...   por fa·*vor* ...
  slow down   vaya más despacio   va·ya mas des·*pa*·thyo
  stop here   pare aquí   pa·re a·*kee*
  wait here   espere aquí   es·*pe*·re a·*kee*

car, motorbike & bicycle hire

I'd like to hire a ...   Quisiera alquilar ...   kee·*sye*·ra al·*kee*·lar ...
  bicycle   una bicicleta   *oo*·na bee·thee·*kle*·ta
  car   un coche   oon *ko*·che
  motorbike   una moto   *oo*·na *mo*·to

with ...	con ...	kon ...
a driver	*chófer*	*cho*·fer
air conditioning	*aire acondicionado*	*ai*·re a·kon·dee·thyo·*na*·do
antifreeze	*anticongelante*	an·tee·kon·khe·*lan*·te
snow chains	*cadenas de nieve*	ka·*de*·nas de *nye*·ve

How much for	*¿Cuánto cuesta*	*kwan*·to *kwes*·ta
... hire?	*el alquiler por ...?*	el al·*kee*·ler por ...
hourly	*hora*	*o*·ra
daily	*día*	*dee*·a
weekly	*semana*	se·*ma*·na

air	*aire* m	*ai*·re
oil	*aceite* m	a·*they*·te
petrol	*gasolina* f	ga·so·*lee*·na
tyres	*neumáticos* f pl	ne·oo·*ma*·tee·kos

I need a mechanic.
Necesito un mecánico.   ne·the·*see*·to oon me·*ka*·nee·ko

I've run out of petrol.
Me he quedado sin gasolina.   me e ke·*da*·do seen ga·so·*lee*·na

I have a flat tyre.
Tengo un pinchazo.   *ten*·go oon peen·*cha*·tho

directions

Where's the ...?	*¿Dónde está/ están ...?* sg/pl	*don*·de es·*ta*/ es·*tan* ...
bank	*el banco* sg	el *ban*·ko
city centre	*el centro de la ciudad* sg	el *then*·tro de la theew·*da*
hotel	*el hotel* sg	el o·*tel*
market	*el mercado* sg	el mer·*ka*·do
police station	*la comisaría* sg	la ko·mee·sa·*ree*·a
post office	*el correos* sg	el ko·*rre*·os
public toilet	*los servicios* pl	los ser·*vee*·thyos
tourist office	*la oficina de turismo* sg	la o·fee·*thee*·na de too·*rees*·mo

Is this the road to (Valladolid)?

¿Se va a (Valladolid) por esta carretera? — se va a (va·lya·do·*lee*) por *es*·ta ka·rre·*te*·ra

Can you show me (on the map)?

¿Me lo puede indicar (en el mapa)? — me lo *pwe*·de een·dee·*kar* (en el *ma*·pa)

What's the address?

¿Cuál es la dirección? — kwal es la dee·rek·*thyon*

How far is it?

¿A cuánta distancia está? — a *kwan*·ta dees·*tan*·thya es·ta

How do I get there?

¿Cómo se llega ahí? — *ko*·mo se *lye*·ga a·*ee*

Turn ...	*Doble ...*	*do*·ble ...
at the corner	*en la esquina*	en la es·*kee*·na
at the traffic lights	*en el semáforo*	en el se·*ma*·fo·ro
left	*a la izquierda*	a la eeth·*kyer*·da
right	*a la iderecha*	a la de·*re*·cha

It's ...	*Está ...*	es·ta ...
behind ...	*detrás de ...*	de·*tras* de ...
far away	*lejos*	*le*·khos
here	*aquí*	a·*kee*
in front of ...	*enfrente de ...*	en·*fren*·te de ...
left	*por la izquierda*	por la eeth·*kyer*·da
near (to ...)	*cerca (de ...)*	*ther*·ka (de ...)
next to ...	*al lado de ...*	al *la*·do de ...
opposite ...	*frente a ...*	*fren*·te a ...
right	*por la derecha*	por la de·*re*·cha
straight ahead	*todo recto*	*to*·do *rrek*·to
there	*ahí*	a·*ee*

by bus	*por autobús*	por ow·to·boos
by taxi	*por taxi*	por *tak*·see
by train	*por tren*	por tren
on foot	*a pie*	a pye

north	*norte* m	*nor*·te
south	*sur* m	soor
east	*este* m	*es*·te
west	*oeste* m	o·*es*·te

signs

Acceso/Salida	ak·*the*·so/sa·*lee*·da	**Entrance/Exit**
Abierto/Cerrado	a·*byer*·to/the·*rra*·do	**Open/Closed**
Hay Lugar	ai loo·*gar*	**Rooms Available**
No Hay Lugar	no ai loo·*gar*	**No Vacancies**
Información	een·for·ma·*thyon*	**Information**
Comisaría	ko·mee·sa·*ree*·a	**Police Station**
de Policía	de po·lee·*thee*·a	
Prohibido	pro·ee·*bee*·do	**Prohibited**
Servicios	ser·*vee*·thyos	**Toilets**
Caballeros	ka·ba·*lye*·ros	**Men**
Señoras	se·*nyo*·ras	**Women**
Caliente/Frío	ka·*lyen*·te/*free*·o	**Hot/Cold**

accommodation

finding accommodation

Where's a ...?	*¿Dónde hay ...?*	don·de ai ...
camping ground	*un terreno de cámping*	oon te·*rre*·no de *kam*·peeng
guesthouse	*una pensión*	*oo*·na pen·*syon*
hotel	*un hotel*	oon o·*tel*
youth hostel	*un albergue juvenil*	oon al·*ber*·ge khoo·ve·*neel*

Can you recommend somewhere ...?	*¿Puede recomendar algún sitio ...?*	pwe·de rre·ko·men·*dar* al·*goon* see·tio ...
cheap	*barato*	ba·*ra*·to
good	*bueno*	*bwe*·no
nearby	*cercano*	ther·*ka*·no

I'd like to book a room, please.
Quisiera reservar una habitación.   kee·*sye*·ra rre·ser·*var* *oo*·na a·bee·ta·*thyon*

I have a reservation.
He hecho una reserva.   e *e*·cho *oo*·na rre·*ser*·va

My name's ...
Me llamo ...   me *lya*·mo ...

accommodation – SPANISH

Do you have a ... room?	¿Tiene una habitación ...?	tye·ne oo·na a·bee·ta·thyon ...
single	individual	een·dee·vee·dwal
double	doble	do·ble
twin	con dos camas	kon dos ka·mas

How much is it per ...?	¿Cuánto cuesta por ...?	kwan·to kwes·ta por ...
night	noche	no·che
person	persona	per·so·na

Can I pay by ...?	¿Puedo pagar con ...?	pwe·do pa·gar con ...
credit card	tarjeta de crédito	tar·khe·ta de kre·dee·to
travellers cheque	cheque de viajero	che·ke de vya·khe·ro

I'd like to stay for (three) nights/weeks.
Quisiera quedarme por (tres) noches/semanas.
kee·sye·ra ke·dar·me por (tres) no·ches/se·ma·nas

From (July 2) to (July 6).
Desde (el dos de julio)
hasta (el seis de julio).
des·de (el dos de khoo·lyo)
as·ta (el seys de khoo·lyo)

Can I see it?
¿Puedo verla?
pwe·do ver·la

Am I allowed to camp here?
¿Se puede acampar aquí?
se pwe·de a·kam·par a·kee

Is there a camp site nearby?
¿Hay un terreno de cámping cercano?
ai oon te·rre·no de kam·peeng ther·ka·no

requests & queries

When/Where's breakfast served?
¿Cuándo/Dónde se sirve el desayuno?
kwan·do/don·de se seer·ve el de·sa·yoo·no

Please wake me at (seven).
Por favor, despiérteme a (las siete).
por fa·vor des·pyer·te·me a (las sye·te)

Could I have my key, please?
¿Me puede dar la llave, por favor?
me pwe·de dar la lya·ve por fa·vor

Can I get another (blanket)?
¿Puede darme otra (manta)?
pwe·de dar·me ot·ra (man·ta)

Is there a/an ...?	¿Hay ...?	ai ...
elevator	ascensor	as·then·sor
safe	una caja fuerte	oo·na ka·kha fwer·te

The room is too ...	Es demasiado ...	es de·ma·sya·do ...
expensive	cara	ka·ra
noisy	ruidosa	rrwee·do·sa
small	pequeña	pe·ke·nya

The ... doesn't work.	No funciona ...	no foon·thyo·na ...
air conditioning	el aire	el ai·re
	acondicionado	a·kon·dee·thyo·na·do
fan	el ventilador	el ven·tee·la·dor
toilet	el retrete	el rre·tre·te

This ... isn't clean.	Esta ... no está limpia.	es·ta ... no es·ta leem·pya
pillow	almohada	al·mwa·da
sheet	sábana	sa·ba·na
towel	toalla	to·a·lya

checking out

What time is checkout?
¿A qué hora hay que dejar   a ke o·ra ai ke de·khar
libre la habitación?   lee·bre la a·bee·ta·thyon

Can I leave my luggage here?
¿Puedo dejar las maletas aquí?   pwe·do de·khar las ma·le·tas a·kee

Could I have ..., please?	¿Me puede dar ..., por favor?	me pwe·de dar ... por fa·vor
my deposit	mi depósito	mee de·po·see·to
my passport	mi pasaporte	mee pa·sa·por·te
my valuables	mis objetos de valor	mees ob·khe·tos de va·lor

communications & banking

the internet

Where's the local Internet café?
¿Dónde hay un cibercafé cercano? — *don*-de ai oon thee-ber-ka-*fe* ther-*ka*-no

How much is it per hour?
¿Cuánto cuesta por hora? — *kwan*-to *kwes*-ta por *o*-ra

I'd like to ...	*Quisiera ...*	kee-*sye*-ra ...
check my email	*revisar mi correo electrónico*	rre-vee-*sar* mee ko-*re*-o e-lek-*tro*-nee-ko
get Internet access	*usar el Internet*	oo-*sar* el *een*-ter-net
use a printer	*usar una impresora*	oo-*sar* oo-na eem-pre-*so*-ra
use a scanner	*usar un escáner*	oo-*sar* oon es-*ka*-ner

mobile/cell phone

I'd like a ...	*Quisiera ...*	kee-*sye*-ra ...
mobile/cell phone for hire	*un móvil para alquilar*	oon *mo*-veel *pa*-ra al-kee-*lar*
SIM card for your network	*una tarjeta SIM para su red*	oo-na tar-*khe*-ta seem *pa*-ra soo rred

What are the rates?
¿Cuál es la tarifa? — kwal es la ta-*ree*-fa

telephone

What's your phone number?
¿Cuál es su/tu número de teléfono? pol/inf — kwal es soo/too *noo*-me-ro de te-*le*-fo-no

The number is ...
El número es ... — el *noo*-me-ro es ...

Where's the nearest public phone?
¿Dónde hay una cabina telefónica? — *don*-de ai *oo*-na ka-*bee*-na te-le-*fo*-nee-ka

I'd like to buy a phonecard.
Quiero comprar una tarjeta telefónica. — *kye*-ro kom-*prar* oo-na tar-*khe*-ta te-le-*fo*-nee-ka

I want to ...	Quiero ...	kye·ro ...
call (Singapore)	hacer una llamada (a Singapur)	a·ther oo·na lya·ma·da (a seen·ga·poor)
make a local call	hacer una llamada local	a·ther oo·na lya·ma·da lo·kal
reverse the charges	hacer una llamada a cobro revertido	a·ther oo·na lya·ma·da a ko·bro rre·ver·tee·do

How much does ... cost?	¿Cuánto cuesta ...?	kwan·to kwes·ta ...
a (three)-minute call	una llamada de (tres) minutos	oo·na lya·ma·da de (tres) mee·noo·tos
each extra minute	cada minuto extra	ka·da mee·noo·to ek·stra

It's (one euro) per (minute).
(Un euro) por (un minuto). (oon e·oo·ro) por (oon mee·noo·to)

post office

I want to send a ...	Quisiera enviar ...	kee·sye·ra en·vee·ar ...
fax	un fax	oon faks
letter	una carta	oo·na kar·ta
parcel	un paquete	oon pa·ke·te
postcard	una postal	oo·na pos·tal

I want to buy ...	Quisiera comprar ...	kee·sye·ra kom·prar ...
an envelope	un sobre	oon so·bre
stamps	sellos	se·lyos

Please send it (to Australia) by ...	Por favor, mándelo (a Australia) por ...	por fa·vor man·de·lo (a ows·tra·lya) por ...
airmail	vía aérea	vee·a a·e·re·a
express mail	correo urgente	ko·rre·o oor·khen·te
registered mail	correo certificado	ko·rre·o ther·tee·fee·ka·do
surface mail	vía terrestre	vee·a te·rres·tre

Is there any mail for me?
¿Hay alguna carta para mí? ai al·goo·na kar·ta pa·ra mee

bank

Where's a/an ...?	¿Dónde hay ...?	don·de ai ...
ATM	un cajero automático	oon ka·khe·ro ow·to·ma·tee·ko o
foreign exchange office	una oficina de cambio	oo·na o·fee·thee·na de kam·byo
I'd like to ...	Me gustaría ...	me goos·ta·ree·a ...
cash a cheque	cambiar un cheque	kam·byar oon che·ke
change a travellers cheque	cobrar un cheque de viajero	ko·brar oon che·ke de vee·a·khe·ro
change money	cambiar dinero	kam·byar dee·ne·ro
get a cash advance	obtener un adelanto	ob·te·ner oon a·de·lan·to
withdraw money	sacar dinero	sa·kar dee·ne·ro
What's the ...?	¿Cuál es ...?	kwal es ...
commission	la comisión	la ko·mee·syon
exchange rate	el tipo de cambio	el tee·po de kam·byo
It's (12) euros.	Es (doce) euros.	es (do·the) e·oo·ros
It's free.	Es gratis.	es gra·tees

What's the charge for that?
¿Cuánto hay que pagar por eso?   kwan·to ai ke pa·gar por e·so

What time does the bank open?
¿A qué hora abre el banco?   a ke o·ra a·bre el ban·ko

Has my money arrived yet?
¿Ya ha llegado mi dinero?   ya a lye·ga·do mee dee·ne·ro

sightseeing

getting in

What time does it open/close?
¿A qué hora abren/cierran?   a ke o·ra ab·ren/thye·rran

What's the admission charge?
¿Cuánto cuesta la entrada?   kwan·to kwes·ta la en·tra·da

Is there a discount for children/students?
¿Hay descuentos para niños/estudiantes?   ai des·kwen·tos pa·ra nee·nyos/es·too·dyan·tes

I'd like a ...	Quisiera ...	kee-*sye*-ra ...
catalogue	un catálogo	oon ka-*ta*-lo-go
guide	una guía	*oo*-na *gee*-a
(local) map	un mapa (de la zona)	oon *ma*-pa (de la *tho*-na)

I'd like to see ...	Me gustaría ver ...	me goos-ta-*ree*-a ver ...
What's that?	¿Qué es eso?	ke es *e*-so
Can I take a photo?	¿Puedo tomar un foto?	*pwe*-do to-*mar* un *fo*-to

tours

When's the next day trip?
¿Cuándo es la próxima   *kwan*-do es la *prok*-see-ma
excursión de un día?   eks-koor-*syon* de oon *dee*-a

When's the next tour?
¿Cuándo es el próximo recorrido?   *kwan*-do es ela *prok*-see-mo rre-ko-*rree*-do

Is ... included?	¿Incluye ...?	een-*kloo*-ye ...
accommodation	alojamiento	a-lo-kha-*myen*-to
the admission charge	entrada	en-*tra*-da
food	comida	ko-*mee*-da
transport	transporte	trans-*por*-te

How long is the tour?
¿Cuánto dura el recorrido?   *kwan*-to *doo*-ra el rre-ko-*rree*-do

What time should we be back?
¿A qué hora tenemos que volver?   a ke *o*-ra te-*ne*-mos ke vol-*ver*

sightseeing

castle	castillo m	kas-*tee*-lyo
cathedral	catedral f	ka-te-*dral*
church	iglesia f	ee-*gle*-sya
main square	plaza mayor f	*pla*-tha ma-*yor*
monastery	monasterio m	mo-na-*ste*-ryo
monument	monumento m	mo-noo-*men*-to
museum	museo m	moo-*se*-o
old city	casco antiguo m	*kas*-ko an-*tee*-gwo
palace	palacio m	pa-*la*-thyo
ruins	ruinas f pl	*rrwee*-nas
stadium	estadio m	es-*ta*-dyo
statues	estatuas f pl	es-*ta*-twas

shopping

enquiries

Where's a ...?	¿Dónde está ...?	don·de es·ta ...
bank	el banco	el ban·ko
bookshop	la librería	la lee·bre·ree·a
camera shop	la tienda de fotografía	la tyen·da de fo·to·gra·fee·a
department store	el centro comercial	el then·tro ko·mer·thyal
grocery store	la tienda de comestibles	la tyen·da de ko·mes·tee·bles
market	el mercado	el mer·ka·do
newsagency	el quiosco	el kyos·ko
supermarket	el supermercado	el soo·per·mer·ka·do

Where can I buy (a padlock)?
¿Dónde puedo comprar (un candado)?
don·de pwe·do kom·prar (oon kan·da·do)

I'm looking for ...
Estoy buscando ...
es·toy boos·kan·do ...

Can I look at it?
¿Puedo verlo?
pwe·do ver·lo

Do you have any others?
¿Tiene otros?
tye·ne o·tros

Does it have a guarantee?
¿Tiene garantía?
tye·ne ga·ran·tee·a

Can I have it sent overseas?
¿Pueden enviarlo por correo a otro país?
pwe·den en·vee·ar·lo por ko·rre·o a o·tro pa·ees

Can I have my ... repaired?
¿Puede reparar mi ... aquí?
pwe·de rre·pa·rar mee ... a·kee

It's faulty.
Es defectuoso.
es de·fek·too·o·so

I'd like …, please.	Quisiera …, por favor.	kee·*sye*·ra … por fa·*vor*
a bag	una bolsa	*oo*·na *bol*·sa
a refund	que me devuelva	ke me de·*vwel*·va
	el dinero	el dee·*ne*·ro
to return this	devolver esto	de·vol·*ver* es·to

paying

How much is it?
  ¿Cuánto cuesta esto?   *kwan*·to *kwes*·ta es·to

Can you write down the price?
  ¿Puede escribir el precio?   *pwe*·de es·kree·*beer* el *pre*·thyo

That's too expensive.
  Es muy caro.   es mooy *ka*·ro

What's your lowest price?
  ¿Cuál es su precio más bajo?   kwal es soo *pre*·thyo mas *ba*·kho

I'll give you (five) euros.
  Te daré (cinco) euros.   te da·*re* (*theen*·ko) e·oo·ros

There's a mistake in the bill.
  Hay un error en la cuenta.   ai oon e·*rror* en la *kwen*·ta

Do you accept …?	¿Aceptan …?	a·*thep*·tan …
credit cards	tarjetas de crédito	tar·*khe*·tas de *kre*·dee·to
debit cards	tarjetas de débito	tar·*khe*·tas de *de*·bee·to
travellers cheques	cheques de viajero	*che*·kes de vya·*khe*·ro

I'd like …, please.	Quisiera …, por favor.	kee·*sye*·ra … por fa·*vor*
a receipt	un recibo	oon rre·*thee*·bo
my change	mi cambio	mee *kam*·byo

clothes & shoes

Can I try it on?	¿Me lo puedo probar?	me lo *pwe*·do pro·*bar*
My size is (40).	Uso la talla (cuarenta).	*oo*·so la *ta*·lya (kwa·*ren*·ta)
It doesn't fit.	No me queda bien.	no me *ke*·da byen

small	pequeño/a m/f	pe·*ke*·nyo/a
medium	mediano/a m/f	me·*dya*·no/a
large	grande m&f	*gran*·de

books & music

I'd like a ...	Quisiera un ...	kee·*sye*·ra oon ...
newspaper	periódico	pe·*ryo*·dee·ko
(in English)	(en inglés)	(en een·*gles*)
pen	bolígrafo	bo·*lee*·gra·fo

Is there an English-language bookshop?
¿Hay alguna librería en inglés?   ai al·*goo*·na lee·bre·*ree*·a en een·*gles*

I'm looking for something by (Enrique Iglesias).
Estoy buscando algo de   es·*toy* boos·*kan*·do *al*·go de
(Enrique Iglesias).   (en·*ree*·ke ee·*gle*·syas)

Can I listen to this?
¿Puedo escuchar esto aquí?   *pwe*·do es·koo·*char* es·to a·*kee*

photography

Can you ...?	¿Puede usted ...?	*pwe*·de oos·*ted* ...
burn a CD from	copiar un disco	ko·*pyar* oon *dees*·ko
my memory card	compacto de esta	kom·*pak*·to de *es*·ta
	tarjeta de memoria	tar·*khe*·ta de me·*mo*·rya
develop this film	revelar este carrete	rre·ve·*lar* es·te ka·*rre*·te
load my film	cargar el carrete	kar·*gar* el ka·*rre*·te

I need a ... film	Necesito película ...	ne·the·*see*·to pe·*lee*·koo·la ...
for this camera.	para esta cámara.	*pa*·ra *es*·ta *ka*·ma·ra
APS	APS	a pe *e*·se
B&W	en blanco y negro	en *blan*·ko y *ne*·gro
colour	en color	en ko·*lor*
slide	para diapositivas	*pa*·ra dya·po·see·*tee*·vas
(200) speed	de sensibilidad	de sen·see·bee·lee·*da*
	(doscientos)	(dos·*thyen*·tos)

When will it be ready?   ¿Cuándo estará listo?   *kwan*·do es·ta·*ra* *lees*·to

meeting people

greetings, goodbyes & introductions

Hello/Hi.	*Hola.*	o·la
Good night.	*Buenas noches.*	bwe·nas no·ches
Goodbye/Bye.	*Adiós.*	a·dyos
See you later.	*Hasta luego.*	as·ta lwe·go
Mr	*Señor*	se·nyor
Mrs	*Señora*	se·nyo·ra
Miss	*Señorita*	se·nyo·ree·ta
How are you?	*¿Qué tal?*	ke tal
Fine, thanks.	*Bien, gracias.*	byen gra·thyas
And you?	*¿Y Usted/tú?* pol/inf	ee oos·te/too
What's your name?	*¿Cómo se llama Usted?* pol	ko·mo se lya·ma oos·te
	¿Cómo te llamas? inf	ko·mo te lya·mas
My name is ...	*Me llamo ...*	me lya·mo ...
I'm pleased to meet you.	*Mucho gusto.*	moo·cho goos·to

This is my ...	*Éste/Ésta es mi ...* m/f	es·te/a es mee ...
boyfriend	*novio*	no·vyo
brother	*hermano*	er·ma·no
daughter	*hija*	ee·kho
father	*padre*	pa·dre
friend	*amigo/a* m/f	a·mee·go/a
girlfriend	*novia*	no·vya
husband	*marido*	ma·ree·do
mother	*madre*	ma·dre
partner (intimate)	*pareja*	pa·re·kha
sister	*hermana*	er·ma·na
son	*hijo*	ee·kho
wife	*esposa*	es·po·sa

Here's my ...	*Éste/Ésta es mi ...* m/f	es·te/a es mee ...
What's your ...?	*¿Cuál es su/tu ...?* pol/inf	kwal es soo/too ...
address	*dirección* f	dee·rek·thyon
email address	*dirección de email* f	dee·rek·thyon de ee·mayl
fax number	*número de fax* m	noo·me·ro de faks
phone number	*número de teléfono* m	noo·me·ro de te·le·fo·no

occupations

What's your occupation?	¿A qué se dedica Usted? pol	a ke se de·dee·ka oos·te
	¿A qué te dedicas? inf	a ke te de·dee·kas
I'm a/an ...	Soy un/una ... m/f	soy oon/oo·na ...
artist	artista m&f	ar·tees·ta
business person	comerciante m&f	ko·mer·thyan·te
farmer	agricultor m	a·gree·kool·tor
	agricultora f	a·gree·kool·to·ra
manual worker	obrero/a m/f	o·bre·ro/a
office worker	oficinista m&f	o·fee·thee·nees·ta
scientist	científico/a m/f	thyen·tee·fee·ko/a
student	estudiante m&f	es·too·dyan·te
tradesperson	artesano/a m/f	ar·te·sa·no/a

background

Where are you from?	¿De dónde es Usted? pol	de don·de es oos·te
	¿De dónde eres? inf	de don·de e·res
I'm from ...	Soy de ...	soy de ...
Australia	Australia	ow·stra·lya
Canada	Canadá	ka·na·da
England	Inglaterra	een·gla·te·rra
New Zealand	Nueva Zelanda	nwe·va the·lan·da
the USA	los Estados Unidos	los es·ta·dos oo·nee·dos
Are you married?	¿Estás casado/a? m/f	es·tas ka·sa·do/a
I'm married.	Estoy casado/a. m/f	es·toy ka·sa·do/a
I'm single.	Soy soltero/a. m/f	soy sol·te·ro/a

age

How old ...?	¿Cuántos años ...?	kwan·tos a·nyos ...
are you	tienes inf	tye·nes
is your daughter	tiene su hija pol	tye·ne soo ee·kha
is your son	tiene su hijo pol	tye·ne soo ee·kho
I'm ... years old.	Tengo ... años.	ten·go ... a·nyos
He/She is ... years old.	Tiene ... años.	tye·ne ... a·nyos

feelings

I'm (not) ...	(No) Tengo ...	(no) ten·go ...
Are you ...?	¿Tiene Usted ...? pol	tye·ne oos·te ...
	¿Tienes ...? inf	tye·nes ...
cold	frío	free·o
hot	calor	ka·lor
hungry	hambre	am·bre
thirsty	sed	se

I'm (not) ...	(No) Estoy ...	(no) es·toy ...
Are you ...?	¿Está Usted ...? pol	es·ta oos·te ...
	¿Estás ...? inf	es·tas ...
happy	feliz m&f	fe·leeth
OK	bien m&f	byen
sad	triste m&f	trees·te
tired	cansado/a m/f	kan·sa·do/a

entertainment

going out

Where can I find ...?	¿Dónde hay ...?	don·de ai ...
clubs	clubs nocturnos	kloobs nok·toor·nos
gay venues	lugares gay	loo·ga·res gai
pubs	bares	ba·res

I feel like going to a/the ...	Tengo ganas de ir ...	ten·go ga·nas de eer ...
concert	a un concierto	a oon kon·thyer·to
movies	al cine	al thee·ne
party	a una fiesta	a oo·na fyes·ta
restaurant	a un restaurante	a oon rres·tow·ran·te
theatre	al teatro	al te·a·tro

interests

Do you like ...	¿Le/Te gusta ...? **pol/inf**	le/te *goos*·ta ...
I (don't) like ...	(No) Me gusta ...	(no) me *goos*·ta ...
art	el arte	el *ar*·te
movies	el cine	el *thee*·ne
reading	leer	le·*er*
sport	el deporte	el de·*por*·te
travelling	viajar	vya·*khar*
Do you like to ...?	¿Le/Te gusta ...? **pol/inf**	le/te *goos*·ta ...
dance	ir a bailar	eer a bai·*lar*
go to concerts	ir a conciertos	eer a kon·*thyer*·tos
listen to music	escuchar música	es·koo·*char* moo·see·ka

food & drink

finding a place to eat

Can you recommend a ...?	¿Puede recomendar un ...?	*pwe*·de rre·ko·men·*dar* oon ...
bar	bar	bar
café	café	ka·*fe*
restaurant	restaurante	rres·tow·*ran*·te
I'd like ..., please.	Quisiera ..., por favor.	kee·*sye*·ra ... por fa·*vor*
a table for (two)	una mesa para (dos)	oo·na *me*·sa *pa*·ra (dos)
the (non)smoking section	(no) fumadores	(no) foo·ma·*do*·res

ordering food

breakfast	desayuno **m**	de·sa·*yoo*·no
lunch	comida **f**	ko·*mee*·da
dinner	almuerzo **m**	al·*mwer*·tho
snack	tentempié **m**	ten·tem·*pye*

What would you recommend?
   ¿Qué recomienda?   ke rre·ko·*myen*·da

I'd like (the) ...	Quisiera ..., por favor.	kee·sye·ra ... por fa·vor
bill	la cuenta	la kwen·ta
drink list	la lista de bebidas	la lees·ta de be·bee·das
menu	el menú	el me·noo
that dish	ese plato	e·se pla·to

drinks

(cup of) coffee ...	(taza de) café ...	(ta·tha de) ka·fe ...
(cup of) tea ...	(taza de) té ...	(ta·tha de) te ...
with milk	con leche	kon le·che
without sugar	sin azúcar	seen a·thoo·kar
(orange) juice	zumo de (naranja) m	zoo·mo de (na·ran·kha)
soft drink	refresco m	rre·fres·ko
... water	agua ...	a·gwa ...
boiled	hervida	er·vee·da
(sparkling) mineral	mineral (con gas)	mee·ne·ral (kon gas)

in the bar

I'll have ...	Para mí ...	pa·ra mee ...
I'll buy you a drink.	Te invito a una copa. inf	le/te een·vee·to a oo·na ko·pa
What would you like?	¿Qué quieres tomar? inf	ke kye·res to·mar
Cheers!	¡Salud!	sa·loo
brandy	coñac m	ko·nyak
cocktail	combinado m	kom·bee·na·do
red-wine punch	sangría f	san·gree·a
a shot of (whisky)	chupito de (güisqui)	choo·pee·to de (gwees·kee)
a ... of beer	una ... de cerveza	oo·na ... de ther·ve·tha
bottle	botella	bo·te·lya
glass	caña	ka·nya
a bottle/glass of	una botella/copa	oo·na bo·te·lya/ko·pa
... wine	de vino ...	de vee·no ...
red	tinto	teen·to
sparkling	espumoso	es·poo·mo·so
white	blanco	blan·ko

self-catering

What's the local speciality?
¿Cuál es la especialidad de la zona?   kwal es la es·pe·thya·lee·*da* de la *tho*·na

What's that?
¿Qué es eso?   ke es *e*·so

How much is (a kilo of cheese)?
¿Cuánto vale (un kilo de queso)?   kwan·to *va*·le (oon *kee*·lo de *ke*·so)

I'd like ...	*Póngame ...*	pon·ga·me ...
(200) grams	*(doscientos) gramos*	(dos·*thyen*·tos) *gra*·mos
(two) kilos	*(dos) kilos*	(dos) *kee*·los
(three) pieces	*(tres) piezas*	(tres) *pye*·thas
(six) slices	*(seis) lonchas*	(seys) *lon*·chas

Less.	*Menos.*	*me*·nos
Enough.	*Basta.*	*ba*·sta
More.	*Más.*	mas

special diets & allergies

Is there a vegetarian restaurant near here?
¿Hay un restaurante   ai oon rres·tow·*ran*·te
vegetariano por aquí?   ve·khe·ta·*rya*·no por a·*kee*

Do you have vegetarian food?
¿Tienen comida vegetariana?   *tye*·nen ko·*mee*·da ve·khe·ta·*rya*·na

Could you prepare a	*¿Me puede preparar*	me *pwe*·de pre·pa·*rar*
meal without ...?	*una comida sin ...?*	oo·na ko·*mee*·da seen ...
butter	*mantequilla*	man·te·*kee*·lya
eggs	*huevos*	*we*·vos
meat stock	*caldo de carne*	*kal*·do de *kar*·ne

I'm allergic to ...	*Soy alérgico/a ...* m/f	soy a·*ler*·khee·ko/a ...
dairy produce	*a los productos*	a los pro·*dook*·tos
	lácteos	*lak*·te·os
gluten	*al gluten*	al *gloo*·ten
MSG	*al glutamato*	al gloo·ta·*ma*·to
	monosódico	mo·no·*so*·dee·ko
nuts	*a las nueces*	a las *nwe*·thes
seafood	*a los mariscos*	a los ma·*rees*·kos

emergencies

basics

Help!	¡Socorro!	so·ko·ro
Stop!	¡Pare!	pa·re
Go away!	¡Váyase!	va·ya·se
Thief!	¡Ladrón!	lad·ron
Fire!	¡Fuego!	fwe·go
Watch out!	¡Cuidado!	kwee·da·do

Call ...!	¡Llame a ...!	lya·me a ...
a doctor	un médico	oon me·dee·ko
an ambulance	una ambulancia	oo·na am·boo·lan·thya
the police	la policía	la po·lee·thee·a

It's an emergency.
Es una emergencia.   es oo·na e·mer·khen·thya

Could you help me, please?
¿Me puede ayudar, por favor?   me pwe·de a·yoo·dar por fa·vor

I have to use the telephone.
Necesito usar el teléfono.   ne·the·see·to oo·sar el te·le·fo·no

I'm lost.
Estoy perdido/a. m/f   es·toy per·dee·do/a

Where are the toilets?
¿Dónde están los servicios?   don·de es·tan los ser·vee·thyos

police

Where's the police station?
¿Dónde está la comisaría?   don·de es·ta la ko·mee·sa·ree·a

I want to report an offence.
Quiero denunciar un delito.   kye·ro de·noon·thyar oon de·lee·to

I have insurance.
Tengo seguro.   ten·go se·goo·ro

I've been assaulted.	He sido asaltado/a. m/f	e see·do a·sal·ta·do/a
I've been raped.	He sido violado/a. m/f	e see·do vee·o·la·do/a
I've been robbed.	Me han robado.	me an rro·ba·do

I've lost my ...	He perdido ...	e per·dee·do ...
backpack	mi mochila	mee mo·chee·la
bags	mis maletas	mees ma·le·tas
credit card	mi tarjeta de	mee tar·khe·ta de
	crédito	kre·dee·to
handbag	mi bolso	mee bol·so
jewellery	mis joyas	mees kho·yas
money	mi dinero	mee dee·ne·ro
passport	mi pasaporte	mee pa·sa·por·te
travellers	mis cheques	mees che·kes de
cheques	de viajero	vya·khe·ro
wallet	mi cartera	mee kar·te·ra
I want to contact	Quiero ponerme en	kye·ro po·ner·me en
my ...	contacto con mi ...	kon·tak·to kon mee ...
consulate	consulado	kon·soo·la·do
embassy	embajada	em·ba·kha·da

health

medical needs

Where's the	¿Dónde está el ...	don·de es·ta el ...
nearest ...?	más cercano?	mas ther·ka·no
dentist	dentista	den·tees·ta
doctor	médico	me·dee·ko
hospital	hospital	os·pee·tal

Where's the nearest (night) pharmacist?
¿Dónde está la farmacia   don·de es·ta la far·ma·thya
(de guardia) más cercana?   (de gwar·dya) mas ther·ka·na

I need a doctor (who speaks English).
Necesito un médico   ne·the·see·to oon me·dee·ko
(que hable inglés).   (ke a·ble een·gles)

Could I see a female doctor?
¿Puede examinarme una   pwe·de ek·sa·mee·nar·me oo·na
médica?   me·dee·ka

I've run out of my medication.
Se me terminaron los   se me ter·mee·na·ron los
medicamentos.   me·dee·ka·men·tos

symptoms, conditions & allergies

| I'm sick. | *Estoy enfermo/a.* m/f | es·*toy* en·*fer*·mo/a |
| It hurts here. | *Me duele aquí.* | me *dwe*·le a·*kee* |

I have (a) ...	*Tengo...*	*ten*·go ...
asthma	*asma*	*as*·ma
bronchitis	*bronquitis*	bron·*kee*·tees
constipation	*estreñimiento*	es·tre·nyee·*myen*·to
cough	*tos*	tos
diarrhoea	*diarrea*	dya·*rre*·a
fever	*fiebre*	*fye*·bre
headache	*dolor de cabeza*	do·*lor* de ka·*be*·tha
heart condition	*una condición*	*oo*·na kon·dee·*thyon*
	cardíaca	kar·*dee*·a·ka
nausea	*náusea*	*now*·se·a
pain	*dolor*	do·*lor*
sore throat	*dolor de garganta*	do·*lor* de gar·*gan*·ta
toothache	*dolor de muelas*	do·*lor* de *mwe*·las

I'm allergic to ...	*Soy alérgico/a a ...* m/f	soy a·*ler*·khee·ko/a a ...
antibiotics	*los antibióticos*	los an·tee·*byo*·tee·kos
anti-	*los anti-*	los *an*·tee·
inflammatories	*inflamatorios*	een·fla·ma·*to*·ryos
aspirin	*la aspirina*	la as·pee·*ree*·na
bees	*las abejas*	las a·*be*·khas
codeine	*la codeina*	la ko·de·*ee*·na
penicillin	*la penicilina*	la pe·nee·thee·*lee*·na

antiseptic	*antiséptico* m	an·tee·*sep*·tee·ko
bandage	*vendaje* m	ven·*da*·khe
condoms	*condones* m pl	kon·*do*·nes
contraceptives	*anticonceptivos* m pl	an·tee·kon·thep·*tee*·vos
diarrhoea medicine	*medicina para diarrea* f	me·dee·*thee*·na *pa*·ra dya·*rre*·a
insect repellent	*repelente de insectos* m	re·pe·*len*·te de een·*sek*·tos
laxatives	*laxantes* m pl	lak·*san*·tes
painkillers	*analgésicos* m pl	a·nal·*khe*·see·kos
rehydration salts	*sales rehidratantes* f pl	*sa*·les re·eed·ra·*tan*·tes
sleeping tablets	*pastillas para dormir* f pl	pas·*tee*·lyas *pa*·ra dor·*meer*

english–spanish dictionary

Spanish nouns in this dictionary, and adjectives affected by gender, have their gender indicated by ⓜ (masculine) or ⓕ (feminine). If it's a plural noun, you'll also see pl. Words are also marked as v (verb), n (noun), a (adjective), pl (plural), sg (singular), inf (informal) and pol (polite) where necessary.

A

accident *accidente* ⓜ ak-thee-*den*-te
accommodation *alojamiento* ⓜ a-lo-kha-*myen*-to
adaptor *adaptador* ⓜ a-dap-ta-*dor*
address *dirección* ⓕ dee-rek-*thyon*
after *después de* des-*pwes* de
air-conditioned *con aire acondicionado*
    kon *ai*-re a-kon-dee-thyo-*na*-do
airplane *avión* ⓜ a-*vyon*
airport *aeropuerto* ⓜ ay-ro-*pwer*-to
alcohol *alcohol* ⓜ al-*col*
all a *todo/a* *to*-do/a
allergy *alergia* ⓕ a-*ler*-khya
ambulance *ambulancia* ⓕ am-boo-*lan*-thya
ankle *tobillo* ⓜ to-*bee*-lyo
and *y* ee
arm *brazo* ⓜ *bra*-tho
ashtray *cenicero* ⓜ the-nee-*the*-ro
ATM *cajero automático* ka-*khe*-ro ow-to-*ma*-tee-ko

B

baby *bebé* ⓜ be-*be*
back (body) *espalda* ⓕ es-*pal*-da
backpack *mochila* ⓕ mo-*chee*-la
bad *malo/a* ⓜ/ⓕ *ma*-lo/a
bag *bolso* ⓜ *bol*-so
baggage claim *recogida de equipajes* ⓕ
    rre-ko-*khee*-da de e-kee-*pa*-khes
bank *banco* ⓜ *ban*-ko
bar *bar* ⓜ bar
bathroom *baño* ⓜ *ba*-nyo
battery (general) *pila* ⓕ *pee*-la
battery (car) *batería* ⓕ ba-te-*ree*-a
beautiful *hermoso/a* ⓜ/ⓕ er-*mo*-so/a
bed *cama* ⓕ *ka*-ma
beer *cerveza* ⓕ ther-*ve*-tha
before *antes* *an*-tes
behind *detrás de* de-*tras* de
bicycle *bicicleta* ⓕ bee-thee-*kle*-ta

big *grande* *gran*-de
bill *cuenta* ⓕ *kwen*-ta
black *negro/a* ⓜ/ⓕ *ne*-gro/a
blanket *manta* ⓕ *man*-ta
blood group *grupo sanguíneo* ⓜ *groo*-po san-*gee*-neo
blue *azul* a-*thool*
boat *barco* ⓜ *bar*-ko
book (make a reservation) v *reservar* rre-ser-*var*
bottle *botella* ⓕ bo-*te*-lya
bottle opener *abrebotellas* ⓕ a-bre-bo-*te*-lyas
boy *chico* ⓜ *chee*-ko
brakes (car) *frenos* ⓜ pl *fre*-nos
breakfast *desayuno* ⓜ des-a-*yoo*-no
broken (faulty) *roto/a* ⓜ/ⓕ *ro*-to/a
bus *autobús* ⓜ ow-to-*boos*
business *negocios* ⓜ pl ne-*go*-thyos
buy *comprar* kom-*prar*

C

café *café* ⓜ ka-*fe*
camera *cámara (fotográfica)* ⓕ
    ka-ma-ra (fo-to-*gra*-fee-ka)
camp site *cámping* ⓜ *kam*-peen
cancel *cancelar* kan-the-*lar*
can opener *abrelatas* ⓕ a-bre-*la*-tas
car *coche* ⓜ *ko*-che
cash *dinero en efectivo* ⓜ dee-*ne*-ro en e-fek-*tee*-vo
cash (a cheque) v *cambiar (un cheque)*
    kam-*byar* (oon *che*-ke)
cell phone *teléfono móvil* ⓜ te-*le*-fo-no *mo*-veel
centre *centro* ⓜ *then*-tro
change (money) v *cambiar* kam-*byar*
cheap *barato/a* ⓜ/ⓕ ba-*ra*-to/a
check (bill) *cuenta* ⓕ *kwen*-ta
check-in *facturación de equipajes* ⓕ
    fak-too-ra-*thyon* de e-kee-*pa*-khes
chest *pecho* ⓜ *pe*-cho
child *niño/a* ⓜ/ⓕ *nee*-nyo/a
cigarette *cigarrillo* ⓜ thee-ga-*ree*-lyo
city *ciudad* ⓕ thee-oo-*da*
clean a *limpio/a* ⓜ/ⓕ *leem*-pyo/a

closed *cerrado/a* m/f the-*rra*-do/a
coffee *café* m ka-*fe*
coins *monedas* f pl mo-*ne*-das
cold a *frío/a* m/f *free*-o/a
collect call *llamada a cobro revertido* f
lya-*ma*-da a *ko*-bro re-ver-*tee*-do
come *venir* ve-*neer*
computer *ordenador* m or-de-na-*dor*
condom *condones* m pl kon-*do*-nes
contact lenses *lentes de contacto* m pl
len-tes de kon-*tak*-to
cook v *cocinar* ko-thee-*nar*
cost *precio* m *pre*-thyo
credit card *tarjeta de crédito* f
tar-*khe*-ta de *kre*-dee-to
cup *taza* f *ta*-tha
currency exchange *cambio de dinero* m
kam-byo de dee-*ne*-ro
customs (immigration) *aduana* f a-*dwa*-na

D

dangerous *peligroso/a* m/f pe-lee-*gro*-so/a
date (time) *fecha* f *fe*-cha
day *día* m *dee*-a
delay *demora* f de-*mo*-ra
dentist *dentista* m/f den-*tees*-ta
depart *salir de* sa-*leer* de
diaper *pañal* m pa-*nyal*
dictionary *diccionario* m deek-thyo-*na*-ryo
dinner *cena* f *the*-na
direct *directo/a* m/f dee-*rek*-to/a
dirty *sucio/a* m/f *soo*-thyo/a
disabled *minusválido/a* m/f mee-noos-*va*-lee-do/a
discount *descuento* m des-*kwen*-to
doctor *doctor/doctora* m/f dok-*tor*/dok-*to*-ra
double bed *cama de matrimonio* f
ka-ma de ma-tree-*mo*-nyo
double room *habitación doble* f a-bee-ta-*thyon do*-ble
drink *bebida* f be-*bee*-da
drive v *conducir* kon-doo-*theer*
drivers licence *carnet de conducir* m
kar-*ne* de kon-doo-*theer*
drugs (illicit) *droga* f *dro*-ga
dummy (pacifier) *chupete* m choo-*pe*-te

E

ear *oreja* f o-*re*-kha
east *este* *es*-te
eat *comer* ko-*mer*

economy class *clase turística* f *kla*-se too-*rees*-tee-ka
electricity *electricidad* f e-lek-tree-thee-*da*
elevator *ascensor* m as-then-*sor*
email *correo electrónico* m ko-rre-o e-lek-*tro*-nee-ko
embassy *embajada* f em-ba-*kha*-da
emergency *emergencia* f e-mer-*khen*-thya
English (language) *inglés* m een-*gles*
entrance *entrada* f en-*tra*-da
evening *noche* f *no*-che
exchange rate *tipo de cambio* f *tee*-po de *kam*-byo
exit *salida* f sa-*lee*-da
expensive *caro/a* m/f *ka*-ro/a
express mail *correo urgente* m ko-rre-o oor-*khen*-te
eye *ojo* m *o*-kho

F

far *lejos* *le*-khos
fast *rápido/a* m/f *rra*-pee-do/a
father *padre* m *pa*-dre
film (camera) *carrete* m ka-*rre*-te
finger *dedo* m *de*-do
first-aid kit *maletín de primeros auxilios* m
ma-le-*teen* de pree-*me*-ros ow-*ksee*-lyos
first class *de primera clase* de pree-*me*-ra *kla*-se
fish *pez* m peth
food *comida* f ko-*mee*-da
foot *pie* m pye
fork *tenedor* m te-ne-*dor*
free (of charge) *gratis* *gra*-tees
friend *amigo/a* m/f a-*mee*-go/a
fruit *fruta* f *froo*-ta
full *lleno/a* m/f *lye*-no/a
funny *gracioso/a* m/f gra-*thyo*-so/a

G

gift *regalo* m rre-*ga*-lo
girl *chica* f *chee*-ka
glass (drinking) *vaso* m *va*-so
glasses *gafas* f pl *ga*-fas
go *ir* eer
good *bueno/a* m/f *bwe*-no/a
green *verde* *ver*-de
guide n *guía* m/f *gee*-a

H

half *mitad* f mee-*tad*
hand *mano* f *ma*-no
handbag *bolso* m *bol*-so

happy *feliz* fe-*leeth*
have *tener* te-*ner*
he *él* el
head *cabeza* ① ka-*be*-tha
heart *corazón* ⓜ ko-ra-*thon*
heat *calor* ka-*lor*
heavy *pesado/a* ⓜ/① pe-*sa*-do/a
help v *ayudar* a-yoo-*dar*
here *aquí* a-*kee*
high *alto/a* ⓜ/① *al*-to/a
highway *autovía* ① ow-to-*vee*-a
hike v *ir de excursión* eer de eks-koor-*syon*
holiday *vacaciones* ① pl va-ka-*thyo*-nes
homosexual *homosexual* ⓜ/① o-mo-se-*kswal*
hospital *hospital* ⓜ os-pee-*tal*
hot *caliente* ka-*lyen*-te
hotel *hotel* ⓜ o-*tel*
hungry *hambriento/a* ⓜ/① am-bree-*en*-to/a
husband *marido* ⓜ ma-*ree*-do

I

I *yo* yo
identification (card) *carnet de identidad* ⓜ kar-*net* de ee-den-tee-*da*
ill *enfermo/a* ⓜ/① en-*fer*-mo/a
important *importante* eem-por-*tan*-te
included *incluido* een-kloo-*ee*-do
injury *herida* ① e-*ree*-da
insurance *seguro* se-*goo*-ro
Internet *Internet* een-ter-*net*
interpreter *intérprete* ⓜ/① een-*ter*-pre-te

J

jewellery *joyas* ① pl *kho*-yas
job *trabajo* ⓜ tra-*ba*-kho

K

key *llave* ① *lya*-ve
kilogram *kilogramo* ① kee-lo-*gra*-mo
kitchen *cocina* ① ko-*thee*-na
knife *cuchillo* ⓜ koo-*chee*-lyo

L

laundry (place) *lavadero* ⓜ la-va-*de*-ro
lawyer *abogado/a* ⓜ/① a-bo-*ga*-do/a
left (direction) *izquierda* ① eeth-*kyer*-da

left-luggage office *consigna* ① kon-*seeg*-na
leg *pierna* ① *pyer*-na
lesbian *lesbiana* ① les-bee-*a*-na
less *menos* *me*-nos
letter (mail) *carta* ① *kar*-ta
lift (elevator) *ascensor* ⓜ as-then-*sor*
light *luz* ① looth
like v *gustar* goos-*tar*
lock *cerradura* ① the-rra-*doo*-ra
long *largo/a* ⓜ/① *lar*-go/a
lost *perdido/a* ⓜ/① per-*dee*-do/a
lost-property office *oficina de objetos perdidos* ① o-fee-*thee*-na de ob-*khe*-tos per-*dee*-dos
love v *querer* ke-*rer*
luggage *equipaje* ⓜ e-kee-*pa*-khe
lunch *almuerzo* ⓜ al-*mwer*-tho

M

mail *correo* ⓜ ko-*rre*-o
man *hombre* ⓜ *om*-bre
map *mapa* ⓜ *ma*-pa
market *mercado* ⓜ mer-*ka*-do
matches *cerillas* ① pl the-*ree*-lyas
meat *carne* ① *kar*-ne
medicine *medicina* ① me-dee-*thee*-na
menu *menú* ⓜ me-*noo*
message *mensaje* ⓜ men-*sa*-khe
milk *leche* ① *le*-che
minute *minuto* ⓜ mee-*noo*-to
mobile phone *teléfono móvil* ⓜ te-*le*-fo-no *mo*-veel
money *dinero* ⓜ dee-*ne*-ro
month *mes* ⓜ mes
morning *mañana* ① ma-*nya*-na
mother *madre* ① *ma*-dre
motorcycle *motocicleta* ① mo-to-thee-*kle*-ta
motorway *autovía* ① ow-to-*vee*-a
mouth *boca* ① *bo*-ka
music *música* ① *moo*-see-ka

N

name *nombre* ⓜ *nom*-bre
napkin *servilleta* ① ser-vee-*lye*-ta
nappy *pañal* ⓜ pa-*nyal*
near *cerca* *ther*-ka
neck *cuello* ⓜ *kwe*-lyo
new *nuevo/a* ⓜ/① *nwe*-vo/a
news *noticias* ① pl no-*tee*-thyas
newspaper *periódico* ⓜ pe-ryo-*dee*-ko

night *noche* ① *no*-che

no *no* no

noisy *ruidoso/a* ⓜ/① rrwee-*do*-so/a

nonsmoking no fumadores no foo-ma-*do*-res

north *norte* ⓜ *nor*-te

nose *nariz* ① na-*reeth*

now *ahora* a-o-ra

number *número* ⓜ *noo*-me-ro

O

oil (engine) *aceite* ⓜ a-*they*-te

old *viejo/a* ⓜ/① *vye*-kho/a

one-way ticket *billete sencillo* bee-*lye*-te sen-*thee*-lyo

open a *abierto/a* ⓜ/① a-*byer*-to/a

outside *exterior* ⓜ eks-te-*ryor*

P

package *paquete* ⓜ pa-*ke*-te

paper *papel* ⓜ pa-*pel*

park (car) v *estacionar* es-ta-thyo-*nar*

passport *pasaporte* ⓜ pa-sa-*por*-te

pay *pagar* pa-*gar*

pen *bolígrafo* ⓜ bo-*lee*-gra-fo

petrol *gasolina* ① ga-so-*lee*-na

pharmacy *farmacia* ① far-*ma*-thya

phonecard *tarjeta de teléfono* ①
tar-*khe*-ta de te-*le*-fo-no

photo *foto* ① *fo*-to

plate *plato* ⓜ *pla*-to

police *policía* ① po-lee-*thee*-a

postcard *postal* ① pos-*tal*

post office *correos* ⓜ ko-*rre*-os

pregnant *embarazada* ① em-ba-ra-*tha*-da

price *precio* ⓜ *pre*-thyo

Q

quiet *tranquilo/a* ⓜ/① tran-*kee*-lo/a

R

rain *lluvia* ① *lyoo*-vya

razor *afeitadora* ① a-fey-ta-*do*-ra

receipt *recibo* ⓜ rre-*thee*-bo

red *rojo/a* ⓜ/① *rro*-kho/a

refund *reembolso* ⓜ rre-em-*bol*-so

registered mail *correo certificado* ⓜ
ko-*rre*-o ther-tee-fee-*ka*-do

rent v *alquilar* al-kee-*lar*

repair v *reparar* rre-pa-*rar*

reservation *reserva* ① rre-*ser*-va

restaurant *restaurante* ⓜ rres-tow-*ran*-te

return v *volver* vol-*ver*

return ticket *billete de ida y vuelta* ⓜ
bee-*lye*-te de ee-da ee *vwel*-ta

right (direction) *derecha* de-*re*-cha

road *carretera* ① ka-rre-*te*-ra

room *habitación* ① a-bee-ta-*thyon*

S

safe a *seguro/a* ⓜ/① se-*goo*-ro/a

sanitary napkin *compresas* ① pl kom-*pre*-sas

seat *asiento* ⓜ a-*syen*-to

send *enviar* en-vee-*ar*

service station *gasolinera* ① ga-so-lee-*ne*-ra

sex *sexo* ⓜ *se*-kso

shampoo *champú* ⓜ cham-*poo*

share (a dorm) *compartir* kom-par-*teer*

shaving cream *espuma de afeitar* ①
es-*poo*-ma de a-fey-*tar*

she *ella* ① *e*-lya

sheet (bed) *sábana* ① *sa*-ba-na

shirt *camisa* ① ka-*mee*-sa

shoes *zapatos* ⓜ pl tha-*pa*-tos

shop *tienda* ① *tyen*-da

short *corto/a* ⓜ/① *kor*-to/a

shower *ducha* ① *doo*-cha

single room *habitación individual* ①
a-bee-ta-*thyon* een-dee-vee-*dwal*

skin *piel* ① pyel

skirt *falda* ① *fal*-da

sleep v *dormir* dor-*meer*

slowly *despacio* des-*pa*-thyo

small *pequeño/a* ⓜ/① pe-*ke*-nyo/a

smoke (cigarettes) v *fumar* foo-*mar*

soap *jabón* ⓜ kha-*bon*

some *alguno/a* ⓜ/① al-*goo*-no/a

soon *pronto* *pron*-to

south *sur* ⓜ soor

souvenir shop *tienda de recuerdos* ①
tyen-da de re-*kwer*-dos

Spain *España* ① es-*pa*-nya

Spanish (language) *español/castellano* ⓜ
es-pa-*nyol*/kas-te-*lya*-no

speak *hablar* a-*blar*

spoon *cuchara* ① koo-*cha*-ra

stamp *sello* ⓜ *se*-lyo

stand-by ticket *billete de lista de espera* m
 bee-*lye*-te de *lees*-ta de es-*pe*-ra
station (train) *estación* f es-ta-*thyon*
stomach *estómago* m es-*to*-ma-go
stop v *parar* pa-*rar*
stop (bus) *parada* f pa-*ra*-da
street *calle* f *ka*-lye
student *estudiante* m/f es-too-*dyan*-te
sun *sol* m sol
sunscreen *crema solar* f *kre*-ma so-*lar*
swim v *nadar* na-*dar*

T

tampons *tampones* m pl tam-*po*-nes
taxi *taxi* m *tak*-see
teaspoon *cucharita* f koo-cha-*ree*-ta
teeth *dientes* m pl *dyen*-tes
telephone *teléfono* m te-*le*-fo-no
television *televisión* f te-le-vee-*syon*
temperature (weather) *temperatura* f
 tem-pe-ra-*too*-ra
tent *tienda (de campaña)* f *tyen*-da (de kam-*pa*-nya)
that (one) *ése/a* m/f *e*-se/a
they *ellos/ellas* m/f *e*-lyos/e-*lyas*
thirsty *sediento/a* m/f se-dee-*en*-to/a
this (one) *éste/a* m/f *es*-te/a
throat *garganta* f gar-*gan*-ta
ticket *billete* m bee-*lye*-te
time *tiempo* m *tyem*-po
tired *cansado/a* m/f kan-*sa*-do/a
tissues *pañuelos de papel* m pl pa-*nywe*-los de pa-*pel*
today *hoy* oy
toilet *servicio* m ser-*vee*-thyo
tomorrow *mañana* ma-*nya*-na
tonight *esta noche* es-ta *no*-che
toothbrush *cepillo de dientes* m the-*pee*-lyo de *dyen*-tes
toothpaste *pasta dentífrica* f *pas*-ta den-*tee*-free-ka
torch (flashlight) *linterna* f leen-*ter*-na
tour *excursión* f eks-koor-*syon*
tourist office *oficina de turismo* f
 o-fee-*thee*-na de too-*rees*-mo
towel *toalla* f to-*a*-lya
train *tren* m tren
translate *traducir* tra-doo-*theer*
travel agency *agencia de viajes* f
 a-*khen*-thya de *vya*-khes
travellers cheque *cheque de viajero* m
 che-ke de vya-*khe*-ro
trousers *pantalones* m pl pan-ta-*lo*-nes

twin beds *dos camas* f pl dos *ka*-mas
tyre *neumático* m ne-oo-*ma*-tee-ko

U

underwear *ropa interior* f *rro*-pa een-te-*ryor*
urgent *urgente* oor-*khen*-te

V

vacant *vacante* va-*kan*-te
vacation *vacaciones* f pl va-ka-*thyo*-nes
vegetable *verdura* f ver-*doo*-ra
vegetarian a *vegetariano/a* m/f ve-khe-ta-*rya*-no/a
visa *visado* m vee-*sa*-do

W

waiter *camarero/a* m/f ka-ma-*re*-ro/a
walk v *caminar* ka-mee-*nar*
wallet *cartera* f kar-*te*-ra
warm a *templado/a* m/f tem-*pla*-do/a
wash (something) *lavar* la-*var*
watch *reloj de pulsera* m rre-*lokh* de pool-*se*-ra
water *agua* f *a*-gwa
we *nosotros/nosotras* m/f no-*so*-tros/ no-*so*-tras
weekend *fin de semana* m feen de se-*ma*-na
west *oeste* m o-es-te
wheelchair *silla de ruedas* f *see*-lya de *rrwe*-das
when *cuando* kwan-do
where *donde* don-de
white *blanco/a* m/f *blan*-ko/a
who *quien* kyen
why *por qué* por ke
wife *esposa* f es-*po*-sa
window *ventana* f ven-*ta*-na
wine *vino* m *vee*-no
with *con* kon
without *sin* seen
woman *mujer* f moo-*kher*
write *escribir* es-kree-*beer*

Y

yellow *amarillo/a* a-ma-*ree*-lyo/a
yes *sí* see
yesterday *ayer* a-*yer*
you sg inf/pol *tú/Usted* too/oos-*te*
you pl *vosotros/vosotras* m/f vo-*so*-tros/vo-*so*-tras

Swedish

swedish alphabet

A a aa	*B b* bey	*C c* sey	*D d* dey	*E e* ey
F f ef	*G g* gey	*H h* hoh	*I i* ee	*J j* yoy
K k koh	*L l* el	*M m* em	*N n* en	*O o* oh
P p pey	*Q q* ku	*R r* er	*S s* es	*T t* tey
U u u	*V v* vey	*W w* *do*·belt vey	*X x* eks	*Y y* ew
Z z set	*Å å* aw	*Ä ä* e	*Ö ö* eu	

■ swedish

about Swedish

The Swedish language (*svenska* sven·ska) gave us *ombudsman* and *smorgasbord*, which just confirms the image of the Swedes as a nation that's good at making the most of life in more ways than one. As a member of the Germanic language family, Swedish shares common roots with English and German. German, in particular, has influenced Swedish in the form of numerous loanwords. However, the closest relatives of Swedish are, of course, the other Scandinavian languages, Danish and Norwegian – all of them descendants of Old Norse, which started branching out from the 9th century and the Viking age.

The oldest inscriptions in Old Norse, dating from the same period, used the runic alphabet and were written on stone or wood. The missionaries who introduced Christianity in the 12th century brought the Roman alphabet (and the custom of writing on parchment) to the emerging Scandinavian languages, but some modification was necessary to represent the specific vowel sounds, so additional letters were eventually developed. The turning point in the evolution of Swedish coincided with the achievement of independence from Danish rule in 1526, when the first translation of the New Testament appeared. The modern literary language was shaped after the first Swedish translation of the whole Bible, known as *Gustav Vasas Bibel* as it was published under the patronage of King Gustav Vasa in 1541.

The standard language or *Rikssvenska* reek·sven·ska (lit: kingdom-Swedish) is based on the central dialects from the area around Stockholm. Some of the rural dialects that are spoken across the country are quite diverse – for example, *Skånska* skawn·ska, spoken in the southern province of Skåne, has flatter vowel sounds (and sounds a lot more like Danish), whereas *Dalmål* daal·mawl, spoken in the central region of Dalarna, has a very up-and-down sound.

Interestingly, Swedish doesn't have official status in Sweden itself, but it does in neighbouring Finland. This is easily explained though – Swedish is the national language of Sweden, spoken by the majority of residents (around 8.5 million), and it simply wasn't felt necessary to enforce its use by law. Finland, on the other hand, was part of Sweden from the mid-14th century until 1809, and Swedish was the language of administration. Today, it shares official status with Finnish and is a mandatory subject in schools, but it's the first language for only about 300,000 people or 6% of Finland's population. PS: any traveller to Sweden should know that the Swedish Chef from the Muppets doesn't really speak Swedish at all.

pronunciation

vowel sounds

Swedish vowel sounds can be either short or long – generally the stressed vowels are long, except when they are followed by double consonants, in which case they are short. The vowels in unstressed syllables are also short.

symbol	english equivalent	swedish example	transliteration
a	run	*glass*	glas
aa	father	*glas*	glaas
ai	aisle	*kaj*	kai
aw	saw	*gå*	gaw
e	bet	*vän*	ven
air	hair	*gärna*	*yair*·na
ee	see	*hit*	heet
eu	nurse	*söt*	seut
ew	ee pronounced with rounded lips	*nytt*	newt
ey	as in 'bet', but longer	*heta*	*hey*·ta
i	hit	*hitta*	*hi*·ta
o	pot	*kopp*	kop
oh	**oh**	*bott*	boht
oo	zoo	*kul*	kool
u	put	*buss*	bus

consonant sounds

Most Swedish consonants sounds are similar to their English counterparts. One exception is the fh sound (a breathy sound pronounced with rounded lips, like saying 'f' and 'w' at the same time), but with a little practice, you'll soon get it right.

symbol	english equivalent	swedish example	transliteration
b	bed	*bil*	beel
ch	cheat	*tjur*	choor
d	dog	*dyr*	dewr
f	fat	*filt*	filt
fh	f pronounced with rounded lips	*sjuk*	fhook
g	go	*gård*	gawrd
h	hat	*hård*	hawrd
k	kit	*kung*	kung
l	lot	*land*	land
m	man	*man*	man
n	not	*nej*	ney
ng	ring	*sång*	sawng
p	pet	*penna*	pe·na
r	red	*rosa*	roh·sa
s	sun	*sol*	sohl
sh	shot	*första*	feush·ta
t	top	*tröja*	tror·ya
v	very	*vit*	veet
y	yes	*jag*	yaag

word stress

In Swedish, stress usually falls on the first syllable in a word, but sometimes it falls on two syllables. It's important to get the stress right, as it can change the meaning of words (eg *anden an*-den 'duck' versus *anden an*-den 'spirit'). Words borrowed from other languages are often stressed on the last syllable (eg *bibliotek* bib·li·o·*tek* 'library'). In this chapter, the stressed syllables are always in italics.

tools

language difficulties

Do you speak English?
Talar du engelska? — taa·lar doo eng·el·ska

Do you understand?
Förstår du? — feur·shtawr doo

I (don't) understand.
Jag förstår (inte). — yaa feur·shtawr (in·te)

What does (snus) mean?
Vad betyder (snus)? — vaad be·tew·der (snoos)

How do you ...? — *Hur ...?* — hoor ...
  pronounce this — *uttalar man detta* — ut·taa·lar man de·ta
  write (spårvagn) — *skrivar man (spårvagn)* — skree·var man (spawr·vangn)

Could you please ...? — *Kan du vara snäll och ...?* — kan doo vaa·ra snel o ...
  repeat that — *upprepa det* — up·rey·pa det
  speak more slowly — *tala lite långsammare* — taa·la lee·te lawng·sa·ma·re
  write it down — *skriva ner det* — skree·va neyr de

essentials

Yes.	*Ja.*	yaa
No.	*Nej.*	ney
Please.	*Tack.*	tak
Thank you (very much).	*Tack (så mycket).*	tak (saw mew·ke)
You're welcome.	*Varsågod.*	var·sha·gohd
Excuse me.	*Ursäkta mig.*	oor·shek·ta mey
Sorry.	*Förlåt.*	feur·lawt

numbers

0	*noll*	nol	16	*sexton*	seks·ton
1	*ett*	et	17	*sjutton*	fhu·ton
2	*två*	tvaw	18	*arton*	ar·ton
3	*tre*	trey	19	*nitton*	ni·ton
4	*fyra*	few·ra	20	*tjugo*	shoo·go
5	*fem*	fem	21	*tjugoett*	shoo·go·et
6	*sex*	seks	22	*tjugotvå*	shoo·go·tvaw
7	*sju*	fhoo	30	*trettio*	tre·tee
8	*åtta*	o·ta	40	*fyrtio*	fewr·tee
9	*nio*	nee·oh	50	*femtio*	fem·tee
10	*tio*	tee·oh	60	*sextio*	seks·tee
11	*elva*	el·va	70	*sjuttio*	fhu·tee
12	*tolv*	tolv	80	*åttio*	o·tee
13	*tretton*	tre·ton	90	*nittio*	ni·tee
14	*fjorton*	fyor·ton	100	*ett hundra*	et hun·dra
15	*femton*	fem·ton	1000	*ett tusen*	et too·sen

time & dates

What time is it?	*Hur mycket är klockan?*	hur mew·ke air klo·kan
It's one o'clock.	*Klockan är en.*	klo·kan air eyn
It's (two) o'clock.	*Klockan är (två).*	klo·kan air (tvaw)
Quarter past (one).	*Kvart över (en).*	kvart eu·ver (eyn)
Half past (one).	*Halv (två).* (lit: half two)	halv (tvaw)
Quarter to (nine).	*Kvart i (nio).*	kvart ee (nee·oh)
At what time ...?	*Hur dags ...?*	hur daks ...
At (10) o'clock.	*Klockan (tio).*	klo·kan (tee·oh)

am	*förmiddagen (f m)*	feur·mi·daa·gen
pm	*eftermiddagen (e m)*	ef·ter·mi·daa·gen

Monday	*måndag*	mawn·daa
Tuesday	*tisdag*	tees·taa
Wednesday	*onsdag*	ohns·daa
Thursday	*torsdag*	torsh·daa
Friday	*fredag*	frey·daa
Saturday	*lördag*	leur·daa
Sunday	*söndag*	seun·daa

January	*januari*	ya·nu·*aa*·ree
February	*februari*	fe·bru·*aa*·ree
March	*mars*	mars
April	*april*	a·*preel*
May	*maj*	mai
June	*juni*	*yoo*·nee
July	*juli*	*yoo*·lee
August	*augusti*	aw·*gus*·tee
September	*september*	sep·*tem*·ber
October	*oktober*	ok·*toh*·ber
November	*november*	noh·*vem*·ber
December	*december*	dey·*sem*·ber

What date is it today?
   Vilket datum är det idag?   *vil*·ket *daa*·tum air de ee·*daag*

It's (15 December).
   Det är (femtonde December).   de air (*fem*·ton·de dey·*sem*·ber)

since (May)	*sedan (maj)*	seyn (mai)
until (June)	*till (juni)*	til (*yoo*·nee)

last ...		
night	*igår kväll*	ee·*gawr* kvel
week	*förra veckan*	*feu*·ra *ve*·kan
month	*förra månaden*	*feu*·ra *maw*·na·den
year	*förra året*	*feu*·ra *aw*·ret

next ...	*nästa ...*	*nes*·ta ...
week	*vecka*	*ve*·ka
month	*månad*	*maw*·nad
year	*år*	awr

yesterday ...	*igår ...*	ee·*gawr* ...
morning	*morse*	*mor*·she
afternoon	*eftermiddag*	*ef*·ter·mi·daag
evening	*kväll*	kvel

tomorrow ...	*imorgon ...*	ee·*mor*·ron ...
morning	*bitti*	*bi*·ti
afternoon	*eftermiddag*	*ef*·ter·mi·daag
evening	*kväll*	kvel

weather

What's the weather like?	*Hur är vädret?*	hur air *vey*·dret
It's...		
cold	*Det är kallt.*	de air kalt
cloudy	*Det är molnigt.*	de air *mol*·nit
hot	*Det är het.*	de air heyt
raining	*Det regnar.*	de *reng*·nar
snowing	*Det snöar.*	de *sneu*·ar
sunny	*Solen skiner.*	*soh*·len *fhee*·ner
warm	*Det är varmt.*	de air varmt
windy	*Det blåser.*	de *blaw*·ser
spring	*vår*	vawr
summer	*sommar*	*so*·mar
autumn	*höst*	heust
winter	*vinter*	*vin*·ter

border crossing

I'm here ...	*Jag är ...*	yaa air ...
in transit	*i transit*	i *tran*·sit
on business	*på affärsresa*	paw a·*fairsh*·rey·sa
on holiday	*på semester*	paw se·*mes*·ter
I'm here for ...	*Jag stannar här ...*	yaa *sta*·nar hair ...
(10) days	*(tio) dagar*	(*tee*·oh) *daa*·gar
(three) weeks	*(tre) veckor*	(trey) *ve*·kor
(two) months	*(två) månader*	(tvaw) *maw*·na·der

I'm going to (Trelleborg).
Jag resar till (Trelleborg). yaa *rey*·sa til (tre·le·*bory*)

I'm staying at the (Grand Hotel).
Jag bor på (Grand Hotell). yaa bor paw (grand hoh·*tel*)

I have nothing to declare.
Jag har ingenting att förtulla. yaa har *ing*·en·ting at feur·*tu*·la

I have something to declare.
Jag har något att förtulla. yaa har *naw*·got at feur·*tu*·la

That's (not) mine.
Det är (inte) min. de air (*in*·te) min

transport

tickets & luggage

Where can I buy a ticket?
Var kan jag köpa en biljett?   var kan yaa *sheu*·pa eyn bil·*yet*

Do I need to book a seat?
Måste man boka?   maw·ste man *boh*·ka

One ... ticket (to Stockholm), please.	*Jag skulle vilja ha en ... (till Stockholm).*	yaa *sku*·le *vil*·ya haa eyn ... (til *stok*·holm)
one-way	*enkelbiljett*	en·kel·bil·*yet*
return	*returbiljett*	re·*toor*·bil·*yet*

I'd like to ... my ticket, please.	*Jag vill gärna ... min biljett.*	yaa vil *yair*·na ... min bil·*yet*
cancel	*upphäva*	up·*hey*·va
change	*ändra*	*en*·dra
collect	*hämta*	*hem*·ta
confirm	*bekräfta*	be·*kref*·ta

I'd like a ... seat, please.	*Jag vill gärna ha en ... plads.*	yaa vil *yair*·na haa eyn ... plads
nonsmoking	*icke-rökande*	*i*·ke·reu·kan·de
smoking	*rökande*	*reu*·kan·de

How much is it?
Hur mycket kostar det?   hoor *mew*·ke *kos*·tar de

Is there air conditioning?
Finns det luft-konditionering?   fins de *luft*·kon·di·fho·*ney*·ring

Is there a toilet?
Finns det en toalett?   fins de eyn toh·aa·*let*

How long does the trip take?
Hur länge undgår resan?   hoor *leng*·e *und*·gawr *rey*·san

Is it a direct route?
Är det en direktförbindelse?   air de eyn dee·*rekt*·feur·bin·del·se

I'd like a luggage locker.
Jag vill gärna få ett låsbara skåp till mit bagage.   yaa vil *yair*·na faw et *laws*·ba·ra skawp til mit ba·*gaash*

My luggage has been ...	Mit bagage är blivit ...	mit ba·*gaash* air *blee*·vit ...
damaged	skadat	*skaa*·dat
lost	förlorat	feur·*loh*·rat
stolen	stulit	*stoo*·lit

getting around

Where does flight (SK403) arrive/depart?

Var ankommar/avgår flyg (SK403)?

var *an*·ko·mar/*aav*·gawr flewg (es koh *few*·ra nol trey)

Where's (the) ...?	Var finns ...?	var fins ...
arrivals hall	ankomsthallen	*an*·komst·ha·len
departures hall	avgångshallen	*aav*·gawngs·ha·len
duty-free shop	en duty-free affär	eyn *dyoo*·tee·*free* a·*fair*
gate (12)	gate (tolv)	gayt (tolv)

Is this the ... to (Stockholm)?	Är den här ... till (Stockholm)?	air den hair ... til (*stok*·holm)
boat	båten	*baw*·ten
bus	bussen	*bu*·sen

Is this the ... to (Stockholm)?	Är det här ... till (Stockholm)?	air de hair ... til (*stok*·holm)
plane	planet	*plaa*·net
train	tåget	*taw*·get

What time's the ... bus?	När går ...?	nair gawr ...
first	första bussen	*feursh*·ta *bu*·sen
last	sista bussen	*sis*·ta *bu*·sen
next	nästa buss	*nes*·ta bus

At what time does it arrive/leave?

Hur dags anländer/avgår den?

hoor daks *an*·len·der/*aav*·gawr deyn

How long will it be delayed?

Hur mycket är det försenat?

hoor *mew*·ket air dey feur·*shey*·nat

What station/stop is this?

Vilken station/hållplats är denna?

vil·ken sta·*fhohn*/*hawl*·plats air *dey*·na

What's the next station/stop?

Vilken är nästa station/hållplats?

vil·ken air *nes*·ta sta·*fhohn*/*hawl*·plats

Does it stop at (Lund)?
Stannar den på (Lund)? — sta·nar deyn paw (lund)

Please tell me when we get to (Linköping).
Kan du säga till när vi kommer — kan doo *say*·ya til nair vee *ko*·mer
till (Linköping)? — til (*lin*·sheu·ping)

How long do we stop here?
Hur länge stannar vi här? — hoor *leng*·e *sta*·nar vee hair

Is this seat available?
Är denna plads ledig? — air *dey*·na plats *ley*·dig

That's my seat.
Det är min plats. — de air min plats

I'd like a taxi ...	*Jag vill gärna få*	yaa vil *yair*·na faw
	en taxi ...	eyn *tak*·see ...
at (9am)	*klockan (nio*	*klo*·kan (*nee*·oh
	på morgonen)	paw *mo*·ro·nen)
now	*nu*	noo
tomorrow	*imorgon*	ee·*mo*·ron

Is this taxi available?
Är denna taxi ledig? — air *dey*·na *tak*·see *ley*·di

How much is it to ...?
Vad kostar det till ...? — vaad *kos*·tar de til ...

Please put the meter on.
Kan du köra på taxametern? — kan doo sheur paw tak·sa·*mey*·tern

Please take me to (this address).
Kan du köra mig till (denna address)? — kan doo *sheu*·ra mey til (*dey*·na a·*dres*)

Please ...	*Kan du ...?*	kan doo ...
slow down	*sakta ner*	*sak*·ta *neyr*
stop here	*stanna här*	*sta*·na hair
wait here	*vänta här*	*ven*·ta hair

car, motorbike & bicycle hire

I'd like to hire a ...	*Jag vill hyra en ...*	yaa vil *hew*·ra eyn ...
bicycle	*cykel*	*sew*·kel
car	*bil*	beel
motorbike	*motorcykel*	*moh*·tor·sew·kel

with ...	med ...	meyd ...
a driver	*chaufför*	fho-*feur*
air conditioning	*luft-konditionering*	luft-kon-di-fho-*ney*-ring
antifreeze	*kylarvätska*	shew-lar-vet-ska
snow chains	*snökedja*	sneu-she-dya

How much for ... hire?	*Hur mycket kostar det ...?*	hoor *mew*-ke *kos*-tar de ...
hourly	*per timma*	peyr *ti*-ma
daily	*per dag*	peyr *daag*
weekly	*per vecka*	peyr *ve*-ka

air	*luft*	luft
oil	*olja*	*ol*-ya
petrol	*bensin*	ben-*seen*
tyres	*däck* n	dek

I need a mechanic.
Jag behöver en mekaniker.
yaa be-*heu*-ver eyn me-*kaa*-ni-ker

I've run out of petrol.
Jag har ingen bensin kvar.
yaa har *ing*-en ben-*seen* kvar

I have a flat tyre.
Jag har fått punktering.
yaa har fawt punk-*tey*-ring

directions

Where's the ...?	*Var ligger ...?*	var li-ger ...
bank	*banken*	*ban*-ken
city centre	*centrum*	*sen*-trum
hotel	*hotellet*	hoh-*te*-let
market	*salutorget*	saa-loo-*tor*-yet
police station	*polisen*	poh-*lee*-sen
post office	*posten*	*pos*-ten
public toilet	*en offentlig toalett*	eyn o-*feynt*-lig toh-aa-*let*
tourist office	*turistinformationen*	too-*rist*-in-for-ma-*fhoh*-nen

Is this the road to (Göteborg)?
Går den här vägen till (Göteborg)?   gawr den hair *vey*·gen til (yeu·te·*bory*)

Can you show me (on the map)?
Kan du visa mig (på kartan)?   kan doo *vee*·sa mey (paw *kar*·tan)

What's the address?
Vilken adress är det?   *vil*·ken a·*dres* air de

How far is it?
Hur långt är det?   hoor *lawngt* air de

How do I get there?
Hur kommer man dit?   hoor *ko*·mar man *deet*

Turn ...	*Sväng ...*	sveng ...
at the corner	*vid hörnet*	veed *heur*·net
at the traffic lights	*vid trafikljuset*	veed tra·*feek*·yoo·set
left/right	*till vänster/höger*	til *ven*·ster/*heu*·ger

It's ...	*Det är ...*	de air ...
behind ...	*bakom ...*	*baa*·kom ...
far away	*långt*	lawngt
here	*här*	hair
in front of ...	*framför ...*	*fram*·feur ...
left	*till vänster*	til *ven*·ster
near (to ...)	*nära (på ...)*	*nair*·ra (paw ...)
next to ...	*bredvid ...*	breyd·*veed* ...
on the corner	*vid hörnet*	veed *heur*·net
opposite ...	*mitt emot ...*	mit ey·*moht* ...
right	*till höger*	til *heu*·ger
straight ahead	*rakt fram*	raakt fram
there	*där*	dair

by boat	*med båt*	me *bawt*
by bus	*med buss*	me *bus*
by taxi	*med taxi*	me *tak*·see
by train	*med tåg*	me *tawg*
on foot	*till fods*	til *fohts*

north	*nord*	nord
south	*syd*	sewd
east	*öst*	eust
west	*väst*	vest

signs

Ingång/Utgång	in-gawng/oot-gawng	Entrance/Exit
Öppet/Stängt	eu-pet/stengt	Open/Closed
Lediga Rum	ley-di-ga rum	Rooms Available
Fullt/Inga Lediga Rum	fult/ing-a ley-di-ga rum	No Vacancies
Information	in-for-ma-fhohn	Information
Polisstation	poh-lees-sta-fhohn	Police Station
Förbjudet	feur-byoo-det	Prohibited
Toaletter	toh-aa-le-ter	Toilets
Herrar	her-ar	Men
Damer	daa-mer	Women
Varm/Kall	varm/kal	Hot/Cold

accommodation

finding accommodation

Where's a ...?	Var finns det ...?	var fins de ...
camping ground	en campingplats	eyn kam-ping-plats
guesthouse	ett gästhus	et yest-hoos
hotel	ett hotell	et hoh-tel
youth hostel	ett vandrarhem	et van-drar-hem

Can you recommend	Kan ni rekommendera	kan nee re-ko-men-dey-ra
somewhere ...?	något ...?	naw-got ...
cheap	billigt	bi-lit
good	bra	braa
nearby	i närheten	ee nair-hey-ten

I'd like to book a room, please.
Jag skulle vilja boka ett rum.   yaa sku-le vil-ya boh-ka et rum

I have a reservation.
Jag har bokat.   yaa har boh-kat

My name's ...
Jag heter ...   yaa hey-ter ...

Do you have a … room?	*Har ni …?*	har nee …
single	*ett enkeltrum*	et *en*·kelt·rum
double	*ett dubbeltrum*	et *du*·belt·rum
twin	*ett rum med*	et rum me
	två sängar	tvaw *seng*·ar

How much is it	*Hur mycket kostar*	hoor *mew*·ket *kos*·tar
per …?	*det per …?*	de peyr …
night	*natt*	nat
person	*person*	*peyr*·shohn

Can I pay by …?	*Tar ni …?*	taar nee …
credit card	*kreditkort*	kre·*deet*·kort
travellers cheque	*resecheckar*	*rey*·se·*she*·kar

I'd like to stay for (two) nights.
Jag tänker stanna (två) dagar.   yaa *ten*·kar *sta*·na (tvaw) *daa*·gar

From (July 2) to (July 6).
Från (annan Juli) till (sjätte Juli).   frawn (*a*·nen *yoo*·lee) til (*fhe*·te *yoo*·lee)

Can I see it?
Kan jag få se rummet?   kan yaa faw se *ru*·met

Am I allowed to camp here?
Får jag campa här?   fawr yaa *kam*·pa hair

Is there a campsite nearby?
Finns det någon campingplats   fins de nawn *kam*·ping·*plats*
i närheten?   ee *nair*·hey·ten

requests & queries

When/Where is breakfast served?
När/Var serveras frukost?   nair/var ser·*vey*·ras *froo*·kost

Please wake me at (seven).
Kan ni väcka mig klockan (sju).   kan nee *ve*·ka mey *klo*·kan (fhoo)

Could I have my key, please?
Jag vill gärna ha min nyckel.   yaa vil *yair*·na haa min *new*·kel

Can I get another (blanket)?
Kan jag få en (filt) till?   kan yaa fawr eyn (filt) *till*

Is there an elevator/a safe?
Finns det en hiss/förvaringsbox?   fins de eyn his/feur·*vaa*·rings·boks

The room is too ...	*Rummet är för ...*	*ru·met air feur ...*
expensive	*dyrt*	dewrt
noisy	*bullrigt*	*bul·rit*
small	*litet*	*lee·tet*

The ... doesn't work.	*... funkar inte.*	*... fun·kar in·te*
air conditioning	*Luftkonditioneringen*	luft·kon·di·fho·ney·ring·en
fan	*Fläkten*	flek·ten
toilet	*Toaletten*	toh·aa·le·ten

This ... isn't clean.	*Denna ... är inte ren.*	*dey·na ... air in·te reyn*
pillow	*kudde*	*ku·de*
sheet	*lakan*	*laa·kan*
towel	*handduk*	*han·duk*

checking out

What time is checkout?
Hur dags måste man checka ut? — hoor daks *maw*·ste man *she*·ka *ut*

Can I leave my luggage here?
Kan jag lämna min bagage här? — kan yaa *lem*·na min ba·*gaash* hair

Could I have my ..., please?	*Kan jag få ...?*	kan yaa fawr ...
deposit	*min depositionsavgift*	min de·poh·si·*fhohns*·aav·yift
passport	*mitt pass*	mit pas
valuables	*mina värdesaker*	*mee*·na *vair*·de·saa·ker

communications & banking

the internet

Where's the local Internet café?
Var finns det lokala Internet kaféet? — var fins de loh·*kaa*·la *in*·ter·net ka·*fey*·et

How much is it per hour?
Hur mycket kostar det per timma? — hoor *mew*·ke *kos*·tar de par *ti*·ma

I'd like to ...	Jag skulle vilja ...	yaa sku·le vil·ya ...
check my email	kolla min e-post	ko·la min ey·post
get Internet access	koppla upp mig till Internetet	kop·la up mey til in·ter·ne·tet
use a printer	använda en printer	an·ven·da eyn prin·ter
use a scanner	använda en scanner	an·ven·da eyn ska·ner

mobile/cell phone

I'd like a ...	Jag skulle vilja ha ...	yaa sku·le vil·ya haa ...
mobile/cell phone for hire	en mobil telefon till hyra	eyn moh·beel te·le·fohn til hew·ra
SIM card for your network	ett sim-kort till detta nätverk	et sim·kort til de·ta neyt·verk

What are the rates?	Vad är prisarna?	vaad air pree·sar·na

telephone

What's your phone number?
Vad är ditt telefonnummer?   vaad air dit te·le·fohn·nu·mer

The number is ...
Numret är ...   num·ret air ...

Where's the nearest public phone?
Var ligger närmaste publiktelefon?   var li·ger nair·ma·ste pub·leek·te·le·fohn

I'd like to buy a phonecard.
Jag skulle vilja ha ett telefonkort.   yaa sku·le vil·ya haa et te·le·fohn·kort

I want to ...	Jag skulle vilja ...	yaa sku·le vil·ya ...
call (Singapore)	ringa till (Singapore)	ring·a til (sing·a·poor)
make a local call	ringa lokalt	ring·a loh·kaalt
reverse the charges	göra ett ba-samtal	yeu·ra et be·aa·sam·taal

How much does ... cost?	Hur mycket kostar ...?	hoor mew·ke kos·tar ...
a (three)-minute call	ett (tre)minuter samtal	et (trey)·mi·noo·te sham·taal
each extra minute	varje extra minut	var·ye eks·tra mi·noot

It's (three) kronor per minute.
(Tre) kronor per minut.   (tre) kroh·nor par mi·noot

post office

I want to send a ...	Jag skulle vilja skicka ett ...	yaa *sku·*le *vil·*ya *fhi·*ka et ...
fax	fax	faks
letter	brev	breyv
parcel	paket	pa·*keyt*
postcard	vykort	vew·kort

I want to buy ...	Jag skulle vilja ha ...	yaa *sku·*le *vil·*ya haa ...
an envelope	kuvert	koo·*ver*
stamps	frimärken	free·mair·ken

Please send it (to Australia) by ...	Var snäll och skicka den (till Australien) ...	var snel o *fhi·*ka deyn (til o·*straa·*lyen) ...
airmail	med flygpost	me *flewg·*post
express mail	express	eks·*pres*
registered mail	som rekommenderat brev	som re·ko·men·*dey·*rat breyv
surface mail	som ytpost	som *ewt·*post

Is there any mail for me?	Finns det post til mig?	fins de post til mey

bank

Where's a/an ...?	Var finns det en ...?	var fins de eyn ...
ATM	bankomat	ban·koh·*maat*
foreign exchange office	utländsk valuta	oot·lensk va·*loo·*ta

I'd like to ...	Jag skulle vilja ...	yaa *sku·*le *vil·*ya ...
arrange a transfer	överföra pengar	eu·ver·fer·ra *peng·*ar
cash a cheque	lösa in en check	*leu·*sa in eyn shek
change a travellers cheque	växla resecheckar	*veks·*la *rey·*se·she·kar
change money	växla pengar	*veks·*la *peng·*ar
get a cash advance	ta ut kontant på mitt bankkort	taa oot kon·*tant* paw mit *bank·*kort
withdraw money	dra ut pengar	draa oot *peng·*ar

What's the ...?	Vad är ...?	vaad air ...
charge for that	belastningen för det	be·*last·*ning·en fer de
exchange rate	växelkursen	*vek·*sel·koor·shen

It's ...	*Det är ...*	de air ...
(25) kronor	*(tjugofem) kronor*	(shoo·go·*fem*) *kroh*·nor
free	*gratis*	*graa*·tis

What time does the bank open?
Hur dags öppnar banken?   hoor daks *eup*·nar *ban*·ken

Has my money arrived yet?
Är mina pengar kommit än?   air *mee*·na *peng*·ar *ko*·mit en

sightseeing

getting in

What time does it open/close?
Hur dags öppnar/stänger de?   hoor daks *eup*·nar/*steng*·ar dom

What's the admission charge?
Hur mycket kostar det i inträde?   hoor *mew*·ke *kos*·tar de i *in*·trey·de

Is there a discount for children/students?
Finns det barnrabatt/studentrabatt?   fins de *barn*·ra·bat/stoo·*dent*·ra·bat

I'd like a ...	*Jag skulle vilja ha en ...*	yaa *sku*·le *vil*·ya *haa* eyn ...
catalogue	*katalog*	ka·ta·*lohg*
guide	*resehandbok*	*rey*·se·hand·bohk
local map	*lokal karta*	loh·*kaal* kar·ta

I'd like to see ...	*Jag skulle vilja se ...*	yaa *sku*·le *vil*·ya se ...
What's that?	*Vad är det?*	vaad air *de*
Can I take a photo?	*Får jag fotografera?*	fawr yaa foh·toh·gra·*fey*·ra

tours

When's the next ...?	*När avgår nästa ...?*	nair *aav*·gawr *nes*·ta ...
day trip	*dagsturen*	*daks*·too·ren
tour	*turen*	*too*·ren

Is ... included?	*Inkluderas ...*	in·kloo·*dey*·ras ...
accommodation	*logi*	lo·*shee*
the admission charge	*inträden*	*in*·trey·den
food	*mat*	maat
transport	*transport*	tran·*sport*

How long is the tour?
Hur länge undgår turen?   hoor *leng*·e *oon*·gawr *too*·ren

What time should we be back?
Hur dags kommer vi tillbaka?   hoor *daks* ko·mar vee til·*baa*·ka

sightseeing

castle	*slott* n	slot
cathedral	*domkyrka*	*dom*·shewr·ka
church	*kyrka*	*shewr*·ka
main square	*stortorget* n	*stor*·tor·yet
monastery	*kloster* n	*klos*·ter
monument	*monument* n	mo·noo·*ment*
museum	*museum/museet* n	moo·*sey*·oom/moo·*sey*·et
old city	*gamla stan*	*gam*·la *staan*
palace	*palats*	pa·*lats*
ruins	*ruiner*	roo·*ee*·ner
stadium	*idrottsplats*	*i*·drots·plats
statues	*statyer*	sta·*tew*·er

shopping

enquiries

Where's a ...?	*Var finns det ...?*	var finns de ...
bank	*en bank*	eyn bank
bookshop	*en bokhandel*	eyn *bohk*·han·del
camera shop	*en fotoaffär*	eyn *fo*·toh·a·fair
department store	*ett varuhus*	et *va*·roo·hus
grocery store	*en livsmedelsaffär*	eyn *leevs*·mey·dels·a·fair
market	*en torghandel*	eyn *tory*·han·del
newsagency	*en pressbyrå*	eyn *pres*·bew·raw
supermarket	*ett snabbköp*	et *snab*·sheup

Where can I buy a (padlock)?
Var kan jag köpa ett (hänglås)?   var kan yaa *sheu*·pa et (*heng*·laws)

I'm looking for ...
Jag letar efter ...   yaa *ley*·tar *ef*·ter ...

Can I look at it?
Får jag se den?   fawr yaa *se* deyn

Do you have any others?
Har ni några andra?   har nee *naw*·ra *an*·dra

Does it have a guarantee?
Har den garanti?   har deyn ga·ran·*tee*

Can I have it sent overseas?
Kan jag få den skickat utomlands?   kan yaa fawr deyn *fhi*·kat *oo*·tom·lants

Can I have (my backpack) repaired?
Kan jag får (min ryggsäck) reparerad?   kan yaa fawr (min *rewg*·sek) re·pa·*rey*·rad

It's faulty.
Den är felaktig.   deyn air *fey*·lak·ti

I'd like ..., please.	*Jag vill gärna ...*	yaa vil *yair*·na ...
a bag	*ha en kasse*	ha eyn *ka*·se
a refund	*få en återbäring*	faw eyn *aw*·ter·bai·ring
to return this	*återlämna denna*	*aw*·ter·lem·na *dey*·na

paying

How much is it?
Hur mycket kostar det?   hoor *mew*·ke *kos*·tar de

Can you write down the price?
Kan du skriva ner priset?   kan du *skree*·va neyr *pree*·set

That's too expensive.
Det är för dyrt.   de air feur *dewrt*

What's your lowest price?
Vad är dit lägste pris?   vaad air dit *leyg*·ste prees

I'll give you (50) kronor.
Jag ger dig (femtio) kronor.   yaa yer dey (*fem*·ti) *kroh*·nor

There's a mistake in the bill.
Det är ett fel på räkningen.   de air et *fel* paw *reyk*·ning·en

Do you accept ...?	Tar ni ...?	tar nee ...
credit cards	kreditkort	kre·*deet*·kort
debit cards	betalkort	be·*taal*·kort
travellers cheques	resecheckar	*rey*·se·she·kar

I'd like ..., please.	Jag vill gärna ha ...	yaa vil *yair*·na ha ...
a receipt	ett kvitto	et *kvi*·to
my change	min växel	min *vek*·sel

clothes & shoes

Can I try it on?	Får jag pröva den?	fawr yaa *preu*·va deyn
My size is (40).	Min storlek är (fyrtio).	min *stor*·leyk air (*fewr*·tee)
It doesn't fit.	Den passar inte.	deyn *pa*·sar *in*·te

small	liten	*lee*·ten
medium	medelstor	*mey*·del·stor
large	stor	stor

books & music

I'd like a ...	Jag skulle vilja ha en ...	yaa *sku*·le *vil*·ya *haa* eyn ...
newspaper (in English)	(engelsk) tidning	(*eng*·elsk) *teed*·ning
pen	penna	*pe*·na

Is there an English-language bookshop?
Finns det an bokhandel — fins de eyn *bohk*·han·del
med böcker på engelska? — me *beu*·ker paw *eng*·el·ska

I'm looking for something by (Henning Mankell).
Jag letar efter något av — yaa *ley*·tar *ef*·ter nawt aav
(Henning Mankell). — (*he*·ning *man*·kel)

Can I listen to this?
Kan jag få höra denna? — kan yaa faw *heu*·ra *dey*·na

photography

Could you ...?	Kan du ...?	kan doo ...
burn a CD from my memory card	bränna en CD från min memory kort	bre·na eyn se·de frawn min me·mo·ree kort
develop this film	framkalla denna filmen	fram·ka·la dey·na fil·men
load my film	ladda film i min kamera	la·da film i min kaa·me·ra

I need a ... film for this camera.	Jag skulle vilja ha en ... till den här kameran.	yaa sku·le vil·ya haa eyn ... til deyn hair kaa·me·ra
APS	APS-film	aa·pe·es·film
B&W	svart-vit film	svart·vit film
colour	färg film	fairg film
slide	dia-film	dee·a·film
(200) speed	(tvåhundra)-film	(tvaw·hund·ra)·film

When will it be ready?	När är den klar?	nair air deyn klaar

meeting people

greetings, goodbyes & introductions

Hello.	Hej.	hey
Hi.	Hejså.	hey·saw
Good night.	Godnatt.	goh·nat
Goodbye.	Adjö./Hej då.	aa·yeu/hey daw
See you later.	Vi ses senare.	vee seys sey·na·re

Mr	herr	her
Mrs	fru	froo
Miss	fröken	freu·ken

How are you?	Hur står det till?	hoor stawr de til
Fine, thanks. And you?	Bra, tack. Och dig?	braa tak o dey
What's your name?	Vad heter du?	vaad hey·ter doo
My name is ...	Jag heter ...	yaa hey·ter ...
I'm pleased to meet you.	Trevligt att träffas.	treyv·lit at tre·fas

This is my ...	Detta är min ...	de·ta air min ...
boyfriend	pojkvän	poyk·ven
brother	bror	bror
daughter	dotter	do·ter
father	far	far
friend	vän/väninna m/f	ven/ve·ni·na
girlfriend	flickvän	flik·ven
husband	man	man
mother	mor	mor
partner (intimate)	partner	part·ner
sister	syster	sews·ter
son	son	sohn
wife	fru	froo

Here's my ...	Här är min ...	hair air min ...
What's your ...?	Vad är din ...?	vaad air din ...
address	adress	a·dres
email address	e-post adress	ey·post a·dres

Here's my ...	Här är mitt ...	hair air mit ...
What's your ...?	Vad är ditt ...?	vaad air dit ...
fax number	fax-nummer	faks·nu·mer
phone number	telefonnummer	te·le·fohn·nu·mer

occupations

What's your occupation?	Vad har du för yrke?	vaad har doo feur ewr·ke

I'm a/an ...	Jag är ...	yaa air ...
artist	konstnär	konst·nair
business person	affärsman	a·fairsh·man
office worker	kontorist	kon·to·rist
scientist	naturvetare	na·toor·vey·ta·re
tradesperson	detaljhandlare	de·taly·hand·la·re

background

Where are you from?	Varifrån kommer du?	var·ee·frawn ko·mer doo
I'm from ...	Jag kommer från ...	yaa ko·mer frawn ...
Australia	Australien	o·straa·lyen
Canada	Kanada	ka·na·da
England	England	eng·land
New Zealand	Nya Zealand	new·a sey·land
the USA	USA	oo·es·aa

Are you married?	Är du gift?	air doo yift
I'm married.	Jag är gift.	yaa air yift
I'm single.	Jag är ogift.	yaa air oh·yift

age

How old ...?	Hur gammal ...?	hoor ga·mal ...
are you	är du	air doo
is your daughter	är din dotter	air din do·ter
is your son	är din son	air din sohn

I'm ... years old.
Jag är ... år gammal.	yaa air ... awr ga·mal

He/She is ... years old.
Han/Hon är ... år gammal.	han/hon air ... awr ga·mal

feelings

I'm (not) ...	Jag är (inte) ...	yaa air (in·te) ...
Are you ...?	Är du ...?	air doo ...
happy	glad	glaad
hot	varm	varm
hungry	hungrig	hung·greeg
sad	ledsen	le·sen
thirsty	törstig	teur·shteeg
tired	trött	treut

Are you cold?	Fryser du?	frew·ser doo
I'm (not) cold.	Jag fryser (inte).	yaa frew·ser (in·te)
Are you OK?	Mår du bra?	mawr doo braa
I'm (not) OK.	Jag mår (inte) bra.	yaa mawr (in·te) braa

entertainment

going out

Where can I find ...?	*Var finns ...?*	var fins ...
clubs	*klubbarna*	*klu*·bar·na
gay venues	*gayklubbarna*	*gay*·klu·bar·na
pubs	*pubbarna*	*pu*·bar·na
I feel like going to a/the ...	*Jag vil gärna gå på ...*	yaa vil *yair*·na gaw paw ...
concert	*konsert*	kon·*seyr*
movies	*bio*	*bee*·oh
party	*fest*	fest
restaurant	*restaurang*	res·taw·*rang*
theatre	*teater*	tee·*ay*·ter

interests

Do you like ...?	*Tycker du om ...?*	*tew*·ker doo om ...
I (don't) like ...	*Jag tycker (inte) om ...*	yaa *tew*·ker (*in*·te) om ...
art	*konst*	konst
cooking	*att laga mat*	at *laa*·ga *maat*
movies	*film*	film
nightclubs	*natklubbar*	*nat*·klu·bar
reading	*att läsa*	at *ley*·sa
shopping	*att shoppa*	at *sho*·pa
sport	*sport*	sport
travelling	*att resa*	at *rey*·sa
Do you like to ...?	*Tycker du om att ...?*	*tew*·ker doo om at ...
dance	*dansa*	*dan*·sa
go to concerts	*gå på konsert*	gaw paw kon·*seyr*
listen to music	*lyssna på musik*	*lews*·na paw moo·*seek*

food & drink

finding a place to eat

Can you recommend a ...?	*Kan du anbefalla en ...?*	kan doo an·be·fa·la eyn ...
bar	*bar*	bar
café	*kafé*	ka·*fey*
restaurant	*restaurang*	res·taw·*rang*
I'd like ..., please.	*... , tack.*	... tak
a table for (four)	*Ett bord för (fyra)*	et bord feur (*few*·ra)
the nonsmoking section	*Rökfria avdelningen*	*reuk*·free·a aav·del·ning·en
the smoking section	*Rökavdelningen*	*reuk*·aav·del·ning·en

ordering food

breakfast	*frukost*	*froo*·kost
lunch	*lunch*	lunsh
dinner	*middag*	*mi*·daa
snack	*mellanmål* n	*me*·lan·mawl
today's special	*dagens rätt*	*daa*·gens ret

What would you recommend?
Vad skulle ni anbefalla?   vaad *sku*·le nee an·be·*fa*·la

I'd like (the) ...	*Jag skulle vilja ha ...*	yaa *sku*·le *vil*·ya haa ...
bill	*räkningen*	*reyk*·ning·en
drink list	*drickslistan*	*driks*·lis·tan
menu	*menyn*	me·*newn*
that dish	*den maträtt*	deyn maat·ret

drinks

(cup of) coffee ...	(en kopp) kaffe ...	(eyn kop) ka·fe ...
(cup of) tea ...	(en kopp) te ...	(eyn kop) tey ...
with milk	*med mjölk*	me myeulk
without sugar	*utan socker*	oo·taan so·ker
(orange) juice	*(apelsin)juice*	(a·pel·seen·)djoos
soft drink	*läsk*	lesk
boiled water	*kokt vatten* n	kohkt va·ten
mineral water	*mineralvatten* n	mi·ne·raal·va·ten
water	*vatten* n	va·ten

in the bar

I'll have ...
Jag vill ha ...   yaa vil haa ...

I'll buy you a drink.
Jag köper dig en drink.   yaa sheu·per dey eyn drink

What would you like?
Vad vill du ha?   vaad vil doo haa

Cheers!
Skål!   skawl

brandy	*brandy*	bran·dee
cocktail	*cocktail*	kok·tayl
cognac	*cognac*	kon·yak
a shot of (whisky)	*2 cl (whiskey)*	tvaw sen·ti·ley·ter (vis·kee)
a ... of beer	*... öl*	... eul
bottle	*en flaska*	eyn flas·ka
glass	*ett glass*	et glaas
a bottle of ...	*en flaska ...*	eyn flas·ka ...
a glass of ...	*ett glas ...*	et glaas ...
red wine	*rödvin*	reud·veen
sparkling wine	*mousserande vin*	moo·sey·ran·de veen
white wine	*vitt vin*	vit veen

self-catering

What's the local speciality?
Vad är den lokala specialiteten?   vaad air deyn loh·*kaa*·la spe·si·a·li·*tey*·ten

What's that?
Vad är det?   vaad air de

How much is (a kilo of cheese)?
Hur mycket kostar (en kilo ost)?   hoor *mew*·ke *kos*·tar (eyn *shee*·loh ohst)

I'd like ...	*Jag vil ha ...*	yaa vil ha ...
(100) grams	*(hundra) gram*	(*hun*·dra) gram
(two) kilos	*(två) kilo*	(*tvaw*) *shee*·loh
(three) pieces	*(tre) styck*	(*trey*) stewk
(six) slices	*(sex) skivor*	(*seks*) *fhee*·vor

Less.	*Mindre.*	*min*·dre
Enough.	*Det räcker.*	de *re*·ker
More.	*Mera.*	*mey*·ra

special diets & allergies

Is there a vegetarian restaurant near here?
Finns det en vegetarisk   fins de eyn ve·ge·*taa*·risk
restaurang i närheten?   res·taw·*rang* ee *nair*·hey·ten

Do you have vegetarian food?
Har ni vegetarisk mat?   har nee ve·ge·*taa*·risk maat

Could you prepare	*Kan ni laga*	kan nee *laa*·ga
a meal without ...?	*en maträtt utan ...?*	eyn *maat*·ret *oo*·tan ...
butter	*smör*	smeur
eggs	*ägg*	eg
meat stock	*köttspad*	*sheut*·spaad

I'm allergic to ...	*Jag är allergisk mot ...*	yaa air al·*leyr*·gisk moht ...
dairy produce	*mejeriprodukter*	me·ye·*ree*·pro·*dook*·ter
gluten	*gluten*	*gloo*·ten
MSG	*MSG*	em·es·*gee*
nuts	*nötter*	*neu*·ter
seafood	*fisk och skaldjur*	fisk o *skaal*·yoor

emergencies

basics

Help!	*Hjälp!*	yelp
Stop!	*Stanna!*	*sta*·na
Go away!	*Försvinn!*	feur·*shvin*
Thief!	*Ta fast tjuven!*	ta fast *shoo*·ven
Fire!	*Elden är lös!*	*el*·den air *leus*
Watch out!	*Se upp!*	se up
Call ...!	*Ring ...!*	ring ...
a doctor	*efter en doktor*	*ef*·ter en *dok*·tor
an ambulance	*efter en ambulans*	*ef*·ter en am·boo·*lans*
the police	*polisen*	poh·*lee*·sen

It's an emergency!
Det är ett nödsituation!   de air et *neud*·si·too·a·fhohn

Could you help me, please?
Kan du hjälpa mig?   kan doo *yel*·pa mai

I have to use the telephone.
Jag måste använda telefonen.   yaa *maws*·te *an*·ven·da te·le·*foh*·nen

I'm lost.
Jag har gått vilse.   yaa har got *vil*·se

Where are the toilets?
Var är toaletten?   var air toh·aa·*le*·ten

police

Where's the police station?
Var är polisstationen?   var air poh·*lees*·sta·*fhoh*·nen

I want to report an offence.
Jag vill anmäla ett brott.   yaa vil *an*·mey·la et brot

I have insurance.
Jag har försäkring.   yaa har feur·*shey*·kring

I've been assaulted.
Jag är blivit utsatt för övervåld.   yaa air *blee*·vit *ut*·sat feur *eu*·ver·vawld

I've been ...	Jag har blivit ...	yaa har *blee*·vit ...
raped	*våldtagen*	*vol*·taa·gen
robbed	*rånad*	*raw*·nad

I've lost my ...	Jag har förlorat ...	yaa har feur·*loh*·rat ...
backpack	*min ryggsäck*	min *rewk*·sek
bags	*mina väskor*	*mee*·na *ves*·kor
credit card	*min kreditkort*	min kre·*deet*·kort
handbag	*min handväska*	min *hand*·ves·ka
jewellery	*mina smycken*	*mee*·na *smew*·ken
money	*mina pengar*	*mee*·na *peng*·ar
passport	*mitt pass*	mit pas
travellers cheques	*mina resecheckar*	*mee*·na *rey*·se·she·kar
wallet	*min plånbok*	min *plawn*·bohk

I want to contact my ...	Jag vill kontakta ...	yaa vil kon·*tak*·ta ...
consulate	*mitt konsulat*	mit kon·soo·*laat*
embassy	*min ambassad*	min am·ba·*saad*

health

medical needs

Where's the nearest ...?	Var är närmaste ...?	var air *nair*·ma·ste ...
dentist	*tandläkaren*	*tand*·ley·ka·ren
doctor	*doktorn*	*dok*·torn
hospital	*sjukhuset*	*fhook*·hu·set
(night) pharmacist	*(natt)apoteket*	(*nat*·)a·poh·*te*·ket

I need a doctor (who speaks English).
Jag behöver en läkare   yaa be·*heu*·ver eyn *ley*·ka·re
(som tular engelska).   (som *taa*·lar *eng*·el·ska)

Could I see a female doctor?
Kan jag få träffa en kvinnlig läkare?   kan yaa faw *tre*·fa eyn *kvin*·li *ley*·ka·re

I've run out of my medication.
Jag har ingen medikament kvar.   yaa har *ing*·en me·di·ka·*ment* kvar

symptoms, conditions & allergies

I'm sick.	Jag är sjuk.	yaa air fhook
It hurts here.	Det gör ont här.	de yeur ont hair
I have nausea.	Jag mår illa.	yaa mawr i·la

I have (a) ...	Jag har ...	yaa haa ...
asthma	astma	ast·maa
bronchitis	bronkit	bron·keet
constipation	förstoppning	feur·shtop·ning
cough	en hosta	eyn hoh·sta
diarrhoea	diarré	dee·a·rey
fever	feber	fey·ber
headache	huvudvärk	hoo·vud·vairk
heart condition	en hjärttillstånd	eyn yairt·til·stawnd
pain	ont	ont
sore throat	ont i halsen	ont ee hal·sen
toothache	tandvärk	tand·verk

I'm allergic to ...	Jag är allergisk mot ...	yaa air a·leyr·gisk moht ...
antibiotics	antibiotika	an·tee·bee·oh·ti·ka
anti-inflammatories	anti-inflammatoriska medel	an·tee·in·fla·ma·toh·ri·ska mey·del
aspirin	magnecyl	mag·ne·sewl
bees	bin	been
codeine	kodein	koh·deen
penicillin	penicillin	pe·ne·si·leen

antiseptic	antiseptiskt medel n	an·tee·sep·tiskt mey·del
bandage	förband n	feur·band
condoms	kondomer	kon·doh·mer
diarrhoea medicine	medel mot diarré n	mey·del moht dee·a·rey
insect repellent	insektsmedel n	in·sekts·mey·del
laxatives	laxermedel n	lak·ser·mey·del
painkillers	smärtstillande medel n	smairt·sti·lan·de mey·del
rehydration salts	vätskeersätt·ningsmedel n	vet·ske·er·set·nings·mey·del
sleeping tablets	sovmedel n	sohv·mey·del

english–swedish dictionary

In this dictionary, words are marked as n (noun), a (adjective), v (verb), sg (singular), pl (plural), inf (informal) and pol (polite) where necessary. Note that Swedish nouns are either masculine, feminine or neuter. Masculine and feminine forms (known as 'common gender') take the indefinite article *en* (a) while the neuter forms take the article *ett* (a). Every Swedish noun needs to be learned with its indefinite article (*en* or *ett*). We've only indicated the neuter nouns with ⓝ after the Swedish word. Note also that the ending 't' is added to adjectives for the neuter form (ie when they accompany indefinite singular nouns). In some cases both forms of the adjective (ie ⓜ & ⓕ form and ⓝ form) are spelled out in full and separated with a slash.

A

accident *olycka* oh-lew-ka
accommodation *husrum* ⓝ hus-rum
adaptor *adapter* a-*dap*-ter
address n *adress* a-dres
after *efter* ef-ter
air-conditioned *luftkonditionerad/luftkonditionerat*
  luft-kon-di-fho-*ney*-rad/luft-kon-di-fho-*ney*-rat
airplane *flygplan* ⓝ flewg-plaan
airport *flygplats* flewg-plats
alcohol *alkohol* al-ko-*hohl*
all *alla* a-la
all (everything) n *allt* alt
allergy *allergi* a-ler-*gee*
ambulance *ambulans* am-bu-*lans*
and *och* ok
ankle *vrist* vrist
arm *arm* arm
ashtray *askfat* ⓝ ask-*faat*
ATM *bankomat* bang-koh-*maat*

B

baby *baby* bey-bee
back (body) *rygg* rewg
backpack *ryggsäck* rewg-sek
bad *dålig(t)* dawr-lig/dawr-lit
bag *väska* ves-ka
baggage claim *bagageavhämtning*
  ba-*gaash*-aav-hemt-ning
bank *bank* bank
bar *bar* baar
bathroom *badrum* ⓝ baad-rum
battery *batteri* ⓝ ba-te-ree
beautiful *vacker(t)* va-ker(t)
bed *säng* seng

beer *öl* ⓝ eul
before *framför* fram-feur
behind *bakom* baa-kom
bicycle *cykel* sew-kel
big *stor(t)* stawr(t)
bill *räkning* reyk-ning
black *svart* svart
blanket *filt* filt
blood group *blodgrupp* blohd-grup
blue *blå(tt)* blaw/blot
boat *båt* bawt
book (make a reservation) v *boka* boh-ka
bottle *flaska* flas-ka
bottle opener *flasköppnare* flask-eup-na-re
boy *pojke* poy-ke
brakes (car) *bromsar* brom-sar
breakfast *frukost* froo-kost
broken (faulty) *sönder* seun-der
bus *buss* bus
(do) business *handla* hand-la
buy *köpa* sheu-pa

C

café *kafé* ⓝ ka-*fey*
camera *kamera* kaa-me-ra
camp site *campingplats* kam-ping-plats
cancel *upphäva* up-hey-va
can opener *burköppnare* burk-eup-na-re
car *bil* beel
cash n *kontant* kon-*tant*
cash (a cheque) v *lösa in (en check)* leu-sa in (eyn shek)
cell phone *mobiltelefon* moh-*beel*-te-le-fohn
centre *center* ⓝ sen-ter
change (money) v *växla (pengar)* veyk-sla (peng-ar)
cheap *billig(t)* bi-lig/bi-lit
check (bill) *räkning* reyk-ning

check-in *incheckning* in-chek-ning
chest *bröst* ⓝ breust
child *barn* ⓝ barn
cigarette *cigarett* si-ga-*ret*
city *storstad* stawr-staad
clean a *ren(t)* reyn(t)
closed *stängd/stängt* stengd/stengt
coffee *kaffe* ⓝ *ka*-fe
coins *mynt* ⓝ mewnt
cold a *kylig(t)* shew-lig/shew-lit
collect call *ba-samtal* ⓝ be-aa-sam-taal
come *komma* ko-ma
computer *dator* daa-tor
condom *kondom* kon-*dohm*
contact lenses *kontaklinser* kon-takt-lin-ser
cook v *laga mat* laa-ga maat
cost n *kostnad* kost-nad
credit card *kreditkort* ⓝ kre-*deet*-kort
cup *kopp* kop
currency exchange *växel* veyk-sel
customs (immigration) *tullen* tu-len

D

dangerous *farlig(t)* far-lig/far-lit
date (time) *datum* ⓝ *daa*-tum
day *dag* daag
delay *dröjsmål* ⓝ *dreuys*-mawl
dentist *tandläkare* tand-ley-ka-re
depart *avresa* aav-rey-sa
diaper *blöja* bleu-ya
dictionary *ordbok* ord-bohk
dinner *middag* mi-daag
direct *direkt* dee-rekt
dirty *smutsig(t)* smut-sig/smut-sit
disabled *handikappad* han-dee-ka-pad
discount n *rabatt* ra-bat
doctor *läkare* ley-ka-re
double bed *dubbelsäng* du-bel-seng
double room *dubbelt rum* ⓝ du-belt rum
drink n *dricka* dri-ka
drive v *köra* sheu-ra
drivers licence *körkort* ⓝ sheur-kort
drug (illicit) *narkotika* nar-koh-ti-ka
dummy (pacifier) *napp* nap

E

ear *öra* eu-ra
east *öst* eust

eat *äta* ey-ta
economy class *ekonomiklass* e-ko-noh-*mee*-klas
electricity *elektricitet* ey-lek-tri-si-*teyt*
elevator *hiss* his
email *e-post* ey-post
embassy *ambassad* am-ba-*saad*
emergency *nödsituation* ⓝ neud-si-too-a-fhohn
English (language) *engelska* eng-el-ska
entrance *ingång* in-gawng
evening *kväll* kvel
exchange rate *växelkurs* veyk-sel-kursh
exit n *utgång* oot-gawng
expensive *dyr(t)* dewr(t)
express mail *expresspost* eks-*pres*-post
eye *öga* ⓝ eu-ga

F

far *långt* lawngt
fast *snabb(t)* snab(t)
father *far* faar
film (camera) *film* film
finger *finger* ⓝ fing-er
first-aid kit *förbandslåda* feur-*bants*-law-da
first class *första klass* feu-shta klas
fish n *fisk* fisk
food *mat* maat
foot *fot* foht
fork *gaffel* ga-fel
free (of charge) *gratis* graa-tis
friend *vän/vänninna* ⓜ/ⓕ ven/ve-*ni*-na
fruit *frukt* frukt
full *fylld/fyllt* fewld/fewlt
funny *rolig(t)* roh-lig/roh-lit

G

gift *gåva* gaw-va
girl *flicka* fli-ka
glass (drinking) *glas* ⓝ glaas
glasses *glasögon* ⓝ glaa-seu-gon
go *åka* aw-ka
good *bra* braa
green *grön(t)* greun(t)
guide n *guide* gaid

H

half n *halv* halv
hand *hand* hand

handbag *handväska* hand-vey-ska
happy *glad* glaad
have *ha* haa
he *han* han
head *huvud* ⓝ hoo-vud
heart *hjärta* yair-ta
heat n *hetta* he-ta
heavy *tung(t)* tung(t)
help v *hjälp* yelp
here *här* hair
high *hög(t)* heug(t)
highway *huvudväg* hoo-vud-veyg
hike v *fotvandra* foht-van-dra
holiday *semester* se-mes-ter
homosexual n&a *homosexuell* hoh-moh-sek-soo-el
hospital *sjukhus* ⓝ fhook-hoos
hot *varm(t)* varm(t)
hotel *hotell* ⓝ hoh-tel
hungry *hungrig(t)* hung-grig/hung-grit
husband *man* man

I

I *jag* yaag
identification (card) *identitetskort* ⓝ
ee-den-ti-teyts-kort
ill *sjuk(t)* fhook(t)
important *viktig(t)* vik-tig/vik-tit
included *inklusiv* in-kloo-seev
injury *skada* skaa-da
insurance *försäkring* feu-shey-kring
Internet *Internet* ⓝ in-ter-net
interpreter *tolk* tolk

J

jewellery *smycke* ⓝ smew-ke
job *arbete* ⓝ aar-bey-te

K

key *nyckel* new-kel
kilogram *kilo(gram)* ⓝ shee-loh(-gram)
kitchen *kök* ⓝ sheuk
knife *kniv* kneev

L

laundry (place) *tvättstuga* tvet-stoo-ga
lawyer *advokat* ad-voh-kaat

left (direction) *vänster* ven-ster
left-luggage office *resgodsinlämning*
reys-gohds-in-lem-ning
leg *ben* ⓝ beyn
lesbian a *lesbisk* lez-bisk
less *mindre* min-dre
letter (mail) *brev* ⓝ breyv
lift (elevator) *hiss* his
light *ljus* ⓝ yoos
like v *tycka om* tew-ka om
lock n *lås* laws
long *lång(t)* lawng(t)
(be) lost (of a person) *vilse* vil-se
(be) lost (of property) *borta* bor-ta
lost-property office *hittegodsexpedition*
hi-te-gohds-eks-pe-di-fhohn
love v *älska* el-ska
luggage *bagage* ⓝ ba-gaash
lunch *lunch* lunsh

M

mail n *post* post
man *man* man
map *karta* kar-ta
market *marknad/torg* ⓝ mark-naad/tory
matches *tändstickor* ten-sti-kor
meat *kött* ⓝ sheut
medicine *medicin* me-di-seen
menu *meny/matsedel* me-new/maat-sey-del
message *bud* ⓝ bood
milk *mjölk* myeulk
minute *minut* mi-noot
mobile phone *mobiltelefon* moh-beel-te-le-fohn
money *pengar* peng-ar
month *månad* maw-nad
morning *morgon* mor-gon
mother *mor* mawr
motorcycle *motorcykel* moh-tor-sew-kel
motorway *motorväg* moh-tor-veyg
mouth *mun* mun
music *musik* moo-seek

N

name *namn* ⓝ namn
napkin *servett* seyr-vet
nappy *blöja* bleu-ya
near *nära* nair-a

neck *hals* hals
new *ny(tt)* new(t)
news *nyheter* new-hey-ter
newspaper *tidning* teed-ning
night *natt* nat
no *nej* ney
noisy *bullrig(t)* bul-rig/bul-rit
nonsmoking *icke-rökande* i·ke-reu-kan-de
north *nord* nord
nose *näsa* ney-sa
now *nu* noo
number *nummer* ⓝ nu-mer

O

oil (engine) *olja* ol-ya
old *gammal(t)* ga-mal(t)
one-way ticket *enkelbiljett* en-kel-bil-yet
open a *öppen/öppet* eu-pen/eu-pet
outside *utanför* oo-tan-feur

P

package *paket* ⓝ pa-keyt
paper *papper* ⓝ pa-per
park (car) v *parkera* par-key-ra
passport *pass* ⓝ pas
pay *betala* be-taa-la
pen *penna* pe-na
petrol *bensin* ben-seen
pharmacy *apotek* ⓝ a-poh-teyk
phonecard *telefonkort* ⓝ tel-le-fohn-kort
photo *foto* ⓝ foh-toh
plate *tallrik* tal-reek
police *polis* poh-lees
postcard *postkort* ⓝ post-kort
post office *posten* pos-ten
pregnant *gravid* gra-veed
price *pris* prees

Q

quiet *stilla* stil-la

R

rain n *regn* rengn
razor *rakhyvel* raak-hew-vel
receipt *kvitto* ⓝ kvi-toh

red *röd/rött* reud/reut
refund n *återbäring* aw-ter-bair-ing
registered mail *värdeförsändelse*
  vair-de-feu-shen-del-se
rent v *hyra* hew-ra
repair v *reparera* re-pa-rey-ra
reservation *beställning* be-stel-ning
restaurant *restaurang* res-taw-rang
return v *återvända* aw-ter-ven-da
return ticket *returbiljett* rey-toor-bil-yet
right (direction) *höger* heu-ger
road *väg* veyg
room *rum* ⓝ rum

S

safe a *trygg(t)* trewg(t)
sanitary napkin *dambinda* daam-bin-da
seat *sittplats* sit-plats
send *skicka* fhi-ka
service station *bensinstation* ben-seen-sta-fhohn
sex *samlag* ⓝ sam-laag
shampoo *schampo* ⓝ fham-poo
share (a dorm) *dela* dey-la
shaving cream *rakkräm* raak-kreym
she *hon* hoon
sheet (bed) *lakan* ⓝ laa-kan
shirt *skjorta* fhor-ta
shoes *skor* skor
shop n *affär* a-fair
short *kort* kort
shower n *dusch* doosh
single room *enkelt rum* ⓝ en-kelt rum
skin *hud* hood
skirt *kjol* shohl
sleep v *sova* soh-va
slowly *sakta* sak-ta
small *liten/litet* lee-ten/lee-tet
smoke (cigarettes) v *röka* reu-ka
soap *tvål* tvawl
some *någon/något* naw-gon/naw-got
soon *snart* snart
south *syd* sewd
souvenir shop *souvenir affär* su-ve-neer a-fair
speak *tala* taa-la
spoon *sked* fheyd
stamp *frimärke* ⓝ free-mair-ke
stand-by ticket *standbybiljett* stand-bai-bil-yet
station (train) *(järnvägs)station* (yairn-veyks-)sta-fhohn

stomach *mage* maa-ge
stop v *stanna/hålla* sta-na/haw-la
stop (bus) n *(buss)hållplats* (bus-)hawl-plats
street *gata* gaa-ta
student *studerande* stoo-dey-ran-de
sun *sol* sohl
sunscreen *solkräm* sohl-kreym
Sweden *Sverige* sve-rya
Swedish (language) *svenska* sven-ska
Swedish a *svensk(t)* svensk(t)
swim v *simma* si-ma

T

tampons *tampong* tam-pong
taxi *taxi* tak-see
teaspoon *tesked* tey-fheyd
teeth *tänder* te-ner
telephone n *telefon* te-le-fohn
television *TV* tey-vey
temperature (weather) *temperatur* tem-pe-ra-toor
tent *tält* ⓝ telt
that (one) *den* ⓜ & ⓣ/*det* ⓝ deyn/dey
they *dem* dom
thirsty *törstig(t)* teush-tig/teush-tit
this (one) *den här* ⓜ & ⓣ/*det här* ⓝ den hair/dey hair
throat *strupe* stroo-pe
ticket *biljett* bil-yet
time *tid* teed
tired *trött* treut
tissues *näsdukar* neys-doo-kar
today *i dag* i daag
toilet *toalett* toh-aa-let
tomorrow *imorgon* ee-mor-ron
tonight *i kväll* ee kvel
toothbrush *tandborste* tand-beu-shte
toothpaste *tandkräm* tand-kreym
torch (flashlight) *ficklampa* fik-lam-pa
tour n *tur* toor
tourist office *turistbyrå* too-rist-bew-raw
towel *badduk* baad-dook
train *tåg* ⓝ tawg
translate *översätta* eu-ve-se-ta
travel agency *resebyrå* rey-se-bew-raw
travellers cheque *resecheck* rey-se-shek
trousers *byxor* bewk-sor
twin beds *två sängar* tvaw seng-ar
tyre *däck* ⓝ dek

U

underwear *underkläder* un-der-kley-der
urgent *angelägen/angeläget*
   an-ye-ley-gen/an-ye-ley-get

V

vacant *ledig(t)* ley-dig/ley-dit
vacation *semester* se-mes-ter
vegetable n *grönsak* greun-saak
vegetarian a *vegetarian* ve-ge-taa-ree-aan
visa *visum* ⓝ vee-sum

W

waiter *servitör* ser-vi-teur
Waiter! *Vaktmästern!* vakt-mes-tern
walk v *gå* gaw
wallet *plånbok* plawn-bohk
warm a *varm(t)* varm(t)
wash (something) *tvätta* tve-ta
watch n *klocka* klo-ka
water *vatten* ⓝ va-ten
we *vi* vee
weekend *helg* hely
west *väst* vest
wheelchair *rullstol* rul-stohl
when *när* nair
where *var* var
white *vit(t)* veet/vit
who *vem* vem
why *varför* var-feur
wife *fru* froo
window *fönster* feun-ster
wine *vin* ⓝ veen
with *med* meyd
without *utan* oo-taan
woman *kvinna* kvi-na
write *skriva* skree-va

Y

yellow *gul(t)* gul(t)
yes *ja* yaa
yesterday *igår* i-gawr
you sg inf *du* doo
you sg pol & pl *ni* nee

Turkish

turkish alphabet

A a a	*B b* be	*C c* je	*Ç ç* che	*D d* de
E e e	*F f* fe	*G g* ge	*Ğ ğ* yu-*moo*·shak ge	*H h* he
I ı uh	*İ i* ee	*J j* zhe	*K k* ke	*L l* le
M m me	*N n* ne	*O o* o	*Ö ö* er	*P p* pe
R r re	*S s* se	*Ş ş* she	*T t* te	*U u* oo
Ü ü ew	*V v* ve	*Y y* ye	*Z z* ze	

■ turkish

TÜRKÇE

about Turkish

Turkish (*Türkçe tewrk·che*) – the language which traces its roots as far back as 3500 BC, has travelled through Central Asia, Persia, North Africa and Europe and been written in both Arabic and Latin script – has left us words like *yogurt*, *horde*, *sequin* and *bridge* (the game) along the way. But how did it transform itself from a nomad's tongue spoken in Mongolia into the language of modern Turkey, with a prestigious interlude as the diplomatic language of the Ottoman Empire?

The first evidence of the Turkish language, which is a member of the Ural-Altaic language family, was found on stone monuments from the 8th century BC, in what's now Outer Mongolia. In the 11th century, the Seljuq clan invaded Asia Minor (Anatolia) and imposed their language on the peoples they ruled. Over time, Arabic and Persian vocabulary was adopted to express artistic and philosophical concepts and Arabic script began to be used. By the 14th century, another clan – the Ottomans – was busy establishing the empire that was to control Eurasia for centuries. In their wake, they left the Turkish language. There were then two levels of Turkish – ornate Ottoman Turkish, with flowery Persian phrases and Arabic honorifics (words showing respect), used for diplomacy, business and art, and the language of the common Turks, which still used 'native' Turkish vocabulary and structures.

When the Ottoman Empire fell in 1922, the military hero, amateur linguist and historian Kemal Atatürk came to power and led the new Republic of Turkey. With the backing of a strong language reform movement, he devised a phonetic Latin script that reflected Turkish sounds more accurately than Arabic script. On 1 November 1928, the new writing system was unveiled: within two months, it was illegal to write Turkish in the old script. In 1932 Atatürk created the *Türk Dil Kurumu* (Turkish Language Society) and gave it the brief of simplifying the Turkish language to its 'pure' form of centuries before. The vocabulary and structure was completely overhauled. As a consequence, Turkish has changed so drastically that even Atatürk's own speeches are barely comprehensible to today's speakers of *öztürkçe* ('pure Turkish').

With 70 million speakers worldwide, Turkish is the official language of Turkey and the Turkish Republic of Northern Cyprus (recognised as a nation only by the Turkish government). Elsewhere, the language is also called *Osmanlı os·man·luh*, and is spoken by large populations in Germany, Bulgaria, Macedonia, Greece and the '-stans' of Central Asia. So start practising and you might soon be complimented with *Ağzına sağlık!* a·zuh·na sa·luhk (lit: health to your mouth) – 'Well said!'

pronunciation

vowel sounds

Most Turkish vowel sounds can be found in English, although in Turkish they're generally shorter and slightly harsher. When you see a double vowel, such as *saat* sa-*at* (hour), you need to pronounce both vowels.

symbol	english equivalent	turkish example	transliteration
a	run	*abide*	a·bee·*de*
ai	aisle	*hayvan*	hai·*van*
ay	say	*ney*	nay
e	bet	*ekmek*	ek·*mek*
ee	see	*ile*	ee·le
eu	nurse	*özel*	eu·*zel*
ew	ee pronounced with rounded lips	*üye*	ew·ye
o	pot	*oda*	o·*da*
oo	zoo	*uçak*	oo·*chak*
uh	ago	*ıslak*	uhs·*lak*

word stress

In Turkish, the stress generally falls on the last syllable of the word. Most two-syllable placenames, however, are stressed on the first syllable (eg *Kıbrıs kuhb*-ruhs), and in three-syllable placenames the stress is usually on the second syllable (eg *İstanbul* ees·*tan*·bool). Another common exception occurs when a verb has a form of the negative marker *me* (*me* me, *ma* ma, *mı* muh, *mi* mee, *mu* moo, or *mü* mew) added to it. In those cases, the stress goes onto the syllable before the marker – eg *gelmiyorlar* gel·*mee*·yor·lar (they're not coming). You don't need to worry too much about this, as the stressed syllable is always in italics in our coloured pronunciation guides.

consonant sounds

Most Turkish consonants sound the same as in English, so they're straightforward to pronounce. The exception is the Turkish r, which is always rolled. Note also that ğ is a silent letter which extends the vowel before it – it acts like the 'gh' combination in 'weigh', and is never pronounced.

symbol	english equivalent	turkish example	transliteration
b	**bed**	*bira*	*bee-ra*
ch	**cheat**	*çanta*	chan-*ta*
d	**dog**	*deniz*	de-*neez*
f	**fat**	*fabrika*	fab-ree-*ka*
g	**go**	*gar*	gar
h	**hat**	*hala*	ha-*la*
j	**joke**	*cadde*	jad-*de*
k	**kit**	*kadın*	ka-*duhn*
l	**lot**	*lider*	lee-*der*
m	**man**	*maç*	mach
n	**not**	*nefis*	ne-*fees*
p	**pet**	*paket*	pa-*ket*
r	**red** (rolled)	*rehber*	reh-*ber*
s	**sun**	*saat*	sa-*at*
sh	**shot**	*şarkı*	shar-*kuh*
t	**top**	*tas*	tas
v	**van** (but softer, between 'v' and 'w')	*vadi*	va-*dee*
y	**yes**	*yarım*	ya-*ruhm*
z	**zero**	*zarf*	zarf
zh	**pleasure**	*jambon*	zham-*bon*

tools

language difficulties

Do you speak English?
İngilizce konuşuyor musunuz?   een·gee·*leez*·je ko·noo·*shoo*·yor moo·soo·*nooz*

Do you understand?
Anlıyor musun?   an·*luh*·yor moo·*soon*

I understand.
Anlıyorum.   an·*luh*·yo·room

I don't understand.
Anlamıyorum.   an·*la*·muh·yo·room

What does (kitap) mean?
(Kitap) ne demektir?   (kee·*tap*) ne de·*mek*·teer

How do you pronounce this?
Bunu nasıl telaffuz edersiniz?   boo·*noo na*·suhl te·laf·*fooz* e·*der*·see·neez

How do you write (yabancı)?
(Yabancı) kelimesini   (ya·ban·*juh*) ke·lee·me·see·*nee*
nasıl yazarsınız?   *na*·suhl ya·*zar*·suh·nuhz

Could you please ...?	*Lütfen ...?*	*lewt*·fen ...
repeat that	*tekrarlar mısınız*	tek·*rar*·lar muh·suh·*nuhz*
speak more	*daha yavaş*	da·*ha* ya·*vash*
slowly	*konuşur musunuz*	ko·noo·*shoor* moo·soo·*nooz*
write it down	*yazar mısınız*	ya·*zar* muh·suh·*nuhz*

essentials

Yes.	*Evet.*	e·*vet*
No.	*Hayır.*	*ha*·yuhr
Please.	*Lütfen.*	*lewt*·fen
Thank you	*(Çok) Teşekkür*	(chok) te·shek·*kewr*
(very much). pol	*ederim.*	e·*de*·reem
Thanks. inf	*Teşekkürler.*	te·shek·kewr·*ler*
You're welcome.	*Birşey değil.*	beer·*shay* de·*eel*
Excuse me.	*Bakar mısınız?*	ba·*kar* muh·suh·*nuhz*
Sorry.	*Özür dilerim.*	eu·*zewr* dee·*le*·reem

numbers

0	*sıfır*	suh-*fuhr*	16	*onaltı*	on-al-*tuh*
1	*bir*	beer	17	*onyedi*	on-ye-*dee*
2	*iki*	ee-*kee*	18	*onsekiz*	on-se-*keez*
3	*üç*	ewch	19	*ondokuz*	on-do-*kooz*
4	*dört*	deurt	20	*yirmi*	yeer-*mee*
5	*beş*	besh	21	*yirmibir*	yeer-*mee*-beer
6	*altı*	al-*tuh*	22	*yirmiiki*	yeer-*mee*-ee-*kee*
7	*yedi*	ye-*dee*	30	*otuz*	o-*tooz*
8	*sekiz*	se-*keez*	40	*kırk*	kuhrk
9	*dokuz*	do-*kooz*	50	*elli*	el-*lee*
10	*on*	on	60	*altmış*	alt-*muhsh*
11	*onbir*	on-beer	70	*yetmiş*	yet-*meesh*
12	*oniki*	on-ee-*kee*	80	*seksen*	sek-*sen*
13	*onüç*	on-ewch	90	*doksan*	dok-*san*
14	*ondört*	on-deurt	100	*yüz*	yewz
15	*onbeş*	on-besh	1000	*bin*	been

time & dates

What time is it?	*Saat kaç?*	sa-*at* kach
It's one o'clock.	*Saat bir.*	sa-*at* beer
It's (10) o'clock.	*Saat (on).*	sa-*at* (on)
Quarter past (10).	*(Onu) çeyrek geçiyor.*	(o-*noo*) chay-*rek* ge-*chee*-yor
Half past (10).	*(On) buçuk.*	(on) boo-*chook*
Quarter to (11).	*(Onbire) çeyrek var.*	(on-bee-*re*) chay-*rek* var
At what time ...?	*Saat kaçta ...?*	sa-*at* kach-*ta* ...
At ...	*Saat ...*	sa-*at* ...
am (morning)	*sabah*	sa-*bah*
pm (afternoon)	*öğleden sonra*	er-le-*den* son-ra
pm (evening)	*gece*	ge-*je*
Monday	*Pazartesi*	pa-*zar*-te-see
Tuesday	*Salı*	sa-*luh*
Wednesday	*Çarşamba*	char-sham-*ba*
Thursday	*Perşembe*	per-shem-*be*
Friday	*Cuma*	joo-*ma*
Saturday	*Cumartesi*	joo-*mar*-te-see
Sunday	*Pazar*	pa-*zar*

January	Ocak	o·jak
February	Şubat	shoo·bat
March	Mart	mart
April	Nisan	nee·san
May	Mayıs	ma·yuhs
June	Haziran	ha·zee·ran
July	Temmuz	tem·mooz
August	Ağustos	a·oos·tos
September	Eylül	ay·lewl
October	Ekim	e·keem
November	Kasım	ka·suhm
December	Aralık	a·ra·luhk

What date is it today?
Bugün ayın kaçı?   boo·gewn a·yuhn ka·chuh

It's (18 October).
(Onsekiz Ekim).   (on·se·keez e·keem)

since (May)	(Mayıs'tan) beri	(ma·yuhs·tan) be·ree
until (June)	(Haziran'a) kadar	(ha·zee·ra·na) ka·dar
yesterday	dün	dewn
today	bugün	boo·gewn
tonight	bu gece	boo ge·je
tomorrow	yarın	ya·ruhn
last/next ...	geçen/gelecek ...	ge·chen/ge·le·jek ...
night	gece	ge·je
week	hafta	haf·ta
month	ay	ai
year	yıl	yuhl
yesterday/tomorrow ...	dün/yarın ...	dewn/ya·ruhn ...
morning	sabah	sa·bah
afternoon	öğleden sonra	eu·le·den son·ra
evening	akşam	ak·sham

weather

What's the weather like?	Hava nasıl?	ha·va na·suhl

It's ...	Hava ...	ha·va ...
cloudy	bulutlu	boo·loot·loo
cold	soğuk	so·ook
hot	sıcak	suh·jak
raining	yağmurlu	ya·moor·loo
snowing	kar yağışı	kar ya·uhsh·luh
sunny	güneşli	gew·nesh·lee
warm	ılık	uh·luhk
windy	rüzgarlı	rewz·gar·luh

spring	ilkbahar	eelk·ba·har
summer	yaz	yaz
autumn	sonbahar	son·ba·har
winter	kış	kuhsh

border crossing

I'm here ...	Ben ...	ben ...
in transit	transit yolcuyum	tran·seet yol·joo·yoom
on business	iş gezisindeyim	eesh ge·zee·seen·de·yeem
on holiday	tatildeyim	ta·teel·de·yeem

I'm here for ...	Ben ... buradayım.	ben ... boo·ra·da·yuhm
(10) days	(on) günlüğüne	(on) gewn·lew·ew·ne
(three) weeks	(üç) haftalığına	(ewch) haf·ta·luh·uh·na
(two) months	(iki) aylığına	(ee·kee) ai·luh·uh·na

I'm going to (Sarıyer).
(Sarıyer'e) gidiyorum.   (sa·ruh·ye·re) gee·dee·yo·room

I'm staying at the (Divan).
(Divan'da) kalıyorum.   (dee·van·da) ka·luh·yo·room

I have nothing to declare.
Beyan edecek hiçbir şeyim yok.   be·yan e·de·jek heech·beer she·yeem yok

I have something to declare.
Beyan edecek bir şeyim var.   be·yan e·de·jek beer she·yeem var

That's (not) mine.
Bu benim (değil).   boo be·neem (de·eel)

transport

tickets & luggage

Where can I buy a ticket?
Nereden bilet alabilirim?   ne·re·den bee·*let* a·*la*·bee·lee·reem

Do I need to book a seat?
Yer ayırtmam gerekli mi?   yer a·yuhrt·*mam* ge·rek·*lee* mee

One ... ticket to (Bostancı), please.	*(Bostancı'ya) ... lütfen.*	*(bos·tan·juh·ya) ... lewt·fen*
one-way	*bir gidiş bileti*	beer gee·*deesh* bee·le·*tee*
return	*gidiş-dönüş bir bilet*	gee·deesh·deu·*newsh* beer bee·*let*

I'd like to ... my ticket, please.	*Biletimi ... istiyorum.*	bee·le·tee·*mee* ... ees·*tee*·yo·room
cancel	*iptal ettirmek*	eep·*tal* et·teer·*mek*
change	*değiştirmek*	de·eesh·teer·*mek*
collect	*almak*	al·*mak*
confirm	*onaylatmak*	o·nai·lat·*mak*

I'd like a ... seat, please.	*... bir yer istiyorum.*	... beer yer ees·*tee*·yo·room
nonsmoking	*Sigara içilmeyen kısımda*	see·*ga*·ra ee·*cheel*·me·yen kuh·suhm·*da*
smoking	*Sigara içilen kısımda*	see·*ga*·ra ee·*chee*·len kuh·suhm·*da*

How much is it?
Şu ne kadar?   shoo ne ka·*dar*

Is there air conditioning?
Klima var mı?   *klee*·ma var muh

Is there a toilet?
Tuvalet var mı?   too·va·*let* var muh

How long does the trip take?
Yolculuk ne kadar sürer?   yol·joo·*look* ne ka·*dar* sew·*rer*

Is it a direct route?
Direk güzergah mı?   dee·*rek* gew·zer·*gah* muh

Where's the luggage locker?
Emanet dolabı nerede?   e·ma·*net* do·la·*buh* ne·re·de

My luggage has been ...	Bagajım ...	ba·ga·*zhuhm* ...
damaged	zarar gördü	za·*rar* geu·*dew*
lost	kayboldu	kai·bol·*doo*
stolen	çalındı	cha·luhn·*duh*

getting around

Where does flight (TK0060) arrive?

(TK0060) sefer	(*te*·ka suh·*fuhr* suh·*fuhr* alt·*muhsh*)
sayılı uçak nereye iniyor?	se·*fer* sa·yuh·*luh* oo·*chak* ne·re·ye ee·*nee*·yor

Where does flight (TK0060) depart?

(TK0060) sefer	(*te*·ka suh·*fuhr* suh·*fuhr* alt·*muhsh*)
sayılı uçak nereden kalkıyor?	se·*fer* sa·yuh·*luh* oo·*chak* ne·re·den kal·*kuh*·yor

Where's (the) ...?	... nerede?	... *ne*·re·de
arrivals hall	Gelen yolcu bölümü	ge·*len* yol·*joo* beu·lew·*mew*
departures hall	Giden yolcu bölümü	gee·*den* yol·*joo* beu·lew·*mew*
duty-free shop	Gümrüksüz satış mağazası	gewm·rewk·*sewz* sa·*tuhsh* ma·a·za·*suh*
gate (12)	(Oniki) numaralı kapı	(on·ee·*kee*) noo·ma·ra·*luh* ka·*puh*

Is this the ... to (Sirkeci)?	(Sirkeci'ye) giden ... bu mu?	(seer·ke·jee·ye) gee·*den* ... boo moo
boat	vapur	va·*poor*
bus	otobüs	o·to·*bews*
plane	uçak	oo·*chak*
train	tren	tren

What time's the ... bus?	... otobüs ne zaman?	... o·to·*bews* ne za·*man*
first	İlk	eelk
last	Son	son
next	Sonraki	son·ra·*kee*

At what time does it arrive/leave?

Ne zaman varır/kalkacak?   ne za·*man* va·*ruhr*/kal·ka·*jak*

How long will it be delayed?

Ne kadar gecikecek?   ne ka·*dar* ge·jee·ke·*jek*

What station/stop is this?
Bu hangi istasyon/durak?   boo *han*·gee ees·tas·*yon/*doo·*rak*

What's the next station/stop?
Sonraki istasyon/durak hangisi?   son·ra·*kee* ees·tas·*yon/*doo·*rak han*·gee·see

Does it stop at (Kadıköy)?
(Kadıköy'de) durur mu?   (ka·*duh*·kay·de) doo·*roor* moo

Please tell me when we get to (Beşiktaş).
(Beşiktaş'a) vardığımızda   (be·*sheek*·ta·sha) var·duh·uh·muhz·*da*
lütfen bana söyleyin.   *lewt*·fen ba·*na* say·*le*·yeen

How long do we stop here?
Burada ne kadar duracağız   boo·ra·*da* ne ka·*dar* doo·ra·ja·uhz

Is this seat available?
Bu koltuk boş mu?   boo kol·*took* bosh moo

That's my seat.
Burası benim yerim.   boo·ra·*suh* be·*neem* ye·*reem*

I'd like a taxi ...   **... bir taksi istiyorum.**   ... beer tak·*see* ees·*tee*·yo·room
  at (9am)   *(Sabah dokuzda)*   (sa·*bah* do·kooz·*da*)
  now   *Hemen*   *he*·men
  tomorrow   *Yarın*   *ya*·ruhn

Is this taxi available?
Bu taksi boş mu?   boo tak·*see* bosh moo

How much is it to ...?
... ne kadar?   ... ne ka·*dar*

Please put the meter on.
Lütfen taksimetreyi   *lewt*·fen tak·*see*·met·re·yee
çalıştırın.   cha·luhsh·*tuh*·ruhn

Please take me to (this address).
Lütfen beni (bu adrese) götürün.   *lewt*·fen be·*nee* (boo ad·re·*se*) geu·*tew*·rewn

Please ...   *Lütfen ...*   *lewt*·fen ...
  slow down   *yavaşlayın*   ya·vash·*la*·yuhn
  stop here   *burada durun*   boo·ra·*da* doo·roon
  wait here   *burada bekleyin*   boo·ra·*da* bek·*le*·yeen

car, motorbike & bicycle hire

I'd like to	Bir ... kiralamak	beer ... kee·ra·la·mak
hire a ...	istiyorum.	ees·tee·yo·room
bicycle	bisiklet	bee·seek·let
car	araba	a·ra·ba
motorbike	motosiklet	mo·to·seek·let

with ...		
a driver	şoförlü	sho·feur·lew
air conditioning	klimalı	klee·ma·luh

How much	... kirası ne	... kee·ra·suh ne
for ... hire?	kadar?	ka·dar
hourly	Saatlık	sa·at·luhk
daily	Günlük	gewn·lewk
weekly	Haftalık	haf·ta·luhk

air	hava	ha·va
oil	yağ	ya
petrol	benzin	ben·zeen
tyres	lastikler	las·teek·ler

I need a mechanic.
Tamirciye ihtiyacım var.   ta·meer·jee·ye eeh·tee·ya·juhm var

I've run out of petrol.
Benzinim bitti.   ben·zee·neem beet·tee

I have a flat tyre.
Lastiğim patladı.   las·tee·eem pat·la·duh

directions

Where's the ...?	... nerede?	... ne·re·de
bank	Banka	ban·ka
city centre	Şehir merkezi	she·heer mer·ke·zee
hotel	Otel	o·tel
market	Pazar yeri	pa·zar ye·ree
police station	Polis karakolu	po·lees ka·ra·ko·loo
post office	Postane	pos·ta·ne
public toilet	Umumi tuvalet	oo·moo·mee too·va·let
tourist office	Turizm bürosu	too·reezm bew·ro·soo

Is this the road to (Taksim)?
(Taksim'e) giden yol bu mu?   (*tak*·see·me) gee·*den* yol boo moo

Can you show me (on the map)?
Bana (haritada)   ba·*na* (ha·ree·ta·*da*)
gösterebilir misiniz?   geus·te·*re*·bee·leer mee·seen·*neez*

What's the address?
Adresi nedir?   ad·re·*see* ne·deer

How far is it?
Ne kadar uzakta?   ne ka·*dar* oo·zak·*ta*

How do I get there?
Oraya nasıl gidebilirim?   o·ra·*ya na*·suhl gee·*de*·bee·lee·reem

Turn ...	... *dön.*	... deun
at the corner	*Köşeden*	keu·she·*den*
at the traffic lights	*Trafik*	tra·*feek*
	ışıklarından	uh·shuhk·la·ruhn·*dan*
left/right	*Sola/Sağa*	so·*la*/sa·*a*

It's ...		
behind ...	... *arkasında.*	... ar·ka·suhn·*da*
far away	*Uzak.*	oo·*zak*
here	*Burada.*	boo·ra·*da*
in front of ...	... *önünde.*	... eu·newn·*de*
left	*Solda.*	sol·*da*
near ...	... *yakınında.*	... ya·kuh·nuhn·*da*
next to ...	... *yanında.*	... ya·nuhn·*da*
on the corner	*Köşede.*	keu·she·*de*
opposite ...	... *karşısında.*	... kar·shuh·suhn·*da*
right	*Sağda.*	sa·*da*
straight ahead	*Tam karşıda.*	tam kar·shuh·*da*
there	*Şurada.*	shoo·ra·*da*

by bus	*otobüslü*	o·to·bews·*lew*
by taxi	*taksili*	tak·see·*lee*
by train	*trenli*	tren·*lee*
on foot	*yürüyerek*	yew·rew·ye·*rek*

north	*kuzey*	koo·*zay*
south	*güney*	gew·*nay*
east	*doğu*	do·*oo*
west	*batı*	ba·*tuh*

signs

Giriş/Çıkış	gee-*reesh*/chuh-*kuhsh*	**Entrance/Exit**
Açık/Kapalı	a-*chuhk*/ka-pa-*luh*	**Open/Closed**
Boş Oda	bosh o-*da*	**Rooms Available**
Boş Yer Yok	bosh yer yok	**No Vacancies**
Danışma	da-nuhsh-*ma*	**Information**
Polis Karakolu	po-*lees* ka-ra-ko-*loo*	**Police Station**
Yasak	ya-*sak*	**Prohibited**
Tuvaletler	too-va-let-*ler*	**Toilets**
Erkek	er-*kek*	**Men**
Kadın	ka-*duhn*	**Women**
Sıcak/Soğuk	suh-*jak*/so-*ook*	**Hot/Cold**

accommodation

finding accommodation

Where's a ...?	Buralarda nerede ... var?	boo-ra-lar-*da* ne-re-de ... var
camping ground	kamp yeri	kamp ye-*ree*
guesthouse	misafirhane	mee-*sa*-feer-ha-ne
hotel	otel	o-*tel*
youth hostel	gençlik hosteli	gench-*leek* hos-te-*lee*
Can you recommend somewhere ...?	... bir yer tavsiye edebilir misiniz?	... beer yer tav-see-*ye* e-de-bee-leer mee-see-*neez*
cheap	Ucuz	oo-*jooz*
good	İyi	ee-*yee*
nearby	Yakın	ya-*kuhn*

I'd like to book a room, please.
Bir oda ayırtmak
istiyorum lütfen.
beer o-*da* a-*yuhrt*-mak
ees-*tee*-yo-room *lewt*-fen

I have a reservation.
Rezervasyonum var.
re-zer-vas-yo-*noom* var

My name's ...
Benim ismim ...
be-*neem* ees-*meem* ...

Do you have a ... room?	... odanız var mı?	... o-da-nuhz var muh
single	Tek kişilik	tek kee-shee-leek
double	İki kişilik	ee-kee kee-shee-leek
twin	Çift yataklı	cheeft ya-tak-luh

How much is it per ...?	... ne kadar?	... ne ka-dar
night	Geceliği	ge-je-lee-ee
person	Kişi başına	kee-shee ba-shuh-na

Can I pay by ...?	... ile ödeyebilir miyim?	... ee-le eu-de-ye-bee-leer mee-yeem
credit card	Kredi kartı	kre-dee kar-tuh
travellers cheque	Seyahat çeki	se-ya-hat che-kee

I'd like to stay for (three) nights.
Kalmak istiyorum (üç) geceliğine. kal-mak ees-tee-yo-room (ewch) ge-je-lee-ee-ne

From (2 July) to (6 July).
(İki Temmuz'dan) (ee-kee tem-mooz-dan)
(altı Temmuz'a) kadar. (al-tuh tem-moo-za) ka-dar

Can I see it?
Görebilir miyim. geu-re-bee-leer mee-yeem

Am I allowed to camp here?
Burada kamp yapabilir miyim? boo-ra-da kamp ya-pa-bee-leer mee-yeem

Where can I find a camping ground?
Kamp alanı nerede? kamp a-la-nuh ne-re-de

requests & queries

When/Where is breakfast served?
Kahvaltı ne zaman/ kah-val-tuh ne za-man/
nerede veriliyor? ne-re-de ve-ree-lee-yor

Please wake me at (seven).
Lütfen beni (yedide) kaldırın. lewt-fen be-nee (ye-dee-de) kal-duh-ruhn

Could I have my key, please?
Anahtarımı alabilir miyim? a-nah-ta-ruh-muh a-la-bee-leer mee-yeem

Can I get another (blanket)?
Başka bir (battaniye) bash-ka beer (bat-ta-nee-ye)
alabilir miyim? a-la-bee-leer mee-yeem

Is there an elevator/a safe?
Asansör/Kasanız var mı? a-san-seur/ka-sa-nuhz var muh

The room is too ...	Çok ...	chok ...
expensive	pahalı	pa·ha·luh
noisy	gürültülü	gew·rewl·tew·lew
small	küçük	kew·chewk

The ... doesn't work.	... çalışmıyor.	... cha·luhsh·muh·yor
air conditioning	Klima	klee·ma
fan	Fan	fan
toilet	Tuvalet	too·va·let

This ... isn't clean.	Bu ... temiz değil.	boo ... te·meez de·eel
pillow	yastık	yas·tuhk
sheet	çarşaf	char·shaf
towel	havlu	hav·loo

checking out

What time is checkout?
Çıkış ne zaman? chuh·kuhsh ne za·man

Can I leave my luggage here?
Eşyalarımı burada esh·ya·la·ruh·muh boo·ra·da
bırakabilir miyim? buh·ra·ka·bee·leer mee·yeem

Could I have	... alabilir	... a·la·bee·leer
my ..., please?	miyim lütfen?	mee·yeem lewt·fen
deposit	Depozitomu	de·po·zee·to·moo
passport	Pasaportumu	pa·sa·por·too·moo
valuables	Değerli eşyalarımı	de·er·lee esh·ya·la·ruh·muh

communications & banking

the internet

Where's the local Internet café?
En yakın internet kafe nerede? en ya·kuhn een·ter·net ka·fe ne·re·de

How much is it per hour?
Saati ne kadar? sa·a·tee ne ka·dar

I'd like to ...	... istiyorum.	... ees·tee·yo·room
check my email	E-postama bakmak	e·pos·ta·ma bak·mak
get Internet access	İnternete girmek	een·ter·ne·te geer·mek
use a printer	Printeri kullanmak	preen·te·ree kool·lan·mak
use a scanner	Tarayıcıyı	ta·ra·yuh·juh·yuh

mobile/cell phone

I'd like a ...	... istiyorum.	... ees·tee·yo·room
mobile/cell	Cep telefonu	jep te·le·fo·noo
phone for hire	kiralamak	kee·ra·la·mak
SIM card for	Buradaki şebeke	boo·ra·da·kee she·be·ke
your network	için SİM kart	ee·cheen seem kart

What are the rates?	Ücret tarifesi nedir?	ewj·ret ta·ree·fe·see ne·deer

telephone

What's your phone number?
Telefon numaranız nedir?
te·le·fon noo·ma·ra·nuhz ne·deer

The number is ...
Telefon numarası ...
te·le·fon noo·ma·ra·suh ...

Where's the nearest public phone?
En yakın telefon
kulübesi nerede?
en ya·kuhn te·le·fon
koo·lew·be·see ne·re·de

I'd like to buy a phonecard.
Telefon kartı almak istiyorum.
te·le·fon kar·tuh al·mak ees·tee·yo·room

I want to ...	... istiyorum.	... ees·tee·yo·room
call (Singapore)	(Singapur'u)	(seen·ga·poo·roo)
	aramak	a·ra·mak
make a local	Yerel bir görüşme	ye·rel beer geu·rewsh·me
call	yapmak	yap·mak
reverse the	Ödemeli görüşme	eu·de·me·lee ger·rewsh·me
charges	yapmak	yap·mak

How much does ... cost?	... ne kadar eder?	... ne ka·dar e·der
a (three)-minute call	(Üç) dakikalık konuşma	(ewch) da·kee·ka·luhk ko·noosh·ma
each extra minute	Her ekstra dakika	her eks·tra da·kee·ka

It's (10) *yeni kuruş* per minute.
Bir dakikası (on) yeni kuruş.   beer da·kee·ka·*suh* (on) ye·*nee* koo·*roosh*

post office

I want to send a ...	Bir ... göndermek istiyorum.	beer ... geun·der·mek ees·tee·yo·room
fax	faks	faks
letter	mektup	mek·toop
parcel	paket	pa·ket
postcard	kartpostal	kart·pos·tal
I want to buy a/an ...	... satın almak istiyorum.	... sa·tuhn al·mak ees·tee·yo·room
envelope	Zarf	zarf
stamp	Pul	pool
Please send it (to Australia) by ...	Lütfen ... (Avustralya'ya) gönderin.	lewt·fen ... (a·voos·tral·ya·ya) geun·de·reen
airmail	hava yoluyla	ha·va yo·looy·la
express mail	ekspres posta	eks·pres pos·ta
registered mail	taahhütlü posta	ta·ah·hewt·lew pos·ta
surface mail	deniz yoluyla	de·neez yo·looy·la
Is there any mail for me?	Bana posta var mı?	ba·na pos·ta var muh

bank

Where's a/an ...?	... nerede var?	... ne·re·de var
ATM	Bankamatik	ban·ka·ma·teek
foreign exchange office	Döviz bürosu	deu·veez bew·ro·soo

I'd like to ...	... istiyorum.	... ees·tee·yo·room
cash a cheque	Çek bozdurmak	chek boz·door·mak
change a travellers cheque	Seyahat çeki bozdurmak	se·ya·hat che·kee boz·door·mak
change money	Para bozdurmak	pa·ra boz·door·mak
get a cash advance	Avans çekmek	a·vans chek·mek
withdraw money	Para çekmek	pa·ra chek·mek

What's the ...?	... nedir?	... ne·deer
charge for that	Ücreti	ewj·re·tee
commission	Komisyon	ko·mees·yon
exchange rate	Döviz kuru	deu·veez koo·roo

It's ...		
(12) euros	(Oniki) euro.	(on·ee·kee) yoo·ro
(25) lira	(Yirmibeş) lira.	(yeer·mee·besh) lee·ra
free	Ücretsiz.	ewj·ret·seez

What time does the bank open?
Banka ne zaman açılıyor? — ban·ka ne za·man a·chuh·luh·yor

Has my money arrived yet?
Param geldi mi? — pa·ram gel·dee mee

sightseeing

getting in

What time does it open/close?
Saat kaçta açılır/kapanır? — sa·at kach·ta a·chuh·luhr/ka·pa·nuhr

What's the admission charge?
Giriş ücreti nedir? — gee·reesh ewj·re·tee ne·deer

Is there a discount for children/students?
Çocuk/Öğrenci indirimi var mı? — cho·jook/eu·ren·jee een·dee·ree·mee var muh

I'd like a ...	... istiyorum.	... ees·tee·yo·room
catalogue	Katalog	ka·ta·log
guide	Rehber	reh·ber
local map	Yerel Harita	ye·rel ha·ree·ta

I'd like to see ...	... görmek istiyorum.	... geur-*mek* ees-*tee*-yo-room
What's that?	Bu nedir?	boo *ne*-deer
Can I take a photo?	Bir fotoğrafınızı	beer fo-to-ra-fuh-nuh-*zuh*
	çekebilir miyim?	che-ke-bee-leer mee-*yeem*

tours

When's the next ...?	Sonraki ... ne zaman?	son-ra-*kee* ... ne za-*man*
day trip	gündüz turu	gewn-*dewz* too-*roo*
tour	tur	toor

Is ... included?	... dahil mi?	... da-*heel* mee
accommodation	Kalacak yer	ka-la-*jak* yer
the admission charge	Giriş	gee-*reesh*
food	Yemek	ye-*mek*
transport	Ulaşım	oo-la-*shuhm*

How long is the tour?
Tur ne kadar sürer?   toor ne ka-*dar* sew-*rer*

What time should we be back?
Saat kaçta dönmeliyiz?   sa-*at* kach-*ta* deun-me-*lee*-yeez

sightseeing

castle	kale	ka-*le*
church	kilise	kee-lee-*se*
main square	meydan	may-*dan*
monument	anıt	a-*nuht*
mosque	cami	ja-*mee*
museum	müze	mew-*ze*
old city	eski şehir	es-kee she-*heer*
palace	saray	sa-*rai*
ruins	harabeler	ha-ra-be-*ler*
stadium	stadyum	stad-*yoom*
statue	heykel	hay-*kel*
Turkish bath	hamam	ha-*mam*

shopping

enquiries

Where's a ...?	... nerede?	... ne·re·de
bank	Banka	ban·ka
bookshop	Kitapçı	kee·tap·chuh
camera shop	Fotoğrafçı	fo·to·raf·chuh
department store	Büyük mağaza	bew·yewk ma·a·za
grocery store	Bakkal	bak·kal
market	Pazar yeri	pa·zar ye·ree
newsagency	Gazete bayii	ga·ze·te ba·yee·ee
supermarket	Süpermarket	sew·per·mar·ket

Where can I buy (a padlock)?
Nereden (asma kilit)   ne·re·den (as·ma kee·leet)
alabilirim?   a·la·bee·lee·reem

I'm looking for ...
... istiyorum.   ... ees·tee·yo·room

Can I look at it?
Bakabilir miyim?   ba·ka·bee·leer mee·yeem

Do you have any others?
Başka var mı?   bash·ka var muh

Does it have a guarantee?
Garantisi var mı?   ga·ran·tee·see var muh

Can I have it sent overseas?
Yurt dışına gönderebilir   yoort duh·shuh·na geun·de·re·bee·leer
misiniz?   mee·see·neez

Can I have my ... repaired?
... burada tamir ettirebilir   ... boo·ra·da ta·meer et·tee·re·bee·leer
miyim?   mee·yeem

It's faulty.
Arızalı.   a·ruh·za·luh

I'd like ..., please.	... istiyorum lütfen.	... ees·tee·yo·room lewt·fen
a bag	Çanta	chan·ta
a refund	Para iadesi	pa·ra ee·a·de·see
to return this	Bunu iade etmek	boo·noo ee·a·de et·mek

paying

How much is it?
Ne kadar?
ne ka·*dar*

Can you write down the price?
Fiyatı yazabilir misiniz?
fee·ya·*tuh* ya·*za*·bee·leer mee·see·*neez*

That's too expensive.
Bu çok pahalı.
boo chok pa·ha·*luh*

Is that your lowest price?
Son fiyatınız bu mu?
son fee·ya·tuh·*nuhz* boo moo

I'll give you (30) lira.
(Otuz) lira veririm.
(o·*tooz*) lee·*ra* ve·*ree*·reem

There's a mistake in the bill.
Hesapta bir yanlışlık var.
he·sap·*ta* beer yan·luhsh·*luhk* var

Do you accept ...?   *... kabul ediyor*   *... ka·bool e·dee·yor*
     musunuz?   moo·soo·*nooz*
     credit cards   *Kredi kartı*   kre·dee kar·*tuh*
     debit cards   *Banka kartı*   ban·ka kar·*tuh*
     travellers cheques   *Seyahat çeki*   se·ya·hat che·kee

I'd like ..., please.   *... istiyorum lütfen.*   *... ees·tee·yo·room lewt·*fen
     a receipt   *Makbuz*   mak·*booz*
     my change   *Paramın üstünü*   pa·ra·*muhn* ews·tew·*new*

clothes & shoes

Can I try it on?   *Deneyebilir miyim?*   de·ne·ye·bee·leer mee·*yeem*
My size is (42).   *(Kırkiki) beden*   (kuhrk·ee·*kee*) be·*den*
     giyiyorum.   gee·yee·yo·room
It doesn't fit.   *Olmuyor.*   ol·moo·yor

small   *küçük*   kew·*chewk*
medium   *orta*   or·*ta*
large   *büyük*   bew·*yewk*

books & music

I'd like a . . .	. . . istiyorum.	. . . ees·tee·yo·room
newspaper	(İngilizce)	(een·gee·leez·je)
(in English)	bir gazete	beer ga·ze·te
pen	Tükenmez kalem	tew·ken·mez ka·lem

Is there an English-language bookshop?
İngilizce yayın satan — een·gee·leez·je ya·yuhn sa·tan
bir dükkan var mı? — beer dewk·kan var muh

I'm looking for something by (Yaşar Kemal).
(Yaşar Kemal'in) albümlerine — (ya·shar ke·mal·een) al·bewm·le·ree·ne
bakmak istiyorum. — bak·mak ees·tee·yo·room

Can I listen to this?
Bunu dinleyebilir miyim? — boo·noo deen·le·ye·bee·leer mee·yeem

photography

Can you . . . ?	. . . misiniz?	. . . mee·see·neez
develop this film	Bu filmi basabilir	boo feel·mee ba·sa·bee·leer
load my film	Filmi makineye	feel·mee ma·kee·ne·ye
	takabilir	ta·ka·bee·leer
transfer photos	Kameramdaki	ka·me·ram·da·kee
from my	fotoğrafları	fo·to·raf·la·ruh
camera to CD	CD'ye aktarabilir	see·dee·ye ak·ta·ra·bee·leer

I need a/an . . . film	Bu kamera için . . .	boo ka·me·ra ee·cheen . . .
for this camera.	film istiyorum.	feelm ees·tee·yo·room
APS	APS	a·pe·se
B&W	siyah-beyaz	see·yah·be·yaz
colour	renkli	renk·lee
slide	slayt	slayt
(200) speed	(ikiyüz) hızlı	(ee·kee·yewz) huhz·luh

When will it be ready?	Ne zaman hazır olur?	ne za·man ha·zuhr o·loor

meeting people

greetings, goodbyes & introductions

Hello.	*Merhaba.*	*mer·ha·ba*
Hi.	*Selam.*	*se·lam*
Good night.	*İyi geceler.*	*ee·yee ge·je·ler*
Goodbye.	*Hoşçakal.* inf	hosh·*cha*·kal
(by person leaving)	*Hoşçakalın.* pol	hosh·*cha*·ka·luhn
Goodbye.	*Güle güle.*	gew·le gew·le
(by person staying)		
See you later.	*Sonra görüşürüz.*	*son*·ra ger·rew·*shew*·rewz
Mr	*Bay*	bai
Mrs/Miss	*Bayan*	ba·*yan*
How are you?	*Nasılsın?* inf	*na*·suhl·suhn
	Nasılsınız? pol	*na*·suhl·suh·nuhz
Fine. And you?	*İyiyim. Ya sen/siz?* inf/pol	ee·*yee*·yeem ya sen/seez
What's your name?	*Adınız ne?* inf	a·duh·*nuhz* ne
	Adınız nedir? pol	a·duh·*nuhz* ne·deer
My name is ...	*Benim adım ...*	be·*neem* a·*duhm* ...
I'm pleased to	*Tanıştığımıza*	ta·nuhsh·tuh·uh·muh·*za*
meet you.	*sevindim.*	se·veen·*deem*
This is my ...	*Bu benim ...*	boo be·*neem* ...
brother	*kardeşim*	kar·de·*sheem*
daughter	*kızım*	kuh·*zuhm*
father	*babayım*	ba·ba·*yuhm*
friend	*arkadaşım*	ar·ka·da·*shuhm*
husband	*kocam*	ko·*jam*
mother	*anneyim*	an·ne·*yeem*
partner (intimate)	*partnerim*	part·ne·*reem*
sister	*kız kardeşim*	kuhz kar·de·*sheem*
son	*oğlum*	o·*loom*
wife	*karım*	ka·*ruhm*
Here's my ...	*İşte benim ...*	eesh·te be·*neem* ...
(email) address	*(e-posta) adresim*	(e·*pos*·ta) ad·re·*seem*
fax number	*faks numaram*	faks noo·ma·*ram*
phone number	*telefon numaram*	te·le·*fon* noo·ma·*ram*

What's your ...?	Sizin ... nedir?	see·zeen ... ne·deer
(email) address	(e·posta) adresiniz	(e·pos·ta) ad·re·see·neez
fax number	faks numaranız	faks noo·ma·ra·nuhz
phone number	telefon numaranız	te·le·fon noo·ma·ra·nuhz

occupations

What's your occupation?	Mesleğiniz nedir? pol	mes·le·ee·neez ne·deer
	Mesleğin nedir? inf	mes·le·een ne·deer
I'm a/an ...	Ben ...	ben ...
artist	sanatçıyım m&f	sa·nat·chuh·yuhm
business person	iş adamıyım m	ish a·da·muh·yuhm
	kadınıyım f	ka·duh·nuh·yuhm
farmer	çiftçiyim m&f	cheeft·chee·yeem
manual worker	işçiyim m&f	eesh·chee·yeem
office worker	memurum m&f	me·moo·room
scientist	bilim adamıyım m&f	bee·leem a·da·muh·yuhm

background

Where are you from?	Nerelisiniz? pol	ne·re·lee·see·neez
	Nerelisin? inf	ne·re·lee·seen
I'm from ...	Ben ...	ben ...
Australia	Avustralya'lıyım	a·voos·tral·ya·luh·yuhm
Canada	Kanada'lıyım	ka·na·da·luh·yuhm
England	İngiltere'liyim	een·geel·te·re·lee·yeem
the USA	Amerika'lıyım	a·me·ree·ka·luh·yuhm
Are you married?	Evli misiniz?	ev·lee mee·see·neez
I'm married/single.	Ben evliyim/bekarım.	ben ev·lee·yeem/be·ka·ruhm

age

How old ...?	Kaç ...?	kach ...
are you	yaşındasın inf	ya·shuhn·da·suhn
is your son	yaşında oğlunuz	ya·shuhn·da o·loo·nooz
is your daughter	yaşında kızınız	ya·shuhn·da kuh·zuh·nuhz
I'm ... years old.	Ben ... yaşındayım.	ben ... ya·shuhn·da·yuhm
He/She is ... years old.	O ... yaşında.	o ... ya·shuhn·da

feelings

I'm/I'm not ...		
cold	Üşüdüm./	ew·shew·dewm/
	Üşümedim.	ew·shew·me·deem
happy	Mutluyum./	moot·loo·yoom/
	Mutlu değilim.	moot·loo de·ee·leem
hot	Sıcakladım./	suh·jak·la·duhm/
	Sıcaklamadım.	suh·jak·la·ma·duhm
hungry	Açım./Aç değilim.	a·chuhm/ach de·ee·leem
sad	Üzgünüm./	ewz·gew·newm/
	Üzgün değilim.	ewz·gewn de·ee·leem
thirsty	Susadım./Susamadım.	soo·sa·duhm/soo·sa·ma·duhm
tired	Yorgunum./	yor·goo·noom/
	Yorgun değilim.	yor·goon de·ee·leem

Are you ...?		
cold	Üşüdün mü?	ew·shew·dewn mew
happy	Mutlu musun?	moot·loo moo·soon
hot	Sıcakladın mı?	suh·jak·la·duhn muh
hungry	Aç mısın?	ach muh·suhn
sad	Üzgün musun?	ewz·gewn moo·soon
thirsty	Susadın mı?	soo·sa·duhn muh
tired	Yorgun musun?	yor·goon moo·soon

entertainment

going out

Where can I find ...?	Buranın ... nerede?	boo·ra·nuhn ... ne·re·de
clubs	kulüpleri	koo·lewp·le·ree
gay venues	gey kulüpleri	gay koo·lewp·le·ree
pubs	birahaneleri	bee·ra·ha·ne·le·ree

I feel like going to a/the ...	... gitmek istiyor.	... geet·mek ees·tee·yor
concert	Konsere	kon·se·re
movies	Sinemaya	see·ne·ma·ya
party	Partiye	par·tee·ye
restaurant	Restorana	res·to·ra·na
theatre	Oyuna	o·yoo·na

interests

Do you like ...?	... sever misin?	... se·*ver* mee·*seen*
I like ...	... seviyorum.	... se·*vee*·yo·room
I don't like ...	... sevmiyorum.	... *sev*·mee·yo·room
art	Sanat	sa·*nat*
movies	Sinemaya gitmeyi	see·ne·ma·*ya* geet·me·*yee*
reading	Okumayı	o·koo·ma·*yuh*
sport	Sporu	spo·*roo*
travelling	Seyahat etmeyi	se·ya·*hat* et·me·*yee*
Do you ...?	... misin/misiniz? inf/pol	... mee·*seen*/mee·see·*neez*
dance	Dans eder	dans e·*der*
go to concerts	Konserlere gider	kon·ser·le·*re* gee·*der*
listen to music	Müzik dinler	mew·*zeek* deen·*ler*

food & drink

finding a place to eat

Can you recommend a ...?	İyi bir ... tavsiye edebilir misiniz?	ee·*yee* beer ... tav·see·*ye* e·*de*·bee·leer mee·see·*neez*
bar	bar	bar
café	kafe	ka·*fe*
restaurant	restoran	res·to·*ran*
I'd like ..., please.	... istiyorum.	... ees·*tee*·yo·room
a table for (five)	(Beş) kişilik bir masa	(besh) kee·shee·*leek* beer ma·*sa*
the nonsmoking section	Sigara içilmeyen bir yer	see·*ga*·ra ee·*cheel*·me·yen beer yer
the smoking section	Sigara içilen bir yer	see·*ga*·ra ee·chee·*len* beer yer

ordering food

breakfast	kahvaltı	kah·val·*tuh*
lunch	öğle yemeği	eu·*le* ye·me·*ee*
dinner	akşam yemeği	ak·*sham* ye·me·*ee*
snack	hafif yemek	ha·*feef* ye·*mek*

What would you recommend?
Ne tavsiye edersiniz? — ne tav·see·ye e·der·see·neez

I'd like (a/the)...	... istiyorum.	... ees·tee·yo·room
bill	Hesabı	he·sa·buh
drink list	İçecek listesini	ee·che·jek lees·te·see·nee
menu	Menüyü	me·new·yew
that dish	Şu yemeği	shoo ye·me·ee

drinks

(cup of) coffee ...	(fincan) kahve ...	(feen·jan) kah·ve ...
(cup of) tea ...	(fincan) çay ...	(feen·jan) chai ...
with milk	sütlü	sewt·lew
without sugar	şekersiz	she·ker·seez
(orange) juice	(portakal) suyu	(por·ta·kal) soo·yoo
soft drink	alkolsüz içecek	al·kol·sewz ee·che·jek
sparkling mineral water	maden sodası	ma·den so·da·suh
still mineral water	maden suyu	ma·den soo·yoo
(hot) water	(sıcak) su	(suh·jak) soo

in the bar

I'll have ...	... alayım.	... a·la·yuhm
I'll buy you a drink.	Sana içecek alayım.	sa·na ee·che·jek a·la·yuhm
What would you like?	Ne alırsınız?	ne a·luhr·suh·nuhz
Cheers!	Şerefe!	she·re·fe
brandy	brendi	bren·dee
cocktail	kokteyl	kok·tayl
cognac	konyak	kon·yak
a shot of (whisky)	bir tek (viski)	beer tek (vees·kee)
a bottle/glass of beer	bir şişe/bardak bira	beer shee·she/bar·dak bee·ra
a bottle/glass	bir şişe/bardak	beer shee·she/bar·dak
of ... wine	... şarap	... sha·rap
red	kırmızı	kuhr·muh·zuh
sparkling	köpüklü	keu·pewk·lew
white	beyaz	be·yaz

self-catering

What's the local speciality?
Bu yöreye has yiyecekler neler?   boo yeu·re·*ye* has yee·ye·jek·*ler* ne·ler

What's that?
Bu nedir?   boo ne·deer

How much (is a kilo of cheese)?
(Bir kilo peynir) Ne kadar?   (beer kee·*lo* pay·*neer*) ne ka·*dar*

I'd like ...	... istiyorum.	... ees·*tee*·yo·room
(200) grams	(İkiyüz) gram	(ee·kee·yewz) gram
(two) kilos	(İki) kilo	(ee·*kee*) kee·*lo*
(three) pieces	(Üç) parça	(ewch) par·*cha*
(six) slices	(Altı) dilim	(al·*tuh*) dee·*leem*

Less.	Daha az.	da·ha az
Enough.	Yeterli.	ye·ter·*lee*
More.	Daha fazla.	da·ha faz·*la*

special diets & allergies

Where's a vegetarian restaurant?
Buralarda vejeteryan restoran var mı?   boo·ra·lar·*da* ve·zhe·ter·*yan* res·to·*ran* var muh

Do you have vegetarian food?
Vejeteryan yiyecekleriniz var mı?   ve·zhe·ter·*yan* yee·ye·jek·le·ree·*neez* var muh

Is it cooked with ...?	İçinde ... var mı?	ee·cheen·*de* ... var muh
butter	tereyağ	te·*re*·ya
eggs	yumurta	yoo·moor·*ta*
meat stock	et suyu	et soo·*yoo*

I'm allergic to ...	... alerjim var.	... a·ler·*zheem* var
dairy produce	Süt ürünlerine	sewt ew·rewn·le·ree·ne
gluten	Glutene	gloo·te·ne
MSG	Mono sodyum glutamata	mo·no sod·yoom gloo·ta·ma·ta
nuts	Çerezlere	che·rez·le·re
seafood	Deniz ürünlerine	de·neez ew·rewn·le·ree·ne

emergencies

basics

Help!	*İmdat!*	*eem*-dat
Stop!	*Dur!*	door
Go away!	*Git burdan!*	geet boor-*dan*
Thief!	*Hırsız var!*	huhr-*suhz* var
Fire!	*Yangın var!*	*yan*-guhn var
Watch out!	*Dikkat et!*	*deek*-kat et

Call …!	… *çağırın!*	… cha-*uh*-ruhn
a doctor	*Doktor*	dok-*tor*
an ambulance	*Ambulans*	am-boo-*lans*
the police	*Polis*	po-*lees*

It's an emergency!
Bu acil bir durum.   boo a-*jeel* beer *doo*-room

Could you help me, please?
Yardım edebilir misiniz lütfen?   yar-*duhm* e-de-bee-leer mee-see-*neez* lewt-fen

Can I use your phone?
Telefonunuzu kullanabilir miyim?   te-le-fe-noo-noo-*zoo* kool-la-*na*-bee-leer mee-*yeem*

I'm lost.
Kayboldum.   kai-bol-*doom*

Where are the toilets?
Tuvaletler nerede?   too-va-let-*ler* ne-re-de

police

Where's the police station?
Polis karakolu nerede?   po-*lees* ka-ra-ko-*loo* ne-re-de

I want to report an offence.
Şikayette bulunmak istiyorum.   shee-ka-yet-*te* boo-loon-*mak* ees-*tee*-yo-room

I have insurance.
Sigortam var.   see-gor-*tam* var

I've been ...	Ben ...	ben ...
assaulted	saldırıya uğradım	sal-duh-ruh-ya oo-ra-duhm
raped	tecavüze uğradım	te-ja-vew-ze oo-ra-duhm
robbed	soyuldum	so-yool-doom

I've lost my ...	... kayıp.	... ka-yuhp
My ... was/were stolen.	... çalındı.	... cha-luhn-duh
backpack	Sırt çantası	suhrt chan-ta-suh
bags	Çantalar	chan-ta-lar
credit card	Kredi kartı	kre-dee kar-tuh
handbag	El çantası	el chan-ta-suh
jewellery	Mücevherler	mew-jev-her-ler
money	Para	pa-ra
passport	Pasaport	pa-sa-port
travellers cheques	Seyahat çekleri	se-ya-hat chek-le-ree
wallet	Cüzdan	jewz-dan

I want to contact	... görüşmek	... geu-rewsh-mek
my ...	istiyorum.	ees-tee-yo-room
consulate	Konsoloslukla	kon-so-los-look-la
embassy	Elçilikle	el-chee-leek-le

health

medical needs

Where's the nearest ...?	En yakın ... nerede?	en ya-kuhn ... ne-re-de
dentist	dişçi	deesh-chee
doctor	doktor	dok-tor
hospital	hastane	has-ta-ne
(night) pharmacist	(nöbetçi) eczane	(neu-bet-chee) ej-za-ne

I need a doctor (who speaks English).
(İngilizce konuşan)   (een-gee-leez-je ko-noo-shan)
Bir doktora ihtiyacım var.   beer dok-to-ra eeh-tee-ya-juhm var

Could I see a female doctor?
Bayan doktora   ba-yan dok-to-ra
görünebilir miyim?   geu-rew-ne-bee-leer mee-yeem

I've run out of my medication.
İlacım bitti.   ee-la-juhm beet-tee

symptoms, conditions & allergies

I'm sick.	Hastayım.	has·ta·yuhm
It hurts here.	Burası ağrıyor.	boo·ra·suh a·ruh·yor
I have a toothache.	Dişim ağrıyor.	dee·sheem a·ruh·yor
I have (a) ...	Bende ... var.	ben·de ... var
asthma	astım	as·tuhm
bronchitis	bronşit	bron·sheet
constipation	kabızlık	ka·buhz·luhk
cough	öksürük	euk·sew·rewk
diarrhoea	ishal	ees·hal
fever	ateş	a·tesh
headache	baş ağrısı	bash a·ruh·suh
heart condition	kalp rahatsızlığı	kalp ra·hat·suhz·luh·uh
nausea	bulantı	boo·lan·tuh
pain	ağrı	a·ruh
sore throat	boğaz ağrısı	bo·az a·ruh·suh
I'm allergic to ...	... alerjim var.	... a·ler·zheem var
antibiotics	Antibiyotiklere	an·tee·bee·yo·teek·le·re
anti- inflammatories	Anti- emflamatuarlara	an·tee- em·fla·ma·too·ar·la·ra
aspirin	Aspirine	as·pee·ree·ne
bees	Arılara	a·ruh·la·ra
codeine	Kodeine	ko·de·ee·ne
penicillin	Penisiline	pe·nee·see·lee·ne
antiseptic	antiseptik	an·tee·sep·teek
bandage	bandaj	ban·dazh
condoms	prezervatifler	pre·zer·va·teef·ler
contraceptives	doğum kontrol hapı	do·oom kon·trol ha·puh
diarrhoea medicine	ishal ilacı	ees·hal ee·la·juh
insect repellent	sinek kovucu	see·nek ko·voo·joo
laxatives	müsil ilacı	mew·seel ee·la·juh
painkillers	ağrı kesici	a·ruh ke·see·jee
rehydration salts	rehidrasyon tuzları	re·heed·ras·yon tooz·la·ruh
sleeping tablets	uyku hapı	ooy·koo ha·puh

english–turkish dictionary

Words in this dictionary are marked as a (adjective), n (noun), v (verb), sg (singular), pl (plural), inf (informal) and pol (polite) where necessary.

A

accident *kaza* ka-*za*
accommodation *kalacak yer* ka-la-*jak* yer
adaptor *adaptör* a-dap-*teur*
address n *adres* ad-*res*
after *sonra* son-*ra*
air conditioning *klima* klee-ma
airplane *uçak* oo-*chak*
airport *havaalanı* ha-va-a-la-*nuh*
alcohol *alkol* al-kol
all *hepsi* hep-see
allergy *alerji* a-ler-*zhee*
ambulance *ambulans* am-boo-*lans*
and *ve* ve
ankle *ayak bileği* a-*yak* bee-le-*ee*
arm *kol* kol
ashtray *kül tablası* kewl tab-la-*suh*
ATM *bankamatik* ban-ka-ma-*teek*

B

baby *bebek* be-*bek*
back (body) *sırt* suhrt
backpack *sırt çantası* suhrt chan-ta-*suh*
bad *kötü* keu-*tew*
bag *çanta* chan-ta
baggage claim *bagaj konveyörü*
   ba-*gazh* kon-ve-yeu-*rew*
bank *banka* ban-ka
bar *bar* bar
bathroom *banyo* ban-yo
battery *pil* peel
beautiful *güzel* gew-*zel*
bed *yatak* ya-*tak*
beer *bira* bee-ra
before *önce* eun-je
behind *arkasında* ar-ka-suhn-*da*
bicycle *bisiklet* bee-seek-*let*
big *büyük* bew-*yewk*
bill *hesap* he-*sap*
black *siyah* see-*yah*
blanket *battaniye* bat-*ta*-nee-ye

blood group *kan grubu* kan goo-roo-*boo*
blue *mavi* ma-vee
boat *vapur* va-poor
book (make a reservation) v *yer ayırtmak*
   yer a-yuhrt-*mak*
bottle *şişe* shee-*she*
bottle opener *şişe açacağı* shee-*she* a-cha-ja-*uh*
boy *oğlan* o-lan
brakes (car) *fren* fren
breakfast *kahvaltı* kah-val-*tuh*
broken (faulty) *bozuk* bo-*zook*
bus *otobüs* o-to-*bews*
business *iş* eesh
buy *satın almak* sa-*tuhn* al-mak

C

café *kafe* ka-fe
camera *kamera* ka-*me*-ra
camp site *kamp yeri* kamp ye-*ree*
cancel *iptal etmek* eep-*tal* et-mek
can opener *konserve açacağı* kon-ser-*ve* a-cha-ja-*uh*
car *araba* a-ra-ba
cash n *nakit* na-*keet*
cash (a cheque) v *(çek) bozdurmak*
   (chek) boz-door-*mak*
cell phone *cep telefonu* jep te-le-fo-*noo*
centre n *merkez* mer-*kez*
change (money) v *bozdurmak* boz-door-*mak*
cheap *ucuz* oo-*jooz*
check (bill) *fatura* fa-*too*-ra
check-in *giriş* gee-*reesh*
chest *göğüs* geu-*ews*
child *çocuk* cho-*jook*
cigarette *sigara* see-*ga*-ra
city *şehir* she-*heer*
clean a *temiz* te-*meez*
closed *kapalı* ka-pa-*luh*
coffee *kahve* kah-ve
coins *madeni para* ma-de-*nee* pa-*ra*
cold a *soğuk* so-*ook*
collect call *ödemeli telefon* eu-de-me-*lee* te-le-*fon*
come *gelmek* gel-*mek*

computer *bilgisayar* beel-gee-sa-*yar*
condom *prezervatif* pre-zer-va-*teef*
contact lenses *kontak lens* kon-*tak* lens
cook v *pişirmek* pee-sheer-*mek*
cost n *fiyat* fee-*yat*
credit card *kredi kartı* kre-dee kar-*tuh*
cup *fincan* feen-*jan*
currency exchange *döviz kuru* deu-*veez* koo-*roo*
customs (immigration) *gümrük* gewm-*rewk*

D

dangerous *tehlikeli* teh-lee-ke-*lee*
date (time) *tarih* ta-*reeh*
day *gün* gewn
delay n *gecikme* ge-jeek-*me*
dentist *dişçi* deesh-*chee*
depart *ayrılmak* ai-ruhl-*mak*
diaper *bebek bezi* be-bek be-*zee*
dictionary *sözlük* seuz-*lewk*
dinner *akşam yemeği* ak-sham ye-me-*ee*
direct *direk* dee-*rek*
dirty *kirli* keer-*lee*
disabled *özürlü* eu-zewr-*lew*
discount n *indirim* een-dee-*reem*
doctor *doktor* dok-*tor*
double bed *iki kişilik yatak* ee-kee kee-shee-*leek* ya-*tak*
double room *iki kişilik oda* ee-kee kee-shee-*leek* o-*da*
drink n *içecek* ee-che-*jek*
drive v *sürmek* sewr-*mek*
drivers licence *ehliyet* eh-lee-*yet*
drugs (illicit) *uyuşturucu* oo-yoosh-too-roo-*joo*
dummy (pacifier) *emzik* em-*zeek*

E

ear *kulak* koo-*lak*
east *doğu* do-*oo*
eat *yemek* ye-*mek*
economy class *ekonomi sınıfı* e-ko-no-*mee* suh-nuh-*fuh*
electricity *elektrik* e-lek-*treek*
elevator *asansör* a-san-*seur*
email *e-posta* e-pos-*ta*
embassy *elçilik* el-chee-*leek*
emergency *acil durum* a-jeel doo-*room*
English (language) *İngilizce* een-gee-*leez*-je
entrance *giriş* gee-*reesh*
evening *akşam* ak-*sham*
exchange rate *döviz kuru* deu-*veez* koo-*roo*
exit n *çıkış* chuh-*kuhsh*

expensive *pahalı* pa-ha-*luh*
express mail *ekspres posta* eks-pres pos-*ta*
eye *göz* geuz

F

far *uzak* oo-*zak*
fast *hızlı* huhz-*luh*
father *baba* ba-*ba*
film (camera) *film* feelm
finger *parmak* par-*mak*
first-aid kit *ilk yardım çantası*
    eelk yar-*duhm* chan-ta-*suh*
first class *birinci sınıf* bee-reen-*jee* suh-*nuhf*
fish n *balık* ba-*luhk*
food *yiyecek* yee-ye-*jek*
foot *ayak* a-*yak*
fork *çatal* cha-*tal*
free (of charge) *ücretsiz* ewj-ret-*seez*
friend *arkadaş* ar-ka-*dash*
fruit *meyve* may-*ve*
full *dolu* do-*loo*
funny *komik* ko-*meek*

G

gift *hediye* he-dee-*ye*
girl *kız* kuhz
glass (drinking) *bardak* bar-*dak*
glasses *gözlük* geuz-*lewk*
go *gitmek* geet-*mek*
good *iyi* ee-*yee*
green *yeşil* ye-*sheel*
guide n *rehber* reh-*ber*

H

half n *yarım* ya-*ruhm*
hand *el* el
handbag *el çantası* el chan-ta-*suh*
happy *mutlu* moot-*loo*
have *sahip olmak* sa-*heep* ol-*mak*
he *o* o
head *baş* bash
heart *kalp* kalp
heat n *ısı* uh-*suh*
heavy *ağır* a-*uhr*
help v *yardım etmek* yar-*duhm* et-*mek*
here *burada* boo-ra-*da*
high *yüksek* yewk-*sek*

highway *otoyol* o-to-yol
hike v *uzun yürüyüşe çıkmak*
  oo-zoon yew-rew-yew-she chuhk-mak
holiday *tatil* ta-teel
homosexual *homoseksüel* ho-mo-sek-sew-el
hospital *hastane* has-ta-ne
hot *sıcak* suh-jak
hotel *otel* o-tel
hungry *aç* ach
husband *koca* ko-ja

I

I *ben* ben
identification (card) *kimlik kartı* keem-leek kar-tuh
ill *hasta* has-ta
important *önemli* eu-nem-lee
included *dahil* da-heel
injury *yara* ya-ra
insurance *sigorta* see-gor-ta
Internet *internet* een-ter-net
interpreter *tercüman* ter-jew-man

J

jewellery *mücevherler* mew-jev-her-ler
job *meslek* mes-lek

K

key *anahtar* a-nah-tar
kilogram *kilogram* kee-log-ram
kitchen *mutfak* moot-fak
knife *bıçak* buh-chak

L

laundry (place) *çamaşırlık* cha-ma-shuhr-luhk
lawyer *avukat* a-voo-kat
left (direction) *sol* sol
left-luggage office *emanet bürosu* e-ma-net bew-ro-soo
leg *bacak* ba-jak
lesbian *lezbiyen* lez-bee-yen
less *daha az* da-ha az
letter (mail) *mektup* mek-toop
lift (elevator) *asansör* a-san-seur
light n *ışık* uh-shuhk
like v *sevmek* sev-mek
lock n *kilit* kee-leet
long *uzun* oo-zoon

lost *kayıp* ka-yuhp
lost-property office *kayıp eşya bürosu*
  ka-yuhp esh-ya bew-ro-soo
love v *aşık olmak* a-shuhk ol-mak
luggage *bagaj* ba-gazh
lunch *öğle yemeği* eu-le ye-me-ee

M

mail n *mektup* mek-toop
man *adam* a-dam
map *harita* ha-ree-ta
market *pazar* pa-zar
matches *kibrit* keeb-reet
meat *et* et
medicine *ilaç* ee-lach
menu *yemek listesi* ye-mek lees-te-see
message *mesaj* me-sazh
milk *süt* sewt
minute *dakika* da-kee-ka
mobile phone *cep telefonu* jep te-le-fo-noo
money *para* pa-ra
month *ay* ai
morning *sabah* sa-bah
mother *anne* an-ne
motorcycle *motosiklet* mo-to-seek-let
motorway *paralı yol* pa-ra-luh yol
mouth *ağız* a-uhz
music *müzik* mew-zeek

N

name *ad* ad
napkin *peçete* pe-che-te
nappy *bebek bezi* be-bek be-zee
near *yakında* ya-kuhn-da
neck *boyun* bo-yoon
new *yeni* ye-nee
news *haberler* ha-ber-ler
newspaper *gazete* ga-ze-te
night *gece* ge-je
no *hayır* ha-yuhr
noisy *gürültülü* gew-rewl-tew-lew
nonsmoking *sigara içilmeyen* see-ga-ra ee-cheel-me-yen
north *kuzey* koo-zay
nose *burun* boo-roon
now *şimdi* sheem-dee
number *sayı* sa-yuh

O

oil (engine) *jağ* ya
old (object/person) *eski/yaşlı* es-kee/yash-luh
one-way ticket *gidiş bilet* gee-deesh bee-let
open a *açık* a-chuhk
outside *dışarıda* duh-sha-ruh-da

P

package *ambalaj* am-ba-lazh
paper *kağıt* ka-uht
park (car) v *park etmek* park et-mek
passport *pasaport* pa-sa-port
pay *ödemek* eu-de-mek
pen *tükenmez kalem* tew-ken-mez ka-lem
petrol *benzin* ben-zeen
pharmacy *eczane* ej-za-ne
phonecard *telefon kartı* te-le-fon kar-tuh
photo *fotoğraf* fo-to-raf
plate *tabak* ta-bak
police *polis* po-lees
postcard *kartpostal* kart-pos-tal
post office *postane* pos-ta-ne
pregnant *hamile* ha-mee-le
price *fiyat* fee-yat

Q

quiet *sakin* sa-keen

R

ain n *yağmur* ya-moor
azor *traş makinesi* trash ma-kee-ne-see
eceipt n *makbuz* mak-booz
d *kırmızı* kuhr-muh-zuh
fund n *para iadesi* pa-ra ee-a-de-see
gistered mail *taahhütlü posta* ta-ah-hewt-lew pos-ta
nt v *kiralamak* kee-ra-la-mak
pair v *tamir etmek* ta-meer et-mek
ervation *rezervasyon* re-zer-vas-yon
taurant *restoran* res-to-ran
urn v *geri dönmek* ge-ree deun-mek
urn ticket *gidiş-dönüş bilet*
ee-deesh-deu-newsh bee-let
t (direction) *doğru yön* do-roo yeun

road *yol* yol
room *oda* o-da

S

safe a *emniyetli* em-nee-yet-lee
sanitary napkin *hijyenik kadın bağı*
heezh-ye-neek ka-duhn ba-uh
seat *yer* yer
send *göndermek* geun-der-mek
service station *benzin istasyonu*
ben-zeen ees-tas-yo-noo
sex *seks* seks
shampoo *şampuan* sham-poo-an
share (a dorm) *paylaşmak* pai-lash-mak
shaving cream *tıraş kremi* tuh-rash kre-mee
she *o* o
sheet (bed) *çarşaf* char-shaf
shirt *gömlek* geum-lek
shoes *ayakkabılar* a-yak-ka-buh-lar
shop n *dükkan* dewk-kan
short *kısa* kuh-sa
shower n *duş* doosh
single room *tek kişilik oda* tek kee-shee-leek o-da
skin *cilt* jeelt
skirt *etek* e-tek
sleep v *uyumak* oo-yoo-mak
slowly *yavaşça* ya-vash-cha
small *küçük* kew-chewk
smoke (cigarettes) v *sigara içmek*
see-ga-ra eech-mek
soap *sabun* sa-boon
some *biraz* bee-raz
soon *yakında* ya-kuhn-da
south *güney* gew-nay
souvenir shop *hediyelik eşya dükkanı*
he-dee-ye-leek esh-ya dewk-ka-nuh
speak *konuşmak* ko-noosh-mak
spoon *kaşık* ka-shuhk
stamp *pul* pool
stand-by ticket *açık bilet* a-chuhk bee-let
station (train) *istasyon* ees-tas-yon
stomach *mide* mee-de
stop v *durmak* door-mak
stop (bus) n *durağı* doo-ra-uh
street *sokak* so-kak
student *öğrenci* eu-ren-jee
sun *güneş* gew-nesh

sunscreen *güneşten koruma kremi* gew-nesh-*ten* ko-roo-ma kre-*mee*
swim v *yüzmek* yewz-*mek*

T

tampons *tamponlar* tam-pon-*lar*
taxi *taksi* tak-*see*
teaspoon *çay kaşığı* chai ka-shuh-*uh*
teeth *dişler* deesh-*ler*
telephone n *telefon* te-le-*fon*
television *televizyon* te-le-veez-*yon*
temperature (weather) *derece* de-re-*je*
tent *çadır* cha-*duhr*
that (one) *şunu/onu* shoo-*noo*/o-*noo*
they *onlar* on-*lar*
thirsty *susamış* soo-sa-*muhsh*
this (one) *bunu* boo-*noo*
throat *boğaz* bo-*az*
ticket *bilet* bee-*let*
time *zaman* za-*man*
tired *yorgun* yor-*goon*
tissues *kağıt mendil* ka-*uht* men-*deel*
today *bugün* boo-*gewn*
toilet *tuvalet* too-va-*let*
tomorrow *yarın* ya-*ruhn*
tonight *bu gece* boo ge-*je*
toothbrush *diş fırçası* deesh fuhr-cha-*suh*
toothpaste *diş macunu* deesh ma-joo-*noo*
torch (flashlight) *el feneri* el fe-ne-*ree*
tour n *tur* toor
tourist office *turizm bürosu* too-*reezm* bew-ro-*soo*
towel *havlu* hav-*loo*
train *tren* tren
translate *çevirmek* che-veer-*mek*
travel agency *seyahat acentesi* seya-*hat* a-jen-te-*see*
travellers cheque *seyahat çeki* se-ya-hat che-*kee*
trousers *pantolon* pan-to-*lon*
twin beds *çift yatak* cheeft ya-*tak*
Turkey *Türkiye* tewr-kee-*ye*
Turkish (language) *Türkçe* tewrk-*che*
Turkish Republic of Northern Cyprus (TRNC)
   Kuzey Kıbrıs Türk Cumhuriyeti (KKTC) koo-*zay* kuhb-*ruhs* tewrk joom-hoo-ree-ye-*tee* (ka-ka-te-je)
twin beds *çift yatak* cheeft ya-*tak*
tyre *lastik* las-*teek*

U

underwear *iç çamaşırı* eech cha-ma-shuh-*ruh*
urgent *acil* a-*jeel*

V

vacant *boş* bosh
vacation *tatil* ta-*teel*
vegetable n *sebze* seb-*ze*
vegetarian a *vejeteryan* ve-zhe-ter-*yan*
visa *vize* vee-*ze*

W

waiter *garson* gar-*son*
walk v *yürümek* yew-rew-*mek*
wallet *cüzdan* jewz-*dan*
warm a *ılık* uh-*luhk*
wash (something) *yıkamak* yuh-ka-*mak*
watch n *saat* sa-*at*
water *su* soo
we *biz* beez
weekend *hafta sonu* haf-*ta* so-*noo*
west *batı* ba-*tuh*
wheelchair *tekerlekli sandalye* te-ker-lek-*lee* san-*dal*-ye
when *ne zaman* ne za-*man*
where *nerede* ne-re-*de*
white *beyaz* be-*yaz*
who *kim* keem
why *neden* ne-*den*
wife *karı* ka-*ruh*
window *pencere* pen-je-*re*
wine *şarap* sha-*rap*
with *ile* ee-*le*
without *-sız/-siz/-suz/-süz* -suhz/-seez/-sooz/-sewz
woman *kadın* ka-*duhn*
write *yazı yazmak* ya-zuh yaz-*mak*

Y

yellow *sarı* sa-*ruh*
yes *evet* e-*vet*
yesterday *dün* dewn
you sg inf *sen* sen
you sg pol & pl *siz* seez